THE
PSYCHOSES:
Family Studies

Sheldon C. Reed, Ph.D.

Carl Hartley, Ph.D.

V. Elving Anderson, Ph.D.

Vivian P. Phillips, B.S.

Nelson A. Johnson, M.S.W.

*with
the
collaboration of*
JOHN C. URBAITIS, M.D.
ROBERT H. ISRAEL, M.D.
ANNA WENDT FINLAYSON

THE DIGHT INSTITUTE FOR HUMAN GENETICS,
UNIVERSITY OF MINNESOTA
and the
WARREN STATE HOSPITAL,
WARREN, PENNSYLVANIA

1973   W. B. SAUNDERS COMPANY—PHILADELPHIA—LONDON—TORONTO

W. B. Saunders Company: West Washington Square
Philadelphia, Pa.   19105

12 Dyott Street
London, WC1A   1DB

833 Oxford Street
Toronto 18, Ontario

Supported by Grant Number MH-02892 of the National Institute of Mental Health and The Minnesota Human Genetics League

The Psychoses: Family Studies   ISBN 0–7216-7507-7

Print No.:   9   8   7   6   5   4   3   2   1

To the Memory
of
Carl Hartley, Ph.D.
April 7, 1887–December 15, 1968

Mental health was a lifelong personal interest of this versatile scientist. The group working on this study at Warren State Hospital was organized and directed by him. His contributions of time and money were indispensable to the completion of our mental health study. We hope that he would be pleased with the finished product, this book.

PREFACE
AND
ACKNOWLEDGMENTS

This book is a study of the relatives of a sample of individuals who were psychotic patients at the Warren State Hospital during the early years of this century. The information was obtained from hundreds of relatives, physicians, psychiatrists, and others who were involved with the families. It is impossible to thank all of these people individually for their help, but we are deeply grateful to them because this book is built upon the data they provided.

The present study, as was the case with a previous one by E. W. and S. C. Reed (1965) on mental retardation, was initiated by Dr. C. B. Davenport, the Director of the Eugenics Records Office at Cold Spring Harbor, New York. The first E.R.O. bulletin on human genetics was published by him in 1911. During the next 25 years about 90 persons received training as field workers in human genetics at the Eugenics Records Office. The field workers were college graduates with majors in sociology, psychology, biology, and other appropriate areas. They were well trained in the techniques of family history taking and pedigree construction. These field workers were then assigned to state institutions such as the State School and Hospital for the mentally retarded at Faribault, Minnesota, and the State Hospital for the mentally ill at Warren, Pennsylvania. It was intended that complete family histories would be obtained for all of the patients in the hospital, one by one. However, it was impossible to reach this goal because of a lack of sufficient personnel to study the families of all the patients.

Family studies were completed for a large enough sample of the patients present in the hospital during the second decade of the twentieth century to provide the starting material for this book. Furthermore, a practical result of the emphasis on family history taking was that record keeping was greatly improved and continues to be of high quality to the present time.

A significant factor in the consistently good record keeping at the Warren State Hospital is that there have been, essentially, only two superintendents during the 54 years encompassed by this study. H. W. Mitchell, M.D., was the Superintendent from 1912 to 1933, while Robert H. Israel, M.D., was the Superintendent from 1935 to 1970. This research project could not have been initiated without its enthusiastic acceptance by Superintendent Mitchell, nor could it have been completed without the patient and firm support of Superintendent Israel during the last 18 years.

The first person assigned to the project at Warren State Hospital was Miss Anna Wendt, who later became Mrs. A. D. Finlayson. Fortunately, she is still alive at the time of the writing of this book and has been of great help in answering our questions about the procedures employed in the early days of the work. She studied the families of 118 patients during 1913 and subsequent years. In 1916 additional families were studied by Miss Ruth Badger. During 1913 the Eugenics Records Office provided Miss Wendt's salary while the hospital provided her subsistence and field expenses. Her salary as well as the other expenses were provided by the hospital for the subsequent years. Copies of the family study data obtained by these research workers were filed at the Eugenics Records Office.

The research data of the Eugenics Records Office were presented to the Dight Institute for Human Genetics of the University of Minnesota in 1948 by the late Dr. Milislav Demerec of the Cold Spring Harbor Laboratory of Quantitative Biology. We appreciate his vision in finding a home for the records obtained by the combined efforts of the 90 field workers. The primary element of the science of genetics is the study of the transmission of traits from generation to generation. Such study is difficult in man for several reasons. One of the greatest difficulties is that of obtaining data for several consecutive generations of people. Consequently, one should never discard human data for which there is even a remote possibility of future use.

In 1949 Dr. Elizabeth Reed started work on the Eugenics Records Office data which had been obtained for mentally retarded patients at the Faribault, Minnesota, State School and Hospital, while Dr. David J. Merrell of the Dight Institute went to the Warren, Pennsylvania, State Hospital and started work on the families previously investigated by Miss Wendt and Miss Badger. Dr. Merrell learned that it would be possible to reactivate the study if someone could be found who could reside permanently at Warren and establish a group of resident field workers there. This would necessitate rather extensive financial support, which was not available then. We thank Dr. Merrell for this valuable pioneering effort.

Dr. Carl Hartley reconnoitered the possibility of reopening the project in 1957. Funds became available on May 1, 1959 from the National Institute of Mental Health to the Dight Institute and the Warren State Hospital, as grant MH–02892. The grants continued on an annual basis until the work was completed in 1967. Naturally, we are extremely grateful for this essential support and also to the Minnesota Human Genetics League for additional financial aid. Dr. Hartley took up residence in Warren and recruited a team of workers there with assistance from the Director of Social Services, Mr. Nelson Johnson, and others.

Some of the members of the team of workers based in Warren, and in other communities who made unusually valuable contributions of their skills were the following, whom we have not previously mentioned: Martha Baker, Margaret Donaldson, Walter Finken, M.D., Peter Francis, M.D., A. L. Halpern, M.D., Helen Heymann, Arthur Hoshino, M.D., Helen Israel, Mary Hartley, Marian Kinkead, Harry Little, M.D., Fred Mack, Leila Mack, Genevieve Murphy, George O'Dea, Patricia O'Dea, E. R. Olivier, Florence Olivier, Louise Peterson, Paul Randolph, James Suess, M.D., Annamarie Towne, Lockwood Towne, M.D., Elizabeth Wendelboe and N. P. Wendelboe, all of Warren, Pennsylvania. Also, Arthur DiVittis, Ph.D. (Torrance, Penna.), Samuel Detwiler (Washington, D.C.), Zoe Friedberg (Los Angeles, Calif.), Ann Petrovich (Polk, Penna.), William Schaefnocker (Bricksville, Ohio), Theodore Stroup (Torrance, Penna.), Archie Sundback (Erie, Penna.), and Terese West (Los Angeles, Calif.).

The reader will not be surprised to learn that all the physicians listed above were psychiatrists attached to the Warren State Hospital who provided diagnoses and reviews of the diagnoses of other physicians. The persons listed in other communities carried out field studies in those areas.

Persons who worked at the Dight Institute on this project and were not listed previously include Magnhild O. Goodman, who contributed hundreds of hours of typing without financial recompense, Elizabeth Reed, Ph.D., William Rice, Robert Selmo, and Bertha Storts.

The authors extend their sincere thanks to each of the many faithful workers acknowledged above, as well as to the hundreds of relatives of the patients, record searchers in vital statistics bureaus, and all the others involved in this study. We also wish to thank Irving Gottesman, Ph.D., for reading this book and for his suggestions. He does not accept our interpretations of the data in all cases.

Finally, we are extremely grateful to the publisher for the great care devoted to the production of this book, and to an anonymous donor whose gift of several thousand dollars helped absorb the cost of publishing the family pedigrees.

SHELDON C. REED

CONTENTS

CHAPTER ONE

INTRODUCTION

It is clear that the content of a psychosis is learned. One cannot believe that he is Napoleon unless he has learned something about the famous Frenchman. But there is something more to a psychosis than the learned content. Every person devotes much of his thought to fantasy, as this is a satisfying activity and often more enjoyable than many real life experiences. Some people find that both their fantasies and their realities become threatening and they develop a fear of both. When they have lost control of both their fantasies and the realities of life they have become so estranged from their environment that they can no longer adapt to it. Their brains no longer work in the same way they did before. They are considered by their peers to be mentally ill.

The content of a person's fantasies and real experiences is stored in the cells of the brain. The cells regulate the way in which the stored material is utilized, presumably in response to external stimuli. It should be remembered that a patient could not display verbal hallucinations without "commands" from the brain cells to the muscles which produce the words of the hallucinations. Each part of the process seems to be extremely complicated and defies complete understanding up to the present time. This is particularly true for the crucial mechanisms which regulate the kinds of thoughts produced and the appropriateness of the resulting actions.

It is surprising that it has been possible to group the psychoses into any kind of taxonomic formulation when we contemplate the fact that no two people of the more than three billion alive today are identical. Even identical twins are not completely alike. However, millions of people are identical for a specific trait. There are millions of people who are identical for the blood antigen A_1; other millions are identical for a particular gene for hair color. The thousands of people who have the same, or a very similar, Mendelian dominant gene for Huntington's chorea are of great interest to us because these unfortunate people develop severe psychoses — often before the choreic motions appear. Thus we see that while no two people are precisely alike, large masses of them are alike for a particular trait. They are alike not only in the perceived expression of the trait but also in the genetics of the trait as a result of their descent from the same ancestors. It follows from this that some persons, and particularly those in the same genetic kinship, will have the same genes for a particular trait, either mental or physical. It should be clear that in one sense all traits are physical traits because all are in some way the products of cellular activity. No one considers psychiatry to be a subdivision of cell biology, but it might lead to faster progress in the area of mental health if more consideration were given to this point.

The study presented in this book is similar to the various family studies on psychotic disorders already in the literature. There are three important reasons why we are adding more data to the literature. The first is that we had a unique opportunity to start with a family study made by a group of workers at the beginning of the century and bring it up to date. The members of the families studied were of more than usual interest to the staff members at the Warren State Hospital, so items about the families were recorded which otherwise would have been ignored and lost. Thus we have a fairly continuous story for as many as five generations of people in relation to mental illness. The second reason for the existence of this book is that we have included the data for concordance or discordance of *other* kinds of mental illness in the relatives of the probands, whereas many studies have neglected this important consideration. The third reason is the obvious one that any careful study of the families of psychotics is of value because psychotic people are of the greatest social concern. The reduction of mental illness is a problem of pressing urgency.

REVIEW OF SOME OF THE LITERATURE

It would be impossible to review all of the literature concerning the relatives of psychotic persons. Therefore, we will consider only some of the publications which seem relevant to the major findings in this area. Later on, during the presentation of our results, there will be frequent references to additional studies which relate to our data. At this point we propose to write a short essay which, we hope, will provide the reader with a comprehension of the contributions made to an understanding of psychotic disorders that have resulted from the family studies of the past. The studies build upon the findings of previous efforts with a greater sophistication of analyses and results as time passes. However, the fundamental concept that psychotic disorders do not appear on a statistically random basis but instead are found in familial aggregations of biologically related people was demonstrated early in this century.

Age is clearly related to the appearance of a psychosis but age *in itself* is not a cause of psychosis; it is the things that go with increasing age that are related to mental illness. Social class has been implicated as being related to the type of mental disorder exhibited. As with age, there may be some components of social class which are prejudicial to good mental health, but these have not been demonstrated to everyone's satisfaction as yet.

The psychotic behavior of a person having the Mendelian dominant gene for Huntington's chorea resembles that seen in some schizophrenic patients, but with Hunting-

ton's chorea there is no reason to suspect that the patient's behavior has any important correlation with his interpersonal relationships with the members of his family or with anyone else. A not unusual experience with Huntington's chorea was that of a patient who insisted that she did not have the family disease and that her "nervousness" was the consequence of her divorce. Everyone else in the family agreed that her divorce was the result of her deteriorating personality and not the other way around.

Great emphasis has been placed on the role of interpersonal relationships in the etiology of psychotic disorders despite the evidence that these are not of great importance in the psychotic behavior of patients with Huntington's chorea, Marie's cerebellar ataxia, and other neurological disorders with a strictly Mendelian type of inheritance. The environment is certainly of importance in Huntington's chorea, but it is clearly an internal environment of cellular physiology that should be investigated for productive results. On the other hand, perhaps the expression of schizophrenia *is* affected by early interpersonal relationships and we will consider this point later on in the book.

EARLY FAMILY STUDIES

It is hard to know where to start our review of the family studies which have contributed to our understanding of the development of the psychotic disorders. We should mention Gregor Mendel, who was the first to comprehend how simple genetics operates. We cannot ignore Francis Galton, who demonstrated the advantages of twin studies for the gross determination of the relative importance of heredity and environment in the variations shown by a given trait. Mendel and Galton made their observations during the second half of the nineteenth century, but it was not until early in the twentieth century that science was sufficiently advanced so that intelligent questions about the etiology of psychotic disorders could be asked. This was partly because no good taxonomies of mental disorders were available. There is still much individual confusion of diagnosis even though a broad general concept of psychotic types has been established. However, Kraft-

Ebing, Kraepelin and Freud had given enough identity to the different psychotic disorders so that by the twentieth century a synthesis of data could begin.

The first family study to attempt to combine Mendelian genetics and some semblance of a taxonomic treatment of psychotic disorders was that by Rosanoff and Orr (1911). The field work for this study was done by Miss Florence Orr, who was the seventeenth field worker to be trained at the Eugenics Records Office at Cold Spring Harbor. Copies of her records are now at the Dight Institute and in excellent condition. Miss Orr was stationed at the King's Park State Hospital, King's Park, New York. Her data were collected on mimeographed forms bound in a booklet with a form for each ancestor and descendant. If the ancestor could not be found, the form for him was left blank. This system stimulated attempts to find all relevant persons for each kinship, a virtue not present in several studies of much more recent vintage. Their 40-page paper opens with a clear description of how Mendelian heredity works.

The second section of their paper opens with the following statements:

In selecting cases our aim has been to exclude all those forms of insanity in the causation of which exogenous factors, such as traumata, alcoholism, and syphilis, are known to play an essential part; and we have also systematically excluded psychoses which occur upon a basis of organic cerebral affections, such as tumors, arteriosclerosis, apoplexy, and the like.

In the actual analysis of the data collected in the course of our investigation the problem in each case was to distinguish, on the basis of information obtained by questioning the relatives, neuropathic states from the normal state and in the case of a neuropathic state to identify, if possible, the special variety.

We have endeavored to reduce the amount of diagnostic error by interviewing personally as many as possible of the nearest relatives of the patients whose pedigrees were being investigated, and by the practice of tracing almost all the families not farther than to the generation of the grandparents, for the farther back our inquiries extended the more scant and more vague was the information which we were able to obtain.

Unfortunately, Rosanoff and Orr had the same passionate belief that the Mendelian recessive gene was the basis of everything abnormal as did Davenport, Goddard and many other early American geneticists.

It is hard for us today to realize what a tremendously exciting concept simple Mendelian genetics was for the biologists of 1910–1930. It is not surprising, then, that after analyzing their data they state, in italics, *"It would seem, then, that the fact of the hereditary transmission of the neuropathic constitution as a recessive trait, in accordance with the Mendelian theory, may be regarded as definitely established."* This was an appropriate and intelligent conclusion at that time and their data did seem to support their contention. For instance, when both parents were affected they found that 54 of 64 offspring were affected. Of the 10 offspring who were not affected, when they should have been according to a single recessive gene theory, they state, "Of these ten one died at the age of thirty-eight years in an accident, during life suffered from asthma; another is described as easy going, is somewhat odd and possibly abnormal in make-up, is twenty-nine years of age; the rest are from eight to twenty-two years of age. In other words, in two of the ten subjects the neuropathic constitution is not positively excluded and the remaining eight have not reached the age of incidence."

Rosanoff and Orr obtained about 40 per cent affected children when one parent was affected and the other was normal. Their data gave higher percentages of affected children than would be obtained today for at least three reasons:

1. They probably selected "loaded" families for study, families biased toward higher percentages of affected individuals.

2. They selected from the resident population of the hospital, which would presumably have a higher proportion of affected relatives than would a random sample of probands who were first admissions. This point will be discussed later.

3. Their diagnostic category of affected persons was too broad as it included what they called epileptic and feeble-minded persons. They recognized that their neuropathic entities were clinically distinct but thought that they were "in some manner related to each other." Studies today may err in the opposite direction and exclude conditions which *are* genetically related to each other.

The next major contribution to our subject is an elegant 172 page book by Ernst Rüdin (1916) entitled *Zur Vererbung und Neuentstehung der Dementia praecox*. It is four times as long as the article by Rosanoff and Orr. Like these authors, Rüdin presents a description of simple Mendelian heredity but in a much more elaborate fashion. He was well aware of the problems of ascertainment of probands in relation to family size, and the fact that the same family may be ascertained through each of the various affected members. He adopted the Weinberg method of correcting for the age of onset of a noncongenital disorder. The greatest advance in Rüdin's book over the previous study is probably the greater sophistication of the diagnostic techniques. Dementia praecox is now separated from the other psychoses and attention is focused on it as the disorder of interest. Fortunately, the other psychoses were included, though separately from the cases of dementia praecox.

Rüdin's series of probands came from the Psychiatric Clinic in Munich. He eliminated siblings under 17 years of age from consideration, subtracted his probands and found that 4.5 per cent of the siblings of his probands also had dementia praecox. In addition, there were 4.1 per cent of the siblings who had other psychoses, so a total of 8.6 per cent of the siblings were psychotic, without age correction. These sibships were all from parents of whom neither one had a psychosis. We wish to point out that the "other psychoses" are practically as frequent as the cases of dementia praecox; this is approximately true of all other careful studies, including the present one.

In Rüdin's sample, where one parent of the proband had dementia praecox and the other was normal, the probands were subtracted, which left 6.2 per cent of the offspring with dementia praecox and 10.3 per cent with "another psychosis," for a total of 16.5 per cent of the siblings of the probands who were psychotic. We see again that the "other psychoses" are exceptionally frequent unless we consider them to have an etiology related to the cases of dementia praecox.

Rüdin realized that his data did not meet the criteria for heredity owing to a single pair of recessive genes and therefore tried to fit his data to the expected ratios for two pairs of genes. One can usually find a ratio to fit one's data by varying the number of pairs of genes included in the formula. Such efforts are not very convincing in most cases and suggest that the problem should be approached in some other way.

One of the classical family studies of schizophrenia *not* involving the use of twin data was the work of Kallmann (1938) at the Herzberge Hospital in Berlin. The 1087 schizophrenic probands represented the total number of schizophrenic case histories which were still available in the archives of the Herzberge Hospital from the first 10 years of its existence (1893–1902). His probands had to have been committed to the hospital during those 10 years, they had to have schizophrenia beyond a doubt, and their disease had to have become manifest before the age of 40.

Kallmann reviewed each of the old case histories and selected the 1087 cases out of about 15,000 as being certainly schizophrenic. This would seem to be a very low proportion of the total hospital population with schizophrenia and therefore probably represented a selection of more severely affected cases than one would find in an average public mental hospital. Kallmann's insistence on an undisputed diagnosis of schizophrenia for resident hospital patients leads us to suspect that there will be a higher percentage of affected relatives than if all first admissions with a functional psychosis had been selected. However, Kallmann was aware of the danger of selecting "loaded" families and apparently avoided this pitfall.

The total number of persons in the Kallmann study was 13,851. Of these, there were the 1087 probands and 3384 descendants of them, including a few great-great-grandchildren. Thus, approximately one-third of the total population of the study was made up of the probands and their descendants. The other two-thirds of the population were parents, siblings, nephews and nieces, and persons who married these blood relatives. There were two sets of relatives for which the information is of great significance because of the completeness of the data and because most of the persons had passed the danger period for the onset of a psychotic disorder. These relatives are the children and siblings of the 1087 probands.

The probands had 2000 children, of whom 1000 either were under age 15 or had died before reaching that age. There were

643 offspring, or almost two-thirds, who were still within the danger period for schizophrenia, and only 357 had passed their forty-fifth year. Of the 1000 offspring who had attained the danger period for schizophrenia, arbitrarily (but appropriately) set as the beginning of the fifteenth year, there were 111, or 11.1 per cent, who were definite or doubtful schizophrenic cases. In addition, there were 326 offspring who were classified as schizoid types, giving a total of 43.7 per cent of the offspring who were not normal. Furthermore, of the 56.3 per cent who were considered to be normal, a rather large number would still have been within the danger period and some would develop schizophrenia at a later time. There is no way of knowing how many of the offspring would have become schizophrenic but it is legitimate to estimate the number of additional cases to be expected by using some age of onset correction.

Kallmann tried various age of onset corrections and preferred the abridged method of Weinberg, which increased the frequency for schizophrenia in the offspring from the 11.1 per cent observed to 16.4 per cent expected in the future. Obviously, the 11.1 per cent is too low. Good descriptions of each of the offspring are included in the book and everyone would agree that these people were mentally ill. Furthermore, some age correction is called for, and the one used is reasonable and should not be greatly in error. There are two statements which would seem to us to be in order concerning these data.

1. The selection of such severe cases of mental disorder for probands may have given a higher percentage of affected offspring than would have occurred had the sample of probands been more representative.

2. The concept that *all* the 437 cases of mental anomalies observed among the 1000 offspring were either schizophrenia or schizoidia is acceptable to us only if it is considered that all persons everywhere who have a functional psychosis belong to the schizophrenic disease complex. It is doubtful whether anyone else would have diagnosed every single one of the 437 persons as being in the schizophrenic disease complex.

Let us now turn to the siblings of Kallmann's schizophrenic probands. There were 230 definite and doubtful schiz-

ophrenics among 2681 living and dead siblings of age 15 or older. This was then a minimal observed value of 8.6 per cent which when age-corrected became 11.5 per cent. Kallmann stated (page 121 of his book) that, "Theoretically the frequency of schizophrenia ought to be greater in the siblings than in the children, if we assume that schizophrenia is a recessive hereditary trait." He realized that his data were the opposite of his theory of recessive heredity, but did not seem embarrassed by the sharp contradiction between his excellent data and his theory.

Let us now survey Kallmann's very important data concerning the half siblings of his probands. These will be of two types: those in which the shared parent of the proband and the half sibling was schizophrenic; and those where the shared parent was not psychotic. In the first instance the half sibling was likely to have similar genetics for schizophrenia compared to the child of the proband, while in the second instance the half sibling would have two normal parents though one of the two also was the parent of a schizophrenic proband. The social class and many environmental factors would have been reasonably similar for the probands and their two types of half siblings, but the genetics of the two types of half siblings would be decidedly different. There were 21 half siblings of Kallmann's probands who shared the schizophrenic parent and of them five, or 24 per cent, were schizophrenic, while of the 57 half siblings for whom the shared parent was normal only one, or 1.8 per cent, was schizophrenic, a very striking difference. The high value of 24 per cent is an age-corrected value and may be compared with the 14.8 per cent of affected full siblings of the probands. Small sample size of the group of 21 half siblings would probably account for the excess of 24 per cent compared with the 14.8 per cent expectation. However, the very large difference between the two types of half siblings seems to be important information regarding the etiology of schizophrenia.

The nephews and nieces of Kallmann's probands were second-degree relatives of the probands and lived at about the same time as the children of the probands. They would share only one-quarter of the genes possessed by the probands and we can predict lower percentages of schizophrenia than those in the probands' sibships. We will not discuss the nephews and nieces here but will present now a summary of the data for the three sets of relatives of the probands, comprising more than 1500 persons of age 15 or older in each set. Even with 1500 or more persons in each of the three sets the size of some of the subsamples is too small to give complete stability to each percentage, but they are useful approximations for any populations in which the probands were rigidly selected for severity of the psychotic disorder. The summary data for the three sets of relatives are presented in Table 1–1. The data have been corrected by the abridged Weinberg method which adds from 25 to 50 per cent to the uncorrected values. Kallmann accepted a base rate or morbid risk for schizophrenia for general populations of about one per cent.

It will be seen in Table 1–1 that only 1.8 per cent of the half siblings of the proband were schizophrenic when the shared parent was not schizophrenic, and similarly only 1.8 per cent of the nieces and nephews of the proband were schizophrenic when neither parent was affected. The two findings of 1.8 per cent affected are probably not significantly different from Kallmann's es-

timate of 1.0 per cent schizophrenia as the base rate for the population. However, the 9.1 per cent affected full siblings of the probands, with both parents normal, is of interest because either the difference between 9.1 and 1.8 per cent is due to genetic differences or else the higher value of 9.1 results from the schizophrenic proband being present and successfully causing schizophrenia to appear in the sibling. The choice here is between a psychogenic effect of the schizophrenic proband upon a sibling, and the presence of genes in the two normal parents which resulted in one or more affected siblings of the proband. The latter mechanism is more appealing to the geneticist, though the difficulty of disentangling the relative effects of heredity and environment is extremely great.

The three categories in Table 1–1 where both parents were schizophrenic gave 63.4, 68.1 and 50.0 per cent schizophrenic offspring while most of the remaining offspring were not normal but had schizoidia, whatever that may be. In addition, there were substantial percentages of what Kallmann called "psychopathologic abnormalities *not* included in the schizophrenic disease-complex." Clearly, there are few really normal persons among the offspring of two schizophrenic parents.

Table 1–1. *Kallmann's Data (1938) for Three Sets of Relatives of His Schizophrenic Probands.*

	AGE CORRECTED PERCENTAGE AFFECTED WITH		
	SCHIZOPHRENIA	SCHIZOIDIA	TOTALS
I. *Children of the Probands*			
1. One parent affected (the proband)	11.9	26.8	38.7
2. Both parents affected	63.4	32.8	96.2
Average Combined Percentage	16.4	32.6	49.0
II. *Siblings of the Probands*			
A. *Full Siblings*			
1. Neither parent affected	9.1	4.4	13.5
2. One parent affected	14.8	10.2	25.0
3. Both parents affected	68.1	23.3	91.4
Average Combined Percentage	11.5	10.5	22.0
B. *Half Siblings*			
1. Shared parent not affected	1.8	2.7	4.5
2. Shared parent affected	24.0	23.1	47.1
Average Combined Percentage	7.6	7.9	15.5
III. *Nieces and Nephews of the Probands*			
1. Neither parent affected	1.8	2.6	4.4
2. One parent affected	21.4	16.8	38.2
3. Both parents affected	50.0	46.2	96.2
Combined Percentage	3.9	6.2	10.1

The next family study which we have selected for comment is that of Böök (1953). This study is of interest from numerous points of view, one of them being personal, in that we had the pleasure of having Jan and Ruth Böök at the Dight Institute during 1950 while they were analyzing the data from their North Swedish population. The work by the Bööks is useful for comparison with that of Franz and Helen Kallmann because the probands for the Kallmann studies originated in very large cities while the Böök probands were from three isolated parishes in Northern Sweden bordering Finland and about 50 miles north of the Arctic Circle (essentially a small rural isolate). There is an advantage in studying an isolate in that there should be less genetic and environmental heterogeneity than in the population of Berlin or New York State.

The three Swedish parishes had a total population of 8981 persons on December 31, 1949. The object of the study was a thorough statistical and genetic analysis of all major neuropsychiatric disorders which occurred in the area between January 1, 1902 and September 1, 1949. There were 347 probands and 17 secondary cases in that time, including a psychotic group, a mentally deficient group and a group of convulsive disorders. On September 1, 1949 there were present 106 psychotic cases, 99 mentally deficient cases and 35 with convulsive disorders. None of these cases was a minor disability, but there were some persons who had recovered. We shall consider only the 106 psychotic persons. The 106 persons had the following diagnoses. There were 93 who had schizophrenia or a similar psychosis, two manic-depressives, three involutional, one senile, two with encephalopathy and five with "other psychoses." The large majority with a schizophreniform-type psychosis is remarkable and perhaps peculiar to this particular isolate. All 93 cases may be genetically fairly homogeneous. This was strikingly demonstrated by the fact that there were only 285 sibships responsible for Böök's 364 probands, and 240 of the sibships could be joined into one large pedigree complex which goes back to 31 ancestral pairs who were living about 1700 to 1750.

The 93 cases of certain or probable schizophrenia included 85 certain and 8 probable schizophrenics. Of the 85 certain

cases, 18 had never had psychiatric treatment or had never been in a mental hospital. It is of interest that 56 of the cases were males and 37 were females. Only 25 per cent of the males were married while a surprising 73 per cent of the females were married. Fecundity of those schizophrenic males and females who did marry was as high as that of normal control persons in the area. Böök states, "The effective selection against the trait schizophrenia was only moderately expressed, the reproductive fitness was estimated at about 70 per cent."

The prevalence of schizophrenia, certain and probable, on September 1, 1949 was 93 cases in the total population of 8981 persons, or almost exactly 1 per cent. More important than this inclusive prevalence figure of 1 per cent is the morbid risk which expresses the probability that a newborn baby subsequently will develop schizophrenia if he lives to be 60 years old. In order to get the morbid risk one has to correct for age and for excess mortality. After Böök had made these necessary corrections there was a morbid risk of about 3 per cent, with no appreciable differences between the two sexes.

We have just seen that there is a probability of 1 per cent of a person having schizophrenia on a certain date in this North Swedish area and a 3 per cent chance that a person will have the disease if he or she survives to be 60 years old. If there is a relative with the disorder, the risk increases significantly for the other genetically related persons in the kinship. Böök found that the morbid risk for parents of the schizophrenic probands was 12.0 ± 2.7 per cent. Table 1–2 gives the morbid risks for parents and for siblings in his material. They agree well with Kallmann's results, shown in Table 1–1. The agreement is especially impressive when one keeps in mind that different methods of age correction were used and that Böök's sample sizes were small. Furthermore, the proband selection was very different; Böök included all persons in his study who were alive and resident in the three North Swedish parishes in 1949 and had any neuropsychiatric problem of major dimensions while Kallmann selected specifically for undeniable schizophrenic cases only, in a hospital population.

Böök showed statistically that there was less than one chance in 1000 that the mor-

Table 1–2. *Böök's Data (1953) for Relatives of His Schizophrenic Probands.*

These figures are the risk of developing schizophrenia by age 60 and are corrected for age and mortality.

	CORRECTED PERCENTAGE WITH SCHIZOPHRENIA
I. *Parents of the Probands*	12.0 ± 2.7
II. *Siblings of the Probands*	
Neither parent affected	7.7 ± 2.6
One parent affected	17.9 ± 7.3
Both parents affected	33.3 (not age corrected)
Average Combined Percentage	9.1 ± 1.9

bid risks shown by the parents and by the siblings of his probands were merely random fluctuations from the 3 per cent morbid risk for any person in his area of study. Thus, there is no question but that schizophrenia is familial, though this finding does not help us to allocate the variance between environmental and genetic factors.

There were only 11 patients who had received original diagnoses of manic-depressive psychosis in Böök's study area. Of these, there were only two whom he regarded as fairly typical manic-depressives. Synopses of these two patients were given in his paper but a diagnosis of schizophrenia instead of manic-depressive psychosis would have been difficult to reject.

Finally, there were three cases with involutional psychosis, one senile psychosis, three cases of acute confusional psychoses during pregnancy, one alcoholic psychosis and two borderline cases. None of these presented anything of interest to our general problem.

A few remarks concerning another most interesting isolate are in order because of the contrast with that of Böök. The study of Eaton and Weil (1953) occurred at the same time as Böök's work and with an equally rural isolate, the Hutterites of the Northern United States and Canada. This group was composed of 8542 persons, practically all descended from 101 married couples and their children who came to the United States between 1874 and 1877. The Hutterites and the North Swedish groups are of the same size, both are rural and without higher education, and both marry only

within their isolate. In both groups descent is from a small number of somewhat related individuals. Under these circumstances, we might expect some genes to become established and spread to some degree within the isolate while other genes would be lost from the group. This process of eventual fixation or elimination of particular genes during the history of a closed group of persons is expected in such populations.

While Böök found only two clear-cut cases of manic-depressive psychosis, Eaton and Weil found 74 cases of what seemed to be manic depression and only 17 cases of schizophrenia in their Hutterite population. It is most interesting that Eaton, a sociologist, and Weil, a psychiatrist, started their study of the Hutterites with the assumption that there would be little mental illness in this group. "They live a simple, rural life, have a harmonious social order and provide every member with a high level of economic security from the womb to the tomb." However, they found instead the highest frequency of depression so far recorded for any population!

The study of Eaton and Weil showed that, while the Hutterite culture could not prevent the appearance of mental disorders, it did provide a highly therapeutic atmosphere for their treatment. The onset of symptoms served as a signal for the entire community to demonstrate support and love for the patients. They received great encouragement and were considered to be ill rather than "crazy." But in this unique culture the prognoses for the patients seem to be about the same as they are in other Caucasian cultures.

MODERN FAMILY STUDIES

We turn now to a modern family study for a large population, rather than an isolate, and one in which all functional psychoses were included. The probands were successive first admissions to the Gaustad psychiatric hospital in Norway and all cases were included, regardless of the severity of the disorder. The sample size is adequate. Thus, the shortcomings of one sort or another found in the earlier family studies have been avoided to a considerable degree. The investigator, Professor Ödegård (1963 and 1972), also had the advantage of being able to check all the names against a complete register of all persons admitted to psychiatric hospitals in Norway since 1916. The values were age-corrected, the weights being based upon the age distribution of all first admissions from functional psychoses to psychiatric hospitals in Norway for 1936–1945. Ödegård found that the base rate for all functional psychoses for Norway was from 3 to 4 per cent. This is a valuable figure which could be used for studies in other countries because it is probably about as accurate as it is possible to obtain at present. There is no good evidence that the base rates vary significantly from country to country for the group of functional psychoses as a whole. The *base rate* is the morbid risk for persons in the danger period, does not include children, and is about three times the *prevalence*, which of course does include all children.

Some of the results of this excellent study by Ödegård (1963) are presented in Table 1–3. The results show without question that there is a familial elevation of the percentage of psychotic relatives among the first degree relatives (parents, sibs, children) of his probands. Note, however, that it is not necessary for the relatives to have the *same* psychosis as the probands, though this will often be the case. The manic-depressive probands had the highest frequency of affected relatives (12.4 per cent) and the paranoid probands the lowest frequency (6.6 per cent) of psychotic relatives but none of the groups is statistically significantly different from the average of 9.7 per cent for the whole material.

Ödegård found the same mass of "minor" mental deviations among the relatives of the probands as did Rosanoff and Orr, Rüdin, and Kallmann, with the morbidity being much higher in the most closely related groups. No other reasonable conclusion can be drawn but that much of what Kallmann called "Schizoidia" is called "Neurosis, Psychopaths, Criminals, Alcoholics and Others" by Ödegård. Naturally, the Schizoidia group and Ödegård's melange do not coincide completely but they must overlap to a great degree because in all studies they loom up as such a large group of the first degree relatives. Had Kallmann's children and siblings of his schizophrenic probands been averaged, there would have been about 14 per cent schizophrenic first degree relatives plus 22 per cent schizoidias. Ödegård's combined functional psychoses in the first degree relatives amounted to 9.7 per cent with an additional 22.6 per cent suffering from his "minor" mental deviations; together these add up to 36 per cent of the first degree relatives in Kallmann's study and 32.3 per cent of Ödegård's first degree relatives. The terminology is clearly different but isn't the biology likely to be similar? What other explanation can be supported than that Kallmann and Ödegård have used different terminology to describe the same phenomena?

We would go one step farther and ask whether there is a biological dichotomy between Kallmann's schizophrenia and schizoidia or whether he has made an arbitrary, though probably useful, cutting point along a graded range of severities of expression of a disease complex.

Ödegård recognizes that a crucial point for the problem of gene specificity is the degree of concordance between probands and psychotic relatives with regard to the clinical diagnosis. If there is one single gene locus for schizophrenia and a different

Table 1–3. *The Frequency of Psychotic Persons Among the First Degree Relatives of Ödegård's Unselected Probands.*

DIAGNOSIS OF PROBAND (Functional Psychosis)	TOTAL FIRST DEGREE RELATIVES	PSYCHOTIC RELATIVES	
		No.	*Per Cent*
Schizophrenia	832	84	10.1
Manic-depressive psychosis	154	19	12.4
Reactive-depression (psychotic)	120	11	9.2
Paranoid psychoses	152	10	6.6
Other functional psychoses	120	9	7.5
Total (all diagnoses)	1378	133	9.7
Expected number of psychotic relatives according to a base rate of 3.8 per cent		51.7	3.8

gene locus for manic-depressive psychosis, the first degree relatives should almost always have the same disorder as the proband. If multifactorial inheritance is the genetic basis for both schizophrenia and manic-depressive psychosis, rather than single gene loci, less agreement would be expected between the diagnoses of probands and relatives. This extremely important problem has not been adequately investigated in any of the previous studies.

There is always the danger of "contamination" of the diagnosis, that is, a tendency for the psychiatrist to give the same diagnosis to the other members of the same family who have a mental illness. Furthermore, the diagnosis of schizophrenia is given in over one-half of all cases of functional psychoses (in the United States), so there will naturally be more cases of schizophrenia present in the relatives of a schizophrenic than any other single type of functional psychosis, on a random basis. Thus a substantial part of the concordance for schizophrenia between the probands and their relatives could be purely coincidental. There is still another type of contamination of diagnosis resulting in dramatic variations in the proportions of schizophrenics to manic-depressives from state to state, from hospital to hospital, and from psychiatrist to psychiatrist. The net effect of this type of contamination would be to increase the diagnostic concordance between a proband and his relatives. Finally, the concordance could be increased owing to purely environmental similarities between first degree relatives which would be greater than the environmental similarities between unrelated families.

We do *not* propose that the clinical diagnoses are invalid or useless. Quite the contrary; patients are obviously very different in their illnesses and can be sorted into broad taxonomic groups. However, if these differences depend upon single independent gene loci we should expect an almost perfect concordance between a proband's diagnosis and that of his relative. Such high concordance did *not* appear in Ödegård's work, even though there was a strong tendency for the diagnosis to be the same in the proband and the psychotic relatives. We are presenting his 1972 data in Table 1–4 in order that the reader may make his own estimate as to whether the agreements between the expected and observed are high enough to support a "one gene–one disease" hypothesis or whether the concordances are actually rather low if one acknowledges the various diagnostic contaminations suggested in the previous paragraph.

The figures in Table 1–4 show beyond a doubt that the agreement between observation and expectation based on random distribution is poor. There is clearly a tendency for proband and relative to have the same diagnosis but the agreement is not very good. In only 512 out of the 824 relatives (62.1 per cent) was their diagnosis the

Table 1–4. *Condensation of Ö. Ödegård's Table 11–IV.*[*]

| | DIAGNOSES IN THE RELATIVES | | | |
DIAGNOSIS IN THE PROBANDS	*Schizophrenic Relative*	*Reactive Psychosis Relative*	*Affective Relative*	*Total*
Schizophrenic proband	426 (375.8)	107 (129.0)	123 (151.3)	656
Reactive psychosis proband	23 (47.0)	39 (16.1)	20 (18.9)	82
Affective proband	23 (49.3)	16 (16.9)	47 (19.8)	86
Total	472	162	190	824

$$\chi^2 = 112.1 \quad d/f = 4 \quad p < .001$$

[*]From Kaplan: *Genetic Factors in Schizophrenia.* 1972, p. 267.

The figures in parentheses are the expectations if no association is present between the diagnoses of the proband and of his relatives.

same as that of the proband. There may be some diagnostic contamination which would give some spurious agreement.

It was possible to calculate the G statistic for the data in Table 1–4. This is similar to the usual Pearsonian correlation. $G = 0.53 \pm 0.05$, and is a correlation too high to be a chance association between the diagnoses of the probands and their relatives. (For a discussion of the applications of the G statistic see Garrison, Anderson and Reed [1968].)

One of the important advances in psychiatric genetics is the departure from the old notion that the relatives of a patient should have the same diagnosis as the patient. It is true that when siblings have a psychosis it is often the same one. But that is *not* the interesting finding; it is the diagnostically discordant sibling pairs that provide the crucial information. In the broad diagnostic groups of Table 1–4 only 62.1 per cent of the relatives had the same diagnosis. The study of Tsuang (1967) compared pairs of siblings who were diagnosed blindly by one person, Dr. Eliot Slater. He found that 41 per cent of the diagnoses of the sibs were alike, whereas 36 per cent of the diagnoses would be expected to be alike on a pure chance basis. The slight concordance of the diagnoses of relatives, in excess of chance agreement, would seem to be fatal to almost any monogenic hypothesis but entirely acceptable on a multigenic hypothesis. Studies of the dizygotic twins have not been helpful in this regard because in almost all cases the probands selected were relatively pure schizophrenics rather than covering the whole range of the functional psychoses.

Another of the non-twin family studies to receive attention is that of Garrone (1962). We include this work not only because it is a modern study but also because an important innovation in it is the extension of the risk period from the usual 45 to 50 year termination to 70 years. He showed that in Geneva, at least, by age 50 a male had achieved 74 per cent of his risk of becoming schizophrenic while a female of age 50 had only passed 62 per cent of her risk. Even at age 70 a person had only passed 95 per cent of the risk if a male, and 97 per cent of the risk for a female. Larson and Nyman (1970) confirmed this important point.

A very important paper which relates to our own study is that of Lindelius and Kay (1970). It is a family study of schizophrenia in rural Sweden which includes all psychotic relatives, not just those with diagnoses of schizophrenia. Their results for the nieces and nephews of the probands, for instance, are practically identical with ours and will be considered in detail in Chapter Nine of this book.

One of the recent projects of the group at the Washington University School of Medicine in St. Louis, Missouri will be considered now. A paper from the group by McCabe, Fowler, Cadoret and Winokur (1971) is of particular interest in relation to the problem of disagreements in diagnoses between probands and relatives. They found that for schizophrenic probands of *poor* prognosis there were 15.1 per cent of their first degree relatives with confirmed or suspected schizophrenia and in addition 4.5 per cent had a confirmed or suspected affective disorder. The schizophrenic probands with *good* prognosis, on the other hand, had only 5.5 per cent of the relatives with schizophrenia and 20.1 per cent with affective disorder. They consider their data to indicate a "very great overlap between good prognosis schizophrenia and schizo-affective disorder." The relatives display a spectrum of disorders running from the pole of schizophrenia to that for the affective disorders. Apparently, the more seriously ill relatives are to be found at the schizophrenic pole and the less seriously ill at the affective disorder pole.

Every family study is different in methodology from the others. Naturally, they all provide somewhat different results. Some studies had probands with a narrow diagnosis of schizophrenia and used this basis consistently for the relatives, as did Hallgren and Sjögren (1959). Others, such as that of Ödegård (1972), included consecutive hospital admissions for all functional psychoses. The combination of a large number of slightly different studies provides a larger population size but a mishmash of results. However, such compilations may demonstrate relationships that are less conspicuous in the individual studies. For instance, Table 28 in Slater and Cowie (1971) emphatically demonstrates that among 8505 siblings of schizophrenic index cases there were 10.2 per cent with schizophrenia, although 13.9 per cent of the 1227 children of the schizophrenic probands were affected. The large sizes of the combined samples lend strength to the conclusion that the frequency of schizophrenia is higher in the children of the probands than in the siblings of the probands. This seems to be a firm finding and argues against a monogenic recessive hypothesis in which siblings should have a higher incidence of schizophrenia than the children of the probands. Nor does the finding support a monogenic dominant hypothesis where siblings and children should show the same incidence. It is slightly favorable to a multigenic system in that greater environmental effects are usually expected, as would seem to be the case here. The excess morbidity in the children compared with the siblings could be the result of the transmission of some environmental factor from parent to offspring.

One of the reasons it is a little hazardous to combine studies from different countries, as did Zerbin-Rüdin (1967), is that the diagnostic concepts vary so greatly from place to place. A very recent study of differences in diagnostic concepts is that of Edwards (1972). This work compared attitudes of British and American psychiatrists concerning symptom importance in the diagnosis of schizophrenia. Thought disorder ranked first among the top 10 symptoms in both countries but there was no agreement in rank order for the other nine. Hallucinations were considered to be of primary importance in the diagnosis by 68.7 per cent of the American psychiatrists but only 25.6 per cent of the British psychiatrists were of this opinion. Classical cases would receive the same diagnosis anywhere in the world but the large mass of patients who deviate from the classical picture of schizophrenia or manic-depressive psychosis are likely to receive different diagnoses in each case from different psychiatrists.

Let us turn now to the twin studies to see if we can get some leverage on the problem of identifying a few of the factors which are transmitted from generation to generation and result in psychotic disorders. We would like most to identify some of the environmental factors involved, as it is probably easier to alter an environment in a desired direction than it is to direct gene mutation in a specific way.

SOME OF THE TWIN STUDIES

Sir Francis Galton was the first to publicize the utility of the comparison of identical (one egg, one sperm) twins with fraternal (two eggs, two sperms) twins for research purposes. Luxenburger (1928) was the first to adapt the twin technique to the study of psychotic disorders. He emphasized the importance of obtaining a complete representative series of twins rather than combining the single cases reported in the literature or asking hospitals to supply the names of patients recalled as being twins. He showed that when these faults exist, the one egg twins almost always are both affected (that is, concordant) and the two egg twins are usually discordant, the proband being affected while the other twin is normal. He showed that for single case reports in the literature, 91 per cent of the monozygotic twins were concordant, but in his representative series only 66.7 per cent of the monozygotic twin pairs were found to have the second member of the pair also affected. Neither value was age-corrected.

We will coin now what might be called Luxenburger's axiom: The greater the bias of the sample, the higher the concordance of the monozygotic twins for the trait being studied. Luxenburger pointed out that the twin pairs should be selected in a defined place and at a defined time and in a completely inclusive fashion. We might add that the original selection should be diagnostically broad enough to include all of the persons who do have the diagnosis in question in order that the mild forms of the disorder not be excluded from the analysis. It is appropriate to separate mild and severe forms in one's tables but it is an error to omit the mild expressions of a disorder from the study. Luxenburger probably committed this last error in his study, at least to the point where he "carefully excluded every case which appeared in any way suspicious or doubtful."

Rosanoff was the first to do an important family study of psychotic disorders and the second to publish a large twin study. Rosanoff et al. (1934) collected 1014 pairs of twins with mental disorders. Of these, 142 pairs represented cases of dementia praecox or schizophrenia in one or both twins of each pair. Rosanoff recognized the validity of Luxenburger's strictures concerning the collection of twin material but it is not clear just how well he observed them in collecting the 142 pairs of twins with schizophrenia. The zygosity of the twins seems to have been determined as well as it was possible to do in 1934.

It is obvious that Rosanoff challenges any unitary diagnostic concept of schizophrenia, as the following quotation illustrates: "It is hardly necessary to labor the point that the so-called schizophrenic psychoses constitute a heterogeneous group. It seems probable that this group contains acute, subacute, chronic, and deteriorating psychoses which bear to one another little or no pathologic or etiologic relationship." Rosanoff had a flourishing psychiatric practice and was personally acquainted with the great differences among schizophrenics. Some of Rosanoff's conclusions are as follows:

1. Hereditary factors seem to play an important part in the etiology of so-called schizophrenic psychoses. This is revealed in the contrast between monozygotic and dizygotic twins with respect to the proportion of cases of both twins of the pair being affected. These proportions were, respectively, 68.3 per cent and 14.9 per cent. No age corrections were made.

2. The hereditary factors are often inadequate to produce a psychosis. This is shown by the cases in which *only one* of the pair of monozygotic twins is affected (31.7 per cent in his study). Rosanoff stated, "It is not unlikely that the percentage of cases of complete discordance is even higher than that indicated by our material. It is a question whether, in gathering our material, we have fully succeeded in avoiding the danger of overloading the collection with cases of both twins affected."

We have found in the family study review that the resident population of a mental hospital ends up with a large proportion of patients who are much more severely affected than all patients at first admission or those who never are admitted to a mental hospital. Rosanoff's solicited twin sample can be assumed to have the highest concordance of all, and any study in which the concordance for identical twins is over 60 per cent (uncorrected) is likely to be significantly biased.

The Swedish twin study of Essen-Möller (1941) was the first one to be correctly designed. His material consisted entirely of consecutive admissions to three mental hospitals and a psychiatric clinic over a period of about 11 years. He investigated all of the twins personally, irrespective of diagnosis, and not just typical cases of specific disorders. No cases were excluded on grounds of uncertain zygosity. The case histories were presented so the reader could make his own diagnoses or at least ponder about any disagreements which seemed to emerge. Essen-Möller paid great attention to the clinical features, giving the possible environmental factors close scrutiny, and attempted to discover what aspects of mental illness were genetically influenced.

Unfortunately, this elegant approach provided only 69 useful pairs of twins of all diagnoses, and only 21 of the 69 pairs were monozygotic. Of the 21 pairs of monozygotic twins only 8 probands were unquestionably schizophrenic. Thus the sample is too small to be statistically decisive, though it is of clinical importance because of the careful personal investigation of the co-twins by Essen-Möller. He did not find any of the co-twins to be psychologically identical to its proband twin, although *none* of the co-twins was normal, including the one who was discordant in 1941 but was discovered later by Kaij (1960) to have developed a clear-cut schizophrenia with two years of hospitalization. This discovery was accidental and part of a study of alcoholism in twins. The chance discovery of this psychotic co-twin who was psychiatrically "normal" when seen at age 29 by Essen-Möller illustrates the need for follow-up of the co-twins until they die or for an appropriate age correction if one is interested in obtaining concordance figures. Essen-Möller (1970) revisited his co-twins, except for one who died shortly after the first examination, and found that 4 of 8 had been admitted to a mental hospital. Furthermore, 6 of 8 had suffered at least mild mental disorder.

The best known family study of psychotic disorders in the United States is the twin-family project carried out in New York State by Franz J. Kallmann, M.D., his wife and their associates. Their efforts have done more than those of any other group to remind American psychiatrists and others that psychotic behavior must be related to one's genetics in some important way.

It is natural that such an influential study should be scrutinized very carefully in detail, but much of the criticism of Kallmann's data has been unscientific and trivial. There is no point to making a big issue out of whether the zygosity of his twins was correct in every instance, because his sample size is so large that reversal of zygosity in several cases would have no significant effect upon his results.

Kallmann's (1946 and 1950) reports make up for their experimental design demerits by the quantity of data. It is almost unbelievable that by the time of the 1950 paper he had collected 1232 psychotic twin index cases and their numerous relatives over a period of only nine years. The 1232 twin index cases included 953 who were schizophrenic, 75 manic-depressives, 96 involutionals and 108 senile psychoses.

In the 1950 paper Kallmann states his taxonomic criteria very clearly and it is appropriate to quote his statement of his commitment:

The classification of *schizophrenia* was extended to include the simple, atypical (mixed, diluted) and pseudoneurotic varieties, the acute confusional states precipitated by extreme stress, and the so-called schizo-affective reaction syndrome, in addition to the usual episodic or progressive (deteriorating) types of hebephrenic, catatonic or paranoid coloring, as distinguishable by a disintegrative bend in personality development. The diagnosis of *manic-depressive psychosis* was restricted to cases showing acute, self-limited and unadulterated mood swings of a manic or depressive variety before the fifth decade of life and no progressive or residual personality disintegration before or following psychotic episodes. Reactive or neurotic (situational) depressions were not included in the survey, while primary menopausal and presenile depressions, agitated anxiety states and other non-periodical forms of depressive behavior in the involutional period (50–69) were in the category of *involutional psychosis*, together with the typical cases of involutional melancholia characterized by agitated depressions with paranoid features. Manifestation of a delusional or depressive syndrome after the age of 70 led to the classification of *senile psychosis*.

Kallmann continues,

The uniform application of this longitudinal scheme of psychiatric diagnosis resulted in the distinct impossibility of finding any pair of monozygotic twin partners, whose clinical symptomatology would have warranted their placement into two different diagnostic categories within the range of psychoses studied.

What does this last statement mean? It would seem to say that a non-periodic depressed monozygotic twin of 69 would be classified as an involutional psychosis and that it would be impossible for the co-twin to become depressed and be classified as a senile psychosis at age 70.

Furthermore, Kallmann states that

In the *dizygotic* sample of index pairs, the only diagnostic discrepancies, overriding the dividing lines between our main groups of psychoses, consist of four opposite-sexed pairs showing varying combinations of schizophrenic, involutional, and senile psychoses. Otherwise, our material offers neither a dizygotic pair with a schizophrenic psychosis in one member and with a manic depressive psychosis in the other nor a single manic depressive index family with an authentic case of schizophrenia among the parents and siblings of the index cases.

It would take a great deal of faith to believe that there would be no single exception to perfect diagnostic concordance in all these hundreds of families in view of Ödegård's family study. We can believe that each of Kallmann's affected persons was mentally ill but it seems unlikely that every one of them would have been concordant had he diagnosed them blind without knowledge of the diagnosis of the proband.

We must not let our criticisms obscure the elegant aspects of Kallmann's work. His project displays the most interesting array of types of sibships imaginable. These are shown in Table 1–5. All five types of siblings could theoretically be raised in the same household with somewhat similar environments. Table 1–5 gives our arrangement of Kallmann's (1953) data for three of his four diagnoses. The two figures in parentheses are estimates, as there were no published data for these two types of step siblings in his book.

The rationale for stating that these data give evidence of the presence of genetic factors in the etiology of the three psychoses is simply that the percentages of affected siblings vary more than common sense would lead one to expect if the variations were entirely dependent upon environmental differences within the family. The percentages for the different kinds of af-

Table 1–5. *Kallmann's (1953) Five Types of Siblings.*

The proband was a twin in each case and the age-corrected percentage of schizophrenia, manic-depressive psychosis or involutional psychosis in the various types of siblings is shown.

	GENETIC CONCORDANCE	SCHIZOPHRENIA	MANIC-DEPRESSIVE PSYCHOSIS	INVOLUTIONAL PSYCHOSIS
MZ twin siblings	100.0	85.8	96.7	60.9
DZ twin siblings	50.0	14.7	26.3	6.9
Ordinary siblings	50.0	14.3	23.0	6.9
Half siblings	25.0	7.0	16.7	4.5
Step siblings	0.0	1.8	(0.8)	(2.0)

fected siblings parallel the known genetic relationships with fidelity. The environmental factors probably also parallel the genetic relationships between the five types of siblings but the proof of this is still to come, whereas the evidence for the genetic relationship, which is the consequence of meiosis, is incontrovertible. The 85.8 per cent chance that a monozygotic twin sibling will develop schizophrenia is 49 times as great as the 1.8 per cent chance that a step sibling will be affected. It is difficult to understand this difference unless the genetic relationship is of importance.

Kallmann's mass of data allows us to come to grips with an important aspect of the relative importance of environmental and genetic factors in the risk for schizophrenia and the other endogenous psychoses. From an *environmental* point of view one would certainly expect that the offspring of two schizophrenic parents should have a greater risk of schizophrenia than a monozygotic co-twin where both parents were normal and the twins were separated for many years. But such was *not* the case. Only 68.1 per cent of the offspring of two schizophrenic parents were expected to develop the disorder, while the expectation for the separated monozygotic co-twin was higher, 77.6 per cent. It should be mentioned that a multigenic hypothesis for schizophrenia would predict something less than 100 per cent of the offspring of two affected parents to have a genetic potentiality for schizophrenia.

A comparison of the data in Kallmann's 1938 study of schizophrenia in the families of German probands with his 1946 New York State families shows no significant differences between the two populations. If adjustments are made for sample size and other design differences, we find only one unexplainable difference among all the studies so far reviewed and that difference involves the diagnostic question of why Kallmann in his two large populations never had a manic-depressive member of a schizophrenic family and vice versa. There is no way of answering this question, except to admit that the diagnosis of psychoses seems to be somewhat a matter of taste — and Kallmann's taste was unique.

Kallmann devoted about half of the 1946 paper and a good portion of his 1953 book to an examination of non-genetic factors that might account for the differences in morbidity between monozygotic and dizygotic twins. No discrete environmental factors could be identified, despite his extensive efforts to do so. The fact remains that for the subsample of 60 monozygotic twin pairs with the most *dissimilar* environments the expectation for concordance was still 65 per cent, while the dizygotic twins with the most similar environments were concordant only 8 per cent of the time.

The next study for discussion is that of Slater (1953). It is a study of twin patients with at least one of the pair being hospitalized in the London area. All probands, whether diagnostically typical or not, were allocated to one of four groups — schizophrenic (156), affective (38), organic (49) and personality disorders or neuroses (52). Even with a sample of this size there were only eight pairs of monozygotic twins in whom the proband twin was in the *affective* group, and four of the eight pairs were concordant. There were 41 pairs of monozygotic twins in whom the proband twin had schizophrenia, and 28 of the co-twins (68 per cent, without age correction) were also schizophrenic. Slater made a careful clinical study of the patients and their first degree relatives. This permitted a study of possible reasons for the discordance of the 13 pairs of monozygotic twins out of the 41 pairs where the proband was schizophrenic.

Rosenthal (1959) and later Gottesman and Shields (1966) reanalyzed Slater's published material from several points of view. Rosenthal found that in the discordant male pairs the future schizophrenic twin had the poorer social and sexual history. Gottesman and Shields pointed out that 3 of the 13 discordant pairs might have been organic cases rather than endogamous schizophrenics, while in 5 more of the 13 the co-twin died several years before the proband twin was admitted to the hospital. Some co-twins may have been borderline cases, suggesting a continuum of schizophrenic psychopathology.

We are particularly interested in Slater's finding that while, for instance, schizophrenia is highest among the relatives of schizophrenics and affective mental illness is highest among the families of the probands in the affective group, the concordances are far from perfect. Like all other workers except Kallmann, Slater finds many diagnostic discordances between the relatives and the probands.

In closing this section on studies of hospitalized twin probands, we should mention that Inouye (1963) found that the data for schizophrenia in Japan agreed nicely with those already cited for Caucasian populations. Inouye's monozygotic twins were 76 per cent concordant for schizophrenia and for the dizygotic twins 22 per cent, with both figures age-corrected. Furthermore, Inouye showed that concordance was highest with the most severely affected twin probands.

NOVEL TWIN STUDIES

We mean both new and unusual in our use of the word "novel" for the twin studies now to be considered. The first of these studies is a large book devoted to the products of a single fertilized egg. The book was edited by Rosenthal (1963) and is entitled *The Genain Quadruplets*. It is the story of identical quadruplet girls concordant for schizophrenia who were studied by Rosenthal and 23 collaborators at the National Institute of Mental Health in Bethesda, Maryland. The four descendants of a single fertilized egg hardly comprise a statistical sample but they are of clinical interest as they were in the public eye since birth and their behavior was well documented.

The father of the quadruplets held down a sinecure job as a petty public official but seldom went to his office; usually he sat around the house and drank beer when it was available. On one occasion he ran around the outside of the house shooting his revolver in order to frighten away imaginary intruders. However, he adjusted to society to the extent of avoiding hospitalization. It was impossible to determine any age of onset for schizophrenia in the quadruplets even though the evidence was detailed and voluminous. The girls were different from other children at an early age and gradually became more so. In Rosenthal's words,

The girls seemed to have had characteristics from a very early age that may best be described as constrictive. They had low energy levels, were rather placid, "sweet," introversive, not very talkative, communicative, or outgoing, and they took little initiative either with respect to general activities or interpersonal relationships. On top of this behavioral pattern was imposed a severely constrictive family regimen, their parents transcending all bounds of reasonableness in this regard. Environmental constriction was heaped upon inherited constriction. When the girls became ill, the predominant feature of their illness was extreme constriction as manifested by catatonic symptoms.

The Genain quadruplets were studied at the National Institute of Mental Health while they were in their twenties. It was found that all four girls and their father, but not their mother, had a 4 to 7 per second occipital slow wave EEG. There was a history of psychiatric disorders in the paternal family but not the maternal family. However, the type of EEG abnormality most frequently reported in schizophrenic groups is not the type found in the Genain family. Nevertheless, the quadruplets displayed the constellation of EEG pattern, enuresis, physical and emotional immaturity and behavioral disorder which may well be a manifestation of a common diathesis of a relatively specific type.

The quadruplets are four women with identical genetics and concordant for schizophrenia. No psychiatrist would have diagnosed them as anything else. The problem of the etiology of schizophrenic subtypes of the four identical genotypes is clarified somewhat here. The father and his mother were paranoid types while the girls all received a diagnosis of catatonia and also of "undifferentiated" schizophrenia. In addition, three of them received diagnoses of hebephrenia or hebephrenic features. At other episodes two of them were thought to have paranoid features. The fact that nearly all the subtypes of schizophrenia were found in the presence of one single genotype indicates that subtype differences in the quadruplets had to have an environmental basis. Even Kallmann did not find any striking concordance between subtypes among relatives. Thus we see that the one genotype present in the quads resulted in different subtypes because of trivial environmental differences previous to different psychotic episodes.

While no definite age at onset could be determined for the quads, they were concordant in that all were diagnosable as schizophrenic while in their late teens or early twenties. There is no question that the development of mental illness in the girls was a gradual process which started very early. The most severely affected girl was the lightest in weight at birth and had the most health problems from the beginning. But their psychological problems began very early also and these were of the type psychologists have thought about but have not elucidated very well. These problems involve the relationships between parent and child, which in this case were particularly stressful because their parents could not enjoy the individual differences which would have appeared if the quads had been fraternal rather than identical quadruplets. Instead, the girls were classified at birth, or soon thereafter, into a hierarchy of four and this peck order was maintained thereafter. We cannot take space to reproduce the information available in Rosenthal's book as to how the girls diverged in personality traits because of the differences in their positions in a psychologically gruesome family situation. These differences in life experience resulted in great differences in the severity and outcome of their schizophrenia. The girl at the bottom of the peck order is severely regressed and a patient in a state hospital, where she will probably stay for the rest of her life. The least severely affected of the four is married and has one child. Life within her new family is apparently endurable but probably not enjoyable. The other two girls are unmarried and vary in their adaptability to society over the years, with little likelihood of a very satisfying future.

We have learned from the Genain quadruplets that wide variations in subtypes of schizophrenia and in severity and outcome of the disease are non-genetic because the quads all had the same genotype.

The study of Kringlen (1966) warns us that the high concordance where the affected proband twins were selected from hospital populations may not be replicated in twin samples selected in other ways. The impression will probably become established that Kringlen examined about 24,000 pairs of twins and personally determined which among them had one or both members affected with a psychosis. This was by no means the case! Kringlen obtained his probands in much the same way that all other investigators have obtained theirs. Each of his proband twins had been seen by another physician and reported as psychotic before Kringlen saw the proband. In other words, the first ascertainment of the psychosis of the proband twin was in all cases made by someone other than Kringlen and reported to the National Register of Psychosis where Kringlen obtained the name of the proband. Kringlen's advantage was that by use of the twin registry he could find those twins in the Psychosis Registry who had *not* been designated as twins by the Psychosis Registry. The major unanswered questions regarding his study are whether the concordance between monozygotic twins is low (31 of 69, or 45 per cent) because of the methodology, or because Scandinavians are different from Germans, Japanese and Swiss, or because of some other unknown reason. Family studies such as those of Böök (1953) and Ödegård (1972) give no hint that the Scandinavians are less psychotic than any other people.

It is our impression that the rather low concordance shown by Kringlen's monozygotic twins results from the less severely ill twins in the population being included in contrast to the early studies composed of severely deteriorated probands who had been hospitalized for many years and who presumably had a heavier genetic loading for the disorder.

A study by Allen, Cohen and Pollin (1972) gives a similarly low concordance of monozygotic twins (43 per cent) in United States military veterans. They were selected for good mental health to some degree at the time of induction into the armed services. These cases, therefore, should display a lesser severity of the disorder than that in the general population. Presumably the concordance would be lower if diagnostic concepts are comparable for the veterans and the general public.

The passage of time has been accompanied by more elegant methodologies being employed in the studies of schizophrenic twins. An excellent example of this improvement is the twin-family project which is being carried out by Gottesman and Shields (1972). Through the foresight of Dr. Eliot Slater, Director of the Medical Research Council's Psychiatric Genetics Research Unit in the United Kingdom, a register of all twins seen at the Maudsley and Bethlem Royal Joint Hospital was kept from 1948 onward. These hospitals are short-stay hospitals with large outpatient departments. The members of the twin population studied by Gottesman and Shields were all consecutive admissions. It was not the same population as that of state hospital type twin studies done by Slater (1953). Gottesman and Shields' sample presumably included all patients who were sick enough to have received a diagnosis of schizophrenia, the great mass of whom were not twins, of course. Those so mildly affected as to fail to receive outpatient attention, at least, were not available for the proband sample. Only same-sexed twins were included in the sample. Zygosity was determined by a combination of blood grouping, fingerprint analysis and resemblance in appearance. Both Gottesman and Shields have had extensive experience in modern zygosity determination and their judgment that no pair was misclassified is presumably valid.

Their series of schizophrenic patients consisted of 62 probands from 57 twin pairs; in five pairs both twins had been patients at the Maudsley Hospital in their own right. There were 30 pairs of male twins and 27 pairs of female twins, an indication that representative samples can be expected to have

about an equal number of schizophrenic males and females. The sample was composed of 24 monozygotic pairs and 33 dizygotic pairs of twins. The twins ranged in age from 19 to 65 with an average age of 37.5 years. Gottesman and Shields expect some of the presently unaffected co-twins to have breakdowns in future years, which should increase the concordance rates to a significant degree. The use of conventional Weinberg age correction raised the concordance rates for the hospitalized patients from 42 to 69 per cent for the monozygotic twins and from 9 to 17 per cent for the dizygotic pairs. However, rather than confuse the reader, they reported the rest of their results without any kind of age correction.

Gottesman and Shields realized the necessity of including other functional psychoses in viewing the co-twins of their twin probands. The probands were selected because of their diagnosis of schizophrenia (Grade 1). So, without necessarily implying a diagnostic continuum, concordance rates were also given for psychiatric hospitalization of any kind (Grades $1+2$), and for any noteworthy degree of personality disruption (Grades $1+2+3$), while "normal" co-twins were given Grade 4. As can be seen in Table 1–6, in 79 per cent of the pairs both co-twins were abnormal, the abnormality ranging from psychiatric hospitalization for schizophrenia to having once been treated by a general practitioner for a transient anxiety state. It is quite remarkable that this diagnostic broadening increased the monozygotic agreement from 42 to 79 per cent, but the increase from 9 to 45 per cent in agreement for the dizygotic twins was proportionally much greater.

We should mention as our final example of novel twin studies the work of Pollin and collaborators (1965 and 1966). They are studying a selected sample of 11 pairs of discordant MZ twins over a long period of time in order to detect the environmental factors which may result in the appearance of schizophrenia. Unfortunately, their sample of 11 pairs of discordant twins is unrepresentative of any usual schizophrenic population. The sample was obtained by inquiring via a form letter whether any psychiatrists or psychiatric institute in the United States knew of families which met their criteria, a method similar to that used by Rosanoff and his collaborators

Table 1–6. *Change in Concordance with Increase in Breadth of Diagnosis.*
(Adapted from Gottesman and Shields, 1966.)

	MONOZYGOTIC PAIRS			DIZYGOTIC PAIRS		
	Number	Per Cent		Number	Per Cent	
Both twins hospitalized for schizophrenia	10	42	} 54	3	9	} 18
Second twin with other psychiatric hospitalization	3	12	} 79	3	9	} 45
Second twin with treated personality disorder	6	25		9	27	
Second twin normal	5	21		18	55	
	24	100		33	100	

in 1934. Rosenthal and Van Dyke (1970) have studied the 11 co-twins and found their mean full-scale IQ on the WAIS to be 130, clearly a group representative of the top social classes. The presence of schizophrenia in the index twins must have contributed to a decrease in their IQs, with a mean of only 109.7.

Our view of Pollin's 11 pairs of twins, which were selected because they were both monozygotic and discordant for frank schizophrenia, is that the environmental factors which pushed one identical twin into schizophrenia were fairly trivial ones that would have had little effect on children with more resistant genotypes.

In concluding our comments on the twin studies, it is clear that the "true" value for concordance between monozygotic twins for psychoses of the schizophrenic, manic-depressive types would be about 50 per cent. The concordance for same-sexed dizygotic twins will be about 15 per cent. There can be no question but that this difference of some 35 per cent is real and of great importance. We are still left, however, without proof as to how much of the difference is environmental and how much is genetic, even in the simplest sense.

OTHER TYPES OF STUDIES

The literature relevant to the etiology of the psychoses has accumulated at an ever-increasing rate during recent years. We will at least mention some of the most relevant papers at this point and defer other articles for consideration later on in the book. We will group the papers according to the areas in which the advances were made.

Adoption Studies. The potentialities of this approach are considerable. Children were placed for adoption because of psychosis in the mother and many years later were scored for mental health. It was found that about 16 per cent of the adopted children became psychotic during their lifetimes. This frequency is not significantly different from the expectation for children reared by their psychotic parent. The conclusion from these results is that the primary etiology for the psychoses studied is perinatal. That is, the causes of the psychoses have produced their effects by the time the child is born or within a few months thereafter. Genetics and deleterious maternal influences seem to be the most likely causes of the later psychotic behavior. This work should concentrate attention on the genetic component and especially should lead to a more intense search for noxious factors affecting the fetus.

The first of the adoption studies which we will consider are those of Heston (1966 and 1967). His courage in initiating this project is commendable. One of us (S.C.R.) once obtained the backing of the National Welfare League to carry out this type of study but other activities prevented initiation of the venture.

Heston's experimental subjects were born between 1915 and 1945 to schizophrenic mothers confined to an Oregon State psychiatric hospital. All apparently normal children born of such mothers during this time span were included if the mother's hospital record specified a diagnosis of schizophrenia or psychosis and the mother and child had been separated from birth. All the babies were discharged from the State hospital within three days of birth to the care of family members or to foundling homes. Children were not included, however, if released to maternal relatives; children released to paternal relatives were accepted. None of the children were returned to suspected schizophrenogenic environments. The starting number of 74 babies ended with 47 experimental subjects mainly because 15 children died before reaching school age. A like number of control subjects were selected from the records of the same foundling homes that received some of the experimental subjects. The control subjects were matched for sex, type of eventual placements (adoptive, foster family or institutional), and for length of time in child care institutions.

Starting in 1964, Heston accounted for all of the original subjects except five persons, all females. Tremendous amounts of information were obtained, since for most subjects the psychiatric assessment included a personal interview, a Minnesota Multiphasic Personality Inventory (MMPI), an IQ test score, the social class of the subject's first home, and the subject's current social class. All the investigations and interviews were conducted by Heston in 14 states and in Canada; this is a remarkable feat. The dossier compiled on each subject, excluding genetic and institutional information, was evaluated blindly and independently by two psychiatrists and also by Heston.

Evaluations of the 47 subjects and 50 controls were based on the Menninger Mental Health-Sickness Rating Scale (MHSRS), which proved highly reliable as a measure of degree of incapacity; the intraclass correlation coefficient between the scores of the raters was 0.94. The results of this study are so unique and of such great importance that we think they should be reproduced here in condensed form as Table 1–7. The effects of having a schizophrenic mother, compared with a nonschizophrenic mother, are extremely pervasive especially when it is remembered that the baby was taken from the mother when three days old and never returned to her nor to a blood relative of hers.

We haven't space for as many comments as we would like to make about these remarkable data but some brief notes will be presented. We see that the schizophrenic mothers produced 5 children who became schizophrenic, 4 who were mentally defi-

Table 1–7. *Heston's Data on Children Separated From Their Schizophrenic Mothers Compared with Matched Controls From Non-Schizophrenic Mothers.*

	CONTROLS	STUDY SUBJECTS
Number	50	47
Mean Age	36.3	35.8
Adopted	19	22
MHSRS, mean	80.1	65.2
Schizophrenia	0	5
Mental deficiency (IQ < 70)	0	4
Sociopathic personality	2	9
Neurotic personality disorder	7	13
Persons spending > 1 year in penal or psychiatric institution	2	11
Total years institutionalized	15	112
Felons	2	7
Social class, first home	4.2	4.5
Social class, present	4.7	5.4
IQ mean	103.7	94.0
Average years in school	12.4	11.6
Children, total	84	71
Divorces, total	7	6
Never married, 30 years age	4	9

(One mentally deficient person was also schizophrenic and a second was sociopathic. Duplication occurs in some entries.)

cient and 9 who developed sociopathic personalities for a total of 18 types of non-adaptive behavior, although 2 of these had 2 of the problems in each case so that there were at least 16 offspring with serious problems compared with only 2 persons with sociopathic personalities produced by the control mothers. Thus 16 out of 47 (34 per cent) of the offspring of the schizophrenic mothers had serious troubles while only 2 out of 50 (4 per cent) of the children of the control mothers were so badly affected. This difference is statistically highly significant ($\chi^2 = 16.2$, p <0.0005).

It is clear that the psychiatric disability in the offspring of the schizophrenic mothers was not restricted to the transmission of the potentiality for schizophrenia. What was transmitted was a potentiality for what Essen-Möller (1941) called a "characterological disorder," a mental instability which can express itself in a wide range of poorly adaptive behavior with a good proportion of it expressed as diagnosed schizophrenia. The 5 schizophrenics in the 47 offspring, or 10.6 per cent without age correction, give as high a frequency in the children of an affected mother as found by Kallmann or any other researcher where the children were not taken from the mother at the end of three days, as was the case for Heston's material.

An unusual type of finding, probably not envisioned by previous researchers, was that 21 of 47 children of schizophrenic mothers, who exhibited no psycho-social impairment, not only were successful adults but in comparison to the control group were more spontaneous when interviewed and had more colorful life histories. "They held the more creative jobs: musician, teacher, home-designer; and followed the more imaginative hobbies: oil painting, music, antique aircraft. Within the experimental group there was much more variability of personality and behavior in all social dimensions." We may add that it is quite possible that Heston's control sample was not truly representative of a "normal" population of children.

It is perhaps these adaptive aspects of some of the variations of the gene complex related to schizophrenia that maintain these genes in the "normal" population. The more pathological gene combinations could result in the severely ill people

who have reproductive rates below replacement values, while the beneficial combinations of the same genes might result in slightly higher reproductive rates than the average. Only a small reproductive advantage for the more frequent, well-adapted genotypes would be necessary to replace the less frequent, poorly adapted genotypes having lower reproductive rates.

A small but valuable set of data can be found in the book by Karlsson (1966) on the biologic basis of schizophrenia. This is a careful study of schizophrenia in Iceland where records are well kept. In Karlsson's investigation one parent was schizophrenic but not both, as far as one could tell. The ascertainment was made through a schizophrenic proband offspring and it is the fate of the siblings, all over 35 years of age, of the proband which concerns us. Of the 119 siblings of a proband with an affected parent, 102 were reared in the parental home and 12 of them (11.8 per cent) became schizophrenic (without any age correction). There were 8 siblings reared by relatives and 2 (25 per cent) became schizophrenic, while 3 of 9 (33 per cent) were reared by non-relatives and were affected. It is astonishing that 5 out of 17 (29 per cent) of the foster reared children became schizophrenic. The only explanation we can think of for the *higher* frequency of schizophrenia in the fostered children compared with those raised in their own home with a schizophrenic parent is that the children who had to be placed in foster homes had much more severely affected parents and thus a heavier genetic load for schizophrenia themselves. All the children in the foster homes were placed there before the age of one year. It is surprising indeed that placement in foster homes had no apparent helpful effect in reducing the expectation of schizophrenia in these high risk children. We are bothered by the small sample size, of course.

Rosenthal (1971) in Denmark obtained results different from those just described for Heston and for Karlsson. The Danish material contained only one hospitalized adoptee (1.3 per cent) in 76 index adoptees. However, 23 others were in the schizophrenic spectrum. The biological parents of the Danish adoptees seem to have been less severely affected than in the other adoption studies.

Kety, Rosenthal, Wender and Schulsinger (1968) found that among 5483 adoptions in the Copenhagen area, there were 33 with an acceptable diagnosis of schizophrenia. These were matched with appropriate controls who had been adopted. There were five or six times as many schizophrenics among the biological relatives of the adopted children who developed schizophrenia as among their relatives by adoption. The biological and adoptive relatives of the controls were no different from each other or from the adoptive relatives of the subjects. This is a kind of "reverse" experiment to that of Heston and confirms it again. Furthermore, it eliminates all environmental factors from fundamental significance in the etiology of schizophrenia *except those with perinatal effects*. In other words, the stage for schizophrenia is set before birth or soon afterwards. Subsequent environmental events are not responsible for the appearance of the psychosis but may be important in the severity of expression of the disorder, and in "triggering" the psychotic episode.

The adoptive studies still do not prove absolutely and without any doubt whatsoever that genetic factors contribute appreciably to the development of schizophrenic illness, but any theory of schizophrenia must give the evidence for genetic factors equal weight with any other type of causation. They definitely prove that the environmental factors are perinatal and presumably prenatal.

The Diagnoses. It is quite likely that there are more than 100 etiologically distinct types of mental retardation. How many etiologically distinct types of psychoses are there? The question cannot be answered, even as an approximation, because the taxonomy of the psychoses is still in a chaotic state.

Snezhnevsky and Vartanyan (1971), in a study of the forms of schizophrenia, list 3 forms of the first order, each with 4 forms of the second order, and each of these 12 has either 2, 3, or 4 forms of the third order. There are patients to be found who fit nicely into each of these 27 third order forms. There is no way of knowing what correlations may exist between the 27 phenotypes of this taxonomy and the possible genetic variants. Furthermore, this 27 phenotype classification is probably accepted *in toto*

only by its two authors. Numerous other ways of classifying the schizophrenias, such as peripheral and nuclear, reactive and process, and so on, have sensible rationales which merit consideration.

There are also efforts to classify the depressive type psychoses in various ways. These have recently received considerable attention, with simple depressions being called unipolar and persons with both manic and depressed states referred to as bipolar cases. The combined data of Angst and Perris (1968) show clearly that there is a higher percentage of affective illness among the parents and siblings of the bipolar probands than is found for unipolar probands. We view their work as primarily a demonstration of a greater severity of expression, and perhaps a heavier genetic loading, in the families of the bipolar probands compared with the families of the unipolar patients.

A study of 193 inpatients diagnosed as bipolar was carried out by Slater, Maxwell and Price (1971), utilizing Slater's ancestral secondary case technique. The distribution of the secondary cases failed to support the hypothesis of major gene transmission. Consequently, if there are genetic differences between bipolar and unipolar patients we should expect them to depend upon numerous pairs of genes rather than upon one major gene pair. The discriminant function analyses of Kendell and Gourlay (1970A) indicate that the depressive illnesses are best regarded as a continuum and that patients are better categorized by their position on the continuum than by an endogenous/reactive dichotomy.

It will be recalled from the discussion of the Genain quadruplets that the one-egg quadruplets were without doubt schizophrenic but all displayed catatonia and the other subtypes of schizophrenia at different times. The genotype for all four girls was identical, which means that this one genotype was capable of initiating various schizophrenic subtypes. Presumably the distinctions between the subtypes resulted from what seemed to be trivial environmental variants, but which produced rather serious behavioral fluctuations.

Everyone would agree that the Genain quadruplets were schizophrenic rather than manic. There would be less agreement concerning the diagnosis for many patients.

There has not been enough effort expended in trying to accommodate the patients who are "schizo-affective" within some diagnostic scheme. Many researchers have either forced such cases into the schizophrenic melange or into the group of affective disorders, or omitted them from consideration. This is a very important problem because, if the existence of intermediate patients is conceded, the traditional concept of manic-depressive illness and schizophrenia as distinct disease entities becomes open to question. Kendell and Gourlay (1970B) tried to determine whether the schizophrenic and affective psychoses are distinct entities with the aid of a discriminant function analysis. They did not succeed in discriminating between the two disorders; that is, there were many patients who might have received either diagnosis and smaller numbers who were "pure" cases of schizophrenia or manic-depressive psychosis. The two disorders seem to form a continuum which is evidence for heterogeneity and multigenic inheritance with, of course, an environmental component.

The cardinal point of this section is that both the schizophrenic and manic-depressive taxa include numerous phenotypes which display the gradations of a spectrum but still allow distinct characterization for some patients. With such an array of heterogeneous phenotypes, it would be unwise to expect any single genotype to account for all of them. The probability that such extensive variability in behavior could result from the alleles at a single gene locus, even with modifying genes, would seem to be extremely small. It seems imperative that any genetic theory of manic-depressive psychosis, for instance, include numerous gene loci in order to accommodate the phenotypic heterogeneity which is observed.

Simplistic Gene Hypotheses. Early students of the genetics of mental retardation, such as Goddard, have been ridiculed because they thought that all mental retardation behaved in a Mendelian recessive fashion and resulted from the homozygous mutant at a single gene locus. We have a not too different body of recent literature stressing dominant inheritance related to one or two gene loci for schizophrenia and for the depressive disorders.

These simplistic gene theories are espoused as a resort to scientific parsimony, but this is false economy if it is in contradiction to the heterogeneity of the genotypes for the psychoses. The phenotypic spectrum of diversity of the psychoses is so vast that one must assume at least modest genetic diversity to initiate the phenotypic heterogeneity. The modern single gene hypotheses attempt to reconcile this contradiction by invoking modifying genes at numerous loci. This provides an instant dilemma because, as the modifying genes assume importance, the "major" gene locus becomes less significant.

When one looks at a trait such as intelligence through the lens of evolution, as did Reed (1965), it is clear that many gene loci must be involved in the expression of the trait. The psychoses must also have had a long evolutionary adaptation, and so could hardly have any simple genetic basis. Nonetheless, there have been numerous recent publications which attempt to fit the family study data to simplistic gene hypotheses.

Karlsson (1966, 1972) envisions two gene loci with dominant behavior as the genetic component of schizophrenia. Heston (1970A, 1970B) thinks that "the same genotype is compatible with either schizophrenic or schizoid disease" and it approximates the expectations resulting from a defect in a single autosomal dominant gene. Winokur, Cadoret, Dorzab and Baker (1971) consider that the genetics of pure depressive disease (unipolar) depends upon a dominant gene locus but that the disorder is sex-limited to females. The proper terminology should be "sex-influenced," not "sex-limited," as 14 per cent of the fathers and 20 per cent of the brothers displayed the illness; these values are only modestly smaller than the 29 per cent for the mothers and 21 per cent of the sisters who were affected. It is quite possible that there was some sex influence present in their material but that is not evidence for any single gene hypothesis.

It is conceivable that psychoses caused by single genes can be isolated from the heterogeneous mass. This has been done in the mental retardation area and for rare psychoses such as Huntington's chorea. However, the majority of cases of mental retardation and the psychoses should have complicated genetics and not single gene explanations.

Multi-gene Hypotheses. Edwards (1960)

has probably been more effective than anyone else in demonstrating that multigenic action can simulate that of a single pair of genes completely. The truth of the matter is that we do not have the tools in human genetics which allow us to distinguish between single locus and multigenic action for continuum traits of high frequency in the population. We can pin down the genetics of discrete blood groups that are of high frequency because of their antigen-antibody reactions and we know that thousands of different genotypes for the blood antigens exist, but we do not know the selective value of a single complete genotype out of all the thousands there must be. Probably we do not understand all the implications for natural selection of the well-studied gene locus for sickle cell anemia. The difficulties with these simple genetic systems warn us that we must expect much greater problems with our variably diagnosed heterogeneous psychoses. Thus we can expect even greater complexity than is found for height, weight or intelligence. Obviously, the psychoses genetically resemble the quantitative trait of intelligence much more than the qualitative blood group loci.

Some investigators object to a multigenic hypothesis on the grounds that this might inhibit the search for a single, unique chemical responsible for most cases of schizophrenia. The variability in phenotypes observed suggests that there is no such unique chemical and that further search for one will not be productive. If the biochemical variability is quantitative, presumably the genetic pattern is quantitative also.

The main problem of quantitative genetics, which rests upon a multigene basis, is that it is so difficult to design experiments which permit its acceptance or rejection. Nonetheless, the practical uses of the multigenic theory in agriculture and with laboratory organisms have established its existence and general attributes unequivocally. The work of Carter (1965) and others has demonstrated the usefulness of quantitative genetics theory for mankind also.

The most ambitious treatment of the quantitative genetics of schizophrenia is that of Gottesman and Shields (1967). They calculated heritabilities for the liability of parents, sibs, and aunts and uncles to schizophrenia and obtained values of from 60 to 80 per cent. These are probably too high because within some families environmental variance is included in the heritabilities obtained. The discordance of schizophrenic co-twins is approximately 50 per cent, which may be the clue to the most useful answer available. In other words, we will probably not be very far from the truth if we assume that about 50 per cent of the variance in the frequency of schizophrenia is genetic and 50 per cent environmental.

One especially interesting feature of the Gottesman and Shields heritability values is that they are about the same for first degree relatives of the probands as for second degree relatives. While their answers cannot be precise with a trait such as schizophrenia, their concepts are the most acceptable to well-trained geneticists. There is room for rare types of schizophrenia with regular Mendelian genetics but geneticists do not expect these to be as frequent as the multigenic variants. The genetic picture for the psychoses is of necessity quite comparable to that for mental retardation. This is because a decrease in reproductive rates, frequency in the population and general social status are about the same for the two constellations of mental disorders and mental retardation.

Ödegård (1972) has always viewed the psychoses as a multigenic situation and states that his "large-scale and long-time clinical investigation has shown us a picture of the functional psychoses as an ocean of individual cases without natural boundaries, but not at all without an orderly pattern. The conventional diagnoses are helpful, as are the degrees of latitude and longitude for navigation, but not as unsurpassable walls erected between two parts of a population."

Twins. Twin studies contribute to our understanding of the environmental factors in a unique way because the genetic component is held constant when two monozygotic twins are compared. Fischer (1971) compared the offspring of schizophrenic monozygotic twins with the offspring of discordant monozygotic twins. The morbidity risk of about 10 to 15 per cent found in the first group of offspring was indistinguishable from that in the second group of offspring. This investigation gave no support to the hypothesis that environmental factors, associated with being reared by a schizophrenic parent, should cause more schizophrenia in the offspring. The fact that the non-schizophrenic twin (environmentally different) produced as many schizophrenic offspring as did the affected monozygotic twin focuses our attention more sharply on the perinatal environmental factors which must be necessary for the later appearance of the psychosis.

The adoption studies localized the primary environmental factors in the perinatal period, and the Fischer twin study shows that the schizophrenic *behavior* of the parent was *not* one of the environmental factors responsible for psychosis in the offspring. What *are* possible perinatal environmental factors which initiate eventual psychotic responses in genetically disposed persons?

High Risk Children. Prospective studies of babies born to schizophrenic *fathers* might be most helpful in demonstrating primary environmental factors in the etiology of the psychosis. Studies of children of schizophrenic fathers and normal mothers would eliminate environmental trauma due to psychosis in the mother; this is the type of study reported on by Mednick and Schulsinger (1968). The adoption studies referred to earlier indicate clearly that the important etiological factors produce their environmental insults by the time of birth or soon thereafter, so studies of adolescent persons could only discover some of the secondary "triggering" factors at best. The difficulty of studying babies before birth is almost overwhelming, but if one hopes to find an answer one must look for it at the right time and place. The proper search design has not been initiated yet.

A step in the right direction has been taken by Anthony (1968), who intends to study children under five years of age who have a high risk because of a schizophrenic parent. His main problem is that of finding mental traits that are measurable in such young children.

Advantages of a Mild Psychosis. It is probable that about 3 per cent of the population develops a severe psychosis before death. The severely psychotic also have a lower marriage rate, with a consequently lower net reproductive rate. Their significant reproductive loss must be compensated for in some way if the frequency of psychosis is to be maintained. There are numerous mechanisms which might maintain the necessary balanced system.

The number of gene loci necessary to maintain the psychoses on the basis of new mutations would have to be large. The number of such loci probably is large. We know that there are certainly more than 100 loci capable of producing mental retardation and it is not unreasonable to assume that there are about as many involved with the psychoses, because the frequency of the psychoses is about the same as that of the retardations. It may not be necessary to search for any other explanation on a genetic basis. Other explanations are available in the literature.

Carter and Watts (1971) seem to have shown that schizophrenics' relatives have a diminished incidence of virus infections compared with control persons' relatives. Possibly the schizophrenics' relatives also had increased fertility. This type of work is promising even though it is difficult to obtain repeatable results.

Kuttner, Lorincz and Swan (1967) hypothesize that a tendency toward schizophrenia offers protection from some of the stresses of social interaction. Only when the disease is moderate or severe would the individual be handicapped. The researchers realize that actual demonstration of the advantageous nature of the mild disorder is not likely to be achieved in the immediate future.

There is no lack of hypotheses to explain the high frequencies of the psychoses but no convincing tests of the hypotheses have appeared yet.

We conclude our introductory review of the literature with strong evidence that psychotic parents transmit a genetic component to their offspring that results in a range of new genetic combinations which interact with environmental factors in utero or soon after birth to produce a continuum from neuro-psycho-social impairment in some, to well-adapted behavior in others. We are considering behavioral traits which have positive or negative adaptive values in different individuals in different circumstances. The psychoses are frequent in the population and probably are a product of our evolution. Under such circumstances it would seem more logical to assume a multigenic pattern rather than a single gene locus of primary importance with modifiers.

Our preference for a multigenic basis for the functional psychoses is, of course, also an endorsement of the diathesis-stress hypothesis of Rosenthal (1963). In all hypotheses of the development of the functional psychoses it is the environmental factors which shape the final expression of the poorly adaptive behavior. In the Genain quadruplets and in Pollin's discordant twins, the environmental factors which resulted in the differences in sub-type diagnoses or even in the appearance of the frank symptoms of the disease seemed to be rather trivial in nature and presumably would be quite ineffective with more resistant genotypes.

THE PURPOSES OF THIS BOOK

What is there that we might learn in addition to the conclusions already obtained from the voluminous literature which we have reviewed?

Our project is unique in that two generations of research workers, separated by a gap of 40 years, have studied from three to five consecutive generations of families with high risks of developing functional psychoses in some of their members. The longitudinal study provided more or less continuous surveillance of 89 kinships for over 50 years and permits us to attempt to answer the following questions:

1. Does mental illness continue to be transmitted from generation to generation in these families?

2. Does the transmission of mental illness pass through people with normal behavior as well as through the affected?

3. What is the frequency of psychoses in our control families and how does it compare with that of the experimental families?

4. Do psychotic mothers have a higher *percentage* of psychotic offspring than do psychotic fathers?

5. Do diagnostic differences between the functional psychoses have etiological validity, or only pragmatic utility?

6. Was there a significant correlation between a psychosis and specific personal relations experienced in childhood? Was the correlation more obvious where a parent was mentally ill compared with families where both parents were apparently healthy?

7. Was there a relationship between the frequency of a psychosis and the social class of the family?

8. What are the fertility patterns of the mentally ill? What maintains the frequency of these poorly adapted behaviors in the population?

9. What do our data tell us about the genetics of the psychoses?

We hope that the reader will be interested in our data from this truly longitudinal study and in the applications of the data to the questions listed above.

CHAPTER TWO

THE METHODOLOGY

SELECTION OF THE SAMPLE

The experimental design for this project was determined to a considerable degree in 1910 by Dr. Charles B. Davenport at the Eugenics Records Office in Cold Spring Harbor, Long Island. Long Island was the source of much of the eugenic thought in America, starting with the classic encounter between George W. Huntington, M.D., while still a boy, and a choreic mother with her affected daughter. He remembered for the rest of his life the shaking, grimacing pair of women shuffling along the roadside. His medical study of chorea years after this chance encounter resulted in his name being attached to the phenotype of this Mendelian dominant trait. Later on, Davenport and Muncey carried out their important study of the spread of this disastrous gene across the continent. It is little wonder that Dr. Davenport had some expectations of obtaining similar results for the psychoses when he sent Miss Florence Orr to work with Dr. Rosanoff at the nearby King's Park State Hospital, and Miss Anna Wendt to work with Dr. H. W. Mitchell at the Warren State Hospital in Warren, Pennsylvania. The dementias of Huntington's chorea patients probably seemed to Davenport to be much like those of the patients with dementia praecox, so the genetics might be similar also.

Davenport knew that if one is to study the genetics of a trait one must observe its transmission from generation to generation because the genetic *mechanism* is revealed best by family studies. The study of twins permits an estimate of the heritability of a trait but usually does not elucidate its genetics. The combination of a study of twins and their relatives is of course better than either by itself, but this was not to come about until many years later with Kallmann's monumental work in New York State. The design of experiment devised by Dr. Davenport to be carried out at the Warren State Hospital was to study the relatives of patients at the hospital in order to determine the frequency of mental aberrations of all kinds among these relatives, presumably demonstrating simple Mendelian heredity.

Miss Anna Wendt, who later became Mrs. A. D. Finlayson, studied the grandparents, parents, aunts and uncles, siblings, children, nephews and nieces of each of 118 patients at the hospital during 1913 and subsequent years. During 1916 additional families were studied by Miss Ruth Badger and in 1925 others were added by Miss O. B. Lee. For the work reported in this book we have utilized 77 of the kinships studied by Miss Wendt and 12 of those studied by Miss Badger, but none of Miss Lee's families. We have added 10 kinships selected by ourselves from the general Warren State Hospital files. These 10 are called the "pretest" kinships and were selected to test our techniques before approaching the descendants of the 89 key kinships collected by Wendt and Badger. Thus there are a total of 99 kinships which provided the data for this book.

The 99 kinships varied in size from the smallest, which was composed of 23 persons, to the largest one with 1907 members. The distribution of the kinships by the number of members in each one is given in

Table 2–1. *Number of Persons Included in Each of Our 99 Kinships.*

Each kinship includes the aunts and uncles of the proband, all descendants of the father and mother of the proband and all persons who married these descendants of the proband's parents.

NUMBER OF PERSONS IN EACH KINSHIP	NUMBER OF KINSHIPS	TOTAL PERSONS
23– 99	52	3225
100– 199	24	3485
200– 399	14	3941
400– 599	4	1817
600– 799	2	1418
800– 999	1	852
1000–1499	1	1149
1500–1999	1	1907
Total	99	17,794
TOTAL CONTROL GROUPS		942
GRAND TOTAL		18,736

Table 2–1. Each kinship included the aunts and uncles of the probands, all descendants of the father and mother of the proband, and all those persons who married the descendants of the proband and his parents.

There were, in addition, 942 persons in the control groups, so that the grand total of all persons enumerated in the study amounted to 18,736 individuals.

Miss Wendt selected her probands from the patients then in the Warren State Hospital without much thought as to the specific diagnosis involved. It should be recalled that in 1913 people were hospitalized because they were "insane" and the precise diagnosis was primarily of medical interest. At that time the general public did not make fine distinctions between the numerous varieties of mental instability, so that alcoholics, neurotics and psychotics were all considered as rather similar specimens of intolerable social misbehavior. They were therefore placed in asylums where they could not impede progress toward what many people thought would be an almost perfect new world within a few generations.

We wished to limit ourselves to probands who had, according to present day diagnostic standards, some kind of "functional" psychosis. Consequently, we retained only 77 of Miss Wendt's original 118 kinships and 12 of those collected by Miss Badger. We rejected probands who were primarily alcoholics, had chronic brain damage, were mentally retarded but not mentally ill and various others who were not relevant to our study. We included five of the 77 probands who were originally unclassified but who clearly had a functional psychosis.

The Warren State Hospital serves the 13 northwestern counties of Pennsylvania, which are predominantly rural with the exception of the one large city of Erie. The terrain is rough and composed of long ridges of very steep hills and was rather difficult to traverse in 1913. Many of the members of these kinships later migrated to Cleveland, California and other parts of the country. We were fortunate to be able to employ social workers in various parts of the country to search out these migrants. They had the same experience as we did in our study of mental retardation (Reed and Reed, 1965); namely, if there were numerous members of a family at the time of the original study it was usually possible to find one or more survivors and to reestablish contact. However, after a lapse of 40 to 50 years the searching difficulties become gradually greater. The larger the original family group the greater the likelihood of finding survivors and descendants.

The reader may be interested in more details about the Warren State Hospital, the area it serves, and the kinds of statistical studies which have been carried out there by others. Numerous studies have been made and one of the most interesting which could serve as an introduction to the others is that of Kramer, Goldstein, Israel and Johnson (1955).

BIASES IN PROBAND SELECTION

All probands were hospitalized. The fact of hospitalization indicates that every proband was sufficiently disturbed so that public assistance was needed. No doubt other equally psychotic individuals were cared for at home or in private institutions, but as a rule our probands must have been more seriously ill than the psychotics who were not under supervision anywhere. Slightly psychotic and mildly psychotic persons were not included in our sample of probands, though such persons must have been present in the 13 counties at that time but were not hospitalized.

Mrs. Finlayson (Miss Wendt) stated that she picked probands who had identifiable relatives, which eliminated drifters, orphans and other persons without local attachments. It is unlikely that this bias is of much importance.

Mrs. Finlayson stated that she picked three or four probands who she knew had other psychotic relatives. She remembered which ones were the "loaded" families and we have treated them separately where appropriate. The proband was the only psychotic member of the family in 24 of the 89 kinships at the time of selection.

It was not realized in 1913 that second or later admissions were likely to have more psychotic relatives than is the case for first admission probands. Consequently, no attention was given to this matter in the proband selection. As a result, we find that 63 of the 89 probands were first admissions between 1912 and 1917, 7 had been admitted earlier, and the remaining 19 were second or subsequent admissions. We should mention the fact that if a sample of probands is to be representative of a hospital population it should include some fraction of second and later admission patients, as they are a legitimate and significant part of the hospital clientele. Our sample seems to be representative of the usual hospital population and the major bias seems to be that it is a selection of hospital patients only. A sample selected from a complete survey of all persons in a given geographic area without regard to previous knowledge of their health, and including those who were in institutions, would be more desirable. Observations on the subjects' descendants could not be made until 50 years or more had passed because we are dealing with psychoses with late ages of onset in many cases.

It is hard to visualize what our sample would have been like had it included all those in the population who were mentally disturbed but not sufficiently disordered to have ever been hospitalized. Where does normality end and psychosis begin? It seems rather unlikely that there is any sharp threshold or truncation. Obviously, when we study probands who are closer to normality we can expect the frequency of psychoses among their relatives to decrease, with proportionately less benefit to be derived from a study where the frequency of disorder becomes very low. Once maximum frequencies of psychoses among the relatives have been found, as in the work of Garrone (1962), or perhaps in that of Kallmann (1950), one could obtain samples with lesser frequencies of psychoses among the relatives by including larger proportions of "psychotic" persons with milder manifestations in the sample of probands, if this would be useful.

A final note about the 10 probands selected as a pre-test sample is needed. The 10 probands were selected arbitrarily from the Warren State Hospital population of patients with a functional psychosis. Six had diagnoses of schizophrenic reaction, paranoid type, and four had manic-depressive reactions. Seven were first admissions and the other three were second or later admissions. Again, probands who had siblings or children, or both, were selected in order that a family study could be made to test our techniques. There was a definite effort to select about equal numbers with diagnoses of manic-depressive psychosis and of schizophrenia, but no attention was paid to whether the relatives had the same mental illness or any mental illness at the time the selection was made.

THE FIELD WORK

Preliminary visits to relatives of a few of our probands were made by Drs. David J. Merrell in 1949 and Carl Hartley in 1957. These visits demonstrated that good cooperation could be obtained from the relatives. The techniques employed included unannounced visits and the use of the names of the Warren State Hospital and of the proband. Mr. Nelson Johnson, M.S.W., has been at the Warren State Hospital since 1939 and was responsible for recruiting other social workers to assist in finding and interviewing the relatives of the probands. He did a great deal of traveling himself and his long acquaintance with the families and the geography of Pennsylvania was extremely valuable.

It was realized that some kind of structured guide for the interviewing would be necessary in order that important data not be omitted. While the interviewers were free to utilize their individual abilities, the crucial items needed were to be listed on the forms as rapidly as possible. Dittoed instructions and examples were provided the interviewers in order that they would know which questions were likely to create resistance and how to avoid it. It is difficult to inquire into the private lives of the relatives of psychotic persons as the fundamental difficulty with the proband has often been that of interpersonal relationships. However, if the interviewer starts with innocuous statistical questions it is not difficult to work up to those which, frankly, invade the person's privacy. The astonishing thing is not that someone occasionally refuses to have his privacy invaded but that many times the subject of the interview seems to benefit from pouring out much more detail than is requested. Probably the major problem in obtaining interviews with the relatives of psychotics is their desire to shield the young from questioning and to prevent them from learning the facts about their own relatives. The chief reason for this is that the older relatives fear that if the younger people learn about their psychotic relatives and worry about mental disorders they will become psychotic also as a result. One can sympathize with this concern and the social workers refrained from approaching such "shielded" persons. Fortunately, the desired information could usually be obtained from other relatives.

Every effort was made to complete the interview within one hour unless the circumstances seemed unusually favorable.

Figure 2–1 is a copy of the form provided each interviewer as a guide for obtaining the usual type of family statistics.

Figure 2–2 is a copy of the screening questions suggested for the interviewer. These are similar to those listed in Eaton and Weil (1955). Contributions to this form were also made by Lockwood Towne, M.D., at Warren.

As soon as the interview was over, the field worker was expected to make further notes as to cooperativeness of the informant, reliability estimates, "closed areas" in the conversation and a thoughtful estimate of the personality of the informant as well as possible signs of mental illness.

In addition to the circumstances of the interview, the field worker was expected to evaluate the socio-economic background of the informant. Inquiries at local social welfare agencies and other such sources of information were often helpful. There was a summary-of-interview form designed to assist the field worker in coordinating all the material obtained about each person. The data were then brought back to the Research Office of the Warren State Hospital for processing.

The subjects interviewed were motivated to cooperate in various ways.

1. When a relative of the subject was in the hospital some news of the patient could be provided which was of interest to the subject and opened the door to frank discussions.

2. Some of the subjects had already become acquainted with the social worker in his official hospital capacity.

3. One of the interviewers had close relatives affected with mental illness and was able to use his own experiences to secure rapport.

4. Many subjects were interested in their family genealogies and hoped to obtain information about their ancestry. It was sometimes possible to provide some information, but the policy was to point out that the information to be obtained from the subject would be held in confidence and therefore it would not be possible to provide information from relatives that was equally confidential.

5. Some subjects were willing to contribute information because of their desire to help in the research on mental disorders. Many knew the importance of research.

6. The excellent reputation of the Warren State Hospital assisted the interviewers in obtaining entrée to the homes of subjects living in northwestern Pennsylvania.

PROCESSING OF THE DATA

It was not possible in some cases to visit relatives of our probands because the network of interviewers was not able to penetrate to every part of the country. Consequently, information had to be obtained by mail questionnaire from inaccessible subjects. Mail questionnaires are satisfactory sources of statistical data if the covering letters are skillfully conceived. Correspondence is not usually a satisfactory way of learning about family relationships

Family No. _____ Gen. No. _____

CONFIDENTIAL INFORMATION CONCERNING CHILDREN OF _____

Source of Information _____ Interviewer _____ Date _____

Please fill in blank spaces below, and make any corrections needed.
List children in order of birth. For each married child use next line below for information about the child's spouse.

FULL NAME	MARITAL STATUS	BIRTH Date Year	EDUCATION Grade Completed	USUAL OCCUPATION	No. of Children	ADDRESS or Place of Death	MEDICAL HISTORY Hospitals or Clinics Reason, Date and Place	OTHER REMARKS If dead, give age, date and cause

Figure 2-1.

Questions about _____and their children

Fam. No. _____

Source of information _____ Interviewer

Gen. No._____

Date_____

First, consider the family while the children were young (under 15 years old)

Please circle answer (DK= don't know)

a. Did either parent die or leave home before the children were grown? Yes No DK
b. Were the parents ever separated? Or ever consider separation? Yes No DK
c. Did any of the children live away from home for some time? Yes No DK
d. Was there friction in the home? Or disagreement about handling the children? Yes No DK
e. Were the parents unfair or partial to any of the children? Yes No DK
f. Were any of the children difficult to handle? Yes No DK

Then, think of those children as they grew up and include their husbands or wives

1. Are there any diseases or conditions which appear to run in the family? Yes No DK
2. Has anyone been sick a lot? Or seemed to need a lot of "doctoring"? Yes No DK
3. Has anyone been especially nervous? Or had a nervous breakdown? Yes No DK
4. Has anyone ever gone to a doctor for his nerves? Yes No DK
5. Has anyone been often depressed or unhappy? Often had blue spells? Yes No DK
6. Has anyone had particular difficulty going through menopause? Yes No DK
7. Has anyone been prominent in the community? Or always had to be on the go? Yes No DK
8. Has anyone lived by himself too much? Or been unable to make friends? Yes No DK
9. Has anyone moved around a lot? Or had difficulty holding a job? Yes No DK
10. Has anyone been a problem in the community? Or had trouble with alcohol? Yes No DK

If any answer is YES, please write name of person(s), briefly tell what happened, how old they were:

Figure 2–2.

though some of the letters were extremely conscientious and provided specific details which were as forthright as anything which could have been obtained in an interview.

The field worker usually assisted in processing the data upon returning to the Research Office at Warren. This experience was helpful to the interviewer in improving his field technique.

The Minnesota study on mental retardation (Reed and Reed, 1965) included all the descendants of the grandparents of the probands and the persons who married these descendants. There were 82,219 persons included in the completed work and all of them resulted from a starting sample of 289 probands, an average of 284 persons per kinship. It would have been desirable to include all the descendants of the grandparents of the 99 Warren, Pennsylvania probands but it was decided instead to include only the descendants of the parents of the probands. This resulted in a total population of 18,736 persons, including controls, an average of 189 persons per kinship, which was once again a sizable population.

The immediate task upon returning from the field was to ensure that all the required members of the kinship had been located. Usually there were many members of a kinship not located on the first trip so that other trips to other places and often by a different worker were necessary. It was generally a matter of several years before all work that could be done on a single kinship was completed.

The Research Office staff made every effort to obtain a copy of the death certificate for each person who had died. This provided not only valuable medical information but also vital addresses for next of kin of the deceased, permitting further field work in some cases. There was also a check in Harrisburg, the state capital, to see if there had been a commitment of the person to any other Pennsylvania institution. Extremely little information, beyond that already known to the field worker, was obtained from the search for commitment records, so this practice was discontinued.

All the information for each person was assembled and every effort was made to obtain all possible records of the person's mental health. If there was any suspicion of mental illness a conscientious ef-fort was made to obtain at least a summary of the physician's opinion about the illness. All physicians and hospitals were cooperative.

There was always the possibility that mental illness was concealed by the subject from his relatives, and of course from us. We have no way of estimating our loss of information of this sort. However, if the illness was this successfully concealed it was of no great concern to society and must have been of a relatively mild variety. A problem of greater importance results from the "accidental" deaths which are of a mysterious nature. A young, unemployed male found asphyxiated in the kitchen of his apartment with two gas jets open could hardly be considered to be the victim of a faulty stove; we are more inclined to consider him to have committed suicide. Each of these cases had to be reviewed individually and we gave a great deal of weight to the opinions of the psychiatrists presently at Warren, even when they were not in agreement with the official death records.

At the time the original study was made by Miss Wendt and Miss Badger it was clear that a fairly large proportion of the severely psychotic had never been hospitalized. In the meantime, social services had been improved to such an extent that the follow-up field workers found extremely few clearly psychotic persons who had never been hospitalized for mental illness.

During the process of assembling the data a pedigree chart was constructed for each kinship. This was usually several feet long and maintained as a roll or scroll. When this was complete for the kinship it was sent along with the documents and records to the Dight Institute for Human Genetics at the University of Minnesota. At the Dight Institute the pedigree chart was redrawn by Mrs. Vivian Phillips and then drawn once more by Mr. Robert Selmo and Mr. William Rice in the compact final form published in this book. A description of the symbols in the pedigrees can be found with the charts in the Appendix.

The data from Warren were assembled in a family history with each member having a number corresponding to that on the pedigree chart. The complete family histories assembled in Minneapolis were then sent to Warren where each member of the family was rechecked by Dr. Hartley and

Mr. Johnson in order to ensure that no pertinent information had been omitted. This complete family history for the kinship was then abstracted by Mrs. Phillips in the form published in the Appendix of this book. The names of the family members were omitted from the abstracts for obvious reasons.

All diagnoses of mental deviation from the normal were reviewed by psychiatrists at the Warren State Hospital. The perplexing problem of diagnosis will be considered now.

THE DIAGNOSIS

Most people would agree that the problem of diagnosis of mental disorders is the soft underbelly of psychiatry. Different psychiatrists often disagree as to the diagnosis for the same person. None of the diagnoses in this study were made by beginners; all were made by psychiatrists with extensive experience. John C. Urbaitis, M.D., the assistant superintendent of the Warren State Hospital, very generously accepted responsibility for the diagnostic procedures used in the data analyses.

The first challenge was that of reviewing the original diagnoses for the probands and their relatives as provided in the early 1900's. A review board of two hospital psychiatrists studied the original staff notes regarding the proband or relative and either accepted the original diagnosis or provided a new one. If the two psychiatrists found that they did not agree on the diagnosis, a third psychiatrist, Lockwood Towne, M.D., then director of research at Warren State Hospital, reviewed the information and if there was still uncertainty as to a firm diagnosis, a final decision was made by Dr. Urbaitis. Dr. Urbaitis has represented the hospital for many years in court cases. Experience in forensic medicine is very helpful in settling upon diagnoses which will withstand the criticism of opposing psychiatrists. Consequently, it is our opinion that the diagnoses included in this project would be acceptable to most psychiatrists. Descriptions of the behavior of the mentally ill persons are included in the family histories in the Appendix in order that others may formulate their own diagnoses if they so desire.

There has been a general change in frequency of the major diagnostic categories of the functional psychoses since 1913. There has been a recognition that the early stages of schizophrenia are often marked by depression, with the appearance of typical schizophrenic features being delayed in some cases for several years. This means that on later review we can expect changes of diagnosis from depression or even from manic-depressive psychosis to schizophrenia, but not in the reverse direction. There was no case in our study of a reversal from what once was considered to be definitely schizophrenia to manic-depressive psychosis. There were many cases in which the review board changed the original diagnosis from the manic-depressive group to schizophrenia. Table 2–2 presents the data for our original 89 probands. There were 43 of the 89 patients who had been classified as schizophrenic and all were left in that category by the reviewers. Five of the 89 were not classified in the original study; four of these were considered to be schizophrenic by the reviewers while one was diagnosed as manic. Some of the 41 patients (46 per cent) with original diagnoses of melancholia, mania and manic-depressive psychosis had their diagnoses changed radically upon review: two were placed in the involutional category and 26 patients were considered to have been schizophrenic. This left only 14 out of 89 (16 per cent) of the total group of original patients in the manic-depressive group after review, including the one patient originally unclassified.

The differentiation between affective disorder and schizophrenia has the fundamental weakness of lack of objectivity. There are no distinctive anatomical or biochemical differences between the two major categories of psychoses. Consequently, diagnosis remains to some degree a matter of personal preference; this is unfortunate and presumably delays progress in treatment as well as the development of comprehensive theories which would account for the presence of the many psychotics among us.

It is probable that the drop in affective disorders from 46 per cent of our sample to 16 per cent, as the result of the decisions of our board of review, resulted from something more fundamental than the change in fashions in psychiatry during the last 50 years. It is now apparent that the early

Table 2–2. *The Original Diagnosis for the Probands as Compared with the Diagnosis Upon Review Many Years Later.*

RESULTS OF RECENT DIAGNOSIS REVIEW

ORIGINAL DIAGNOSIS (1912–1917)	Involutional Psychotic Reaction	Affective Reaction (Manic-depressive)			Not Spec.	Schizophrenic Reaction					TOTAL
		Manic	De-pressed	Other		Simple	Hebe-phrenic	Cata-tonic	Para-noid	Schizo-affec-tive	
Unclassified		1			1			1	2		5
Melancholia									3		3
Mania		1						1	3	1	6
Manic-depressive											
Type not specified				2				1	2		5
Manic		2						4		1	7
Depressed	2		5						3		10
Mixed, circular		1		2					4	3	10
Paranoia									2		2
Dementia praecox											
Type not specified							1	9	13		23
Hebephrenic						1			4		5
Catatonic								3			3
Paranoid									10		10
Total	2	5	5	4	1	1	1	19	46	5	89

stages of schizophrenia are often indistinguishable from the affective disorders.

Clark and Mallett (1963) carried out a follow-up study of schizophrenia and depression in young adults. They followed a group of 186 patients for a period of three years. This was a rather brief period but even so it showed the trend to shift the diagnosis along the axis from affective toward schizophrenic behavior. Approximately 70 per cent of the schizophrenic group required admission to a mental hospital within the three year period and 93 per cent of these readmissions were again diagnosed as schizophrenic. Of the depressive group, 20 per cent required readmission and about two-thirds again had depressive illnesses, but *one-third were diagnosed as schizophrenic.* Apparently, their small "schizo-affective" group occupied an intermediate position. All 186 patients were admitted for the first time, and almost always for the readmission, to the Maudsley Hospital in London, so we assume that their diagnoses would be acceptable to most psychiatrists. The 186 patients were all under the age of 30 and had on discharge from their first admission a diagnosis of schizophrenia in 86 cases, depression in 82 cases and schizo-af-

fective disorder in 18 cases. This is a much higher proportion of diagnoses of depression than would be given in most hospitals in the United States and probably represents a difference in concepts of diagnosis rather than any basic psychological differences between the patients in the two countries. The fact that the diagnosis of the same patient could vary from country to country, hospital to hospital, and psychiatrist to psychiatrist does not mean that the proband is not ill but does demonstrate the fundamental lack of invariant diagnostic criteria.

The reader may have noticed in Table 2–2 that 46 of the 73 probands with schizophrenic reaction were listed as being of the paranoid subtype. This is 63 per cent of the schizophrenics with this subtype. It differs sharply from Kallmann's (1938) German sample, in which only 160 out of 1087 schizophrenic probands (15 per cent) were of the paranoid subtype. However, Kallmann required as his criterion of selection that the schizophrenia in all of his probands must have become manifest before the age of 40. He introduced this bias deliberately in order to reassure himself that there were only schizophrenics in his sample beyond the possibility of doubt. He realized that this action biased his sample against the paranoid subtype and against mildness of the schizophrenia.

The large difference in the proportion of paranoid schizophrenia in Kallmann's German population compared with that in our study is not only the result of Kallmann's deliberate sampling procedure but probably also due to a preference in diagnosis of the Warren State Hospital Review Board. Paranoid schizophrenia seems to have been their "diagnosis of choice."

The personal factors entering into the diagnosis of the subtypes of schizophrenia are best illustrated by the even greater difference in the proportions of hebephrenic probands in the Kallmann and Warren studies. In the German population of probands, 493 out of 1087 were diagnosed as hebephrenic, or almost 50 per cent, while only one of the 73 Warren probands with schizophrenia had a diagnosis of the hebephrenic subtype. Why this astonishing difference? One answer would seem to be that the same patient would be diagnosed differently as a result of differences in the psychiatrists. To one psychiatrist the deviant behavior of importance may be the silliness and inappropriate verbalization leading to the diagnosis of hebephrenia, while another psychiatrist might consider the same patient a paranoid schizophrenic because he is overly religious and suspects that he is being poisoned.

It is quite possible that the subtypes of schizophrenia are largely the products of environmental factors. Each of the Genain quadruplets (Rosenthal 1963) displayed at least three of the different subtypes of schizophrenia at different times *in spite of their genetic identity.* We have no alternative but to conclude that while different patients belong to different subtypes of schizophrenia, the subtypes result mostly from environmental rather than genetic differences. However, it is possible that particular combinations of genes result in a greater potentiality for some subtypes of schizophrenia than for others.

In our formal diagnosis for all patients we have used the 1952 Diagnostic and Statistical Manual for Mental Disorders of the American Psychiatric Association, Washington, D.C. In our discussion we have tried to conform to the terminology of the manual. However, sometimes it is useful to deviate to some degree from such static taxonomies, so we hope the reader will be tolerant of our semantic inconsistencies.

CHAPTER THREE

THE PROBANDS

The purpose of this chapter is to describe the probands in order to detect the biases which relate to them, to measure the variability they display and to learn more, if we can, about the nature of their disorders. The Appendix includes a description of each of the probands and should be helpful in obtaining a picture of the personal characteristics of each proband. In this chapter we will group the probands in various ways intended to demonstrate their similarities to, and differences from, other samples from the Warren State Hospital population.

The geneticist thinks of the proband as a person displaying a particular trait and as a basic item of a sample which has been selected in order to satisfy specific experimental requirements. The proband is the central figure in the pedigree by virtue of the design of the experiment and not because he had numerous children or was a particularly conspicuous member of the family.

Detailed annual reports were issued by the Warren State Hospital that provide useful statistics for the years during which our probands were selected for study by the original investigators. During 1912, for example, there was a total of 374 admissions, comprising 205 males and 169 females, or 56.8 per cent males. These were included in a total of 8089 admissions—4596 males and 3493 females—recorded from the time the hospital was opened until the end of 1912.

The alleged causes of insanity for the 8089 admissions included some rather astonishing etiological items. There were 27 cases reputed to result from typhoid fever, one from nostalgia, two from overjoy and 201 from overexertion; there were also 111 drug addicts, 137 cases said to be due to masturbation and 63 to heat stroke.

Fortunately, the forms of disease for the 395 cases admitted during 1911 and for those thereafter bear more resemblance to modern terminology. The diagnosis of choice in 1911 was manic-depressive psychosis. Thus 181 of the 395 admissions, or 46 per cent, fell into this one category. In addition, there were 9 cases of undifferentiated depression. Oddly enough, the "sin" of alcoholism was credited with only 22 victims and paresis with only 14 cases. Dementia praecox and paranoia accounted for only 52, or 13 per cent, of the admissions during 1911. The term "schizophrenia" had not appeared in the 1916 report but the frequency of manic-depressive psychosis dropped from 46 per cent to 19 per cent of all admissions during these five years while dementia praecox and paranoia rose from 13 to 20 per cent in the same period. This period from 1911 to 1916 was when the trend toward fewer diagnoses of manic-depressive psychoses and more of schizophrenia began, at least at the Warren State Hospital. The fact that such a large change in diagnostic types occurred within only five years indicates that the change was probably in the taxonomic concepts of the psychiatrists rather than in the psychopathology of the patients. During 1911 some 252 of the 395 admissions, or 64 per cent, were apparently of the "functional" psychosis categories. This proportion did not change much from 1911 through 1916.

We might expect that our probands would have a short life expectancy because of their mental disorder and the possible health hazards of living in an institution. It

Table 3–1. *Age of Probands at Death or at Last Report.*

	NUMBER OF PROBANDS	
AGE	Age at Death	Living at Last Report
20–29	4	
30–39	6	
40–49	12	
50–59	18	1
60–69	17	3
70–79	26	3
80–89	7	
90 or over	2	
Total	92	7
Mean	61.6	68.9

can be seen from Table 3–1 that the patients had long lives, 9 of the 99 having been 80 years old or more at the time of death. The 10 pre-test cases included here confound the averages because a greater proportion of them are from more recent times. Presumably there is a bias for longevity in our group of probands in that young patients who died soon after admission to the hospital would be less likely to be included in our sample. Our conclusion from these data is that mental disorder does not reduce life expectancy to any catastrophic degree. This conclusion is subjective, as it would be difficult to obtain a valid control sample.

TIME OF ADMISSION

The 99 probands of our study comprised three sub-samples in regard to when they were first admitted to the Warren State Hospital. The first group of 26 patients had been admitted to Warren before the study began in 1912. The second group of 63 patients were admitted during the progress of the study from 1912 through 1917. The final group of 10 probands were the pre-test cases selected during the second phase of the study and all were admitted between 1926 and 1953. Of the 99 probands, 77 were only admitted to Warren once, while 22 were admitted two or more times. The Warren Annual Report for 1912 showed that 311 of the 374 admissions for that year, or 83 per cent, were first admissions. This is not significantly different from the 77 per cent of our probands who were first admissions.

THE SEX RATIO

It will be recalled that 4596 of the 8089 admissions to Warren from its opening through 1912 were males. This is 56.8 per cent males. However, only 40 of our 99 probands (40.4 per cent) were men and the difference between the two samples is statistically highly significant. The discrepancy in the sex ratio becomes even more striking when we note that of the 89 probands selected by the Misses Wendt and Badger only 32, or 36 per cent, were males. What are the reasons for this obvious bias? We don't know the reasons for it but can speculate as follows:

1. The Misses Wendt and Badger, being unmarried females, probably preferred to visit the women's wards to interview patients rather than the men's wards. Perhaps they were not aware of their preference but they were probably more comfortable when working with women patients.

2. The 10 more recent pre-test cases were selected by Dr. Hartley and Mr. Johnson, both married males. They selected 8 males and only 2 females.

3. We see that the women interviewers selected a majority of women patients to be their probands while the men interviewers selected a majority of male patients as their probands. This is the first suggestion, as far as we know, that the sex of the person who selects the sample biases the sex ratio of the sample. Probably this bias would be at the subconscious level in some cases but in others it would be recognized and accepted as being a practical procedure.

We were not aware of this possible source of bias in our mental retardation study (Reed and Reed, 1965) in which the probands, originally selected by Miss Curial, were 47.7 per cent men and 52.3 per cent women. Professor Penrose (1938) presented a sample of retardates, presumably selected by him, composed of 56.5 per cent males and 43.5 per cent females. Here also the majority of probands are of the same sex as the person who selected them. Presumably these sex biases would be avoided if only consecutive admissions were selected.

THE DIAGNOSIS

It will be recalled from Chapter Two that 41 of the 89 probands selected by 1917 were diagnosed as having an affective type of psychosis. Upon review of the records in the 1960's, only 14 of the 41 were left in the affective reaction category (Table 2–2). Because of this striking shift in diagnostic concepts, which occurred at Warren between 1910 and 1920, it was decided that the records for *all* patients who were first admitted to Warren from 1912 through 1917 would be reviewed by Dr. Urbaitis. Thus we can compare our probands, the 63 who were first admitted from 1912 through 1917, with the rest of the patients who were first admitted during the same years. We can compare our 63 probands with 535 non-probands first admitted at the same time period. These are a selected sample also in that only "functional" psychoses were included in the non-proband group. In order to make the reviewing feasible it was necessary to restrict the detailed review to every fifth one of the schizophrenic non-probands. The number of schizophrenic non-proband cases which were reviewed was then multiplied by five and added to the rest of the cases.

When we look at our 63 probands as to diagnosis after review, we see that there were 55 (12.7 per cent) schizophrenics and 8 with affective reactions. The 535 non-probands included 455 schizophrenics, 52 patients (10.3 per cent) with affective disorders and 28 patients with other functional psychoses. The difference between these two distributions is not statistically significant. The fundamental difference, if there is one, is the selection of a higher proportion of patients with affective disorders in the proband sample.

The selection of a higher proportion of probands with affective disorders than was present in the rest of the Warren population was probably deliberate and necessary in order to make a study of the affective disorders possible from a statistical standpoint. Even this effort leaves us with a smaller sample of probands with affective disorders than we would like to have. There were 4 of 10 of the pre-test probands with affective disorders and the bias here was intentional, for without this deliberate selection there might have been no case of affective reaction among the 10 probands.

Let us return to the sex ratio of the probands now that we have been introduced to the non-proband group. Of the 63 probands selected from the 1912 to 1917

population only 21, or 33.3 per cent, were males. However, 285, or 53.3 per cent, of the 535 non-probands were males. This difference is statistically highly significant ($p < 0.005$) and is convincing evidence for the hypothesis that the interviewer has a tendency to select probands of his or her own sex.

AGE AT FIRST ADMISSION

We will now introduce extensive data from another sample of patients that will provide some useful comparisons for our investigation of the biases which affected the selection of our probands.

Mr. Nelson Johnson and his assistants compiled data in 1960 on the 5000 consecutive first admissions to the Warren State Hospital between November 7, 1953 and December 31, 1959. These were the last 5000 first admissions up to January, 1960 and the data were obtained for use in making decisions about admissions policies and budget requests as determined by the characteristics of the patients being admitted at that time. The 5000 patients were not listed in his study according to diagnosis and are from a later time period than our probands. However, several comparisons can be made between the 5000 patient sample, the 535 non-probands of 1912 to 1917 and our 99 probands.

In Table 3–2 we see that our 99 probands were younger at first admission than the 535 non-probands and very much

Table 3–2. *Age of the Warren Population of 5000, the 535 Non-Probands, and of our 99 Probands at First Admission to Warren State Hospital.*

AGE	THE 5000 PATIENTS (Per Cent)	THE 535 NON-PROBANDS (Per Cent)	THE 99 PROBANDS (Per Cent)
Under 20	5.6	3.2	13
20–29	12.6	29.7	30
30–39	16.7	23.6	16
40–49	14.9	22.2	19
50–59	13.4	18.1	17
60–69	12.3	3.0	2
70–79	14.0	0.2	2
80 and Over	10.5	0.0	0
	100.0	100.0	99
Mean (years)	51.3	38.3	36.1

younger than the 5000 patient sample. Only 4 per cent of our 99 probands were 60 or over at first admission, while 36.8 per cent of the sample of 5000 were 60 years of age or older. It is of greater significance that 43 per cent of our probands were admitted when less than 30 years old, while only 28.2 per cent of the 5000 patients were under 30. It is clear that the patients admitted in the late fifties were very much older than either the probands or non-probands of the early 1900's. This increase in geriatric mental problems would be expected in view of the great increase in the average age of the United States population over several decades. However, there may also have been a change in the cultural pattern which includes more frequent hospitalization of the elderly persons with mental derangements now than was the case early in the century.

COUNTY OF RESIDENCE

The county of residence of the 5000 patients and the 99 probands is not significantly different for these two samples. Approximately 30 per cent of each sample resided in Erie County, which includes the large city of Erie, while the remaining 70 per cent of the patients resided in towns or rural areas. Our sample of 99 probands is too small for further subdivision. The data are given in Table 3–3.

BIRTH ORDER

A comparison of the birth order of the 5000 patients and our 99 probands is given in Table 3–4. It is clear that the two samples

Table 3–3. *County of Residence of the Warren Population of 5000 and of Our 99 Probands at First Admission.*

COUNTY	THE 5000 PATIENTS (Per Cent)	THE 99 PROBANDS (Per Cent)
Erie	27.9	31
Warren	8.0	6
Other 11 counties	63.1	62
Non-residents	1.0	0
	100.0	99

Table 3–4. *Position of Birth in Family of the Warren Population of 5000 and of Our 99 Probands.*

BIRTH ORDER	THE 5000 PATIENTS (Per Cent)	THE 99 PROBANDS Study Subjects	Expected (Per Cent)
1st	24.0	16	18.2
2nd	19.5	24	18.2
3rd	14.1	16	16.7
4th	9.9	10	13.0
5th	7.6	11	10.7
6th	5.0	8	8.1
7th	3.4	5	5.8
8th	2.2	2	4.0
9th or more	2.9	7	5.1
Unknown	11.4	0	0
	100.0	99	99.8

do not differ significantly from each other. A test for deviations from random birth order is routine for this type of problem. Therefore, we made an internal test of the expectations for our 99 probands to see whether the birth orders departed from the values calculated on the basis of the size of the sibship of which the patient was a member.

For the evaluation of birth order among the probands all half sibs were included, but all half or full sibs who died at two years of age or less were excluded. This was thought to provide the most reasonable test of possible psychogenic factors within the family setting that were related to birth order.

The expected distribution of birth order was calculated based on the assumption that the order of the probands would be expected to be distributed equally in all positions within each sibship size. The difference between the observed and expected distributions was relatively small and was not statistically significant.

NUMBER OF LIVING SIBLINGS

Our 99 probands were born in the generation before the 5000 patients and would be in larger families than the 5000 patients because of the larger family sizes of the earlier generations. There was also a bias in selecting the probands toward larger sibships since the geneticist cannot study the siblings when the proband is an only child. None of the 99 probands was an only child. The average family size, excluding the proband, was 4.4 siblings, and it was 3.9 siblings for the non-proband. Thus the bias presumably introduced by selection for larger numbers of siblings of our probands could not have been larger than one-half a child, a seemingly inconsequential bias as far as the etiology of mental disorders is concerned.

SCHOOLING

The majority of our probands and of the 5000 patient sample were from rural areas and hence it is not surprising that 60 per cent of our probands and 49.8 per cent of the larger sample completed only eight grades or less of school. The difference of about 10 per cent between the two samples is again probably due to our probands having been born in the preceding generation when high school and college attendance was less popular than in more recent times. These data are given in Table 3–6.

A satisfactory comparison of the two groups of patients with the remaining population of Pennsylvania is not possible because the patients are of different age cohorts. However, a look at the state

Table 3–6. *Highest Grade of School Completed of the Warren Population of 5000 and of Our 99 Probands.*

GRADE OF SCHOOL	THE 5000 PATIENTS (Per Cent)	THE 99 PROBANDS (Per Cent)
None	3.0	1
1–4	6.9	12
5–8	39.9	47
9–11	17.2	11
12	18.5	10
13–15	4.1	8
16 or more	2.4	1
Unknown	8.0	9
	100.0	99
Median (omitting unknown)	7.6 grades	6.7 grades

population for 1940 and 1950 in regard to educational attainment shows the distributions to be very similar to that of the 5000 patients. It is possible to conclude that the education of our probands was not grossly inferior to that of their normal age cohorts.

MARITAL STATUS

The data in Table 3–7 are the first which show a difference between our 99 probands and the 5000 patients that is probably of importance. The fact that 46 per cent of our probands were single at the time of first admission, compared with only 25.3 per cent of the 5000 patients who were unmarried, probably means that more of our probands were more seriously ill than was the case for the Warren Hospital population as a whole. This seems to be a reasonable assumption in view of the high proportion of 46 per cent of our 99 probands who were not married at first admission. Naturally, the earlier the onset and the more serious the disorder, the less likely it is that the person would be married at the time of the first admission. It means also that in selecting the group of 99 probands with "functional" psychoses we obtained the more seriously ill patients as compared with the entire population in a mental hospital, which would include alcoholics, senile dementias and others who would have been fairly healthy at the usual age of marriage.

The 535 non-probands were selected

Table 3–5. *Number of Living Siblings of the Warren Population of 5000, of the 535 Non-Probands, and of Our 99 Probands at First Admission.*

NUMBER SIBLINGS OF PROBAND	THE 5000 PATIENTS (Per Cent)	535 NON-PROBANDS (Per Cent)	THE 99 PROBANDS (Per Cent)
None	12.4	3.9	0
1	16.0	9.3	6
2	16.7	24.9	16
3	14.0	10.7	15
4	10.3	13.3	19
5	8.1	13.1	14
6	6.1	9.9	13
7	3.9	5.4	7
8	2.7	5.2	4
9 or more	3.8	4.3	5
Unknown	6.0	0.0	0
	100.0	100.0	99
Mean number of siblings	3.1	3.9	4.4

Table 3–7. *Marital Status of the Warren Population of 5000, the 535 Non-Probands, and of Our 99 Probands at First Admission. (Ten of the 99 probands married after their first admission.)*

MARITAL STATUS	THE 5000 PATIENTS (Per Cent)	535 NON-PROBANDS (Per Cent)	THE 99 PROBANDS (Per Cent)
Single	25.3	40.9	46
Married	46.0	46.4	43
Divorced or separated	10.4	6.5	3
Widowed	18.0	6.2	7
Other	0.3	0	0
	100.0	100.0	99

Table 3–8. *Number of Marriages of the Warren Population of 5000 and of Our Probands.*

NUMBER OF MARRIAGES	THE 5000 PATIENTS (Per Cent)	THE 99 PROBANDS (Per Cent) At First Admission	THE 99 PROBANDS (Per Cent) At Last Information
None	25.3	46	36
Married once	61.0	52	52
Married more than once	12.3	1	11
Unknown	1.4	0	0
	100.0	99	99

for a "functional" psychosis and resemble the 99 probands more than the whole Warren population of 5000 consecutive patients in having over 40 per cent single persons.

We see in the heading for Table 3–7 that 10 of our 99 probands married after their first admission to Warren State Hospital. Thus, roughly 20 per cent of probands who married at all did so after their first admission to the hospital. Presumably they made at least a partial recovery from their illness before their release from the hospital. This would be indicated not only by the fact that they left the hospital but also by the fact that they then were married.

In Table 3–8 it is clear that our probands are also different from the 5000 patient population at the time of first admission in that only one proband, or 1 per cent, had married more than once compared with 12.3 per cent of the 5000 patients. However, our last information about our 99 probands, almost all of whom are now deceased, shows 11 per cent to have married more than once, so they are probably not much different in respect to multiple marriages from the Warren Hospital population as a whole.

It should be emphasized again that our 99 probands were definitely different from the 5000 patient sample in that at least 10 per cent more of the 99 proband group never married at any time. The most likely reason for this is simply that they were more seriously ill than the Warren Hospital population as a whole. They were also much younger at admission.

Table 3–9 contains the same informa-

tion about our 99 probands, all of whom at last information were either deceased or quite old, but tabulated according to the sex of the proband. There was twice the percentage of single males compared with females and naturally twice as many married females as males. The principle here is the same as it was for the mentally retarded (Reed and Reed, 1965) in that the mentally ill or mentally retarded woman is more marriageable than the affected male. This may mean that women are less seriously ill than men but it is more likely that the phenomenon is due to poorer social adjustment of males compared with females with the same clinical degree of illness. Stated another way, a normal man is more likely to marry a mentally disadvantaged woman than is a normal woman to marry a mentally disadvantaged man.

We can find out more about the marriages of our probands by looking at the mental health of their spouses. It can be seen in Table 3–10 that the 63 probands who married had a total of 75 spouses. Unfortunately, we don't know the mental status of 13 of the spouses. These were

Table 3–9. *Marital History of Our 99 Probands at Last Information.*

MARITAL HISTORY	MALE PROBANDS No.	MALE PROBANDS Per Cent	FEMALE PROBANDS No.	FEMALE PROBANDS Per Cent	TOTALS No.	TOTALS Per Cent
Single	21	52.5	15	25.4	36	36.4
Married once	15	37.5	37	62.7	52	52.5
Married more than once	4	10.0	7	11.9	11	11.1
Totals	40	100.0	59	100.0	99	100.0

Table 3-10. *Mental Health of the Spouses of Our 63 Married Probands.*

	MALE PROBANDS		FEMALE PROBANDS		TOTALS	
	No.	*Per Cent*	No.	*Per Cent*	No.	*Per Cent*
Spouse with "functional" psychosis (proved or probable)	2	8.7	0	0.0	2	2.7
Spouse with other mental disorder	3	13.0	19	36.5	22	29.4
Spouse without any of the above	11	47.9	27	52.0	38	50.6
Spouse unknown as to mental health	7	30.4	6	11.5	13	17.3
Totals (including remarriages)	23	100.0	52	100.0	75	100.0

mostly the spouses of earlier marriages; naturally, it was difficult to obtain information about them as usually it was unknown to the more recent spouse and other relatives.

Table 3-10 is illuminating in that the percentage of spouses with "functional" psychoses is probably no higher than expected by chance. There is no convincing evidence of positive assortative marriage for schizophrenia or manic-depressive psychosis either here or in the literature (Erlenmeyer-Kimling and Paradowski, 1966), which is in sharp contrast to the highly significant assortative marriage for degree of intelligence and for educational attainment (Garrison, Anderson and Reed, 1968). It is possible that the 29.4 per cent of the spouses with "other mental disorders" is higher than chance expectation. It is difficult to determine what the expectation is in the normal population for "other mental disorders," which is a conglomeration of poorly defined ailments such as the various neuroses and different manifestations not included in the functional psychoses.

REPRODUCTION OF THE SAMPLES OF PATIENTS

It is well known that psychotic persons who are ill enough to be hospitalized do not replace themselves in the population. Their deficit in children may be due in part to their removal from the reproductive pool while in the hospital but obviously their lower reproductive rate cannot be entirely separable from the severity of their illness and must have some correlation with it. At least 2.2 children per person are necessary at present to replace the individual and his spouse in the population. In pioneer communities the greater hazards and higher mortality required a larger number of children per family than 2.2 to maintain the population size. In Pennsylvania, at the time our patients were of reproductive age, the number of children per person must have averaged better than four or even five. We saw in Table 3-5 that our probands themselves had 4.4 *living* siblings at the time the probands were first admitted to the Warren State Hospital. Consequently, when we look at the number of living children of our 99 probands and the Warren 5000 patient sample we see in Table 3-11 that the 5000 patient sample averaged 1.8 children while the 99 probands averaged 1.5 children each. In none of the three samples was the average of 2.2 children necessary for replacement achieved.

The question of paramount importance in regard to the reproduction of psychotics is that related to population dynamics. Why is it that we have more admissions to the state hospitals each year when the psychotics of one generation are not replacing themselves in the next generation? We will consider this question in detail when we

Table 3-11. *Number of Living Children of the Warren Population of 5000, the 535 Non-Probands, and of Our 99 Probands at First Admission.*

NUMBER LIVING CHILDREN	THE 5000 PATIENTS *(Per Cent)*	535 NON-PROBANDS *(Per Cent)*	THE 99 PROBANDS *(Per Cent)*
None	39.4	59.8	52
1	14.7	7.9	11
2	15.4	12.9	10
3	11.7	4.7	14
4	6.5	5.2	3
5	4.3	4.5	2
6	2.5	3.7	2
7	1.7	0.9	4
8	0.9	0	0
9 or more	1.6	0.4	1
Unknown	1.3	0	0
	100.0	100.0	99
Mean no. living children	1.8	1.2	1.5

consider the genetic mechanisms involved with mental disorders.

CONSANGUINITY

Seven of the 99 probands were the products of consanguineous marriages, five were from first cousins, one from a first cousin once removed and one from a second cousin marriage. The average inbreeding coefficient (F) is 0.00363 for the 99 probands, which is higher than normal. Ordinarily, we expect to find less than 1 per cent of a group of people to have consanguineous parentage. Four of these 7 probands were clearly schizophrenic (2 catatonic and 2 paranoid), while the other three were diagnosed at various times as having schizophrenic, manic-depressive psychosis or involutional psychosis.

The 7 probands had an average of 6.6 siblings. Of the 46 sibs, 6 (13.0 per cent) were also psychotic and 12 others (26.1 per cent) had some other mental disorder. Thus 39.1 per cent of the siblings of these 7 consanguineous probands did not have normal mental health, compared with 43.6 per cent of the non-consanguineous siblings of the probands.

The usual view of consanguineous matings is that they bring about homozygosity in the offspring of those recessive genes carried by both parents. However, Reed and Reed (1965) found that it was the mental retardation which resulted in the excess of consanguineous unions to a greater degree than chance expectation. The mentally defective person, whether retarded or with thought disorder, has a severely limited population from which to choose a mate and therefore is much more likely to marry a blood relative. Therefore, we should expect the consanguineous parents of our seven probands to be mentally ill in most of the cases. We find this to be true. Two of the seven probands had one parent psychotic and the other parent had a psychoneurotic or personality disorder. Four more probands had one normal parent, while the other parent was psychoneurotic or had a personality disorder. For only one proband of the seven were both parents reported to have normal mental health.

Thus our principle that the consanguineous marriages are frequently the primary result of the mental defect and produce mentally defective children is upheld. In the Reed and Reed (1965) study of mental retardation it was found that 8 per cent of the probands had consanguineous parents, while 7 per cent of the Warren probands with psychoses had consanguineous parents. This close agreement is probably not mainly coincidence but instead a rather reliable index of the percentage of consanguinity to be expected among the parents of hospitalized patients with serious mental difficulties.

ILLEGITIMATE BIRTHS

Only one of the 99 probands produced an illegitimate child. The baby died shortly after birth and is not included, of course, in the total of 143 children born to the 99 probands who survived to 15 years of age. The reader may be surprised that the illegitimacy rate turned out to be less than 1 per cent whereas for 289 mentally retarded probands there were 37 illegitimate children (37.4 per cent) of 99 children in the Reed and Reed (1965) study. The sharp distinction between the mentally disordered and the mentally retarded in their illegitimacy rates illustrates the difference in behavior of the two groups of affected persons. The mentally retarded are handicapped throughout life and less often have normal marriages with legitimate children; they are likely to have unstable relationships and occasional illegitimate children. The mentally disordered, on the other hand, may have a late age of onset and remissions, so they were more likely to be married and have legitimate children than were the retarded probands. Stevens (1969) found that before their first admission 7.4 per cent of her 622 British white schizophrenics had at least one illegitimate birth. This is probably closer to what we might have found if we had had a larger sample of psychotic probands.

TWINNING

About 2 of 85 births are members of twin pairs in the United States. Two of our 99 probands were born as members of twin pairs, which is in agreement with expectation. However, the other twin died within a few months of birth in both cases and thus twinning seems to have had no significance in our sample of 99 probands.

LENGTH OF RESIDENCE

The 99 probands were in the Warren State Hospital for a total of 1093.2 years. This total would have to be increased somewhat to account for the 7 probands still there at the time of writing. This is an average of 11 years per patient. Fortunately, the length of residence is decreasing for present-day admissions as the result of the introduction of tranquilizers and other new therapeutic techniques. It is interesting that the length of residence for our probands is only 11 years while the average residence of the mentally retarded at the Faribault State School and Hospital was 25 years, or over twice as long, as shown by Reed and Reed (1965). The retarded are admitted to the hospital at a much younger average age than the psychotic patients, which is the main reason for their longer residence there.

SUMMARY

This chapter described some attributes of the 99 probands, each with a psychosis, who were selected as the starting points for this study. They are compared with the 535 patients with functional psychoses who were admitted to the Warren State Hospital between 1912 and 1917, and with a complete sample of 5000 consecutive admissions to Warren State Hospital between November 7, 1953 and December 31, 1959. In general, the 99 probands were much like the larger sample of 5000 unselected consecutive patients, even though the 99 probands were admitted to Warren about one generation earlier than the 5000 patients.

Some of the noteworthy characteristics of our 99 probands are as follows:

1. The probands were much younger at first admission (average 36.1 years) than the sample of 5000 patients (average 51.3 years). This probably means that there were more schizophrenics among our probands than in the complete sample of admissions, and it is certainly clear that geriatric cases were omitted from our selected probands.

2. Of the 99 probands, 77 were admitted to Warren only once while 22 were admitted two or more times.

3. Only 40 of our 99 probands were males. This 40.4 per cent males is, statistically, highly significant as it is lower than the 56.8 per cent males among the 8089 admissions to Warren from its opening through 1912. Probably the major reason for the shortage of males was that the interviewing of the probands by Miss Wendt in the women's wards was preferred by her to interviews with men patients. This suggests that the sex of the person who selects the sample may bias the sex ratio of the sample.

4. The average age at first admission of our probands was 36.1 years. This is much younger than the average age of 51.3 years for the 5000 patient sample. Presumably the major difference is due to the much larger proportion of geriatric admissions in recent times because of the greater average age of the population now.

5. There was no evidence for any birth order effect.

6. Our probands had 4.4 living siblings while the non-probands had 3.9 living siblings at time of first admission. Apparently our probands came from slightly larger families than the non-proband patients.

7. A significant difference between the two populations is that of the greater disadvantage of our probands in obtaining mates. About 25 per cent of the 5000 patient group were single at first admission, while 46 per cent of our 99 probands had not married at first admission to the Warren State Hospital. This probably means that our probands were more seriously ill than the patients at Warren as a whole. It is clear that our male probands were at twice as great a disadvantage in obtaining mates as the female probands; 52.5 per cent of the male probands never married, while 25.4 per cent of the females never married.

8. The 99 probands averaged 1.5 children, while the 5000 patients averaged only 1.8 children. In neither case is this average high enough for replacement of the patient and spouse in the next generation.

9. Seven of the 99 probands were the products of consanguineous parentage. This is higher than normal consanguinity rates and probably means that many of the parents of the probands were also mentally disturbed. This was found to be the case. For only 1 proband of the 7 were both parents reported to have normal mental health.

10. The 99 probands were in the Warren State Hospital for a total of 1093.2 years, an average of 11 years per patient.

CHAPTER FOUR

THE PROBANDS' PARENTS, SIBLINGS, AND CHILDREN

In this chapter we will restrict ourselves to the parents, siblings and children of the probands. These are all of the first degree relatives of the proband and all share 50 per cent of their genes, as an average, with the proband.

Our probands will be subdivided in various ways in this chapter with the expectation that insights as to relevant genetic or environmental factors might emerge.

The 10 pre-test probands will be omitted from many of the analyses because they were our practice cases from which we learned how to follow up families better so that we would not waste or spoil any of the valuable material from our original 89 families which had been investigated so carefully about 50 years previously. Furthermore, the pre-test probands intentionally included an over-sampling of cases of manic-depressive psychosis in order to include a few cases of this less-frequent type of disorder.

Table 4–1 shows the 99 probands according to whether they were first admitted to Warren from 1912 through 1917 or whether they were admitted prior to 1912 for the first time. The pre-test probands were subsequent admissions since 1917 and have younger children. It has been mentioned in the previous paragraph that 4 of 10 pre-test cases were diagnosed as affective reaction, which is an excess of this diagnosis in relation to schizophrenia in most hospitals. It may be seen in Table 4–1 that while the review of the original diagnoses decreased greatly the proportion of effective reaction probands in both the first admissions group (1912 to 1917) and in the prior to 1912 admissions group, there is probably still an excess of this type of diagnosis present in the total sample compared with that in the hospital population as a whole. The excess of affective reaction probands is greatest in the pre-test group, next greatest in the prior admissions group and least nu-

Table 4–1. *The 99 Probands According to Time of First Admission and Type of Diagnosis After Recent Review by a Group of Psychiatrists.*

	FIRST ADMISSION 1912–1917	PRIOR ADMISSION	SUB-TOTALS	PRE-TEST	TOTALS
Affective reaction	8	6	14	4	18
Affective reaction changed to schizophrenia*	20	12	32	0	32
Schizophrenic reaction	35	8	43	6	49
Totals	63	26	89	10	99

*Includes 2 probands who were changed from "depressed" to "involutional psychotic reaction."

merous in the first admissions from 1912 to 1917 group.

There are striking and perplexing variations in the percentages of proved and probable psychosis in the relatives of the probands as shown in Table 4–2. Before considering the data it should be mentioned that all of the first degree relatives were investigated carefully and only 20 of the 881 (2.3 per cent) of the parents, siblings and children had to be classified as having unknown mental health.

The combination of all psychoses in one category in Table 4–2 and the tables immediately following was deliberate. Later on there will be separations of the data into subdivisions of the psychoses, such as schizophrenia and manic-depressive psychosis. Our intention is to present the data in various ways and at this point we wish them to be all-inclusive, that is, with all clearly psychotic persons counted as such. This gives a different picture from later tables in which, for example, only schizophrenia is included, the persons with different psychoses being excluded.

The fact that two generations of research workers were involved in collecting the data means that most all of the individuals shown in this chapter were either old or dead when the study ended so that an age correction would not have changed the results greatly. Later on, considerable attention will be given to the calculation of age corrections for the more recent generations of the kinships of the study.

Thus, in the present chapter we will present the data in a more global form with refinements to follow in later chapters.

The first problem is that of the pre-test group, which lowers the percentages of affected persons of all categories and provides a nonsense answer of zero per cent of the children with any kind of psychosis. One of the reasons for this nonsense answer for the children is that there were only 18 of them which is too small a sample to be useful. Finally, the whole pre-test group was given less careful individual attention simply because it was included only as a vehicle for testing data forms, interview techniques and other necessary preliminary maneuvers. Consequently, the pre-test data will be omitted from tables where they cannot be clearly separated from the other material.

Probably the most striking feature of Table 4–2 is the high frequency of psychoses and other mental disorders in the relatives of the probands admitted prior to 1912 when compared with the probands who were first admitted between 1912 to 1917. The most reasonable explanation of this difference would be that the early workers selected probands with "loaded" family histories from the population of patients who had their first admissions to Warren before 1912. We do not have any direct evidence, however, that such a bias in the selection of probands was practiced.

The values in Table 4–2 for the first degree relatives of the probands who were admitted between 1912 to 1917 are in reasonably good agreement with those expected from the family studies of Kallmann and others previously cited. However, there is one striking incongruity which needs comment. It can be seen that the frequency of "other mental disorders" is 45.2 per cent in the parents of the 1912 to 1917 probands and 44.2 per cent in the parents of the probands admitted prior to 1912. Both of these percentages are about twice as high as the frequencies of "other mental disorders" in the siblings and children of the probands. What explanations are possible for this statistically highly significant difference? We cannot answer this question with any certainty and can only suggest what seem to be reasonable possibilities to account for the high frequency of the "other disorder" category in the parents compared with siblings and children of the probands. Three possible explanations are the following:

1. A causal explanation would be that persons are more likely to become part of a study if one or both parents are themselves afflicted with some mental difficulty, particularly of the "other mental disorder" type. This would be because such parents produce a disproportionately high percentage of psychotic offspring.

2. If assortative marriage is important between persons with various "other mental disorders," we might find an excess of such marriages in the parents of our probands.

3. There may well have been an ascertainment bias in that interviewers were more likely to select probands who had one or both parents with "other mental disorders." This bias, if it was present, may not have been a conscious one.

Table 4-2. *Mental Health of the First Degree Relatives of the Probands by Admission Group, Excluding Those Under 15 Years of Age.*

MENTAL HEALTH OF RELATIVES	PROBANDS WITH FIRST ADMISSION 1912–1917 N=63			PROBANDS ADMITTED PRIOR TO 1912 N=26			PRE-TEST PROBANDS N=10			ALL PROBANDS N=99		
	Parents	*Sibs*	*Children*	*Parents*	*Sibs*	*Children*	*Parents*	*Sibs*	*Children*	*Parents*	*Sibs*	*Children*
Functional psychosis	9	31	11	8	26	11	1	1	0	18	58	22
Probable psychosis	8	14	3	6	14	2	2	1	0	16	29	5
Other mental disorder	57	85	21	23	30	18	3	5	0	83	120	39
Without the above (or unknown)	52	200	64	15	63	24	14	41	18	81	304	106
Totals	126	330	99	52	133	55	20	48	18	198	511	172
Psychosis (including probable) Per Cent	13.5	13.6	14.1	26.9	30.1	23.6	15.0	4.2	0.0	17.2	17.0	15.7
Other mental disorder Per Cent	45.2	25.8	21.2	44.2	22.6	32.7	15.0	10.4	0.0	41.9	23.5	22.7
Total psychotic and other disorders Per Cent	58.7	39.4	35.3	71.1	52.7	56.3	30.0	14.6	0.0	59.1	40.5	38.4
Mean age	69.3	62.8	52.9	69.5	63.2	57.4	64.8	62.0	43.9	68.9	62.9	53.3

We are not able to evaluate the relative importance of these three explanations for the high frequency of "other mental disorders" in the parents of our probands at this point in our analysis. This category of mental defects is of great significance in any study of the etiology of the psychoses and we will give the subject consideration later.

The "other mental disorders" (with the corresponding code numbers from the 1952 manual of the American Psychiatric Association) are psychotic reactions to arteriosclerosis (15.01) or to senility (17.11), psychoneurotic disorders (40), and personality disorders (50 to 54). The latter group includes schizoid personality, compulsive personality, sociopathic personality disturbance, alcoholism and some other patterns of behavior which are not frank psychoses but which are not normal either. A listing of all categories included in the "other mental disorders" is given in Table 7–24.

THE PARENTS

We expect to find a higher frequency of psychotic disorders in the parents of our probands than there would be on a chance basis. Such an excess does not permit any discrimination between the relative importance of heredity and environment in regard to the etiology of psychoses. However, some leverage might be obtained by comparing the frequencies of the affected parent of each sex. These data are in Table 4–3.

The mother of the proband had a proved or probable psychosis in 20.3 per cent of the cases while the father was affected in 14.5 per cent of the 89 probands.

However, there was a slight excess of "other psychotic disorders" among the fathers (46.2 per cent) when compared with the mothers (43.9 per cent) of the probands. The combined difference is only slightly in the direction of an excess for affected mothers and is not statistically significant. Thus we tried to obtain a leverage in relation to a genetic-environmental distinction without success. The most striking finding in the table is that only 16 of the 89 probands (18 per cent) were offspring of parents both of whom were free of detectable mental disorders. Some readers may be surprised that only 18 per cent of the probands had both parents free of mental disorders, functional or other, yet the study of Srole et al. (1961), "Mental Health in the Metropolis," indicated that only about 18 per cent of the population of midtown Manhattan were free of mental difficulties of some sort. Consequently, significantly less than 18 per cent of children born to residents of midtown Manhattan would have both parents free of mental difficulties. If marriage were random in relation to mental health, only $(0.18)^2$ of the marriages, or 3 per cent, would be between two mentally healthy persons. The Manhattan study included large numbers of people with neuroses and other mental quirks which would be excluded from our categories of functional psychosis, though some of them would have been included in our "other mental disorders" group. The Manhattan study emphasizes again the importance of the diagnostic criteria in describing and interpreting the results of mental health studies. It also shows clearly that diagnostic boundaries are not discrete and that the completely normal

Table 4–3. *The Presence of Proved and Probable Functional Psychoses and Other Mental Disorders in the Parents of the 89 Original Probands. Pre-Test Probands Omitted.*

DIAGNOSIS OF FATHER	DIAGNOSIS OF MOTHER			
	Functional Psychosis No. (Per Cent)	*Other Mental Disorder No. (Per Cent)*	*Without Mental Disorder No. (Per Cent)*	*Totals No. (Per Cent)*
Functional psychosis	3(3.4)	8(9.0)	2(2.1)	13(14.5)
Other mental disorder	12(13.5)	15(16.9)	14(15.8)	41(46.2)
Without mental disorder	3(3.4)	16(18.0)	16(18.0)	35(39.4)
Totals	18(20.3)	39(43.9)	32(35.9)	89(100.1)

fraction of the population is a surprisingly small group at one end of an apparently continuous curve of mental health variants.

It should be mentioned that while only 18.0 per cent of our probands had both parents apparently free of mental disorder, between 35 and 40 per cent of the parents as individuals were without mental disorder, a figure which is twice as high as the 18 per cent of the Manhattan population. The difference is probably due in large part to the extremely inclusive diagnostic criteria employed by the Manhattan investigators.

THE AUNTS AND UNCLES

The aunts and uncles are second degree relatives of our probands. They are also the siblings of the parents of our probands. The aunts and uncles are of interest to us because they could provide evidence as to possible bias in the selection of our probands with "loaded" families. Our results will not be generally applicable if many probands were selected who had a disproportionately large percentage of psychotic relatives (loaded pedigrees). We have already seen in Table 4–2 that there were unusually high percentages of probable and proved psychosis in the first degree relatives of the probands who were admitted to Warren prior to 1912, but for the larger group of probands admitted from 1912 through 1917 the frequencies of psychoses in the first degree relatives were in the range of values found by other authors. Generally

accepted values for first degree relatives of psychotic probands are in the range of 12 to 18 per cent of proved and probable psychosis when age-corrected.

The aunts and uncles are second degree relatives of the probands and therefore might be expected to display a range of values half as great, that is, from 6 to 9 per cent of proved and probable psychosis. However, in some cases the aunts and uncles are siblings of psychotic parents of our probands so, in essence, they are first degree relatives of a psychotic person. Nonetheless, the aunts and uncles as a group should have a lower frequency of psychosis than that found in the first degree relatives of the proband but the frequency should not be as low as 50 per cent of the value for the first degree relatives of the proband.

Table 4–4 presents the data for the aunts and uncles according to the diagnostic group of each parent of the proband. It can be seen that when the parent was psychotic there were 12.8 per cent of the aunts and uncles with a psychosis, whereas if the parent was not affected only about half as many (6.7 per cent) of the aunts and uncles were psychotic. There were also 21.6 per cent of the aunts and uncles with other mental disorders if the proband's parent was psychotic and only 10 per cent with other mental disorders if the parent was not affected. These low values for psychosis (6.7 per cent) and for other mental disorders (10 per cent) in the aunts and uncles, when the respective parent is not affected, would seem to indicate that there were not many

Table 4–4. *Mental Health of the Aunts and Uncles of our Probands. Data for the 1912–1917 Admissions and the Admissions Prior to 1912 Were Similar and Have Been Pooled Here.*

| | MENTAL HEALTH OF AUNTS AND UNCLES (PARENTS' SIBS) | | | | |
Parents' Mental Health	Proved and Probable Psychosis No. (Per Cent)	Other Mental Disorder No. (Per Cent)	Not Affected No. (Per Cent)	Unknown as to Mental Health No. (Per Cent)	Totals No. (Per Cent)
Proved and probable psychosis	16(12.8)	27(21.6)	73(58.4)	9(7.2)	125(100)
Other mental disorder	25(5.8)	60(13.8)	289(66.6)	60(13.8)	434(100)
Not affected	25(6.7)	37(10.0)	254(68.5)	55(14.8)	371(100)
Totals	66(7.1)	124(13.3)	616(66.2)	124(13.3)	930(100)

Table 4–5. *Mental Health of the Siblings of the 89 Probands When Classified According to the Sex and Mental Health of Their Parents.*

Mental Health of Parents		FULL SIBLINGS OF THE PROBANDS			
		1. Psychosis No. (Per Cent)	2. Other Mental Disorder No. (Per Cent)	3. (Cols. 1&2) Psychosis and Other Disorder No. (Per Cent)	4. Total Siblings (incl. Unaffected)
Mother	Father				
Psychotic	Psychotic	4(36.4)	2(18.2)	6(54.6)	11
Other disorder	Psychotic	5(13.5)	12(32.4)	17(45.9)	37
Unaffected	Psychotic	0(0.0)	0(0.0)	0(0.0)	5
Psychotic	Other disorder	28(44.4)	14(22.2)	42(66.6)	63
Other disorder	Other disorder	18(20.2)	23(25.8)	41(46.0)	89
Unaffected	Other disorder	7(9.6)	18(24.7)	25(34.3)	73
Psychotic	Unaffected	6(26.1)	5(21.7)	11(47.8)	23
Other disorder	Unaffected	9(12.2)	19(25.7)	28(37.9)	74
Unaffected	Unaffected	8(9.1)	22(25.0)	30(34.1)	88
Totals		85(18.4)	115(24.8)	200(43.2)	463

loaded families selected. There is no excess of affected persons in the group of aunts and uncles, compared with expectation for families that were not loaded.

THE SIBLINGS OF THE PROBAND

The reader may remember that in Table 4–2 there was an excessively large percentage (30.1 per cent) of the siblings of the probands with a proved or probable psychosis for the probands admitted prior to 1912. The value of 13.6 per cent of proved and probable psychosis for the siblings of the probands admitted from 1912 to 1917 is, however, well within the range of values expected from the review of the literature. The possible biases in selection of the two groups of probands have been discussed and need not be considered again here. The contention that the values from a particular study are higher or lower than those from other studies is not very helpful in resolving the basic problems of the origins of mental illnesses. It is quite possible that a strongly biased sample might provide insights which would be overlooked in more strictly representative populations. The reader is warned that what follows results from combining the two samples in which the proband was admitted prior to 1912 or from 1912 to 1917. An important advantage of combining the two groups of families is that the numbers in

different subdivisions will usually be large enough to give significant answers to our questions.

One of the first questions we wish to ask is that of what proportions of the full siblings of the probands have psychoses or other mental disorders for each of the types of marriages possible when the parents are classified as to sex and the state of their mental health. These data are given in Table 4–5 and will be recombined in various ways in Tables 4–6 and 4–7.

The problem of small sample size is obvious in Table 4–5, in which there are only a total of 11 siblings of our 3 probands with both parents psychotic. Fortunately, we have larger samples for all other classifications except where the father was psychotic and the mother unaffected (with only 5 siblings available). It is interesting that there were 23 siblings in the reciprocal marriage of unaffected fathers and psychotic mothers.

Another observation of interest obtained from Table 4–5 is that only 88 of the total of 463 siblings (19 per cent) of our probands were from marriages where both parents were unaffected by some mental disorder or psychosis. It is clear that the parents of the siblings of our probands are in much worse mental health than parents in the general population.

It is important to point out the large and orderly decrease in the percentages of psychotic siblings that drops sharply in relation to the better mental health of the mother, as shown in Column 1 of Table 4–5. It can be seen that the mental health of the father is held constant in this comparison. If we were to rearrange the lines of the table so that the mental health of the mother is held constant there would be no orderly relationship between the percentages of psychosis in the siblings and the mental health of the father. This is an important finding because other studies have not made this type of analysis. It is amazing that a distinction between whether the affected parent was the father or the mother has been made so seldom in previous research. There has been much attention devoted to the "psychogenic" mothers but little statistical evidence of the existence of them as an important factor in the production of the next generation of psychotic persons. We will return to this topic shortly.

In Column 2 of Table 4–5 it is apparent that the percentage of "other mental disorders" is relatively constant and in the range of 20 to 25 per cent for the siblings from each type of parental combination. It is not clear to us why the value for other mental disorders in the siblings should be so constant. Why should 25 per cent of the siblings have "other mental disorders" when both parents are unaffected (bottom of Table 4–5)? Why also should 9.1 per cent of the siblings of the proband be psychotic when both parents are unaffected? We will

return to these questions after we have seen the data for these same types of marriages for other relatives of our probands.

Table 4–6 is merely a summary of the data in Table 4–5. This is provided to demonstrate the expected decrease in percentage of psychosis in the siblings from the 30.9 per cent when one or both parents were psychotic to the 20.2 per cent of psychosis when both parents had "other mental disorders" but did not have a functional psychosis, at least according to their diagnoses. Clearly the "other mental disorders" are related to the psychoses because when both parents had these disorders, 20.2 per cent of their offspring, in addition to the proband, were frankly psychotic.

It is also of importance to note in Table 4–6 that even when both parents of our probands were classified as unaffected there was still a total of 34.1 per cent of the siblings of the proband with psychoses or other mental disorders. If the parents were actually both phenotypically unaffected the logical conclusion is that they carried heredity which in new combinations in their offspring (the probands and their siblings) resulted in the 34.1 per cent of poor mental health observed in the siblings. It is clear that psychotics do not appear at random in the population.

Summary Table 4–7 brings us back to the problem of the effect of the sex of the parent on the mental health of the siblings

Table 4–6. *Summary Table for the Siblings of the 89 Probands When Classified According to the Mental Health of Their Parents.*

	FULL SIBLINGS OF THE PROBANDS			
Mental Health of Parents	1. Psychosis No. (Per Cent)	2. Other Mental Disorder No. (Per Cent)	3. (Cols. 1&2) Psychosis and Other Disorder No. (Per Cent)	4. Total Siblings (incl. Unaffected)
One or both parents psychotic	43(30.9)	33(23.7)	76(54.6)	139
Both with other mental disorder	18(20.2)	23(25.8)	41(46.0)	89
One parent with other disorder, one unaffected	16(10.9)	37(25.2)	53(36.1)	147
Both parents unaffected	8(9.1)	22(25.0)	30(34.1)	88
Totals	85(18.4)	115(24.8)	200(43.2)	463

Table 4–7. *Summary Table for the Siblings of the 89 Probands When Classified According to the Sex and Mental Health of the Parent.*

Mental Health of One Parent	1. Psychosis No. (Per Cent)	2. Other Mental Disorder No. (Per Cent)	3. (Cols. 1&2) Psychosis and Other Disorder No. (Per Cent)	4. Total Siblings (incl. Unaffected)
	FULL SIBLINGS OF THE PROBANDS (Each sibling is entered twice)			
Mother psychotic	38(39.2)	21(21.6)	59(60.8)	97
Father psychotic	9(17.0)	14(26.4)	23(43.4)	53
Mother other mental disorder	32(16.0)	54(27.0)	86(43.0)	200
Father other mental disorder	53(23.6)	55(24.4)	108(48.0)	225
Mother unaffected	15(9.0)	40(24.1)	55(33.1)	166
Father unaffected	23(12.4)	46(24.9)	69(37.3)	185

of the proband. We see there that 38 of the 463 siblings were psychotic (8.2 per cent) and had a psychotic mother, while only 9 of the 463 (1.9 per cent) were psychotic and had a psychotic father. Of these 9 there were 4 who had a psychotic mother as well as a psychotic father so only 5 of the 463 siblings were psychotic and had just a father who was psychotic. There were 85 psychotic siblings produced by all the various types of marriages and 34 of the 85 (40.0 per cent) had a psychotic mother while only 5 (5.9 per cent) had a psychotic father and 4 (4.8 per cent) had both parents psychotic.

It will be of great interest to see whether this striking maternal effect persists when we come to the other groups of the relatives of the probands.

Let us note again the constant, and still unexplained, high percentage of "other mental disorders" among the siblings from each type of marriage, as shown in Table 4–7.

THE HALF SIBLINGS OF THE PROBANDS

The half siblings of the probands are of great interest because, while they share only one-quarter of their genes with the probands, they share a rather similar environment as they are often reared for much of their childhood in the same household with the probands. If the parent who is shared by the proband and his half siblings is psychotic, the half siblings should have about the same environment as the proband and his full siblings. The "psychogenic" parent is the same for full siblings, half siblings and the proband. The genetic potentiality for psychosis should be decreased for the half siblings of probands compared with the full siblings because of the expected genetic differences for psychosis in the two parents which are *not* shared by the two sets of children.

We have only 9 children where the shared parent was psychotic as shown in Table 4–8. Thus our sample size is too small to provide much resolution of our problem. However, the fact that only 1 of the 31 half siblings was psychotic is in agreement with the idea that the frequency of psychosis in half siblings should be lower than that in full siblings.

We find that the frequency of "other mental disorders" in the half siblings is 32.3 per cent, which is higher than in the full siblings (24.8 per cent). This increase in other mental disorders in the half siblings, if a reality, might result from the fact that in every case where there are half siblings there has been a broken home. However, the broken homes do not increase the frequency of psychosis in the half siblings compared with that in the full siblings in

Table 4–8. *The Half Siblings of the 89 Probands Classified According to the Mental Health of the Parent Shared with the Proband.*

	HALF SIBLINGS OF THE PROBAND			
Mental Health of Shared Parent	*1. Psychosis No. (Per Cent)*	*2. Other Mental Disorder No. (Per Cent)*	*3. (Cols. 1&2) Psychosis and Other Disorder No. (Per Cent)*	*4. Total Half Siblings (incl. Unaffected)*
Psychotic	1(11.1)	4(44.4)	5(55.5)	9
Other mental disorder	0(0.0)	5(26.3)	5(26.3)	19
Unaffected	0(0.0)	1(33.3)	1(33.3)	3
Totals	1(3.2)	10(32.3)	11(35.5)	31

our sample. We have seen that the frequency of psychosis in the full siblings is about twice that in the half siblings when the shared parent is psychotic. Where the shared parent was *not* psychotic, none of the 22 half siblings in our small sample was psychotic.

Two important considerations seem to emerge from these observations, although the sample is too small to establish them.

1. When the shared parent is psychotic only about half as many of the half siblings are affected as full siblings. This probably indicates a genetic difference for psychosis between the parents who are not shared and are not psychotic. Any psychogenic effect from the shared psychotic parent should be the same for both types of siblings.

2. Broken homes do not seem to increase the frequency of psychosis.

THE CHILDREN OF THE PROBANDS

We will expect to find a high frequency of psychosis and other mental disorders in the children of the probands because at least one parent of the children, the proband, is psychotic. There were 154 children of our probands who had survived to the age of 15. At the time of the follow-up study the average age of the 154 children was about 55 years. Even so an age correction would add an appreciable percentage of psychosis and other mental disorders to the values given in Table 4–9. An appropriate age correction for the children will be provided later but we can get along without it at this point.

The sample of 154 children of our probands is not a large one but seems to be adequate for comparison with the 463 siblings set forth in Tables 4–5, 4–6 and 4–7. The agreement of the totals of Tables 4–9 and 4–5 could hardly be closer. It can be seen that 17.5 per cent of the children of the probands were psychotic compared with 18.4 per cent of the siblings of the probands. Even closer agreement is present between the 25.3 per cent of other mental disorders in the children and the 24.8 per cent of other mental disorders in the siblings. The combined values for psychoses and other mental disorders are 42.8 per cent for the children and 43.2 per cent for the siblings, only one-half of 1 per cent difference.

The comparison of the frequency of a trait in the proband's siblings and children is of value in attempting to determine what genetic mechanism is involved in the development of the trait. If a single pair of recessive genes were the basis for the trait we would expect a higher frequency of affected siblings than affected children of the proband. Our data show the frequencies of psychoses and other mental disorders to be about the same in both siblings and children. Simple recessive heredity is thus eliminated as the primary basis for the mental ill-health of our group of persons. It is of course possible that mental illness in an occasional family is the result of simple, recessive heredity but there is no evidence that this is so in a significant proportion of the families of our study. We cannot distinguish whether there is a single dominant gene with reduced penetrance primarily responsible for the mental illness in our families or whether there is more than one gene locus (that is, multigenic or polygenic inheritance) involved. However, in view of the high frequency throughout the world of a highly variable population of clinically different mental disorders, it seems to be extremely probable that multigenic heredity is present. The environmental component of the variance complicates the analysis and reduces drastically any expectations of detecting a simple single gene locus as the basis for mental disorders in any significant proportion of the families, even if such a simple mechanism exists.

The reader may recall from Table 4–7 that when the mother was psychotic the siblings of the probands were psychotic in 39.2 per cent of the cases, whereas if the father was the psychotic parent only 17.0 per cent of the siblings were psychotic. In the present case, where we are interested in the children of the probands, the data can be assembled from Table 4–9 in regard to the sex of the psychotic parent. The same data are summarized in Table 4–10. It can be seen that 20.7 per cent of the children of psychotic mothers were psychotic, while only 13.3 per cent of the children of psychotic fathers were likewise psychotic. We see that in both the siblings and the children of the probands a strikingly higher percentage of

psychotic offspring were produced by psychotic mothers than by psychotic fathers.

The relationship of sex of parent to the psychotic children becomes even more spectacular when we note in Table 4–9 that 21 (77.7 per cent) of the 27 psychotic children had a psychotic proband as their mother, and only 4 (14.8 per cent) had a psychotic father, while 2 (7.4 per cent) of the 27 had the misfortune to have both proband parents psychotic. This information indicates (as did the data from the siblings) that psychotic women produce a much larger proportion of the psychotic persons in the next generation than are produced by psychotic men. This result depends upon two factors, namely that more psychotic women reproduce than psychotic men, and secondly, that the psychotic women have twice the percentage of children who become psychotic as do men.

The present study is the first to clearly establish on a quantitative basis a maternal effect related to the development of psychoses. Our study *cannot* be considered to establish the existence of the "psychogenic mother" in the sense that the epithet usually has been employed. Our maternal effect, that is, the "psychogenic-mother effect," seems to be primarily the consequence of the different genotypes of the fathers and mothers acting through the dif-

Table 4–9. *Mental Health of the Children of the 89 Probands Classified According to the Sex and the Mental Health of Their Parents. At Least One Parent, the Proband, was Psychotic in Every Case.*

Mental Health of Parents		CHILDREN OF THE PROBANDS			
Mother	Father	1. Psychosis No. (Per Cent)	2. Other Mental Disorder No. (Per Cent)	3. (Cols. 1&2) Psychosis and Other Disorder No. (Per Cent)	4. Total Children (incl. Unaffected)
Psychotic	Psychotic	2(100.0)	0	2(100.0)	2
Other disorder	Psychotic	1(7.7)	5(38.5)	6(46.2)	13
Unaffected	Psychotic	3(10.0)	6(20.0)	9(30.0)	30
Psychotic	Other disorder	14(27.5)	20(39.2)	34(66.7)	51
Psychotic	Unaffected	7(12.1)	8(13.8)	15(25.9)	58
Totals		27(17.5)	39(25.3)	66(42.8)	154

Table 4–10. *Summary Table for the Children of the 89 Probands When Classified According to the Sex and Mental Health of the Parent.*

	CHILDREN OF THE PROBANDS (Each child is entered twice)			
Mental Health of One Parent	*1. Psychosis No. (Per Cent)*	*2. Other Mental Disorder No. (Per Cent)*	*3. (Cols. 1&2) Psychosis and Other Disorder No. (Per Cent)*	*4. Total Children (incl. Unaffected)*
Mother psychotic	23(20.7)	28(25.2)	51(45.9)	111
Father psychotic	6(13.3)	11(24.4)	17(37.8)	45
Mother other mental disorder	1(7.7)	5(38.5)	6(46.2)	13
Father other mental disorder	14(27.5)	20(39.2)	34(66.7)	51
Mother unaffected	3(10.0)	6(20.0)	9(30.0)	30
Father unaffected	7(12.1)	8(13.8)	15(25.9)	58

ferential reproduction of the two sexes of psychotic parents.

The following two hypotheses occur to us as possible explanations of the maternal effect just established:

1. More of the psychotic females reproduce than do psychotic males. Firm evidence of this will be presented in the chapter on fertility, and it is established in the literature. Probably more of the severely ill psychotic women reproduce than is the case for men. Thus the average genotype of the reproducing woman may be more heavily loaded for the genetic potential psychoses than the average reproducing male genotype. That is, the psychotic reproducing woman has a greater genetic potential for psychotic offspring than the psychotic male. We are assuming that our psychoses are multigenic and that expression occurs at the same threshold in males and females since the general frequency of psychoses is about the same for both sexes. The above hypothesis does not require any specific psychogenic behavior of the mother. The social or environmental aspects of this hypothesis rest upon the greater ability of psychotic women to obtain mates than is the case for psychotic males. Their greater genetic loading for psychoses would explain a large part of their higher percentage of psychotic offspring than is observed for psychotic fathers.

2. There is a "psychogenic" effect resulting from the presence of a psychotic mother in the household. This is the conventional hypothesis that the psychogenic mother subjects some of her children, but not others, to a "double-bind," or in some other way teaches them to become psychotic. The adoption studies of Heston (1966 and 1968) in which children of schizophrenic mothers were separated from them at the age of three days and reared by other women, cast doubt upon this hypothesis because the separated children became psychotic in 16 per cent (age-corrected) of the cases. This is about the same morbid risk as found by Kallmann and numerous other workers for children of schizophrenic mothers. Nonetheless, the fact that identical twins are not always concordant for schizophrenia proves that experiential environmental factors are crucial in the development of the disorder, or in its failure to develop in many cases.

What can we conclude about these two hypotheses? That more psychotic women succeed in reproducing than do psychotic men is factual. A reproductive excess for women is also present in the mentally retarded (see Reed and Reed [1965]). As the incidence of psychosis is about the same in men and women, and a greater proportion of the psychotic women reproduce, we can assume that the average genetic loading is greater in the psychotic women. Consequently, the women produce a higher percentage of psychotic children than do the men. The genetic aspect of the phenomenon seems to be a reality. The environmental factors involved are less easily identified. It is obvious that a mother does not have to be psychotic to produce psychotic children, but apparently it helps. Furthermore, about three-quarters of the children of psychotic mothers are *not* psychotic. Unfortunately, we cannot measure the added risk of psychosis to the child resulting from the environmental contribution of a psychotic mother compared with a non-psychotic mother with any precision. However, we can make a very rough estimate as to the relative importance of the psychogenic behavior of the psychotic mother in the development of psychosis in her offspring. We will derive this estimate later in this chapter.

The above seems to be well integrated and highly logical. The major problem with it all is that it has not been discovered previously. Why did not Kallmann (1938) find a higher risk for the children of his psychotic mothers compared with children of psychotic fathers? He did not score the siblings of his probands, or the nieces and nephews, in relation to both sex and mental health of their parents. However, as Slater (1968) has pointed out, it is apparently possible to extract the data for the children of Kallmann's 1938 probands and no appreciable difference in percentage of schizophrenic children was produced by the female probands compared with the male probands. We do not know why our data are in disagreement with those obtained by Kallmann. Future work by others should clarify this very important point.

THE ADOPTION PROBLEM

The extremely important studies of Heston (1966 and 1968) with children of schizophrenic mothers who were taken from their ill mothers and raised by other women showed that about 16 per cent of these children could be expected to develop schizophrenia before death.

Karlsson (1966) found that in Iceland 12 out of 102 (12 per cent) of the siblings of his index cases with one psychotic parent developed schizophrenia. The 17 similarly produced siblings who were reared by persons other than their parents included 5 (30 per cent) with schizophrenia.

The results obtained in an adoption study by Rosenthal (1971) in Denmark are of great interest though difficult to compare with our own material or with that of Heston or Karlsson. The difficulties result primarily from the method of selection of the sample by the various authors and in the different diagnostic criteria employed. Rosenthal had 32 children with a psychotic parent who were placed for adoption at an average age of about 6 months. The follow-up of the 32 children showed 12 (37.5 per cent) with a "spectrum diagnosis" which was usually a "borderline schizophrenia," though 3 of the 12 were considered to be schizophrenic and one a manic-depressive psychotic person. The control group of 67 "children" also included 12 (17.8 per cent) with a "spectrum diagnosis." We don't know what to make of this high frequency of borderline psychotics in Rosenthal's control group of adoptees without a psychotic parent.

Let us turn to our own results which are in some ways more interesting than those cited above.

We chose to make an arbitrary classification of the children of our 89 psychotic probands as to whether they were separated from their psychotic proband parent before the age of 6 years or whether they stayed with the proband beyond the age of 6. The cutting point of 6 years was selected as the school entering age with the hope that the children of the probands might have a more normal life after entering school and also that the sample size for the group separated from the psychotic proband before age 6 would be as large as possible for statistical considerations.

The results of separating the 154 children of the psychotic probands, previously given in Table 4-9, into two groups, depending upon whether the child was separated from the psychotic proband parent before the child was 6 years old or whether the child stayed indefinitely with the psychotic parent, were quite striking. The results of this dichotomy are shown in Table 4-11.

We can confirm Heston's findings that children separated from their psychotic parent at an early age later develop a psychosis in a high percentage of cases and add

Table 4–11. *The 154 Children of the 89 Probands Classified According to the Sex of the Proband and Whether or Not the Child was Separated from the Proband Parent Before the Child was Six Years Old.*

	CHILDREN OF THE PROBANDS			
	1. Psychosis No. (Per Cent)	*2.* Other Mental Disorder No. (Per Cent)	*3. (Cols. 1&2)* Psychosis and Other Disorder No. (Per Cent)	*4.* Total Children (incl. Unaffected)
A. *Separated Before Six Years*				
Proband mother	5(27.8)	8(44.4)	13(72.2)	18
Proband father	1(33.3)	0(0.0)	1(33.3)	3
Sub-totals	6(28.6)	8(38.1)	14(66.7)	21
B. *Not Separated Before Six Years*				
Proband mother	17(18.5)	20(21.7)	37(40.2)	92
Proband father	4(9.8)	11(26.8)	15(36.6)	41
Sub-totals	21(15.8)	31(23.3)	52(39.1)	133
Grand Totals	27(17.5)	39(25.3)	66(42.8)	154

the very interesting finding that 28.5 per cent of those separated from the psychotic parent before six years of age developed a psychosis, while of those staying with the psychotic proband parent only 15.8 per cent developed a psychosis.

How can we explain the finding that almost twice as high a percentage of the children separated from the psychotic parent developed a psychosis eventually when compared with the children who were *not* separated from the psychotic parent?

All the children separated from their mothers by age six were, of course, products of broken homes. However, welfare agencies do not expect anything approaching 28.5 per cent of the children they place to develop a psychosis. Thus broken homes and psychogenic influences in the new homes should not be expected to account for this increase in the percentage of psychosis over the 15.8 per cent in the children who were *not* separated from their psychotic proband parent. One explanation, which seems reasonable to us, is that the probands who had to give away their children were more severely ill than those who were able

to keep their children. Presumably the more severely ill transmitted a heavier genetic load for psychosis to their children that later resulted in a higher frequency of the disorders in these children, even though they had been removed to a new environment. Not all the affected children were removed at birth so there could also have been a greater psychogenic effect produced by the more seriously ill proband on the children in the years before age six.

It can be seen in Table 4–11 that the frequency of other mental disorders was also higher in the children separated from the psychotic parent before age 6 than in the rest of the children of the probands. Finally, in Column 3 of Table 4–11 we see that 14 of the 21 children (66.7 per cent) who were separated from the psychotic parent before the age of 6 were either psychotic or had some other mental disorder by the time this study ended. The remaining 133 children of the probands showed only a total of 39.1 per cent of psychosis or other mental disorder and the difference between the two groups is statistically significant ($\chi^2 = 5.61$, d.f. = 1, p < 0.05).

Because of the great importance of the results for the children who were separated from the psychotic proband before they were 6 years old we will present condensed material from the extensive files we have concerning these "children," who by the time of this study were of middle or old age or deceased.

CHARACTERISTICS OF THE SEPARATED CHILDREN

One of the most important problems in the etiology of the psychoses is that of what is transmitted to the psychotic "child" from the parent and what experiences of the child contribute to the development of his psychosis. It is now very clear that a child of a psychotic parent has at least as high a risk of developing a psychosis if removed from the parent as the child who is not removed from the household of the psychotic parent. This seemingly paradoxical situation might be the result of the more serious illness of the parent from which the child had to be separated. It may be that the separated child has a heavier genetic loading for psychosis received from the more seriously ill parent. We propose to outline below the characteristics of the 21 separated children and their psychotic parents. The reader should consult the Appendix of this book for more details about these families. The Appendix is a condensation of the data but it is hoped that no biases were introduced by the omission of many details because of space limitations.

WSH 22. This child (number 33 on the chart) had little contact with his mother, who was considered to be "peculiar" when a child. She (number 29, the proband) became insanely jealous of her husband during the pregnancy and expressed suicidal and homicidal tendencies. She was committed to Warren State Hospital about one year after the birth of the boy (33), following a suicide attempt. Her diagnosis was dementia praecox, paranoid type. The boy was cared for by relatives until committed to Polk State Hospital at age 9 with an IQ of 53. Later he became abusive and delusional and at age 47 was transferred to a mental hospital and then to Warren. His diagnosis was that of schizophrenic reaction, paranoid

type. It is clear that the proband's sibship was very heavily loaded for schizophrenia (read the whole history, WSH 22).

WSH 30. Six children of the proband were placed in different homes at ages from 5 weeks to 3 years. The proband (number 24 on the chart) had a 6 year history of periodic attacks of mania prior to her first admission to Warren. She had seven subsequent hospitalizations, all less than 2 years in duration except for the last which was from 1912 until her death in 1930. The early diagnoses were various types of mania as she had no periods of depression. Diagnosis on review was that of a schizophrenic reaction, schizo-affective type. She married at 19 years of age and had 12 children and 3 miscarriages. Because of her illness and her husband's irresponsibility, the children were placed for adoption or forced to become self-supporting at a very young age. The six children who were placed for adoption were as follows:

1. Number 36 on the chart was placed at birth. When young she was described as "stubborn, easily excitable and not inclined to communicate her troubles or show her grief." She was unable to get along with her first husband and was very hostile toward her second husband. She was interviewed at age 77 and was classified as having a possible personality trait disturbance.

2. Number 40. He was placed for adoption in infancy. He was reportedly hospitalized at a mental hospital but no records could be located. At age 23 years, the last time any family member heard from him, he stated in a letter that he was very nervous. He was classified as a probable psychoneurotic reaction.

3. Number 42. She was adopted at age 9 months in a "good home with every possible advantage." As a child she was neat and industrious but abnormally sensitive and had prolonged crying spells. By age 14 she was promiscuous and had two illegitimate children before admission to Warren. She was hospitalized three times, the last at age 25. She was still at Warren at age 69. There is a large amount of evidence indicating her to be schizophrenic without question. Classification: schizophrenic reaction, catatonic type.

4. Number 44. He was in the county home sometime before age 5. He was considered "a little touched" at age 20 when he

wanted to marry a 60-year-old woman. He had three wives but only one child. At age 67 he was not well organized but functioned fairly well. Classification: possible personality trait disturbance, schizoid personality.

5. Number 47. He was placed in the county home at age 3. At 16 his personality changed and he developed persecutory delusions and began to wander around at night. He was sent to Warren State Hospital where he deteriorated rapidly and died at age 28. Schizophrenic reaction, catatonic type.

6. Number 48. He was adopted at age 5 weeks and no unusual behavior occurred until age 16 when he began hallucinating. He was admitted to Warren but recovered and was not readmitted for 13 years. He was paroled 6 months later and for 30 years has been working as a janitor. He married but has no children. Classification: schizophrenic reaction, paranoid type.

WSH 39.   This patient, number 37, was mentally retarded, had seizures, and was hospitalized at Warren State Hospital at age 22 with dementia praecox, paranoid type. Her three children were taken by her sister at the time she was hospitalized. The children were 4 years of age, 2 years of age and 8 weeks at the time. She remained in the hospital for eight years and had no further influence on the children. All three children, Numbers 43, 46 and 48, developed normally and 43 and 46 were still normal at ages 50 and 49, but Number 48 died of bronchopneumonia at age 17. She was normal at the time of death.

WSH 52.   Patient was considered well until age 22 when she set fire to her house and developed delusions, became unruly and had to be sent to Warren where she stayed until she died of tuberculosis at age 33. She had three children before hospitalization:

1. Number 36. Little is known of the whereabouts of this child after the home was broken up because of her mother's hospitalization. The child would have been 3 years old at that time. She may have lived with her father from time to time. Later she had a child by him. She had two temporary marriages and at age 51 was a foreman in a bubble gum factory. Classification: transient situational personality disorder.

2. Number 39. She was placed at age 2 years, along with her infant sister, number

41, in the same home and they took the name of their foster parents. At age 55 the psychiatrist who saw her considered her to have a schizophrenic reaction of chronic undifferentiated type, with somatic delusions and paranoid ideation. She was on public assistance but not hospitalized up to the time of the investigation.

3. Number 41. She was placed as an infant along with her sister, number 39. She was normal, married a normal man and had six children. She died at age 43 of a cerebral hemorrhage.

WSH 58.   The proband had numerous hospitalizations and remissions with a final classification of schizophrenic reaction, paranoid type. She had 7 children of whom only one was considered to be normal (number 53) and he was killed at age 19 when trying to open a keg of powder he had stolen. See the Appendix for the descriptions of the schizophrenia in the 5 affected children. The last child (number 60) was seven years younger than the next oldest and from the age of 2 years was raised by a "coarse, ignorant woman who lived in a dirty miner's shanty." This daughter was reported to be "scattered and difficult to follow in conversation" from the age of 37 years. The interviewer described her to be easily distracted and rambling at 67 years of age. Classification: probable personality pattern disturbance.

WSH 63.   The proband is the father in this case and was diagnosed at review as having the paranoid type of schizophrenia. However, the mother developed schizophrenia at about age 60 and was also committed to Warren with a diagnosis of schizophrenia, paranoid type. They had only one son, number 40, who had no contact with his father after he was four years old. The son was hospitalized twice for psychosis and was classified as schizophrenic reaction, paranoid type.

WSH 71.   The proband was a male with a schizophrenic reaction, catatonic type. He had two children, numbers 28 and 29, but nothing is known as to who reared them or their whereabouts or their mental health at any time. For present purposes we have scored them as normals in determining our percentage of affected children of our probands. Neither child had any appreciable contact with the father as the marriage was unsuccessful and the patient separated from his wife soon after the birth of the second child.

WSH 83. The proband was hospitalized at Warren on four different occasions. Her classification was that of a schizophrenic reaction, catatonic type. She was married to her first cousin once removed and had two sons by him. He seemed to be a normal man but died at age 26 of tuberculosis. Six months later his wife (the patient) was hospitalized and the two sons were placed with his parents, who reared them from the ages of three and five years.

1. The older son (31 on the chart) was 52 years of age at interview. He was described as "brilliant, well-liked, happy-go-lucky and generally successful but depressed when sick." He was asthmatic but not neurotic and has received no treatment for mental or emotional problems.

2. The second son (33 on the chart) is a successful farmer and carpenter-contractor. He suffered a "nervous breakdown," remained in bed for two weeks and gradually resumed activities with complete recovery in one year. He was "very religious" but was considered well at the interview when he was 50 years old. He was classified as possibly having functional psychosis with a psychotic-depressive reaction.

WSH 98. The proband (number 28) was hospitalized at Warren at age 26 and died one year later. Her classification was that of schizophrenic reaction, catatonic type. She had two daughters.

1. The older (number 47) was four years old when her mother was hospitalized. She lived with her paternal grandmother and later with her maternal aunt. She drowned in a boating accident at age 38. However, her sex life seems to have been rather chaotic and she was classified as having a sociopathic personality disturbance.

2. The second daughter was 2 years old when she went to live with her grandmother, along with her older sister. She was married at 16 years of age but later separated from her husband. She has received medication for "nerves" on two occasions and was classified as having an adult situational reaction.

Let us summarize our impressions of the general situation which resulted from separating the 21 children from their 9 psychotic parents before they were 6 years old.

All 9 parents (probands) received final classifications of schizophrenia. There were 7 female and 2 male parents. The 6 of the 21 children who became psychotic were 4 boys and 2 girls. The 6 affected children all had diagnoses of schizophrenia and all but one were hospitalized for their psychoses. They were taken from the psychotic parent by the ages of 5 weeks, 9 months, 1 year, 2 years, 3 years and 4 years. Their ages of hospitalization for their schizophrenia were by 14 years, 16, 16, 25, and 47, with one undetermined because of lack of hospitalization. Presumably their ages of onset were less than their ages at hospitalization. It is probable, from these relatively young ages of onset, that the children were more severely ill than the general run of schizophrenics. It is clear that their parents were also severely ill and it seems unreasonable to deny the probability of a strong genetic influence on the development of the schizophrenia in these six children.

It is an important and striking discovery that fairly early separation from the schizophrenic parent failed to protect the child from developing schizophrenia when a sufficient genetic background for the disorder was present in him. It is difficult to rule out the possibility that the schizophrenic mother "infects" the child in utero with some schizophrenogenic virus or biochemical but our result showing late age of onset for some siblings and children of our probands does *not* support this idea, as will be seen in the next chapter.

The evidence from Heston, Karlsson, and this book seems to be sufficient to establish the point beyond question that children who are separated from their psychotic parent become psychotic at least as frequently, and perhaps even more frequently, than those who are left with their psychotic parent. It becomes difficult therefore to visualize any large "psychogenic" effect of the mothers upon their children who were raised by other women. The excess of psychotic children produced by psychotic mothers compared with those produced by psychotic fathers seems to be largely the result of characteristics of the psychotic mothers which affect the child before birth, and it will be remembered that the children in the Heston study were separated by the end of the third day after birth because of an Oregon state law which required this for psychotic women giving birth to a child in an institution.

What weight can we ascribe to the experiential factors of a psychological nature responsible for the development of psychoses in the children of psychotic mothers, contrasted with those of psychotic fathers? The adoption studies make it difficult to assign any substantial weight to the "double-bind" or other psychogenic effects previously assumed to be characteristic of psychotic mothers. The maternal effect seems to be *prenatal*, which is an important concept! The prenatal effect seems to be that of the greater genetic loading of the psychotic mothers. We have definite evidence of the greater genetic loading of the psychotic mothers compared with the cases where it is the father who is psychotic. It is essential that this concept be pursued in future research. In addition there could be a biochemical (hormonal?) effect of the mother upon the embryo in utero and such lines of research would seem to offer considerable promise.

Our conclusion is that the excess of psychotic children produced by mothers results from prenatal influences. A genetic potential for psychosis that is greater in the psychotic mother than in the psychotic father is the only factor we have been able to identify as a possible explanation for the maternal effect which we have established. It should be remembered that none of the adopted children were psychotic at birth and that some internal or external environmental factors must have been responsible for the "triggering" or initiation of symptoms in those children who later became mentally ill. These postnatal environmental factors have not been clearly identified yet but presumably are of the kinds suggested by Rosenthal (1963) as a result of his and his colleagues' careful studies of the Genain quadruplets.

SUMMARY

This chapter is primarily an analysis of the mental health of the first degree relatives of the 89 probands, the sample selected between 1910 and 1917. We have evaluated the original findings and extended the investigation up to the late 1960's.

There is evidence in this chapter that both genetic and prenatal maternal factors are important in the etiology of the functional psychoses. We have been able to establish the existence of the "psychogenic mother" on a quantitative basis for the first time. However, the psychogenic mother seems to exert her effect more through her heavier genetic loading for psychosis than in any other single way. Some of the major findings of this chapter are the following:

1. The mother of the proband had a proved or probable psychosis in 20.3 per cent of the cases while only 14.5 per cent of the probands had a father with a proved or probable psychosis. There is an extremely high frequency of "other mental disorders" among both the mothers (43.9 per cent) and the fathers (46.2 per cent) of the probands. Thus we find that 64.2 per cent of the mothers and 60.7 per cent of the fathers of the probands had a serious mental problem, with values much higher than those in the general population.

2. The siblings of our probands are a selected group in the sense that their parents proved themselves to be capable of having psychotic offspring when they produced the probands. We would expect a higher percentage of psychotics among the siblings than among the children of the probands, if simple recessive genetic mechanisms were of major importance. However, the difference of 0.9 per cent between the percentage of psychosis in the full siblings (18.4 per cent) and in the children (17.5 per cent) of the probands is not statistically significant. Our male probands had a total of six psychotic sons and no psychotic daughters, which is evidence that genetic sex-linkage is not an important mechanism in the etiology of our psychoses. Remaining alternatives are single dominant gene loci (with considerable lack of penetrance) or multigenic heredity; the latter seems to be the more reasonable hypothesis to consider in relation to relatively frequent traits such as the psychoses.

3. When the mother of the proband was psychotic, 39.2 per cent of the proband's full siblings were also psychotic. If the proband's father was psychotic, only 17.0 per cent of the siblings were psychotic. Similar data for the children and for the nieces and nephews of the probands show clearly that

psychotic mothers produce about twice as many psychotic offspring as do psychotic fathers. This maternal effect seems to be firmly established. Two possible explanations for the maternal effect suggest themselves and both may contribute significantly to it.

A. The frequencies of the female and male psychotics in the population seem to be about the same. A larger proportion of the psychotic females marry and reproduce than do psychotic males. Presumably this means that more severely ill females have offspring and give them a heavier genetic loading for psychosis than do psychotic males.

B. The psychotic mother exerts a psychogenic effect upon some, though not all, of her offspring. She would do this by placing some offspring in "double-binds," by constricting their social development or by some other mental pressure which contributes to the development of psychosis in some of her offspring. However, the data from children who were taken from their psychotic mothers and reared by other presumably normal women provide little, if any, support for this "double-bind" concept as the explanation for the maternal effect.

4. The half siblings of the proband are of great interest because sometimes they share the psychotic parent with the proband and the full siblings. The half siblings with a shared psychotic parent seem to have a lower frequency of psychosis than the full siblings. The shared psychotic parent is the same person for both half siblings and full siblings and a lower frequency of psychosis in the half siblings would seem to indicate that the non-shared parents were genetically different in their capacity to produce psychotic offspring. The half siblings for whom the shared parent is *not* psychotic apparently have no greater expectation of developing a psychosis than persons in the general population.

5. We would expect to find a high frequency of psychosis in the children of the probands because at least one parent of the children, the proband, is psychotic. Actually, the percentage of psychosis (17.5 per cent) in the children is about the same as that in the full siblings of the probands (18.4 per cent). This lack of difference sheds light upon the mechanism of heredity involved with the psychoses of our probands. It permits us to reject simple recessive heredity at a single gene locus as being of importance. The most likely alternative is that the genetic prerequisite for the development of a psychosis usually is multigenic in nature. Gottesman and Shields (1967) came to this conclusion as a result of twin-family studies with schizophrenia.

6. Our probands produced 154 children who survived beyond the age of 15 years. Because of the mental illness of the parents, 21 of the 154 children were removed from their parents by age 6 years. Of the 21 children removed from their psychotic parent there were 6 (28.6 per cent) who received unequivocal diagnoses of schizophrenia. Of the 133 children not separated from their psychotic parent only 15.8 per cent became psychotic.

It was surprising, at first, that a higher percentage of the children separated from their psychotic parent became psychotic than was the case for the children who remained with the psychotic parent. A reasonable explanation of this finding is that the parents of the 21 children who had to be taken away from them were more severely ill and had a heavier genetic load for psychoses than the parents who were able to care for their children in spite of their mental illness.

CHAPTER FIVE

THE CALCULATION OF AGE CORRECTIONS

In any condition with delayed age at onset, some form of age adjustment is essential. An initial assumption is that individuals differ early in life with respect to the likelihood of developing the condition. A variety of genetic and environmental factors may be involved.

Several sources of bias can be identified: (1) Potentially affected persons may be subject to higher risk of death, even before any signs of the condition can be detected. There is no way of detecting or adjusting for this type of bias short of new techniques for earlier detection of the trait. (2) Affected persons may be subject to higher risk of death than the unaffected after the condition is expressed and begins to influence the subsequent health history. (3) All persons are subject to death from other unrelated causes, with the result that potentially affected persons would have been identified as affected *only if* they had lived longer. Corrections can be made for this last type of bias if we are willing to assume that the uncompleted life experience of those who died early would have replicated the pattern observed in those followed to later age. The basic discussions of these issues appear in Weinberg (1915; 1925), in Larsson and Sjögren (1954) and in Nyholm and Helweg-Larsen (1954).

We wanted to choose a procedure which would: (1) use as much of the information available as possible; (2) involve a relatively simple procedure for computation, which will be easy to explain and to adapt for other studies if desired; (3) keep the number of assumptions to a minimum; and (4) permit a graphic display of results.

A given group of relatives is treated as a *cohort* of individuals followed from some early age (before which the risk of psychosis is low) until death or the time of the study. We wish to estimate the risk (at the entering age) of developing a psychotic disorder prior to any older designated age. We do not want to use the "risk prior to death" since the mortality risks probably vary from one sample to another. The risk "given survival to age X" is more interesting as an estimate of the "predisposition" for the disorder.

There are basically two different ways of estimating this "morbid risk." 1. The number of individuals in the cohort can be reduced to the number of persons considered "fully exposed to risk." To do this one can use Weinberg's "short method" which counts one-half of the persons within a selected risk period and all persons older than the upper age limit. As Larsson and Sjögren (1954) pointed out, the adequacy of this method depends primarily upon the wise choice of age limits for the risk period. A refinement of the Weinberg procedure uses data on the distribution by age at onset in some general population to provide estimates for each age interval of the proportion of the risk period already completed. The number of persons in each age interval for the study population is multiplied by the corresponding weight, and summed to yield a total number fully exposed to risk (Bezugsziffer). This latter method assumes that the age-specific incidence rates in the general population are proportional to those in the sample being studied. We preferred not to make the assumptions required for either variant of this general approach. 2. A different method, which we prefer, uses only the data for the sample being studied. The number of persons developing psychosis within an age interval is divided by the calculated number of persons who were living in that interval, providing an age-specific incidence rate. The rates for all age intervals are then used to estimate the cumulative risk of developing psychosis, assuming that all persons were to survive to age 85. The method of calculation is the same as that used by Hagnell (1966), except that his incidence rates were derived from a *current* population while we used a *cohort*.

At this point, these definitions may be needed:

1. Age means age at last birthday.
2. Age at last report:
    (a) Those who died: Age at death.
    (b) Those who were living at last information, but whose status at the time of study was unknown: Age at last information.
    (c) Those living at time of study: Age at interview.
3. Age at first hospitalization: Age at first hospitalization for psychotic disorder (or other mental illness where indicated).
4. Age at onset: Age at first clear indication of psychotic behavior, estimated retrospectively after diagnosis was established.

The calculations of mean age were based on tabulations in 5-year age intervals. The tables presented here are mainly in 10-year intervals for convenience.

The age experience is started at 15 years. One full sibling had onset of psychosis at age 13. One child of a proband developed psychosis at age 14. Both of these will be tabulated in the 15 to 24 interval. No full niece or nephew became psychotic before 15.

Let us now illustrate the approach we have chosen with reference to the data for full siblings. Among the full siblings of the probands only 13 (2.8 per cent) had been lost from observation (Table 5–1). Among the psychotic siblings significantly fewer were living than among the remainder of the siblings ($\chi^2 = 14.8$, d/f = 1, P less than .001). There were 23 psychotic siblings who had attempted suicide, and for 10 of these the attempt was successful. When the 10 deaths by suicide are excluded, there remained 9 living psychotic siblings out of 75 (12.0 per cent). Thus the excess mortality among psychotic siblings is not explained fully by suicide.

The age distributions of the siblings (at last report) is shown in Table 5–2. The mean age for the psychotic siblings (whether living or dead) is lower than for the non-psychotic. It is clear that psychosis and death should be treated as competing risks (as in Kinch, Gittlesohn and Doyle, 1964) if one wishes to explore the meaning of such age differences. We have chosen to disregard the point at this time.

The age distributions for the living and dead siblings (psychotic and non-psychotic combined) are shown in Figure 5–1. One of the major potential advantages of starting with probands hospitalized about 1915 is that many of the close relatives would have lived through the "period of risk" for psychosis. It may seem somewhat surprising to find that a fair proportion of the siblings (27.4 per cent) were still living in the 1960's. Of the 322 who died at a known age, 157 (48.8 per cent) died under age 65.

Table 5–1. *Status of Full Siblings at Time of Study, by Their Mental Health.*

Status at Time of Study	Psychotic No. (Per Cent)	Other Disorder No. (Per Cent)	Unaffected No. (Per Cent)	Total No. (Per Cent)
Living	9 (10.6)	31 (26.9)	87 (33.1)	127 (27.4)
Lost from observation	0	4 (3.5)	9 (3.4)	13 (2.8)
Dead	76 (89.4)	80 (69.6)	167 (63.5)	323 (69.8)
	85 (100.0)	115 (100.0)	263 (100.0)	463 (100.0)

Table 5–2. *Age of Full Siblings at Last Report, by Mental Health and Status at Time of Study.*

Age at Last Report	PSYCHOTIC SIBLINGS[1]			NOT PSYCHOTIC				ALL SIBLINGS			
	Living at Time of Study	Dead	Total Psychotic	Living at Time of Study	Lost from Observation	Dead	Total not Psychotic	Living at Time of Study	Lost from Observation	Dead	Total All Sibs
15–24		2	2		1	21	22		1	23	24
25–34		9	9		2	25	27		2	34	36
35–44		9	9	1	1	13	15	1	1	22	24
45–54	1	9	10	6	2	21	29	7	2	30	39
55–64	2	19	21	24	2	29	55	26	2	48	76
65–74	6	12	18	44		65	109	50		77	127
75–84		14	14	38		53	91	38		67	105
85–94		2	2	5		16	21	5		18	23
95–99						3	3			3	3
Total age known	9	76	85	118	8	246	372	127	8	322	457
Age unknown					5	1	6		5	1	6
Grand total	9	76	85	118	13	247	378	127	13	323	463
Mean age (years)	64.2	58.2	58.8	70.9	42.5	61.1	63.8	70.4	42.5	60.2	62.9

[1]No psychotic sibs were lost from observation.

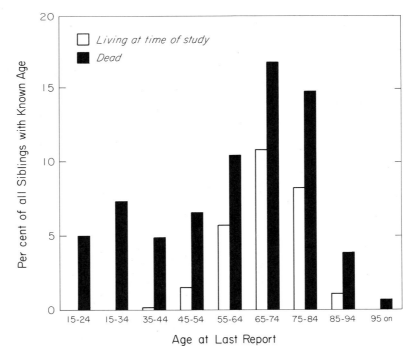

Figure 5–1. Age of full siblings of the probands by status (living or dead) at the time of the study.

Table 5–3. *Information about Hospitalization and Age at Onset of Psychosis Among Full Siblings.*

	AGE AT ONSET KNOWN	AGE AT ONSET NOT KNOWN	TOTALS No. (Per Cent)
Hospitalized for psychosis	48	6	54 (63.5)
Not hospitalized	12	19	31 (36.5)
Totals	60	25	85 (100.0)

Further information concerning the psychotic siblings is shown in Table 5–3. A comparison with other first degree relatives follows:

PSYCHOTIC RELATIVES	HOSPITALIZED	AGE AT ONSET KNOWN
Full siblings	63.5%	70.6%
Children	70.4%	51.9%
Full nieces and nephews	82.0%	75.4%

The age distribution for the psychotic siblings is shown in Table 5–4. The age at onset was known for 60 individuals (mean age = 34.9). The age *at first hospitalization* was reported for 54 persons (mean age = 41.4). These values may be compared with the mean age *at last report* for all 85 psychotic siblings of 58.8 years (Table 5–2).

The age adjustment procedure requires age-specific incidence rates, which in turn should be based upon *age at first diagnosis of psychotic disorder.* We do not have pre-

cisely that kind of information, so some compromises must be made. Age at onset may be earlier than age at first diagnosis. An observer seeing the person at the time of "onset" might not have reported psychosis. On the other hand, when neither age at onset or at hospitalization was available, as in 19 out of 85 siblings (22.4 per cent), the age at last report usually will be too high. We have chosen to use the youngest age available for each psychotic individual, as indicated in the last column of Table 5–4.

We are now ready to describe the age-correction procedure (Table 5–5). The calculated number of persons living in the 15 to 24 age interval (and each successive interval) is the sum of three numbers:

All those followed into older age intervals	413.0
All becoming psychotic in the 15–24 interval	22.0
One-half the non-psychotic with age at last report in the 15 to 24 interval	11.0
Calculated number in age interval	446.0

The last of the three numbers may need some further explanation. There were 22

Table 5–4. *Age of Psychotic Full Siblings at Onset or at Hospitalization for Psychosis or at Last Report.*

Age of Siblings	AGE AT ONSET AND AT HOSPITALIZATION KNOWN[1] Age at Onset	Age at First Hospitaliza-tion	AGE AT ONSET UNKNOWN Age at First Hospitaliza-tion	NOT HOSPITALIZED AGE AT ONSET KNOWN Age at Onset	NOT HOSPITALIZED AGE AT ONSET UNKNOWN Age at Last Report	ALL PSYCHOTIC SIBLINGS Youngest Age[2]
15–24	14	8	2	5	1	22
25–34	13	13	0	3	2	18
35–44	7	6	2	2	3	14
45–54	7	11	2	2	2	13
55–64	5	5	0	0	6	11
65–74	2	5	0	0	2	4
75–84	0	0	0	0	3	3
Totals	48	48	6	12	19	85
Mean age	36.0	41.9	37.5	30.4	54.9	39.6

[1]The same 48 persons are shown in these two columns, first by age at onset, then by age at first hospitalization.
[2]Age at onset of psychosis, or at first hospitalization or at last report (youngest age available).

Table 5–5. *Cumulative Risk of Psychosis Among Siblings of the Probands.*

Age Interval	NUMBER OF SIBLINGS Psychotic[1] a	Other Dis-order[2] b	Un-affected[2] c	Total d	CALCULATED NUMBER IN AGE INTERVAL e	PSYCHOSIS RATE (10 YEAR) (Per Cent) f	CUMULATIVE RISK OF PSYCHOSIS[3] (To End of Interval) (Per Cent)
15–24	22	4	18	44	446.0	4.9 ± 1.0	4.9 ± 1.0
25–34	18	6	21	45	399.5	4.5 ± 1.0	9.2 ± 1.4
35–44	14	6	9	29	360.5	3.9 ± 1.0	12.7 ± 1.6
45–54	13	8	21	42	324.5	4.0 ± 1.1	16.2 ± 1.8
55–64	11	15	40	66	269.5	4.1 ± 1.2	19.7 ± 2.0
65–74	4	41	68	113	176.5	2.3 ± 1.1	21.5 ± 2.2
75–84	3	26	65	94	72.5	4.1 ± 2.3	24.7 ± 2.8
85–94		7	14	21	13.5		
95–99			3	3	1.5		
Total, age known	85	113	259	457			
Age not known		2	4	6			
Grand totals	85	115	263	463			

[1]Age at onset of psychosis, or at first hospitalization or at last report (youngest age available).
[2]Age at last report.
[3]Method of calculation shown in Table 5–6.

non-psychotic siblings whose age at last report was in the 15 to 24 interval. In this particular age group, 21 had died and one was lost from observation (Table 5–2); in some of the older groups a fraction were still living at the time of this study. Some were under observation for only a few months while others were under observation for almost 10 years. If we assume that the 22 siblings are equally distributed by age over the 10-year interval, the calculated number under observation for the *entire* 10-year period is one-half that number, or 11.

The results are shown graphically in Figure 5–2. The height of each column represents the calculated number of persons assumed to have been observed throughout the age interval. The psychosis rate is thus the black portion, depicted as a percentage of the height of each column. Similarly, the psychosis rate in Table 5–5 is calculated from a to e.

The calculation of cumulative risk requires several intervening steps (Table 5–6). Column f (Table 5–6) is the same as the psychosis rate in Table 5–5, except that the values are expressed in proportions rather than in percentages. A simple *addition* of

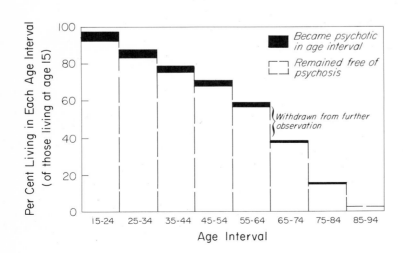

Figure 5–2. Life experience of the full siblings of the probands.

the values in Column f would result in a total of .278. This procedure would be incorrect, however, since it assumes that a person becoming psychotic in one age interval could be counted as having another first diagnosis of psychosis at some later age. To avoid this problem, it is necessary to calculate for each age interval the probability of remaining *free* of psychosis, then *multiply* these probabilities, and finally subtract from one. The final result (Column i in Table 5–6) shows a cumulative risk of .247 by age 85.

The cumulative risk for psychosis among siblings is plotted in Figure 5–3. The uncorrected line represents the cumulative number with psychosis in Column a (Table 5–5) divided by the total number of siblings with known age (457). The relationship between these two curves is as follows:

	Age Adjusted (Per Cent)	Uncorrected (Per Cent)	Adjusted/ Uncorrected
Age 45	12.7	11.8	1.08
Age 65	19.7	17.1	1.15
Age 85	24.7	18.6	1.33

An estimate using the Weinberg short method (counting all psychotic persons at any age and all non-psychotics aged 45 or over, but only one-half of the non-psychotic persons aged 15 to 44 years) would be 20.0 per cent. Using one-half of the non-psychotic persons aged 15 to 64 years yields an estimate of 22.2 per cent, which is similar to the value as determined by our cumulative risk method to the end of life. This coincidence indicates that the Weinberg and our

method *can* give almost identical values, depending upon the choice of risk period.

The standard errors were estimated following the procedure used by Hagnell (1966) and the formulae at the bottom of Table 5–6. The 10-year psychosis rates are plotted in Figure 5–4. The values for the different age intervals are surprisingly similar.

The cumulative risks with the standard errors are plotted in Figure 5–5. This type of figure will be used later to compare cumulative risks for different groups at any desired age.

AGE CORRECTIONS FOR THE CHILDREN

We have illustrated the method of our choice for making the necessary age corrections for the full siblings of our probands. It should suffice to present the data for the children of the probands without much comment. The raw data for the children of the probands are presented in Table 5–7 and Table 5–8. Even though the probands were selected in the second decade of this century, the average age of all "children" at the time of the follow-up was only 54.5 years and 54 per cent of them were still alive in the 1960's. Figure 5–6 is a graph of the vital statistics given in Table 5–7.

The cumulative risks of psychoses developing in the children of the probands are given in Table 5–9. The risks are slightly higher than those for siblings of the probands in each age interval, but they are

Table 5–6. *Method for Calculation of Cumulative Risk.*

AGE INTERVAL	PSYCHOSIS RATE (10 YEAR) f	PSYCHOSIS-FREE g	CUMULATIVE PROBABILITY PSYCHOSIS-FREE h	CUMULATIVE RISK OF PSYCHOSIS i	USED IN CALCULATION OF STANDARD ERRORS j	k
15–24	.049	.951	.951	.049	.000116	.000116
25–34	.045	.955	.908	.092	.000118	.000234
35–44	.039	.961	.873	.127	.000112	.000347
45–54	.040	.960	.838	.162	.000129	.000475
55–64	.041	.959	.803	.197	.000158	.000633
65–74	.023	.977	.785	.215	.000131	.000764
75–84	.041	.959	.753	.247	.000595	.001360

$f = a/e$ (from Table 5–5) $i = 1 - h$ S.E. $(f) = g\sqrt{j}$

$g = 1 - f$ $j = f/eg$ S.E. $(i) = h\sqrt{k}$

$h_x = (g_1) \times (g_2) \ldots (g_x)$ $k_x = j_1 + j_2 + \ldots j_x$

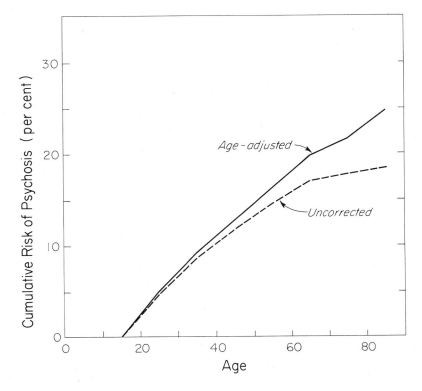

Figure 5–3. Cumulative risk of psychosis in the full siblings compared with their values without age correction.

more remarkable for their similarities than for their differences (see Table 5–5 for the comparison). The fact that the final cumulative risks for both the siblings (24.7 per cent) and the children of the probands (26.2 per cent) are about the same would be expected for a multigenic etiology but it is difficult to reconcile it with an important environmental etiology because all of the children of the probands had at least one

psychotic parent while the siblings of the probands seldom had a psychotic parent.

In Figure 5–8 we see the gradually increasing spread between the cumulative risk for the children of our probands when an age correction has been made compared with the uncorrected data. It is noteworthy that neither in the siblings (Figure 5–3) nor in the children does the age correction assume much importance, in relation to the

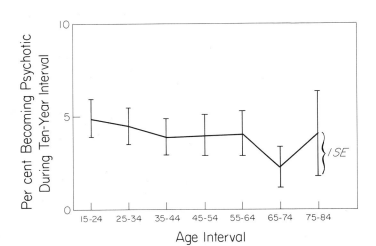

Figure 5–4. Ten year psychosis rates among full siblings of the probands.

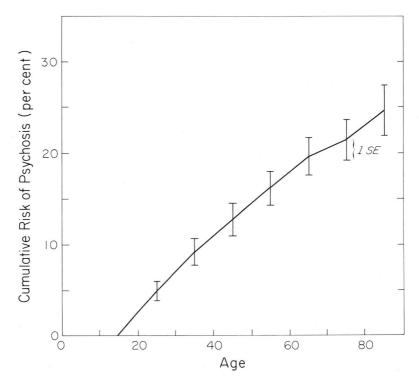

Figure 5–5. Cumulative risk of a psychosis in the full siblings of the probands.

Table 5–7. *Age of Children at Last Report by Mental Health and Status at Time of Study.*

Age at Last Report	PSYCHOTIC CHILDREN[1]			NOT PSYCHOTIC				ALL CHILDREN			
	Living at Time of Study	Dead	Total Psychotic	Living at Time of Study	Lost from Observation	Dead	Total Not Psychotic	Living at Time of Study	Lost from Observation	Dead	Total All Children
15–24					1	7	8		1	7	8
25–34		1	1	6	1	8	15	6	1	9	16
35–44	7	3	10	5		6	11	12		9	21
45–54	3	2	5	17		6	23	20		8	28
55–64	3	3	6	10		11	21	13		14	27
65–74	1	3	4	18		8	26	19		11	30
75–84	1		1	11		5	16	12		5	17
85–94				1			1	1			1
Total age known	15	12	27	68	2	51	121	83	2	63	148
Age unknown	–	–	–	–	5	1	6	–	5	1	6
Grand total	15	12	27	68	7	52	127	83	7	64	154
Mean age (years)	51.8	52.5	52.1	59.7	–	49.9	55.0	58.3	–	50.4	54.5

[1]No psychotic children were lost from observation.

Table 5–8. *Age of Psychotic Children at Onset or at Hospitalization for Psychosis or at Last Report.*

Age of Children	AGE AT ONSET AND AT HOSPITALIZATION KNOWN[1]		AGE AT ONSET UNKNOWN	NOT HOSPITALIZED AGE AT ONSET KNOWN	NOT HOSPITALIZED AGE AT ONSET UNKNOWN	ALL PSYCHOTIC SIBLINGS
	Age at Onset	*Age at First Hospital-ization*	*Age at First Hospital-ization*	*Age at Onset*	*Age at Last Report*	*Youngest Age*[2]
15–24	9	7	2	1		12
25–34	1	1	5			6
35–44	1	1			1	2
45–54	1	3			1	2
55–64				1	3	4
65–74						0
75–84					1	1
Totals	12	12	7	2	6	27
Mean age	22.9	29.2	25.4	40.0	43.8	32.7

[1] The same 12 persons are shown in the first two columns.
[2] Age at onset of psychosis, or at first hospitalization or at last report (youngest age available).

uncorrected age-risk curve, until the populations are 55 years of age and older. This is because even the probands' "children" were over 50 years old; they had thus survived much of the risk period for a psychosis by the time our study was completed. The gap between the age-adjusted and the uncorrected risk curves becomes greater with ages over 50 because the death rate increases rapidly while the risk of developing a psychosis in the survivors does not change much.

SUMMARY

In any condition with a variable age at onset some form of age adjustment is essential for accurate interpretation of the data. The method developed here uses only the

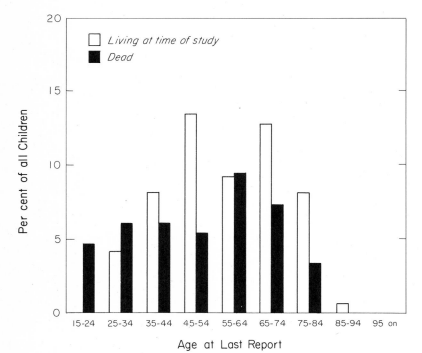

Figure 5–6. Age distribution of the children of the probands by status (living or dead) at the time of the study.

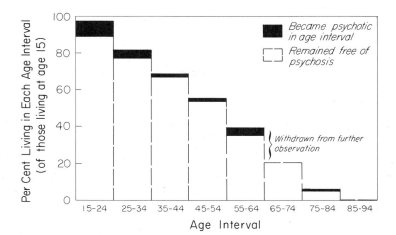

Figure 5–7. Life experience of the children of the probands.

data from the sample being studied. A cohort, such as the siblings of our probands, was selected and the age correction was made in the following way:

The number of siblings developing psychosis within an age interval (10 years) is divided by the calculated number of siblings who were living in that interval, to provide an age-specific incidence rate. The rates for all age intervals (from ages 15 to 85) are then used to estimate the cumulative risk of developing a psychosis, assuming that all the siblings were to survive to age 85.

In the study of the age corrections for siblings and children of the probands the following points of interest emerged:

1. Among the psychotic siblings significantly fewer were living than was the case for the non-psychotic siblings ($\chi^2 = 14.8$, $p < 0.001$). More of the psychotic siblings had died but they died at only slightly younger ages than the non-psychotic siblings. However, 44.4 per cent of the psychotic children had died compared with 42.2 per cent deaths for the non-psychotic children, and the psychotic children were slightly older at death than the non-psy-

Table 5–9. *Cumulative Risk of Psychosis Among Children.*

	NUMBER OF CHILDREN				CALCULATED NUMBER IN AGE INTERVAL *e*	PSYCHOSIS RATE (10 YEAR) (Per Cent) *f*	CUMULATIVE RISK OF PSYCHOSIS[3] (TO END OF INTERVAL) (Per Cent)
Age Interval	Psychotic[1] *a*	Other Disorder[2] *b*	Unaffected[2] *c*	Total *d*			
15–24	12	3	5	20	144.0	8.3 ± 2.3	8.3 ± 2.3
25–34	6	7	8	21	120.5	5.0 ± 2.0	12.9 ± 2.8
35–44	2	2	9	13	101.5	2.0 ± 1.4	14.6 ± 3.0
45–54	2	6	17	25	82.5	2.4 ± 1.7	16.7 ± 3.3
55–64	4	4	17	25	58.5	6.8 ± 3.3	22.4 ± 4.1
65–74	0	9	17	26	31.0 ⎫		
75–84	1	7	9	17	10.0 ⎬ 20.5*	4.9 ± 4.8	26.2 ± 5.4
85–94	0	1	0	1	0.5 ⎭		
Total, age known	27	39	82	148			
Age not known	0	0	6	6			
Grand totals	27	39	88	154			

[1] Age at onset of psychosis, or at first hospitalization or at last report (youngest age available).
[2] Age at last report.
[3] Method of calculation shown in Table 5–6.
* A 20-year rate.

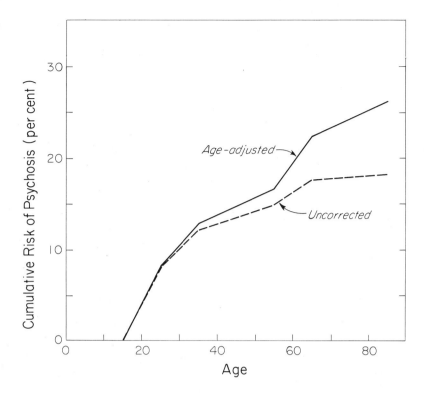

Figure 5–8. Cumulative risk of psychosis in the children of the probands compared with their values without age correction.

chotic children. In view of the deaths from suicide and of the presumed lower viability of the psychotics who passed their last years in state hospitals, it is not surprising to find a greater mortality among the psychotics than among the non-psychotics. We will return to this problem in the next chapter when we deal with the nieces and nephews.

2. The siblings of our probands showed a remarkably constant risk of becoming psychotic at all 10-year age intervals. The age intervals with adequate numbers of siblings present showed that a little more than 4 per cent of them received a diagnosis of a psychosis in each of the 10-year periods or almost half of 1 per cent of the siblings per year. Consequently, if all of the 457 siblings of our probands had survived until age 85, about one-quarter of them (24.7 ± 2.8 per cent) would have developed a psychosis. The uncorrected curve of actual cases shows that of the 457 siblings followed from age 15 there were 85 or 18.6 per cent who did develop a psychosis at some time during their lives. With complete survival we would have expected about 113 psychotics instead of the 85 observed. Thus 75 per cent of the siblings who could have been ex-

pected to develop a psychosis if all had lived to age 85 were diagnosed as such.

3. The 10-year interval risks for the children were individually more variable than those for the siblings but also averaged a little more than a 4 per cent risk for each 10-year interval. Presumably the increase in variability for the 10-year risks was the result of the smaller sample sizes for the children compared with the siblings. The final cumulative risk for the children, had all of them lived to age 85, would have been 26.2 ± 5.4 per cent, which is not significantly different from the 24.7 ± 2.8 per cent determination for the siblings that a psychosis would be developed and recorded by us. The uncorrected curve of observed cases shows that, of the 148 children followed from age 15, there were 27, or 18.2 per cent, who did develop a psychosis at some time during their lives. Our results for siblings and children seem to be practically identical. This almost embarrassingly good agreement of the risks for siblings and children of the probands leaves us groping for an explanation as to what kinds of environmental effects could be so similar in the two different generations.

CHAPTER SIX

OTHER GROUPS OF RELATIVES

We have presented data for the parents, siblings and children of the probands that are of primary significance because they are the first degree relatives of the probands. These relatives all share, on the average, half of their genes with the probands in each comparison of a relative and a proband. Only identical twins are genetically more closely related than first degree relatives and identical twins have a disadvantage in that we cannot obtain much evidence from them as to the mechanism of heredity which is responsible for the transmission of the genes for the trait of interest.

If we consider the nieces and nephews of the probands, the common heredity is one-fourth, on the average. However, some of the nieces and nephews will have had a psychotic parent and these should show es-

sentially the same frequencies of psychoses as the children of the probands. Apparently the environments are not much different as far as the development of the psychoses are concerned. The results in Tables 6–1 and 6–2 for the nieces and nephews with a psychotic parent are very similar both in sample size and in percentages with a psychosis to the results for the children of the probands (see Table 4–10).

It is obvious that we would expect only half as many psychotic nieces and nephews as psychotic children of the probands. In Table 6–1 we see that 5.8 per cent of the nieces and nephews were psychotic compared with the 17.5 per cent psychotic children. Actually one-third, not one-half, as many nieces and nephews were psychotic as children of the probands. This defi-

Table 6–1. *Mental Health of the Full Nieces and Nephews of the Probands When Classified According to the Sex and the Mental Health of Their Parents. (Excluding Those Who Died Before 15 Years of Age.)*

		FULL NIECES AND NEPHEWS OF THE PROBANDS			
		1.	2.	3. (Cols. 1 & 2)	4.
Mental Health of Parents		*Psychosis*	*Other Mental Disorder*	*Psychosis and Other Disorder*	*Total Nieces and Nephews (incl. Un-affected)*
Mother	*Father*	No. (Per Cent)	No. (Per Cent)	No. (Per Cent)	
Psychotic	Psychotic	1(100.0)	0	1(100.0)	1
Other disorder	Psychotic	1(5.6)	8(44.4)	9(50.0)	18
Unaffected	Psychotic	5(9.3)	7(13.0)	12(22.3)	54
Psychotic	Other disorder	4(22.2)	1(5.6)	5(27.8)	18
Other disorder	Other disorder	6(7.3)	23(28.0)	29(35.3)	82
Unaffected	Other disorder	7(4.0)	25(14.1)	32(18.1)	177
Psychotic	Unaffected	15(16.3)	15(16.3)	30(32.6)	92
Other disorder	Unaffected	7(6.4)	18(16.5)	25(22.9)	109
Unaffected	Unaffected	15(3.0)	46(9.2)	61(12.2)	500
		61(5.8)	143(13.6)	204(19.4)	1051

Table 6–2. *Summary Table for the Full Nieces and Nephews of the Probands Classified According to the Sex and Mental Health of Each Parent.*

| | FULL NIECES AND NEPHEWS OF THE PROBANDS (Each child is entered twice.) | | | |
	1. Psychosis No. (Per Cent)	2. Other Mental Disorders No. (Per Cent)	3. (Cols. 1 & 2) Psychosis and Other Disorder No. (Per Cent)	4. Total Nieces and Nephews (incl. Un-affected)
Mother psychotic	20(18.0)	16(14.4)	36(32.4)	111
Father psychotic	7(9.6)	15(20.5)	22(30.1)	73
Mother other mental disorder	14(6.7)	49(23.4)	63(30.1)	209
Father other mental disorder	17(6.1)	49(17.7)	66(23.8)	277
Mother unaffected	27(3.7)	78(10.7)	105(14.4)	731
Father unaffected	37(5.3)	79(11.3)	116(16.6)	701

ciency, if real and not the result of less reliable ascertainment, is characteristic of traits showing a multigenic etiology. Both the children of probands and the siblings of probands may reflect a "loading" bias present in the selection of the probands and thus would tend to have higher frequencies of psychoses than a sample free from a genetic loading bias. The nieces and nephews would have less selection bias than the siblings and children and therefore would be expected to have lower frequencies of psychoses than the siblings of the probands, for whom there could be greater selection bias.

It is certainly remarkable that the percentages of psychoses and "other mental disorders" turn out to be so precisely correlated with the genetic relationships be-

tween the groups of relatives involved. We are compelled to acknowledge the role of environmental factors in the development of the psychoses because of the discordance observed between identical twins. However, the genetic evidence given above would seem to indicate that the relevant environmental factors are almost universally present. The environmental differences accounting for the discordance of identical twins seem to be relatively trivial because they are so commonplace that they defy specific identification at the present time.

It is interesting to present the 1051 nieces and nephews classified as to the mental health of the parents considered as couples rather than individuals. This material (Table 6–3) is the same as that in the previous two tables but it demonstrates bet-

Table 6–3. *The Full Nieces and Nephews of the Probands Classified According to the Mental Health of the Parents.*

| | FULL NIECES AND NEPHEWS OF THE PROBANDS | | | |
	1. Psychosis No. (Per Cent)	2. Other Mental Disorders No. (Per Cent)	3. Sum (Cols. 1 & 2) No. (Per Cent)	4. Total Nieces and Nephews (incl. Un-affected)
One or both parents psychotic	26(14.2)	31(16.9)	57(31.1)	183
Both with other mental disorder	6(7.3)	23(28.0)	29(35.3)	82
One parent with other disorder, one unaffected	14(4.9)	43(15.0)	57(19.9)	286
Both parents unaffected	15(3.0)	46(9.2)	61(12.2)	500
Totals	61(5.8)	143(13.6)	204(19.4)	1051

ter the decrease in psychosis in the nieces and nephews as the mental health of the parents, as a couple, improves.

The nieces and nephews have the same genetic relationship to the probands as do the aunts and uncles of the probands. The data for the aunts and uncles are in Table 4–4 and show that 7.1 per cent of them had a psychosis compared with the 5.8 per cent in the nieces and nephews of the probands. The frequency of "other mental disorders" among the aunts and uncles was 13.3 per cent, compared with 13.6 per cent in the nieces and nephews. There were 930 aunts and uncles and 1051 nieces and nephews of the probands. The aunts and uncles of the probands are, of course, the great aunts and great uncles of the nieces and nephews of the probands. There is a long generation gap between the great aunts and great uncles of the probands' nieces and nephews and one could have expected the environments of these widely separated generations to be greatly different in respect to the development of psychoses. Yet the percentages of both psychoses and the "other mental disorders" are practically identical for these two groups of relatives of the probands; this is in accord with the identity, or at least the similarity, of the genetic components assumed for the two groups of relatives as far as the psychoses are concerned.

AGE CORRECTIONS FOR THE NIECES AND NEPHEWS

The data for the nieces and nephews will be presented in the same format as those for the children of the probands. The mean age of the nieces and nephews of the probands at the time of the termination of the study was 50.5 years, as shown in Table 6–4. The average age for the children of the probands (Table 5–7) was 54.5 years, so these two groups of relatives were similar both in their mean ages and in their chronological existence. There is a difference in that the *psychotic* nieces and nephews had a greater mean age than the non-psychotic nieces and nephews, whereas the opposite situation held in the case of the children. However, these differences are not large and probably do not have any biological significance.

If the reader will look at Figures 5–6 and 6–1, he will see that the proportion of the nieces and nephews still living at the close of the study was much higher than the proportion of the children who were still alive at the end of the study. This was unexpected, as the average ages for the two groups of relatives were similar. An analysis of the situation revealed that the distinction was not whether a person was in the niece and nephew group compared with the children, but whether the parent of the person

Table 6–4. *Age of Nieces and Nephews at Last Report by Mental Health and Status at Time of Study.*

	PSYCHOTIC NIECES AND NEPHEWS					NOT PSYCHOTIC					ALL NIECES AND NEPHEWS			
Age at Last Report	Living at Time of Study	Lost from Obser-vation	Dead	Total Psychotic	Living at Time of Study	Lost from Obser-vation	Dead	Total Not Psychotic	Living at Time of Study	Lost from Obser-vation	Dead	Total
15–24	1		4	5	29		37	66	30		41	71
25–34	3			3	83	4	29	116	86	4	29	119
35–44	4			4	168	2	39	209	172	2	39	213
45–54	7	1	7	15	167	3	32	202	174	4	39	217
55–64	5		5	10	128		52	180	133		57	190
65–74	3		8	11	83		40	123	86		48	134
75–84	1		6	7	41		26	67	42		32	74
85–94	1		5	6	3		7	10	4		12	16
95–99							1	1			1	1
Total age known	25	1	35	61	702	9	263	974	727	10	298	1035
Age un-known						15	1	16		15	1	16
Grand total	25	1	35	61	702	24	264	990	727	25	299	1051
Mean age (years)	52.7	—	53.9	53.4	50.1	37.5	51.4	50.4	50.2	39.0	51.7	50.5

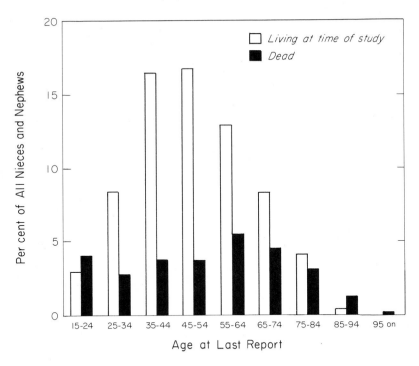

Figure 6–1. Age distribution of the nieces and nephews of the probands by status at the time of study.

was psychotic or not psychotic. All of the children of the probands had a psychotic parent and their average year of birth was 1897.8. The average year of birth for the nieces and nephews who had a psychotic parent was 1895.4±1.7 years. There was no statistically significant difference between these two groups. However, the nieces and nephews who had neither parent psychotic had an average birth year of 1907±0.7. The difference between these last two groups is 12.2 ± 1.9 years, which is statistically highly significant, with a probability of less than 1 chance in 1000 that the difference is due to sampling error.

Presumably the reason that the nieces and nephews who had a psychotic parent were born before those without a psychotic parent is, on the average, simply that the psychotic parents usually completed their reproduction before hospitalization, but the non-psychotic parents continued to reproduce for many years while a large number of the psychotic parents were hospitalized and not reproducing.

The raw data for the nieces and nephews of the probands as to age at onset, age at hospitalization and age at last report are

given in Table 6–5 and may be compared with the data for the children of the probands shown in Table 5–8. The fact that the youngest age (last column of the two tables) is less for the children than for the nieces and nephews, if a biological reality rather than just a sampling difference, may be because many of the nieces and nephews had non-psychotic parents while all the children of the probands had a psychotic parent.

We are interested in the cumulative-risk figures for all nieces and nephews and these may be found in Table 6–6. They are age-corrected, and on a multigenic hypothesis we would expect the risk figures for the nieces and nephews to be about one-half the size of those for the children, as shown in Table 5–9. The numbers are rather small for the children but our expectations for a multigenic hypothesis are confirmed in general, at least for the older age groups.

The reader may think that the cumulative-risk figures for the nieces and nephews shown in Table 6–6 are too high to be realistic. There are at least two reasons why they are this high:

1. The parents of the nieces and neph-

Table 6–5. *Age of Psychotic Nieces and Nephews at Onset or at Hospitalization for Psychosis or at Last Report.*

| AGE | AGE AT ONSET AND AT HOSPITALIZATION KNOWN[1] | | AGE AT ONSET UNKNOWN | NOT HOSPITALIZED AGE AT ONSET KNOWN | NOT HOSPITALIZED AGE AT ONSET UNKNOWN | ALL PSYCHOTIC NIECES AND NEPHEWS |
	Age at Onset	*Age at First Hospital-ization*	*Age at First Hospital-ization*	*Age at Onset*	*Age at Last Report*	*Youngest Age[2]*
15–24	13	10	2	2		17
25–34	14	14	4			18
35–44	8	4			2	10
45–54	4	8	1	1	1	7
55–64	1	3			2	3
65–74	2	3			1	3
75–84	1	1			2	3
Totals	43	43	7	3	8	61
Mean age	34.2	38.0	31.1	30.8	59.4	37.0

[1] The same 43 persons are shown in the first two columns.
[2] Age at onset of psychosis, or at first hospitalization or at last report (the youngest age available).

ews are, of course, the siblings of our probands. Of the 1051 nieces and nephews, there were 183 who had one or both parents psychotic and only 500 of them had both parents unaffected. Thus, about half of the nieces and nephews had at least one parent with some mental disorder or a psychosis; therefore, we expect the risks, after age correction, to be high.

2. The cumulative risk of psychosis for any group of elderly people is high. In Table 6–8 it can be seen that the risk for persons surviving to age 75 is 6.1 per cent. These control persons are not genetically related to our probands and the risk figure should be characteristic of "normal" populations of white persons not living in the center cities of this country.

Table 6–6. *Cumulative Risk of Psychosis Among Nieces and Nephews.*

| Age Interval | NUMBER OF NIECES AND NEPHEWS | | | | CALCULATED NUMBER IN AGE INTERVAL | PSYCHOSIS RATE (10 YEAR) | CUMULATIVE RISK OF PSYCHOSIS[3] (TO END OF INTERVAL) |
	Psychotic[1] a	*Other Dis-order[2]* b	*Un-affected[2]* c	*Total* d	e	*(Per Cent)* f	*(Per Cent)*
15–24	17	5	61	83	1002.0	1.7 ± 0.4	1.7 ± 0.4
25–34	18	11	104	133	894.5	1.8 ± 0.4	3.5 ± 0.6
35–44	10	20	189	219	714.5	1.4 ± 0.4	4.8 ± 0.7
45–54	7	27	174	208	499.5	1.4 ± 0.5	6.2 ± 0.9
55–64	3	31	151	185	301.0	1.0 ± 0.6	7.1 ± 1.0
65–74	3	29	94	126	145.5	2.1 ± 1.2	9.0 ± 1.5
75–84	3	14	53	70	47.5	6.3 ± 3.5	14.8 ± 3.5
85–94		4	6	10	6.0		
95–99		1	0	1	0.5		
Total, age known	61	142	832	1035			
Age not known	0	1	15	16			
Grand totals	61	143	847	1051			

[1] Age at onset of psychosis, or at first hospitalization or at last report (youngest age available).
[2] Age at last report.
[3] Method of calculation shown in Table 5–6.

CONTROL GROUP

It was obvious to us when designing the study that the group of individuals which would be the largest and also the most interesting from the genetic point of view would be Generation IV (the children of the probands, and the nieces and nephews). They would be relatively old (well along in their exposure to risk of psychosis), would be less subject to selection bias than the probands and the siblings of probands and could be sorted according to the various combinations of mental health in their parents. It was for Generation IV, therefore, that a control group would be most desirable.

We considered carefully the possibility of using morbidity data to calculate expected rates for psychosis. Several good morbidity studies for the Warren State Hospital area have been prepared for other purposes, and these would have been helpful. On the other hand, this approach has several disadvantages:

1. Such data would have to be organized in a cohort fashion so that we could follow persons born in different calendar years through successively older age intervals.

2. Such data generally would not include non-hospitalized cases of psychosis.

3. The individuals in Generation IV may not be a representative sample of the general population from which such data would be drawn.

For these reasons we selected a control strategy that had been used for an earlier Dight Institute study on breast cancer (Anderson, Goodman, and Reed, 1958), namely, siblings of spouses. Marriages tend to be assortative for socio-economic reasons and for other factors that may influence the development of mental disorders. The spouses themselves are biased in several ways that make them unsuitable for control purposes: (1) There may be assortative marriage for

mental illness; and (2) unmarried persons (having different risks for psychosis) are excluded. The siblings of the spouses are not subject to these restrictions. Individuals without siblings would not be included, but we considered this to be a less-critical problem.

To have traced all siblings of all spouses would have been an excessively time-consuming task. Therefore, arbitrary rules were established to select a representative 20 per cent sample of sibships within Generation IV. When a given sibship was identified, an effort was made to obtain information about the siblings of all persons who had married into the family. In the case of divorce the information usually was not available, but whenever the names of siblings for a given spouse were obtained that sibship was included in the control sample.

In Generation IV there was a total of 1107 persons who married. For 226 of these (20.4 per cent) the siblings of one or more spouses were included in the control group. The 1107 persons had a total of 1292 spouses, and the siblings of 242 spouses (18.7 per cent) were used as controls. Thus the 20 per cent sampling plan was met reasonably well.

The collection of data followed the same procedures as for the members of Generation IV. There was a deliberate attempt to find several informants for each control sibship in order to increase the overall adequacy of the data. Some idea of the resulting comparability can be seen in the statistics below.

In some control sibships two or more persons had married into the family being studied. In tabulating the results the standard proband method was employed, using each spouse (marrying into the family) as a proband and counting all siblings. The mental health of the spouses and of the control is shown in Table 6–7. Comparing the number with psychosis in the two groups, $\chi^2 = 6.6$, with P less than .05. We have no ex-

	Children	Nieces and Nephews	Control Group
Number surviving to age 15	154	1051	913
Mean age (of survivors to 15)	54.5 years	50.5 years	51.5 years
Age unknown	3.9%	1.5%	5.6%
Mental health unknown	4.5%	2.3%	2.4%

Table 6–7. *Mental Health of the Spouses in Generation IV and the Control Group.*

	1. PSYCHOSIS No. (Per Cent)	2. OTHER MENTAL DISORDER No. (Per Cent)	3. SUM (COLS. 1 & 2) No. (Per Cent)	4. TOTAL (INCL. UNAFFECTED)
Spouses in Generation IV	15 (1.2)	124 (9.6)	139 (10.8)	1292
Control group (siblings of a sample of spouses)	24 (2.6)	38 (4.2)	62 (6.8)	913

planation for this difference between the 1.2 per cent of psychosis in the spouses and the 2.6 per cent in the sample of siblings of spouses, if it is a real difference. The age-adjusted cumulative risk for psychosis in the control group is calculated in Table 6–8.

For purposes of comparison we have tabulated in Table 6–9 the data for those nieces and nephews who had unaffected parents (having no psychosis or other mental disorder). Note that three older age intervals are combined in order to avoid an inflated psychosis rate in the 75 to 84 year interval based on the small population therein. It is clear that the risks for psychosis are very similar to those in the control group.

An additional comparison is possible by using the data from the survey by Hagnell (1966). Some explanation is necessary, how-

ever, since his data were collected in a different manner. A specified population was studied in the year 1947 and those free from psychosis were identified. Ten years later the same population was surveyed to find those who had developed some type of mental problem. Thus, Hagnell's study provides *current* data for a population at various ages followed for 10 years, while we have *cohort* data for persons followed for successive 10-year periods throughout their lifetime. To use Hagnell's data for comparison we made the simplifying assumption that his group of individuals aged 10 to 19 years (with a mean age of 15), if followed for 10 years, would be equivalent to following a cohort from age 15 through 24. The cumulative risks from Hagnell's study are plotted in Figure 6–2 together with the lines from our control group and the nieces and neph-

Table 6–8. *Cumulative Risk of Psychosis for the Control Group.*

Age Interval	Psychotic[1] a	NUMBER OF CONTROLS Other Dis- order[2] b	Un- affected[2] c	Total d	CALCULATED NUMBER IN AGE INTERVAL e	PSYCHOSIS RATE (10 YEAR) (Per Cent) f	CUMULATIVE RISK OF PSYCHOSIS[3] (TO END OF INTERVAL) (Per Cent)
15–24	1	1	38	40	842.5	0.1 ± 0.1	0.1 ± 0.1
25–34	3	2	99	104	771.5	0.4 ± 0.2	0.5 ± 0.3
35–44	13	10	172	195	627.0	2.1 ± 0.6	2.6 ± 0.6
45–54	1	5	162	168	439.5	0.2 ± 0.2	2.8 ± 0.7
55–64	3	8	157	168	272.5	1.1 ± 0.6	3.9 ± 0.9
65–74	3	7	107	117	130.0	2.3 ± 1.3	6.1 ± 1.5
75–84		2	61	63	38.5		
85–94		1	6	7	3.5		
Total, age known	24	36	802	862			
Age not known		1	50	51			
Grand totals	24	37	852	913			

[1]Age at onset of psychosis, or at first hospitalization or at last report (youngest age available).
[2]Age at last report.
[3]Method of calculation shown in Table 5–6.

Table 6–9. *Cumulative Risk of Psychosis Among Nieces and Nephews with Unaffected Parents.*

| | NUMBER OF NIECES AND NEPHEWS | | | | CALCULATED NUMBER IN AGE INTERVAL *e* | PSYCHOSIS RATE (10 YEAR) (Per Cent) *f* | CUMULATIVE RISK OF PSYCHOSIS[3] (TO END OF INTERVAL) (Per Cent) |
Age Interval	Psychotic[1] *a*	Other Dis-order[2] *b*	Un-affected[2] *c*	Total *d*			
15–24	4	4	35	43	470.5	0.9 ± 0.4	0.9 ± 0.4
25–34	3	3	54	60	418.5	0.7 ± 0.4	1.6 ± 0.6
35–44	5	10	113	128	325.5	1.5 ± 0.7	3.1 ± 0.9
45–54	1	6	89	96	211.5	0.5 ± 0.5	3.5 ± 1.0
55–64	0	13	73	86	120.0 ⎫		
65–74	1	8	40	49	53.0 ⎬ 62.7	3.2 ± 2.2*	6.6 ± 2.3
75–84	1	3	23	27	15.0 ⎭		
85–94			1	1			
Total, age known	15	47	428	490			
Age not known			10	10			
Grand totals	15	47	438	500			

[1] Age at onset of psychosis, or at first hospitalization or at last report (youngest age available).
[2] Age at last report.
[3] Method of calculation shown in Table 5–6.
* A 30-year rate.

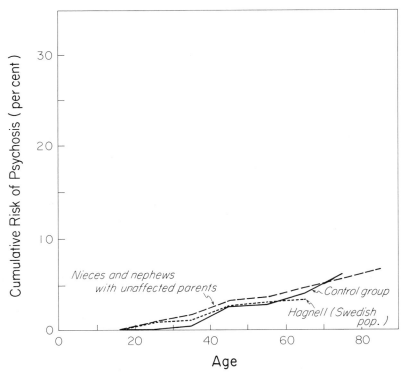

Figure 6–2. Psychosis in three control samples.

ews with unaffected parents. The overall correspondence of the three groups is surprisingly close. We would expect the nieces and nephews from *unaffected* parents to have a small genetic loading for psychosis, so their curve should be slightly higher than the two control group curves, and it is.

A large advantage derived from our good-sized population of nephews and nieces is that this group can be subdivided in regard to the mental health of the parents more extensively than is the case for the children of the probands who, of course, always have at least one psychotic parent. Thus nieces and nephews of the proband would have only half as many genes for psychosis as the children of the probands as an average value. However, some of the nieces and nephews will have a psychotic parent (who is a sibling of the proband) and in these cases the cumulative risk figures should be about the same as those for the children. The data in Table 6–10 show this to be the case. The final cumulative risk figure for the nieces and nephews with a psychotic parent of 21.5 per cent predicts that the person will become psychotic by age 85 if he survives that long, while the similar figure for the children of the probands is 26.2 per cent.

Later on we will consider the meaning

of the diagnosis for the group of persons who have "other mental disorders." At the moment we will only say that they seem to have a genetic potential for the development of psychoses. This is demonstrated by the data in Table 6–11, where we see a final cumulative risk of 11.2 per cent for the nieces and nephews with neither parent psychotic but having at least one parent with some "other mental disorder." This figure is intermediate between that for the nieces and nephews with an affected parent and those with both parents unaffected. A graphic presentation of the cumulative risk curves for the groups of relatives we have discussed is provided in Figure 6–3.

We see that the curve for the children in Figure 6–3 is consistently higher than that for either the siblings or the nieces and nephews with psychotic parents. The differences between the children, the siblings and the nephews and nieces with a psychotic parent, whatever their causation, are too small to be of importance, and they are not statistically significant. The similarities are the important finding because, on the average, these three groups of relatives must have similar genotypes for their psychoses. Presumably the same kinds of environmental factors were also present in all three groups of relatives.

Table 6–10. *Cumulative Risk of Psychosis Among Nieces and Nephews with Psychotic Parent.*

| Age Interval | NUMBER OF NIECES AND NEPHEWS | | | | CALCULATED NUMBER IN AGE INTERVAL *e* | PSYCHOSIS RATE (10 YEAR) (Per Cent) *f* | CUMULATIVE RISK OF PSYCHOSIS[3] (TO END OF INTERVAL) (Per Cent) |
	Psychotic[1] *a*	Other Disorder[2] *b*	Unaffected[2] *c*	Total *d*			
15–24	7	0	8	15	177.0	4.0 ± 1.5	4.0 ± 1.5
25–34	11	3	16	30	156.5	7.0 ± 2.0	10.7 ± 2.4
35–44	3	1	14	18	128.5	2.3 ± 1.3	12.8 ± 2.6
45–54	2	5	20	27	105.5	1.9 ± 1.3	14.4 ± 2.8
55–64	1	3	26	30	76.5	1.3 ± 1.3	15.6 ± 3.0
65–74	0	13	25	38	42.0 ⎫ 28.5	7.0±4.8°	21.5 ± 4.9
75–84	2	5	11	18	15.0 ⎭		
85–94		1	4	5	2.5		
Total, age known	26	31	124	181			
Age not known			2	2			
Grand totals	26	31	126	183			

[1] Age at onset of psychosis, or at first hospitalization or at last report (youngest age available).
[2] Age at last report.
[3] Method of calculation shown in Table 5–6.
° A 20-year rate.

Table 6–11. *Cumulative Risk of Psychosis Among Nieces and Nephews with Neither Parent Psychotic But at Least One Parent Having Some Other Mental Disorder.*

	NUMBER OF NIECES AND NEPHEWS				CALCULATED NUMBER IN AGE INTERVAL *e*	PSYCHOSIS RATE (10 YEAR) (Per Cent) *f*	CUMULATIVE RISK OF PSYCHOSIS[3] (TO END OF INTERVAL) (Per Cent)
Age Interval	Psychotic[1] *a*	Other Disorder[2] *b*	Unaffected[2] *c*	Total *d*			
15–24	6	1	18	25	354.5	1.7 ± 0.7	1.7 ± 0.7
25–34	4	5	34	43	319.5	1.3 ± 0.6	2.9 ± 0.9
35–44	2	9	62	73	260.5	0.8 ± 0.5	3.7 ± 1.0
45–54	4	16	65	85	182.5	2.2 ± 1.1	5.8 ± 1.5
55–64	2	15	52	69	104.5	1.9 ± 1.3	7.6 ± 1.9
65–74	2	8	29	39	50.5	4.0 ± 2.7	11.2 ± 3.1
75–84		6	19	25	17.5		
85–94		3	1	4	3.0		
95–99		1		1	0.5		
Total, age known	20	64	280	364			
Age not known		1	3	4			
Grand totals	20	65	283	368			

[1]Age at last report.
[2]Age at onset of psychosis, or at first hospitalization or at last report (youngest age available).
[3]Method of calculation shown in Table 5–6.

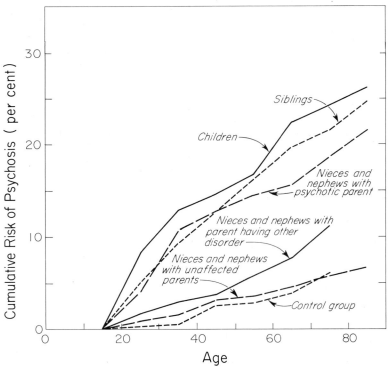

Figure 6–3. Cumulative risk of psychosis in various groups of relatives and the unrelated control group.

We apologize for Figure 6–3 in that six curves in one figure are slightly confusing. However, it is important to see how the three categories of nieces and nephews relate to each other and to the other relatives and to the control group. The total group of nieces and nephews is divided into the three categories which do not overlap and where

1. one or both of their parents had a psychosis,
2. neither parent was psychotic but one or both parents had an "other mental disorder," and
3. both parents were unaffected.

COMBINED DATA

Up to this point we have been looking at groups of relatives separately. It may now be of interest to make appropriate combinations of the data. For example, the data for nieces and nephews of the probands can be combined with the data for children of the probands as long as the information is sorted according to the mental health of the parents. The results are shown in Table 6–12. The main advantage of combining the data for the children and the nieces and nephews is the increase in the sample size with the increased statistical significance of the combined results. If we combine rows 4 and 5 of Table 6–12, we find that there are 40 psychotic and 179 not psychotic offspring of psychotic mothers and not psychotic fathers. The reciprocal union of not psychotic mothers and psychotic fathers (rows 2 and 3) produced only 10 psychotic offspring out of 115 offspring. The χ^2 value for this compari-

son is equal to 5.42, with 1 degree of freedom and $p = < 0.05$. Thus the children combined with the nieces and nephews provide statistically significant evidence that psychotic mothers have a higher percentage of psychotic offspring than do psychotic fathers.

This important finding can be tested further by adding the data from the siblings of the probands to the above data. When this is done there are 74 psychotic offspring of 305 from psychotic mothers, compared with 15 psychotic offspring of 157 from psychotic fathers. The χ^2 value is now 14.4 with 1 degree of freedom and $p = < 0.01$. Thus there are consistent data from three groups of relatives with a statistically highly significant χ^2 for the combined data. It seems to be established that psychotic mothers have a higher percentage of psychotic offspring than is the case for psychotic fathers. We are left with the unanswered question as to why this relationship has not been found in previous family studies of the psychoses.

Let us return to a consideration of the cumulative risks for the children of the probands plus the nieces and nephews with a psychotic parent that are shown in Figure 6–4. For comparison the curve is shown for the control group plus the nieces and nephews with unaffected parents.

The remaining curve in this figure will need some additional explanation. It is possible to identify among the nieces and nephews those who have a psychotic *sibling*. In a sibship with one person psychotic, it is only the non-psychotics who are counted. With two or more affected persons in a sibship, all the persons are counted. If the usual "proband method" is applied,

Table 6–12. *Combined Data for the Children of the Probands and the Nieces and Nephews with One or Both Parents Psychotic.*

Mother	Father	1. PSYCHOSIS No. (Per Cent)	2. OTHER MENTAL DISORDER No. (Per Cent)	3. SUM (COLS. 1 & 2) No. (Per Cent)	4. TOTALS (INCL. UN-AFFECTED)
Psychotic	Psychotic	3(100.0)	0	3(100.0)	3
Other disorder	Psychotic	2(6.5)	13(41.9)	15(48.4)	31
Unaffected	Psychotic	8(9.5)	13(15.5)	21(25.0)	84
Psychotic	Other disorder	18(26.1)	21(30.4)	39(56.5)	69
Psychotic	Unaffected	22(14.7)	23(15.3)	45(30.0)	150
Totals		53(15.7)	70(20.8)	123(36.5)	337

each person is counted once for each psychotic sibling. There were 160 nieces and nephews with a psychotic sibling, and of these 21 (13.1 per cent) were themselves psychotic. The cumulative risk to age 85 was 30.1 per cent (counting each person once) and 31.0 per cent using the proband method. Neither of these values is significantly different from the 24.7 cumulative risk for siblings of the probands. The age distribution obtained by single counting of the nieces and nephews with psychotic siblings was combined with the data for siblings of the probands to calculate the third line in Figure 6–4.

These combined populations have the further advantage of yielding somewhat larger samples as a basis for comparing the 10-year psychosis rates in these different groups at the various age intervals. The results are shown in Figure 6–5.

At first we were puzzled by the high rate in the control group for the 35 to 44 interval as compared with the younger and older ages. On the other hand, the data from Hagnell (1966) were very similar. The com-

ponents of these rates by separate diagnostic categories will be evaluated in the next chapter.

The curves in Figure 6–5 generate several observations:

1. The rates for children and siblings are significantly higher than those for the control group in the 15 to 34 age period. This may have some implications for age-adjustment procedures using a "Bezugsziffer" derived from the age distribution of psychosis in some general population. Such a method may produce misleading results if the age-specific rates in a group of relatives follow a pattern which is different from that in the general population.

2. The rates for children are somewhat higher than those for siblings during the 15 to 34 age period and somewhat lower during the 35 to 54 period. However, the differences are not statistically significant at any point. It is perhaps surprising that the curve for the children is *not* consistently higher as they always have a psychotic parent while the siblings have a psychotic parent only in a minority of the cases. Ge-

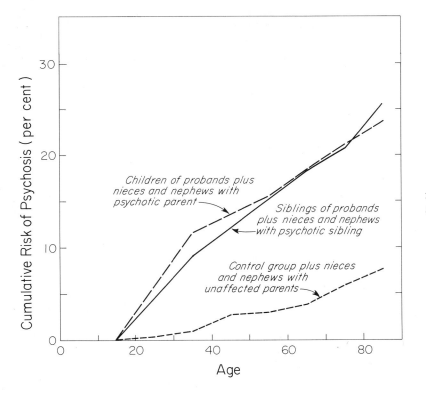

Figure 6–4. Cumulative risks of psychosis in various groups of persons.

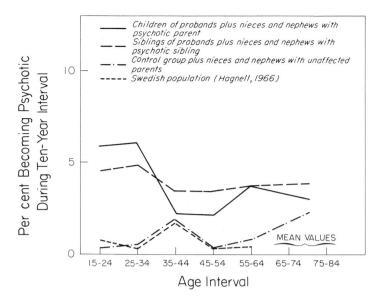

Figure 6–5. Ten year psychosis rates for various groups of persons.

netic expectations for the two curves are the same and the curves are statistically indistinguishable.

OTHER RELATIVES

The persons shown in a specific generation on the pedigree chart are more or less synchronous in time. They are not genetically equivalent, however. For instance, the grandchildren of the probands are part of Generation V and share one-quarter of their genes with their proband grandparent, while the grandnieces and grandnephews are also part of Generation V but have only one-eighth of their genes in common with the probands, on the average. The children of the half nieces and half nephews are also part of Generation V but share only one-sixteenth of their genes with the probands. Such distant relatives are not usually studied by geneticists but they are of value here in that they are far from the family environments of the probands. However, if the parent is psychotic they are similar genetically to the children of the probands and so should give similar frequencies of psychotic persons. The Generation V relatives, such as the grandchildren of the probands, will be much younger than the Generation IV relatives, so that the ages of onset for psychotic disorders will not have been reached as often in Generation V as in Generation IV. We would expect low frequencies of psychoses in the relatives in Generation V both because of their genetic distance from the probands and their relatively young ages. About half of the Generation V persons were between 15 and 35 years of age; the other half were over 35. However, even the older half of the persons still have many years to live at risk. Children under 15 are omitted here as elsewhere.

The data for these relatives in Generation V are given in Table 6–13. The fact that only 1.7 per cent of the 1966 relatives of Generation V were psychotic is primarily because of their genetic distance from the probands and their young ages. The data in Table 6–13 are useful only for comparisons of the different types of marriages. Once again there was a higher percentage of psychotic offspring (5.0 per cent) when the mother was psychotic, contrasted with 3.4 per cent when the father was the psychotic partner. It would not be meaningful to make a single cumulative risk curve for the combined data in Table 6–13 as there are three different genetic relationships included with a different sized sample of people in each category. Naturally, if each genetic category were age-corrected separately we would have much higher expected frequencies of psychoses than the observed value of 1.7 per cent psychoses for the combined data without age correction.

Table 6–13. *The Combined Data for the Relatives in Generation V. These Relatives Share One-Quarter, One-Eighth or One-Sixteenth of Their Genes with the Proband in Their Kinship.*

Mother	Father	1. PSYCHOSIS No. (Per Cent)	2. OTHER MENTAL DISORDER No. (Per Cent)	3. SUM (COLS. 1 & 2) No. (Per Cent)	4. TOTALS (INCL. UN- AFFECTED)
Psychotic	Psychotic	2(22.2)	2(22.2)	4(44.4)	9
Other	Psychotic	0	2(20.0)	2(20.0)	10
Unaffected	Psychotic	2(4.1)	3(6.1)	5(10.2)	49
Psychotic	Other	0	6(50.0)	6(50.0)	12
Other	Other	3(2.3)	32(24.6)	35(26.9)	130
Unaffected	Other	8(3.1)	27(10.5)	35(13.6)	258
Psychotic	Unaffected	3(6.3)	10(20.8)	13(27.1)	48
Other	Unaffected	4(2.7)	22(15.1)	26(17.8)	146
Unaffected	Unaffected	11(0.8)	58(4.4)	69(5.2)	1304
Totals		33(1.7)	162(8.2)	195(9.9)	1966

Finally, the fact that the frequencies of psychoses in these distant relatives is not substantially greater than in the controls, except when the parent is psychotic, is not surprising. The data from these distant relatives are useful mainly because they confirm findings such as the higher frequency of psychosis in the children of psychotic mothers compared with the children of psychotic fathers observed in the close relatives of the probands.

One of the most important observations of this book is that in a sample of psychotic persons we can expect more women than men to become parents and, in addition, the psychotic mothers have a higher percentage of psychotic offspring than do the psychotic fathers. No other study has produced strictly comparable data nor is there any other study where there are several generations which provide a test of the consistency of the higher proportion of psychotic children produced by psychotic mothers compared with psychotic fathers. We have one more generation, that of the aunts and uncles of the probands, in which the test of consistency can be made. The data are presented in Table 6–14. It can be seen that when the mother (of the aunts and uncles) was psychotic and the father was not psychotic there were 7 psychotic aunts and uncles in 52, or 13.5 per cent, but if the father was psychotic and the mother was not psychotic there were 3 psychotic aunts and uncles out of 31, or 9.7 per cent. The difference is consistent with that found in all the other groups of relatives.

There are only 834 aunts and uncles

Table 6–14. *Mental Health of the Aunts and Uncles of the Probands, According to the Sex and Mental Health of the Parents of the Aunt or Uncle.*

Mother	Father	1. PSYCHOSIS No. (Per Cent)	2. OTHER MENTAL DISORDER No. (Per Cent)	3. SUM (COLS. 1 & 2) No. (Per Cent)	4. TOTALS (INCL. UN- AFFECTED)
Psychotic	Psychotic	2(18.2)	2(18.2)	4(36.4)	11
Other disorder	Psychotic	2(10.0)	3(15.0)	5(25.0)	20
Unaffected	Psychotic	1(9.1)	5(45.5)	6(54.6)	11
Psychotic	Other disorder	3(23.1)	2(15.4)	5(38.5)	13
Other disorder	Other disorder	7(12.3)	12(21.1)	19(33.4)	57
Unaffected	Other disorder	15(13.6)	33(30.0)	48(43.6)	110
Psychotic	Unaffected	4(10.3)	7(17.9)	11(28.2)	39
Other disorder	Unaffected	7(7.1)	14(14.3)	21(21.4)	98
Unaffected	Unaffected	25(5.3)	49(10.3)	74(15.6)	475
Totals		66(7.9)	127(15.2)	193(23.1)	834

shown in Table 6–14 while there are 930 in Table 4–4. The difference results from the omission of those aunts and uncles from Table 6–14 whose parents were of unknown mental health.

It is now appropriate to combine all five groups of relatives to get a final figure for the higher frequency of psychosis in the offspring of psychotic mothers compared with the offspring from psychotic fathers. The 20.1 per cent psychotic offspring of the psychotic mothers is over twice the 8.1 per cent produced by the psychotic fathers, as shown in Table 6–15. We find for the four-fold table obtained that $\chi^2 = 17.0$, with 1 degree of freedom, and the probability that the difference between the two frequencies of psychosis is due to chance is less than 1 chance in 1000. The combination of complete consistency for all five groups of relatives and the high χ^2 value of 17.0 would seem to leave no doubt that psychotic mothers demonstrate a higher frequency of psychosis in their offspring than do psychotic fathers. This is one of the most important findings of our study and has highly significant implications for the mental health of subsequent generations.

SUMMARY

Geneticists usually restrict studies of traits like the psychoses to the first degree relatives of the selected probands. This is partly because of the expense involved in searching for the large numbers of more distant relatives and partly because of the lower frequencies of the trait to be expected in these genetically more distant relatives. The combination of these two disadvantages is often enough to prevent the collection of data from second and third degree relatives. The present study is unique among the family studies of the psychoses in that two groups of workers, some 45 years apart, studied the same families and in this way were able to get satisfactory data from second and third degree relatives. The data from the more distant relatives permit essentially independent tests of the findings obtained from the first degree relatives.

1. The group of nieces and nephews are second degree relatives and obviously should have only one-half (or less) the percentage of psychoses found in the children of the probands. The nieces and nephews were psychotic in 5.8 per cent of the cases while 17.5 per cent of the children of the probands were psychotic. The more interesting finding is that when the mother of the nieces and nephews was psychotic, 18.0 per cent of her offspring (the nieces and nephews) were also psychotic. When the father was psychotic only 9.6 per cent of the nieces and nephews were psychotic. Comparable figures for the children of the probands are 20.7 per cent psychotic when the mother (proband) was psychotic and 13.3 per cent psychotic children when the father was the psychotic proband.

2. Another interesting comparison is that of the 7.1 per cent of the aunts and uncles who were psychotic (Table 4–4) with the 5.8 per cent of the nieces and nephews of the probands who were psychotic. The two groups are genetically of the same

Table 6–15. *Summary of All Our Data Concerning the Percentage of Psychotic Offspring Produced by Psychotic Mothers Compared with Psychotic Fathers.*

	MOTHER PSYCHOTIC FATHER NOT PSYCHOTIC No. (Per Cent)	FATHER PSYCHOTIC MOTHER NOT PSYCHOTIC No. (Per Cent)
Aunts and uncles of the probands	7 of 52 (13.5)	3 of 31 (9.7)
Siblings of the probands	34 of 86 (39.5)	5 of 42 (11.9)
Children of the probands	21 of 109 (19.3)	4 of 43 (9.3)
Nieces and nephews of the probands	19 of 110 (17.3)	6 of 72 (8.3)
More distant relatives of the probands (Generation V)	3 of 60 (5.0)	2 of 59 (3.4)
Totals°	84 of 417 (20.1)	20 of 247 (8.1)

° $\chi^2 = 17.0$, d.f. = 1, p < 0.001.
Data from Tables 4–5, 4–9, 6–1, 6–13 and 6–14.

relationship to the proband but the aunts and uncles are of Generation II and might show some selection bias while the nieces and nephews of the probands are of Generation IV, thus separated in chronology, and one might assume that their environments would be different. However, the similar percentages of psychosis in both groups show that the genetics and the environments of the two sets of relatives were about the same. The difference represents the maximum bias which could have been present in the selection of the families to be studied. The aunts and uncles would have been old enough to have developed their psychoses, while nieces and nephews of the probands would have been children or still not born at the time of the original study. Clearly, the selection bias was not large enough to affect our conclusions in any significant way.

3. Consideration of possible controls for the study led to the use of the siblings of the spouses of the persons in Generation IV. There were 1107 persons in Generation IV who married. The siblings of 242 selected spouses of the 1107 married persons were utilized. There were 913 siblings of the 242 spouses and 2.6 per cent of these control siblings were psychotic. The cumulative risk for psychosis in the controls if all had lived to be 75 years old was 6.1 per cent. There can have been little bias in the selection of our control sample, which provides confidence in the values of 2.5 per cent observed psychosis and 6.1 cumulative risk to age 75 for our "normal" population.

4. This chapter presented data for the more distant relatives of the probands who provide additional data in regard to the two findings that more psychotic women have offspring than psychotic men and that the psychotic women also have a higher percentage of psychotic offspring than do psychotic men. The five different groups of relatives (Table 6–15) were all consistent in demonstrating both of these findings. Psychotic mothers produced 417 children of whom 84, or 20.1 per cent, were psychotic, while psychotic fathers had only 247 children of whom 20, or 8.1 per cent, were psychotic. The χ^2 value for these differences is 17.0 with 1 degree of freedom and the chance that the association is due to random sampling is less than 1 in 1000. There are no really similar data in the literature with which to compare this striking finding that about twice as many of the children of the psychotic women are psychotic also, compared with the children of the psychotic men.

CHAPTER SEVEN

THE TAXONOMIC PROBLEM
(DIAGNOSIS)

A diagnosis is desirable for the proper management of any patient. Fortunately, many patients get better even when they are given an incorrect diagnosis and the wrong treatment. The taxonomic problem is unusually acute for the mental disorders because of the difficulty of making the correct diagnosis. And when correct, the diagnosis may have to be changed to a different one, which may also be correct at a later time in the life of the patient. The less-than-perfect reliability and validity of the psychiatric diagnosis seem to be well established.

There are psychologists and psychiatrists who seem to be confident of their own ability to make the correct diagnosis in each case but they often disagree with the equally confident diagnoses of their peers.

In the real world many more labels of mental disorders are bestowed by relatives, the police, judges, social workers and other decision makers than by psychiatrists; it will always be that way because the mentally ill are ubiquitous while psychiatrists are scarce.

The literature on the general problems of psychiatric diagnoses is vast and there is no need to review it here. However, the reader is referred to one intriguing little paper by Nathan, Andberg, Behan and Patch (1969) as an illustration of the diversity of diagnostic labels given to one patient when observed by 32 health professionals, including a Harvard Medical School professor of psychiatry. There was no question but that the 36-year-old male patient was mentally ill. Two of the observers declined to make a diagnosis, while the remaining 30 observers conferred 14 diagnostic labels which ranged from paranoid schizophrenia to temporal lobe epilepsy to combinations such as "depressive reaction and temporal lobe epilepsy." Presumably it would make some difference to the patient which of the 14 diagnostic labels were accepted as the basis for his treatment. Fortunately, most patients are not this difficult to diagnose.

In a family study of any mental disorder one *must* give consideration to the diagnoses of mental problems in the relatives of the proband. The exclusion of all diagnoses except the one held by the proband must result in an incomplete picture of the complexity of the mental disorder. It is not scientifically permissible to intentionally omit a large part of the possibly relevant data. It is clear from the tables in previous chapters that even the diagnoses of "other mental disorders" are relevant in some important way to the functional psychoses, such as schizophrenia and manic-depressive psychosis. It will be one of the functions of this chapter to at least describe some of the taxonomic relationships of the various diagnoses of mental disorders as found among the relatives in our families.

DIAGNOSIS ACCORDING TO THE SEX OF THE PSYCHOTIC PARENT

The data in Table 6–15 showed clearly and consistently that psychotic mothers gave rise to a higher percentage of psychotic offspring than did psychotic fathers. Those data were not age-corrected. When the age

91

corrections are made and shown as cumulative risks we obtain striking curves which do not overlap and which become increasingly separated with age. Tables 7–1 and 7–2 contain the cumulative risk figures for the siblings of our probands classified according to whether the psychotic parent of the sibling was the father or the mother. The cumulative risk for a sibling, if its mother was psychotic, was 51.5 per cent by age 85, which is a surprisingly high value. Figure 7–1 shows the cumulative risk curves, plus and minus one standard error, for the data in Tables 7–1 and 7–2. The difference between the two curves at age 65 is 24.2 ± 7.8 per cent and is highly significant (p = <.01).

The cumulative risk figures for the siblings of the probands show the differences in percentages with psychosis, depending upon whether it was the mother or father who was psychotic, more clearly than any of the other five groupings in Table 6–15. The cumulative risk provides the expected percentage of psychotic persons in a group of relatives on the assumption that each member of the group lives to be 85 years old. Naturally, most of the relatives in the group die before they reach 85 and so escape receiving a diagnosis of mental disorder which they might have gotten later on if they had lived long enough. The cumulative risk curves are very useful as they show so clearly that the frequencies of mental disorders increase at rather constant rates with age, that is, the curves do not form a plateau and remain there. The combination

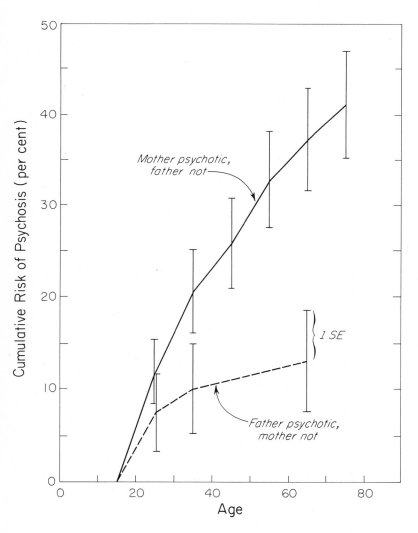

Figure 7–1. Psychosis in siblings with psychotic mother or father.

Table 7–1. *Cumulative Risk of Psychosis Among Siblings with Mother Psychotic and Father Not Psychotic.*

Age Interval	NUMBER OF SIBLINGS Psychotic[1] a	Other Disorder[2] b	Unaffected[2] c	Total d	CALCULATED NUMBER IN AGE INTERVAL e	PSYCHOSIS RATE (10 YEAR) (Per Cent) f	CUMULATIVE RISK OF PSYCHOSIS[3] (TO END OF INTERVAL) (Per Cent)
15–24	10	1	1	12	84.0	11.9 ± 3.5	11.9 ± 3.5
25–34	7	1	4	12	70.5	9.9 ± 3.6	20.7 ± 4.5
35–44	4	1	1	6	60.0	6.7 ± 3.2	25.9 ± 4.9
45–54	5	2	0	7	54.0	9.3 ± 3.9	32.8 ± 5.3
55–64	3	2	4	9	45.0	6.7 ± 3.7	37.3 ± 5.6
65–74	2	5	7	14	33.0	6.1 ± 4.2	41.1 ± 5.8
75–84	3	4	12	19	17.0	17.6 ± 9.2	51.5 ± 7.3
85 plus	–	3	3	6			
Total, age known	34	19	32	85			
Age not known	0	0	1	1			
Grand total	34	19	33	86			

[1]Age at onset of psychosis, or at first hospitalization or at last report (youngest age available).
[2]Age at last report.
[3]Method of calculation shown in Table 5–6.

of the data for the children and for the nieces and nephews of the probands provides a substantial sample size and strongly reinforces the conclusions derived from the data for the siblings of the probands. Thus, in Tables 7–3 and 7–4 and Figure 7–2 we see the gradual separation of the two cumulative risk curves, with a final expectation of 28.4 per cent psychosis in the offspring of psychotic mothers compared with an expectation of 10.9 per cent psychosis in the offspring of psychotic fathers. The curves for

Table 7–2. *Cumulative Risk of Psychosis Among Siblings with Father Psychotic and Mother Not Psychotic.*

Age Interval	NUMBER OF SIBLINGS Psychotic[1] a	Other Disorder[2] b	Unaffected[2] c	Total d	CALCULATED NUMBER IN AGE INTERVAL e	PSYCHOSIS RATE (10 YEAR) (Per Cent) f	CUMULATIVE RISK OF PSYCHOSIS[3] (TO END OF INTERVAL) (Per Cent)
15–24	3			3	40.0	7.5 ± 4.2	7.5 ± 4.2
25–34	1		3	4	35.5	2.8 ± 2.8	10.1 ± 4.8
35–44		1		1	32.5 ⎫		
45–54		1	1	2	31.0 ⎬ 30.2		
55–64	1	2	4	7	27.0 ⎭	3.3 ± 3.3*	13.1 ± 5.5
65–74		4	8	12	17.0		
75–84		3	6	9	6.5		
85–94		1	1	2	1.0		
Total, age known	5	12	23	40			
Age not known			2	2			
Grand total	5	12	25	42			

[1]Age at onset of psychosis, or at first hospitalization or at last report (youngest age available).
[2]Age at last report.
[3]Method of calculation shown in Table 5–6.
*A 30-year rate.

Table 7–3. *Cumulative Risk of Psychosis Among Children, Nieces and Nephews with Mother Psychotic, Father Not.*

Age Interval	NUMBER OF INDIVIDUALS WITH PSYCHOTIC MOTHER Psychotic[1] a	Other Disorder[2] b	Unaffected[2] c	Total d	CALCULATED NUMBER IN AGE INTERVAL e	PSYCHOSIS RATE (10 YEAR) (Per Cent) f	CUMULATIVE RISK OF PSYCHOSIS[3] (TO END OF INTERVAL) (Per Cent)
15–24	13	2	10	25	211.0	6.2 ± 1.7	6.2 ± 1.7
25–34	12	6	12	30	183.0	6.6 ± 1.8	12.3 ± 2.3
35–44	5	2	14	21	154.0	3.2 ± 1.4	15.2 ± 2.6
45–54	4	10	27	41	122.5	3.3 ± 1.6	17.9 ± 2.8
55–64	3	5	26	34	84.5	3.6 ± 2.0	20.8 ± 3.2
65–74	0	10	30	40	46.0 ⎫		
75–84	3	7	11	21	17.0 ⎬ 31.5	9.5 ± 5.2*	28.4 ± 5.0
85–94	0	2	3	5	2.5 ⎭		
Total, age known	40	44	133	217			
Age not known			2	2			
Grand total	40	44	135	219			

[1]Age at onset of psychosis, or at first hospitalization or at last report (youngest age available).
[2]Age at last report.
[3]Method of calculation shown in Table 5–6.
*A 20-year rate.

the offspring of psychotic fathers terminate before age 85 because of small sample sizes and lower risks than those for the offspring of psychotic mothers.

Similar curves could be provided for the other three groups of relatives shown in table 6–15 but it is not necessary to do so. There can be no reasonable doubt that there is a highly significant difference between the percentages of psychotic offspring pro-

Table 7–4. *Cumulative Risk of Psychosis Among Children, Nieces and Nephews with Father Psychotic, Mother Not.*

Age Interval	NUMBER OF INDIVIDUALS WITH PSYCHOTIC FATHER Psychotic[1] a	Other Disorder[2] b	Unaffected[2] c	Total d	CALCULATED NUMBER IN AGE INTERVAL e	PSYCHOSIS RATE (10 YEAR) (Per Cent) f	CUMULATIVE RISK OF PSYCHOSIS[3] (TO END OF INTERVAL) (Per Cent)
15–24	5	1	3	9	107.0	4.7 ± 2.0	4.7 ± 2.0
25–34	3	4	12	19	92.0	3.3 ± 1.9	7.8 ± 2.6
35–44	0	1	9	10	76.0 ⎫		
45–54	1	1	10	12	65.5 ⎬ 70.8	1.4 ± 1.4*	9.1 ± 2.9
55–64	1	2	17	20	49.5	2.0 ± 2.0	10.9 ± 3.4
65–74	0	12	12	24	27.0		
75–84	0	5	9	14	8.0		
85–94	0	0	1	1	0.5		
Total, age known	10	26	73	109			
Age not known			6	6			
Grand total	10	26	79	115			

[1]Age at onset of psychosis, or at first hospitalization or at last report (youngest age available).
[2]Age at last report.
[3]Method of calculation shown in Table 5–6.
*A 20-year rate.

duced by psychotic mothers compared with those produced by psychotic fathers.

A warning must be given that the striking cumulative risk shown in Table 7–1 and Figure 7–1 for the siblings of the proband where the mother was psychotic and the father was not psychotic is much higher than the risk for any other group of relatives of the proband. This cumulative risk figure of 51.5 per cent for the siblings of the probands with a psychotic mother is 23.1 per cent higher than the comparable figure for the combined children and nephews and nieces shown in Table 7–3 and Figure 7–2. The difference of 23.1 per cent is accounted for by the large number of psychotic siblings in 4 of the 16 kinships where the proband had an affective disorder. The problem contributed by these four "loaded" families will be considered in the next several pages but the question they raise should be pointed out without delay.

We are now ready to arrange our data by the cumulative risk method according to the diagnosis of the parent as well as the sex of the parent. The results in Tables 7–5 and 7–6 show the frequency of schizophrenia among siblings of the proband whose

mother or father, respectively, also had a label of schizophrenia. The sample size for the siblings is small but it is large enough to show the difference in results when the siblings of the proband who had a schizophrenic mother are compared with those who had a schizophrenic father. The same kind of results are obtained when we combine the data for the children of the probands with those for the nieces and nephews of the probands. It should be remembered that when we combine data for the children who are first degree relatives of the probands with data for the nieces and nephews who are second degree relatives we might expect to get lower risk figures than for the siblings who are first degree relatives of the probands. However, the nieces and nephews in Tables 7–7 and 7–8 all had a psychotic parent, so for these nieces and nephews the genetic and environmental factors would be about the same as for first degree relatives, that is, about the same as for the children and siblings of the probands. The cumulative risk curves, combining the data shown in the four Tables 7–5 through 7–8, are presented in Figure 7–3.

There is a sharp difference in the risks

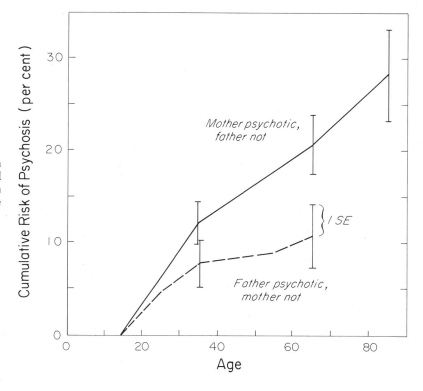

Figure 7–2. Psychosis in the children, nieces, and nephews, depending upon whether the mother or the father was psychotic.

Table 7–5. *Cumulative Risk of Schizophrenia Among Siblings Having Schizophrenic Mother, Non-Psychotic Father.*

Age Interval	NUMBER OF SIBLINGS Schizo-phrenic[1] a	Other Dis-order[2] b	Un-affected[3] c	Total d	CALCULATED NUMBER IN AGE INTERVAL e	SCHIZO-PHRENIA RATE (10 YEAR) (Per Cent) f	CUMULATIVE RISK OF SCHIZOPHRENIA[4] (TO END OF INTERVAL) (Per Cent)
15–24	5	2	1	8	67.5	7.4 ± 3.2	7.4 ± 3.2
25–34	4	1	3	8	59.0	6.8 ± 3.3	13.7 ± 4.2
35–44	2	1	1	4	52.0	3.8 ± 2.7	17.0 ± 4.7
45–54	1	6		7	46.0	2.2 ± 2.2	18.8 ± 4.9
55–64		5	2	7	38.5 ⎫		
65–74	1	5	8	14	28.5 ⎬ 26.8	7.5 ± 5.1°	24.9 ± 6.1
75–84	1	6	9	16	13.5 ⎭		
85–94		4	1	5	2.5		
Total, age known	14	30	25	69			
Age not known			1	1			
Grand total	14	30	26	70			

[1] Age at onset of schizophrenia, or at first hospitalization or at last report (youngest age available).
[2] For this table, the column includes those with affective psychosis or psychosis not otherwise specified, in addition to those with other mental disorder, by age at last report.
[3] Age at last report.
[4] Method of calculation shown in Table 5–6.
° A 30-year rate.

Table 7–6. *Cumulative Risk of Schizophrenia Among Siblings Having Schizophrenic Father, Non-Psychotic Mother.*

Age Interval	NUMBER OF SIBLINGS Schizo-phrenic[1] a	Other Dis-order[2] b	Un-affected[3] c	Total d	CALCULATED NUMBER IN AGE INTERVAL e	SCHIZO-PHRENIA RATE (Per Cent) f	CUMULATIVE RISK OF SCHIZOPHRENIA[4] (TO END OF INTERVAL) (Per Cent)
15–24	1			1	28.0	3.6 ± 3.5	3.6 ± 3.5
25–34	1		2	3	26.0	3.8 ± 3.8	7.3 ± 5.0
35–44		1		1	23.5		
45–54		1		1	22.5		
55–64		2	4	6	19.0		
65–74		3	6	9	11.5		
75–84		2	3	5	4.5		
85–94		1	1	2	1.0		
Total, age known	2	10	16	28			
Age not known							
Grand total	2	10	16	28			

[1] Age at onset of schizophrenia, or at first hospitalization or at last report (youngest age available).
[2] For this table, the column includes those with affective psychosis or psychosis not otherwise specified, in addition to those with other mental disorder, by age at last report.
[3] Age at last report.
[4] Method of calculation shown in Table 5–6.

Table 7–7. *Cumulative Risk of Schizophrenia Among Children, Nieces and Nephews with Schizophrenic Mother, Non-Psychotic Father.*

Age Interval	NUMBER OF CHILDREN, NIECES AND NEPHEWS				CALCULATED NUMBER IN AGE INTERVAL *e*	SCHIZO-PHRENIA RATE (10 YEAR) (Per Cent) *f*	CUMULATIVE RISK OF SCHIZOPHRENIA[4] (TO END OF INTERVAL) (Per Cent)
	Schizo-phrenic[1] *a*	Other Dis-order[2] *b*	Un-affected[3] *c*	Total *d*			
15–24	11	2	7	20	140.5	7.8 ± 2.3	7.8 ± 2.3
25–34	12	6	8	26	118.0	10.2 ± 2.8	17.2 ± 3.3
35–44	4	3	5	12	95.0	4.2 ± 2.1	20.7 ± 3.6
45–54	2	7	16	25	75.5	2.6 ± 1.8	22.8 ± 3.8
55–64	2	5	13	20	53.0	3.8 ± 2.6	25.7 ± 4.2
65–74		9	19	28	28.0		
75–84		6	4	10	9.0		
85–94		2	2	4	2.0		
Total, age known	31	40	74	145			
Age not known			2	2			
Grand total	31	40	76	147			

[1]Age at onset of schizophrenia, or at first hospitalization or at last report (youngest age available).
[2]For this table, the column includes those with affective psychosis or psychosis not otherwise specified, in addition to those with other mental disorder, by age at last report.
[3]Age at last report.
[4]Method of calculation shown in Table 5–6.

Table 7–8. *Cumulative Risk of Schizophrenia Among Children, Nieces and Nephews with Schizophrenic Father, Non-Psychotic Mother.*

Age Interval	NUMBER OF CHILDREN, NIECES AND NEPHEWS				CALCULATED NUMBER IN AGE INTERVAL *e*	SCHIZO-PHRENIA RATE (10 YEAR) (Per Cent) *f*	CUMULATIVE RISK OF SCHIZOPHRENIA[4] (TO END OF INTERVAL) (Per Cent)
	Schizo-phrenic[1] *a*	Other Dis-order[2] *b*	Un-affected[3] *c*	Total *d*			
15–24	2			2	39.0	5.1 ± 3.5	5.1 ± 3.5
25–34	1	1	8	10	32.5	3.1 ± 3.0	8.0 ± 4.5
35–44		1	5	6	24.0		
45–54		1	2	3	19.5		
55–64		0	9	9	13.5		
65–74		4	3	7	5.5		
75–84		1	1	2	1.0		
85–94							
Total, age known	3	8	28	39			
Age not known			6	6			
Grand total	3	8	34	45			

[1]Age at onset of schizophrenia, or at first hospitalization or at last report (youngest age available).
[2]For this table, the column includes those with affective psychosis or psychosis not otherwise specified, in addition to those with other mental disorder, by age at last report.
[3]Age at last report.
[4]Method of calculation shown in Table 5–6.

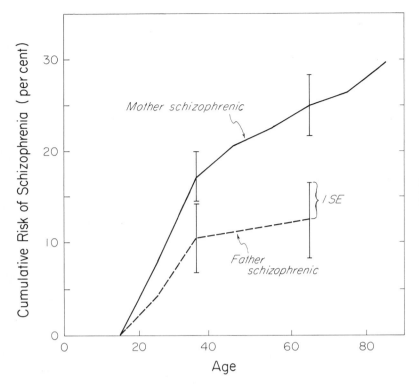

Figure 7–3. Schizophrenia in the siblings, children, nieces, and nephews, depending upon whether the mother or the father was schizophrenic.

for the various groups of offspring of schizophrenic mothers compared with the offspring of schizophrenic fathers.

We would like to provide the same type of curves for the risks for siblings, children and nieces and nephews where the mother or the father had an affective psychosis. Unfortunately, the sample sizes are too small to permit the construction of cumulative risk curves for the affective disorders. Nonetheless, there are data of sufficient interest to be presented in tabular form in Table 7–10.

DIAGNOSES IN THE PROBANDS AND THEIR RELATIVES

Tables 7–9 and 7–10 show in detail the diagnostic labels for the various mental problems found in the parents, siblings, children and the whole group of nephews and nieces of the schizophrenic and the affective probands. Several interesting facts may be observed.

1. The 73 schizophrenic probands had 100 first degree relatives with some sort of psychosis. There were 16, or 16.0 per cent,

of the 100 psychotic relatives who received the manic-depressive label and they were distributed over all three groups of relatives. The diagnoses for the 16 manic-depressive relatives have been made, and also reviewed, by competent psychiatrists. The implication of the observation that 16 of the 100 psychotic first degree relatives of the schizophrenic probands had manic-depressive psychoses is clearly that schizophrenia and manic-depressive psychosis are not etiologically unrelated. No doubt the two groups of people are behaving differently and should have different labels but it cannot be denied that the two groups have some basic etiological relationship.

2. The same point is made again in Table 7–10. There were 43 psychotic first degree relatives of the 16 affective probands. There were 27 of the 43 psychotic relatives, or 62.8 per cent, who obtained a label of schizophrenia; only 3, or 7.0 per cent, of the 43 psychotic relatives of the 16 affective probands had a diagnosis of manic-depressive psychosis. None of the 46 children of the 16 probands with an affective psychosis also had an affective psychosis.

Indeed only 2 of the 46 children had a psychosis and they were both schizophrenic. The fact that 62.8 per cent of the psychotic first degree relatives of our 16 affective probands were schizophrenic should dispel any idea that schizophrenia and manic-depressive psychosis are etiologically unrelated to each other. The presence of a significant number of affective psychoses among the relatives of the schizophrenic probands and a huge majority of schizophrenic relatives of our affective probands must mean that the two diagnostically distinct disorders share at least part of a common basic etiology.

3. The first degree relatives of the affective probands had a higher proportion with psychoses (23.9 per cent) than did the first degree relatives of the schizophrenic probands (16.3 per cent). This comes about partly because the siblings of the schizophrenic probands had *less* schizophrenia (8.3 per cent) than was present in the siblings of the affective probands (19.6 per

cent) with a χ^2 of 10.5 and $p < 0.01$. This large difference would not seem to have a rational basis and suggests that there might be a bias which would account for part of it. One of the original workers, Mrs. Finlayson, thought that families WSH 48 and 73 were selected because of their numerous psychotic relatives. We consider families WSH 15 and 92 also to have an unusually large number of psychotic siblings of each proband. These four families appear to have been selected because they were "loaded" with psychotic siblings and presumably were therefore of greater interest to the investigator.

If we remove the 4 "loaded" families from the 16 families in which the proband had an affective psychosis, the number of schizophrenic siblings decreases from 20 to 11. The data of Table 7–10 that remain after excluding the four "loaded" families are given in Table 7–11. It can be seen that after the exclusion, the percentages of the various groups of relatives with the various

Table 7–9. *Diagnosis of Psychosis and Other Mental Disorders Among the Relatives of the 73 Schizophrenic Probands.*

DIAGNOSIS IN THE RELATIVES	NUMBER IN EACH GROUP OF RELATIVES			TOTAL FIRST DEGREE RELATIVES No. (Per Cent)	NIECES AND NEPHEWS No. (Per Cent)
	Parents No. (Per Cent)	Siblings No. (Per Cent)	Children No. (Per Cent)		
A. *Psychosis*					
Involutional	1(0.7)	4(1.1)	0	5(0.8)	1(0.1)
Manic-depressive	2(1.4)	11(3.0)	3(2.8)	16(2.6)	2(0.3)
Schizophrenic	16(11.0)	30(8.3)	21(19.4)	67(10.9)	29(3.8)
Psychotic NOS*	4(2.7)	7(1.9)	1(0.9)	12(2.0)	5(0.7)
Sub-total	23(15.8)	52(14.3)	25(23.1)	100(16.3)	37(4.9)
B. *Other Mental Disorder*					
Personality pattern disturbance**	9(6.2)	17(4.7)	3(2.8)	29(4.7)	5(0.7)
Alcoholism	3(2.1)	10(2.8)	4(3.7)	17(2.8)	20(2.6)
Other personality disorder	31(21.2)	35(9.7)	12(11.1)	78(12.7)	33(4.4)
Psychoneurosis	17(11.6)	31(8.6)	6(5.6)	54(8.8)	38(5.0)
Chronic brain syndrome	9(6.2)	6(1.7)	1(0.9)	16(2.6)	4(0.5)
Less duplications	−3(−2.1)	−3(−0.8)	0	−6(−1.0)	−4(−0.5)
Sub-total	66(45.2)	96(26.7)	26(24.1)	188(30.6)	96(12.7)
C. *Without the Above (Normal?)*	57(39.0)	213(59.0)	57(52.8)	327(53.2)	625(82.5)
Grand total	146(100.0)	361(100.0)	108(100.0)	615(100.1)	758(100.1)

*NOS = Not otherwise specified.
**Including schizoid personality.

Table 7–10. *Diagnosis of Psychosis and Other Mental Disorders Among the Relatives of the 16 Affective Probands.*

| DIAGNOSIS IN THE RELATIVES | NUMBER IN EACH GROUP OF RELATIVES | | | TOTAL FIRST DEGREE RELATIVES No. (Per Cent) | NIECES AND NEPHEWS No. (Per Cent) |
	Parents No. (Per Cent)	Siblings No. (Per Cent)	Children No. (Per Cent)		
A. Psychosis					
Involutional	0	0	0	0	2(0.7)
Manic-depressive	1(3.1)	2(2.0)	0	3(1.7)	2(0.7)
Schizophrenic	5(15.6)	20(19.6)	2(4.3)	27(15.0)	17(6.0)
Psychotic NOS°	2(6.3)	11(10.8)	0	13(7.2)	3(1.1)
Sub-total	8(25.0)	33(32.4)	2(4.3)	43(23.9)	24(8.5)
B. Other Mental Disorder					
Personality pattern disturbance°°	3(9.4)	2(2.0)	1(2.2)	6(3.3)	4(1.4)
Alcoholism	2(6.3)	2(2.0)	0	4(2.2)	10(3.6)
Other personality disorder	6(18.8)	12(11.8)	9(19.6)	27(15.0)	19(6.8)
Psychoneurosis	2(6.3)	4(3.9)	2(4.3)	8(4.4)	10(3.6)
Chronic brain syndrome	1(3.1)	0	3(6.5)	4(2.2)	6(2.1)
Less duplications	0	−1(−1.0)	−2(−4.3)	−3(−1.7)	−2(−0.7)
Sub-total	14(43.9)	19(18.7)	13(28.3)	46(25.4)	47(16.8)
C. Without the Above (Normal?)	10(31.2)	50(49.0)	31(67.4)	91(50.6)	210(74.7)
Grand total	32(100.1)	102(100.1)	46(100.0)	180(99.9)	281(100.0)

°NOS = Not otherwise specified.
°°Including schizoid personality.

Table 7–11. *Diagnosis of Psychosis Among the Relatives of the 12 "Unbiased" Affective Probands, Excluding the Four "Loaded" Families, Numbers WSH 15, 48, 73 and 92.*

| DIAGNOSIS IN THE RELATIVES | NUMBER IN EACH GROUP OF RELATIVES | | | TOTAL FIRST DEGREE RELATIVES No. (Per Cent) | NIECES AND NEPHEWS No. (Per Cent) |
	Parents No. (Per Cent)	Siblings No. (Per Cent)	Children No. (Per Cent)		
A. Psychosis					
Involutional	0	0	0	0	2(1.2)
Manic-depressive	1(4.2)	0	0	1(0.9)	1(0.6)
Schizophrenic	2(8.3)	6(9.0)	2(8.3)	10(8.7)	6(3.6)
Psychotic NOS°	2(8.3)	2(3.0)	0	4(3.5)	2(1.2)
Sub-total	5(20.8)	8(12.0)	2(8.3)	15(13.1)	11(6.6)
B. Other Mental Disorder	9(37.5)	13(19.4)	3(12.5)	25(21.7)	24(14.5)
C. Without the Above	10(41.7)	46(68.7)	19(79.2)	75(65.2)	130(78.8)
Grand total	24(100.0)	67(100.1)	24(100.0)	115(100.0)	165(99.9)

°Not otherwise specified.

psychoses are not significantly different from those shown for the relatives of the 73 schizophrenic probands in Table 7–9.

It may be entirely a coincidence that all four of our "loaded" families had a manic-depressive psychosis proband, although we do not consider any of the 73 kinships with a schizophrenic proband to have been selected because of an excess of psychotic relatives. On the other hand, there may be some significance in this odd bias. It could have been present in other research studies on the affective disorders and might account for the higher percentages of psychoses found in the relatives of probands with an affective disorder when compared with the relatives of schizophrenic probands. When we excluded our four "loaded" families from the data we found there were no longer any significant differences in the frequencies of psychotic relatives for the two sets of probands. Compare Tables 7–9 and 7–11.

It is important to see what effect the exclusion of the four "loaded" families has upon the finding shown in Summary Table 6–15 that 20.1 per cent of the offspring of psychotic mothers were psychotic and only 8.1 per cent of the offspring of the psychotic fathers were likewise psychotic. The removal of the four "loaded" families markedly reduces χ^2 to 5.2, p <0.05 from the χ^2 of 17.0, p <0.001 which was shown in Table 6–15. However, all five categories of relatives show a consistent excess in the percentage of offspring of psychotic mothers compared with psychotic fathers.

A comparison of Tables 7–10 and 7–11 shows that the four "loaded" kinships did not produce greater than average percentages of psychotic relatives in the generations maturing after the original sample of probands was selected. This seems to indicate that the high percentage of psychotic siblings of the four probands was coincidental rather than the result of unusually high genetic or environmental loading since both of these latter phenomena could be expected to be transmitted to subsequent generations if they had been present.

It should be pointed out that the "loaded" families were useful in that they were responsible for our noticing the tendency of psychotic mothers to have a higher percentage of psychotic offspring than do psychotic fathers. Geneticists learned long ago to treasure their exceptions.

4. The exclusion of the four "loaded" kinships removed some of the data supporting the finding that psychotic mothers produce a higher percentage of psychotic offspring than do psychotic fathers. However, as shown in Table 7–12, all five groups of relatives of the probands are consistent in showing a higher percentage of psychotic offspring from psychotic mothers than from psychotic fathers. The greatest difference is shown in the data for the siblings of the probands both before (Figure 7–1) and after (Figure 7–4) the exclusion was made. The data for Figure 7–4 are provided in Table 7–13 for the psychotic mothers while the data for the psychotic fathers are unchanged from those in Table 7–2. It is clear that the exclusion of the four "loaded" families reduced the cumulative risk of a psychosis in the siblings having psychotic mothers by one-half, but it had no effect upon the siblings with psychotic fathers. The difference that remains is confined to the older

Table 7–12. *The Revision of Summary Table 6–15 After the Exclusion of All Relatives of the Probands in the Four "Loaded" Kinships, Numbers WSH 15, 48, 73 and 92.*

| | FREQUENCY OF PSYCHOSIS IN GROUP BY SEX OF PSYCHOTIC PARENT | |
| | Mother Psychotic Father Not Psychotic No. (Per Cent) | Father Psychotic Mother Not Psychotic No. (Per Cent) |
Group of Relatives		
Aunts and uncles of the probands	7 of 49(14.3)	3 of 31(9.7)
Siblings	14 of 62(22.6)	5 of 42(11.9)
Children	21 of 107(19.6)	4 of 23(17.4)
Nieces and nephews	11 of 71(15.5)	4 of 34(11.8)
More distant relatives	3 of 48(6.3)	0 of 44(0.0)
Total°	56 of 337(16.6)	16 of 174(9.2)

°$\chi^2 = 5.2$, d.f. = 1, p = <0.05.

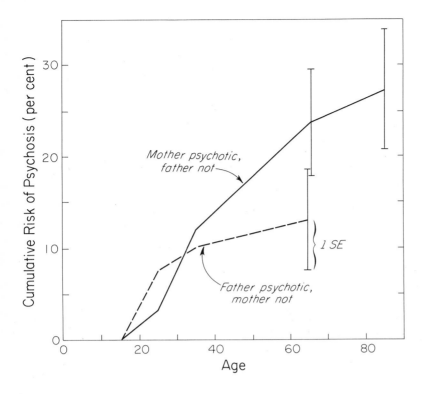

Figure 7–4. Psychosis in siblings with psychotic mother or father (excluding four loaded families).

ages and suggests that the failure of all previous investigators to find a difference between the offspring with a psychotic mother compared with those from a psychotic father came about because there was no follow-up of the offspring into the older ages where the differences become important. Age correction cannot compensate for lack of information at the older ages, and an actual follow-up is the only way by which the information can be obtained.

5. The exclusion of the four "loaded" kinships removes 25 of the 33 psychotic siblings of the 4 affective psychosis probands, 3 of the probands' 8 psychotic parents, none of their 2 psychotic children and 13 of their 24 psychotic nieces and nephews. This is a substantial deletion of psychotic relatives of the affective probands and probably resulted in an over-correction of the data. However, it does nothing to diminish the lack of correlation between the diagnosis of the proband and any of his relatives. Table 7–14 has been constructed in order to summarize the data for relatives of the affective and schizophrenic probands according to diagnosis.

It is easy to demonstrate the absence of any significant correlation between the diagnosis of the proband and his relatives as given in Table 7–14 by a four-fold table as follows:

	Schizophrenic Proband	Affective Proband	Total
Schizophrenic relative	80	14	94
Affective relative	21	3	24
Total	101	17	118

$\chi^2 = 0.09$, d.f. = 1, p = >0.7.

Let us look at the data in a different way. The relatives of the proband (his siblings, children and so forth) can be classified according to the diagnosis of their parent rather than that of the proband. The resulting values are presented in Table 7–15. It is both striking and strange that no affective parent had an affective offspring as evidenced by the zeros in the first row of the table. It is clear that there is a complete lack of association between the diagnosis of the parent and that of the offspring in this case, presumably due to the small sample size.

Table 7–13. *Cumulative Risk of Psychosis Among Siblings with Mother Psychotic and Father Not Psychotic, after Exclusion of the Four "Loaded" Families.*

Age Interval	NUMBER OF SIBLINGS Psychotic[1] a	Other Disorder[2] b	Un-affected[2] c	Total d	CALCULATED NUMBER IN AGE INTERVAL e	PSYCHOSIS RATE (10 YEAR) (Per Cent) f	CUMULATIVE RISK OF PSYCHOSIS[3] (TO END OF INTERVAL) (Per Cent)
15–24	2	1	1	4	60.0	3.3 ± 2.3	3.3 ± 2.3
25–34	5	1	2	8	55.5	9.0 ± 3.8	12.0 ± 4.3
35–44	2	1	1	4	48.0	4.2 ± 2.9	15.7 ± 4.8
45–54	2	2	0	4	44.0	4.5 ± 3.1	19.5 ± 5.3
55–64	2	2	3	7	38.5	5.2 ± 3.6	23.7 ± 5.8
65–74	0	5	7	12	28.0 ⎫		
75–84	1	4	11	16	14.5 ⎬ 21.2	$4.7 \pm 4.6°$	27.3 ± 6.5
85–100	0	3	3	6	3.0 ⎭		
Total, age known	14	19	28	61			
Age not known	0	0	1	1			
Grand total	14	19	29	62			

[1]Age at onset of psychosis, or at first hospitalization or at last report (youngest age available).
[2]Age at last report.
[3]Method of calculation shown in Table 5–6.
°A 20-year rate.

The fact that there was no correlation between our probands and their relatives in regard to diagnosis has important implications for other family studies. It is clear that different states in the United States have astonishingly different diagnostic practices which supposedly result in large part from the different psychiatric concepts of those who bestow the labels rather than from differences in the patients. Many patients have an array of signs which would permit decidedly different diagnoses depending upon the weight given to particular manifestations. In a family study it would be natural to weight the signs in the direction of the psychiatrist's concepts, which in turn would be related to the psychosis he chose to study. Furthermore, where the study is restricted to one psychosis, other diagnoses in relatives are included in the category of those not affected (with the specific psychosis) and therefore counted as normal

Table 7–14. *The Diagnoses in the Major Groups of Relatives of the Affective Psychosis and Schizophrenic Probands after Exclusion of the Four "Loaded" Kinships.*

Diagnosis in Relatives	SIBLINGS Affective Proband No. (Per Cent)	Schizophrenic Proband No. (Per Cent)	CHILDREN Affective Proband No. (Per Cent)	Schizophrenic Proband No. (Per Cent)	NIECES AND NEPHEWS Affective Proband No. (Per Cent)	Schizophrenic Proband No. (Per Cent)
Affective	0	15(4.1)	0	3(2.8)	3(1.8)	3(0.4)
Schizophrenic	6(9.0)	30(8.3)	2(8.3)	21(19.4)	6(3.6)	29(3.8)
Psychosis NOS°	2(3.0)	7(1.9)	0	1(0.9)	2(1.2)	5(0.7)
Sub-total	8(12.0)	52(14.3)	2(8.3)	25(23.1)	11(6.6)	37(4.9)
Other disorder	13(19.4)	96(26.7)	3(12.5)	26(24.1)	24(14.5)	96(12.7)
Without the above	46(68.7)	213(59.0)	19(79.2)	57(52.8)	130(78.8)	625(82.5)
Grand total	67(100.1)	361(100.0)	24(100.0)	108(100.0)	165(99.9)	758(100.1)

°Not otherwise specified.

Table 7–15. *The Diagnoses in the Major Groups of Relatives of the Probands According to the Diagnosis in the Parent of the Relative After the Exclusion of the Four "Loaded" Kinships and of Those Persons with Both Parents Psychotic.*

Diagnosis in Relatives	SIBLINGS		CHILDREN		NIECES AND NEPHEWS		ALL THREE GROUPS COMBINED	
	Affective Parent No. (Per Cent)	Schizo-phrenic Parent No. (Per Cent)	Affective Parent No. (Per Cent)	Schizo-phrenic Parent No. (Per Cent)	Affective Parent No. (Per Cent)	Schizo-phrenic Parent No. (Per Cent)	Affective Parent No. (Per Cent)	Schizo-phrenic Parent No. (Per Cent)
Affective	0	2(2.8)	0	3(2.8)	0	2(4.7)	0	7(3.2)
Schizophrenic	1(7.7)	6(8.3)	2(8.3)	19(17.9)	2(6.5)	8(18.6)	5(7.4)	33(14.9)
Psychosis NOS	2(15.4)	2(2.8)	0	1(0.9)	2(6.5)	0	4(5.9)	3(1.4)
Sub-total	3(23.1)	10(13.9)	2(8.3)	23(21.6)	4(13.0)	10(23.3)	9(13.3)	43(19.5)
Other disorder	1(7.7)	26(36.1)	3(12.5)	26(24.5)	2(6.5)	6(14.0)	6(8.8)	58(26.2)
Without the above	9(69.2)	36(50.0)	19(79.2)	57(53.8)	25(80.6)	27(62.8)	53(77.9)	120(54.3)
Total	13(100.0)	72(100.0)	24(100.0)	106(99.9)	31(100.1)	43(100.0)	68(100.0)	221(100.0)

persons or placed in some ambiguous group such as the "schizoidias." In our own study, the deviants from the schizophrenic or manic-depressive psychosis diagnoses are placed in the category of "other mental disorders" but these procedures make the genetic analysis very difficult. Our study also has an important advantage in that many of the diagnoses were made by psychiatrists who could not have anticipated that anyone would use the information for a family study many years later.

It is hardly necessary to point out that identical twins not only have the same genotype but usually fairly similar environments. Consequently, there should be high correlations between the diagnoses for these twins. However, there should be appreciable frequencies of schizophrenic relatives when we have identical twins with manic-depressive psychosis. Some studies have excluded these schizophrenic relatives from the groups of affected relatives or have diagnosed them as manic-depressives since every schizophrenic has times of depression which would permit a diagnosis of depression.

We had the pleasure of a visit from the world famous psychiatrist, Erik Strömgren, M.D., of Aarhus University, Denmark, some time ago. He wondered whether there were any cases in our study where a clearly schizophrenic person had produced an offspring who was clearly affected with manic-depressive psychosis. We could not give a positive answer to this because there are very few persons in our study who seem to us "clearly" to be candidates for the diagnosis of manic-depressive psychosis. There are only three cases where it seems certain that there was a schizophrenic parent with a clearly manic-depressive offspring. These three cases have the following numbers:

Schizophrenic Parent	Manic-Depressive Offspring
WSH 48(38)	WSH 48(107)
WSH 57(29)	WSH 57(52)
WSH 73(10)	WSH 73(27)

There were several other cases in which there seemed to be a schizophrenic parent and a manic-depressive offspring but there were signs which made one or the other diagnosis somewhat equivocal. Unfortunately, the symptoms in a large number of the psychotic persons in this study were so varied that the diagnosis could easily shift toward whatever direction conformed with the concepts of the particular psychiatrist involved. The basic mental illness was obvious in every case but the label bestowed could be determined by a majority vote of the staff psychiatrists.

The fact that our affective psychosis probands had only 2 children of 45 who developed a psychosis (both schizophrenic) has been mentioned. There is only one additional case where a clearly manic-depressive person produced a schizophrenic child. These three parent-offspring combinations are as follows:

Manic-Depressive Parent	Schizophrenic Offspring
WSH 35(25)	WSH 35(46)
WSH 81(23)	WSH 81(45)
WSH 74(37)	WSH 74(66)

There is, of course, a long list of cases where a clearly schizophrenic parent produced a clearly schizophrenic offspring. The functional psychoses are mental disorders of a heterogeneous nature that usually have some signs which may be called schizophrenic—if a label must be applied to the person. Various sub-type labels, such as catatonia, may be useful for practical purposes but the labels would not seem to us to be of genetic significance. It should be recalled that the Genain quadruplets showed various sub-types of schizophrenia during their lives. The girls were genetically identical so the sub-types they showed at different times in their lives should have been the result of different environmental variables, often of a trivial nature. For a consideration of possible environmental differences of a psychoanalytic sort between two of the quadruplets see Stierlin (1972).

6. The fact that the proportion of relatives with a diagnosis of affective psychosis was *not* significantly associated with these diagnoses in the probands has numerous implications which will be examined later on. It is useful now to compare the data in the several tables with those for our unrelated controls and for a rather similar group, the nephews and nieces with both parents unaffected (normal). The figures for these two groups are given in Table 7–16. These control values for siblings of persons who married into our kinships in Generation IV do not provide cumulative risk figures to age 85 but they do give the expected values for a population with an average age of about 55 years.

We see that the base rates in our control population are in good agreement with what might be expected for the general population. The diagnosis of schizophrenia was 5 to 10 times more common than that of affective psychosis. This ratio is probably representative of the diagnostic preferences of the present Warren State Hospital psychiatric staff. It differs greatly from the ratio

Table 7–16.   *Diagnosis of Psychosis and Other Mental Disorders Among the Control Group and the Nieces and Nephews with Unaffected Parents.*

| | NUMBER IN EACH GROUP | | |
| | Control Group No. (Per Cent) | Nieces and Nephews with Both Parents Unaffected No. (Per Cent) | Combined Totals No. (Per Cent) |
Diagnosis			
A. Psychosis			
Involutional	1(0.1)	0	1(0.1)
Manic-depressive	2(0.2)	0	2(0.1)
Schizophrenic	14(1.5)	14(2.8)	28(2.0)
Psychotic NOS°	7(0.8)	1(0.2)	8(0.6)
Sub-total	24(2.6)	15(3.0)	39(2.8)
B. Other Mental Disorder			
Personality pattern disturbance°°	3(0.3)	1(0.2)	4(0.3)
Alcoholism	9(1.0)	7(1.4)	16(1.1)
Other personality disorder	14(1.5)	18(3.6)	32(2.3)
Psychoneurosis	9(1.0)	19(3.8)	28(2.0)
Chronic brain syndrome	2(0.2)	3(0.6)	5(0.4)
Less duplications	0	−2(−0.4)	−2(−0.1)
Sub-total	37(4.0)	46(9.2)	83(6.0)
C. Without the above	852(93.3)	439(87.8)	1291(91.4)
Grand total	913(99.9)	500(100.0)	1413(100.2)

°NOS = Not otherwise specified.
°°Including schizoid personality.

found in some other psychiatric hospitals, such as the one in St. Louis reported upon by Winokur and Pitts (1965), in which 366 of 748 consecutive admissions (48.9 per cent) had a diagnosis of an affective disorder. It is doubtful that the patients in the Warren, Pennsylvania area behave that much differently than those around St. Louis. The only conclusion that seems reasonable to us is that the difference is not in the two groups of patients but rather in the diagnostic concepts and practices of the two groups of psychiatrists.

In Table 7–9 of those relatives with a specific type of psychosis, there are 96 diagnoses of schizophrenia (80 per cent) to 24 of affective disorders (20 per cent) in the relatives of the 73 schizophrenic probands, but in Table 7–10 there are 44 diagnoses of schizophrenia (86.3 per cent) to 7 of affective disorders (13.7 per cent) in the relatives of the 16 affective probands. This is a nonsignificant difference as $\chi^2 = 0.9$ and p = > 0.3. It indicates at least that there was no "contamination" of the diagnosis of the relatives by the knowledge of the diagnosis of the proband. There were about 4 diagnoses of schizophrenia to each one for an affective disorder in the relatives of both groups of probands. Clearly there is no significant correlation between the diagnosis of the proband and those of his relatives.

The best data, in our opinion, for a demonstration of the correlation between the diagnoses of probands and of their relatives are those of Ödegård (1972). He finds a correlation between the diagnoses of his index patients and those of their relatives. We might have expected to find a similar correlation in our material but did not do so. We have no explanation for our failure to find an association between the diagnoses of the probands and of their relatives except that perhaps our sample size of 118 persons is too small. (See Table 1–4 and accompanying text.)

SEX OF THE PSYCHOTIC RELATIVES RELATED TO THE SEX OF THE PROBAND

There is no evidence in our study of genetic sex-linkage. That is, there is no evidence of more affected sons than daughters from affected mothers nor a deficiency of affected sons from affected fathers. One might expect that the psychotic mother might have a harmful influence on either her sons or her daughters which would result, for instance, in a higher rate of psychosis in sons compared with daughters. However, the differences turned out to be trivial and they had no statistical significance. The raw data, excluding the four loaded kinships and the offspring with both parents psychotic, are given in Table 7–17.

While there seems to be no relationship between the sex of a psychotic parent and the sex of the psychotic offspring, we do find a relationship between the sex of the proband and the sex of the psychotic sibling. By combining the data in Table 7–17 for the male and female probands we find that the 85 probands had 41 psychotic siblings (19.5 per cent) of the same sex and 19 psychotic siblings (8.7 per cent) of the opposite sex. The difference of 10.8 per cent is statistically highly significant ($\chi^2 = 10.4$, d.f. = 1, p = < 0.01).

When we looked at the schizophrenic probands and their schizophrenic siblings alone we found the same 2:1 ratio of same sex schizophrenic siblings (20, or 11.0 per cent) to opposite sex schizophrenic siblings (9, or 5.0 per cent) as was found for all psychoses combined, but due to the smaller sample size the difference of 6 per cent is only statistically significant ($\chi^2 = 4.3$, d.f. = 1, p = < 0.05).

Returning to the data for the siblings with all psychoses considered together and in which there were 41 psychotic siblings with the same sex as the proband and only 19 of the opposite sex, the cumulative risk figures for the same sex and opposite sex siblings are shown in Tables 7–18, 7–19 and Figure 7–5.

There seems to be no doubt that the two curves are different from each other (difference at age 65 is 9.9 per cent ± 3.8 per cent with p = < .01) and we should now determine whether this difference is also present in the children and the nieces and nephews of the probands. That is, taking each psychotic child of the proband or niece or nephew we can compare the sex of this psychotic child with the sex of each psychotic sibling he may have. There were 35 same sexed psychotic siblings in a total of 148, or 23.6 per cent, and 34 opposite sexed siblings from a total of 133, or 25.6 per cent, including the unaffected in both cases.

Table 7–17. *Sex of the Psychotic Relatives Related to the Sex of the Proband.*
Sons and Daughters with Both Parents Psychotic, as well as the Four "Loaded" Kinships,
Were Excluded.

Male Proband	1. PSYCHOSIS No. (Per Cent)	2. OTHER MENTAL DISORDER No. (Per Cent)	3. SUM (COLS. 1 AND 2) No. (Per Cent)	4. TOTAL (INCL. UNAFFECTED)
Father	4(13.8)	11(37.9)	15(51.7)	29
Mother	5(17.2)	14(48.3)	19(65.5)	29
Brother	13(17.6)	11(14.9)	24(32.5)	74
Sister	8(11.0)	18(24.7)	26(35.7)	73
Son	4(23.5)	1(5.9)	5(29.4)	17
Daughter	0	1(16.7)	1(16.7)	6
Total	34(14.9)	56(24.6)	90(39.5)	228
Female Proband				
Father	9(16.1)	26(46.4)	35(62.5)	56
Mother	10(17.9)	24(42.9)	34(60.8)	56
Brother	11(7.6)	42(29.0)	53(36.6)	145
Sister	28(20.6)	38(27.9)	66(48.5)	136
Son	11(19.0)	12(20.7)	23(39.7)	58
Daughter	10(20.4)	15(30.6)	25(51.0)	49
Total	79(15.8)	157(31.4)	236(47.2)	500

There is no statistically significant difference for this comparison and no support for the previous finding of a sex concordance for the psychotic siblings of the proband. The failure to confirm the sex concordance of the psychotic siblings of the probands when we looked at the psychotic children and nieces and nephews of the probands casts doubt on the reality of the finding in the siblings. There is nothing that

Table 7–18. *Cumulative Risk of Psychosis Among Same Sex Siblings of the Probands*
Excluding the Four "Loaded" Families.

Age Interval	NUMBER OF SAME SEX SIBLINGS Psychotic[1] a	Other Disorder[2] b	Unaffected[2] c	Total d	CALCULATED NUMBER IN AGE INTERVAL e	PSYCHOSIS RATE (10 YEAR) (Per Cent) f	CUMULATIVE RISK OF PSYCHOSIS[3] (TO END OF INTERVAL) (Per Cent)
15–24	9	1	8	18	203.5	4.4 ± 1.4	4.4 ± 1.4
25–34	10	3	7	20	185.0	5.4 ± 1.7	9.6 ± 2.1
35–44	8	2	4	14	167.0	4.8 ± 1.7	13.9 ± 2.5
45–54	6	3	7	16	151.0	4.0 ± 1.6	17.3 ± 2.8
55–64	5	6	20	31	127.0	3.9 ± 1.7	20.6 ± 3.0
65–74	2	17	34	53	83.5	2.4 ± 1.7	22.5 ± 3.2
75–84	1	15	28	44	34.5	2.9 ± 2.9	24.7 ± 3.8
85–94		2	10	12	6.0		
Total, age known	41	49	118	208			
Age not known	0	0	2	2			
Grand total	41	49	120	210			

[1]Age at onset of psychosis, or at first hospitalization or at last report (youngest age available).
[2]Age at last report.
[3]Method of calculation shown in Table 5–6.

Table 7–19. *Cumulative Risk of Psychosis Among Opposite Sex Siblings of the Probands, Excluding the Four "Loaded" Families.*

| Age Interval | NUMBER OF OPPOSITE SEX SIBLINGS | | | | CALCULATED NUMBER IN AGE INTERVAL *e* | PSYCHOSIS RATE (10 YEAR) (Per Cent) *f* | CUMULATIVE RISK OF PSYCHOSIS[3] (TO END OF INTERVAL) (Per Cent) |
	Psychotic[1] *a*	Other Dis- order[2] *b*	Un- affected[2] *c*	Total *d*			
15–24	4	3	10	17	208.5	1.9 ± 0.9	1.9 ± 0.9
25–34	5	2	12	19	191.0	2.6 ± 1.2	4.5 ± 1.5
35–44	3	4	5	12	174.5	1.7 ± 1.0	6.1 ± 1.7
45–54	3	5	14	22	157.5	1.9 ± 1.1	7.9 ± 2.0
55–64	4	8	19	31	131.5	3.0 ± 1.5	10.7 ± 2.4
65–74		23	34	57	85.5		
75–84		11	36	47	33.5		
85–100		3	7	10	5.0		
Total, age known	19	59	137	215			
Age not known	0	1	2	3			
Grand total	19	60	139	218			

[1] Age at onset of psychosis, or at first hospitalization or at last report (youngest age available).
[2] Age at last report.
[3] Method of calculation shown in Table 5–6.

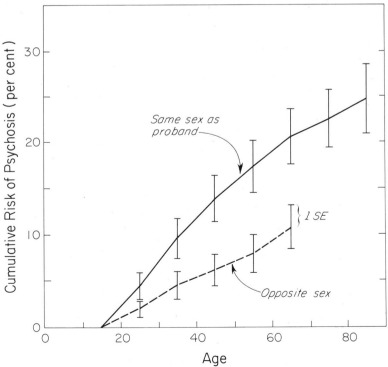

Figure 7–5. Psychosis in siblings who are of the same sex as the proband and in siblings of opposite sex from the proband.

can be done other than to leave the matter as an open question about the explanation of the sex concordance between the proband and his or her psychotic siblings.

AGE OF ONSET AND DIAGNOSIS

It is a general taxonomic convention that the psychiatrist is reluctant to classify young people as having manic-depressive psychosis or those with late age of onset as having schizophrenia. The person with late age of onset presents an additional problem as he may have been "peculiar" all his life although the crisis which resulted in a definite label for him just happened to have occurred at a late age rather than a younger age. Extraneous episodes may be responsible for exacerbating an unstable psychic condition which the person and his relatives had failed to recognize previously.

We are interested in the question as to whether there is an association between age of onset and genetic loading and we will look at the problem by comparing the age of onset in the schizophrenic probands with various groups of relatives. In Table 7–20 we have divided the 73 schizophrenic probands into three groups according to the age of onset and then classified their parents and siblings according to diagnosis. The 17 probands with age of onset under 20 had 20.6 per cent of their parents with a psychosis whereas the 21 probands with age at onset of 30 or over had only 9.5 per cent of their parents with a psychosis. There seems

to be an association between early onset in the proband and a higher percentage of psychosis among his parents, though this comparison of the youngest and oldest ages of onset does not give a statistically significant difference ($\chi^2 = 1.9$, p = <0.2). Even if there were a statistically highly significant difference this would not be proof that persons with early onset have a heavier genetic loading, but it would support that concept.

We are also interested in the possible correlation between the age of onset in schizophrenic parents and their schizophrenic offspring. The data in Table 7–21 show an apparent relationship between the ages of onset of parents and their offspring. The Pearsonian correlation for the 27 pairs of comparisons was $r = +0.06$. Obviously this correlation coefficient is not significantly different from zero. A scatter diagram for the 27 comparisons showed a cluster of 24 of the pairs with a correlation coefficient of $r = +0.39$, p = <0.1, but 3 pairs were far out of line and reduced the correlation for all 27 to $r = +0.06$.

The 27 pairs of comparisons of age of onset for parent and offspring provide an important comment on the old idea of "anticipation." Numerous studies have purported to show for various diseases that the age of onset is earlier in the child than in the parent. Such findings had statistical significance but there is no case where any biological causation of the phenomenon has been demonstrated. Anticipation seems to be a statistical artifact resulting from the fact that parents must survive long enough to repro-

Table 7–20. *Association Between the Age of Onset of Schizophrenia in the Proband with the Frequency of Psychosis in the Parents and Siblings.*

Diagnosis in Relatives	17 SCHIZOPHRENIC PROBANDS WITH ONSET BEFORE 20		35 SCHIZOPHRENIC PROBANDS WITH ONSET AGE 20–29		21 SCHIZOPHRENIC PROBANDS WITH ONSET 30 OR OLDER	
	Parents No. (Per Cent)	*Siblings No. (Per Cent)*	*Parents No. (Per Cent)*	*Siblings No. (Per Cent)*	*Parents No. (Per Cent)*	*Siblings No. (Per Cent)*
Involutional	0	1(1.3)	1(1.4)	3(1.7)	0	0
Manic-depressive	0	2(2.7)	1(1.4)	6(3.4)	1(2.4)	3(2.8)
Schizophrenia	5(14.7)	6(8.0)	8(11.4)	17(9.5)	3(7.1)	7(6.5)
Psychosis NOS	2(5.9)	2(2.7)	2(2.9)	3(1.7)	0	2(1.9)
Sub-total	7(20.6)	11(14.7)	12(17.1)	29(16.3)	4(9.5)	12(11.2)
Other disorders	16(47.0)	18(24.1)	35(49.9)	51(28.4)	15(35.8)	27(25.1)
Without the above	11(32.4)	46(61.3)	23(32.9)	99(55.3)	23(54.8)	68(63.6)
Total	34(100.0)	75(100.0)	70(99.9)	179(100.0)	42(100.1)	107(99.9)

Table 7-21. *The Correlation Between the Age of Onset for Schizophrenic Children, Nieces and Nephews with a Schizophrenic Parent, Excluding Four "Loaded" Kinships and Persons with Both Parents Schizophrenic.*

Diagnosis in Offspring	PARENT WITH ONSET OF SCHIZOPHRENIA BEFORE 20 No. (Per Cent)	PARENT WITH ONSET OF SCHIZOPHRENIA AGE 20–29 No. (Per Cent)	PARENT WITH ONSET OF SCHIZOPHRENIA 30 OR OLDER No. (Per Cent)
Schizophrenia onset before 20	4 ⎫	1 ⎫	2 ⎫
Onset 20–29	1 ⎬ 6(27.3)	7 ⎬ 12(18.5)	3 ⎬ 9(14.5)
Onset 30 or older	1 ⎭	4 ⎭	4 ⎭
Affective psychoses or psychosis NOS	2(9.1)	3(4.6)	1(1.6)
Sub-total	8(36.4)	15(23.1)	10(16.1)
Other disorders	6(27.3)	15(23.0)	11(17.8)
Without the above	8(36.4)	35(53.8)	41(66.1)
Total	22(100.1)	65(99.9)	62(100.0)

duce while their children only have to survive long enough to receive their diagnostic labels. Psychotic disorders could show anticipation if the children were not followed to the end of their risk periods. The average age of onset of the parent for the 27 pairs was 24.3 years while the average age of onset of schizophrenia in the 27 offspring was 27.5 years. There is no evidence of anticipation here.

OTHER MENTAL DISORDERS

Every careful family study of a functional psychosis has found a significant group of relatives of the proband with a similar psychosis as well as another group of relatives who suffer from what have been called schizoidias, or another similar term, indicating that the relatives have serious mental problems but they do not fall into one of the conventional taxonomic pigeon holes. In our study we are calling this group the "other mental disorders" or "other disorders" in the tables and text. This group of other disorders is even more difficult to classify than the frank psychoses. A person with the label of "personality pattern disturbance" may also have chronic alcoholism and it may be almost impossible to decide which of these psychological problems is the more damaging to the person. We will count the person twice in our tables if he had two of the other mental disorders and then subtract one person as a duplication at the end of the table in order to come out

with the actual number of persons in the study, but at the same time each type of other mental disorder will be accounted for in the body of the table.

Our classification of "other mental disorders" adheres to the categories listed in the *Diagnostic and Statistical Manual of Mental Disorders* published by the American Psychiatric Association in 1952. The five major categories into which our "other mental disorders" were placed were the psychoneurotic reactions (40), the personality disorders, including personality pattern disturbance (50), personality trait disturbance (51), sociopathic personality disturbance (52) and the transient situational personality disorders (54). Each of the five categories has numerous subdivisions, such as schizoid personality (50.1), paranoid personality (50.3) and alcoholism (addiction) (52.3). Some persons express more than one of these behavioral traits and have been scored for each one, with a number subtracted from the tables to correct for the multiple scoring. There is a more recent edition of the APA Manual (1968) with a different numbering system but the characteristics of each subdivision remain about the same.

We have also included chronic brain syndrome associated with circulatory disturbance (15) and chronic brain syndrome associated with senile and presenile brain disease (17) on the grounds that these anomalies might result in some cases from genotypes similar to those responsible for the functional psychoses. That is, there may be a genetic commonality which is basic to both the "other mental disorders" and the psychoses.

The reader may have noticed in the many tables which have been presented that there is a rather constant ratio between the frequency of psychoses and the frequency of other mental disorders for each group of relatives. For instance, in Table 4–2 it can be seen that 148 (16.8 per cent) of the 881 parents, siblings and children had a psychosis while 242 (27.4 per cent) of the first degree relatives had some other mental disorder. Although the first degree relatives have a little less than twice the frequency of other mental disorders as they have psychoses, one might expect that this ratio would change in other groups of relatives but it does not seem to change significantly. The data for the nephews and nieces illustrate this point very well, as shown in Table 7–22. There were 5.7 per cent of the 1050 nieces and nephews with a psychosis and 13.7 per cent with an other mental disorder, again about twice as many other disorders as psychoses.

Kallmann (1938) and others have recog-

nized a clear relationship between the psychoses and other mental disorders. He called them schizoidias or schizoform psychopaths. As an example, Kallmann found 9.1 per cent of the children of his schizophrenic probands had schizophrenia and another 17.6 per cent of the children were schizoform psychopaths. This last figure did not include chronic alcoholics, as far as we know. In our Table 7–9 for the 73 schizophrenic probands, 10.9 per cent of the first degree relatives had schizophrenia, which is in agreement with Kallmann's data. However, 30.6 per cent of the first degree relatives in Table 7–9 had some other mental disorder. This value is much higher than Kallmann's 17.6 per cent of schizoform psychopaths but we have intentionally included a wider range of disorders in our category than did Kallmann. However, Heston (1970) thinks that about one-third of the first degree relatives of schizophrenics are schizoid personalities, which is the same order of magnitude as our other mental disorders. Heston thinks that about one-sixth of the first degree relatives of a schizophrenic proband have schizo-

Table 7–22. *The Nieces and Nephews of the Probands According to the Diagnosis of the Parent. (One Case with Both Parents Psychotic is Excluded.)*

	ONE PARENT PSYCHOTIC			NEITHER PARENT PSYCHOTIC			
	Parent Affective No. (Per Cent)	*Parent Schizophrenic No. (Per Cent)*	*Parent Psychotic NOS No. (Per Cent)*	*Both Parents Other Disorder No. (Per Cent)*	*One Parent Other Disorder No. (Per Cent)*	*Both Parents Unaffected No. (Per Cent)*	*Total No. (Per Cent)*
A. Psychosis							
Involutional	0	1(1.2)	0	0	2(0.7)	0	3(0.3)
Manic-depressive	0	2(2.3)	0	0	2(0.7)	0	4(0.4)
Schizophrenic	2(5.0)	15(17.4)	3(5.4)	1(1.2)	10(3.5)	14(2.8)	45(4.3)
Psychotic NOS	2(5.0)	0	0	5(6.1)	0	1(0.2)	8(0.8)
Sub-total	4(10.0)	18(20.9)	3(5.4)	6(7.3)	14(4.9)	15(3.0)	60(5.7)
B. Other Mental Disorders							
Personality pattern disturbance	0	3(3.5)	0	3(3.7)	5(1.7)	1(0.2)	12(1.1)
Alcoholism	0	5(5.8)	1(1.8)	7(8.5)	12(4.2)	7(1.4)	32(3.0)
Other personality disorder	4(10.0)	6(7.0)	3(5.4)	7(8.5)	15(5.2)	18(3.6)	53(5.1)
Psychoneurosis	3(7.5)	1(1.2)	4(7.1)	5(6.1)	12(4.2)	19(3.8)	44(4.2)
Chronic brain syndrome	0	0	2(3.6)	3(3.7)	1(0.3)	3(0.6)	9(0.9)
Less duplications	0	0	0	−2(−2.4)	−2(−0.7)	−2(−0.4)	−6(−0.6)
Sub-total	7(17.5)	15(17.5)	10(17.9)	23(28.1)	43(14.9)	46(9.2)	144(13.7)
C. Without the above	29(72.5)	53(61.6)	43(76.8)	53(64.6)	229(80.1)	439(87.8)	846(80.6)
Grand total	40(100.0)	86(100.0)	56(100.1)	82(100.0)	286(99.9)	500(100.0)	1050(100.0)

Table 7–23.　*The Combined Data for the Children and the Nieces and Nephews of the Probands.
Data From Tables 6–3, 6–12 and 7–16.*

	PSYCHOSIS			OTHER MENTAL DISORDER			Total Number
Diagnosis in Parents	*Number*	*Per Cent*	*Relative Risk*[1]	*Number*	*Per Cent*	*Relative Risk*[1]	*Number (incl. Un- affected)*
Psychosis × other disorder	20	(20.0)	7.7***	34	(34.0)	8.3***	100
Psychosis × unaffected	30	(12.8)	4.9***	36	(15.4)	3.8***	234
Both with other disorder	6	(7.3)	2.8*	23	(28.0)	6.8***	82
Other disorder × unaffected	14	(4.9)	1.9	43	(15.0)	3.7***	286
Both unaffected	15	(3.0)	1.2	46	(9.2)	2.2***	500
Control group	24	(2.6)	1.0	37	(4.1)	1.0	913

[1] The per cent rate for each group divided by the corresponding rate for the control group.
* As compared with the control rate, P = <.01.
*** As compared with the control rate, P = <.001.

phrenia, which gives a 2:1 ratio of schiz- oid persons to schizophrenics. Our 2:1 ratio of other mental disorders to psychoses is a generalization resulting from averaging somewhat independent situations and thus is useful only to emphasize that there are practically always more relatives at every degree of relationship with some other mental disorder than with a psychosis.

Every investigator has found that psy- chotic persons produce more psychotic off- spring than do normal persons. It is natural to expect that specific psychoses, such as manic-depressive psychoses, would show agreement for diagnosis between parents and offspring. Those who studied only one disorder, such as schizophrenia, found agreement and, incredibly, sometimes no cases of disagreement between the diag- noses of parents and offspring. However, in our study, where no restriction to any one diagnostic type was present, we did not find any concordance for specific diagnoses of the psychoses in parents and offspring. But there is, of course, a strong association be- tween the presence of a psychosis in a parent with a psychosis in an offspring.

We have shown that the category of other mental disorders is related to the psy- choses in some way. In our families there is an average ratio of about two cases of some other mental disorder to each psychotic. The problem now is whether there is an as- sociation for other mental disorders be- tween parent and offspring. Our best data regarding this question are the combined values for the children and the nieces and nephews of the probands. We will compare

the relative risks for the combined children and nieces and nephews with the risks in the control population. The original data are in Tables 6–3, 6–12 and 7–16 and are brought together in Table 7–23. It is clear that the relative risk of some other mental disorder is high when the parent is psychot- ic as well as when another mental disorder is present in the parent. Table 7–23 yields probabilities of less than 0.001 for all cat- egories of offspring with other mental dis- orders in relation to the control population. There is thus a strong association between other mental disorders in parents and off- spring. The table also shows a substantial percentage of psychosis (7.3 per cent) when both parents have some other mental dis- order, indicating a basic gene pool for both the group of psychotic persons and those with some other mental disorder. A lighter loading of genes for mental disorder would result in a phenotype which receives a label of other mental disorder, while a heavier loading of the same or similar genes would result in a psychosis.

The genetic relationship between the other mental disorders and the psychoses is probably not that of a single gene locus type as envisioned by Kallmann and others. However, the reality of the relationship, whatever it may be, seems to be well es- tablished by all investigators, including us.

This last observation raises the ques- tion as to whether the other mental dis- orders are pre-psychotics in any substantial fraction of cases. We looked at the psychotic nieces and nephews to see what proportion would have been classified as having some other mental disorder prior to their diagnosis of a psychosis. In 5 cases the psychosis was present before age 20 so these 5 plus 4 retarded psychotics and 1 with an unknown age of onset of the psychosis can be excluded because they do not contribute useful information. There are 36 remaining cases with ages of onset between 25 and 74 for their psychosis. There are 11 cases of the 36 (30.5 per cent) in which a diagnosis of other mental disorder would have been appropriate before the diagnosis of their psychosis. What this means is that these 11 persons deviated from normal behavior for some time before they were ill enough to warrant the label of a psychosis. The pedigree numbers of these 11 persons are given here in case the reader is interested in the development of their mental disorders. The numbers are WSH 15–37, 29–122, 48–97, 48–100, 55–46, 67–74, 84–73, 84–82, 89–53, 92–61 and 97–42.

The combined data for the children and the nieces and nephews of the probands are our best sample for a study of the sub-types of other mental disorders. We expect to find the highest percentage of other mental disorders in the offspring of two psychotic parents. However, we had only three children, all psychotic, from this type of mating. The next highest risk group is where one parent was psychotic and the other had some other mental disorder. In this case it was found that 20 per cent of the offspring had a psychotic disorder and an additional 34.0 per cent had some other mental disorder, a total of 54.0 per cent. The data for the various matings and the sub-types of the other mental disorders are given in Tables 7–24 and 7–25.

Tables 7–24 and 7–25 are necessarily more complicated than we would like to have them. They are still not the most complete breakdowns into sub-types that are possible but we think they include the significant values. The only really surprising item in the tables is the dearth of offspring with a schizoid diagnosis. Our psychiatrists seem to have been generous with the diagnosis of schizophrenia but extremely parsimonious with the schizoid diagnosis. This diagnosis of schizoid personality was not

Table 7–24. *Summary Table of the Psychotic Disorders and the Sub-types of the Other Mental Disorders Present in the Children Combined with the Nephews and Nieces. (Continued in Table 7–25.)*

DIAGNOSIS IN CHILDREN, NEPHEWS, AND NIECES. (1952 APA CODE NUMBER IN PARENTHESIS)	NUMBER OF CHILDREN AND NEPHEWS AND NIECES BY DIAGNOSIS OF PARENTS		
	Parents, Psychosis by Other Disorder No. (Per Cent)	*Parents, Psychosis by Unaffected No. (Per Cent)*	*Both Parents Other Disorder No. (Per Cent)*
Total Psychotic Disorders (20–23)	20(20.0)	30(12.8)	6(7.3)
Personality disorders (50–53)			
Personality pattern disturbance (50)			
Schizoid (50.1)	1(1.0)	1(0.4)	3(3.7)
Other than schizoid	1(1.0)	1(0.4)	0
Personality trait disturbance (51)	2(2.0)	1(0.4)	1(1.2)
Sociopathic personality disturbance (52)			
Alcoholism (52.3)	3(3.0)	5(2.1)	7(8.5)
Other than alcoholism	11(11.0)	4(1.7)	3(3.7)
Personality disorder NOS*	5(5.0)	8(3.4)	3(3.7)
Transient situational personality disorders (54)	2(2.0)	0	0
Psychoneurotic disorders (40)	7(7.0)	13(5.6)	5(6.1)
Psychotic reactions to arteriosclerosis or senility (15.01 and 17.11)	3(3.0)	4(1.7)	3(3.7)
Less duplications	−1(−1.0)	−1(−0.4)	−2(−2.4)
Total other mental disorders (excluding the psychotics)	34(34.0)	36(15.3)	23(28.2)
Unaffected	46(46.0)	168(71.9)	53(64.5)
Total number of persons	100(100.0)	234(100.0)	82(100.0)

*NOS = Not otherwise specified.

Table 7–25. *Continuation of the Summary Table of the Psychotic Disorders and the Sub-types of the Other Mental Disorders Present in the Children Combined with the Nephews and Nieces.*

DIAGNOSIS IN CHILDREN, NEPHEWS AND NIECES. (1952 APA CODE NUMBER IN PARENTHESIS)	NUMBER OF CHILDREN AND NEPHEWS AND NIECES BY DIAGNOSIS OF PARENTS		
	Parents, Other Disorder by Unaffected No. (Per Cent)	*Both Parents Unaffected* No. (Per Cent)	*Control Group* No. (Per Cent)
Total Psychotic Disorders (20–23)	14(4.9)	15(3.0)	24(2.6)
Personality disorders (50–53)			
Personality pattern disturbance (50)			
Schizoid (50.1)	1(0.3)	0	0
Other than schizoid	4(1.4)	1(0.2)	3(0.3)
Personality trait disturbance (51)	2(0.7)	0	2(0.2)
Sociopathic personality disturbance (52)			
Alcoholism (52.3)	12(4.2)	7(1.4)	9(1.0)
Other than alcoholism	7(2.4)	5(1.0)	6(0.7)
Personality disorder NOS*	4(1.4)	6(1.2)	1(0.1)
Transient situational personality disorders (54)	2(0.7)	7(1.4)	5(0.5)
Psychoneurotic disorders (40)	12(4.2)	19(3.8)	9(1.0)
Psychotic reactions to arteriosclerosis or senility (15.01 and 17.11)	1(0.3)	3(0.6)	2(0.2)
Less duplications	−2(−0.7)	−2(−0.4)	0
Total other mental disorders (excluding the psychotics)	43(14.9)	46(9.2)	37(4.0)
Unaffected	229(80.2)	439(87.8)	852(93.4)
Total number of persons	286(100.0)	500(100.0)	913(100.0)

*NOS = Not otherwise specified.

given to any of the 913 controls and to only 6 (0.5 per cent) of the combined group of children and nieces and nephews.

The question now arises as to what sub-type diagnoses were conferred by the psychiatrists in place of the schizoidia or schizoform psychopath labels used by Kallmann. The labels our psychiatrists favored were primarily those of "other sociopathic personality disturbances", "personality disorder not otherwise specified" and "psychoneurotic disorder." It is clear that the psychiatrists were in agreement that a mental disturbance was present, but, except for the psychoneurotics, they did not wish to bestow a very specific label, at least not as specific as "schizoid." This preference of our cooperating psychiatrists for a less rigid taxonomy is probably beneficial as it is so extremely difficult to determine the true mental status of the persons with behavioral aberrations which are not as extreme as a psychosis but at the same time show a variety of behaviors which are socially unacceptable.

A good illustration of the softness of the diagnosis for the other mental disorders is provided by the largest single category of 11 (11 per cent) offspring in which one parent had a psychosis and the second parent was classified as having an other mental disorder. The diagnosis for each of these 11 offspring was that of a sociopathic personality disturbance other than addictive alcoholism. What were these 11 persons like? They all shared the characteristic of lack of social success but seemed to have little definite pathology. For instance, WSH 48–166 was a male of social class V who "had wanderlust, when young drank to excess, stole and was sexually immoral." His wife said, "He was quick-tempered, quite talkative, and always threatened to desert his family when there was any trouble." He left home when his children were 4 and 2 years old and went west. He died in an Oregon logging camp at age 27. The reason for the diagnosis of sociopathic personality disturbance is that the fellow failed to behave as his peers expected him to do. He was not psychotic but on the other hand he was individually not as well adapted to society as the large majority of other persons in his kinship and his community. The other 10 persons had similar sociopathic behaviors, particularly as young adults. Most of them seemed to have reasonably stable lives as they became older though one developed a presenile brain disease.

The second largest category of other mental disorders was the 8.5 per cent of the offspring who had both parents with an other mental disorder and an addictive alcoholism. All of the values for alcoholism, including the 1 per cent in the controls, seem rather low to us and do not seem to require further discussion.

A final word about the "other mental disorders" category. This is composed of a heterogeneous group of socially maladapted persons. Some of the persons with such disorders later develop a frank psychosis; most of them do not. The striking finding in all good family studies is the relatively constant relationship between the percentage of psychoses in any group of relatives of the proband and the percentage of other mental disorders in the same group of relatives. For each group of relatives there are approximately twice as many persons having one of the other mental disorders as there are persons with a psychosis. The fact that the psychoses and the other mental disorders vary in a fairly constant ratio from one group of relatives to the next group would seem to have considerable significance for the etiology of the array of mental disorders. It suggests a common basic component or cause of both the psychoses and the other mental disorders.

SUMMARY

This chapter makes no attempt to authenticate or define the various diagnoses provided for persons with mental disorders. There seems to be some kind of etiological relationship between schizophrenia and manic-depressive psychosis in the members of the same kinships. Many of the other mental disorders also have some kind of etiological relationship to each other and to the psychoses. This does *not* mean that *all* mental disorders have a common etiology; it does mean that a substantial proportion of the disorders have a similar basic etiology.

We envision a common genetic etiology which would depend upon a single autosomal dominant gene basic to *most* of the disorders or a multigenic basis which would be somewhat different in each person. In all cases there would be additional minor genetic modifiers and important environmental factors which would account for the variations in the expression of the disorders. This concept will be presented in greater depth later on in the book but relevant evidence from this chapter includes the following:

1. The calculation of the cumulative risk figures, that is, corrections for age of onset, for the relatives of the probands showed in a very striking way that psychotic mothers produce a higher percentage of psychotic offspring than do psychotic fathers. A sub-sample composed of the schizophrenic mothers only and their schizophrenic offspring again demonstrated a striking excess of schizophrenic offspring when compared with the percentage produced by the schizophrenic fathers. An example of the results obtained after cumulative risk calculations have been made gives an expected risk of psychosis of 27.3 ± 6.5 per cent for the siblings, if all reached 85 years of age and had a psychotic mother, while the siblings with a psychotic father had a risk of developing a psychosis of only 13.1 ± 5.5 per cent. (The differences were less obvious at younger ages.) The failure of other investigators to find higher percentages of psychotic offspring produced by psychotic mothers compared with psychotic fathers is probably the result of younger ages of their samples and the failure to make the age of onset corrections which would have revealed the difference between the two groups of offspring.

The immediate speculation as to the main reasons for the difference, if it is universally valid, would be that of an environmental influence provided by the mother. However, the evidence from the adoption studies and data to be presented in the next chapter suggest that greater genetic loading of the psychotic mothers is an important factor also.

2. The agreement (or disagreement) of the diagnosis of the proband with those of his relatives should provide information about the etiology of the mental disorders involved. We found that the 73 schiz-

ophrenic probands had 16 of their 100 psychotic first degree relatives with a label of an affective psychosis. The 16 probands with an affective disorder had 27 of their 43 psychotic relatives with a diagnosis of schizophrenia. Thus 62.8 per cent of the psychotic relatives of the affective probands were schizophrenic while only 3 or 7.0 per cent of the psychotic relatives had a diagnosis of manic-depressive psychosis. We were surprised to find that there was *no significant association* between the diagnosis of the proband and those given to his relatives.

The failure of the relatives of the probands to show the same diagnoses as the probands or their other relatives indicates a lack of specificity of the etiological factors resulting in the disorders within each family. Nonetheless, the relatives have high frequencies of mental disorders which are in rough agreement with their genetic relationships to the probands. This predictable relationship does not in itself prove that there is a genetic basis for a basic mental disorder but it is in agreement with genetic expectations.

3. There is no evidence of genetic sex-linkage in our study. There were 41 psychotic siblings of the same sex as the proband and only 19 of the opposite sex. However, this difference was not substantiated by any of the other degrees of relationship.

4. The 17 schizophrenic probands with age of onset under 20 had 20.6 per cent of their parents with a psychosis, whereas the 21 probands with an age of onset of 30 or over had only 9.5 per cent of their parents with a psychosis. This would seem to indicate a correlation between early onset and heavier genetic loading for schizophrenia. However, as $\chi^2 = 1.9$, $p = <0.2$, this fails to give statistical significance to the comparison shown above. There seems to be an association between early age of onset and heavier genetic loading but our sample size is too small to provide statistical proof that such an association exists.

5. Every good family study of the functional psychoses has demonstrated a group of relatives who suffer from what have been called the schizoidias, or some similar term. In our study this group of mental problems

is called the "other mental disorders." There is a ratio of approximately two relatives with some "other mental disorder" to each relative with a psychosis. The 2:1 ratio holds fairly constant for first, second and third degree relatives. The ratio is demonstrated in the relatives of the affective disorder probands as clearly as in the relatives of the schizophrenics.

In about one-third of the persons who eventually received a diagnosis of a frank psychosis the behavior previous to the time of the diagnosis was of the type which would be labeled "other mental disorder." While some of the persons with "other mental disorder" are pre-psychotics, not all can be classified as such. It is not possible to determine which of the other mental disorders are etiologically related to the psychosis even though the 2:1 ratio in the various groups of relatives suggests that some extremely important relationship exists.

6. The family study technique, in which independent diagnoses for various relatives of a proband are obtained, has great usefulness as a test of the specificity of the etiological homogeneity or heterogeneity of the disorders. Our family data show that the diagnosis of a psychosis may have operational value for treatment and other purposes, but it does not seem to have precise etiological significance. Thus, a diagnosis of affective disorder does *not* exclude schizophrenia from the relatives in our sample; actually, there is a higher probability that the relative will receive a diagnosis of schizophrenia than one of affective disorder. It is clear from our data that schizophrenia, the affective psychoses and some of the other mental disorders have an etiological relationship. The basic etiological component shared by the relatives might be one or more genes which result in mental disorder, the diagnostic characteristics of which would be determined by other genetic and environmental factors.

7. The lack of a high correlation between the diagnoses of our probands and their relatives is strong evidence that a multigenic system is present rather than a single gene locus for schizophrenia and an independent single gene locus responsible for manic-depressive psychosis.

CHAPTER EIGHT

FERTILITY

It is generally accepted that schizophrenic persons have a lower fertility than their unaffected siblings and the general population. It is also well known that schizophrenic males have a lower fertility than schizophrenic females. Numerous questions remain as to how these differences come about. The implications of the fertility differences are of great interest in regard to future generations. A major advantage of our study is the opportunity to trace at least one complete generation from the parents to their offspring, until the offspring have died or reached old age. When this is done it is possible to show that the differences in the numbers of psychotic offspring produced by schizophrenic females and males are due to the joint effects of at least two variables: (1) the proportion of schizophrenic females reproducing is higher than for schizophrenic males; and (2) the risk of schizophrenia is higher for each child of a schizophrenic female.

This chapter will be concerned with the effects of the various variables upon fertility rates as they influence population dynamics.

REPRODUCTIVE EXPERIENCE OF THE SCHIZOPHRENIC PERSON

Our data are in agreement with other investigators in demonstrating a lower fertility of schizophrenic persons than either their unaffected siblings or a control population. It could hardly be otherwise in view of the prolonged hospitalization of many of the schizophrenics. Hospitalization is not the only reason for the lower fertility of the mentally disordered, as we shall see later on.

We will look at the reproductive experience of the schizophrenic probands and their siblings, taking the sexes separately. In Table 8–1 we see that there were 66 female probands and sisters with schizophrenia. Only 64 per cent of them reproduced compared with 83 per cent of their unaffected sisters. The male probands did much worse since only 27 per cent of them and their schizophrenic brothers reproduced. Even the unaffected brothers did rather poorly as only 63 per cent were known to have offspring. See Figures 8–1, 8–2, and 8–3.

A brief description of the methodology used in constructing Figures 8–1, 8–2 and 8–3 may be useful. The data for schizophrenic females were examined separately for three groups of them: probands, sisters, and females in Generation IV (children, nieces and nephews). The differences were not great, so the data were pooled and are given in Table 8–2. For each age interval the calculated number is the sum of persons living to older ages plus one-half of those last observed within the interval. The live births were tabulated by the age of the schizophrenic female at the birth of the child. The last column shows the age-specific live birth rates.

Looking at Table 8–1 again it may be seen that of the 144 liveborn children produced by the schizophrenic females only 79 per cent survived to age 15 or older compared with higher survival rates for the other three groups in the table. Apparently the children of schizophrenic mothers are at a disadvantage in terms of Darwinian fitness in regard to survival to age 15 ($\chi^2 = 9.5$, p = <0.01 for the comparison with unaffected sisters' children).

Table 8–1. *Reproductive Experience of Schizophrenics.*

	FEMALES		MALES	
Group	*Schizophrenic (Probands and Sisters)*	*Unaffected Sisters*	*Schizophrenic (Probands and Brothers)*	*Unaffected Brothers*
Age 15 or older	66	93	37*	113
Those who reproduced (Number and Per Cent of above)	42 (64)	77 (83)	10 (27)	71 (63)
Liveborn children of persons above	144	297	32	258
Children surviving to age 15 (Number and Per Cent of liveborn)	114 (79)	267 (90)	30 (94)	228 (88)
Mental health of children (Number and Per Cent)				
Schizophrenia	24 (21)	5 (2)	4 (13)	9 (4)
Manic-depressive psychosis	3 (3)	1	1 (3)	0
Psychosis NOS**	1 (1)	0	0	0
Other mental health problem	33 (29)	30 (11)	3 (10)	22 (10)
Unaffected	53 (46)	231 (87)	22 (73)	197 (86)
Total	114(100)	267(100)	30(99)	228(100)

*Including two males who married schizophrenic wives. Each couple produced one child (who developed schizophrenia).

**NOS = Not otherwise specified.

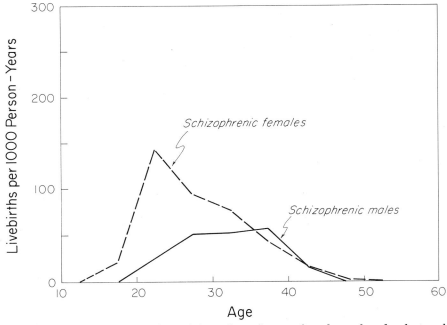

Figure 8–1. The much higher fertility of the schizophrenic female probands, their schizophrenic sisters, daughters, and nieces compared with the schizophrenic male probands, their schizophrenic brothers, sons, and nephews.

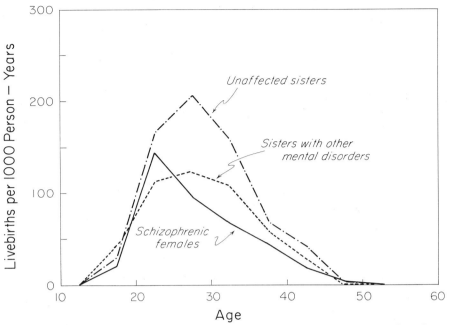

Figure 8–2. Fertility of three groups of related females. The schizophrenic females include the schizophrenic probands, sisters, daughters, and nieces.

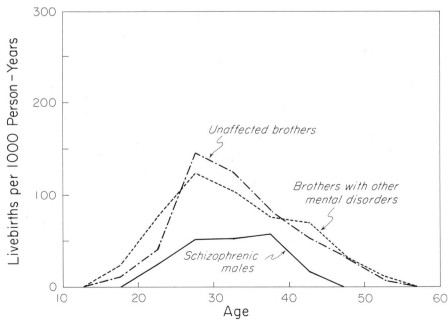

Figure 8–3. Fertility of three groups of related males. The schizophrenic males include the schizophrenic probands, brothers, sons, and nephews.

Table 8–2. *Age-Specific Live Birth Rates for Schizophrenic Females. (Female Probands Plus Schizophrenic Sisters, Daughters, and Nieces of Schizophrenic Probands.)*

| Age Interval | SCHIZOPHRENIC FEMALES | | LIVE BIRTHS | |
	Number of Persons by Age at Last Report	Calculated Number in Age Interval	Number of Live Births to Persons in Age Interval	Number of Live Births per 1000 Person-Years
15–19	0	86.0	9	20.9
20–24	2	85.0	61	143.5
25–29	3	82.5	39	94.5
30–34	6	78.0	26	66.7
35–39	4	73.0	16	43.8
40–44	7	67.5	6	17.8
45–49	3	62.5	1	3.2
50–54	11	55.5		
55–59	7	46.5		
60 and over	43			
Total, age known	86		158	

The children of the schizophrenic mothers are also at a great disadvantage from a second point of view. Table 8–1 shows that 25 per cent of these children developed a psychosis, while only 16 per cent of the children of the male schizophrenics developed schizophrenia or manic-depressive psychosis. When the other mental disorders are included the distinction between the children of female and male schizophrenics becomes even more striking. Only 46 per cent of the children of the schizophrenic females were *unaffected*, while 73 per cent of the children of the schizophrenic males were *unaffected*.

FERTILITY AND RISK TO CHILDREN CONSIDERED SIMULTANEOUSLY

It will be interesting to combine the two disadvantages of the lower fertility of schizophrenic persons with the higher risk their children have of developing schizophrenia. These calculations are presented in Table 8–3. The first line of the table comes from Table 8–1. The second and third lines show that schizophrenic females produce slightly fewer children than their unaffected sisters and they have a clearly lower proportion of their children surviving to age 15. However, in line 4 we see that the

Table 8–3. *Combined Effect of Reproductive Rate and Risk of Schizophrenia in Offspring.*

| | FEMALES | | MALES | |
	Schizophrenic (Probands and Sisters)	Unaffected (Sisters)	Schizophrenic (Probands and Brothers)	Unaffected (Brothers)
1. Proportion ever reproducing	0.64	0.83	0.27	0.63
2. Liveborn children per reproducing individual	3.43	3.86	3.20	3.63
3. Proportion of liveborn surviving to age 15	0.79	0.90	0.94	0.88
4. Net number of surviving children per individual ($1 \times 2 \times 3$)	1.73	2.88	0.81	2.01
5. Risk of schizophrenia per child	0.21	0.02	0.13	0.04
6. Net number of schizophrenic children per individual (4×5)	0.36	0.06	0.11	0.08
7. Net number of children, without any mental disorder, per individual (line 4 times per cent unaffected of Table 8–1)	0.80	2.51	0.59	1.73

net survival is by far the lowest per schizophrenic male (0.81 children), while the value for the schizophrenic female (1.73 children) is also much lower than those for the unaffected siblings. Line 6 shows that the schizophrenic female produces from four to six times as many schizophrenic children (0.36) as each of the other three types of persons. Line 7 is found by multiplying the percentage of unaffected persons in Table 8–1 by line 4 of Table 8–3. The figures show nicely that the Darwinian fitness of the schizophrenic male is lowest, followed by the schizophrenic female. Neither the male nor female schizophrenic approaches a replacement value for itself in terms of psychotic offspring, which would be more than one child per patient.

It is perhaps surprising that the net number of unaffected children per schizophrenic woman is only modestly higher (0.80) than the number for schizophrenic males (0.59) in view of the higher fertility of the schizophrenic woman; however, there is the greater risk of mental disturbance in the woman's children which decreases her proportion of unaffected children.

A similar pattern can be seen in the data for mental retardation. A new tabulation of the data of Reed and Reed (1965) shows (in Table 8–4) the net number of retarded children of retarded females to be 0.31 per

woman and only 0.10 retarded children per retarded male. Line 7 shows that while the retarded females who reproduced had 4.04 children each the number of non-retarded children for all retarded females who survived to age two was only 1.34, while the retarded males had only 0.81 non-retarded children each.

A comparison of Tables 8–3 and 8–4 shows schizophrenic males who reproduced had 3.20 children each while the mentally retarded males who reproduced had 4.30 children each. The net numbers of *unaffected* children per male were respectively 0.59 and 0.81. Higher but comparable values were observed for schizophrenic and mentally retarded women. The comparison seems to indicate that schizophrenia is almost twice as disadvantageous as mental retardation in relation to reproductive fitness. Such estimates are exceedingly rough but permit interesting speculations.

FERTILITY, MATERNAL EFFECT AND DIAGNOSIS

Erlenmeyer-Kimling, et al. (1969) studied changes in the fertility rates of schizophrenic patients in the New York State hospital system. They found that patients of both sexes and of all age groups in the 1954–1956 period showed increases in marital

Table 8–4. *Combined Effect of Sex Difference, Reproductive Rate and Risk of Mental Retardation in Offspring.*[1]

| | SISTERS OF PROBANDS | | BROTHERS OF PROBANDS | |
	Mentally Retarded	*Not Retarded*	*Mentally Retarded*	*Not Retarded*
Number of individuals	144	365	186	352
Those who reproduced	68	268	44	212
Number of children	275	966	189	780
Children surviving two or more years	238	899	166	739
Mentally retarded children	45	19	18	22
1. Proportion ever reproducing	0.47	0.73	0.24	0.60
2. Children per reproducing individual	4.04	3.60	4.30	3.68
3. Proportion surviving	0.87	0.93	0.88	0.95
4. Net number of surviving children per individual $(1 \times 2 \times 3)$	1.65	2.44	0.91	2.10
5. Risk of retardation per child	0.189	0.021	0.108	0.030
6. Net number of retarded children per individual (4×5)	0.31	0.05	0.10	0.06
7. Net number of non-retarded children (line 4 minus line 6)	1.34	2.39	0.81	2.04

[1]Based on data from Reed and Reed (1965).

rates, in fertile marriages and in overall reproductive rates, compared to 1934–1936 patients. The increases evident at admission continued to hold at the end of a five to eight year standard evaluation interval following admission. Our results are like theirs in that women schizophrenics are more fertile than male schizophrenics. However, their samples were less fertile than ours, which is probably due to our sample being more rural in origin and from an earlier period in time when reproductive rates were higher. Erlenmeyer-Kimling et al. would not have been likely to notice a higher risk for schizophrenia in the offspring of schizophrenic mothers compared with those from schizophrenic fathers because the widening differences in the cumulative risk curves do not become significant until after about age 35 in the offspring. See Figure 7–3 and Tables 7–7 and 7–8 as a reminder of the kinds of data we have for schizophrenia. There seems to be general agreement that schizophrenic persons are less fertile than their unaffected siblings and the general population. There is also

agreement that schizophrenic males are less fertile than schizophrenic females.

Our finding that the risk per child of developing a psychosis when the mother is schizophrenic is greater than when the father is schizophrenic has not been adequately investigated by other workers. There are data in Tables 33 through 37 of Kallmann's (1938) study showing that schizophrenic females had 620 children aged 15 or over and of these children 69 (11.1 per cent) were schizophrenic (definite and doubtful diagnoses). The schizophrenic males had 380 children of whom 42 (11.1 per cent) were schizophrenic. We have no explanation for the absence of any difference between the two groups of children.

It is of great interest that Stenstedt (1959) apparently found a strikingly higher risk of manic-depressive psychosis among the offspring of manic-depressive mothers compared with the risk of manic-depressive psychosis in the offspring of affected fathers. The cumulative risk curves for the two groups of offspring (constructed by us from his data) are shown in Figure 8–4.

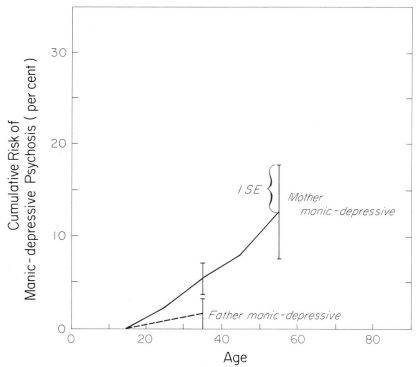

Figure 8–4. Cumulative risk curves for offspring of manic-depressive mothers and of manic-depressive fathers. Curves constructed from Stenstedt's 1959 data.

Our own data for the functional psychoses, other than schizophrenia, also show differences similar to Stenstedt's. Our mothers with a frank psychosis, other than schizophrenia, had 105 children and of them 16 (15.2 per cent) developed a psychosis. The fathers with a frank psychosis, other than schizophrenia, had 83 children of whom 8 (9.6 per cent) developed a psychosis.

The monograph by Angst (1966) on the depressive psychoses has no data on the children of the probands that we can use but it does give the sex of the psychotic parent of the proband. His data seem to show that about 5 per cent of his probands had a psychotic father, 13 per cent had a psychotic mother and 82 per cent had neither parent with a frank psychosis. Similar data from Stenstedt (1959) for manic-depressive probands indicate that about 4 per cent had a psychotic father and 9 per cent had a psychotic mother.

Alanen (1958) found that 1.3 per cent of his schizophrenic probands had a schizophrenic father and 7.2 per cent of the probands had a schizophrenic mother. Essen-Möller (1963) accepted the finding that, "Among parents of schizophrenic probands, mothers are definitely more often schizophrenic than are fathers, in fact about twice as frequent." Essen-Möller thought that the "surplus of mothers can probably wholly be accounted for by statistical biases." Apparently he thinks that as the parent does not enter observation until the moment of birth of the future proband, the remaining risk period for females is about twice that for males. However, in our study and in Stenstedt's there is a greater risk per child of a psychotic mother than of a psychotic father. Thus, we present an additional explanation of the accepted observation that the psychotic proband has an affected mother about twice as frequently as an affected father. Our own schizophrenic probands had both parents with schizophrenia in 1.4 per cent of the cases, 6.8 per cent had a schizophrenic father, 12.3 per cent a schizophrenic mother and for 79.5 per cent neither parent had schizophrenia (though many had some other psychosis or other mental disorder).

By far the largest sample is the material collected by Penrose (1945) from hospitals in Ontario. Of an unknown total of schizophrenic patients, 44 had a schizophrenic father and 106 had a schizophrenic mother, showing again that there are more than twice as many schizophrenics with a schizophrenic mother as with a schizophrenic father.

It is clear that a greater number of persons with the schizophrenias and with the depressive psychoses are the offspring of psychotic mothers than of psychotic fathers. There are at least three hypotheses that account, individually or in combination, for the excess of affected offspring produced by psychotic mothers.

1. Numerous authors, including Alanen (1958), have demonstrated that the relative fertility of female psychotics is greater than that of male psychotics.

2. The risk period for the parent to become psychotic, after the birth of the proband, is longer for females than for males. This hypothesis has been emphasized by Essen-Möller (1963). In this case the psychotic offspring is selected as the proband.

3. The risk of developing a psychosis is greater per child for the child of a psychotic mother than for the child of a psychotic father. Kallmann did not find this to be the case but it seems to be a reasonable assumption and the data of Stenstedt (1959) for manic-depressive psychosis and ours for the schizophrenias and the other psychoses support the hypothesis. In this case the parent is selected as the proband.

In view of the above hypotheses, we can expect to find for any group of probands with a functional psychosis that a significant excess of them will have a psychotic mother compared with those having a psychotic father, regardless of the relative emphasis placed on any of the three hypotheses. The "maternal effect," whether or not it is the result of greater genetic liability of psychotic mothers, is more evidence of the similarities of the etiology of the schizophrenias and the affective disorders.

One should find a maternal effect in other conditions which obviously have a multigenic etiology, such as mental retardation. Reed and Reed (1965, p. 41) reported this finding for mental retardation. They found that mentally retarded mothers (fathers not retarded) had 313 children of whom 60 (19.4 per cent) were retarded, while the mentally retarded fathers (mothers not retarded) produced 341 children of whom 31 (9.1 per cent) were retarded. The difference is statistically highly significant ($\chi^2 = 13.01$, p <0.01). These values are only slightly higher than those from the 219 children, nieces and nephews of psychotic mothers of whom 40 (18.3 per cent) were psychotic, while the 115 children, nieces and nephews of psychotic fathers included 10 (8.7 per cent) who were psychotic ($\chi^2 = 5.4$, p <0.05). This close agreement must be coincidental but it also may be an indication of a general characteristic of multigenic, heterogeneous traits such as personality, intelligence and mental disorders. The ability of women suffering from more severe expressions of these defects to obtain mates and reproduce may be similar for each group of traits and display comparable maternal effects as a result of their greater genetic liability when compared with the affected fathers. We suggest that a search be made for maternal effects resulting from a greater genetic liability in the reproducing women with other mental and physical traits presumed to be of multigenic origin.

A POPULATION DYNAMICS MODEL

It may be helpful to set up a hypothetical population to study the effects of these variables of fertility and morbid risks on population dynamics. We start with an imaginary population of 100,000 persons as shown in the first line of Table 8–5. We assume a rate of 2.0 per cent for schizophrenia in the population. Deming's (1968) data for New York state showed the risk at age 15 of being eventually hospitalized for schizophrenia to be 1 in 35 (2.9 per cent) for males and 1 in 30 for females. The other rates in Table 8–5 repeat those given in Table 8–3 in order to give consistent development of our model. It can be seen that 15.3 per cent of the schizophrenics in the whole population would be expected to have a schizophrenic mother and a nonschizophrenic father, while 4.5 per cent would come from the reciprocal mating. The great majority (80.2 per cent) would be expected to have both parents without schizophrenia.

We are not as much interested in the precise estimation of the values as in the more general implications of this type of model, including the following concepts:

1. The majority of schizophrenic persons will be produced in families with both parents having normal mental health. This would be true even if the category of other mental disorders were introduced.

2. If the risk of schizophrenia per child were identical for offspring of schizophrenic males and females, we should still find more schizophrenic offspring having a schizophrenic mother than a schizophrenic father. The latter difference would arise from

Table 8–5. *Hypothetical Population Illustrating Effect of Reproductive Rates and Risk of Schizophrenia in Offspring.*

| | SCHIZOPHRENIC | | UNAFFECTED | |
	Females	*Males*	*Sexes Combined*	*Total*
Initial number[1]	1000	1000	98,000	100,000
Proportion reproducing	0.64	0.27	0.72	
Individuals reproducing	640	270	70,560	71,470
Pairs reproducing[2]	640	270	34,825	35,735
Liveborn children per pair	3.43	3.20	3.75	
Number liveborn children	2195	864	130,594	133,653
Proportion surviving to 15	0.79	0.94	0.89	
Number surviving to 15	1734	812	116,229	118,775
Risk of schizophrenia per child	0.210	0.130	0.016°	0.020°
Number of schizophrenic children	364	106	1906°	2376°
Distribution of schizophrenic children	15.3%	4.5%	80.2%	100%

[1]Assuming 2 per cent schizophrenia in both generations.
[2]Assuming that schizophrenics mate only with unaffected.
°Arbitrarily set to result in 2 per cent schizophrenia for the whole generation.

the higher fertility of schizophrenic females. It should be obvious that the retrospective finding of more schizophrenic mothers than fathers is never sufficient evidence for a maternal influence upon the behavior of children.

3. The possible effects of medical intervention should be tested in such a model. Therapeutic medication for schizophrenic females could have at least three effects: (a) increase fertility, (b) introduce a new intrauterine drug effect upon the fetus (Werboff and Gottlieb, 1963), and (c) possibly reduce the postnatal risk of schizophrenia for the child. Each of these parameters would have to be assessed before we could determine whether the net effect would be beneficial or detrimental.

4. This type of model makes some straightforward assumptions which are testable. Clear evidence that one of these assumptions is wrong will lead to the modification (and improvement) of the model.

The model provided in Table 8–5 shows that 19.8 per cent of the schizophrenic persons in the hypothetical population would have one schizophrenic parent. How does this calculated figure of 19.8 per cent compare with our observations? We cannot use the children of our probands because they all had a schizophrenic parent in keeping with the design of the experiment. There were 770 nieces and nephews of the probands of whom 29 or 3.8 per cent were diagnosed as schizophrenic. Of the 29 schizophrenic nieces and nephews there were 7 or 24.1 per cent who had a schizophrenic parent. This is higher than the model predicts but the reason for the discrepancy seems to be that all 770 nephews and nieces had at least one schizophrenic aunt or uncle, namely, the proband. This usually would not have been the case for the "hypothetical" schizophrenic children of the model population.

The model shown in Table 8–5 indicates that 19.8 per cent of the present generation of schizophrenic persons might have been produced by a schizophrenic parent. An obvious speculation is that if none of the schizophrenics in the previous generation had reproduced, the frequency of the disorder in the present generation should have been reduced by the 19.8 per cent. However, many schizophrenics would have pro-

duced some children before the onset of their disorder, so it is completely unlikely that any decrease as large as 19.8 per cent would actually happen even under the most extreme program of negative eugenics which one could imagine.

A much more likely possibility is that a higher proportion of schizophrenics will reproduce in the future than was the case in the past. Advances in therapy have decreased the length of hospitalization for schizophrenia most dramatically. Evidence of improved reproduction of schizophrenic persons has been provided by Erlenmeyer-Kimling (1969). We can anticipate the maximum increase in reproduction which would result if all schizophrenics did as well as their normal siblings.

We can rework our model on the assumption that the schizophrenic women and men reproduce at the same rate as their non-schizophrenic siblings. Thus, the absolute conceivable maximum percentage of schizophrenic offspring who might be produced by a schizophrenic parent can be predicted from our revised model.

It can be seen from Table 8–5A that the average proportion of siblings of our schizophrenic persons who reproduced was 72 per cent. The average number of surviving children of each sibling who reproduced was 3.3. The predictions as to the maximum proportion of schizophrenic persons of the next generation who could be produced by those of the present generation are shown in the bottom line of the table.

We see that if all schizophrenic persons of one generation reproduced at the same rate as their non-affected siblings and their children survived as well as those of their siblings, then 30.7 per cent of the schizophrenic persons of the next generation would have been produced by a schizophrenic parent. This is an increase from the 19.8 per cent of our "real life" model of Table 8–5. It is an increase of 55 per cent as a result of the assumption that the schizophrenic persons would do as well in reproduction as their normal siblings.

The broad limits between which the production of schizophrenic offspring by a schizophrenic parent might fluctuate are firmly established by our models. In eugenic terminology, the maximum economy would have been about a 19.8 per cent reduction in

Table 8–5A. *Hypothetical Population Assuming that Schizophrenics Would Reproduce at the Same Rate as Their Siblings.*

| | SCHIZOPHRENIC | | UNAFFECTED | |
	Females	*Males*	*Sexes Combined*	*Total*
Initial numbers*	1000	1000	98,000	100,000
Proportion reproducing	0.72	0.72	0.72	
Individuals reproducing	720	720	70,560	72,000
Pairs reproducing	720	720	34,560	36,000
Surviving children per reproducing pair (calculated from Table 8–5)	3.33	3.33	3.33	
Number surviving children	2398	2398	115,085	119,881
Risk of schizophrenia per child	0.21	0.13	0.016	0.022**
Number of schizophrenic children	504	312	1841	2657
Distribution of schizophrenic children	19.0%	11.7%	69.3%	100.0%

30.7%

*Arbitrarily set to result in 2 per cent schizophrenia.

**Total below, divided by that above, or $\dfrac{2657}{119,881} = 0.022$

schizophrenia if none of the previous generation of schizophrenics had reproduced. No one expects a reduction of this amount, particularly since many children are born before the onset of schizophrenia occurs in the parent.

The opposite extreme, where every schizophrenic person is as prolific as his normal siblings, would result in the production of 30.7 per cent of the schizophrenic offspring by a schizophrenic parent of the previous generation. Our population may be tending in this direction as a result of better medical treatment but it is highly unlikely that such a high value will be achieved. Even if it were, the percentage of schizophrenia in the whole population would only increase from our base rate of 2 per cent to 2.2 per cent in one generation, though this is a 10 per cent increase.

Changes in the reproductive rates of psychotic persons will presumably be reflected by proportional changes in the gene pool for psychoses. Naturally, eugenicists would be distraught at any increase in the frequency of genes for the psychoses but this would be more than balanced by the reduction in the actual suffering from the miseries of the mental disorders as the result of the treatment which simultaneously improved the psychotics' fertility.

It is incredible, in view of the tremendous literature concerning the presumed effect of the mother on the appearance of schizophrenia in her offspring as evidenced by the work of Lidz et al. (1965) and of many others, that no one has ever investigated the obvious implication of these theories from a family-study viewpoint. Kallmann (1938) did not comment on this effect and his data do not support it, though our data do. We have shown that Stenstedt's (1959) data show a clear difference for the two sexes of parents for manic-depressive psychosis (see Figure 8–4). However, we could find no other data for manic-depressive psychosis that permit an analysis of the percentage of psychosis among children produced by a psychotic mother distinguished from the psychotic children of a psychotic father.

Thus, there are no substantial data which support our finding of a greater effect of the psychotic mother compared with the psychotic father, except Stenstedt's, and few disputing it, except Kallmann's, which is an astonishing paucity of information considering the importance of the question. One can restate the question from the following provocative point of view. If the schizophrenic mother does *not* have a higher percentage of schizophrenic offspring than does the schizophrenic father, why should anyone expect an unaffected mother to have a higher percentage of schizophrenic offspring than an unaffected father?

It is sometimes helpful to consider other models which could provide some insight concerning the problems at hand. The situation regarding mental retardation presents some parallels to that for the psychoses. It is true that the psychoses are not congenital in expression, as are the various kinds of mental retardation, and there are no remissions for the retarded. However, both situations are genetically complex and in both fertility is significantly higher in women than in men.

Therefore, let us return to the data for mental retardation in Reed and Reed (1965). A flow-sheet similar to Table 8–5 for schizophrenia can be constructed for mental retardation. The hypothetical population shown in Table 8–6 starts with an unequal number of males and females with retardation because an excess of males is well established in the literature. We are assuming that 2.5 per cent of both the parent and offspring generations have IQ values of less than 70. It is interesting that about 17 per cent of the retarded children had a retarded parent while 19.8 per cent of the schizophrenic children had a schizophrenic parent. Is this striking similarity between the 17 per cent for mental retardation and the 19.8 per cent for schizophrenia only coincidence or is it to some extent a consequence of the population dynamics for similar heterogeneous groups of defects with important genetic and environmental components? It is also of interest that there is extreme similarity in the production of

12 per cent mental retardation by mentally retarded mothers and 5 per cent by retarded fathers while 15.3 per cent of the schizophrenic offspring were produced by schizophrenic mothers and 4.5 per cent by schizophrenic fathers. We have mentioned before that the value of 15.3 per cent for the schizophrenic mothers may be too high owing to sampling error. However, the general correspondence between the data for mental retardation and schizophrenia is extremely interesting.

The utilization of population models such as those shown in Tables 8–5 and 8–6 is a concept-checking device of great value. This is particularly well illustrated by the results shown in Table 8–6 for mental retardation. Reed and Reed (1965) found that 33.1 per cent of the retarded children born to the first cousins of a proband had a retarded parent. They concluded that at least one-third of the retarded children in the general population would similarly have a retarded parent. Our new model shows that this conclusion was incorrect; only 17 per cent of the children in the hypothetical population of Table 8–6 turned out to have a retarded parent.

The reason for the disagreement between the prediction from the first cousin data and the answer given by the model became clear as a result of the construction of the model. In pedigree material from a family study there will be a substantial de-

Table 8–6. *Hypothetical Population Illustrating Effect of Sex Difference in Reproductive Rates and Risk of Mental Retardation in the Offspring.*

	RETARDED Females	Males	NOT RETARDED Sexes Combined	TOTAL
Initial numbers (2.5 per cent retardation)	1090	1410	97,500	100,000
Proportion reproducing	0.47	0.24	0.67	
Individuals reproducing	512	338	65,325	66,175
Pairs reproducing	512	338	32,238	33,088
Children per pair	4.04	4.30	3.64	
Number of children	2068	1453	117,346	
Proportion surviving	0.87	0.88	0.94	
Number surviving	1799	1279	110,305	113,383
Risk of retardation per child	0.189	0.108	0.0214*	0.025*
Number retarded children	340	138	2357*	2835*
Distribution of retarded children	12%	5%	83%	
	17%			

[1] Data based on Reed and Reed (1965).

*Arbitrarily set to result in 2.5 per cent retardation for the whole generation.

crease in the frequency of the trait for each degree of relationship that we move away from the proband until the frequency of the trait in the distant relatives becomes indistinguishable from that in the general population. Consequently, the closer the relationship of the retarded child to the proband, the greater the chance that the child will have a retarded parent. The converse is *not* true because the chance that a retarded person will have a retarded child should be about the same regardless of the relationship to the proband. For example, all children of the proband have a 100 per cent chance of having a retarded parent but the risk of having a retarded child was 16.3 per cent for the probands of the Reed and Reed family study. For the retarded children of first cousins the risk of a retarded parent was 33.1 per cent but the risk that a retarded first cousin would have a retarded child was 16.2 per cent (excluding children with unknown mental status), the same as for the children of the probands. At more distant relationships the risk that a retarded child would have a retarded parent should be about the same as the risk that a retarded parent would expect for retardation in the child. The risk in the general population for both parent-child relationships would be about that shown in the model, Table 8–6, which is 17 per cent (at a population frequency of 2.5 per cent of mental retardation).

We then wondered if there is any systematic relationship between two of these variables: (1) the risk of retardation for offspring of retarded persons; and (2) the proportion of the retarded who have a retarded parent. The relationship can be explored most easily for a population in equilibrium (with respect to population size and frequency of retardation) having the same net reproductive rates for normal and retarded individuals (and for males as compared with females), and with the risk of retardation the same for offspring of retarded males or females. A general statement of the situation is shown in Table 8–7 (which assumes that all persons marry and that all couples average two children each), along with an example using specific values for x and y. The value for x equals the frequency of the trait in the population and the value for y equals the risk of the trait for children of affected persons. The value of y has no

necessary relationship to the value of x; thus, the model is not limited to any specific pattern of genotype-environment interaction.

In the specific illustration there are 2000 affected offspring. Of these, there are 300 with an affected mother (or 15 per cent of the mothers). Similarly, there are 300 with an affected father (or 15 per cent of the fathers). Thus, when parents are counted, the frequency in the parents (15 per cent) is the same as the risk for the offspring ($y = 15$ per cent).

The situation becomes different, however, when we focus on the offspring and ask what proportion of the affected offspring have an affected parent of either sex (mother or father). Since each affected offspring has two parents, either of whom could be affected, the proportion of affected offspring having an affected parent is 600 out of 2000 (30 per cent, or $2y$).

The percentages discussed in the preceding two paragraphs do not depend upon the value of x (the frequency of the trait in the population). All that is required is that the population be in equilibrium, with x remaining the same for each generation.

We can now check our data to see how they agree with the generalization generated in Table 8–7. In the hypothetical population for retardation (Table 8–6) the average risk of retardation for offspring of a retarded mother or father (y) would be 15.5 per cent. We would therefore expect that the proportion of retarded children having a retarded mother or father would be 31 per cent ($2y$), but the calculations in Table 8–6 produce an estimate of 17 per cent.

Essen-Möller (1959) pointed out that an adjustment for relative fertility becomes necessary in this type of situation. The net fertility can be calculated by dividing the net number of surviving children (line 4 in Table 8–4) for the retarded females by the net number for the retarded sisters (and similarly for males). The results of such an adjustment are as follows:

	Retarded Females	*Retarded Males*
1. Relative fertility	0.68	0.43
2. Risk of retardation per child	0.189	0.108
Product of the above (1 × 2)	0.129	0.046

.175

Table 8–7. *Comparison of the Risk for Offspring of Affected Individuals with the Proportion of Affected Individuals Having an Affected Parent. Demonstrated for a Generalized Population and for a Situation with x = .02 and y = .15.*

	GENERALIZED POPULATION				POPULATION OF 100,000 WITH x = .02 AND y = .15[3]			
	Affected Female	*Affected Male*	*Normal Persons*	*Total*	*Affected Female*	*Affected Male*	*Normal Persons*	*Total*
Initial number	$\dfrac{Nx}{2}$	$\dfrac{Nx}{2}$	$N(1-x)$	N	1000	1000	98,000	100,000
Pairs reproducing[1]	$\dfrac{Nx}{2}$	$\dfrac{Nx}{2}$	$\dfrac{N(1-2x)}{2}$	$\dfrac{N}{2}$	1000	1000	48,000	50,000
Number of offspring[2]	Nx	Nx	$N(1-2x)$	N	2000	2000	96,000	100,000
Risk of trait per offspring	y	y	$\dfrac{x(1-2y)}{(1-2x)}$	x	.15	.15	.0146	.02
Number affected offspring	Nxy	Nxy	$Nx(1-2y)$	Nx	300	300	1400	2000
Proportion of affected offspring having affected parent	$\dfrac{Nxy + Nxy}{Nx} = 2y$				$\dfrac{600}{2000} = .30$			

[1]Assuming no matings between two affected persons.
[2]Assuming two children per mating.
[3]Let x = the frequency of the trait in the general population, y = the risk of the trait among offspring of affected parents.

The results now compare closely with the percentages at the bottom of Table 8–6. A similar adjustment for relative fertility leads to a close fit between the predicted values for schizophrenia and those shown on the bottom line of Table 8–5.

It appears proper to conclude that in the general population the probability that an affected child (having a multigenic trait) would have an affected mother is approximately equal to the risk of the trait appearing in the child of affected women multiplied by the relative fertility of affected women. A similar relationship would hold for the affected children of affected men. The probability that an affected child would have an affected parent of either sex is approximately the sum of the separate probabilities of having an affected mother and an affected father.

There is the further implication that if all affected persons in a large general population failed to reproduce, the frequency of the trait in the next generation would be reduced by about the percentage of affected children produced by affected parents.

Thus, if all schizophrenics in one generation failed to reproduce we could expect about 19 per cent fewer schizophrenics in the next generation. If all the mentally retarded (IQ = 69 cut-off point) of one generation failed to reproduce, then we could expect a reduction of about 16 per cent in the number of retardates in the following generation.

EFFECTS OF ONSET OF DISEASE AND HOSPITALIZATION ON FERTILITY

It is obvious that any prolonged hospitalization would reduce fertility of the patient, and early onset of the illness should also reduce fertility, particularly if the patient continues to deteriorate. The question of interest is that of how important these effects on fertility seem to be.

We will use the same schizophrenic persons, the probands, their schizophrenic siblings, children, nephews and nieces as were used for the fertility curves shown earlier. There were the following number of schizophrenic persons:

	Females	Males
Ever hospitalized	78	62
Never hospitalized	8	5
	86	67
For those hospitalized:		
Mean age of onset	28.5	26.5
Mean age at first hospitalization	33.4	29.3

There were 158 live births produced by the 86 schizophrenic females shown above (or 1.8 children per female) and 60 children of the 67 schizophrenic males (or 0.9 children per schizophrenic male), both of which are less than the 2.2 children usually considered necessary for replacement of the parental generation involved. The results, by age of the schizophrenic person at the time of producing the children, and by the course of the disease (with reference to onset and hospitalization), are shown in Table 8–8.

It is now necessary to devise some method for calculating the expected numbers of children for comparison with the totals shown in Table 8–8. The first step is to find the number of person-years of life experience for the schizophrenic females and males for each age interval and time period in the course of the disease. The person-years for the total group of females (shown in Table 8–9) are calculated from the data in Table 8–2 by multiplying the calculated number in each age interval by five (the number of years in the interval). The partitioning of the life experience into the three time periods (with reference to onset and hospitalization) is based on a year-by-year tabulation of the data.

The next step is to divide the actual numbers of live births shown in Table 8–8 by the calculated number of person-years of life experience given in Table 8–9. This provides the calculated number of live births per 1000 person-years for the schizophrenic persons. The live birth rates for the unaffected sisters and brothers of the schizophrenic persons are included for comparison and all are shown in Table 8–10.

It can be seen in Table 8–10 that the schizophrenic females were more fertile than their unaffected sisters only in the 20–24 year age group and then only in the period from "onset to first hospital admission." The point of interest, however, is that the schizophrenic females in the period from "onset to first hospital admission" had significantly higher fertility than in either the "before onset" or "after first hospital admission" periods.

It is easy to understand why the fertility in the period "after first hospital admission" is the lowest. Some of the person-years for

Table 8–8. *Number of Live Births to Schizophrenic Probands (Plus Their Schizophrenic Siblings, Children, Nieces and Nephews) by Sex and Age as Related to Age at Onset and at First Hospitalization.*

Age Interval	LIVE BIRTHS TO SCHIZOPHRENIC FEMALES				LIVE BIRTHS TO SCHIZOPHRENIC MALES			
	Before Onset	Onset to First Hospital Admission[1]	After First Hospital Admission	Total	Before Onset	Onset to First Hospital Admission[1]	After First Hospital Admission	Total
15–19	8	1		9				0
20–24	28	27	6	61	3	4	1	8
25–29	18	17	4	39	3	4	9	16
30–34	7	15	4	26	5	5	6	16
35–39	2	4	10	16	5	3	8	16
40–44	1	4	1	6	2	2		4
45–49			1	1				0
Totals	64	68	26	158	18	18	24	60

[1]Including the year of age at onset or at first hospitalization and one additional year before onset and one additional year after first hospitalization (or for those never hospitalized, the interval from one year before onset until death).

Table 8–9. *Person-Years of Life Experience for Schizophrenic Probands (Plus Their Schizophrenic Siblings, Children, Nieces and Nephews) by Sex and Age as Related to Age at Onset and at First Hospitalization.*

| | PERSON-YEARS FOR SCHIZOPHRENIC FEMALES | | | | PERSON-YEARS FOR SCHIZOPHRENIC MALES | | | |
Age Interval	*Before Onset*	*Onset to First Hospital Admission*[1]	*After First Hospital Admission*	*Total Group*	*Before Onset*	*Onset to First Hospital Admission*[1]	*After First Hospital Admission*	*Total Group*
15–19	357	68	5	430	269	57	9	335
20–24	259	115	51	425	188	74	63	325
25–29	184	113	115.5	412.5	111	83	116	310
30–34	121	123	146	390	65	59	178.5	302.5
35–39	94	93	178	365	48	46	183.5	277.5
40–44	55	90	192.5	337.5	40	35	157.5	232.5
45–49	25	69	218.5	312.5	29	28	138	195
50–54	16	52	209.5	277.5	24	16	122.5	162.5
55–59	11	42	179.5	232.5	10	24	91	125

[1]Including the year of age at onset or at first hospitalization and one additional year before onset and one additional year after first hospitalization (or for those never hospitalized, the interval from one year before onset until death).

Table 8–10. *Number of Live Births per 1000 Person-Years for Schizophrenic Probands (Plus Their Schizophrenic Siblings, Children, Nieces and Nephews) by Sex and Age as Related to Age at Onset and at First Hospitalization, and for Their Unaffected Siblings.*

| | NUMBER OF LIVE BIRTHS PER 1000 PERSON-YEARS | | | | | | | | | |
| | SCHIZOPHRENIC FEMALES | | | | UNAF-FECTED SISTERS | SCHIZOPHRENIC MALES | | | | UNAF-FECTED BROTHERS |
Age Interval	*Before Onset*	*Onset to First Hospital Admission*[1]	*After First Hospital Admission*	*Total Group*		*Before Onset*	*Onset to First Hospital Admission*[1]	*After First Hospital Admission*	*Total Group*	
15–19	22.4	14.7		20.9	30.5					11.0
20–24	108.1	234.8	117.6	143.5	165.5	16.0	54.1	15.9	24.6	40.0
25–29	97.8	150.4	34.6	94.5	206.0	27.0	48.2	77.6	51.6	146.0
30–34	57.9	122.0	27.4	66.7	156.5	76.9	84.7	33.6	52.9	125.0
35–39	21.3	43.0	56.2	43.8	69.2	104.2	65.2	43.6	57.7	83.4
40–44	18.2	44.4	5.2	17.8	42.1	50.0	57.1		17.2	54.6
45–49				4.6	3.2	2.7				34.1
50–54										9.5
55–59										7.7

[1]Including the year of age at onset or at first hospitalization and one additional year before onset and one additional year after first hospitalization (or for those never hospitalized, the interval from one year before onset until death).

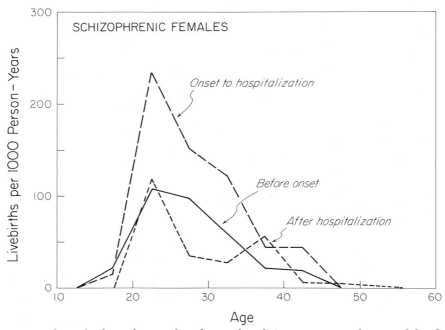

Figure 8–5.   Fertility of schizophrenic females with reference to time of onset of the disorder and to time of hospitalization.

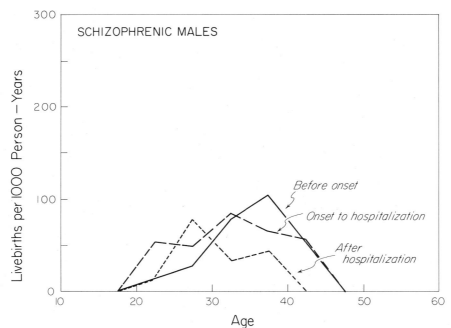

Figure 8–6.   Fertility of schizophrenic males with reference to time of onset of the disorder and to time of hospitalization.

these schizophrenics were spent in the hospital, which lowers fertility. It is not clear why the fertility rates for the schizophrenic females who reproduced before their onset were lower than for the schizophrenic females who reproduced between the time of onset and their first hospitalization. The following explanations suggest themselves:

1. The higher fertility is the result of some bias unique to our sample and has no biological significance.

2. Pregnancy precipitated the psychosis or brought a pre-existing psychosis to medical attention.

3. The onset of psychosis increased sexual activity until hospitalization reduced or terminated reproduction. This seems to us to be the most attractive speculation.

We can now compare the numbers of children produced by schizophrenic females and males with the calculated numbers obtained by applying the live birth rates in Table 8–10 to the distribution of person-years for each group in Table 8–9. The results are shown in Table 8–11 and confirm the observation that schizophrenic females are more fertile in the period from onset to first hospital admission than in either of the other time periods. The differences between the time periods for the females give $\chi^2 = 21.6$, d/f = 2 and P <0.001. The differences for males are in the same direction but are not of statistical significance, $\chi^2 = 3.7$, d/f = 2, P <0.20. If the females in the "onset to first admission period" are actually more fertile than the "before onset" females, we have identified a factor of

practical importance. Presumably hospitalization immediately after onset (diagnosis) would be doubly beneficial, not only for more intensive treatment but also to prevent reproduction at a time when prognosis is still uncertain.

A further analysis of the data showed that the higher schizophrenic female fertility in the period from onset to first hospital admission was restricted to those families in which the schizophrenic proband had a different original diagnosis (unclassified psychosis, melancholia, mania or manic-depressive) than the final one of schizophrenia as shown in Table 2–2. The lifetime fertility of the various groups is shown in Table 8–12, along with the mean numbers of children expected if their entire lives had shown the age-specific live birth rates for the three periods (with respect to onset and hospitalization). For comparison, the expected mean numbers of children based on the rates from unaffected siblings are shown.

This observation leads to the conclusion that schizophrenic females who show early affective signs may have a fertility potential different from that shown by other schizophrenic females (see Stevens, 1969). When we look at the risks for schizophrenia among their children, however, the two groups are alike. (For this comparison the children of the schizophrenic daughters and nieces must be excluded since many were too young to have developed schizophrenia). The schizophrenic females in Group A (probands with original diagnosis

Table 8–11. *Observed and Expected Numbers of Live Births to Schizophrenic Probands (Plus Their Schizophrenic Siblings, Children, Nieces and Nephews) Related to Three Reproductive Periods.*

| Reproductive Period | NUMBER OF LIVE BIRTHS TO SCHIZOPHRENICS | | | |
| | *Schizophrenic Females* | | *Schizophrenic Males* | |
	Observed No.	*Expected*[2] No.	*Observed* No.	*Expected*[2] No.
Before onset of schizophrenia	64	75.3	18	17.2
Onset to first hospitalization[1]	68	42.7	18	12.5
After first hospital admission	26	40.0	24	30.3
Totals	158	158.0	60	60.0

[1] Including the year of age at onset or at first hospitalization and one additional year before onset and one additional year after first hospitalization (or for those never hospitalized, the interval from one year before onset until death).

[2] Calculated by applying the live birth rates for each subgroup (from Table 8–10) to the distribution of person-years for the total groups of schizophrenic females and males (from Table 8–9).

Table 8–12. *Observed and Expected Mean Numbers of Liveborn Children for Schizophrenic Males and Females.*

	MEAN NUMBER OF LIVEBORN CHILDREN			
	Schizophrenic Females[1]			*Schizophrenic Males* (N = 67)
	Group A (N = 37)	*Group B* (N = 49)	*A + B* (N = 86)	
Observed mean numbers	1.53	2.06	1.84	0.90
Expected mean numbers[2] if entire life had shown age-specific live birth rates from:				
I. Period before onset	1.57	1.47	1.54	1.16
II. Period from onset to first hospitalization[3]	1.72	3.03	2.87	1.34
I plus II combined	(1.66)	(2.26)	(2.08)	(1.20)
III. Period after first hospitalization	0.78	1.47	1.15	0.77
IV. Unaffected siblings			3.14	2.16

[1] Group A females are from those families in which the proband was originally diagnosed as schizophrenic. Group B females are from those families in which the proband originally had an affective diagnosis but was classified as schizophrenic upon diagnosis review.

[2] Calculated by applying the age specific rates from the respective sub-groups in Table 8–10 to the distribution of total person-years from Table 8–9. (The data for group A and B females separately are based on unpublished tabulations.)

[3] Including the year of age of onset or at first hospitalization and one additional year before onset and one additional year after hospitalization (or for those never hospitalized, the interval from one year before onset until death).

of schizophrenia) had 44 children surviving to age 15 of whom 10 (22.7 per cent) became schizophrenic, while the schizophrenic females in Group B had 70 children surviving to age 15 of whom 14 (20.0 per cent) became schizophrenic. This contrast between fertility and risk of schizophrenia among children suggests that differences in phenotype (fertility) can be seen between two groups with similar genetic constitution (as seen in risk to children).

ASSORTATIVE MARRIAGES

Excellent data concerning the possibility of assortative marriage of psychotics are those of Erlenmeyer-Kimling and Paradowski (1966). They reported 2706 schizophrenic index cases of whom 26, or about 1 per cent, were known to have married another schizophrenic. This would be the expectation on chance alone and is evidence against assortative marriage as being of significance for schizophrenia. Rosenthal (1970) pointed out that with a 1 per cent frequency of schizophrenia, we could expect that 1 in 10,000 marriages in the whole

population should be between two schizophrenics. However, we have no data which would permit us to test his observation.

Stevens (1969) found that 11 of 440 (2.5 per cent) married schizophrenic women had husbands who were also mentally ill, while 4.9 per cent of the 386 married women with affective disorders had a mentally ill husband. These figures were based solely on cases in which there was very definite evidence of mental disorder in the husband and do not include unstable and peculiar personalities.

Thus there is no evidence of extensive assortative marriage between psychotic persons. This is contrary to the situation for mental retardation where assortative marriage is of great importance (see Reed and Reed, 1965; also Garrison, Anderson and Reed, 1968). Our data, given in Table 8–13, similarly are negative as far as assortative marriages between psychotic persons are concerned. The most obvious aspect of Table 8–13 is that only 9 husbands or wives out of 381, or 2.4 per cent, had any kind of functional psychosis. In view of an expectation of 2.5 per cent schizophrenia in the general population, we see no evidence of positive assortative mating between psychotic persons.

When we turn to column 2 of Table 8–13 we see high percentages of other mental disorders in the spouses of our schizophrenic probands and their schizophrenic siblings. We usually expect to find about twice as many persons in the category of other mental disorders as in the psychotic group. In the table, we see at the bottom that 28.4 per cent of the spouses had some other mental disorder compared with 4.1 per cent who had a psychosis, or seven times as many instead of twice as many. Looking again at the bottom two lines of the table, we see that not only are there seven times more other mental disorders than psychoses in the spouses but a second very important comparison is also shown, as there were 28.4 per cent of the spouses of the schizophrenics with other mental disorder, while only 13.8 per cent of the spouses of the *unaffected* siblings had some other

mental disorder. This last comparison is highly statistically significant ($\chi^2 = 7.8$, $p = <0.01$) and is evidence that psychotic persons marry persons with other mental disorder more often than expected by chance. That is, there is positive assortative marriage between persons with schizophrenia and persons with other mental disorder (though not with a psychosis). Even the spouses of the unaffected siblings had a high percentage (13.8) of other mental disorder, compared with our usual control figures.

The finding that psychotic persons tend to marry persons with other mental disorder more often than expected by chance has not been reported before. Presumably the more frequent than chance marriages of these types of affected persons indicate some similarities in their behavioral characteristics that attract them to each other.

Planansky and Johnson (1967) found that pre-schizophrenic men had a cluster of passive characteristics which seemed to be

Table 8–13. *Assortative Marriages (Mental Health of Spouses of Schizophrenic Probands and of Their Schizophrenic Siblings).*

	MENTAL HEALTH OF WIVES OR HUSBANDS			
	1. Psychosis No. (Per Cent)	2. Other Mental Disorder No. (Per Cent)	(Cols. 1 and 2) Psychosis and Other Disorders No. (Per Cent)	Total (incl. Unaffected)
Wives of:				
1. Schizophrenic males (probands plus brothers)	2(14.3)	2(14.3)	4(28.6)	14
2. Brothers with affective or unspecified psychosis	0	3(50.0)	3(50.0)	6
3. Brothers with other mental disorders	1(2.4)	7(16.7)	8(19.1)	42
4. Unaffected brothers	2(2.0)	10(9.8)	12(11.8)	102
5. *Subtotals*	5(3.0)	22(13.4)	27(16.4)	164
Husbands of:				
6. Schizophrenic females (probands plus sisters)	1(1.7)	19(31.7)	20(33.4)	60
7. Sisters with affective or unspecified psychosis	0	3(21.4)	3(21.4)	14
8. Sisters with other mental disorders	2(4.1)	12(24.5)	14(28.6)	49
9. Unaffected sisters	1(1.1)	17(18.1)	18(19.2)	94
10. *Sub-totals*	4(1.8)	51(23.5)	55(25.3)	217
Spouses of schizophrenic (lines 1 and 6)	3(4.1)	21(28.4)	24(32.5)	74
Spouses of unaffected siblings (lines 4 and 9)	3(1.5)	27(13.8)	30(15.3)	196

preferentially attractive to some women but not others. The women who were attracted to the schizophrenic patients were different from other women but there was no information as to whether they had some other mental disorder more often than might be expected on a chance basis.

THE OTHER MENTAL DISORDERS

The data in this chapter have been mostly related to schizophrenic probands and their relatives. We have fewer probands with affective disorders and do not wish to make comparable tables for them because the sample sizes become too small. Furthermore, the data for the affective probands and their relatives appear to be similar to those for the schizophrenics and would therefore be redundant. However, because of the relationship of the other mental disorders to the psychoses, whatever it may be, it seems worthwhile to present a table which gives a treatment of the data similar to that in Table 8–3. Therefore we have arranged the data as shown in Table 8–14.

We see in the first line of the table that both the sisters and the brothers (of the schizophrenic probands) who have some other mental disorder were less likely to reproduce than were their unaffected siblings. The difference was statistically significant ($\chi^2 = 4.1$, p <0.05) only for the sisters and not for the brothers. The proportion of unaffected sisters who reproduced (0.83) is different from the proportion of unaffected brothers who reproduced (0.63) as $\chi^2 = 10.1$, p$=<0.01$. Presumably this difference is either the result of some bias in ascertainment or just a random fluctuation.

Three conclusions may be drawn from the data in Table 8–14. The first is that women with other mental disorder do almost as poorly in reproduction, when compared with their unaffected sisters, as do the schizophrenic women. The second conclusion is that the risk for a psychosis and for other mental disorder seems to be higher in the offspring of mothers with other mental disorder than in the offspring of fathers with other mental disorder. This agrees with the difference in risks for the offspring with psychotic mothers compared with psychotic fathers. Finally, the combined risks for psychosis and other mental disorder, lines 5 and 6, for the offspring of affected mothers,

Table 8–14. *Combined Effect of Reproductive Rate and Risk of Psychosis in the Offspring of Persons with an "Other Mental Disorder" (Only Those from the Kinships with a Schizophrenic Proband).*

Variable	SISTERS Other Mental Disorder	Unaffected	BROTHERS Other Mental Disorder	Unaffected
1. Proportion ever reproducing	0.68	0.83	0.60	0.63
2. Liveborn children per reproducing individual	3.53	3.86	4.00	3.63
3. Proportion of liveborn surviving to age 15	0.91	0.90	0.89	0.88
4. Net number of surviving children per individual ($1 \times 2 \times 3$)	2.18	2.88	2.14	2.01
5. Risk of psychosis per child	0.06	0.02	0.04	0.04
6. Risk of other mental disorder per child	0.21	0.12	0.14	0.10
7. Net number of psychotic children per person (4×5)	0.13	0.06	0.09	0.08
8. Net number of other mental disorder offspring (4×6)	0.46	0.35	0.30	0.20
9. Net number of children, without any mental disorder	1.59	2.47	1.75	1.73

compared with those from their unaffected sisters, are clearly higher ($\chi^2 = 9.1$, p = <0.01).

SUMMARY

The topic of the fertility of people with functional psychoses and with other mental disorders is of considerable interest in regard to population dynamics. Who are the parents of the psychotic persons inside and outside our hospitals? Are the children of psychotic parents as likely to survive to age 15 as the children of non-psychotic parents? There are numerous questions like these for which we have at least partial answers. Some of the important items are the following:

1. Only 64 per cent of the schizophrenic women and 27 per cent of schizophrenic men age 15 or older ever reproduce. The schizophrenic person is at a sharp reproductive disadvantage in comparison with unaffected persons. The schizophrenic male is at a much greater reproductive disadvantage than the schizophrenic female. The advent of tranquilizers has reduced this disadvantage considerably for both sexes.

2. It can be seen in Table 8–3 that only 79 per cent of the children born to schizophrenic mothers survived to age 15. This is compared with the 90 per cent survival of the children of the unaffected sisters. The difference is statistically highly significant, $\chi^2 = 9.5$, p = <0.01. We do not have any evidence as to what fates befell the children who died young but perhaps their deaths resulted from inadequate care due to the mental illness of the mother.

3. The combined effect of lowered reproduction of the schizophrenic person and the production of psychotic offspring reduces the net number of normal offspring of the schizophrenic individual. Thus the average number of unaffected offspring (without a psychosis or other mental disorder) from schizophrenic females was only 0.80 and from schizophrenic males 0.59. This is well below the 1.00 offspring necessary to replace the schizophrenic person and provides no replacement for the spouse. The conventional estimate is that a person should have 2.2 children in order to replace himself and his spouse in the next generation. Obviously, our psychotic persons do not approach this minimum.

The failure of the schizophrenic person to be replaced in the next generation by the minimal number of offspring indicates a continuing loss of genes related to the disorder. However, the lost genes are probably replaced from other sources. Furthermore, the use of tranquilizers and other therapeutic treatments which reduce the disadvantage in reproduction of the patient should result in some increase in the frequency of the genes for schizophrenia.

4. A population dynamics model for schizophrenics suggests that 15.3 per cent of them should have a schizophrenic mother and 4.5 per cent a schizophrenic father, while the remaining 80.2 per cent of the schizophrenics should have two non-schizophrenic parents. Direct observations of the 770 nieces and nephews of our study showed that 24.1 per cent of those with schizophrenia also had a schizophrenic parent. This is higher than the 19.8 per cent predicted by the model but the excess depends upon the fact that all the nieces and nephews had a schizophrenic aunt or uncle also, that is, the proband.

A similar model was constructed for the data on mental retardation (Reed and Reed, 1965) with the calculated value of retarded children having a retarded mother being 12 per cent and those with a retarded father being 5 per cent. This total of 17.0 per cent of retarded children expected to have one retarded parent is of the same magnitude as the 19.8 per cent of the schizophrenic persons expected to have a schizophrenic parent. Is this similarity between the 17.0 per cent and 19.8 per cent only coincidence or is it to some extent a consequence of the population dynamics of such heterogeneous groups of defects with important genetic and environmental components?

The interesting implication of the model building exercise is that if all schizophrenics in one generation failed to reproduce we would expect just under 20 per cent fewer schizophrenics in the next generation. If all the mentally retarded of one generation failed to reproduce we could expect a reduction of about 16 per cent in the number of retardates in the following generation.

5. We found that one group of females who had their diagnoses changed from an affective disorder to schizophrenia by the review board were more fertile than those with an unchanged diagnosis of schizophrenia. The females with a final diagnosis of schizophrenia were more fertile in the period between the onset of their disease and first hospitalization than either before onset or in the period after first hospitalization. One possibility is that onset of psychoses increased sexual activity until first hospitalization reduced or terminated reproduction.

6. No strong evidence for the assortative marriage of functional psychotics was obtained. However, the spouses of the schizophrenic persons did have some other mental disorder in 28.4 per cent of the cases, which is a much higher frequency than expected by chance. Our control group had only 4.1 per cent of its members in the category of other mental disorders. The other mental disorders as a group seem to be related to the functional psychoses in some way. This, then, is convincing evidence of assortative marriage between persons with a psychosis and some other mental disorder.

7. Mothers with some other mental disorder produce more offspring with a psychosis (0.13 psychotic children per person) than do their unaffected sisters (0.06 psychotic children per person). The differences are in the same direction for the fathers with some other mental disorder compared with their unaffected brothers. This is further evidence of some relationship between the etiology of the psychoses and that of the group of other mental disorders.

CHAPTER NINE

ATTEMPTS TO EVALUATE THE ROLE OF GENETICS IN MENTAL HEALTH

The reason for selecting such a broad title for this chapter is partly to emphasize that the problems in understanding the genetics of the psychoses extend to most mental traits and are basic to the degree of mental health every person possesses. The literature review at the beginning of this book was concerned with family study attempts to evaluate the role of genetics in the etiology of the psychoses. The reader may request the evidence which leads one to expect genetics to be involved in the development of any psychoses. Therefore, a few observations may be helpful at this point.

1. There isn't any reason why "mental" traits should be any different from "physical" traits as far as the relative effects of genetic and environmental factors are concerned. Studies of persons deficient for chromosome segments or with an extra chromosome demonstrate clearly the necessity for a normal chromosome complement if a normal person, both mentally and physically, is to eventuate.

2. The adoptive placement of the children produced by psychotic mothers did not prevent the appearance of about the same percentage (16 per cent) of psychosis in these children as would have occurred if they had remained with their psychotic mother. Thus the important factors must have been present around or before the time of birth. Genetics presents a strong claim for consideration when a trait or the precursors of it are present at birth. This does *not* mean that all congenital traits have a strong genetic basis but it has shifted the consensus in that direction for the psychoses.

3. Numerous mental traits are known which have simple genetic types of inheritance, an excellent example of this being the Mendelian dominant type of porphyria where the metabolic error in porphyrin metabolism is correlated with, and in some way causes, mental derangement.

4. The substantially greater concordance of identical twins for psychotic disorders, when compared with fraternal twins, is favorable to a genetic basis for the psychoses.

5. The incidence of psychosis in the relatives of patients is inversely related to the degree of relationship. The heritabilities (the proportion of the variance due to genetics) seem to be about the same for the different degrees of blood relationship. These findings agree with the expectations based on an important genetic component in the etiology of the psychoses.

There is no unequivocal proof that genetics has an important role in the development of the "functional" psychoses. The ultimate answer awaits us, though the mass of evidence briefly mentioned above justifies the expectation that an important genetic component will be elucidated more precisely. The difficulty in making an evaluation of genetic and environmental factors for the psychoses is that, while environmental factors are clearly of great importance as demonstrated by the large *discordance* of identical twins, they also remain to be described. The environmental factors are numerous and subtle in their effects; there is little known as to how any of them contribute to the onset of mental disorder.

One of the most frequently invoked environmental factors is social class. Obviously, social class is not a single environmental factor but is instead a conglomeration of them. However, a great deal of argument has ensued as to the relationship between social class and the etiology of mental disorders and our research contributes something to this argument. Let us survey the social class problem.

SOCIAL CLASS AND THE PSYCHOSES

One of the major debates in the mental health area centers on the issue of a social class relationship to the psychoses. The question is whether the excess of psychosis in the bottom social class is the effect of the deleterious conditions present there or whether persons who develop a psychosis while members of higher social classes migrate down to the bottom social class and thus increase the frequency of mental illness in it.

Among the important studies which imply that the mentally ill in the bottom social class are the product of their adversity is the Yale project of Hollingshead and Redlich (1958) followed by Myers and Roberts (1959). Among studies which indicate migration of the psychotic persons into the bottom social class concomitant with the development of their disorders is that of Lindelius and Kay (1970). They found that the occupational groups of the fathers of the probands did not differ from those in the general population. A gross defect in many of the studies of social class relationship to the psychoses results from the lack of satisfactory information about the social class of the parents of the patients. Obviously a mentally ill person will be unemployed during his illness, if it is severe enough to be incapacitating. When he is unemployed his social class rating drops automatically by definition. Consequently, some downward drift is inevitable for all of the severely ill if the illness persists. Not all of the mentally ill are unemployed at the time any study is made so there is always going to be considerable uncontrolled variation in data concerned with the social class–psychosis problem.

The interesting study of Turner and Wagonfeld (1967) showed that more schiz-ophrenics than normals have been downwardly mobile. Furthermore, this downward mobility did not come about because of a loss of occupational position that had once been achieved but reflected their failure ever to have achieved as high an occupational level as did most men of their social class origins. Schizophrenics born in the bottom social class cannot drift any further downward. The hospitalized patient will be unemployed and presumably functioned poorly before admission or he would not have needed help; it seems logically impossible for the severely ill to avoid a drop in social class unless already a member of the bottom class. But what is the situation for the mentally impaired who have not been hospitalized?

There are the astonishing findings of the Leightons (1963) in Nova Scotia that about one-third of the entire population suffered significant psychiatric impairment and those of Srole et al. (1962) which showed that about one-quarter of the residents of a section of Manhattan Island were mentally impaired. These residents were not all schizophrenic by any means and their mental problems were such that sharp diagnoses and taxonomic distinctions could not be made in many cases. The implication we obtain from these studies is that the severely mentally ill are the members at one end of a relatively normal curve of mental health. Does this curve of mental health rest upon multiple social and genetic factors just as does the normal curve of intelligence?

Social class, in the literal sense, has nothing to do with mental illness but rather some of the components of social class are involved and these specific components have not yet been identified. Furthermore, the components do not affect all members of a particular family in equal measure as evidenced by the discordances in mental illness shown by the two members of a pair of identical twins. The high frequency of mental disorders in the offspring of schizophrenic mothers, where the offspring have been placed for adoption, adds to the mystery of how social class is related to the etiology of schizophrenia. Clausen (1968) does not think that schizophrenia is *directly* engendered by a person being at the bottom of the heap. The reviews by Clausen (1968) and by Kohn (1968) should be studied by everyone who is interested in the relationship of social class to the frequency of schizophrenia.

We have used the Hollingshead and Redlich (1958) system for scoring social class in our project. Social class I is the professional group with substantial income and top social status. Class V lacks money, skills, status, education and almost everything else that is enjoyed by the majority of the normal population. The other classes are gradations between I and V, with the clearest distinction being between classes IV and V. It is possible to combine classes I through IV for comparison with class V because of the distinction between the bottom two classes. The difficulties of assigning women to particular social classes should be obvious and we found this to be so difficult that only males were included in our analyses. Only two components of the system were used, educational attainment and occupation, because of the difficulty involved in making decisions about items such as community status. It was not too difficult, however, to decide whether a male was in class V, or in some class above V in most cases. It must be remembered throughout that the use of the Hollingshead and Redlich system is statistically awkward because the lower the social class observed, the higher the numerical rating (lowest social class is the highest number, V).

The most useful group of persons for our consideration of social class is the group in the fourth generation, composed of the sons and nephews of the original probands. It can be seen that in Table 9–1 there were only 27 psychotic sons and nephews (out of 40) for whom social class was known. Scoring was possible for higher percentages of the males with other mental disorders and for the unaffected.

We found a very large difference between the social class distribution of the psychotic sons and nephews and the *unaffected* sons and nephews. Utilizing the material in Table 9–1, we have the following selected segment of the data which gives a χ^2 of 55.6 with one degree of freedom, p = <0.0001.

	Psychotic Sons and Nephews	Unaffected Sons and Nephews	Total (Without the Other Mental Disorders)
Social Class			
I through IV	6	283	289
V	21	50	71

A similar sub-section of data for the other mental disorders as compared with their unaffected siblings generated a χ^2 of only 4.8 and is therefore of little interest.

The very large and statistically highly significant χ^2 of 55.6, p = < 0.0001 seems to indicate unequivocally that the psychotic sons and nephews had a distinctly lower social class rating than did their unaffected siblings. The psychotic sons and nephews were also rated lower than their siblings with other mental disorders, the latter group averaging nearer to the unaffected siblings than to the psychotics, which seems reasonable.

It should be of interest to see what social class ratings were given to the control

Table 9–1. *Social Class of the Sons and Nephews According to Their Mental Health (Excluding the Four "Loaded" Families).*

Social Class of Sons and Nephews	MENTAL HEALTH OF SONS AND NEPHEWS			
	Psychosis No. (Per Cent)	Other Disorders No. (Per Cent)	Unaffected No. (Per Cent)	Total
I	0	3(4.1)	25(5.7)	28(5.1)
II	0	1(1.4)	35(8.0)	36(6.5)
III	1(2.5)	10(13.7)	96(21.9)	107(19.4)
IV	5(12.5)	27(37.0)	127(29.0)	159(28.9)
V	21(52.5)	15(20.5)	50(11.4)	86(15.6)
Not stated	13(32.5)	17(23.3)	105(24.0)	135(24.5)
Total	40(100.0)	73(100.0)	438(100.0)	551(100.0)
Mean social class (excluding "not stated")	4.74 ± 0.10	3.89 ± 0.13	3.43 ± 0.06	3.57 ± 0.05

Table 9-2. *Social Class and Mental Health of the Control Males (Excluding the Four "Loaded" Families).*

Social Class of Controls	MENTAL HEALTH OF CONTROL MALES			
	Psychotic No. (Per Cent)	*Other Disorders* No. (Per Cent)	*Unaffected* No. (Per Cent)	*Total* No. (Per Cent)
I	0	1(3.0)	7(1.5)	8(1.6)
II	1(12.5)	2(6.1)	26(5.5)	29(5.6)
III	1(12.5)	5(15.2)	60(12.6)	66(12.8)
IV	2(25.0)	11(33.3)	158(33.3)	171(33.1)
V	2(25.0)	12(36.4)	72(15.2)	86(16.7)
Not stated	2(25.0)	2(6.1)	152(32.0)	156(30.2)
Total	8(100.0)	33(100.1)	475(100.1)	516(100.0)
Mean social class (excluding "not stated")	3.83 ± 0.48	4.00 ± 0.19	3.81 ± 0.05	3.83 ± 0.05

males. These are all genetically unrelated to the psychotic probands and entered our pedigrees as men who married nieces of our psychotic probands. The ratings for the control population (presented in Table 9–2) are difficult to interpret because of the small sample sizes of the psychotic and other mental disorder groups. However, as was the case for Table 9–1, the control males with psychoses and other mental disorders had worse social class ratings than their unaffected siblings. The differences between the different groups of control males are small and not statistically significant; furthermore, there were only six males with a psychosis for whom the social class was known in the whole control sample of males.

We cannot conclude that the much lower social class rating (4.74 ± 0.10) of our psychotic sons and nephews is *entirely* the result of their psychoses. It is quite likely that their low social class is "transmitted" from their parents to some extent. A rearrangement of the 551 sons and nephews according to the mental health of their parents gives the results shown in Table 9–3. In the first two columns of the table, where a parent had a psychosis or other mental disorder, the social class rating of the sons and nephews is distinctly lower than if the parents were both unaffected. The difference is statistically highly significant (difference $= 0.58 \pm 0.10$, p $= <0.001$). It is clear that when parents have mental problems the social class rating of their children is lowered. If some of their children in turn have mental problems, we can expect the social class rating to be lowered even more for the psychotic offspring.

Table 9-3. *Social Class of the Sons and Nephews According to the Mental Health of Their Parents (Excluding Four "Loaded" Families).*

Social Class of Sons and Nephews	*Parent(s) Psychotic* No. (Per cent)	*Parent(s) with Other Disorder* No. (Per Cent)	*Parents Unaffected* No. (Per Cent)	*Total* No. (Per Cent)
I	2(1.5)	5(3.0)	21(8.4)	28(5.1)
II	9(6.7)	5(3.0)	22(8.8)	36(6.5)
III	20(14.8)	30(18.2)	57(22.7)	107(19.4)
IV	40(29.6)	54(32.7)	65(25.9)	159(28.9)
V	27(20.0)	35(21.2)	24(9.6)	86(15.6)
Not stated	37(27.4)	36(21.8)	62(24.7)	135(24.5)
Total	135(100.0)	165(99.9)	251(100.1)	551(100.0)
Mean social class (excluding "not stated")	3.83 ± 0.10	3.84 ± 0.09	3.26 ± 0.08	3.57 ± 0.05

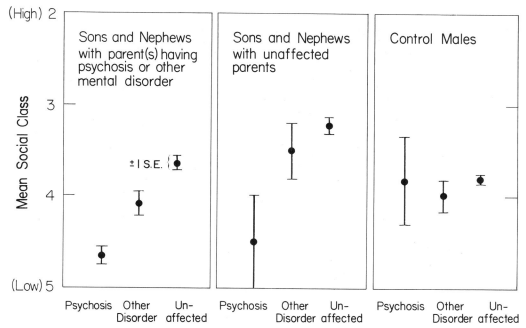

Figure 9–1.   Mean social class of sons and nephews by their own mental health and mental health of their parents, compared with control data.

The expectation that the psychotic sons and nephews of psychotic parents will have the lowest social class ratings is realized and is shown in Table 9–4 and graphically in Figure 9–1, which combines the data in Tables 9–2 and 9–4. It is clear from Table 9–4 and Figure 9–1 that both the illness of the son or nephew and the illness of the parent contribute significantly to lowering the social class accorded to the psychotic son or nephew. Can we evaluate, very approximately, the drop in social class due to the mental problem in the patient compared with that resulting from having a parent with a mental problem?

It is apparent from Table 9–4 that only

Table 9–4.   *Social Class and Mental Health of the Sons and Nephews (Excluding Four "Loaded" Families) According to the Mental Health of Their Parents.*

Social Class of Sons and Nephews	ONE OR BOTH PARENTS WITH PSYCHOSIS OR OTHER MENTAL DISORDER			BOTH PARENTS UNAFFECTED		
	Sons and Nephews with Psychosis No. (Per Cent)	*Sons and Nephews with Other Disorder No. (Per Cent)*	*Unaffected Sons and Nephews No. (Per Cent)*	*Sons and Nephews with Psychosis No. (Per Cent)*	*Sons and Nephews with Other Disorder No. (Per Cent)*	*Unaffected Sons and Nephews No. (Per Cent)*
I	0	0	7(3.3)	0	3(12.5)	18(8.0)
II	0	1(2.0)	13(6.1)	0	0	22(9.8)
III	1(2.7)	7(14.3)	42(19.6)	0	3(12.5)	54(24.1)
IV	4(10.8)	18(36.7)	72(33.6)	1(33.3)	9(37.5)	55(24.6)
V	20(54.1)	12(24.5)	30(14.0)	1(33.3)	3(12.5)	20(8.9)
Not stated	12(32.4)	11(22.4)	50(23.4)	1(33.3)	6(25.0)	55(24.6)
Total	37(100.0)	49(99.9)	214(100.0)	3(99.9)	24(100.0)	224(100.0)
Mean social class (excluding "not stated")	4.76 ± 0.10	4.08 ± 0.13	3.64 ± 0.08	4.50 ± 0.50	3.50 ± 0.31	3.22 ± 0.09

two of the psychotic sons and nephews with known social class had both parents unaffected. This weak point, due to small sample size, forces us to combine the sons and nephews having a psychosis with those having other mental disorders to obtain more stable sample sizes. When this was done we obtained an estimate of the drop of 13 per cent in social class ratings due to mental problems in the parents, and a drop of 22 per cent resulting from psychosis or other mental disorders in the sons and nephews themselves. The combination of the index changes due to mental problems both in the parents and in the sons and nephews adds up to 35 per cent, which is also obtained separately when we take the group where parents and offspring were both psychotic and compare them with the social class average for unaffected parents and unaffected sons and nephews. These results are shown in Table 9–5.

One answer we obtain from Table 9–5 is that the drop in social class is almost twice as great if the person himself is psychotic, compared with the drop (increased rating index) caused if the parent is psychotic. However, it is extremely important to point out that the psychotic parent lowers the social class of the *unaffected* offspring by 13 per cent; this leads to a large total amount of change (downward) of social class because there are so many unaffected offspring of the psychotic parent to be af-fected, in addition to the psychotic offspring.

Our data seem to demonstrate unequivocally that a person's psychosis lowers his social class, which supports the "drift" theory accounting for the excess of psychotics in the bottom social class. Apparently this accounts for about two-thirds of the total effect. The lower social class of the psychotic parent into which the psychotic offspring was born would seem to account for the remaining third of the social class depression related to a psychosis. These estimates from our data must be used by others with caution because, as is always the case with the psychoses, the data are less precise than the theories invoked to explain what the data mean. Nonetheless, we do seem to have learned that the excess of psychosis in the bottom social class is the result of "drift" to a greater degree than it is the effect of the bottom social class environment in producing psychoses.

The adoption studies, which were reviewed earlier, indicated rather precisely that the maternal effect on the etiology of schizophrenia was mostly perinatal. There was little opportunity left for social class effects on the children after the perinatal period, other than as the "trivial" precipitating factors which allow the schizophrenic predisposition to become expressed in a severe enough form to result in medical or social treatment of the person.

Table 9–5. *Effects of the Mental Health of Parents Upon Social Class of Sons and Nephews.*[*]

PARENTS	SONS AND NEPHEWS	MEAN SOCIAL CLASS	CHANGE IN MEAN SOCIAL CLASS
Both unaffected	Unaffected	3.22 ± 0.09	13%
One or both with psychosis or other mental disorder	Unaffected	3.64 ± 0.08	
All parents (affected and unaffected)	Unaffected	3.43 ± 0.05	22%
All parents	Psychosis or other mental disorder	4.17 ± 0.11	
Both unaffected	Unaffected	3.22 ± 0.09	35%
One or both with psychosis or other mental disorder	Psychosis or other mental disorder	4.35 ± 0.10	
One or both with psychosis or other mental disorder	Unaffected	3.64 ± 0.08	20%
One or both with psychosis or other mental disorder	Psychosis or other mental disorder	4.35 ± 0.10	

[*]Based on rearrangements of data from Table 9–4.

The demonstration that a psychosis may lower a person's social class below that of his parents is very important and we hope that it will be tested by other research groups. It seems reasonable to assume that the psychotic person fails to achieve the higher social class of his parents and siblings because of personality and intellectual deficiencies present in the earliest years that become more damaging with the passing of time.

GENETIC TESTS FOR THE PSYCHOSES

We have finally come to the section of the book where our intuitions and skills as professional geneticists are challenged to the fullest. Everyone would agree wholeheartedly that there could hardly be a more difficult subject than that of the genetics of the psychoses. It would seem self-evident that one of the major problems is that of genetic heterogeneity for the different psychoses. The earliest geneticists could have been pardoned for thinking that there was only one gene for "insanity" but all of the work in the whole discipline of genetics since the rediscovery of Mendelism has revealed an increased heterogeneity and complexity of the genetics for every trait which has been examined carefully.

Let us try to make some estimates as to the magnitude of the heterogeneity involved with the psychoses in general. One of our major problems will be, of course, the confusion always present because of diagnostic differences that may be large enough to obscure the heterogeneity which must be present.

Heterogeneity for Overall Risk of a Psychosis (Unrelated to Diagnostic Difficulties)

It is evident that the Mendelian dominant gene for Huntington's chorea, which permits psychotic behavior in some of those who have it, is *not* present in the usual schizophrenic patient. However, it is conceivable that genes responsible for schizophrenia might exacerbate the psychotic behavior of the person with Huntington's chorea. There is no evidence whatever for this speculation, and we have never seen it

proposed elsewhere, but it is a possibility if there are large numbers of genes related to schizophrenia. That is, one can conceive of a set of genes which when present in one person permits the development of schizophrenia. Different members of this set of genes are probably scattered throughout the general population and perhaps everyone has a few of them present. There might be an interaction between the "normal" quota of schizophrenia genes available in the person and the dominant gene for Huntington's disease, resulting in psychotic behavior which would not be expressed otherwise. This digression is offered merely as a mind-opener to stimulate thoughts as to the probable complexity of genetic interactions which lead to mental disorders.

Those who accept any genetic basis for the psychoses, even an exceedingly weak one, probably would assume that there are genetic differences between classic schizophrenic and manic-depressive patients. Presumably there are genetic differences between unipolar and bipolar affective disorders even if these two should differ mainly in severity. Indeed, perhaps one of our greatest problems is that everyone is genetically different from everyone else, except of course for multiple births originating from one zygote. Consequently, there has to be genetic heterogeneity for any trait and especially for complicated ones such as the schizophrenias. What we would like to know now is how significant is the genetic heterogeneity for the psychoses. Are there techniques which would provide any insight into the extent and importance of the heterogeneity which we assume is present?

Isolated Probands

It is probable that the probands who received a diagnosis of schizophrenia were genetically different from those who were considered to have an affective disorder. If this was the case, it is possible that there would be a significantly different percentage of the schizophrenic probands who had no parent or full sibling with a psychosis compared with the percentage of affective disorder probands without a parent or sibling demonstrating a psychosis. In genetic studies one should always determine the percentage of probands who are "isolated" in the sense that they have no first degree relatives with the same trait as the probands. This percentage sets the upper limit of phenocopies which could be expected, though not all or perhaps any of the "isolated" probands would be phenocopies. Table 9–6 shows that the percentages of probands who had no psychosis among their parents or full siblings do not differ statistically for the three diagnostic types into which the 89 probands were divided.

Another way of testing the isolated probands is according to sex. We found that 37.5 per cent of the male probands had no parent or full sibling with a psychosis while 38.6 per cent of the female probands were similarly isolated. Thus, there is no clue obtained from the isolated probands of any heterogeneity affecting diagnosis or sex of the patients. In fact, we found no evidence of the presence of phenocopies for the psychoses. Phenocopies could exist but we could not demonstrate them with our statistical tests.

Consanguinity

One possible way of detecting genetic heterogeneity would be to find a specific type of psychosis present among the siblings produced by consanguineous parents. This would be difficult to demonstrate with our data as the diagnoses are too fluid for this purpose. While 7 of our probands were from consanguineous parents, only 6 of their 46 siblings (13 per cent) were psychotic. This sample size is too small to provide any significant information about genetic heterogeneity.

Distribution within Families

In the analyses which follow we have abided by a few concepts expected to provide consistency in the statistical treatments and to reduce sampling bias.

We will use the data from Generation IV as our test population; the persons in this generation are the children and the nieces and nephews of the probands. This permits complete ascertainment of the sample through the parents without any bias regarding the mental health of the members of Generation IV. The people in Generation IV have a high mean age which obviates the need for age corrections. The loaded families can be combined with the main body of data as they do not differ significantly in Generation IV from the remainder. We wished to test whether the risk for psychosis was essentially the same among the various families within a specific parental mating type, or whether there may have been a low risk in some families and a higher risk in the remaining families. For this purpose it is essential to tabulate the sibships by size of sibship and by number affected, as shown in Table 9–7.

In those sibships with neither parent affected the overall frequency of psychosis was 4.2 per cent (35 out of 836). Of the 252 sibships there were 223 with no one developing a psychosis. If the risk of psychosis were evenly distributed over all sibships of a given sibship size, the expected number of sibships with none psychotic would be the probability of remaining psychosis-free (.958) raised to the power of the sibship size and then multiplied by the number of sibships. For example, of the 49 sibships with size three, 43.1 would be expected to have

Table 9–6. *The Percentages of "Isolated" Probands When Divided into Three Diagnostic Groups.*

DIAGNOSIS OF PROBANDS	NUMBER OF PROBANDS	ISOLATED PROBANDS° Number	ISOLATED PROBANDS° Per Cent
Affective psychosis	16	5	31.2
Paranoid schizophrenia	46	18	39.1
Other schizophrenias	27	11	40.7
Totals	89	34	38.2

$\chi^2 = 0.4$, d.f. $= 2$, p $= >0.8$.
°The probands were isolated in that they had no parent or sibling with a psychosis. Their children were not included because of the fertility difference between male and female probands.

Table 9–7. *Distribution of Psychotic Persons within Sibships by Presence or Absence of Psychosis in Parents.*

| | NUMBER OF PSYCHOTIC PERSONS IN EACH SIBSHIP | | | | | | | | | | | |
| | NEITHER PARENT PSYCHOTIC[2] | | | | | ONE PARENT PSYCHOTIC[3] | | | | | | |
SIBSHIP SIZE[1]	None	One	Two	Three	Total	None	One	Two	Three	Four	Five	Total
One	55	2	—	—	57	11	7	—	—	—	—	18
Two	46	5	0	—	51	23	2	1	—	—	—	26
Three	45	3	1	0	49	13	8	2	0	—	—	23
Four	31	6	1	0	38	7	3	0	1	0	—	11
Five	16	3	1	0	20	4	1	0	0	0	0	5
Six	9	2	0	0	11	1	1	1	0	0	0	3
Seven	9	0	0	1	10	5	0	0	0	0	1	6
Eight	6	2	0	0	8	0	1	1	0	1	0	3
Nine	5	0	1	0	6	0	0	0	0	1	0	1
Ten	0	0	0	0	0	1	0	0	0	0	0	1
Eleven	0	0	0	0	0	0	1	0	0	0	0	1
Twelve	1	1	0	0	2	0	0	0	0	0	0	0
Totals												
Sibships	223	24	4	1	252	65	24	5	1	2	1	98
Siblings	708	100	21	7	836	195	77	22	4	17	7	322
Psychotic	—	24	8	3	35	—	24	10	3	8	5	50

[1] Excluding those under age 15 and those with mental health unknown.
[2] Nieces and nephews (of the probands) with neither parent psychotic.
[3] Children of the probands plus nieces and nephews with one parent psychotic.

none psychotic. When the expectations are summed over the entire distribution, there are 219.6 expected to have none psychotic as compared with 223 observed ($\chi^2 = 0.4$, d/f = 1, p > .50), thus providing no evidence for a significant proportion of "low risk" families.

Among sibships with one psychotic parent, the frequency of psychosis was 15.5 per cent (50 out of 322). Using .845 as the probability of remaining psychosis-free, the expected number of sibships with none psychotic is 59.6, as compared with 65 observed ($\chi^2 = 1.2$, d/f = 1, p > .20). Once again, there is no evidence for a significant proportion of low-risk families.

A second way of analyzing the data in Table 9–7 is to estimate the frequency of psychosis among siblings of a psychotic. The persons in Generation IV have been identified by a complete ascertainment procedure (through parents, without reference to the presence or absence of psychosis in the offspring). Thus it is appropriate to use the simple method of "discarding the recessive singletons" developed by Li and Mantel (1968). The numerator of our estimate is the total number psychotic (35) minus the number psychotic in sibships with only one affected (24). The denominator is the total number of siblings (836) minus those in sibships with none psychotic (708) and the number psychotic in sibships with only one affected (24). The estimated frequency of psychosis among siblings of a psychotic is thus:

$$\frac{35 - 24}{836 - 708 - 24} = \frac{11}{104} = 10.6\%$$

This method can be extended to estimate the risk of psychosis among siblings of two affected individuals. The results of this analysis of data in Table 9–7 are shown in Table 9–8 and in Figure 9–2. A third approach to the data uses the methods developed by Crittenden (1961) and Falconer (1965) to test the hypothesis of a multigenic basis for a trait.

Let us illustrate with the data for neither parent psychotic from Table 9–8. We have a base population rate of 4.2 per cent psychosis when neither parent was affected, and a frequency of 10.6 per cent among siblings of one psychotic person. Using these two rates and the tables from Falconer (1965), a heritability estimate of .45 ± .17 is obtained. Note that the base rate and the rate for sibs of affected were based on the same defined population. Most estimates of

Table 9–8. *Frequency of Psychosis within Sibships by Presence or Absence of Psychosis in Parents.*

TYPE OF ESTIMATE	NEITHER PARENT PSYCHOTIC[1]	ONE PARENT PSYCHOTIC[2]	NIECES AND NEPHEWS[3]
Overall frequency	35/836 = .042 ± .007	50/322 = .155 ± .020	60/1014 = .059 ± .007
Frequency among siblings of one affected	11/104 = .106 ± .039	26/103 = .252 ± .050	21/158 = .133 ± .034
Frequency among siblings of two affected[4]	3/20 = .150	16/40 = .400	7/35 = .200
Estimated risk for siblings of two affected (on multigenic model)	.172	.327	.204
Heritability	.45 ± .17	.45 ± .20	.45 ± .14

[1] Nieces and nephews (of the probands) with neither parent psychotic.
[2] Children of the probands plus nieces and nephews, with one parent psychotic.
[3] Nieces and nephews with neither or with one parent psychotic.
[4] The variance of this type of estimate has not been investigated.

heritability use two different population samples which may not be at all comparable in age distribution, diagnostic criteria or exhaustiveness of investigation. It appears reasonable to conclude that familial clustering accounts for 45 per cent of the variance for psychosis in this population. We cannot estimate from these data alone what part of the 45 per cent might result from nongenetic familial factors, but at least we have eliminated the environmental effect of having a psychotic parent by looking only at the sibships with neither parent psychotic. Note that the heritability estimate is significantly different from zero.

Morton (1967) pointed out that an estimate of heritability can exceed one, but a significant excess over one indicates major genes (genes with major phenotypic effect) or an important interfamily environmental variation. Our estimate of .45 obviously does not enter this range.

Finally, it is possible to use the heritability of .45 and the two frequencies of 4.2 per cent and 10.6 per cent to estimate the risk for siblings of two psychotic persons on the assumption of a multigenic basis for the condition (Morton, 1967). The predicted risk of 17.2 per cent is obviously close to the frequency of 15 per cent estimated from the data. The small sample size remaining, however, does not permit a conclusion. If the predicted risk had been significantly higher than the risk estimated from the data, such a finding could be considered evidence for a major gene effect. Once again, we fail to find such evidence.

There have been further refinements in the methods of study (Morton, Lee, Elston and Lew, 1970; Smith, 1971), but they do not appear to alter the basic interpretation above. In addition, it should be clear that we view heritability estimates as interesting but not sufficient to resolve the problems of genetic–environment interaction.

The second column in Table 9–8 shows the results for the sample of children, nieces and nephews with one parent psychotic. The heritability estimate turns out to be the same as for the preceding column, indicating that a fair amount of familial clustering

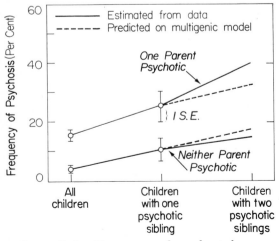

Figure 9–2. Frequency of psychosis by mental health of parents and of siblings.

remains even in this mating type. The increasing risk for siblings of one and of two psychotics would not be expected for simple dominant inheritance, even with reduced penetrance.

The distribution within families of *schizophrenia* rather than all psychoses is shown in Table 9–9. Among the 59 sibships with one schizophrenic parent there were 38 with no schizophrenic children as compared with 33.9 expected if the risk is equal for all such families ($\chi^2 = 1.2$, d/f = 1, p >0.20). There is no evidence for an excess of families with low risk for schizophrenia in the sub-sample with a schizophrenic parent.

Other estimates based upon these data are shown in Table 9–10. For purposes of comparison the frequency of *schizophrenia* is also shown for nieces and nephews with neither parent psychotic and for all nieces and nephews (excluding those with both parents psychotic, those under age 15 and those with mental health unknown). Our interpretation of these data is essentially the same as for Table 9–8. The heritabilities for schizophrenia alone were not significantly higher than those for the whole group of

psychoses. This could be interpreted as evidence for multigenic heredity for schizophrenia as well as the other psychoses.

It is possible to carry out a similar type of analysis for the "other mental disorders." In order to reduce the confounding effect of psychosis in parents, it appeared best to look only at the nieces and nephews with neither parent psychotic. The results are shown in the second column of Table 9–11, with the data for psychosis in the same sample presented for comparison in the first column.

The estimate of heritability for other mental disorders is significantly different from zero, indicating a significant familial clustering. The estimate is somewhat lower than for psychosis, however. When psychosis and the other mental disorders are considered jointly, as though all were manifestations of the same trait, the estimate of heritability is reduced further. This latter observation, however, is not a rigorous test of the hypothesis (Heston, 1970) that the other disorders are expressions of the same genetic background that leads to schizophrenia.

Within this sample of nieces and neph-

Table 9–9. *Distribution of Schizophrenic Persons within Sibships by Presence of Schizophrenia or other Psychotic Disorders in Parents.*

| | NUMBER OF SCHIZOPHRENIC PERSONS IN EACH SIBSHIP | | | | | | | | | |
| | ONE PARENT WITH AFFECTIVE DISORDER OR PSYCHOSIS NOS | | | ONE PARENT SCHIZOPHRENIC | | | | | | |
SIBSHIP SIZE	None	One	Total	None	One	Two	Three	Four	Five	Total
One	3	1	4	9	5					14
Two	9	1	10	14	2	—				16
Three	6	4	10	8	3	2	—			13
Four	4	1	5	3	2	1	—	—		6
Five	3	0	3	2	0	0	0	0	0	2
Six	1	0	1	0	1	1	0	0	0	2
Seven	4	0	4	1	0	0	0	0	1	2
Eight	1	0	1	0	1	0	0	1	0	2
Nine	0	0	0	0	0	0	1	0	0	1
Ten	1	0	1	0	0	0	0	0	0	0
Eleven	0	0	0	1	0	0	0	0	0	1
Totals										
Sibships	32	7	39	38	14	4	1	1	1	59
Siblings	122	19	141	101	40	16	9	8	7	181
Schizophrenic	—	7	7	—	14	8	3	4	5	34

[1] Excluding those under age 15 and those with mental health unknown.

[2] Children of the affective probands plus nieces and nephews with one parent having affective disorder or psychosis not otherwise specified.

[3] Children of the schizophrenic probands plus nieces and nephews with one schizophrenic parent.

Table 9–10. *Frequency of Schizophrenia within Sibships by Presence or Absence of Schizophrenia or Other Psychotic Disorders in Parents.*

TYPE OF ESTIMATE	NEITHER PARENT PSYCHOTIC[1]	ONE PARENT WITH AFFECTING DISORDER OR PSYCHOSIS NOS[2]	ONE PARENT SCHIZOPHRENIC	NIECES AND NEPHEWS[3]
Overall frequency	25/836 = .030 ± .006	7/141 = .050 ± .018	34/181 = .188 ± .029	45/1014 = .044 ± .006
Frequency among siblings of one schizophrenic	7/72 = .097 ± .036	none	20/66 = .303 ± .064	13/111 = .117 ± .039
Frequency among siblings of two schizophrenics[4]	3/10 = .300	none	12/32 = .375	7/19 = .368
Estimated risk for siblings of two schizophrenics (on multigenic model)	.170		.383	.190
Heritability	.51 ± .19		.51 ± .26	.49 ± .16

[1] Nieces and nephews (of the probands) with neither parent psychotic.
[2] Children of the probands plus nieces and nephews with parents as indicated.
[3] Nieces and nephews with neither or with one parent psychotic.
[4] The variance of this type of estimate has not been investigated.

ews with neither parent psychotic we can examine the effect of the breadth of diagnosis upon heritability estimates, as shown in Figure 9–3. The evidence is weak, since the estimates are not significantly different from each other. Nevertheless, there is a suggestion that familial clustering is highest when only the verified cases of schizophrenia are considered. A narrower limitation to paranoid schizophrenia or broader groupings lead to lower estimates.

Some comment on our view of "heritability" may be appropriate. This type of estimate can be a useful tool if its limitations are kept in mind. Only two items of data enter into the calculations—the frequency of the trait among specified relatives or probands, and the frequency in some comparison population. Usually the comparison data are taken from other studies involving a different age distribution of subjects, different intensity of investigation and different diagnostic criteria. The data sources may be disparate enough to bias the heritabilities seriously. For this reason, we have preferred to generate both items of data from the same sample as described above.

Table 9–11. *Frequency of Psychosis and Other Mental Disorders within Sibships Among Nieces and Nephews with Neither Parent Psychotic.*

Type of Estimate	TRAIT UNDER CONSIDERATION		
	Psychosis Only	*Other Mental Disorders Only*	*Psychosis and Other Mental Disorders Combined**
Overall frequency	35/836 = .042 ± .007	112/836 = .134 ± .012	147/836 = .176 ± .013
Frequency among siblings of one affected	11/104 = .106 ± .039	57/286 = .199 ± .029	81/350 = .231 ± .027
Frequency among siblings of two affected	3/20 = .150	23/99 = .232	37/136 = .272
Estimated risk for siblings of two affected (on multigenic basis)	.172	.256	.279
Hereditability	.45 ± .17	.33 ± .12	.27 ± .12

* In this column psychosis plus other mental disorders are treated as a single trait. The second line gives the frequency of either psychosis or other mental disorder among the siblings of each affected person with psychosis or other mental disorder.

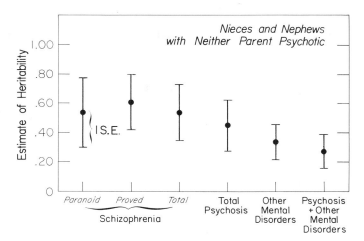

Figure 9–3. Estimates of heritability for diagnostic categories of varying breadth, among nieces and nephews with neither parent psychotic.

A more serious factor is that heritability calculations usually assume randomized environments. This restriction is appropriate for plant and animal breeding, but it is very difficult to collect data for human traits that will permit a separation of genetic and environmental components. This problem is the focus of considerable interest (Smith, 1970; Jinks and Fulker, 1970; Gottesman and Shields, 1972; and Smith et al., 1972). Meanwhile, we prefer to consider heritability estimates as crude measures of "familial clustering," rather than as adequate measures of genetic contribution.

There is the further problem that with common traits (like the psychotic disorders) it has proved very difficult to distinguish between single-locus and multigenic hypotheses (Smith, 1971B). All that we can say at this point is that we have utilized several types of tests in looking for evidence of single loci with major phenotypic effect and have failed to find such evidence.

This study is one of the few which have relatively adequate data available for three or more generations. We have already analyzed Generation IV members by the mental health status of their parents, which had a large effect. We now wish to learn whether there is an additional effect of the mental health status of the grandparents and of the aunts and uncles on the people in Generation IV. The study design provided this information for only one side of each family, the side related to the proband and not to the spouse of the proband.

The data for grandparents, aunts and uncles are shown in Table 9–12. It seems clear that there is only a modest effect of the psychotic grandparent which is not of statistical significance. The effect of psychosis in the *parent* is sufficient by itself to influence the frequency of psychosis among the offspring without much extra effect from the grandparents.

The possible effect of psychosis in aunts and uncles is also shown in Table 9–12. When a parent is psychotic, the variation in the number of psychotic aunts or uncles probably has little effect on the frequency of psychosis in the offspring. However, when neither parent is psychotic, the information from aunts and uncles does appear to show a consistent relationship; that is, the greater the number of aunts and uncles with psychoses, the higher the percentage of affected children, nieces and nephews. The steady rise in the percentage of affected children, which is proportional to the increase in the number of psychotic aunts and uncles, where neither parent is affected is shown at the bottom of Table 9–12. This rise is evidence for a multigenic mechanism of heredity rather than simple dominance or recessiveness.

The data for the nieces and nephews, with neither parent psychotic, were combined in relation to the grandparents, aunts and uncles as shown in Table 9–13. When the grandparent was psychotic and three to eight of the aunts and uncles were also psychotic, we find that 10.3 per cent of the nieces and nephews were psychotic. This is significantly higher than the 2.6 per cent

Table 9–12. *Possible Effects of Grandparents and of Aunts and Uncles upon the Frequency of Psychosis in the Children and the Nephews and Nieces of the Probands.*

| | CHILDREN, NIECES AND NEPHEWS | |
	Total Number	*Psychotic Number (Per Cent)*
One Parent Psychotic		
Grandparents not psychotic	172	28(16.3)
Grandparent(s) psychotic	150	22(14.7)
	322	50(15.5)
0–2 psychotic aunts and uncles	180	34(18.9)
3–8 psychotic aunts and uncles	142	16(11.3)
	322	50(15.5)
Neither Parent Psychotic		
Grandparents not psychotic	580	20(3.4)
Grandparent(s) psychotic	256	15(5.9)
	836	35(4.2)
One psychotic aunt or uncle	412	6(1.5)
Two psychotic aunts and uncles	239	12(5.0)
Three psychotic aunts and uncles	58	5(8.6)
Four or more psychotic aunts and uncles	127	12(9.4)
	836	35(4.2)

psychotic nieces and nephews where no grandparents and only one or two aunts or uncles were psychotic. The effect is mainly due to the aunts and uncles and only slightly to the grandparents. This increase in psychosis is obscured, as shown in the upper part of Table 9–12, when the niece or nephew has a psychotic parent.

There are a few family lines among our kinships which showed five successive generations of mental disorder but they do not tell us much. In our large study of some 18,000 persons it would be difficult to calculate how many five generational lines of successive psychotic persons would be expected by coincidence. But we do have our smaller sample of 1158 persons which encompasses the nieces, nephews and children of our 89 probands. Among the 1158 persons, 22 or 1.9 per cent had at least one parent and one grandparent with a psychosis, giving three successive generations of mental disorder. All the affected persons in these generations are shown in Table 9–14.

The reader may be impressed with the preponderance of diagnoses of schizophrenia and of the sub-type of paranoid

Table 9–13. *Frequency of Psychosis Among Nieces and Nephews with Neither Parent Psychotic by Psychosis Among Grandparents and Aunts and Uncles.*

| | 1–2 PSYCHOTIC AUNTS AND UNCLES | | 3–8 PSYCHOTIC AUNTS AND UNCLES | | COMBINED[1] | |
	Total Number	*Psychotic Number (Per Cent)*	*Total Number*	*Psychotic Number (Per Cent)*	*Total Number*	*Psychotic Number (Per Cent)*
Grandparents not psychotic	492	13(2.6)	88	7(8.0)	580	20(3.4)
Grandparent(s) psychotic	159	5(3.1)	97	10(10.3)	256	15(5.9)
Combined[2]	651	18(2.8)	185	17(9.2)	836	35(4.2)

[1] Testing the effect of psychosis in grandparents, $\chi^2 = 2.9$, d/f = 1, P > .05.
[2] Testing the effect of psychosis in aunts and uncles, $\chi^2 = 14.8$, d/f = 1, P < .001.

Table 9–14.   *Diagnostic Classifications for Persons Involved in Three Successive Generations of Psychotic Disorders.*

DIAGNOSIS FOR EACH PERSON, BY GENERATION, IDENTIFICATION NUMBER AND SEX

Family Number	Generation II (Grandparents of Gen. IV)	Generation III (Parents of Gen. IV)	Generation IV
WSH 15	8 F Schizophrenia, paranoid	15 F Psychosis	37 F Schizophrenia, catatonic
		33 F Probable psychosis..........................	86 M Schizophrenia, paranoid
		35 F Schizophrenia, catatonic	97 F Schizophrenia, paranoid
WSH 20	9 F Schizophrenia, paranoid	24 F Schizophrenia, paranoid	41 F Probable schizophrenia
WSH 22	10 M Probable psychosis	20 F Schizophrenia, catatonic	30 M Schizophrenia, paranoid
		29 F Schizophrenia, paranoid	33 M Schizophrenia, paranoid
WSH 30	5 M Probable psychosis............	24 F Schizophrenia, schizo-affective	28 M Probable psychosis
			42 F Schizophrenia, catatonic
			47 M Schizophrenia, catatonic
			48 M Schizophrenia, paranoid
WSH 38	12 F Possible schizophrenia	21 F Schizophrenia, paranoid	37 M Schizophrenia, catatonic
WSH 46	14 M Probable schizophrenia	29 F Schizophrenia, paranoid	65 M Schizophrenia, paranoid
			67 M Schizophrenia, paranoid
WSH 50	14 F Probable schizophrenia	30 F Manic-depressive	{50 F Probable psychosis
			{51 F Probable psychosis
		41 F Schizophrenia, paranoid ....101 M Possible manic-depressive	
WSH 73	10 F Schizophrenia	23 F Schizophrenia	76 F Schizophrenia, paranoid
WSH 92	8 F Schizophrenia, paranoid	20 F Probable schizophrenia	61 M Schizophrenia, paranoid
WSH 94	16 F Schizophrenia, catatonic	25 F Schizophrenia, catatonic	47 M Schizophrenia, paranoid
			51 M Schizophrenia
			53 F Schizophrenia, catatonic
			57 M Schizophrenia, paranoid

F = Female   M = Male

schizophrenia. This expresses, in part, the preference of Pennsylvania psychiatrists for the paranoid schizophrenia label, and in part the fact that schizophrenia is the most frequent of the functional psychoses in all countries. It is an interesting peculiarity of our data that there is no manic-depressive person who was a grandparent of any one of our 22 psychotic persons in Generation IV as shown in Table 9–14. There isn't any question but that those who received an affective disorder diagnosis behaved differently than those persons with schizophrenia. We will look at this difference now.

Genetic Heterogeneity

In the earlier chapters we have presented the data in terms of total functional psychoses with little separation of the psychoses into specific diagnoses. All the persons given a diagnosis of psychosis were mentally ill but there would be no unanimous agreement as to the correct diagnosis for every one of them. However, if we wish to try to demonstrate genetic heterogeneity among the psychoses diagnostic labels will have to be used, even if they are not acceptable to everyone for specific patients.

Our first effort will involve separating those psychotic persons with a label of schizophrenia from the rest of the functional psychoses. If the schizophrenic siblings and children are significantly different in some way from the siblings and children with other kinds of psychoses, we would consider the difference to be evidence of genetic heterogeneity.

In Chapter Six, Figure 6–4, we showed that the cumulative risk curves for functional psychoses of all kinds were the same for the children of a psychotic person as for the siblings of a psychotic person. When we separate the data according to the diagnostic label the picture is sharply different from that in Figure 6–4. The breakdown into three diagnostic categories is shown in Table 9–15.

Some of the same data as those in Table 9–15 are in Table 7–15 but in a different form. The present table illustrates several important points which indicate genetic heterogeneity between the three diagnostic groups.

1. The siblings of schizophrenics were psychotic in about the same frequency (14.7 per cent) as the siblings of the persons with affective disorders (11.0 per cent). But this is *not* evidence of genetic heterogeneity.

Table 9–15. *Psychosis in Siblings or Offspring of Psychotic Persons.*

DIAGNOSIS IN SIBLINGS OR OFFSPRING	SIBLINGS OF SCHIZOPHRENICS		OFFSPRING OF SCHIZOPHRENICS		SIBLINGS OF AFFECTIVES[1]		OFFSPRING OF AFFECTIVES		CONTROLS	
	No.	(Per Cent)	No.	(Per Cent)	No.	(Per Cent)	No.	(Per Cent)	No.	(Per Cent)
Schizophrenia	43	9.3	34	18.8	8	8.8	4	4.7	28	2.1
Affective	17	3.7	6	3.3	0	0.0	0	0.0	7	0.5
Psychosis NOS[2]	8	1.7	1	0.6	2	2.2	2	2.3	13	1.0
Unaffected	396	85.3	140	77.3	81	89.0	80	93.0	1299	96.4
Totals	464	100.0	181	100.0	91	100.0	86	100.0	1347	100.0

[1]Excluding four loaded families.
[2]NOS = Psychosis, not otherwise specified.

2. The offspring of schizophrenics, however, were psychotic three times as often (22.7 per cent) as the offspring of persons with an affective disorder (7.0 per cent). This is a sharp difference in the genetic behavior of the affective parents and the schizophrenic parents as evidenced by the frequencies of psychoses in their offspring. This would seem to be good evidence of genetic heterogeneity between the schizophrenic and affective disorders.

3. It seems to be firmly established in the literature that there is a higher frequency of schizophrenia in the offspring of a schizophrenic than among the siblings of a schizophrenic. The reader may recall the previous citation of Table 28 from Slater and Cowie (1971) which showed 13.9 per cent of 1227 children of schizophrenics to have schizophrenia while only 10.2 per cent of 8505 siblings of a schizophrenic were so affected. We will return to this difference in risks for children and siblings shortly.

There has been interest in recent years in the separation of the affective disorders into unipolar and bipolar groupings. This dichotomy could be primarily a difference in severity of the disorder with a multigenic basis but, nonetheless, it would represent a genetic heterogeneity of the kind we have been considering. The data for these studies are somewhat confusing but the reader is referred to the recent paper of Mendlewicz et al. (1972) if more information is desired. Whatever the interpretations of all the studies of the functional psychoses may be, the presence of genetic heterogeneity seems to be unquestionable. Its form and substance remain ephemeral.

More Model Building

Quantitative genetics did not make much progress in the area of human genetics until recent years. It was not until after the model building of Edwards, Falconer, Smith and others had developed that one could begin to test predictions and heritabilities for the different kinds of relatives with human traits assumed to be quantitative in nature.

The paper by Smith (1971A) allows one to derive the recurrence risk of a condition with multifactorial inheritance in any family presented. While we are not interested in the risks for an individual family at this point, we wish to call attention to Smith's Table 1 and his Figure 3. The application of most interest to us would be that for schizophrenia, with an assumed population frequency of a little greater than 1 per cent and a heritability of about 50 per cent. We find in Smith's Table 1 for one affected sibling—but normal parents—a risk of 3.9 per cent for the next child, while the risk to the next child if one parent—but no sibling—is affected is 4.3 per cent. Perusal of Smith's table shows that in this case, and in all others, the risk to the child of an affected parent is greater than the risk to the child with an affected sibling but normal parents. Very little has been made of this point in the literature. Usually, it has been assumed that the risk to the child with normal parents—but one affected sibling—would be the same as that for a child with an affected parent and no siblings. Clearly, this is not true. The collected data from Slater and Cowie (1971), originally assembled by

Zerbin-Rüdin (1967), show that an affected parent presents a greater risk to a child than an affected sibling. Penrose (1969) demonstrated that the parent-child and sib-sib correlation surfaces, for traits determined by perfectly additive genes, differ from one another.

Smith's Table 1 demonstrates the above point very clearly but his Figure 3 does not agree with his table in this respect. There is only one curve given, number 7, for one parent affected or one sibling affected. Apparently this one curve represents the risk for offspring of affected and the risk for siblings of one affected, combining the different possible mating types of parents in the proportions that would be found in the general population. Combined risks of this type clearly are not appropriate, however, for situations involving assortative mating or variations in fertility among the several mating types.

We have used the data in Smith's Table 1 to produce the curves shown in Figure 9–4, using the heritability value of 50 per cent.

The curves show the risk to children and siblings of various combinations of affected parents or siblings, depending upon the population frequency assumed for any multigenic disorder. Naturally, population frequencies above 3 or 4 per cent are not relevant for schizophrenia. Using our Figure 9–4 allows us to test the fit of our data to these completely independent predictions. It is clear that our frequencies of schizophrenic persons in Table 9–16 are about twice as high as expected from the predictions. This is a fundamental discrepancy which invites some explanation. If we look at Smith's Figure 3 for a population frequency of 2.0 per cent and heritability of 80 per cent we find much better agreement with our observed data. This implies that our heritabilities, which we found to be about 50 per cent, were too low. Another explanation is that too many genetically unrelated disorders may have been included under the label of schizophrenia, thus giving us observed values which combine several multigenic or monogenic traits that

Figure 9–4. Recurrence risks for a multigenic trait with heritability of 0.50, by number of parents and siblings affected.

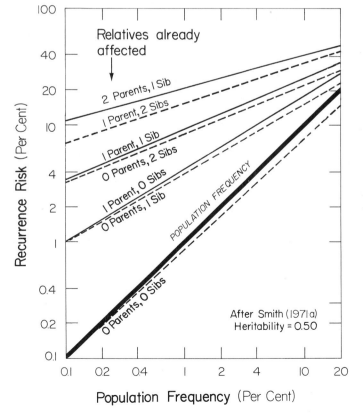

Table 9-16. *Comparison of Our Data for Schizophrenia Only (from Table 9-10) with the Predictions Obtained from Smith's Calculations as Shown in Figure 9-4.*

	OBSERVED DATA *(Per Cent)*	PREDICTED (2 PER CENT SCHIZOPHRENIA IN POPULATION) *(Per Cent)*	PREDICTED (3 PER CENT SCHIZOPHRENIA IN POPULATION) *(Per Cent)*
Frequency among persons with one sibling but neither parent schizophrenic	9.7	5.8	7.5
Frequency among siblings with one sibling and one parent schizophrenic	30.3	12.6	15.0
Frequency among siblings of two schizophrenics but neither parent schizophrenic	30.0	11.2	13.2
Frequency among siblings of two schizophrenics with one parent schizophrenic	37.5	19.0	22.0

are too high for any one individual disorder now grouped under the heading of schizophrenia.

A different way to approach the problem of expected risks for siblings and for children is to set up a model with known genetic parameters. To keep the model simple we made the following assumptions:

1. No environmental contribution (heritability = 1.0).

2. Effect of genes equal and additive (no dominance or epistasis).

3. Five gene loci.

4. Two alleles at each locus, namely A and A', B and B', C and C', D and D', E and E'.

5. The frequencies of the "prime" alleles (leading to the defect) set at 1/3 and the frequency of the alternative alleles at 2/3 for each locus.

6. A population frequency of the defect close to 2 per cent (which was accomplished by considering those with seven or more "prime" alleles affected).

7. Random mating.

The distribution of persons in a general population by number of "prime" alleles is shown in Table 9-17. The distribution is skewed because the allele frequencies were set at 1/3 and 2/3. The mean number of prime alleles is 3.33 for the general population, 3.26 for those not affected and 7.19 for the affected. The frequency of the affected in the general population is 1965 out of 100,000 (essentially 2 per cent).

The skewed nature of this distribution has an interesting possible implication for the equilibrium process, which maintains the frequency of psychotic disorders in the population in spite of a reduced fertility. A slight reproductive disadvantage involving the large number with unaffected genotypes at the left end of the curve could balance the more serious disadvantage for the small number of affected persons at the other end, without requiring high mutation rates as an explanation.

All possible matings in the population were then considered and the allelic combinations in first-born children were calculated (see Table 9-18). In this process a distinction was made between parental genotypes that could produce only one type of gamete (such as A'A'BBC'C'DDEE) and genotypes with the same number of prime alleles that could produce several types of gametes (such as A'AB'BC'CD'DEE). For each parental mating type we could calculate the number of such matings in the population and the proportion of children affected.

We then considered the second-born children for those matings that had produced an affected child the first time. This provides an estimate of recurrence risk among siblings of affected, separated by parental mating type.

The main point that emerges from the calculations in Table 9-18 is that the risk for children of one affected parent (15.9 per cent) is higher than for siblings of an affected child with normal parents (12.1 per cent). These percentages would vary with the parameters introduced but a difference in the risk to the offspring of one affected parent compared with that for the siblings of an affected child should persist.

The same point can be made in a different way. The mean "loading" for a normal person is 3.26 and for an affected person

Table 9–17. *Hypothetical Distribution of Individuals by Number of Alleles Leading to Defect.*

	DISTRIBUTION OF INDIVIDUALS			
Number of "Prime" Alleles	*General Population*	*Normal Persons*	*Affected Persons*	*Normal Parents of Affected*°
None	1734	1734		
One	8671	8671		
Two	19,509	19,509		8
Three	26,012	26,012		90
Four	22,761	22,761		312
Five	13,656	13,656		487
Six	5690	5690		428
Seven	1626		1626	
Eight	305		305	
Nine	34		34	
Ten	2		2	
Totals	100,000	98,033	1967	1325
Mean Number	3.33	3.26	7.19	4.93

°Restricted to matings with both parents normal.

Table 9–18. *Risks to Children in Hypothetical Model by Parental Mating Type.*

		FIRST-BORN CHILDREN			SECOND-BORN SIBLINGS OF AFFECTED		
Status of Parents	*Number of Matings*	*Total Number*	*Affected Number*	*(Per Cent)*	*Total Number*	*Affected Number*	*(Per Cent)*
Both affected	39	39	29	74.4	29	22	75.9
One affected	3855	3855	613	15.9°	613	195	31.8
Neither affected	96,106	96,106	1325	1.4	1325	160	12.1°
Totals	100,000	100,000	1967	2.0	1967	377	19.2

°These two values, 15.9 per cent and 12.1 per cent, are the important ones for comparison.

it is 7.19 (Table 9–17). Thus, in a mating of normal x affected, the mean midparent value would be 5.22. On the other hand, when two normal parents produce an affected child, the mean loading of each normal parent is 4.93, which would lead to a lower estimated risk for defect among second-born children (siblings of an affected).

We conclude this chapter without having provided an absolute and final answer for any of the numerous questions which have been asked. One would not expect final answers for such a complicated subject as the genetics of the functional psychoses. However, we have clarified several points to some degree. Our data seem to demonstrate that a person's psychosis lowers his social class, which supports the "drift" theory accounting for the excess of psychotics in the bottom social class. Furthermore, it is clear that the psychotic parent lowered the social class of the unaffected offspring as well as the psychotic offspring. There is no evidence that social class *causes* schizophrenia, or even contributes to its onset.

We failed to find any evidence for phenocopies (non-genetic cases) of psychoses; there was no evidence of any excess of "low risk" families. We found heritabilities of about 50 per cent for schizophrenia, which we refer to as "clustering" within families. The steady rise in the percentage of affected offspring, which is proportional to the increase in the number of psychotic aunts and uncles, is evidence for a multigenic mechanism of heredity rather than simple dominance or recessiveness. Finally, the offspring of schizophrenics were psychotic three times as often (22.7 per cent) as the offspring of persons with an affective disorder (7.0 per cent). This seems to be good evidence of genetic heterogeneity between the schizophrenic and affective disorders.

SUMMARY

This is the crucial chapter. We were forced to come to grips with the problem of which kind of genetic mechanism seems to be the most likely basis for the genetic predisposition to the psychoses. However, before we take up our final challenge we should look at the environmental contributions to the problem. Social class is a reflection of environmental factors, both advantageous and disadvantageous. It mirrors a conglomerate of environmental effects each of which defies identification. However, social class can be measured in an approximate fashion and thus provides one way of estimating the net effect of the various environmental factors contributing to the expression of the psychotic phenotype.

It proved to be so difficult to assign women to particular social classes that we included only males in our analyses. The social class system used is statistically awkward because the lower the social class observed, the higher the numerical rating; the lowest social class has the highest number, V.

1. Our results showed unequivocally ($\chi^2 = 55.6$, p = <0.0001) that the psychotic sons and nephews of the probands had a distinctly lower social class rating (4.74 ± 0.10) than did their unaffected siblings (3.43 ± 0.05). The siblings with other mental disorders had an intermediate social class rating (3.89 ± 0.13), as might be expected. Furthermore, the drop in social class is almost twice as great if the person himself is psychotic compared with the drop caused if the parent is psychotic.

The social class rating is 35 per cent lower for these persons who are psychotic and have a psychotic parent (4.35 ± 0.10) than for the unaffected relatives with unaffected parents (3.22 ± 0.09). These data strongly support the "drift" theory to account for the observed large excess of psychotics found in the bottom social class. That is, the psychotics drop down to the lower social classes because of their disorder rather than their psychoses being caused by noxious environmental factors concentrated in the lower social classes. Put another way, our data indicated that the psychoses are correlated with lower social class but are not caused by the lower social class environments.

Let us now turn to our major interest, the genetic mechanisms underlying the psychoses.

2. There are at least three large complications which make the search for the genetic mechanism or mechanisms basic to the psychoses so extraordinarily difficult to carry out. One of these complications is the

variable age of onset of the psychoses. Another is the uncertainty of the diagnosis in many cases. Finally, there is the problem of the probable genetic heterogeneity present in the whole group of functional psychoses. Presumably a person with a classic case of schizophrenia has a different set of genes related to his disorder than does a person with a classic case of manic-depressive psychosis.

Our first test was for sample heterogeneity; that is, were there more low risk families than would be expected for the frequency of psychosis present in the whole sample? We did not find any evidence of an excess of low risk families. Low risk families are those in which the development of a psychosis in a specific individual resulted from a rare combination of events (genetic or environmental) such that the risk for a sibling or a child would be about the same as the risk for the general population. If there were a large proportion of low risk families, they could be detected as a greater number of sibships with none affected than would be expected by chance alone.

We then looked at the distribution of psychosis within sibships, given that at least one person per sibship was affected. Clustering of psychotic persons within particular families can be the result of environmental or genetic factors common to that family. An estimate of this clustering is the heritability percentage. The heritability estimates turned out to be remarkably consistent even though their standard errors were relatively large. The heritabilities ranged from 45 to 51 per cent for various related groups of offspring and siblings. We do have some clustering of the psychotics within families having one or more affected children.

The distribution of psychosis within families was compatible with a multigenic mechanism, but not with a single-locus mechanism. We cannot exclude rare single-locus traits that could account for a small fraction of the cases, but can with some assurance conclude that one or more of such single-locus conditions cannot account for the majority of cases.

The heritabilities vary, however, with the breadth of diagnostic categories considered. Among the nieces and nephews with neither parent psychotic we obtained the highest heritability (0.61 ± 0.19) when the

analysis was restricted to proved schizophrenia, while the lowest heritability (0.27 ± 0.12) resulted when all psychoses and other mental disorders were combined as one trait.

3. The greatest single factor resulting in the presence of a psychosis in a person is a psychosis in his parent. If neither parent is psychotic, we find that the greater the number of aunts and uncles with psychosis, the higher the percentage of affected offspring. This is evidence for a multigenic mechanism of heredity rather than simple dominance or recessiveness.

4. Those persons who received a diagnosis of an affective disorder seemed to be genetically different from those who were considered to be schizophrenic. For instance, the offspring of schizophrenics were psychotic three times as often (22.7 per cent) as the offspring of affective disorder parents (7.0 per cent). This difference in ability to transmit a psychosis by the schizophrenic parent and by the affective disorder parents would seem to be evidence of genetic heterogeneity between the two groups of psychoses. The difference might be purely quantitative and not a qualitative genetic difference. It may be that schizophrenics have both a worse environment and a heavier genetic loading which they transmit more frequently than do persons with an affective disorder.

5. A genetic model was constructed which is enlightening from several points of view. It is generally useful for any trait with a frequency of about 2 per cent in the general population, on the assumption of multigenic inheritance. It also assumes in this specific case that there are five loci involved and that the frequency of the "prime" alleles (responsible for the defect) is set at 1/3 and the frequency of the alternative alleles at 2/3 for each one. The model shows that as a result of gene segregation the risk for children of one affected parent (15.9 per cent) is higher than for siblings of an affected child with normal parents (12.1 per cent). These percentages would vary with the parameters introduced but a difference in the risk to the offspring of one affected parent compared with that for the siblings of an affected child should persist.

The model also shows (Table 9–17) that when the frequency of the alleles predisposing to the defect is less than 50 per cent at each locus there will be a substantial skewness toward the right end of the curve in the direction of genotypes with the defect. However, if these unaffected genotypes at the left end of the curve suffered any slight disadvantage as compared with the much more numerous heterozygotes clustered around the center of the curve, then the population equilibrium could be maintained without the aid of new mutations to the genes producing the serious defect.

We emphasize this concept that if the alleles for a multigenic trait are each at less than 50 per cent in frequency only a slight disadvantage to the homozygous persons at the other end of the sharply skewed curve is necessary to maintain an equilibrium without the assistance of new mutations.

CHAPTER TEN

CONCLUSIONS

This chapter will repeat our major findings for the benefit of those who like to read the last chapter of a book first. We will also attempt to provide a comprehensive synthesis concerning the biological basis for the psychoses.

The unique feature of our study is that it includes more generations of psychotic and well persons than any other and thus provides the great advantage of starting several generations back in time and then ascertaining patients, such as psychotic nieces and nephews of our probands, through their parents. It is thus possible to identify biases and adjust for them. Not only have families been completed but most of the early generations of persons have died, which reduced the need for age corrections and allowed us to test the utility of age corrections.

THE PROBANDS

It is extremely difficult to select a set of probands that can be considered representative of the psychotic persons in the general population. The admission policies of a given hospital tend to be selective, and other selective factors (both planned and unplanned) enter into the choice of a sample of probands from within the hospital pool. We made three basic choices in defining our probands:

1. We accepted all persons from the initial Warren State Hospital sample for whom the more recent diagnostic review indicated the presence of a psychotic disorder. Through analysis of the data we then attempted to identify possible biasing fac-tors that might influence the final interpretations.

2. We studied all forms of psychotic disorder in the sample at the same time. This strategy permits comparison between diagnostic groups that would be impossible if only one category were considered.

3. Cases with mixed clinical signs were included and were placed in what was thought to be the most appropriate diagnostic category. This contrasts with the strategy of studying only the extreme or "typical" cases. Our choice was based on the assumption that, on any genetic hypothesis, the psychotic relatives of "typical" cases would tend to resemble the probands in their behavior patterns. The inclusion of intermediate cases with mixed symptomatology is essential for a more realistic view of the genetic basis for psychotic disorders, even though the results may appear more complex and difficult to interpret.

The average age at first admission of our probands was 36.1 years. This is much younger than the average age of 51.3 years for the 5000 patient sample not included in the study. The rather young age of admission of our probands indicates that few geriatric cases were included and that the majority of the probands must have been correctly diagnosed as schizophrenic.

There was no evidence of any birth order effect among our probands.

Our probands had 4.4 siblings but only 1.5 children at the end of their reproductive periods. This average of 1.5 children is not high enough for replacement of the patient and his or her spouse in the next generation.

Seven of the 99 probands were the products of consanguineous parentage. This is a higher than usual consanguinity rate and suggests that many of the consanguineous parents were also mentally disturbed. In fact, only 1 proband of the 7 had both parents with normal mental health.

THE PROBANDS' PARENTS, SIBLINGS, AND CHILDREN

The mother of the proband had a proved or probable psychosis in 20.3 per cent of the cases, while only 14.5 per cent of the probands had an affected father. There was an extremely high frequency of "other mental disorders" among the parents of the probands. Thus we find that 64.2 per cent of the mothers and 60.7 per cent of the fathers of the probands had a serious mental problem.

Our male probands had a total of six psychotic sons and no psychotic daughters, which is evidence that genetic sex-linkage is *not* an important mechanism in the etiology of our psychotic persons.

Psychotic mothers produced about twice as high a percentage of psychotic offspring (20.1 per cent) as did psychotic fathers (8.1 per cent). This maternal effect had not been established previously in the literature. One reasonable explanation of the maternal effect could result from the established fact that a larger proportion of all psychotic females marry and reproduce than do psychotic males. Presumably this means that more severely ill females have offspring and give them a heavier genetic loading for psychosis than is the case for psychotic males. This is one of our most important findings.

The half siblings of the proband sometimes share the psychotic parent with the proband and the full siblings of the proband. The half siblings with a shared psychotic parent had a lower frequency of psychosis (11.1 per cent) than the full siblings (18.4 per cent), which would seem to indicate that the non-shared parents were genetically different in their capacity to produce psychotic offspring. None of the 22 half siblings for whom the shared parent was *not* psychotic was affected with a psychosis.

Our probands produced 154 children who survived beyond the age of 15 years. There were 21 children who were removed from their psychotic parent by age 6 years.

Of these children there were 6 (28.6 per cent) who received unequivocal diagnoses of schizophrenia during their lives. Of the 133 children not separated from their psychotic parent only 15.8 per cent became psychotic. It was surprising that a higher percentage of the children separated from their psychotic parent became psychotic than was the case for the children who remained with the psychotic parent. A plausible explanation of this finding is that the parents of the 21 children who had to be removed were more severely ill and transmitted a heavier genetic load for psychoses than the parents who were able to care for their children despite mental illness.

THE CALCULATION OF AGE CORRECTION

In any condition with delayed age at onset some form of age adjustment is essential. We do *not* want to use the "risk prior to death" because the "risk given survival to age X" is more interesting as an estimate of the predisposition for the disorder. The latter method showed that the siblings and children of our probands had a remarkably similar risk of becoming psychotic at all 10-year age intervals.

If all of the 457 siblings of our probands had survived until age 85, about one quarter (24.7 ± 2.8 per cent) would have developed a psychosis. Not all did survive until age 85, of course, and many died before developing the disorder. There were 18.6 per cent of the siblings who did develop a psychosis at some time during their lives. This is 75 per cent of those who could have been expected to develop a psychosis if all siblings had lived to age 85. Clearly there was a need for the age correction though age corrections do not replace the need for adequate data.

THE MATERNAL EFFECT

The group of nieces and nephews of our probands are a very useful group and are chronologically contemporaneous with the probands' children. They are second degree relatives of the probands and should have one half (or less) the percentage of psychoses found in the children of the probands. The nieces and nephews were psychotic in only 5.8 per cent of the cases while we could expect 8.8 per cent to be affected (half of the 17.5 per cent of the psychotic children of the probands). Most of this difference comes about because only about half of the psychotic siblings of the proband reproduce at all, while most of the normal siblings do reproduce. Thus, the "deficiency" of psychotic nephews and nieces is the result of low fertility of the psychotic siblings rather than environmental differences between children and nieces and nephews.

All five different groups of relatives were consistent in demonstrating the maternal effect. Adding the groups, the psychotic mothers produced 417 children, of whom 84 or 20.1 per cent were psychotic, while psychotic fathers had only 247 children, of whom 20, or 8.1 per cent, were psychotic. The χ^2 value for these differences is 17.0 with 1 degree of freedom and the chance that the association is due to random sampling is less than 1 in 1000. (See Table 6–15.)

It is perhaps our most striking finding that about twice as many of the children of the psychotic mothers are also psychotic compared with the children of psychotic fathers.

POPULATION DYNAMICS

Only 79 per cent of the children born to schizophrenic mothers survived to age 15 compared with the 90 per cent survival of the children of their unaffected sisters.

Only 64 per cent of the schizophrenic women and 27 per cent of the schizophrenic men ever reproduced.

The combined effect of lowered survival of the children of schizophrenic mothers, of lowered reproduction of the schizophrenic person and the production of psychotic offspring reduces the net number of normal offspring of the schizophrenic individual. Thus the average number of unaffected offspring from schizophrenic females was only 0.80 persons and from schizophrenic males, 0.59. The conventional estimate is that a person should have 2.2 children in order to replace himself and his spouse in the next generation. Obviously, our psychotic persons do not approach this

minimum, even if their psychotic children are added to the figures given above.

A population dynamics model generated from our data for schizophrenics suggests that 15.3 per cent of them should have a schizophrenic mother and 4.5 per cent a schizophrenic father, while the remaining 80.2 per cent of the schizophrenics should have two non-schizophrenic parents. Direct observations of the 770 nieces and nephews of our study showed that 24.1 per cent of those with schizophrenia had a schizophrenic parent. This is higher than the 19.8 per cent predicted by the model but the excess presumably depends upon the fact that all the nieces and nephews had a schizophrenic aunt or uncle, namely, the proband.

The interesting implications of the model building exercise are that if all schizophrenics in one generation failed to reproduce we would expect just under 20 per cent fewer schizophrenics in the next generation. This reduction would result in the assumed population frequency of 2 per cent schizophrenia dropping to 1.6 per cent schizophrenia in the next generation. If, on the other hand, the schizophrenic persons reproduced at the same rate as their unaffected siblings, we would expect 30.7 per cent of the schizophrenic persons of the next generation to have been produced by a schizophrenic parent. However, it would only increase the population frequency of schizophrenia from 2.0 per cent to 2.2 per cent.

SOCIAL CLASS

The psychotic sons and nephews of the probands had a strikingly lower social class rating (4.74 ± 0.10) than did their unaffected siblings (3.43 ± 0.05). The rating is statistically awkward because the lower the social class observed, the higher the numerical rating.

The social class rating is 35 per cent lower for those persons who are psychotic and have a psychotic parent than for the unaffected relatives with unaffected parents. Our data strongly support the "drift" theory to account for our observed large excess of psychotics found in the bottom social class. Our data suggest that the psychoses are correlated with lower social class but are not caused by the lower social class environments.

HETEROGENEITY

Low risk families are those in which the development of a psychosis in a specific individual resulted from a rare combination of events (environmental or genetic) such that the risk for a sibling or a child would be about the same as the risk for the general population. If there were a large proportion of low risk families, they could be detected as a greater number of sibships with none affected than would be expected by chance alone. We did not find any excess of low risk families.

We did find clustering of psychotic persons within particular families. An estimate of the clustering is the heritability percentage. The heritabilities ranged from 45 to 61 per cent for various related groups of offspring and siblings, for the psychoses. The clustering of psychosis within families was compatible with a multigenic mechanism but not with a single locus mechanism. We cannot exclude rare single locus traits that could account for a small fraction of the cases but can conclude, with some assurance, that one or more of such single-locus conditions cannot account for the majority of cases.

The heritabilities vary when the classifications are made in relation to diagnosis. We obtained the highest heritability (0.61 ± 0.19) for nieces and nephews where neither parent was psychotic but where the affected nieces and nephews were proved schizophrenics. For the same group the heritability was 0.54 ± 0.24 when the diagnosis in the nieces and nephews was paranoid schizophrenia. The lowest heritability (0.27 ± 0.12) was found in this same group of persons when the affected nieces and nephews included all those with a psychosis of any sort as well as those with other mental disorders (see Figure 9–3).

We also found that, when neither parent is psychotic, the percentage of psychotic offspring increased in proportion to the increase in the percentage of psychotic aunts and uncles. This relationship is evidence for a multigenic mechanism of heredity rather than simple dominance or recessiveness.

GENETIC HETEROGENEITY

Those persons who received a diagnosis of an affective disorder seemed to be genetically different from those who were considered to be schizophrenic. For instance, the offspring of schizophrenics were psychotic 3 times as often as the offspring of affective disorder parents (7.0 per cent). This difference in the ability to transmit a psychosis by the two types of psychotic parents would seem to be evidence of genetic heterogeneity between the two psychoses.

An important aspect of the problem of genetic heterogeneity is the possibility that there is one major gene locus involved with schizophrenia and another independent gene locus responsible for manic-depressive psychosis. This would be the traditional viewpoint and is the simplest one. However, it seems likely that this classic picture is an oversimplification and if that is the case it does not contribute to our understanding of the psychoses.

One of the important techniques which could detect a major gene locus for a psychosis is that of Slater, who reasoned that if secondary cases of the psychosis were distributed very preponderantly on either the paternal or maternal side of the family a single dominant gene would be involved. If the secondary cases were on both sides of the family, then multigenic inheritance would be more probable. The method makes no allowance for clustering on one side of the family resulting from a common environmental cause and it would be somewhat dependent on the frequency of the trait in the population. However, using this method, Tsuang (1971) found some indication that a major gene might be involved with schizophrenia. But Slater, Maxwell and Price (1971) found no excess of unilateral secondary cases in bipolar affective disorders. The bipolar affective disorders are synonymous with the usual concept of manic-depressive psychosis. Slater et al. not only failed to find any excess of unilateral cases but instead had a deficiency of them which almost reached statistical significance.

The failure to find any evidence for an excess of unilateral cases for manic-depressive psychosis was also experienced by Perris (1971). Thus the evidence indicates a multigenic basis for manic-depressive psychosis (bipolar) rather than a single important dominant gene.

SEX LINKAGE

In view of the above, it seems inconsistent to find claims in the popular press (*Newsweek,* August 28, 1972) that manic-depressive psychosis depends upon a gene on the X chromosome and that it is linked with the Xg^a antigen and/or color blindness. We will remain open to conversion when the data appear in some scientific journal but it seems much more likely that sex influence is present rather than sex linkage. The genes for color blindness and the Xg^a antigen are very far apart on the X chromosome, which means that no gene could show *close* linkage with both markers, only with one or the other.

BIOCHEMISTRY

A full understanding of the contribution of genetic factors to any trait would involve the biochemical steps from genes to gene products to the phenotype. Yet this has proved extremely difficult to demonstrate for the psychotic disorders. Why is this so? We have considered here the later onset cases which show few or no problems in childhood, suggesting that we are not dealing with gross biochemical defects. Many affected individuals show periods of recovery, suggesting that the genetic problem may involve a diminished response to stress (a reduced plasticity in the face of environmental stress), and this more subtle difficulty would be harder to trace biochemically. If there are single-locus causes of some of the psychotic disorders the mode of inheritance is probably dominant, and there has been very little success in finding biochemical explanations for dominant disorders. It appears probable that most of the genetic factors leading to psychoses may involve biochemical processes intrinsic to the brain, and thus not readily accessible to research. It is not surprising that progress has been slow.

Advances in the therapeutic uses of various chemicals have been of the greatest importance. The tremendous practical value of the tranquilizers needs no reiteration here. The usefulness of lithium for some cases of hypomania seems to be well established.

It is not at all clear, however, what the successful use of lithium tells us about genetic specificity. The lithium ion apparently has some effect on the deamination of norepinephrine, according to the review by Himwich (1971), but lithium also affects a number of other cellular processes. There is no evidence as yet that the patients suffer from a defect in lithium metabolism that is corrected by the therapy. It seems more likely that the effect of lithium is related to the specificity of symptoms rather than to genetic specificity. Thus lithium might be successful in the treatment of several conditions with different etiology, but in addition it might be useful for only a fraction of cases arising from one specific etiology. Further research will be needed before response to lithium therapy can be used as an aid in testing genetic hypotheses.

Our view of the genetics of the psychotic disorders is that there may be some rarer sub-types, each resulting from a different major gene, whereas the majority of cases have a multigenic basis involving a number of gene loci. What are the implications of this view for biochemical hypotheses? It seems unlikely that a single biochemical explanation will be found; therefore, evidence for multiple biochemical mechanisms will be obscured if data from individual subjects are pooled. We would urge that special attention be given to biochemical studies in multiplex families (those with two or more affected siblings). An observation that two psychotic siblings both display an unusual biochemical finding would suggest the possibility of a simple genetic basis for their disorders, even if none or only a few of the other cases had similar results.

Finally, a multigenic basis does not make biochemical studies impossible. The level of a specific metabolite (such as a neurotransmitter) could be influenced by several (to many) genetic loci. Studies of quantitative variation in affected siblings could provide evidence for genetic control long before the effect of individual genes can be specified. Thus, the biochemistry of psychotic disorders may be simpler than their genetics.

MAINTENANCE OF THE PSYCHOSES IN THE GENERAL POPULATION

Let us reiterate the axiom that our behavior is the result of both our environment and our heredity in varying degrees. It is clear that psychotic people do not reproduce at a rate high enough to replace themselves in the population. We have seen from our model (Table 8–5) that about 80 per cent of the schizophrenic persons in the population had normal parents. Thus, the majority of the psychotic persons in the next generation will be produced by normal parents. In this way the population maintains an approximately constant proportion of psychotic persons from generation to generation. The question as to how this equilibrium is maintained is most intriguing.

The poor reproductive performance of the psychotic person results in the loss of genes disposing toward the psychoses each generation, which must be replaced in some way in order to maintain a constant frequency of the psychosis from generation to generation. There are at least two major hypotheses designed to account for the necessary replacement of the genes lost each generation for common traits such as diabetes, mental retardation and the psychoses. Brief descriptions of the two hypotheses follow:

1. New Mutations. There are at least three loci each of which, when homozygous, produces albinism in man (Witkop et al., 1972). The most reasonable rationale for the continuation of albinism over the generations at a constant frequency is that losses of the genes for albinism are restored by new mutations. The different types of albinism are sufficiently rare so that conventional mutation rates are adequate to maintain the gene frequencies of the various genes for albinism at their present frequencies.

This hypothesis of gene replacement by new mutations at acceptable mutation rates would be adequate to explain the maintenance of the psychoses in the population if there are enough independent gene loci involved, each causing a psychosis by itself. This would require perhaps 10 to 20 separate psychoses with each depending for its expression upon the action at a single gene locus, plus environmental factors, of course. It is entirely within the bounds of common sense to assume that 10 to 20 separately determined psychoses do exist. It

is generally accepted that there are several etiologically distinct types of schizophrenia, and the unipolar and bipolar types of affective disorders seem to have been differentiated from each other. Thus, if sufficient genetic heterogeneity is present, conventional mutation rates would be adequate to maintain the functional psychoses in the population at their present frequencies. This is a very attractive hypothesis.

There is a large problem here concerning the definition of multigenic traits. Are we talking about many independent gene loci, each of which can produce an affected person by itself (genetic heterogeneity), or are we talking about a trait that depends upon the *interaction* of several independent gene loci, no one of which by itself could initiate the psychosis? Presumably both kinds of multigenic inheritance are involved for different psychoses; many of these are called schizophrenia for lack of a good differential diagnosis at the present time. The two kinds of multigenic inheritance are referred to as megaphenic (major genes) and microphenic (continuous variation) by Morton (1967).

2. Balanced Equilibrium. The second hypothesis rejects the idea that the population frequency of psychoses is maintained as the result entirely of new mutations but instead suggests that there is a genetic equilibrium of multigenes predisposing to the disorder in the psychotic person. Accumulation of the opposite alleles would result in some other type of disorder, but the reproductive disadvantage of these non-psychotic homozygous persons need not be large because there will be many more of them in the population. Table 9–17 showed clearly the skewness which results when the frequencies of the alleles predisposing to psychosis are each less than 50 per cent. If both ends of the curve of gene combinations are at some disadvantage no new mutations need be invoked in order to maintain equilibrium. This is also a very attractive hypothesis and is in accord with a quantitative genetics viewpoint. Other hypotheses and combinations of the two just given could be provided. However, such proliferation would not be helpful because we cannot distinguish between any of them with presently available techniques.

Both hypotheses are multigenic in that the first rests upon genetic heterogeneity for numerous independent gene loci which result in a psychosis that is clinically similar to several other psychoses. The second hypothesis assumes the interaction of many gene loci in the production of a psychotic individual and each different genetic loading results in a clinically different psychosis in every affected person.

A SYNTHESIS OF THE DATA

Our final task is that of trying to select the relevant data that can be fitted together to provide a plausible hypothesis which would account for the etiology of the psychoses in general. The fact that a psychosis in a patient is not present at birth but develops partly as a result of various life experiences obscures the genetic component in each family pedigree. Thus, the psychoses are unfavorable material for genetic analysis. However, it would be hard to find any traits that are more distressing to humanity than the psychoses, so it is well worth searching for clues that might stimulate further research into the etiology of the mental disorders.

The evidence for an important genetic component in the development of the psychoses is substantial and has been confirmed by numerous workers in various parts of the world. A few of the important pieces of evidence pointing to the existence of a genetic component are these:

1. Identical twins are concordant for a functional psychosis in about 50 per cent of the cases. Fraternal twins are concordant in about 15 per cent of the cases. The large difference in concordance between the two types of twins must be correlated in part with the well-known genetic fact that both identical twins have the same genotype while fraternal twins have very different genotypes. Furthermore, full siblings develop psychoses about as often as fraternal twins even though born in different years. Full siblings, half siblings and step siblings display frequencies of psychoses that are proportional to their genetic relationship to the proband. On the other hand, no relationship has been found between the length of time that the various kinds of siblings were nurtured by the proband and their frequency of psychoses.

2. We found that psychotic mothers produced about twice the percentage of psychotic offspring produced by psychotic fathers. This maternal effect may result from a higher genetic component for the psychoses being present in the psychotic females who reproduced compared with the psychotic males who reproduced.

3. The adoption studies show that children of psychotic mothers eventually develop the same or a higher percentage of psychoses when raised in adoptive homes as when raised by their psychotic mother in their own homes.

4. The heritabilities, which measure the clustering of psychoses within families and reflect genetic similarities to a significant degree, are about the same for the siblings of the probands and for the nieces and nephews regardless of whether one or neither parent was affected. The fact that the heritabilities were only about 50 per cent indicates the great importance of environmental factors of some kind. Perhaps the environmental factors are trivial random chance type fluctuations which have small effects individually. One should also bear in mind that the environmental factors may more often be internal physiological phenomena rather than external personality incidents.

These data indicate to us that genetic factors are necessary for the onset of a psychosis but, in most persons, are not sufficient to initiate the reaction. If it is granted that we are the product of our genetics and environment in both sickness and health, and that we have demonstrated a genetic basis for the psychoses, the next question concerns the genetic mechanisms responsible for the potential psychoses. It is difficult to answer this question for any trait that develops after birth and shows substantial discordance in identical twins. Both of these obfuscations result from environmental happenings.

The consensus among geneticists is that traits which are subject to such vagaries of the environment are multigenic in their determination. This concept is not just a camouflage for our ignorance but is a reasonable assumption in view of the millions of years over which the genotype has been subject to mutation and natural selection. It is not genetic realism to accept the hypothesis that only one or two gene loci are involved in a significant way with the development of the psychoses.

Smith (1971B) has demonstrated the great difficulty of distinguishing between a multigenic hypothesis and a single-locus partially dominant gene (with modifiers) model by genetic testing for traits like the psychoses. If we consider the psychoses to be a group of disorders in the same way that one understands mental retardation to be a group of independent defects, certainly numerous gene loci must be involved. It is impossible to determine at present whether several major genes each produce a specific psychosis or whether many minor genes interact to produce the psychosis. It is reasonable to assume that both types of multigenic heredity are involved in the wide range of psychotic behaviors.

There is evidence from Ödegård (1972) and others, as well as from the present study, that the most frequent diagnostic categories of schizophrenia and manic-depressive psychosis rest *in part* upon a common genotype involving more than one gene locus. It must be clear to everyone who has worked with psychotic persons that there are no sharp boundaries between schizophrenia, manic-depressive psychosis and normality for many persons. Even hospitalized patients are not always easy to diagnose, though their hospitalization distinguishes them from normal persons. It is quite clear that the psychoses are continuous traits. The heterogeneous diagnostic patterns found in the relatives of psychotic persons demonstrate not only diagnostic difficulties but also underlying genetic heterogeneity. For instance, the psychotic relatives of our affective disorder probands had a higher probability of receiving a diagnosis of schizophrenia than of an affective disorder. This is evidence against a belief that there is one major gene locus for schizophrenia and an independent major gene locus for the affective disorders. A much more attractive hypothesis, in our opinion, is that there are numerous gene loci responsible for the potentiality of a psychosis. Various combinations of the alleles at these loci would result in semicontinuous variation from one diagnosis to another. Some of the loci involved could be common to all psychoses, while others would be present only in one specific diagnosis. Only a few of the genes involved are assumed to be major genes.

Our espousal of multigenic quantitative inheritance for the psychoses will not be satisfying to geneticists with a nostalgia for simple Mendelian genetics. However, our experience as human geneticists and the data generated in relation to the functional psychoses have convinced us that there is no simple genetic basis for the psychoses. The acceptance of a multigenic basis for the psychoses would be discouraging for those looking for discrete genetic linkages or metabolic errors related to specific psychoses, except in rare kinships, but it may speed our eventual understanding of the etiology of the psychoses and their relationships to each other.

What is needed is research planned for the specific purpose of studying the multigenic mode of inheritance. Quantitative geneticists who have studied body size in laboratory animals have found it easy to state the problem, but very difficult to find unequivocal answers. Nonetheless, their problem is our problem and perhaps we can cooperate in finding some of the answers.

Our most practical findings resulted from model building related to population dynamics. If all schizophrenics, for instance, in one generation failed to reproduce, we would expect just under 20 per cent fewer schizophrenics in the next generation. We know that neither event will occur. Indeed, there will be some cases where two schizophrenics will reproduce and there is a risk of about 40 to 50 per cent that each child would develop a psychosis at some time during life. This is a high risk that most people would not care to take. One perplexing question which psychiatrists and others face in relation to the marriage of a psychotic person is whether reproduction is appropriate for this person. If reproduction seems to involve unreasonable risks, what steps, if any, should be taken to intervene in the situation? Ordinarily, genetic counseling is provided only upon the initiative of the people desiring it. It may be useful to all concerned, however, for the psychiatrist, social worker or parent to suggest genetic counseling for retarded or psychotic persons because of the nature of their disorders. Intervention of this type is perilous and could lead to undesirable psychological trauma. But if properly done and with a successful outcome, counseling that results in the prevention of reproduction may be of great benefit to the psychotic person, the close relatives and society.

REFERENCES

Alanen, Y. O. 1968. From the mothers of schizophrenic patients to interactional family dynamics. In D. Rosenthal and S. S. Kety (Eds.). *The transmission of schizophrenia.* Pergamon Press, London, pp. 201–212.

Allen, M. G., S. Cohen, and W. Pollin. 1972. Schizophrenia in veteran twins: a diagnostic review. Am. J. Psychiat. *128*: 939–945.

Angst, J. 1966. Zur äteologie und nosologie endogener depressiver psychosen. Mono. aus dem Ges. der Neurol. u. Psychiat. 112.

Angst, J. and C. Perris. 1968. Zur nosologie endogener depressionen Vergleich der Ergebuisse Zweier Untersuchungen. Arch. f. Psychiat. u. Zeit. f. d. ges. Neurol. *210*: 373–386.

Anthony, E. J. 1971. The developmental precursors of adult schizophrenia. In D. Rosenthal and S. S. Kety (Eds.). *The transmission of schizophrenia.* Pergamon Press, London, pp. 293–316.

Baxter, J. C. 1966. Family relationship variables in schizophrenia. Acta Psychiat. Scand. *42*: 362–391.

Böök, J. A. 1953. A genetic and neuropsychiatric investigation of a North-Swedish population. Acta Genet. *4*: 1–100, 345–414.

Carter, C. O. 1965. The incidence of common congenital malformations. In A. G. Steinberg and A. G. Bearn (Eds.) *Progress in medical genetics.* Grune & Stratton, New York, *4*: 59–84.

Carter, M. and C. A. H. Watts. 1971. Possible biological advantages among schizophrenics' relatives. Brit. J. Psychiat. *118*: 453–460.

Clark, J. A. and B. L. Mallett. 1963. A follow-up study of schizophrenia and depression in young adults. Brit. J. Psych. *109*: 491–499.

Clausen, J. A. 1968. Interpersonal factors in the transmission of schizophrenia. In D. Rosenthal and S. S. Kety (Eds.). *The transmission of schizophrenia.* Pergamon Press, London, pp. 251–266.

Crittenden, L. B. 1961. An interpretation of familial aggregation based on multiple genetic and environmental factors. Ann. N. Y. Acad. Sci. *91*: 769–780.

Dahl, N. L. and J. Ödegård. 1956. On hereditary factors in functional psychoses. Acta Psychiat. Suppl. 106, 320–335.

Deming, W. E. 1968. A recursion formula for the proportion of persons having a first admission as schizophrenic. Behavioral Sci. *13*: 467–476.

Eaton, J. W. and R. J. Weil. 1953. The mental health of the Hutterites. Scient. Am. *189*: 31–37.

Eaton, J. W. and R. J. Weil. 1955. *Culture and mental disorders.* Free Press, Glencoe, Ill., 254 pp.

Edwards, G. 1972. Diagnosis of schizophrenia: an Anglo-American comparison. Brit. J. Psychiat. *120*: 385–390.

Edwards, J. H. 1969. Familial predisposition in man. Brit. Med. Bull. *25*: 58–64.

Erlenmeyer-Kimling, L. and W. Paradowski. 1966. Selection and schizophrenia. Amer. Nat. *100*: 651–665.

Erlenmeyer-Kimling, L., S. Nicol, J. D. Rainer, and W. E. Deming. 1969. Changes in fertility rates of schizophrenic patients in New York State. Amer. J. Psychiat. *125*: 916–927.

Essen-Möller, E. 1941. Psychiatrische untersuchungen an einer Serie von Zwillingen. Acta Psychiat. Scand. Suppl. *23*: 1–200.

Essen-Möller, E. 1959. Mating and fertility patterns in families with schizophrenia. Eugen. Quart. *6*: 127–142.

Essen-Möller, E. 1963. Uber die schizophreniehaufigkeit bei Muttern von Schizophrenan. Schweiz. Archiv. Neurol. Neurochir. Psychiat. *91*: 260–266.

Essen-Möller, E. 1970. Twenty-one psychiatric cases and their MZ cotwins. A thirty years' follow-up. Acta Genet. Med. Gemellol. *19*: 315–317.

Falconer, D. S. 1965. The inheritance of liability to certain diseases, estimated from the incidence among relatives. Ann. Hum. Genet. (Lond.). *29*: 51–76.

Falconer, D. S. 1967. The inheritance of liability to diseases with variable age of onset, with particular reference to diabetes mellitus. Ann. Hum. Genet. (Lond.). *31*: 1–20.

Fischer, M. 1971. Psychoses in the offspring of schizophrenic monozygotic twins and their normal cotwins. Brit. J. Psychiat. *118*: 43–52.

Garrison, R. J., V. E. Anderson, and S. C. Reed. 1968. Assortative marriage. Eugen. Quart. *15*: 113–127.

Garrone, G. 1962. Étude statistique et génétique de la schizophrénie à Genève de 1901 à 1950. J. Génét. Hum. *11*: 89–219.

Gottesman, I. I. and J. Shields. 1966. Contributions of twin studies to perspectives on schizophrenia In Progr. Exp. Personality Res. *3*: 1–84.

Gottesman, I. I. and J. Shields, 1967. A polygenic theory of schizophrenia. Proc. Nat. Acad. Sci. *58*: 199–205.

Gottesman, I. I. and J. Shields, 1972. *Schizophrenia and genetics—a twin study vantage point.* Academic Press, New York.

Hagnell, Olle. 1966. A prospective of the incidence of mental disorder. Svenska Bokförlaget (Norstedts) Bonniers, Stockholm.

Hallgren, B. and T. Sjogren. 1959. A clinical and genetico-statistical study of schizophrenia and low-grade mental deficiency in a large Swedish rural population. Acta Psychiat. Scand. Suppl. *140*: 7–65.

Heston, L. L. 1966. Psychiatric disorders in foster home reared children of schizophrenic mothers. Brit Jour. Psychiat. *112*: 819–825.

Heston, L. L., D. D. Denney, and I. B. Pauly. 1966. The adult adjustment of persons institutionalized as children. Brit. J. Psychiat. *112*: 1103–1110.

Heston, L. L. and D. D. Denney. 1968. Interactions between early life experience and biological factors in schizophrenia. In D. Rosenthal and S. S. Kety (Eds.). *The transmission of schizophrenia.* Pergamon Press, London, pp. 363–376.

Heston, L. L. 1970A. The genetics of schizophrenic and schizoid disease. Sci. *167*: 249–256.

Heston, L. L. 1970B. Dialogue: schizophrenia. Sci. *168*: 420–421.

Himwich, H. E., 1971. *Biochemistry, schizophrenias and affective illnesses.* Williams & Wilkins Co., Baltimore.

Hollingshead, A. B. and F. C. Redlich. 1958. *Social class and mental illness: a community study.* John Wiley & Sons, New York, pp. 1–442.

Inouye, E. 1963. Similarity and dissimilarity of schizophrenia in twins. Univ. of Toronto Press, Proc. Third World Congress of Psychiat. *1*: 524–530.

Inouye, E. 1966. About K. Planansky's "Schizoidness

in twins." Acta Genet. Med. Gemenol. 15:442–443.

Jinks, J. L. and D. W. Fulker. 1970. Comparison of the biometrical, genetical, MAVA, and classical approaches to the analysis of human behavior. Psychol. Bull. 73:311–349.

Kaij, L. 1960. Alcoholism in twins. Almquist and Witsell, Stockholm.

Kallmann, F. J. 1938. *The genetics of schizophrenia.* J. J. Augustin, New York, 291 pp.

Kallmann, F. J. 1946. The genetic theory of schizophrenia: an analysis of 691 schizophrenic twin index families. Am. J. Psychiat., 103:309–322.

Kallmann, F. J. 1950. The genetics of psychoses: an analysis of 1232 twin index families. Congres International de Psychiatrie, Rapports VI. 1–27. Hermann, Paris.

Kallmann, F. J. 1953. *Heredity in health and mental disorder.* W. W. Norton & Co., New York, pp. 1–315.

Kallmann, F. J. 1959. The genetics of mental illness. In S. Arieti (Ed.). *American handbook of psychiatry.* Basic Books, New York.

Kallmann, F. J. and B. Roth. 1956. Genetic aspects of preadolescent schizophrenia. Amer. J. Psychiat. 112:599–606.

Kallmann, F. J., A. Falek, M. Hurzeler, and L. Erlenmeyer-Kimling. 1964. The developmental aspects of children with two schizophrenic parents. Psychiat. Res. Rep. Amer. Psychiat. Assoc. 19:136–145.

Karlsson, J. L. 1966. *The biologic basis of schizophrenia.* Charles C Thomas, Springfield, Ill.

Karlsson, J. L. 1972. A two-locus hypothesis for inheritance of schizophrenia. In A. R. Kaplan (Ed.). *Genetic factors in "schizophrenia."* Charles C Thomas, Springfield, Ill., pp. 246–255.

Kendall, R. E. and J. Gourlay. 1970A. The clinical distinction between psychotic and neurotic depressions. Brit. J. Psychiat. 117:257–260.

Kendall, R. E. and J. Gourlay. 1970B. The clinical distinction between the affective psychoses and schizophrenia. Brit. J. Psychiat. 117:261–266.

Kety, S. S. 1967. Current biochemical approaches to schizophrenia. New Eng. J. Med. 276:325–331.

Kety, S. S., D. Rosenthal, P. Wener, and F. Schulsinger. 1968. The types and prevalence of mental illness in the biological and adoptive families of adopted schizophrenics. In D. Rosenthal and S. S. Kety (Eds.). *The transmission of schizophrenia.* Pergamon Press, London, pp. 345–362.

Kinch, S. H., A. M. Gittesohn, and J. T. Doyle. 1964. Application of a life table analysis in a prospective study of degenerative cardiovascular disease. J. Chron. Dis. 17:503–514.

Kohn, M. L. 1968. Social class and schizophrenia: a critical review. In D. Rosenthal and S. S. Kety (Eds.). *The transmission of schizophrenia.* Pergamon Press, London, pp. 155–174.

Kramer, M., H. Goldstein, R. H. Israel, and N. A. Johnson. 1955. A historical study of the disposition of first admissions to a state mental hospital. Public Health Monograph No. 32. pp. 1–25. Public Health Service Publication No. 445. U. S. Government Printing Office.

Kringlen, E. 1966. Schizophrenia in twins. An epidemiological-clinical study. Psychiatry. 29:172–184.

Kringlen, E. 1968. *Heredity and environment in the functional psychoses.* Universitetsforlaget, Oslo, pp. 1–201.

Kuttner, R. E., A. B. Lorincz, and D. A. Swan. 1967. The schizophrenia gene and social evolution. Psychol. Rep. 20:407–412.

Larson, C. A. and G. E. Nyman. 1970. Age of onset in schizophrenia. Hum. Hered. 20:241–247.

Larsson, T. and T. Sjögren. 1954. A methodological psychiatric and statistical study of a large Swedish rural population. Acta Psych. et Neurol. Scand. Suppl. 89. pp. 1–250.

Leighton, D. C., et al. 1963. *The character of danger: Psychiatric symptoms in selected communities.* Basic Books, New York.

Li, C. C. and N. Mantel. 1968. A simple method of estimating the segregation ratio under complete ascertainment. Am. J. Hum. Genet. 20:61–81.

Lidz, T., S. Fleck, and A. R. Cornelison. 1965. *Schizophrenia and the family.* International Universities Press, Inc., New York.

Lindelius, R. and D. W. K. Kay. 1970. A study of schizophrenia. A clinical, prognostic and family investigation. Acta Psychiat. Scand. Suppl. 216, pp. 9–125.

Luxenburger, H. 1928. Vorlaufiger Bericht uber psychiatrische Serienuntersuchungen an Zwillingen. A. ges. Neurol. Psychiat. 116:297–326.

McCabe, M. S., R. C. Fowler, R. J. Cadoret, and George Winokur. 1972. Familial differences in schizophrenia with good and poor prognosis. Psych. Med. 1:326–332.

Mednick, S. A. and F. Schulsinger. 1968. Some premorbid characteristics related to breakdown in children with schizophrenic mothers. In D. Rosenthal and S. S. Kety (Eds.). *The transmission of schizophrenia.* Pergamon Press, London, pp. 267–291.

Mendlewicz, J., R. R. Fieve, J. D. Rainer, and J. L. Fleiss. 1972. Manic-depressive illness: a comparative study of patients with and without a family history. Brit. J. Psychiat. 120:523–530.

Morton, N. E. 1967. The detection of major genes under additive continuous variation. Am. J. Hum. Genet. 19:23–34.

Morton, N. E., S. Yee, R. C. Elston, and Ruth Lew. 1970. Discontinuity and quasi-continuity: alternative hypotheses of multifactorial inheritance. Clin. Genet. 1:81–94.

Myers, J. K. and B. H. Roberts. 1959. *Family and class dynamics in mental illness.* John Wiley and Sons, Inc., New York, pp. 1–291.

Nathan, P. E., M. M. Andberg, P. O. Behan, and V. D. Patch, 1969. Thirty-two observers and one patient: a study of diagnostic reliability. Jour. Clin. Psychol. 25:9–15.

Neel, J. V., S. S. Fajans, J. W. Conn, and R. T. Davidson. 1965. Diabetes mellitus. In J. V. Neel, M. W. Shaw, and W. J. Schull (Eds.). Genetics and the epidemiology of chronic diseases. Public Health Service Publication No. 1163. Washington, D. C. pp. 105–132.

Nyholm, M. and H. F. Helweg-Larsen. 1954. On the computation of morbid risk (disease expectancy). Acta Genet. et. Statist. Med. 5:25–38.

Ödegård, Ö. 1963. The psychiatric disease entities in the light of a genetic investigation. Acta Psychiat. Scand. 39:Suppl. 169, pp. 94–104.

Ödegård, Ö. 1972. The multifactorial theory of inheritance in predisposition to schizophrenia. In A. R. Kaplan (Ed.). Genetic factors in "schizophrenia." Charles C Thomas, Springfield, Ill., pp. 256–275.

Penrose, L. S. 1938. A clinical and genetic study of 1280 cases of mental defect. His Majesty's Stationery Office, London.

Penrose, L. S. 1944. Mental illness in husband and wife; a contribution to the study of assortative mating in man. Psychiat. Quart. Suppl. 18:161–166.

Penrose, L. S. 1945. Survey of cases of familial mental illness. Digest of Neurol. & Psychiat. (Hartford Inst. of Living) Series 13, p. 644.

Penrose, L. S. 1969. Effects of additive genes at many loci compared with those of a set of alleles at one locus in parent-child and sib correlations Ann. Hum. Genet. (Lond.). 33:15–21.

Perris, C. 1971. Abnormality on paternal and maternal sides: observations in bipolar (manic-depressive) and unipolar depressive psychoses. Brit. J. Psychiat. 118:207–210.

Planansky, K. and R. Johnson. 1967. Mate selection in schizophrenia. Acta Psychiat. Scand. 43:397–409.

Pollin, W., J. R. Stabenau, and J. Tupin. 1965. Family studies with identical twins discordant for schizophrenia. Psychiat. 28:60–78.

Pollin, W., J. R. Stabenau, L. Mosher, and J. Tupin. 1966. Life history differences in identical twins discordant for schizophrenia. Amer. J. Orthopsychiat. 36:492–509.

Reed, E. W. and S. C. Reed. 1965. *Mental retardation: a family study.* W. B. Saunders Co., Philadelphia.

Reed, S. C. 1965. The evolution of human intelligence. Am. Sci. 53:317–326.

Rosanoff, A. J. and F. Orr. 1911. A study of heredity in insanity in the light of the Mendelian theory. Am. J. Insanity 68:221–261.

Rosanoff, A. J., L. M. Handy, I. R. Plesset, and S. Brush. 1934. The etiology of so-called schizophrenic psychoses. With special reference to their occurrence in twins. Am. J. Psychiat. 91:247–286.

Rosenthal, D. 1959. Some factors associated with concordance and discordance with respect to schizophrenia in monozygotic twins. J. Nerv. Ment. Dis. 129:1–10.

Rosenthal, D. 1961. Sex distribution and the severity of illness among samples of schizophrenic twins. J. Psychiat. Res. 1:26–36.

Rosenthal, D. (Ed.). 1963. *The Genain quadruplets.* Basic Books, New York.

Rosenthal, D. 1971. Two adoption studies of heredity in the schizophrenic disorders. In M. Bleuler and J. Angst (Eds.). *The origin of schizophrenia.* Hans Huber, Bern. pp. 21–34.

Rosenthal, D., P. Wender, S. Kety, F. Schulsinger, J. Welner, and L. Östergaard. 1968. Schizophrenics' offspring reared in adoptive homes. In D. Rosenthal and S. S. Kety (Eds.). *The transmission of schizophrenia.* Pergamon Press, London, pp. 377–391.

Rosenthal, D. 1970. *Genetic theory and abnormal behavior.* McGraw Hill Book Company, New York, 183 pp.

Rosenthal, D. and J. Van Dyke. 1970. The use of monozygotic twins discordant as to schizophrenia in the search for an inherited characterological defect. Acta psychiat. Scand. Suppl. 219:183–189.

Rüdin, E. 1961. Studien über Vererbung und Entstehung geistiger Storungen. T. Zur Vererburg und Neuentstehung der Dementia praecox. Julius Springer, Berlin.

Slater, E. (with the assistance of J. Shields). 1953. Psychotic and neurotic illnesses in twins. Medical Research Council special report series No. 278, Her Majesty's Stationery Office, London.

Slater, E. 1958. The monogenic theory of schizophrenia. Act. Genet. Stat. Med. 8:50–56.

Slater, E. 1968. A review of earlier evidence on genetic factors in schizophrenia. In D. Rosenthal and S. S. Kety (Eds.). *The transmission of schizophrenia.* Pergamon Press, London, pp. 15-26.

Slater, E. J. Maxwell, and J. S. Price. 1971. Distribution of ancestral secondary cases in bipolar affective disorders. Brit. J. Psychiat. 118:215–218.

Slater, E. and V. Cowie. 1971. *The genetics of mental disorders.* Oxford Univ. Press, London.

Smith, C. 1970. Heritability of liability and concordance in MZ twins. Ann. Hum. Genet. (Lond.). 34:85–91.

Smith, C. 1971A. Recurrence risks for multifactorial inheritance. Am. J. Hum. Genet. 23:578–588.

Smith, C. 1971B. Discriminating between different modes of inheritance in genetic disease. Clinical Genetics 2:303–314.

Smith, C., D. S. Falconer, and L. J. P. Duncan. 1972. A statistical and genetical study of diabetes. II. Heritability of liability. Ann. Hum. Genet. (Lond.). 35:281–299.

Snezhnevsky, A. V. and M. Vartanyan. 1971. The forms of schizophrenia and their biological correlates. In H. E. Himwich, (Ed.). *Biochemistry, schizophrenias and affective illnesses.* Williams and Wilkins Co., Baltimore.

Stabenau, J. R. and W. Pollin. 1969. Early characteristics of monozygotic twins discordant for schizophrenia. Arch. Gen. Psychiat. 17:723–734.

Stenstedt, A. 1959. *Involutional melancholia.* Ejnar Munksgaard, Copenhagen.

Stevens, B. C. 1969. Marriage and fertility of women suffering from schizophrenia or affective disorders. Oxford Univ. Press, London.

Stierlin, H. 1972. The impact of relational vicissitudes on the life course of one schizophrenic quadruplet. In A. R. Kaplan (Ed.). *Genetic factors in "schizophrenia."* Charles C Thomas, pp. 451–463.

Strole, L., T. S. Langner, S. T. Michael, M. K. Opler, and T. A. C. Rennie. 1962. *Mental health in the metropolis.* McGraw-Hill, New York.

Strömgren, E. 1938. Beiträge zur psychiatrischen Erblehre. Acta psychiat. Kbh., Suppl. 19, 259 pp.

Tienari, P. 1971. Schizophrenia and monozygotic twins. Psychiatria Fennica 1971, pp. 97–104.

Tsuang, M. -T. 1967. A study of pairs of sibs both hospitalized for mental disorder. Brit. J. Psychiat. 113:283–300.

Tsuang, M. T. 1971. Abnormality on paternal and maternal sides in Chinese schizophrenics. Brit. J. Psychiat. 118:211–214.

Turner, R. J. and M. Wagonfeld. 1967. Occupational mobility and schizophrenia, an assessment of the social causation and social selection hypotheses. Am. Soc. Rev. 32:104–113.

Weinberg, W. 1915. Zur korrektur des einflusses der lebensdauer und todesaulese auf die ergebnisse bestimmter kreuzungen. Arch. Ross. u. Gesell 11:434–444.

Weinberg, W. 1925. Methoden und technik der statistik mit besonderer berücksichtigung der sozial-biologie. Handbuch der Sozialen Hygiene und Gezundheitsfürsorge. *1*:71–148.

Werboff, J. and J. S. Gottlieb. 1963. Drugs in pregnancy: behavioral teratology. Obstet. Gynec. Survey *18*:420–423.

Winokur, G. and F. N. Pitts, Jr. 1965. Affective disorder: VI. A family history study of prevalences, sex differences and possible genetic factors. J. Psychiat. Res. 3:113–123.

Winokur, G., R. Cadoret, J. Dorzab, and M. Baker. 1971. Depressive disease: A genetic study. Arch. Gen. Psychiat. 24:135–144.

Winokur, G., J. Morrison, J. Clancy, and R. Crowe. 1972. The Iowa 500. II. A blind family history comparison of mania, depression and schizophrenia. Arch. Gen. Psychiat. 27:462–464.

Witkop, C. J., Jr., J. G. White, W. E. Nance, and R. E. Umber. 1972. Mutations in the melanin pigment system in man resulting in features of oculocutaneous albinism. In V. Riley. (Ed.). *Pigmentation: Its genesis and biologic control.* Appleton-Century-Crofts, New York, pp. 359–377.

Zerbin-Rudin, E. 1967. Endogene psychosen. In P. E. Becker (Ed.). Humangenetic, ein kurzes Handbuck Vol. V12. Stuttgart: Thieme, pp. 446–557.

APPENDIX

KEY TO SYMBOLS

M	F	
■	●	With functional psychosis
◩	◓	Probably with functional psychosis
▨	⊘	Possibly with functional psychosis Psychoneurotic disorder (or probably or possibly so) Personality disorder (or probably or possibly so) Psychotic reaction to senility or to arteriosclerosis (or probably or possibly so)
□	○	Without the above
◨	⊘	Unknown as to mental health
	◇	Unknown as to sex and mental health
	⬤	Death at age two years or less
	╱	Hospitalized in a psychiatric hospital or ward
	P	Proband
	S	Suicide or suicide attempt
	✻	Siblings used as controls
	□━○	Consanguineous union
	□┈○	Illegitimate union
	□─○	Presently childless or unknown as to children
	□┳○	Had no children
	□┳○	Had children, number unknown
	□╫○	Separated or divorced

Roman numerals — indicate generations

Arabic numerals above symbol — indicate individuals

Arabic numerals below symbol — indicate age at
                                               last information

W S H — Kinship number

Material below continuous dotted line obtained
      since original study

INTRODUCTION

In this book we are following the pattern established in the earlier work about mental retardation (Reed and Reed, 1965) by including a large appendix. This strategy presents the basic data for the use of other investigators in order to test hypotheses that had not occurred to us. Furthermore, it permits identification of specific families or individuals who might be benefited by further examination and study.

The study comprises 18,736 individuals who are members of 99 kinships. In the pedigree drawings which follow, the proband is always shown in Generation III and is designated by the letter *P*. The grandparents are in Generation I, and the parents, aunts and uncles are in Generation II. All known descendants of the parents are included. Large kinships are presented in several sections, with the continuations indicated by wavy lines.

For each person the number above and to the right identifies the individual, while the number below the circle or square is the age at last report. The persons above the dashed line are those who were known prior to the recent follow-up. The presence of psychosis or other mental disorder is indicated on the pedigree drawing by the type of symbol, as explained in the Key to Symbols. The criteria for diagnosis are discussed in Section E of Chapter II.

The drawings also present information about controls, which were selected by the procedure described in Chapter VI. The "control probands" are a sample of the persons who married into the families at the level of Generation IV. Each control proband is indicated in the main family pedigree by an asterisk and is shown again in a control drawing together with his or her siblings. The "control group" is composed only of the siblings of the control probands.

The pedigree drawing for each kinship is followed by brief summaries of the information available for those persons having some condition of particular relevance for the study. In a few instances there is a description of a condition which may be of interest but which does not fit one of the categories designated for symbols; thus, there may be a summary statement but a blank symbol. The diagnostic language follows the 1952 Diagnostic and Statistical Manual for Mental Disorders published by the American Psychiatric Association.

PRETEST FAMILIES

Ten probands were selected from the Warren State Hospital files in order to test the techniques of data collection. Eight were first admitted in the period 1926–1937, one was first admitted in 1945 and another in 1953. The data from these pretest families are included in the analyses in Chapter III but not in subsequent chapters.

A brief family summary for each of the proband's families accompanies the 10 pedigree charts. In four of the kinships there were no psychotic relatives of the probands.

Kinships 1 through 10 are included in this section.

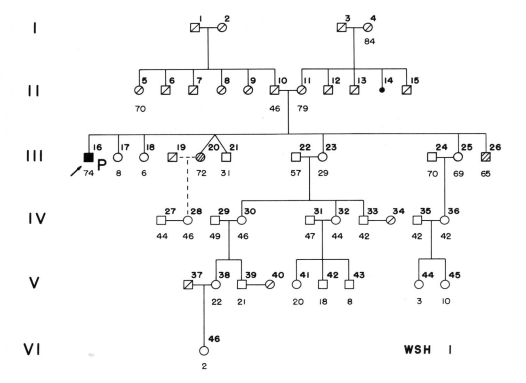

WSH I

WSH 1: The Proband

Proband (16), born 1879; died at age 74 years of coronary occlusion. He was described as "of peculiar mental make-up all his life" but at age 46 years, for one year prior to admission to a state mental hospital, he underwent an emotional reaction characterized by many delusional ideas, auditory hallucinations and paranoid ideas of persecution and reference. He was hospitalized from February until May of 1926, then was recommitted on 3/11/28 as his paranoid traits had extended, alcoholic excesses were reported, and because he persisted in paying unwanted attention to a young girl. He was paroled in June but was recommitted in September, 1928 and remained at the state hospital until his death in 1953. Diagnosis was dementia praecox. His bizarre ideas of reference and persecution persisted; he was auditorily and probably visually hallucinated. Classification: Schizophrenic reaction — paranoid type.

Siblings

Sister (20), born 1887. At age 72 years was still working as a switchboard operator. She was described in mid-life as "nervous . . . flies off the handle now and then." Classification: Probable personality disorder.

Brother (26), born 1894. At age 65 he was a retired laborer who reportedly at one time had "nervous spells." He underwent surgery for crossed eyes; the eye became infected, resulting in eye trouble for most of his life. Classification: Possible other situational personality disturbance.

Family Summary

The proband had a psychotic disorder; a brother and a sister perhaps had personality disorders.

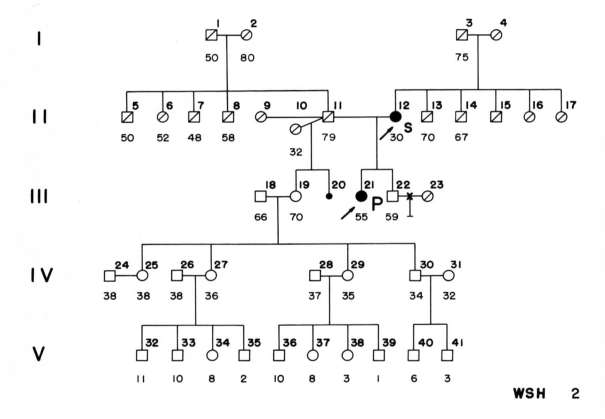

WSH   2

WSH 2: The Proband

Proband (21), born 1898; died at age 55 years of cerebral embolus at a state hospital. She had four hospitalizations at Warren State Hospital: the first from March until April, 1926, with a diagnosis of schizophrenia, the second from May until September, 1936, with a diagnosis of dementia praecox — paranoid type, the third from October, 1950, until June, 1951, and the fourth from April, 1953, until her death in August of the same year. Symptoms began at age 19 years; until then she was a "bright, alert sociable girl." At each hospitalization affect was diminished, she was subject to severe temper outbursts and there was a lack of insight into her condition (she believed her illness to be caused by unknown persons poisoning her food). While hospitalized the symptoms would subside enough for her to get along outside the hospital for a time with supervision. Classification: Schizophrenic reaction — paranoid type.

Parents

Mother (12), born 1874; died at age 30 years of suicide by hanging while a patient at Warren State Hospital. In 1893 she was hospitalized at Warren State Hospital for two months with excitement and nervousness. In 1903 she was again hospitalized for a few weeks with a diagnosis of acute melancholia. She was again admitted to Warren State Hospital on 2/8/1904, with a diagnosis of acute melancholia; she committed suicide during this hospitalization. Hospital notes stated that she always had an uncontrollable temper. She was described as very nervous and depressed and as very concerned about how "bad" and "awful" she was. Classification: Manic-depressive reaction — depressed type.

Family Summary

The proband and her mother had psychotic disorders.

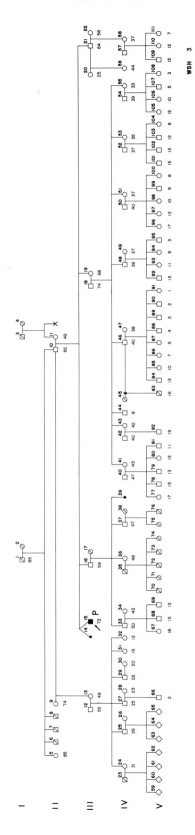

WSH 3

WSH 3: The Proband

Proband (15), born 1878; died at age 72 years of coronary thrombosis at Warren State Hospital. He was a piano teacher who had always been considered "moody" and a "queer character." After the death of his father he became depressed and restless and began a trip to Oklahoma which was interrupted in Chicago by his illness. He spent three weeks in a sanitarium in Illinois before his transfer to Warren State Hospital on 4/20/1933, where he remained until 2/19/1934. He had five subsequent hospitalizations at Warren State Hospital in 1934, 1937, 1938, 1942 and 1944. He never re-mained out of the hospital for more than a few months at a time. The hospital notes consistently describe him as a homosexual type with musical sublimation. He was generally withdrawn, had mood swings, inappropriate affect, blocking and somatic delusions. The original diagnosis was that of a psychopathic personality. A later diagnosis of dementia praecox, simple type, was made. Classification: Schizophrenic reaction—paranoid type.

Family Summary

The proband was the only person designated as psychotic in this pedigree.

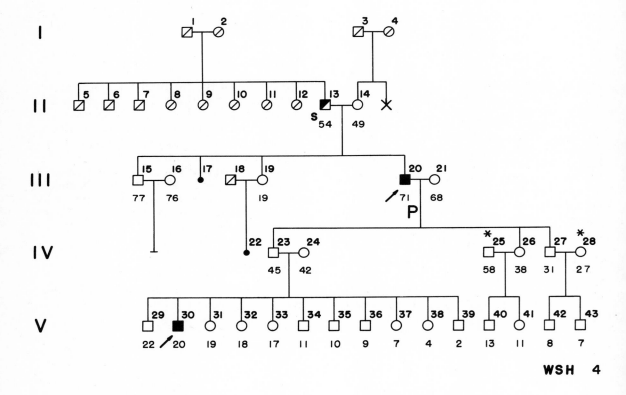

WSH   4

WSH 4: The Proband

Proband (20), born 1889. He was hospitalized at a state hospital from November, 1935, until January, 1936, with a diagnosis of dementia praecox, paranoid type, because of his bizarre thinking and behavior and his visual and auditory hallucinations. For two months before hospitalization he had vague somatic complaints; the mental break came one night when he awoke in an agitated state believing God had spoken to him. Improvement was gradual and he was never rehospitalized. At 71 years he was still working as a secretary and accountant. Classification: Schizophrenic reaction—paranoid type.

Grandchildren

Grandson (30), born 1939. He had a normal infancy and early childhood. The first grade was repeated and at grade six he became "firm and rigid" and at grade seven was placed in a special class. During this year he began stealing and would occasionally sit idle for hours and talk to himself. He was seen at a mental health clinic in April, 1953, where he was diagnosed as schizophrenic reaction, type unclassified, and referred to a state hospital where he was hospitalized from July, 1953, to July, 1954. At admission he had facial grimaces, auditory hallucinations and dissociated thinking. He received psychotherapy and schooling and was discharged as improved on 7/3/1955. He was seen at a child guidance clinic in 1957, where the psychiatrist considered him hallucinated and still disturbed. Classification: Schizophrenic reaction—childhood type.

Parents

Father (13); died at age 54 years of suicide. He was described as "a heavy drinker with a violent temper." Classification: Probably with functional psychosis.

Family Summary

The proband and a grandson had psychotic disorders and the father probably so.

Controls

None noteworthy.

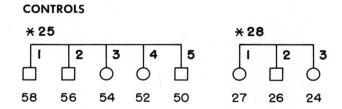

WSH 4

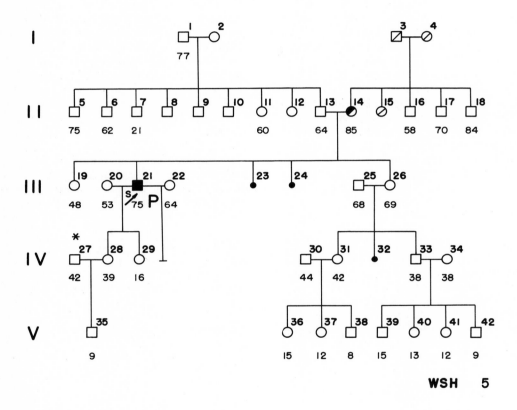

WSH   5

WSH 5: The Proband

Proband (21), born 1886; died at age 75 years of pneumonia at a state mental hospital. He was hospitalized on 9/24/1935, with a diagnosis of psychoneurosis, reactive depression, after losing his job of three decades as a planing mill manager. He was ordinarily a "good mixer" although somewhat "quick-tempered and set in his ways." After the job loss he became indecisive, worried, had insomnia and could not concentrate. While hospitalized he improved considerably and was paroled on 6/2/1938. In October, 1938, he made a suicide attempt at home and was returned to the hospital where he remained until 1941. The history of cyclic depression and overactive state related by his wife at this admission suggested a diagnosis of manic-depressive reaction. In January, 1960, he was again hospitalized because of confusion, poor memory, blunting of affect and lowering of emotional tone. A diagnosis of chronic brain syndrome associated with arteriosclerosis was made. He remained at the hospital until his death. Classification: Manic-depressive reaction — other; Also, chronic brain syndrome associated with cerebral arteriosclerosis.

Parents

Mother (14), born 1854; died at age 85 years of myocarditis due to arteriosclerosis, mental. She reportedly had a nervous breakdown and was depressed, although not hospitalized, at the time of menopause. Classification: Probably with functional psychosis — involutional psychotic reaction.

Family Summary

The proband was psychotic and his mother probably so. Each was also classified as with chronic brain syndrome associated with cerebral arteriosclerosis.

Controls

None noteworthy.

CONTROLS

W S H   5

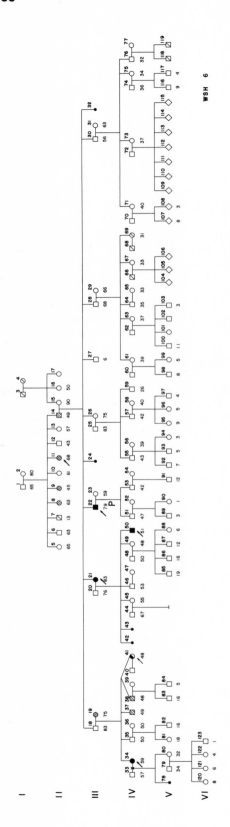

WSH 6

WSH 6: The Proband

Proband (22), born 1879; died at age 70 years of a coronary occlusion at Warren State Hospital. His first period of depression occurred in 1915 when he was greatly worried by a business venture; he recovered as business conditions improved and was not treated for a depression. He worked as a machinist until age 42 years, then became a furniture salesman. In early 1930 his employer introduced high pressure methods of selling at his furniture company. He became irritable and nervous and quit work in August, 1930. He did not seek other employment but became progressively more depressed until hospitalization at Warren State Hospital from January until June, 1932, with a diagnosis of manic-depressive psychosis, mild depression. He had three subsequent hospitalizations at Warren State Hospital from May, 1934, until March, 1937; from September, 1945, until April, 1946, and from September, 1946, until his death in June, 1949. The episodes of depression were characterized by "fussing, sympathizing with self, gloomy talk of the future, sleeping days and sleeplessness at night." Classification: Manic-depressive reaction—other.

Parents

Father (14), born 1848; died at age 49 years of apoplexy. He was described as "extremely nervous and worried a great deal . . . was quick-tempered and irritable." Classification: Probable psychoneurotic disorder.

Aunts and Uncles

Paternal aunt (8), born 1869; at age 63 was well and a housewife. She reportedly was "excitable for a short period at the age of twenty-five" but had no trouble after that. Classification: Probable other transient situational personality disturbance.

Paternal aunt (9). Following an operation at age 45 years she was "depressed and worried for about a year." Classification: Probable psychoneurotic disorder — depressive reaction.

Paternal aunt (11), born 1858; died at age 68 years at a state mental hospital where she had been diagnosed as senile psychosis with cerebral arteriosclerosis. Her mental disturbance, which began about four years before admission on 8/20/1926, was characterized by a general lack of interest, confusion, memory defect and depression. Classification: Chronic brain syndrome associated with cerebral arteriosclerosis.

Siblings

(19) wife of brother (18), born 1876; died at age 75 years of acute cardiac decompensation. She was described as "a strict disciplinarian who endeavored to dominate the lives of her children." The death certificate lists "senile psychosis" as a contributory cause of death. Classification: Chronic brain syndrome of senium.

Sister (21), born 1877; died at age 83 years of coronary thrombosis. As a youth she was slightly seclusive in nature. She later became a school teacher. The first real symptoms of mental disturbance occurred in November, 1907, when she became nervous and destructive and was confined in a mental hospital for seven months. Subsequent hospitalizations were at Warren State Hospital from 11/15/1908 until 10/31/1909, and from 1/29/1912 until 9/8/1914, each with a diagnosis of recurrent mania. She was readmitted to Warren State Hospital in July, 1941, and remained there until her death in 1961. Her psychosis showed a deteriorative course characterized by systematized delusions of persecution, reference, diminished affect, no insight and hyper-religiosity. The concluding diagnosis at Warren State Hospital was dementia praecox, paranoid type. Classification: Schizophrenic reaction—paranoid type.

Nieces and Nephews

Niece (34), born 1905. Early development was normal. Her mental illness began in 1933 when "her brain suddenly turned white," she became depressed and took aspirin "by the hundreds." She also suffered from severe anxiety and sleeplessness. She was not treated until 1946, when she received shock treatments at an Ohio hospital. After release in 1947, she resumed her old pattern of behavior and was admitted to a mental hospital for metrazol treatments. She returned home, again became upset and was taken to a nursing home. It was about this time that she had a pre-frontal lobotomy, following which she began to drink moderately, but after five years began to drink to excess and became a public nuisance. At home she neglected her housework, was profane, obscene, untidy, paranoid and noisy. On 7/9/1953 she was admitted to a state mental hospital with a diagnosis of schizophrenic reaction—paranoid type, where she was still a patient, condition unimproved, at age 59 years. Classification: Schizophrenic reaction—paranoid type.

Nephew (37), born 1910. He at age 49 years was a paper mill worker who reportedly was "violent when drunk," although he had no history of treatment for alcoholism. Classification: Probable sociopathic personality disturbance—alcoholism (addiction).

Nephew (38), born 1911, a butcher who reportedly "gets violent" when inebriated. Classification: Probable sociopathic personality disturbance—alcoholism (addiction).

Niece (41), born 1911. She had a history of drinking to excess as well as a history of electroshock treatments in 1945 at a mental hospital. In 1957 she had a hallucinatory episode for which she was not treated. Classification: Probably with functional psychosis.

Nephew (50), born 1913. He was born while his mother was on parole from a state mental hospital and lived at home for two years after his birth. From that time on he lived in orphanages and with various foster families. He always failed to adjust to his environment. In 1932 he was apprehended for robbery and striking a policeman with a wrench. During the arrest he was shot several times in the leg. After a month of treatment in a general hospital he was hospitalized at a state mental hospital from June until November, 1932, with a diagnosis of without psychosis—psychopathic personality. He spent his time day-dreaming and reading detective stories. There was some blunting of general emotional reaction but no evidence of psychosis. After a prison term he re-entered high school and on 6/25/1935, castrated himself to "improve his intelligence." Subsequently, he was again admitted to the same mental hospital, where a diagnosis of dementia praecox was made. He was paroled in 1939, incarcerated at a Federal Reformatory in 1940 and 1941, then admitted to a state mental hospital where he was still a patient at age 51 years. Classification: Schizophrenic reaction.

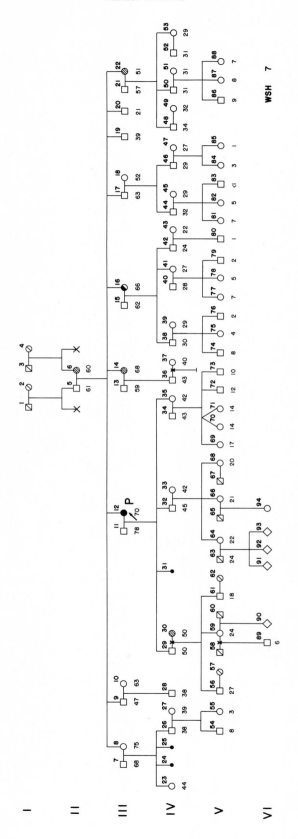

WSH 7

Family Summary

The proband, a sister, a niece and a nephew had psychotic disorders and another niece probably so. The father and a paternal aunt were probably neurotic. Personality disorders were found in a paternal aunt and in two nephews. A paternal aunt was hospitalized with a diagnosis of chronic brain syndrome associated with cerebral arteriosclerosis; the wife of a brother was classified as chronic brain syndrome of senium.

WSH 7: The Proband

Proband (12), born 1894; died at age 70 years of arteriosclerosis and diabetes. She was described as a "rather tense, anxious" individual, although lively and sociable, who had a mild five-month depression in 1912, following the birth of her first child. The next depression, during which she feared suicide and was greatly agitated, began about six weeks prior to her first admission to a state hospital on 6/5/1945, with a diagnosis of involutional psychosis, melancholia, later changed to manic-depressive reaction, mixed type. She remained at the hospital until September, 1945. The second hospitalization was during July and August, 1956, again with a diagnosis of manic-depressed reaction, mixed type. The second admission followed two years of severe intermittent depression, hyperactivity, insomnia and fear of suicide. On 7/28/1964, she was readmitted to the hospital because of hallucinations, disorientation, confusion and parkinsonism, which developed in 1962. A diagnosis of chronic brain syndrome associated with cerebral arteriosclerosis was made. She remained agitated and confused until her death. Classification: Manic-depressive reaction—other; also, chronic brain syndrome associated with cerebral arteriosclerosis.

Children

(30) wife of son (29), born 1914; reportedly "complains all the time of sickness" for which there is no medical basis. Classification: Possible psychoneurotic disorder.

Parents

Mother (6), died at age 60 years, cause of death unknown. She was described as "a worrier, a hard worker" and as "happy and strict." Classification: Possible psychoneurotic disorder.

Siblings

Sister (14), born 1896. She reportedly was depressed at one time but was not hospitalized. In 1964 she was described as "a widow, nervous, takes tranquilizers." She was cooperative when interviewed. Classification: Probable psychoneurotic disorder.

Sister (16), born 1898. She was hospitalized at a mental hospital from 1/12/1928 until 9/9/1928, reportedly for "nerves"; however, the hospital stated that there was nothing in her chart to indicate a mental disturbance. She did have a period of emotional disturbance beginning about 1940 and lasting three or four years, during which time she was excessively emotional and depressed. At this time she cried a great deal, had various somatic complaints and presented a general picture of agitation and depression. She recovered fully and was well at age 66 years. Classification: Probably with functional psychosis, psychotic-depressive reaction.

Sister (22), born 1912. She was interviewed at age 51 years and described as "flighty, nervous and tense." At first she refused to give information as she thought the interviewer was from the "revenue department." Classification: Probable psychoneurotic disorder.

Family Summary

The proband had a psychotic disorder and her sister probably so. The mother, two sisters and the wife of a son were probably or possibly neurotic.

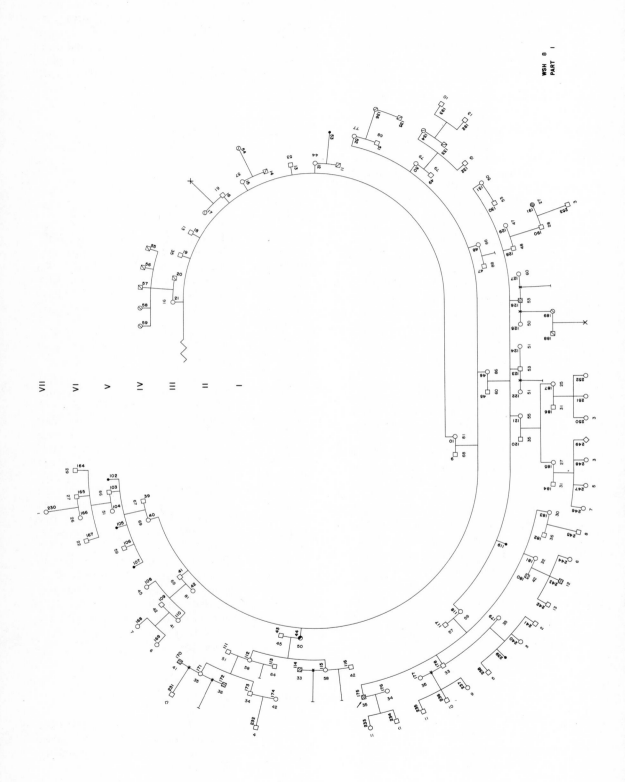

WSH 8
PART 1

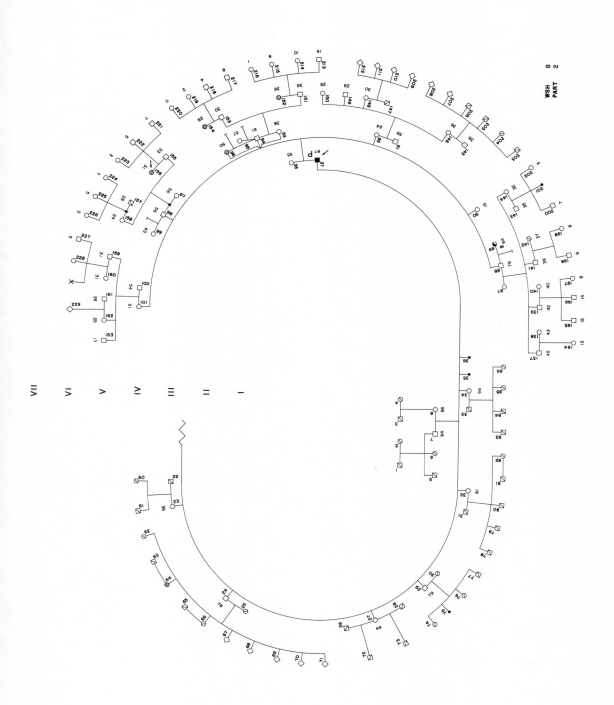

WSH 8: The Proband

The proband (37), born 1867; died at age 87 years of myocardial infarction with arteriosclerotic heart disease. He had a history of intoxication at least once a week throughout his adult life. In September, 1935, he was admitted to a state mental hospital. Mental changes were observed over several years and, following the death of his daughter-in-law in 1935, he became particularly disturbed. At admission he was cheerful, almost euphoric, rambling in his conversation and poorly oriented. He was discharged, much improved, on 1/11/1936, but was readmitted in October. He was again considered over-productive, rambling and believed he was "one of God's chosen people." He was transferred to Warren State Hospital on 2/2/1937, with a diagnosis of psychosis due to disturbance of circulation, cerebral arteriosclerosis, where he remained until death. While at Warren State Hospital he spoke of bizarre experiences which were interpreted as visual and auditory hallucinosis. Classification: Schizophrenic reaction — paranoid type.

Children

(89) wife of son (88), born 1884; suicided at age 64 years. She was reportedly "perturbed before her death, and somewhat depressed, but had no trouble before that." Classification: Probably with functional psychosis, involutional psychotic reaction or psychotic-depressive reaction.

(96) wife of son (94), born 1900; died at age 50 years of obstruction of the bowels. She was reportedly "a drug addict; her syringe and other equipment for the use of drugs were discovered after she died." Classification: Probable sociopathic personality disturbance — drug addiction.

Grandchildren

(152) wife of grandson (151), born 1923. At age 34 years, following the birth of her last baby, she had a "nervous attack." Classification: Probable psychoneurotic disorder.

(154) wife of grandson (153), born 1930. She was hospitalized at a general hospital for seven days in April, 1952, with hysteria and hyperthyroidism. At age 29 years an interviewer described her as "interested and helpful." Classification: Psychoneurotic disorder.

(156) wife of grandson (155), born 1928. She was hospitalized at a mental hospital on 5/20/1957 with a diagnosis of reactive depression. On 6/1/1957 she was transferred to a general hospital where she spent three months. Diagnosis at the second hospital was psychoneurosis, depressive reaction. Classification: Psychoneurotic disorder — depressive reaction.

Nieces and Nephews

Niece (44), born 1876; died at age 20 years of "a nervous disorder." She became extremely depressed after the death of her husband. She reportedly "took no interest in anything" and "grieved herself to death." Classification: Probably with functional psychosis, psychotic-depressive reaction.

Niece (64). When interviewed in 1959 she was resentful, refused to give information and called her sisters advising them not to cooperate. Classification: Possible personality disorder.

Distant Relatives

(114) husband of grandniece (115), born 1897. He was divorced in 1930 because of his promiscuity. Classification: Possible sociopathic personality disturbance.

Grandnephew (126), born 1907. He was an alcoholic who "became wild when intoxicated." Classification: Sociopathic personality disturbance — alcoholism (addiction).

(170) husband of great-grandniece (171), born 1919. He was an alcoholic. Classification: Sociopathic personality disturbance — alcoholism (addiction).

(172) husband of great-grandniece (171), born 1924. He was an unemployed alcoholic whom his physician described as a psychopath. Classification: Sociopathic personality disturbance — alcoholism (addiction).

Great-grandnephew (175), born 1925. He reportedly was a "problem child when younger." He was sentenced to a penitentiary for larceny in 1949 and subsequently hospitalized at a Veterans Administration hospital for a short time with a diagnosis of conversion reaction with psychogenic headaches and mild anxiety. He was discharged as improved and was described as "O.K." at age 35 years. Classification: Probable sociopathic personality disturbance.

(180) husband of great-grandniece (181), born 1918. He reportedly was "very nervous" after World War II. Classification: Probable psychoneurotic disorder.

(191) wife of great-grandnephew (190), born 1953. She reportedly was "nervous and jumpy" before the birth of her baby but was better after its birth. Classification: Probable psychoneurotic disorder.

Great-great-grandnephew (243), born 1943. He was described as "shy, preoccupied and nervous." Classification: Probable psychoneurotic disorder.

Family Summary

The proband had a psychotic disorder and was hospitalized; a niece and the wife of a son had probable psychotic disorders. Neurotics included a great-great-grandnephew, the wives of three grandsons, the wife of a great-grandnephew and the husband of a great-grandniece. A niece, the wife of a son, a grandnephew, the husband of a grandniece, the husbands of two great-grandnieces, and a great-grandnephew had personality disorders. The great-grandnephew was hospitalized for treatment.

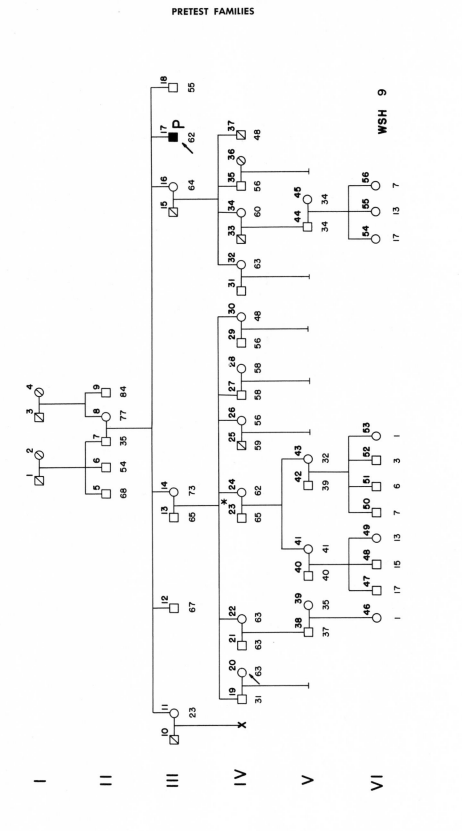

WSH 9: The Proband

Proband (17), born 1876; died at age 62 years of chronic myocardial infarction at Warren State Hospital. He was a wanderer most of his life and worked only occasionally as a painter. He was alcoholic for a time, but had not used alcohol for the two years previous to his admission to Warren State Hospital in August, 1934. He also had periods when he was talkative and silly. The severe attack of overactivity for which he was hospitalized first resulted in a trip to jail and later commitment. At Warren State Hospital he was cheerful, talkative, euphoric; showed mild flight of ideas and some evidence of psychomotor hyperactivity. Diagnosis was manic-depressive—manic type. He escaped but was soon committed to a different state hospital, where he remained for three months. He was again admitted to Warren State Hospital on 7/28/1936, with a diagnosis of manic-depressive psychosis, manic type, and remained there until he died two years later. Classification: Manic-depressive reaction—manic type.

Nieces and Nephews

(20) wife of nephew (19), born 1901. She was an epileptic whose attacks were characterized by confusion, but not psychosis, until about one month before her mother died in early 1949. At this time she became more confused and believed that she was hypnotized with electrical current going through her tongue. At the time of her mother's death she became "hysterical" and refused to eat or sleep. She lived with her mother after her husband was accidentally burned to death following six years of marriage. Epileptic seizures began at age 11 years and there was a history of St. Vitus dance as a child. Her parents separated when she was nine years of age and she was reared by her maternal grandparents. At age 16 years she had tuberculosis. Admission to a state mental hospital was on 3/2/1949, with a diagnosis of without psychosis, convulsive disorder, epilepsy. She was paroled on 8/14/1949, but returned on 3/26/1953. Three years later she was transferred to a county home where she maintained herself by employment at the home as a housemother. Classification: Chronic brain syndrome associated with convulsive disorder with psychotic reaction.

Family Summary

The proband had a psychotic disorder; the wife of a nephew had a psychotic reaction associated with a convulsive disorder.

Controls

None noteworthy.

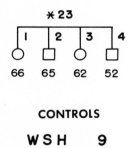

CONTROLS

W S H   9

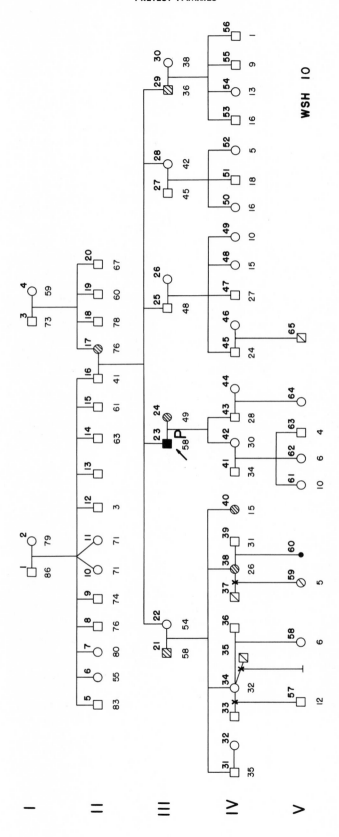

WSH 10

WSH 10: The Proband

Proband (23), born 1908. At age 58 years he was on parole from Warren State Hospital and working as a construction laborer and watchman. He was described as being fairly well adjusted, although excessively moralistic, inclined to worry and averse to trying new things or admitting he was wrong in any matter, until age 40 years when he became depressed, melancholic and believed he had killed his wife. He was treated at a mental hospital with a series of shock treatments and returned home after three months, where he remained well for one year. He then became hyperactive, assaulted his wife, and was treated with shock treatments at another mental hospital. The third psychotic episode, during which he was overactive, overtalkative, hyper-irritable, and fired from his job, was untreated and within a month he was well. In July, 1943, he again became irritable, sleepless, antagonistic toward his wife, homicidal and suicidal. He was hospitalized at Warren State Hospital on 7/14/1953, with a diagnosis of manic-depressive, manic phase. Discharge from Warren State Hospital was in October. He was again at Warren State Hospital from November, 1955, until January, 1956, and from August until December, 1960. Diagnosis at each hospitalization was manic-depressive psychosis, either manic or depressive phase; however, because of the paranoid delusions and inappropriate affect, the possibility of schizophrenia was not excluded. Classification: Schizophrenic reaction—paranoid type.

(24) wife of proband (23), born 1911. When she gave the proband's Warren State Hospital admission history she was described as "rather nervous" and "very upset by the proband's actions." The proband accused her of nagging and belittling him before others, although this was not observed in interview with both the proband and his wife. She worked to help their son through college and continued to visit him in the hospital when he said he didn't care to see her. At the 1966 interview she described herself as nervous and was observed to domineer. Classification: probable transient situational personality disorder—adult situational reaction.

Parents

Mother (17), born 1883. She was described as "rather nervous" by family members. When interviewed she was cooperative and informative. She was critical of the proband's wife and commented that the wife was partly responsible for the proband's mental difficulties. However, the proband's wife described the mother as over-protective and partly responsible for his psychotic breaks. Classification: Possible psychoneurotic disorder.

Siblings

(21) husband of sister (22), born 1901. He reportedly was "accident prone" and had a "poor home attitude" toward his children. Classification: Possible psychoneurotic disorder.

Brother (29), born 1923. He was described as "a worrier with inferiority feelings." When interviewed at age 36 years he seemed relaxed and reasonable. Classification: Possible psychoneurotic disorder.

Nieces and Nephews

Niece (38), born 1933. At age 26 years she had deserted her husband who was trying to locate her by her Social Security number. As an adolescent she was in a juvenile home. The child born to her first marriage was awarded to the husband and raised by his parents. The child born to the second marriage suffered a broken leg in a fall from a table and while hospitalized contracted a virus which proved fatal. She blamed herself for this baby's death. Although described as "very intelligent and a good worker" (she was a secretary) she was also described as "a rover . . . moved around a lot and had many jobs . . . seemed to get into trouble." She was also described as "very nervous." She had periods of migraines and restlessness, hyperactivity and sleeplessness, as well as rather heavy depression. Classification: Probable personality pattern disturbance—cyclothymic personality.

Niece (40), born 1943. At age 15 years she was described as "highly nervous—

seemed depressed and hard to understand."
She was advised by her school counselor to
seek medical attention for her nervousness
and depression. Classification: Probable
psychoneurotic disorder.

Family Summary

The proband had a psychotic disorder.
The mother, a brother, a niece and a sister's
husband were neurotic. The proband's wife
and a niece had personality disorders.

AFFECTIVE PSYCHOSIS

There were 16 probands with a diagnosis of affective psychosis at the time of reclassification (see Table 2–2). The diagnostic statements in the 1912–1917 period were psychosis (unclassified), mania and manic-depressive. Upon recent reclassification there were two with involutional psychotic reaction and 14 with affective psychosis.

Of these kinships, four appeared to have an unusually high frequency of psychosis among individuals in Generation III (siblings of the proband). These were designated as "loaded" kinships, since it is possible (although by no means certain) that the strong family history may have attracted the attention of the original field workers. In certain of the tables these four kinships are treated separately.

Brief family summaries accompany the pedigree charts for this group. It is quite clear that families tend to be larger in this group than in the others.

The four "loaded" kinships are WSH 15, 48, 73, and 92. Other kinships in this group are WSH 12, 19, 26, 27, 28, 29, 35, 38, 79, 81, 87, and 90.

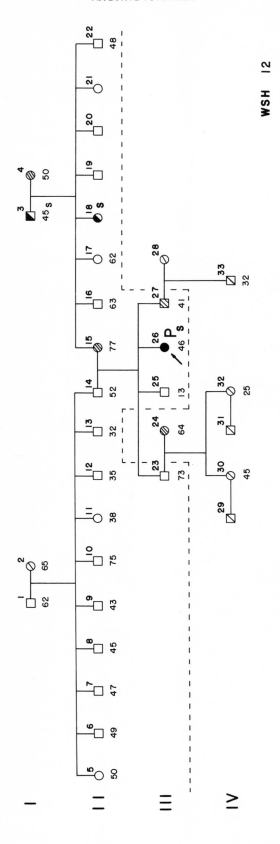

WSH 12

WSH 12: The Proband

Proband (26), born 1895; died at age 46 years of pneumonia and barbiturate poisoning. Her brother reported that the death was a suicide. In childhood she was sensitive and high-strung. As she grew older she became quite independent and outspoken. She worked hard at business during the day but was "impelled by some inward force to excitement after working hours." Shortly after her father's death, when she was 21 years of age, she became depressed, then began drinking. Her behavior became more aberrant; she became very untruthful, extravagant and unreasonable. She was hospitalized awhile later at a mental hospital because of her profane, obscene talk and erotic behavior. Admission to Warren State Hospital was on 12/15/1916, with a diagnosis of manic-depressive psychosis, manic phase, double form. She was discharged as restored in April, 1917. Classification: Manic-depressive reaction—manic type.

Grandparents

Maternal grandfather (3); died at age 45 years of suicide by drowning. The proband's Warren State Hospital case history stated that he "drowned himself while insane at age 45." Another source described him as a "quiet, meek man" who was "nagged to death" by his wife. Classification: With functional psychosis.

Maternal grandmother (4); died at age 65 years of heart trouble. She was described as "very nervous" and "high-strung." Classification: Probable psychoneurotic disorder.

Parents

Mother (15), born 1865; died at age 77 years of uremia. At age 13 years she had "chorea and was very nervous." The proband's Warren State Hospital record described (15) as "nervous and hysterical." Classification: Psychoneurotic disorder.

Aunts and Uncles

Maternal aunt (18), died of suicide by asphyxiation at an estimated age of 55 years. She was "quite broken down nervously" at the time of her death. Classification: Probably with functional psychosis.

Siblings

(24) wife of brother (23), born 1900. Her husband divorced and remarried her, but refused to give the interviewer the reasons for the divorce. She was cooperative when interviewed although nervous and in what seemed to be a chronic anxiety state. Classification: Psychoneurotic disorder—anxiety reaction.

Brother (27), born 1897; died at age 41 years of endocarditis. He had St. Vitus dance from age 14 to 18 years. Although he regained his health, he was very "nervous and quick-tempered" and "quite like his mother in disposition." Classification: Probable psychoneurotic disorder.

Family Summary

The proband and the maternal grandmother had psychotic disorders and a maternal aunt probably so. The maternal grandmother, the mother, a brother and the wife of a brother were neurotic.

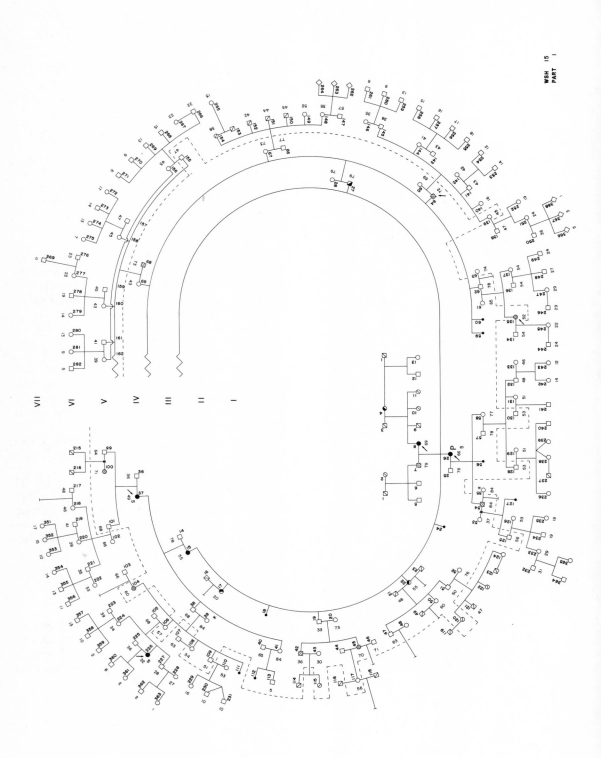

WSH 15
PART I

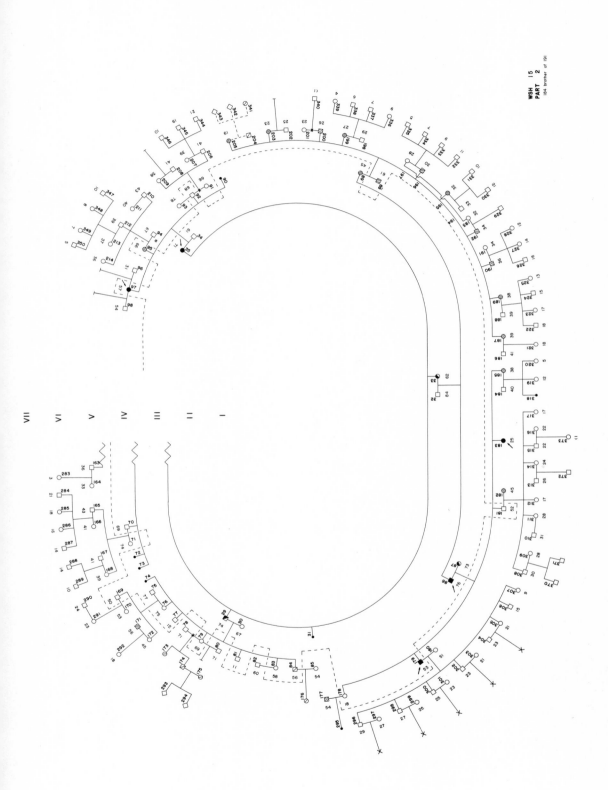

WSH 15
PART 2
(84 brother of 191)

WSH 15: The Proband

The proband (26), born 1860; died at age 66 years of cancer. She was hospitalized the first time at Warren State Hospital from 5/8/1900 until 10/3/1900. For one year previous to hospitalization she was "gloomy and discouraged"; she felt condemned and was despondent. She was well until February, 1915, when she began worrying over unimportant details, was self-accusatory, and emotionally unstable, and in April, 1915, she attempted suicide with Paris green. She spent three months in a private sanitarium, then was readmitted to Warren State Hospital on 10/14/1916. She remained at Warren State Hospital until 11/19/1917, diagnosed as manic-depressive, depressed type, second attack. Third hospitalization at Warren State Hospital was on 4/1/1926, with another attack of depression. She died later that year while still hospitalized. Classification: Manic-depressive reaction—depressed type.

Children

Son (54), born 1879. At age 84 years he reportedly had "senile impairment and difficulty in recalling names and dates." Classification: Chronic brain syndrome of senium.

Grandparents

Maternal grandmother (4); unknown except that she reportedly "was insane." Classification: Probably with functional psychosis.

Parents

Father (7), died at age 79 years of "stomach trouble." He was described as "harsh and cruel to his wife" and as "an ugly dispositioned man." He was also described as "surly, fault-finding and stingy." At one time he owned a large farm which he lost through a lawsuit. Classification: Probable personality disorder.

Mother (8), born 1832; died at age 69 years, cause of death unknown. She reportedly "was insane for forty years." She was hospitalized at Warren State Hospital with a diagnosis of periodic mania from 4/10/1895 until 4/16/1896. The hospital described her as "generally incoherent, antagonistic to her husband, destructive to her clothing . . . confused, quite talkative," and said she had "exaltation of feelings." At discharge she was in the same mental and physical condition she was in at admission. Classification: Schizophrenic reaction—paranoid type.

Siblings

Sister (15), born 1848; died at age 55 years of diabetes. She reportedly was "insane for several years" and was "mentally deranged 10–12 years before her death; she was very childish." Classification: With functional psychosis.

Sister (17), born 1850; died in childbirth at age 20 years. Some family members reported her as "insane." Classification: Possibly with functional psychosis.

Sister (22), born 1857; died at age 55 years of carcinoma of the breast. She reportedly "was insane." Her religious beliefs did not allow medical attention in her terminal illness. Classification: Probably with functional psychosis.

Brother (27), born 1863; died at age 79 years of pneumonia. He was considered to be "insane" by his family. He was forced to marry his wife and was put under bonds to support her but eventually "ran away with another woman." Classification: Probably with functional psychosis.

Brother (29), born 1865; died at age 74 years, cause of death unknown. He reportedly "was insane at one time." Classification: Probably with functional psychosis.

Sister (33), born 1868; died at age 62 years of carcinoma. She was described by various individuals as "somewhat nervous," as "psychotic for most of her married life" and as a "reticent, unsociable woman who was considered insane because of her peculiarities which developed after her marriage; she did not dress herself well nor keep her home up well." Classification: Probably with functional psychosis.

Sister (35), born 1873; died at age 71 years of cardiac failure. She was admitted to Warren State Hospital on 7/4/1895, with a diagnosis of puerperal mania. She had been in poor health since the birth of her first child three years before admission. The onset of psychotic symptoms was about one week before admission when she became fearful and generally confused as well as "dull, sad, worried" and uncommunicative. She was released, apparently improved, on 1/22/1896. She was again hospitalized at Warren State Hospital from 11/18/1943 until February, 1944. She reportedly had a persecution complex concerning religion and involving her neighbors and physicians. She was also irritable, noisy, combative and resistive. When placed in a cold pack she thought she was going to be killed. Diagnosis at this hospitalization was manic-depressive reaction, manic type. Classification: Schizophrenic reaction — catatonic type.

Nieces and Nephews

Niece (37), born 1866; died at age 49 years at Warren State Hospital of chronic myocarditis. She was described as "naturally nervous, excitable and inclined to worry." In November, 1912, following menopause, she became depressed, agitated, restless, auto-accusatory and attempted suicide three times. She was admitted to Warren State Hospital in December, 1914. Previous to admission to Warren State Hospital she spent a total of 20 months in three private mental hospitals. For a year before admission she kept up an almost constant auto-monologia when awake and for six months she was denudative, untidy and resistive to attention. Diagnosis at Warren State Hospital was manic-depressive, depressive phase, involutional type. She showed no improvement at Warren State Hospital and remained there until her death in 1915. Classification: Schizophrenic reaction — catatonic type.

Nephew (42), born 1885; died at age 36 years of peritonitis. He was described as a lawyer who was "very bright" but he "was a heavy drinker . . . he became worthless after he began drinking." Classification: Sociopathic personality disturbance — alcoholism (addiction).

Niece (45), born 1892; died at age 70 years, cause of death unknown. She was described as "a highstrung, active, nervous woman with good insight." Classification: Probable psychoneurotic disorder.

Nephew (64), born 1888; died at age 72 years at Warren State Hospital of pneumonia. He was normal until 1959, when he suffered a stroke. He then became incoherent,

disoriented, was at times combative, thought he lived on a farm and imagined he stepped on animals. He was hospitalized at Warren State Hospital on 2/24/1960, and died within a year. Classification: Chronic brain syndrome associated with cerebral arteriosclerosis.

(68) husband of niece (69), born 1883; died at age 73 years of a cerebral hemorrhage. He was an invalid for several years following a stroke and had terminal mental changes after the stroke. Classification: Chronic brain syndrome of senium.

Nephew (86), born 1887. At age 44 years he developed the belief that his wife was poisoning him and believed that an electronic machine was controlling all his actions. About 10 years later his "peculiar" ideas became more acute; he became indifferent and apathetic and was hospitalized at Warren State Hospital from 5/28/1941 until 11/5/1941, with a diagnosis of dementia praecox. At age 76 the level of his intoxication during an attempted interview made it impossible to estimate his mental health status. Classification: Schizophrenic reaction — paranoid type.

(87) wife of nephew (86), born 1890. When interviewed at age 73 years she was described as "talkative, pleasant and jovial"; however, she was too intoxicated for the interviewer to make an estimate of her mental status. The living conditions were deplorable; the house was a shack with no running water; apparently it was never cleaned. Classification: Probably with functional psychosis.

(88) husband of niece (89), born 1902. He was described as heavily alcoholic, shiftless and abusive to his wife. He "moved around with his children." Classification: Sociopathic personality disturbance — alcoholism (addiction).

Niece (89), born 1904; died at age 45 years of a stroke. She was described as "peculiar, bashful, self-conscious and very strange acting at times." Classification: Probable personality disorder.

Niece (95), born 1897. When interviewed at age 66 years she was at first very cautious, then steadily more talkative. The interviewer stated that (95) always kept the house locked, the blinds closed and that she refused to answer the door until the interviewer went to the back door, even though the appointment had been made and (95) was not at all deaf. Relatives had not expected her to cooperate with the interviewer. Classification: Probable personality disorder.

Niece (97), born 1906. She was hospitalized at Warren State Hospital from May until August, 1939, after she developed the belief that efforts were being made to poison her and she jumped through a second story window to escape her persecutors. She also thought she was being watched and often laughed in response to her auditory hallucinations. Her hallucinations were readily admitted and she discussed them freely. Improvement at Warren State Hospital was continual and she was never rehospitalized. Diagnosis and classification: Schizophrenic reaction—paranoid type.

Distant Relatives

(100) wife of grandnephew (99), born 1892. An interview was attempted but she refused to admit the interviewer. She first gave ill health as a reason for refusal, then later stated firmly that she wanted no part of the project. Her voice and facial tensions were strained and tense. Classification: Possible psychoneurotic disorder.

Grandniece (104), born 1903. She was described as an "intelligent, fine person" who developed laryngitis while teaching school and, contrary to doctor's advice, remained in school in order to give special tutoring to some of her duller students. Subsequently, she lost her voice for five years and nine months, during which time she "could not say a single word." Her friends were amazed, however, that she could sing in the church choir when the minister urged her to do so. When her speaking voice returned, she resumed teaching. She received no psychiatric care. Classification: Possible psychoneurotic disorder—conversion reaction.

Grandniece (135), born 1912. She had polio at age six years and as a result, always limped. She was hospitalized from 11/17/1954 until 11/25/1954, with the diagnosis of (1) menopausal syndrome and (2) glandular dysfunction. She had shock treatments. At admission she complained of "headache, nerves, hot flashes and was unable to sleep." At age 41 years she was described as "at times still suspicious, fault finding and irritable." Classification: Proba-

ble transient situational personality disturbance—adjustment reaction of late life.

(171) husband of grandniece (172), born 1908. He reportedly was "shell shocked" during World War II and was hospitalized in army hospitals in England and North Carolina. He was under continuous medical care for his nerves. Classification: Probable psychoneurotic disorder.

(177) husband of grandniece (178), born 1906; died at age 54 years, cause of death unknown. He reportedly "didn't use his life well." Classification: Possible personality disorder.

Grandnephew (179), born 1910. He was admitted to a state mental hospital on 3/8/1960. At admission he was extremely excited, restless, agitated and expressed the delusion that he was being persecuted. He received electroshock therapy and was released on 9/9/1960. Diagnosis and classification: Schizophrenic reaction—paranoid type.

(182) wife of grandnephew (181), born 1918. When interviewed at age 45 years, she complained of her illness, then insisted on completing the interview. She had recurring, undiagnosed headaches for which spinal taps and a craniotomy had been suggested. Classification: Probable psychoneurotic disorder.

Grandniece (183), born 1920; died at age 25 years at Warren State Hospital of acute myocarditis. She was a midget whose seclusive tendencies became exaggerated in 1941. She later began to "ask forgiveness for imaginary sins" and "stared into space." Shortly before admission to Warren State Hospital on 2/20/1943, she became mute and disoriented. On admittance she was hallucinated both visually and auditorily and was self-accusatory in the religious sphere. She refused all nourishment and was tube-fed daily. Diagnosis was dementia praecox—catatonic type. Classification: Schizophrenic reaction—catatonic type.

Grandniece (185), born 1925. When interviewed at age 38 years she was described as tense, nervous and worried about the insanity in her family. She also appeared "brisk and efficient." Classification: Psychoneurotic disorder.

Grandniece (187), born 1924. She was raised by her grandmother. At age 39 years she stated that all her siblings "were very insecure during childhood and had downgraded each other all the time." As adults they were "all nervous and jealous of each other." She was an outpatient at a general hospital in February, 1954. She sought psychiatric help because of her "temper, jealousy and insecurity." Diagnosis at the hospital was phobic conversion and depressive reaction. Classification: Psychoneurotic disorder.

Grandniece (189), born 1925. She was described as "insecure and nervous" and jealous of her siblings. Classification: Possible psychoneurotic disorder.

Grandnephew (190), born 1927; described as "insecure and nervous." Classification: Possible psychoneurotic disorder.

Grandnephew (192), born 1929. He was described as "insecure and nervous." Classification: Possible psychoneurotic disorder.

Grandniece (195), born 1931. She was described as "insecure and nervous." Classification: Possible psychoneurotic disorder.

Grandnephew (196), born 1933; described as "nervous and insecure." Classification: Possible psychoneurotic disorder.

Grandniece (199), born 1936; described as "insecure and nervous." Classification: Possible psychoneurotic disorder.

Grandnephew (200), born 1937; described as "nervous and insecure." Classification: Possible psychoneurotic disorder.

Grandniece (203), born 1940; described as "nervous" and "insecure." Classification: Possible psychoneurotic disorder.

Grandniece (205), born 1944. At age 19 years she had had three illegitimate children by one man. She was described as "insecure" and "nervous." Classification: Possible psychoneurotic disorder.

Great-grandniece (226) and (410) in WSH 4. Born 1930, a nurse whose last place of residence was in England. In 1954, following the birth of her first child, she became depressed and attempted suicide by slashing her wrist. One week later she again attempted suicide, this time with gas. She had four sessions with a psychiatrist and apparently made a good adjustment until 1957, when she became preoccupied with religion and manifested many grandiose and paranoid delusions. She was hospitalized from 3/25/1957 until 5/23/1957 at a general hospital with a diagnosis of schizophrenic reaction, paranoid type. Then she was well until 2/10/1959, when she again developed symptoms of sleeplessness, inappropriate behavior, confusion of thought and paranoid ideas. Again she was hospitalized, first at a general hospital on 3/8/1959, and 10 days later she was transferred to a mental hospital. She improved to a point of almost complete remission and was discharged on 4/18/1959. Her child, who was mentally retarded, caused her a great deal of anxiety but once the child was institutionalized she remained well.

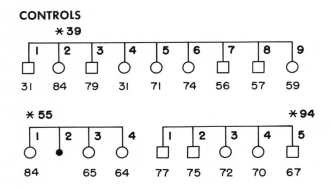

WSH   15

Some family members reported that she was "nervous" long before the birth of her first child, but there was no mention of symptoms of psychosis. Classification: Schizophrenic reaction—paranoid type.

Family Summary

Those who had psychotic disorders, or probable or possible psychotic disorders, were the proband, the maternal grandmother, the mother, five sisters, two brothers, two nieces, a nephew, a grandniece, a grandnephew and a great-grandniece and the wife of a nephew. A son died of senile impairment and was classified as chronic brain syndrome of senium. The husband of a niece also received this classification. A nephew was hospitalized with chronic brain syndrome associated with arteriosclerosis. The father, a nephew, two nieces, a niece's husband, a grandniece and the husband of a grandniece had personality disorders. Neurotics included a niece, eight grandnieces, four grandnephews, the wives of two grandnephews and the husband of a grandniece.

Controls

None noteworthy.

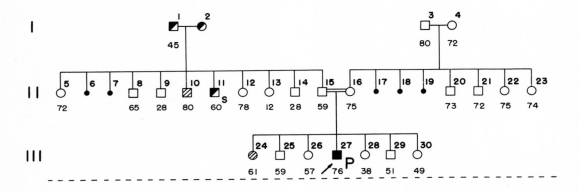

WSH 19: The Proband

Proband (27), born 1860; died at age 76 years of chronic myocarditis. He was described as "sociable, jolly and good-natured but an extremist and overenthusiastic" until age 46 years. He also displayed good judgment and made a good livelihood until then, when he became peculiar, began making poor investments and developed grandiose schemes for making money. He became irritable toward his siblings and attempted to start legal proceedings against them. It was almost 10 years after the onset of his illness when he was committed to a state hospital on 4/25/1916, after he became violent toward his sister. At the time of admission his condition was characterized by "expansive delusions, irritability, defective judgment and dementia." He had tremulous speech and some euphoria. There were two tentative diagnoses at the state hospital: (1) general paralysis of the insane (dependent on evidence of serologic examinations not reported as outcome) and (2) manic-depressive insanity, hypomanic phase. He escaped from the hospital on 5/20/1917, and was never rehospitalized. Classification: Manic-depressive psychosis —manic type.

Grandparents

Paternal grandfather (1), committed suicide at about age 45 years. At the time he was worried and depressed about his wife and about the prospect of another child. Classification: Probably with functional psychosis, psychotic-depressive reaction.

Paternal grandmother (2), died of "old age"; age at death unknown. She was described as a "disagreeable, scolding woman" who was "impossible" to live with as she grew older and was, therefore, committed to a state hospital (no record located). Classification: Probably with functional psychosis.

Aunts and Uncles

Paternal uncle (10), born 1837. When in his 80's he had been "blind for several years" as well as "childish and forgetful." Classification: Possible chronic brain syndrome of senium.

Paternal uncle (11), committed suicide at about age 60 years. He had become "depressed and worried" after the death of his wife. Classification: Probably with functional psychosis, psychotic-depressive reaction.

Siblings

Sister (24), born 1854. At age 61 years she was described as "a very peculiar woman—emotional, unstable, very jealous." She lived a secluded life on the "old homestead." Classification: Probable personality pattern disturbance—schizoid personality.

Family Summary

The proband had a psychotic disorder; the paternal grandparents and a paternal uncle probably so. A paternal uncle was classified as possible chronic brain syndrome of senium. A sister was classified as a probable personality disorder.

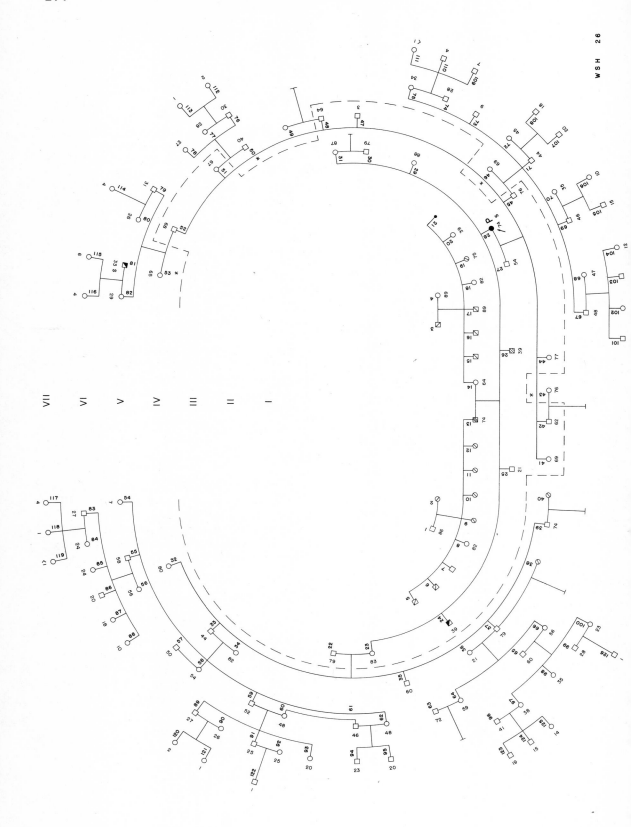

WSH 26

WSH 26: The Proband

Proband (28), born 1855; died at age 74 years of carcinoma of the colon. She worked as a nurse-companion, then learned the tailor's trade previous to her marriage at age 24 years. Ten days after her marriage she was admitted to a mental hospital in a period of excitement which followed a depressed phase. She was returned home but only remained a week or two when she again became depressed and was returned to the hospital for an additional three months. She recovered and was normal for six years, then developed a depression which lasted for one year. At the end of the depression she became excited and was committed to the same hospital for the third time, where she remained for six weeks. She had two more depressions and one more hospitalization before admission to Warren State Hospital on 12/4/1915, with a diagnosis of manic-depressive psychosis, mixed type. She attempted suicide on two occasions while depressed. While excited she was very active and happy, unable to sleep, talked excessively and was very distractible. There was no evidence of hallucinations or delusions. She was never readmitted after her parole from Warren State Hospital on 10/12/1916. Classification: Manic-depressive reaction—other.

Grandchildren

(81) husband of granddaughter (82), born 1928; died at age 33 years of a self-inflicted gunshot wound. Although he had never received psychiatric care he was worried about financial matters at the time of his suicide. Classification: Probably with functional psychosis.

Parents

Father (13), born 1814; died at age 74 years, cause of death unknown. He was a hotel owner and later a laborer; he was described as "a heavy drinker of the spree type." While intoxicated he showed a marked change of mood. His alcoholic habits caused the family to break up for a period of several years. At age 50 years he had an episode of alcoholic hallucinosis and was kept in jail for six months. After age 65 years he no longer drank. Classification: Sociopathic personality disturbance—alcoholism (addiction); Also, acute brain syndrome associated with alcohol intoxication.

Siblings

Brother (24), born 1849, an artist who died at age 39 years of lead poisoning. He was described as peculiar, "a drinker," subject to periods of depression, and a possible suicide. Classification: Probably with functional psychosis, schizophrenic reaction—simple type.

Brother (26), born 1853; died at age 39 years of a "clot on the brain." He was described as a "spree alcoholic." Classification: Sociopathic personality disturbance—alcoholism (addiction).

Family Summary

The proband was psychotic and a brother and the husband of a granddaughter probably so. The father had an episode of alcoholic psychosis and was an alcoholic. A brother was possibly alcoholic.

Controls

Sister (6) of (53), born 1893. She was a housewife with 13 children. She was hospitalized from 5/6/1958 until 6/5/1958, for a "nervous breakdown." Symptoms began in June, 1957, with depression and personality changes which became more pronounced; however, she was never suicidal nor hallucinated. She responded well to electroshock treatments and had regained normal perspective at discharge. Classification: Psychoneurotic disorder—depressive reaction.

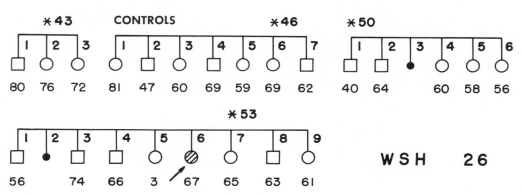

WSH 26

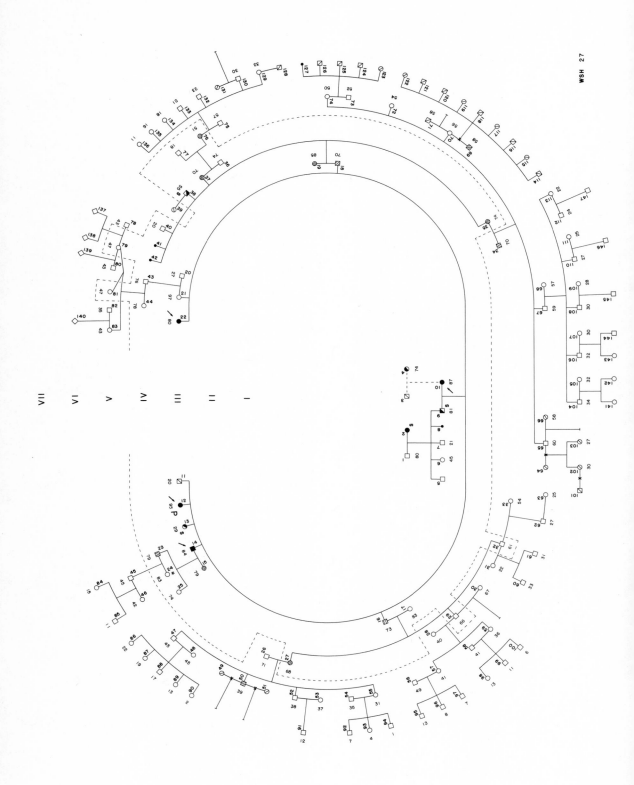

WSH 27: The Proband

Proband (12), born 1845; died at age 95 years of generalized arteriosclerosis and chronic myocarditis. She was first admitted to Warren State Hospital, along with her mother and sister (22), on 11/9/1897, at age 52 years, about nine years after her first manic attack. The second attack, during which she was noisy, violent and had to be restrained, began three weeks before admission to Warren State Hospital, where she improved slightly, then became depressed. She reportedly never entertained ideas of suicide but stated that her earliest recollections were those of not wanting to live. On 9/26/1900, she was transferred to a county home but became so excited that she returned to Warren State Hospital on 10/15/1900. She remained at Warren State Hospital until 1/16/1930, when she was again transferred to the county home. She got along well at the county home for about 10 years, then became deluded, hallucinated, denudative and so difficult to manage that she was admitted to a state mental hospital, where she died one month later. Diagnosis at Warren State Hospital was manic-depressive psychosis. Classification: Manic-depressive reaction — mixed type.

Grandparents

Paternal grandmother (2), died of suicide by hanging, age at death unknown. She was reportedly very fond of city life and became very depressed when her husband moved to the country. Classification: With functional psychosis.

Maternal grandmother (4), born 1800; died at age 71 years, cause of death unknown. When a young woman she began to have "scolding spells" during which she was restless, irritable, fault finding and would want to work all night; however, she was never deluded or hallucinated. She worked as a cook but was unable to work during these excited periods. Classification: Probably with functional psychosis, manic-depressive reaction.

Parents

Father (9), born 1815; died at age 81 years, cause of death unknown. He was described as very impatient, self-willed, a rigid man who was friendly if things went smoothly but who threatened to leave home or commit suicide if things did not go as he liked. He actually attempted suicide once by arsenic poisoning after an argument with his mother-in-law. He was very religious, very set in his political views and would not associate with people who differed from him. As he grew older he became childish and more impatient. Classification: Probably with functional psychosis; Also, chronic brain syndrome of senium.

Mother (10), born 1823; died at age 87 years at Warren State Hospital of erysipelas. Her first mental illness occurred at age 64 years when she became depressed, believed she had killed everyone and wanted to die. She had always felt that she "couldn't be saved" because she was illegitimate and felt that she was to blame "for everything that happened in the world." She remained ill, claiming to be wicked and begging to be killed, for 10 years and was finally admitted to Warren State Hospital on 11/9/1897, along with her two daughters, the proband (12) and (22). She remained at Warren State Hospital until her death. Hospital notes described her as worried, anxious, depressed and noisy. Classification: Psychotic-depressive reaction.

Siblings

Sister (13), born 1847; died at age 29 years of suicide by arsenic poisoning. She was described as "odd and unsociable." She made several unsuccessful suicide attempts in the year previous to her death. Classification: Probably with functional psychosis, schizophrenic reaction.

Brother (14), born 1849; died at age 84 years, cause of death unknown. He was described as a "high-tempered emotional" man who had three distinct attacks of excitement. The first occurred at age 48 years while he was being treated for pleurisy. He became excited, talkative, hyper-religious and was sent to Warren State Hospital, where he recovered in two weeks. After his return home he was abnormally quiet for a few months, then became normal and remained well for eight years. He then developed pleurisy again, became excited but recovered at home in a few days. His third and last episode was in 1907, when he became very destructive and was again hospitalized at Warren State Hospital. He recovered in two weeks and remained well until his death. Classification: Schizophrenic reaction — catatonic type.

(15) wife of brother (14), born 1850; died at age 79 years of "old age." She was described as "reserved, not very friendly nor of a particularly cheerful nature." Classification: Possible personality disorder.

Brother (16), born 1852; died at age 73 years from injuries received from a horse kick. He completed grade 10 and was a farmer and Baptist minister who was described as a "narrow, prejudiced, dictatorial man who was over-emotional and who alienated his congregation by his bitter attitude against liquor." Classification: Possible personality disorder.

Brother (18), born 1855; died at age 70 years, cause of death unknown. He was described as a mental defective who also was "excitable, very conceited, slightly paranoid and very quick-tempered." Classification: Possible personality disorder.

(19) wife of brother (18), born 1870; died at age 85 years of "old age." She was described as "a feeble-minded woman of an ugly, resentful nature." Classification: Possible personality disorder.

Sister (22), born 1861. She was admitted to Warren State Hospital in November, 1897, with her mother and the proband. The onset of symptoms occurred at age 35 years, the same year she was admitted to Warren State Hospital, when she became silly, simple, confused and hallucinated. Diagnosis at Warren was acute mania. At age 69 years she was transferred to a county home where she was still living at age 80 years. Classification: Schizophrenic reaction — chronic undifferentiated type.

Nieces and Nephews

Nephew (23), born 1883; described in early years as a "gloomy, pious man who wrote religious papers." At age 73 years his physician described him as hypochondriacal. Classification: Psychoneurotic reaction — other.

Niece (27), born 1894; described at age 68 years as "always sick," arthritic and nervous and excitable. Classification: Probable psychoneurotic disorder.

(34) husband of niece (35), born 1884; died at age 70 years of hypertensive heart disease. He was once jailed for wife-beating. Classification: Personality disorder.

Niece (35), born 1890. In 1922 she had a stroke and was cared for in a county home for many years. At age 74 years she was a patient in a nursing home and reported to be very confused. Classification: Chronic brain syndrome of senium.

Niece (37), born 1891; died at age 70 years of cerebral hemorrhage. At age 70 years, a family member stated, "Her mind isn't just right . . . odd . . . eccentric. She takes things from stores and houses." Classification: Probable personality pattern disturbance — schizoid personality.

Nephew (38), born 1895; suicided at age 55 years by shooting. Classification: Probably with functional psychosis.

Distant Relatives

Grandnephew (50), born 1923; described at age 39 years as nervous, unsociable, maladjusted and under psychiatric care. Classification: Probable psychoneurotic disorder.

(69) husband of grandniece (70). He reportedly "drank a lot." Classification: Probable sociopathic personality disturbance — alcoholism (addiction).

Grandniece (76), born 1912. She was interviewed at age 51 years and described as sullen, resentful and suspicious in manner, speech and facial expression. She refused to give information about her family. Classification: Personality pattern disturbance — paranoid personality.

Family Summary

The proband, the mother, the paternal grandmother and a sister had psychotic disorders, and the father, the maternal grandmother, a sister and a nephew probably so. A niece was classified as chronic brain syn-

CONTROLS
*** 24**

```
    |1    |2    |3    |4    |5    |6
    ○     ○     ○     □     □     □
    83    60    80
```

W S H   2 7

drome of senium, which was also an additional diagnosis of the father. Personality disorders were found in two brothers, two wives of brothers, a niece, a grandniece, and in the husbands of a niece and of a grand-

niece. A nephew, a niece and a grand-nephew were neurotic.

Controls

None noteworthy.

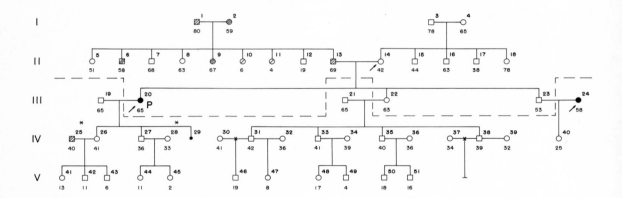

WSH   28

WSH 28: The Proband

Proband (20), born 1896. She worked as a domestic until the first symptoms of mental illness appeared in 1915. At this time she showed unusual irritability and destroyed some furniture in the home in which she was employed. She was first admitted to a state mental hospital for about six weeks, then admitted to Warren State Hospital on 12/9/1915, with a diagnosis of manic-depressive, manic phase. At admission she was "noisy, sang, pounded the furniture, clapped her hands and talked incessantly, using considerable profanity." She began to improve in January, 1916, and was discharged 5/15/1916. She was married after her discharge from Warren State Hospital and was never rehospitalized. When interviewed at age 65 years she was described as obese but mentally normal. Classification: Manic-depressive reaction—manic type.

Children

(25) husband of daughter (26), born 1921 in Sweden. He was described at age 40 years as "very fat...nervous...high strung" and under a doctor's care for his obesity and nervousness. Classification: Probable psychoneurotic disorder.

Grandparents

Paternal grandfather (1), born 1830. At last information, in his early 80's, he was showing "some evidences of senile mental breakdown." He was described as "temperate and thrifty" and made enough money to provide each of his children with a house and a lot. Classification: Possible chronic brain syndrome of senium.

Paternal grandmother (2), born 1844; died at age 59 years of pneumonia. She was described as a "disagreeable, domineering woman who was extremely penurious." Classification: Possible personality disorder.

Parents

Father (13), born 1870; died at age 69 years of acute myocarditis. He inherited a good farm from his father which he neglected badly; he drank heavily until he was struck by a trolley while intoxicated, then became a total abstainer. He reportedly always treated his family well and provided the immediate necessities of life for them, but was also described as "a braggart, egotistical and sensual." Classification: Probable personality disorder.

Mother (14), born 1874; died at age 42 years of myocardial degeneration. She became ill in July, 1915, with an uncompensated mitral valve lesion and albuminuria. Later she became delirious and was admitted to a state mental hospital because of her heart condition. She was later removed to the psychiatric ward because of her screaming and disturbance of other patients. The records state "a diagnosis of an exhaustion psychosis showing amentia syndrome was very evident." She was discharged in January, 1916, and returned two days before her death. Classification: Probable acute brain syndrome associated with circulatory disturbance.

Aunts and Uncles

Paternal uncle (6), born 1864; died at age 58 years of apoplexy. He was described as an alcoholic who "lived the life of a tramp." He deserted both his wives. Classification: Sociopathic personality disturbance—alcoholism (addiction).

Paternal aunt (9), born 1874; died at age 67 years of a coronary occlusion. She was married but had no children and was a "hotel worker." She described herself as "very nervous" at the time of menopause. Classification: Probable psychoneurotic disorder.

Siblings

(24) wife of brother (23), born 1902 in Ireland. She was hospitalized at a state mental hospital from 12/10/1945 until 1/20/1946, with paranoid psychosis. In 1950 she received 11 shock treatments as an outpatient and remained well until her daughter decided to become an airline hostess. She was readmitted to the hospital on 11/14/1957, the day her daughter left to go on duty. The hospital records state

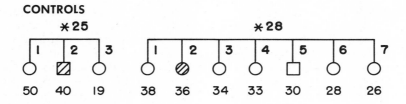

WSH   28

that she had many paranoid ideas and was diagnosed as "depressive reaction with some paranoid ideas." She was given six shock treatments and discharged five weeks later as improved. When interviewed at age 58 years she stated flatly that there was "no mental illness in the family." Classification: Schizophrenic reaction — paranoid type.

Family Summary

The proband and a brother's wife had psychotic illnesses. The mother was hospitalized with a psychotic reaction to circulatory disturbance. Personality disorders were found in the paternal grandmother, the father and in a paternal uncle. A paternal aunt and the husband of a daughter were neurotic. The paternal grandfather was classified as chronic brain syndrome of senium.

Controls

See family pedigree, person 25.

Sister (2) of (28), born 1925. At age 36 years she was described as married with four children and as an alcoholic. Classification: Sociopathic personality disturbance — alcoholism (addiction).

WSH 29: The Proband

The proband (34), born 1845; died at age 79 years of acute cardiac dilatation at Warren State Hospital. She was described as "naturally lively and sociable, but jealous, hypochondriacal and extremely quick-tempered." She married at age 21 years and was considered a "malicious gossip, a child beater and had peculiar notions about her food." She had five distinct depressions before her admission to Warren State Hospital on 8/20/1915. The first occurred one month after the birth of her fourth child and lasted several months; the next two followed the births of the sixth and seventh children and the fourth attack, which lasted eight years, began in 1905. The fifth attack began in January, 1915. During the attacks she was hypochondriacal, apprehensive and had many depressive delusions. She threatened suicide a great deal, but made few attempts. She remained at Warren State Hospital the first time for two months and was much improved when discharged. For five years she lived alone, then moved in with her daughter. After she moved she became nervous, cross, threatening, imagined her food was poisoned, and in general was "odd and queer" and was readmitted to Warren State Hospital on 6/5/1924, where she died two months later. Diagnoses at Warren State Hospital were manic-depressive insanity, depressed phase, and manic-depressive psychosis, cyclothymic type. Classification: Manic-depressive reaction—depressed type.

Children

Daughter (94), born 1871; died at age 69 years of chronic myocarditis. In 1916 she was described by her physician as "peculiar ... a very quick temper and not very good reasoning faculties." She was described as emotionally unstable by an interviewer at that time. At age 69 years she had no apparent difficulties. Classification: Probable personality disorder.

(96) husband of daughter (97), born 1875; died at age 82 years at Warren State Hospital of renal tract infection and senile debility. In 1916 he was described as a "drunken-good-for-nothing." He and (97) were married but a few years. Admission to Warren State Hospital was on 9/25/1954, following an arrest for indecent assault on a young girl. At admission he was confused, disoriented, forgetful and hallucinated. His memory began to fail about one year before admission and became much worse in August, 1954, following an accident in which he fell and struck his head. Diagnosis at Warren State Hospital was chronic brain syndrome due to senile changes of the brain. Classification: Chronic brain syndrome of senium and sociopathic personality disturbance—alcoholism (addiction).

Daughter (97), born 1879; died at age 81 years of arteriosclerotic heart disease. She was described as "always ornery" and was always "a hard person to get along with ... not very well liked by her relatives." She had a "hot temper" but was not violent. Classification: Possible personality disorder.

(101) husband of daughter (102), born 1877. At age 84 years he was described as "friendly but very forgetful for both past and present events." His memory began failing at age 82 years. Classification: Probable chronic brain syndrome of senium.

(54) mother of illegitimate child of son (103), born 1879; died at age 52 years "suddenly," exact cause of death unknown. She "kept house" for various men after her husband's death and had at least three illegitimate children. She was also described as "irresponsible and undependable." Classification: Sociopathic personality disturbance.

Grandchildren

Granddaughter (273), born 1896; died at age 65 years of pulmonary edema and cancer of the breast. She lived with her mother and maternal grandparents after the divorce of her parents until her mother remarried. She and her first husband were divorced because of her infidelity. Classification: Possible personality disorder.

Granddaughter (277), born 1903. She was described as "wild" when young and at age 58 years as "flighty." Her manner was "superficial and affected" at interview. Classification: Probable personality disorder.

(286) wife of grandson (284), born 1928.

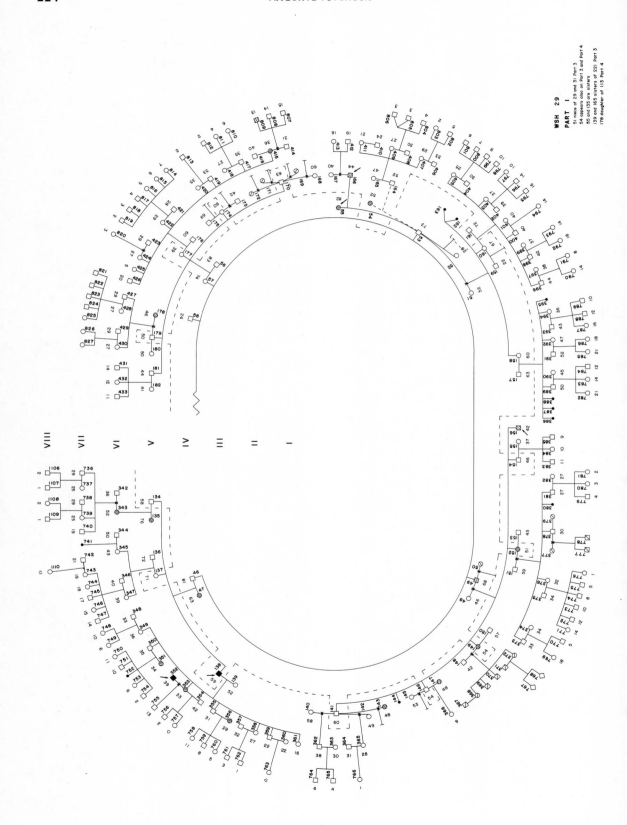

WSH 29
PART I

51 niece of 29 and 31 Part 3
54 appears also on Part 3 and Part 4
55 and 135 are sisters
139 and 165 sisters of 221 Part 3
178 daughter of 115 Part 4

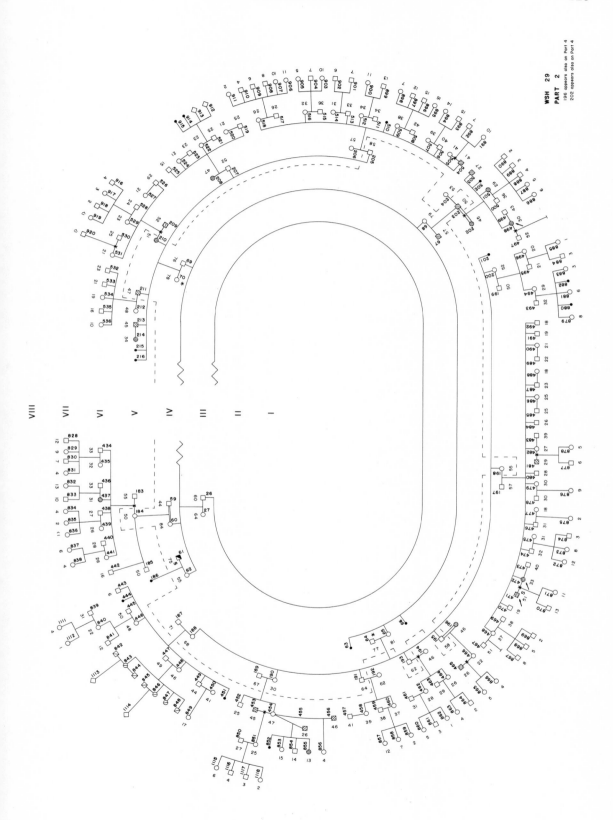

WSH   29
PART   2
196 appears also on Part 4
202 appears also on Part 4

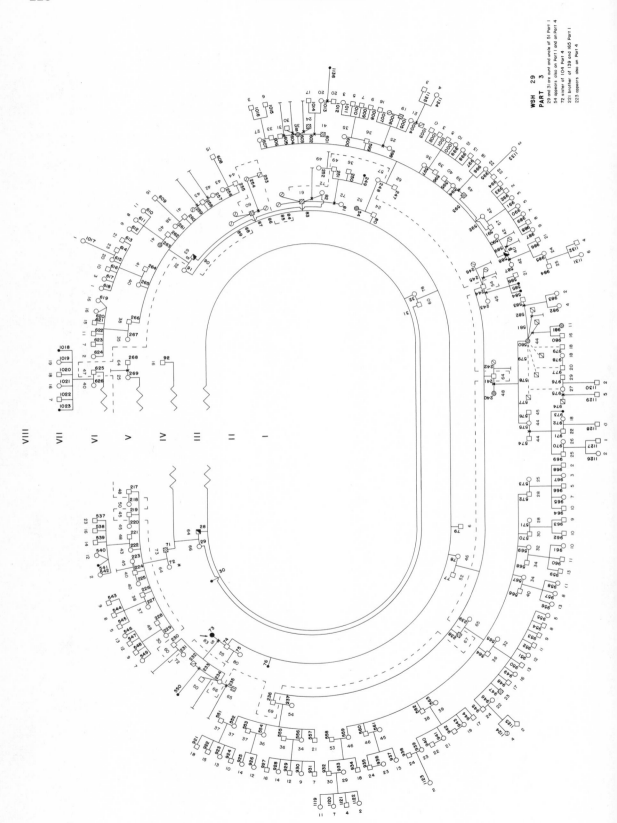

WSH 29
PART 3

29 and 31 are aunt and uncle of 51 Part 1
54 appears also on Part 1 and on Part 4
72 sister of 104 Part 4
221 brother of 139 and 165 Part 1
225 appears also on Part 4

At age 34 years she was described as very unstable, promiscuous and an alcoholic (she was arrested for alcoholism). Classification: Sociopathic personality disturbance.

Granddaughter (196), born 1915; described as "always thin, nervous, precise" and a worrier. Classification: Probable psychoneurotic disorder.

Great-Grandchildren

Great-grandson (629), born 1916. In November of 1943 he became tense and jealous and expressed delusions of infidelity and persecution and was admitted to a state mental hospital in January, 1944, where he remained until June. He was hospitalized at the same hospital from March, 1945, until December, 1947. He received 14 electroshock treatments and was released in January, 1948. He became increasingly untidy, expressed vague delusions of persecution and was subsequently admitted to Warren State Hospital on 3/7/1949, where he was diagnosed as dementia praecox, paranoid type. He was given 41 electroshock treatments and was paroled, slightly improved, on 6/18/1950. He was able to secure work for only 10 weeks of the next 14 months and in April, 1951, his wife left him to live with her parents. He often visited her to effect a reconciliation and on 8/21/1951, he struck her and beat up a cousin who came to her rescue. He was jailed and recommitted to Warren State Hospital where he was still a patient at age 44 years. Diagnosis at Warren State Hospital and classification: Schizophrenic reaction—paranoid type.

Great-grandson (631), born 1913; died at age 36 years of a crushed chest suffered in an accident. He was described as "irresponsible" and as a wanderer who often left home without explanation. The Warren State Hospital abstract of his son's record described him as "apparently psychopathic" and "openly unfaithful to his wife." Classification: Probable personality disorder.

Great-granddaughter (202), born 1916. She was interviewed at age 45 years and was described as mentally retarded and very inadequate. She had ulcers and described herself as nervous. A psychiatrist noted, in her son's records, that "the mother made a paranoid impression." Classification: Probable psychoneurotic disorder.

Great-grandson (635), born 1940. At age 12 years he was committed to a state training school for stealing and was seen at the Warren State Hospital Clinic a year later because of "emotional maladjustment" and "hurting little girls." At age 20 years he married a woman with five children and at age 22 was considered normal. Classification: Transient situational disorder—adjustment reaction of adolescence.

(654) wife of great-grandson (653), born 1926. At age 35 years she described herself as "nervous and depressed at times" because she had had seven operations in the past two years for malignant tumors of the spine. Classification: Possible transient situational personality disorder—gross stress reaction.

(465) husband of great-granddaughter (466), born 1935; described as irresponsible, abusive and "hard to get along with." Classification: Personality trait disturbance—emotionally unstable personality.

Great-Great-Grandchildren

Great-great-grandson (1030), born 1934. He was referred to the Warren State Hospital Clinic at age 11 years for aggressive behavior both in and out of school and for stealing. His father, described as a psychopath, had recently deserted his family. He had enjoyed school and was apparently more or less a leader until the family moved, changing community and school. It was recommended that the boy be returned to his former community, or if that was impossible, to be given intensive psychotherapy. No psychotherapy was done and at age 27 years he was reportedly well adjusted. Classification: Transient situational personality disorder—adjustment reaction of childhood.

Great-great-granddaughter (498), born 1932. She was raised amid marked marital strife and in the worst possible living quarters and was "wild and undisciplined as a child." She got along poorly in the children's home where she was placed after her parents separated, and seduced the young children into sex play. She was then placed in a foster home with her sister, where she got along well until their brother was also placed in the home. Soon after the brother's placement she began stealing food and eating gluttonously. She was returned to the children's home where she became indifferent and withdrawn and was subsequently hospitalized at a state mental hospital on 1/25/1947, with a diagnosis of primary behavior disorder, conduct disturbance. She escaped on 6/20/1948, and was admitted to Warren State Hospital on 7/28/1948, where she remained three months. At Warren State Hospital she did show some flattening of affect but at times expressed fairly normal emotional content. Classification: Sociopathic personality disturbance — antisocial reaction.

Great-great-granddaughter (501), born 1933; described as "nervous." Classification: Possible psychoneurotic disorder.

Great-great-grandson (503), born 1935. He was in and out of correctional institutions from age 12 years on and at age 27 years was serving a sentence for burglary and larceny. Classification: Sociopathic personality disturbance — antisocial reaction.

Great-great-grandson (1034), born 1942. He was described as a "good boy" but mentally retarded. He was treated for an eye defect which the eye clinic reported was possibly due to nervousness. Classification: Possible psychoneurotic disorder.

Great-great-grandson (1035), born 1944. At age 18 years he was at a correction school. He was always a problem to his parents as he had "temper tantrums, mean spells" and was unreasonably jealous of his siblings. At age five years he set fire to the bed next to the crib where his six-year-old brother was sleeping. At age eight years he set fire to an outhouse at his home. On 7/6/1953 his parents brought him to the Warren State Hospital Clinic for evaluation. He was described as mischievous and hostile and diagnosed as anxiety reaction of childhood. In March and April, 1956, he set fire to a barn and later to his parents' home. From April until June, 1956, he was at a private correctional camp, then at a second camp where he set fire to the dog kennels. On 7/7/1956 he was committed to a correctional school. The consulting psychiatrist considered him a very disturbed youngster

and, because of his pre-occupation with fire and overt sexual advances to other boys, he was transferred to a mental hospital for four months. He was diagnosed as an aggressive delinquent with the perversion of pyromania, with regression, and the possibility of psychosis in the future. He was transferred to Warren State Hospital on 4/22/1957, where he remained until 3/24/1959. At Warren State Hospital he was shy, seclusive, had hallucinations which told him to set fires, and was diagnosed as schizophrenic reaction, chronic undifferentiated type. He was apparently in good remission at the time of parole, but soon had trouble at home and in the community (stealing, sexual aggressiveness and passing bad checks) and was readmitted to Warren State Hospital on 7/16/1959, with a diagnosis of schizophrenic reaction, residual type, with sociopathic behavior. On 3/24/1960, when in good remission and not in need of hospital care, he was committed to a correctional school, where he remained. Classification: Sociopathic personality disturbance — antisocial reaction.

Grandparents

Maternal grandmother (4), described as "bad-tempered, ugly, full of mean tricks and thought to be a witch." Classification: Probable personality disorder.

Parents

Father (14), born 1812; died at age 69 years of pneumonia. He was described as ordinarily a "quiet, easy-going man, sociable and talkative" who was "crazy mad" and "out of his head" when angry. He "often knocked his wife down in one of these rages." He was reportedly "crazy when he came home from the war." Classification: Probable personality disorder.

Mother (15), born 1822; died at age 88 years of senility. She was described as "always a very peculiar woman, markedly hypochondriacal . . . of a discontented, suspicious, jealous nature . . . would try to overhear conversations, thought her children

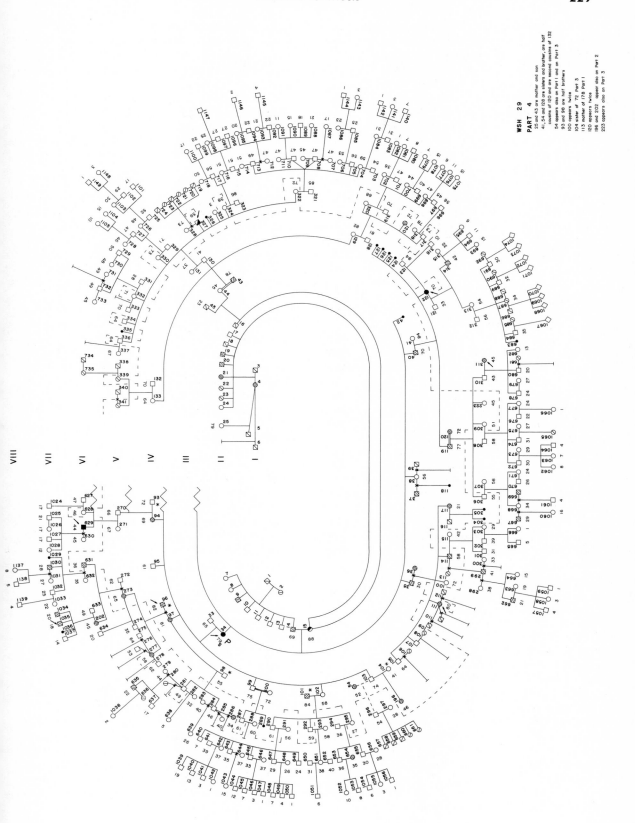

WSH 29
PART 4

25 and 43 are mother and son
41, 54 and 128 are sisters and brother, are half
cousins of 120 and are second cousins of 132
54 appears also on Part 1 and on Part 3
93 and 98 are half brothers
100 appears twice
104 sister of 72 Part 3
113 mother of 178 Part 1
120 appears twice
196 and 202 appear also on Part 2
223 appears also on Part 3

were slighting her, looked on the dark side of life and was afraid to be alone ... was fiery-tempered" and verbally and physically abusive to her children. She "fancied she had every new disease she heard of" and whenever anyone died she "took to her bed and declared she would be the next to pass away." About 20 years before death she became addicted to morphine and occasionally, after taking a large dose of morphine, would be visually and auditorily hallucinated for several days. When not under the influence of morphine she would sing to herself and read from the Bible. The last two weeks before her death she was "exceedingly noisy and ugly." Classification: Probably with functional psychosis.

Aunts and Uncles

Paternal uncle (9), reportedly an excessive drinker who, when intoxicated, was "ugly and dangerous." Classification: Probable sociopathic personality disturbance—alcoholism (addiction).

Maternal uncle (19); described as "contrary, peculiar and a heavy drinker." Classification: Probable sociopathic personality disturbance—alcoholism (addiction).

Maternal uncle (20); described as a heavy drinker for many years. He became more temperate in old age. Classification: Possible sociopathic personality disturbance—alcoholism (addiction).

Maternal uncle (21); described as "snobbish, disagreeable and hard to get along with; also used morphine." Classification: Probable personality disorder.

Siblings

Brother (28), born 1841; died at age 64 years of apoplexy. He had a stroke at age 51 years and another at 57 years, which left him helpless, speechless and with marked mental impairment. In his early years he was alcoholic. He always had a violent temper and reportedly "when angry would smash things and be ready to strike a man dead if he happened to have an axe in his hand." Classification: Probably with functional psychosis.

Brother (35); died at age 30 years from the effects of a head injury received one year previously. He was a "drifter" who drank to excess, and was aggressive when intoxicated. Classification: Sociopathic personality disturbance—alcoholism (addiction).

(36) wife of brother (35); described as a "licentious woman" who deserted (35), and became a "well-known madam" in Erie, Pennsylvania. Classification: Sociopathic personality disturbance—antisocial reaction.

(37) husband of sister (38), born 1860; age at death unknown. He was described as a "vagrant" and as a "tramp and no good." Classification: Possible personality disorder.

Brother (40), born 1861; died at age 70 years of kidney and heart ailments. He was described as "unstable." Classification: Possible personality disorder.

(43) husband of maternal half-sister (44), born 1838. At age 78 years he showed evidence of senile changes and, because of his poor memory and lack of knowledge, was unable to cooperate with the interviewer. Classification: Possible chronic brain syndrome of senium.

Nieces and Nephews

(47) wife of nephew (46), born 1866; died at age 63 years of a cerebral hemorrhage. She reportedly had "fierce, unprovoked rages" during which she was noisy and physically and verbally abusive. She also had "sick headaches" and was "complaining but with no specific illness." Classification: Probable psychoneurotic disorder.

Nephew (49), born 1867; died at age 68 years of a cerebral hemorrhage. He was described as "charming, capable but also irresponsible, undependable and promiscuous." Classification: Probable sociopathic personality disturbance.

(54) mother of illegitimate child by nephew (53). See children of the proband.

(55) wife of nephew (53), born 1879. Her natural disposition was described as "likeable, kind and generous." She began drinking in 1945 after the death of her husband and gradually increased the amount until she was consuming two quarts daily in 1958. In December, 1958, she was injured in an explosion and was unconscious for 1½

days, followed by retrograde amnesia of the accident. After that she became indifferent to her housework and appearance and depressed with some memory impairment. She was admitted to Warren State Hospital on 10/20/59, where she remained. Diagnosis was chronic brain syndrome associated with senile brain disease, mild. Classification: Chronic brain syndrome of senium.

(61) husband of niece (62), born 1863; died at age 75 years of suicide by drowning. He was in good physical and mental health for most of his life, but became despondent after the death of his wife. Classification: Probably with functional psychosis.

(67) husband of niece (68), born 1889; died at age 57 years, cause of death unknown. He was described as "irresponsible and alcoholic." Classification: Sociopathic personality disturbance—alcoholism (addiction).

Nephew (71), born 1888; described as "slovenly in his habits and appearance, drank constantly and refused to eat." At age 73 years he was unable to care for himself and was in a county home. Classification: Sociopathic personality disturbance—alcoholism (addiction).

(73) wife of nephew (74), born 1861; died at age 83 years of cancer of the stomach at Warren State Hospital. She and (74) were divorced in 1904, following which she worried greatly. There were slight, progressive mental changes which became more positive in 1919, when she attempted suicide. She then became mute, untidy, resistive and ugly and was admitted to Warren State Hospital on 4/10/1920, where she remained until November, 1927, when she was paroled into the custody of her daughter. Diagnosis at Warren State Hospital was psychosis associated with arteriosclerosis. Because of her agitation and general mental deterioration it was impossible for relatives to give her adequate care at home and she was readmitted to Warren State Hospital, where she remained until death. Diagnosis at the second admission was provisionally the same as at the previous admission or, as an alternative, manic-depressive psychosis, depressed phase. Classification: Schizophrenic reaction—chronic undifferentiated type.

(54) wife of nephew (80). See children of the proband.

Nephew (83), born 1887; died at age 61 years of unknown causes. He was described as "undependable and shiftless." He deserted his first wife when she was pregnant with their second child and later married three more times. Classification: Possible personality disorder.

Nephew (87), born 1891; died at age 60 years, cause of death unknown. He was described as "irresponsible" and "not very stable." Classification: Probable sociopathic personality disturbance.

(90) husband of niece (91), born 1890; died at age 63 years of a self-inflicted gunshot wound to the head. He had asthma and hay fever and worried unreasonably about his health. His family saw no signs of anxiety or depression before his suicide, although neighbors insisted that they had seen such signs. Classification: Probably with functional psychosis.

Niece (111), born 1879; died at age 80 years of myocardial infarction and generalized arteriosclerosis. She grew up with her mother who was a "madam," was described as "promiscuous and no good" and had a violent temper. She was admitted to Warren State Hospital on 11/21/1955 because she was confused, restless and disoriented. Symptoms of mental deterioration began about one year before hospitalization. Diagnosis at Warren State Hospital was chronic brain syndrome associated with senility. Classification: Chronic brain syndrome of senium and sociopathic personality disturbance.

Nephew (114), born 1885; died at age 58 years of an "accidental death." He lived with his paternal grandparents after the separation of his parents. He was described as "no good, a wanderer and as an alcoholic." He "ran off with a married woman and changed his name." Classification: Sociopathic personality disturbance—alcoholism (addiction).

Niece (117); died at age 21 years of tuberculosis. She lived with her mother, a "madam," after her parents separated and was described as "probably promiscuous." Classification: Possible personality disorder.

Nephew (119), born 1883. At age 77 years was described as "senile and forgetful." Classification: Chronic brain syndrome of senium.

(120) wife of nephew (119). See distant relatives.

Niece (122), born 1887; died at age 70

years of cerebral hemorrhage at Warren State Hospital, where she had been since age 68 years (admission was on 7/2/1955). She was always a rigid, nagging type of person with fixed ideas, but about two years before admission to Warren State Hospital she became nervous, weak, exhausted, irritable and lost interest in her personal appearance. About a month before admission she became hallucinated, denudative, confused and paranoid (thought her husband was trying to kill her). Diagnosis at Warren State Hospital was involutional psychotic reaction. She remained hallucinated, evasive and very flat in affect while at Warren State Hospital. Classification: Involutional psychotic reaction.

Distant Relatives

(135) wife of grandnephew (134), born 1886. At age 76 years she was described by her family as "sharp, critical, suspicious, peculiar, unpredictable and quick-tempered." She refused to answer the door to the interviewer. Classification: Probable personality pattern disturbance—paranoid personality.

Grandnephew (138), born 1903. In 1943 his right leg was crushed in an accident at work. Osteomyelitis developed and he was unable to work for eight years. He abused his wife and children and at one time was arrested for wife beating. He was admitted to a state mental hospital on 7/5/1956 because of his paranoid ideas and because he was emotionally unstable. He had a violent temper, threatened members of his family with loaded guns and knives and was preoccupied with his paranoid delusions regarding his wife's infidelity. Diagnosis at the hospital was paranoid schizophrenia. He remained hospitalized until 11/25/1958, when he was given a leave of absence and went home, much improved, to live with his wife. Classification: Schizophrenic reaction—paranoid type.

(143) wife of grandnephew (141), born 1912; died at age 48 years of cancer and alcoholism. Classification: Sociopathic personality disturbance—alcoholism (addiction).

(147) wife of grandnephew (146), born 1914; reportedly "peculiar" and a member of Alcoholics Anonymous. Classification: Sociopathic personality disturbance—alcoholism (addiction).

Grandniece (149), born 1908; described as "difficult." She moved frequently because of her promiscuity. Classification: Sociopathic personality disturbance—dyssocial reaction.

Grandniece (152), born 1911; described as an alcoholic who, when she and her husband were divorced, did not care to keep the children and they were awarded to the paternal grandparents. Classification: Probable sociopathic personality disturbance—alcoholism (addiction).

Grandnephew (156), born 1920. He was raised by a cousin until she and her husband separated when (156) was 17 years of age. He enlisted in the Navy at age 19 years, saw considerable combat, sustained a cerebral concussion, contracted malaria and developed generalized nervousness with gross tremor of the hands. He was discharged from the Navy in October, 1943, with a diagnosis of psychoneurosis after a month's hospitalization. In June, 1946, he applied for admission to a veterans administration hospital because of "black-outs," restlessness, depression and "drinking." In early October he was apprehended by the police for stealing a pair of shoes which he insisted he stole during a "black-out" and was subsequently admitted to a state mental hospital, with a diagnosis of psychoneurosis, anxiety hysteria, and also personality disorder due to trauma. In addition he had a "bout of intoxication" superimposed on the other conditions. At age 42 years he was considered a "wanderer" and treated with disregard by his family. Classification: Psychoneurotic disorder—anxiety reaction.

Grandnephew (166), born 1918. He was hospitalized at a state mental hospital from 7/7/1959 until 7/14/1961 because of his chronic alcoholism and neglect of his aged mother. His drinking became a problem in 1956, he was divorced in 1957 and released from his job because of absenteeism in 1958. While hospitalized he steadfastly refuted his alcoholism and appeared to be a pathological liar. He was friendly, charming and expansive—rather typically alcoholic—

when interviewed in October, 1961. Classification: Sociopathic personality disturbance — alcoholism (addiction).

(178) wife of grandnephew (179), born 1914. She deserted her husband and family in 1939 and at age 46 years was reported to be nervous and alcoholic. Classification: Probable sociopathic personality disturbance — alcoholism (addiction).

(196) wife of grandnephew (195). See proband's grandchildren.

(202) wife of grandnephew (203). See proband's great-grandchildren.

Grandnephew (203), born 1908; described as an irresponsible alcoholic who seldom worked and at one time was incarcerated at a state correctional institution. Classification: Sociopathic personality disturbance — alcoholism (addiction).

(208) wife of grandnephew (207), born 1913. She was under a physician's care at the time of menopause because she was "worried." Classification: Possible transient situational adjustment disorder — adjustment reaction of late life.

(209) husband of grandniece (210), born 1908. He was described as an alcoholic and an unfaithful husband. He and his wife were frequently separated because of his problems. Classification: Sociopathic personality disturbance — alcoholism (addiction).

Grandniece (210), born 1909. Reportedly her mother rejected her emotionally and physically and favored her four brothers. She was not allowed to live at home nor to continue school except through the aid of a children's service bureau. At age 51 years she and her mother seemed to have an amicable relationship. Classification: Transient situational personality disorder — adjustment reaction of adolescence.

Grandnephew (211), born 1913. When a young man he was jailed on a drunk and disorderly charge but after that was orderly and responsible. Classification: Possible other transient situational personality disturbance.

Grandnephew (213), born 1915. He changed jobs frequently and was described as "spoiled" and "irresponsible." He married for the first time at age 38 years. Classification: Personality pattern disturbance — inadequate personality.

(214) wife of grandnephew (213), born

1926. She had "numerous operations" and "worried a great deal." Classification: Possible other transient situational personality disturbance.

(235) husband of grandniece (234), born 1895; described as an alcoholic. Classification: Sociopathic personality disturbance — alcoholism (addiction).

Grandnephew (238), born 1894; died at age 67 years of cerebral arteriosclerosis. He was "always overweight and alcoholic." In 1957 he had an episode of hallucinosis and was difficult to manage. In the year preceding his death he was excitable, noisy and profane, but was not hospitalized. Classification: Sociopathic personality disturbance — alcoholism (addiction); Acute brain syndrome associated with alcohol intoxication; Chronic brain syndrome of senium.

(240) wife of grandnephew (241), born 1900; described as "a drug addict who died in the city hospital." She was 48 years of age when she died. Classification: Sociopathic personality disturbance — drug addiction.

(263) wife of grandnephew (262), born 1921. At age 41 years she was described as under "doctor's care for nerves" and as "depressed, listless and inattentive due to menopause." Classification: Probable transient situational personality disorder — adjustment reaction of late life.

Grandnephew (299), born 1920; described at age 41 years as rather like his father and as an alcoholic. Classification: Sociopathic personality disturbance — alcoholism (addiction).

(311) wife of grandnephew (310), born 1919. She had psychiatric consultation and hospitalization for diagnosis only for nervousness and hypochondriacal complaints. Classification: Probable psychoneurotic disorder.

Grandnephew (314), born 1918. He was reportedly subject to temper tantrums. Classification: Probable personality trait disturbance — emotionally unstable personality.

Half grandniece (120), born 1888; described at age 72 years as senile and forgetful. Classification: Possible chronic brain syndrome of senium.

Half grandnephew (327), born 1889; died at age 59 years, cause of death unknown. He had a "mental breakdown" following World War I and reportedly was hospitalized somewhere in New York. His parents died when he was nine years of age and he was raised by relatives. Classification: Probably with functional psychosis.

Great-grandniece (343), born 1910. She made a good economic and social adjustment after her divorce. Although considered "sharp, critical and odd" by family members, she was overtalkative and anxious to create a good impression when interviewed at age 52 years. Classification: Possible personality disorder.

(351) See below.

(352) husband of great-grandniece (353), born 1923. He was hospitalized at a state mental hospital from 8/1/1956 until 11/20/1956 because of nervous tension, heavy drinking and expressions of a suicidal wish. He believed that his wife was trying to poison him and had paranoid delusions regarding her infidelity. Just previous to admission he tried to choke his wife. He used alcohol excessively and believed he had cancer of the lungs. While hospitalized he had a series of electroshock treatments and was not hospitalized again. Diagnosis at the hospital and classification: Schizophrenic reaction—paranoid type.

(351) wife of great-grandnephew (350), born 1928. At age 34 years a skilled laborer described as "very reserved—pleasant, but hard to know." At age 33 years she sought medical advice because of nervousness which her physician attributed to overwork. Classification: Possible personality disorder.

Great-grandniece (353), born 1929. She was described as "run down and nervous" during her first marriage but was well and happily married at age 33 years. Classification: Transient situational personality disorder—adult situational reaction.

(356) wife of great-grandnephew (355), born 1933. She and her husband received marital counseling four years before the study and decided to remain together "for the sake of the children." She was described as "emotionally immature, demanding and very jealous." She also had a violent temper and was at times verbally and physically abusive. At interview she and her husband were cooperative and gave factual information clearly and concisely but spent a great deal of interview time in verbal conflict and pointless conversation. Classification: Probable personality trait disturbance—emotionally unstable personality.

Great-grandniece (415), born 1926; described as "very restless, gay, irresponsible, never wanted to stay in one place." She left her husband and three children in 1953 "to wander." After her second marriage in 1961 she assumed responsibility for her children and "seemed to have settled down." Classification: Personality disorder.

Great-grandniece (437), born 1929; reportedly "worried a lot." Classification: Possible psychoneurotic disorder.

(453) husband of great-grandniece (454), born 1917. He was an alcoholic but quit drinking and became very religious and critical. Classification: Sociopathic personality disturbance—alcoholism (addiction).

(455) husband of great-grandniece (454), born 1925; described as an alcoholic whose drinking caused a great deal of marital friction. Classification: Sociopathic personality disturbance—alcoholism (addiction).

(456) husband of great-grandniece (454), born 1917; died at age 46 years from asphyxiation. He was a physician who was described as "very active" and had changed positions at various times. Classification: Probable sociopathic personality disturbance.

(465) husband of great-grandniece (466). See proband's great-grandchildren.

(471) husband of great-grandniece (472), born 1910. He was an illegitimate child who was adopted at age seven weeks. He was always a behavior problem and lied and stole from his foster parents. It was because of truancy and stealing that he was committed to a state training school. He developed signs of mental disturbance after the death of his foster mother, when he became indifferent, unkempt and had sexual problems. He was admitted to Warren State Hospital on 12/19/1938, following a suicide attempt. Diagnosis at Warren State Hospital was primary behavior disorder. He was discharged on 4/18/1939, and sent to a CCC camp where he remained but a short time before he deserted and began to wander around the country. He was arrested in Chicago for vagrancy and, because of his peculiar behavior, was hospitalized at a mental hospital and transferred to Warren State Hospital on 5/1/1941. He was described as completely oriented but with considerable conflict and confusion

and with some sexual disturbance. Diagnosis at this admission was dementia praecox, simple type. Discharge from Warren State Hospital was on 3/8/1942, but in October, 1942, he was committed to a correctional institution as the result of his assault on a woman and released on 4/28/1947. In February, 1948, he was arrested for nonsupport of his wife (whom he had married in 1936) and for assault, battery and attempted rape which occurred 11/27/1947. While jailed he attempted suicide and was again admitted to Warren State Hospital where he remained a short time. Diagnosis at this admission was without psychosis, psychopathic personality. At age 51 years his whereabouts and mental health status were unknown. Classification: Sociopathic personality disturbance — antisocial reaction.

(472) wife of great-grandnephew (471), born 1928. She was described as "good-natured" and with "a sunny disposition." She made friends easily and got along well with employers and co-workers. Her marriage to (471) was always unhappy because of his infidelity and sexual demands. When she asked for a divorce he locked her in the apartment with him and refused to let her out. In order to get out she said that she heard voices and made a suicide attempt. He took her to a physician's office and they were both subsequently hospitalized at a state mental hospital where she remained until 7/27/1947. She was described as "somewhat flattened" and as having defective judgment. Diagnosis was without psychosis. At age 33 years she was described by an interviewer as very happy with her second husband. Classification: Probable personality pattern disturbance — inadequate personality.

(481) husband of great-grandniece (482), born 1927. He and his wife were divorced because of his alcoholism and infidelity. Classification: Sociopathic personality disturbance — alcoholism (addiction).

Great-grandnephew (504), born 1921. He and his wife were separated. She charged that he was a transvestite. Classification: Sociopathic personality disturbance — sexual deviation.

Great-grandniece (580), born 1920; described as "promiscuous, drank to excess, retarded and a prostitute." She was married and divorced three times with four legitimate and three illegitimate children. Classi-

fication: Sociopathic personality disturbance.

Great-grandnephew (588), born 1919; suicided at age 40 years with carbon monoxide gas. He was depressed for more than a year before his death because of lack of employment as a heavy equipment operator and because of the death of his mother. Classification: Probably with functional psychosis.

(593) husband of great-grandniece (594), born 1913. At age 49 years he was described as an unemployed maintenance man who had sclerosis of the liver because of his heavy drinking, although he hadn't had a drink for almost a year. Classification: Possible sociopathic personality disturbance — alcoholism (addiction).

(601) husband of great-grandniece (603), born 1921. He and (603) were divorced after 12 years of marriage because of his drinking. Classification: Sociopathic personality disturbance — alcoholism (addiction).

(602) husband of great-grandniece (603), born 1929. He and (603) were divorced after one year of marriage because of his alcoholism. Classification: Sociopathic personality disturbance — alcoholism (addiction).

Great-grandniece (603), born 1927; described as "restless, dissatisfied and very reckless." She attempted suicide several times. She also "dramatized" and had "no feeling for her children." Classification: Probable personality trait disturbance — emotionally unstable personality.

Great-grandnephew (662), born 1940; described as "like his father and grandfather — undependable." Classification: Probable sociopathic personality disturbance.

(667) husband of great-grandniece (668), born 1917; described as an alcoholic "but not as serious as (669)." Classification: Possible sociopathic personality disturbance — alcoholism (addiction).

(669) husband of great-grandniece (668); described as a tavern owner and an alcoholic. Classification: Sociopathic personality disturbance — alcoholism (addiction).

Great-great-grandnephew (809), born 1948. He was left by his mother, in 1953, at a children's home. After her remarriage in 1961, she assumed responsibility for him. At age 13 years he was described as "off in his own little world — school work was off."

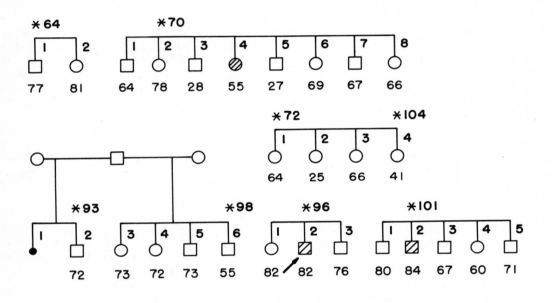

CONTROLS   **W S H   29**

Classification: Probable transient situational personality disorder — adjustment reaction of childhood.

Great-great-grandniece (855), born 1951. At age 13 years she ran away from home and was referred to the juvenile court. Classification: Probable transient situational personality disorder — adjustment reaction of adolescence.

Great-great-grandnephew (947), born 1941. He had been arrested for drunkenness but had no history of treatment for alcoholism. Classification: Sociopathic personality disturbance — alcoholism (addiction).

Great-great-grandniece (981), born 1953. As an 11-year-old she was too nervous to do her school work. Her IQ score was above average. Classification: Possible psychoneurotic disorder.

Great-great-grandniece (1005), born 1945. A 19-year-old who, in early adolescence, was a disciplinary problem and a ward of Juvenile Court. Classification: Probable transient situational personality disorder.

Family Summary

The proband, the mother, a great-grandson, a brother, a niece, the wife of a nephew, the husbands of two nieces, a grandnephew, a half-grandnephew, a great-grandnephew and the husband of a great-grandniece had psychotic disorders, or probably or possibly so. Personality disorders were found in the father, two daughters, two granddaughters, the maternal grandmother, two great-grandsons, three great-great-grandsons, a great-great-granddaughter, one paternal uncle, three maternal uncles, two brothers, four nephews, two nieces, three grandnieces, seven grandnephews, five great-grandnieces, two great-grandnephews, a great-great-grandniece

and in a great-great-grandniece and in a great-great-grandnephew. Also classified as with personality disorders were the husband of a daughter, the mother of a son's illegitimate child, the wife of a grandson, the wife of a great-grandson and the husband of a great-granddaughter, the wife of a brother, the husband of a sister, the husband of a niece, the wives of eight grandnephews, two husbands of grandnieces, the wives of two great-grandnephews and the husbands of 10 grandnieces. Twenty-six of the 73 persons classified under personality disorders were alcoholic and two of the alcoholics were also classified as chronic brain syndrome of senium. One personality disorder (non-alcoholic) was also chronic brain syndrome of senium. A niece, the husband of a daughter, the wife of a nephew, the husband of a maternal half sister, a nephew and a half grandniece were classified as chronic brain syndrome of senium only. A granddaughter, a great-granddaughter, a great-great-granddaughter, a great-great-grandson, a grandnephew, a great-grandniece, the wife of a nephew, the wife of a grandnephew and a great-great-grandniece were neurotic.

Controls

Sister (4) of (70), born 1887; died at age 55 years of acute cardiac luetic aortitis. Her family reported that she was depressed following the death of her daughter at age nine years and again following the death of her husband shortly before her own demise. Her physician stated that although she had "a very bad heart" she was not unduly anxious about her health and she was never treated for depression. Classification: Probable psychoneurotic disorder — depressive reaction.

See family pedigree, person 96.

See family pedigree, person 101.

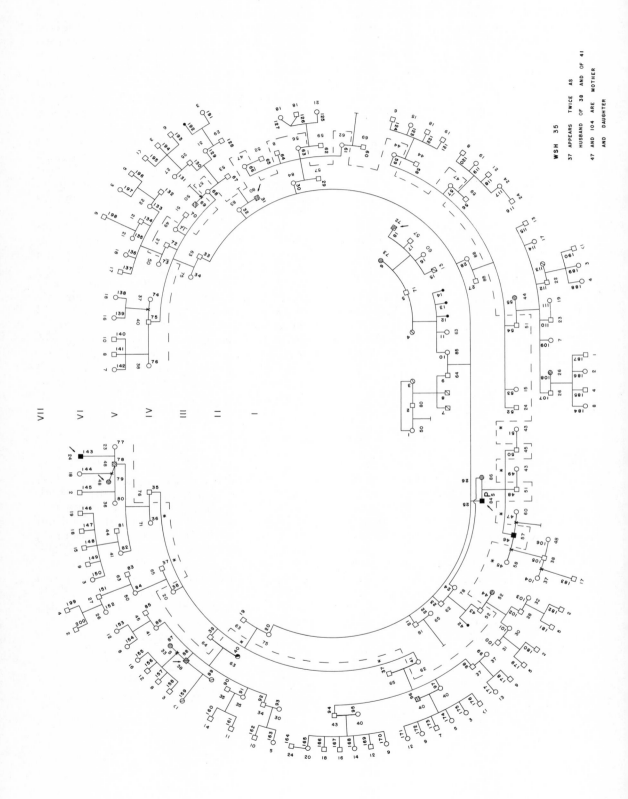

WSH 35

37 APPEARS TWICE AS

HUSBAND OF 38 AND OF 41

47 AND 104 ARE MOTHER

AND DAUGHTER

WSH 35: The Proband

Proband (25), born 1870; died at age 84 years of a cerebral hemorrhage. He was described as "even-tempered, but easily hurt and very tenderhearted" until about five years before his hospitalization at Warren State Hospital when, during the winter months, he became depressed, melancholy, apprehensive, unoccupied and entertained some persecutory delusions. Two years later he had another depression. After that he was subject to short periods of depression. From February until July, 1915, his depression gradually grew worse until he was committed to Warren State Hospital on 7/28/1915, with a diagnosis of manic-depressive insanity—involutional type. After a hospital stay of six months he was released against advice as unimproved. He made at least one suicidal attempt by cutting his throat. Only the prompt action of his wife, who held the wound together until help arrived, saved his life. From the time of release from Warren State Hospital until his death he remained seclusive and depressed and unable to cope with his farm work. Classification: Manic-depressive reaction—depressed type.

(26) wife of proband (25), born 1873; died at age 86 years of an intestinal obstruction. A few family members "blamed her for the patient's mental condition," although the majority described her as "friendly, cheerful and neighborly." She was senile for seven years prior to her death. Classification: Chronic brain syndrome of senium.

Children

Son (46), born 1903. He completed grade 12 and was a plumber by trade but, when interviewed, he had no inside plumbing of any kind in his ramshackle dwelling. He was described as a healthy child but all informants described him as mentally ill as an adult. He never got along with his father and had no friends because of his argumentative nature. He caused mild disturbance in any gathering of which he was a part, although he was never arrested for the disturbance. When interviewed at age 57 years by a psychiatrist from Warren State Hospital, a diagnosis of schizophrenic reaction, paranoid type, was made with "no hesitation." His residence was "indescribably dirty." On knowing the cause of the interviewer's visit he became hostile and aggressive and expressed "a lot of delusional material of a paranoid nature." He looked "wild and inappropriate" and accused the interviewer of poisoning fertilizers and showed the interviewer a jar of fruit which had been poisoned. The interviewer stated, "He shook hands when I left—which was soon after I arrived." Classification: Schizophrenic reaction—paranoid type.

Grandparents

(6) wife of maternal grandfather (5), born 1823; died at age 73 years of a rupture. She was described as "quite a nervous, excitable, loud woman." Classification: Possible personality disorder.

Aunts and Uncles

Maternal half uncle (18), born 1861; died at age 72 years of a coronary thrombosis at Warren State Hospital. He was a successful farm owner who was entirely normal until about age 65 years when a mental change was noted. The gradual change persisted and on 2/28/1930, he was hospitalized at Warren State Hospital with senile psychosis, paranoid type, with an associated arteriosclerosis. The commitment certificate stated "threatens to kill members of his family, especially his wife. Ideas of great wealth . . . sexually unbalanced . . . ." Classification: Chronic brain syndrome of senium.

Siblings

(31) husband of sister (32), born 1875; died at age 80 years of uremia and arteriosclerosis. He farmed although he was trained to be a teacher and worked in Puerto Rico for five years as a supervisory principal of schools and as a missionary. At about age 70 years his memory began to show impairment but he was almost 80 years of age when he became confused for time, place and date, began to wander from home and could no longer recognize acquaintances. He would occasionally cry. He was admitted to Warren State Hospital on 11/22/1955, with a diagnosis of chronic brain syndrome

associated with arteriosclerosis, where he died before the end of the year. Classification: Chronic brain syndrome associated with cerebral arteriosclerosis.

Nieces and Nephews

(40) wife of nephew (39), born 1898. She was described as having always been nervous and as "doctoring" a great deal. For many years she was very withdrawn and, at age 62 years, attempts were made to interview her; however, it could not be determined whether she was out or merely refused to come to the door. Her neighbor and long-time friend felt that the latter was quite likely. About a year later the same neighbor described her as "non-complaining and quite sociable" because of "shots or tranquilizers." Classification: Probably with functional psychosis, schizophrenic reaction—chronic undifferentiated type.

(44) wife of nephew (43), born 1907. She was a school teacher who, at age 52 years, worked as a skilled laborer. At age 36 years she had an episode of fainting spells during which she thought "her heart had stopped beating." She also complained of indigestion, nervousness and shortness of breath. All clinical findings were negative and a diagnosis of hysteria was made. The condition lasted for three years and did not recur. Classification: Psychoneurotic reaction—other.

(55) wife of nephew (54). Between the ages of 40 and 44 she appeared to go through periods of mild emotional depression. She suffered from a hypothyroid condition and it was believed that the depressive reaction was associated with the hypothyroidism. Classification: Psychoneurotic disorder—depressed reaction.

(69) husband of niece (68); described as a laborer with a very poor work record and as an alcoholic. He disappeared at age 50 years when his wife was admitted to a tuberculosis hospital. Classification: Sociopathic personality disturbance—alcoholism (addiction).

Distant Relatives

Grandnephew (78), born 1912. During the difficulties of his second marriage he had very brief periods of depression which his family felt were justified. Classification: Transient situational personality disturbance—adult situational reaction.

(79) wife of grandnephew (78), born 1912. While married to (78) she was rather restless and dissatisfied and frequently left him. She was also "given to extremes of temper" and at times was assaultive. Previous to her marriage to (78) she was married and had one child; she has married and separated again since their divorce. Classification: Personality trait disturbance.

(87) wife of grandnephew (88), born 1924. At age 33 years she took an overdose of sleeping pills in a suicide attempt and was subsequently hospitalized with the diagnosis of depressive reaction. She had a very unsettled childhood in that her parents separated and she lived at various times with her own mother, her stepmother, who showed favoritism to her own children, and at the home of a maternal uncle. She married at age 16 years and later separated from her alcoholic husband. Her fourth child was born after the separation although she maintained that the child belonged to her ex-husband. Classification: Psychoneurotic disorder—depressive reaction.

Grandnephew (88), born 1921. He was reportedly hospitalized for alcoholism in 1959. He deserted his wife and three children in 1956 and at last information had married a very religious woman who was a restaurant owner and "will not allow" him to drink. One family member suggested that he had a character change after a head injury which resulted in a scalp laceration in 1952. Classification: Sociopathic personality disturbance—alcoholism (addiction).

(96) husband of grandniece (97), born 1919. He was a laborer with a poor work record who was described as "shiftless and alcoholic." Classification: Sociopathic personality disturbance—alcoholism (addiction).

(108) wife of grandnephew (107), born 1933. She reportedly became ill in 1955 after a spinal anesthetic. The symptoms of insomnia, weight loss, numbness of face and forehead that did not follow nerve distribution, hearing loss and sense of pressure in her head were originally diagnosed as a

pituitary insufficiency. When referred to a neurosurgeon no organic pathology was found. She was interviewed by a Warren State Hospital psychiatrist who concluded that she suffered mild to moderate depressions following childbirth in 1951. Classification: Psychoneurotic disorder – depressive reaction.

Great-grandnephew (143), born 1936. He was admitted to a state mental hospital on 12/31/1957. His mother died five days after his birth. He made his home with his paternal grandparents until his father remarried when he was four years of age. Adjustment to the stepmother was difficult and he soon returned to the home of the grandparents. After eight years his father was divorced and remarried but (143) preferred to remain with the grandparents. He had social difficulties in school and was considered shy and bashful. About one year before admission to the hospital he developed psychosomatic complaints, became hyperactive, developed bizarre delusions and auditory and visual hallucinations. He had periods during which he was ugly and disagreeable. A leave of absence was approved after a full course of electroshock treatments and at age 24 years he was in excellent remission and making a good adjustment. Classification: Schizophrenic reaction – paranoid type.

Family Summary

The proband, his son and a great-grandnephew had psychotic disorders; the wife of a nephew probably so. Personality disorders were found in two grandnephews, a wife of the maternal grandfather, the husband of a niece, the wife of a grandnephew and in the husband of a grandniece. The wives of two nephews and the wives of two grandnephews were neurotic. The wife of the proband and a maternal half uncle were classified as chronic brain syndrome of senium and a sister's husband was hospitalized with a psychotic reaction to arteriosclerosis.

Controls

Sister (3) of (37), born 1880; died at age 71 years, cause of death unknown. She was "nervous" and restless during the last years of her life, necessitating confinement to a rest home for custodial care. Classification: Probable chronic brain syndrome of senium.

Brother (4) of (37); died at age 39 years, cause of death unknown. He was "nervous" as a result of his World War I experiences although his nervous problem was never described. Classification: Probable transient situational personality disturbance – gross stress reaction.

See family pedigree, person 40.

Brother (2) of (40), born 1903. He was described as always "wilful and disobedient" both in childhood and adolescence. He deserted his first wife during her second pregnancy and had no contact with the children until they approached adulthood. He moved frequently, always working as a gas station operator. Classification: Probable sociopathic personality disturbance.

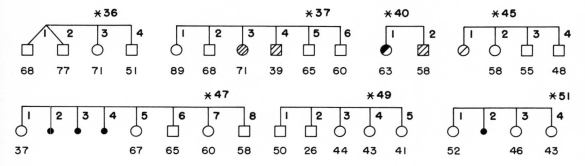

CONTROLS W S H 3 5

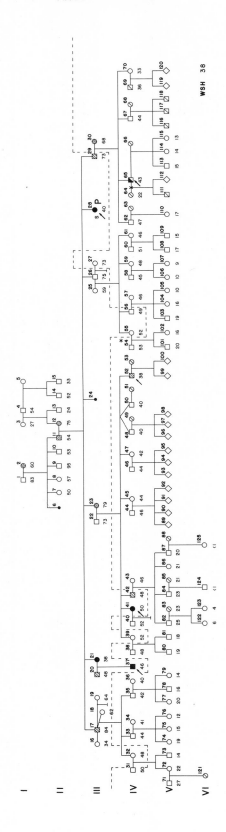

WSH 38: The Proband

The proband (28), born 1889; died at age 40 years of cystitis with pelvic abscess. She was a normally "ambitious, talkative, friendly girl" who, at age 13 years, developed a depression which lasted one year. She made one suicide attempt by taking arsenic during this depression. Four years later she spent two months in a sanitarium with another depression. At discharge she was much improved and remained well for two years. She then suddenly became "noisy, violent, talkative and restless," necessitating admission to Warren State Hospital on 7/9/1909, where she had alternating moods of depression and excitement. In July, 1912, she went home, although depressed. At home she was hallucinated (would search for her father, who was deceased) but remained manageable until July, 1915, when she developed another period of excitement and was rehospitalized at Warren State Hospital for a year with a diagnosis of manic-depressive psychosis, manic phase. She was at home for four years before her next hospitalization on 7/30/1920. This episode, of two years' duration, was characterized by "hyperactivity, flight of ideas, distractibility and generally treacherous attitude." She got along well for several years until she was hospitalized for a bladder infection. While physically ill she became excited and hyperactive, requiring another admission to Warren State Hospital with a diagnosis of manic-depressive psychosis. She was discharged after one year at Warren State Hospital and died at home a short time later. Classification: With functional psychosis, manic-depressive reaction — mixed type.

Grandparents

Paternal grandmother (2), born 1822; died at age 60 years, immediate cause of death unknown. She reportedly took morphine "for years" after it was prescribed for persistent diarrhea. The morphine addiction was cured but she was an invalid for many years before her death because of obesity (nearly 300 pounds). Classification: Psychoneurotic disorder.

Parents

Father (11), born 1856; died at age 54 years of apoplexy. Described as the most peculiar member of what was otherwise considered a normal family. He lived at his father's home for several years after his marriage until his father bought a farm for him. He was so homesick in his own home that he would "walk up and down and cry like a baby." He shortly moved to a small shack near his old home and visited his parents every day. He always worried excessively over trivial matters. Classification: Personality pattern disturbance — inadequate personality.

Mother (12), born 1855; died at age 75 years, cause of death unknown. At age 13 years she developed "prolonged outbreaks of laughing and crying" and became "very cross and ill-tempered." After a remission of these symptoms at about age 16 years she was in bed for a year with acute pains and severe headaches. While in bed she became very despondent and thereafter had what was described as "a depressive tendency" and much insomnia. Later she was a slovenly housekeeper, overly religious, "stubborn and domineering" and described as "decidedly neurotic." Classification: Possibly with functional psychosis — schizophrenic reaction.

Siblings

Brother (17), born 1879. When interviewed at age 84 years he was a resident of a nursing home and was very helpful until he became too tired to participate in the interview. As a youth he was "regarded as rather peculiar" but the "peculiarities" disappeared as he grew older. Classification: Possible transient situational personality disturbance — adjustment reaction of adolescence.

(20) husband of sister (21), born 1886. When a young man he worked "steadily" (at odd jobs) but reportedly was "peculiar" and had "periods when he wants to kill himself." A cryptic interview note said "no good, beat wife to death"; however, information on the wife (21) stated that the wife's assailant was her husband's girl friend.

Classification: Probable psychoneurotic disorder.

Sister (21), born 1881; died at age 38 years of the effects of a beating. She was described as "peculiar" with "hysterical" spells, "delusions of persecution" in that she believed that her deceased father had been "raised from the dead." Her brother reported that "a woman jumped on (21), beat her, and a week later she died." The alleged assailant was her husband's (20) girl friend; the victim's mother objected to having charges brought against the assailant. Classification: With functional psychosis, schizophrenic reaction — paranoid type.

Sister (23), born 1883; retired teacher and practical nurse who at age 79 years was still in good physical and mental health. As a young woman she was "considered quiet, shy, sensitive and quite peculiar... went from store to store asking people if she could pray for them. Then, regardless of whether their answer was 'yes' or was 'no,' she would kneel and begin to pray." Classification: Probable personality disorder.

Brother (29), born 1891; a retired farmer-laborer who was described at age 73 years as extremely nervous and high-strung. Classification: Probable psychoneurotic disorder.

(30) wife of brother (29), born 1896; described at age 68 years in case history of her son (65) as "nervous, has poor health." Classification: Possible psychoneurotic disorder.

Nieces and Nephews

Nephew (37), born 1914; died at age 46 years of malnutrition at a New York State hospital. At age 20 years, while a college student, he suddenly became confused, excited and delusional and was hospitalized at a city hospital, from which he soon escaped only to be picked up by the police and taken to a state mental hospital. At admission he exhibited vague paranoid delusional ideas about fires, his impending murder, and about the medicine containing poison. The agitation and fearfulness continued with only temporary response to ECT. He once attacked a fellow patient, claiming that voices told him to kill this patient for putting poison in his food. He was hospitalized for 312 months; diagnosis was dementia praecox, catatonic type. Classification: Schizophrenic reaction — catatonic type.

Niece (41), born 1912. At age 50 years she was an out-patient at Buffalo State Hospital, where she had recently been hospitalized, and appeared "improved, relaxed and pleasant" at last information. She was a registered nurse by profession and was described as "a good nurse." Her two children were adopted because she had undergone a hysterectomy while of child-bearing age. At age 45 she was treated by a psychiatrist for severe depression. Two years later she was hospitalized at a general hospital for psychiatric symptoms but refused psychiatric care. She remained at home after discharge but temper tantrums, rages, overactivity and agitation necessitated hospitalization. The hospital diagnosis was manic-depressive psychosis, manic type. There was one more short hospitalization just previous to the interview at age 50 years. Classification: Manic-depressive reaction — other.

Nephew (42), born 1914; at 48 years a successful store owner who reportedly had depressed periods for which he never received treatment and "they passed off." Classification: Probable psychoneurotic disorder.

Nephew (52), born 1924. At last information he was 38 years of age and worked as a laborer. He had a history of hospitalization at a general hospital for psychiatric treatment. Diagnosis was inadequate personality and he was discharged as recovered. Classification: Personality pattern disturbance — inadequate personality.

Nephew (65), born 1918; employment (laborer) was sporadic. From boyhood he was "very nervous" and "overactive" and encountered "frequent difficulties in the community": he had stolen chickens, merchandise and finally a car, for which offense he was jailed for 17 days. He was imprisoned a second time for five months for stealing livestock. Admission to a state mental hospital was at age 24 years; he was described as "restless and emotionally unbalanced" and exhibited "uncontrollable temper." He had somato-psychic delusions pertaining to his ears (thought they were continuously discharging). A diagnosis of dementia praecox, simple type, was made "although his behavior is that of a constitu-

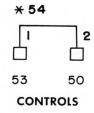

✳ 54

| 1 | 2 |

53   50

CONTROLS

W S H   3 8

tional psychopathic personality . . . his emotional instability and blunted affect are more suggestive of dementia praecox." Duodenal ulcer was also diagnosed. He escaped after two months and remained unhospitalized for 19 years. The second hospitalization, which was at a second state mental hospital was because of "excitement with rage reactions, destructiveness and paranoid accusations." His wife took him home without consent of the hospital in less than a month. Classification: Probably with functional psychosis.

Family Summary

The proband, a sister, her son (the proband's nephew), and a niece were psychotic, another nephew probably so, and the proband's mother possibly so; all except the sister and mother were hospitalized with their psychotic illness. Another nephew was hospitalized with a personality disorder. The father, a brother, a sister and another nephew were classified as with personality disorders. The paternal grandmother, a brother, the brother's wife and a sister's husband were neurotic.

Controls

None noteworthy.

(*Text continued on page 252.*)

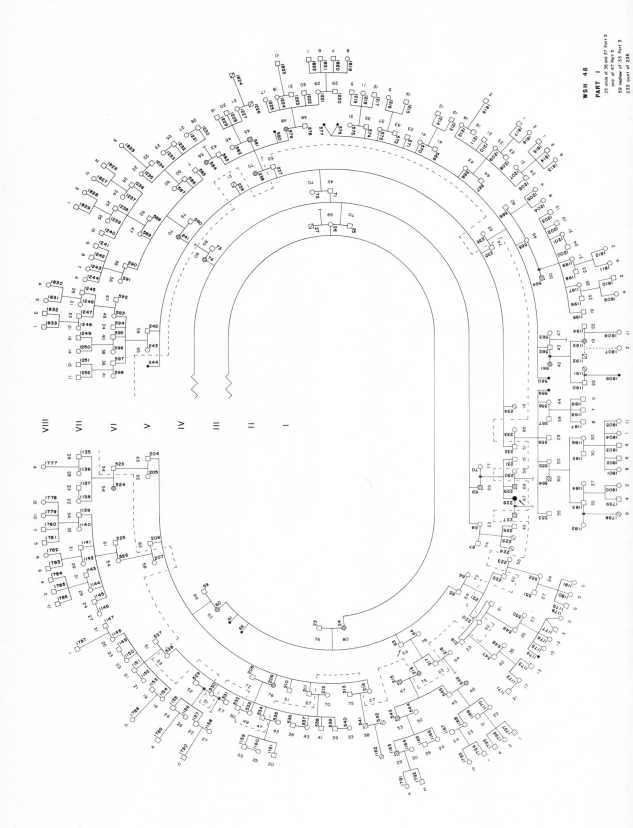

WSH 48

PART 1

25 uncle of 36 and 37 Part 3
and of 47 Part 5
59 nephew of 33 Part 5
233 aunt of 226

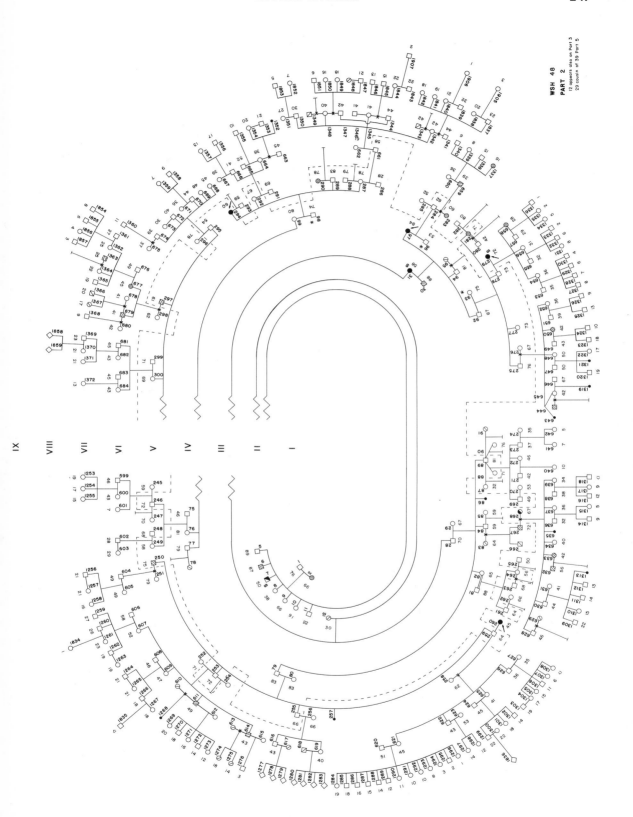

WSH 48
PART 2
12 appears also on Part 3
29 cousin of 39 Part 5

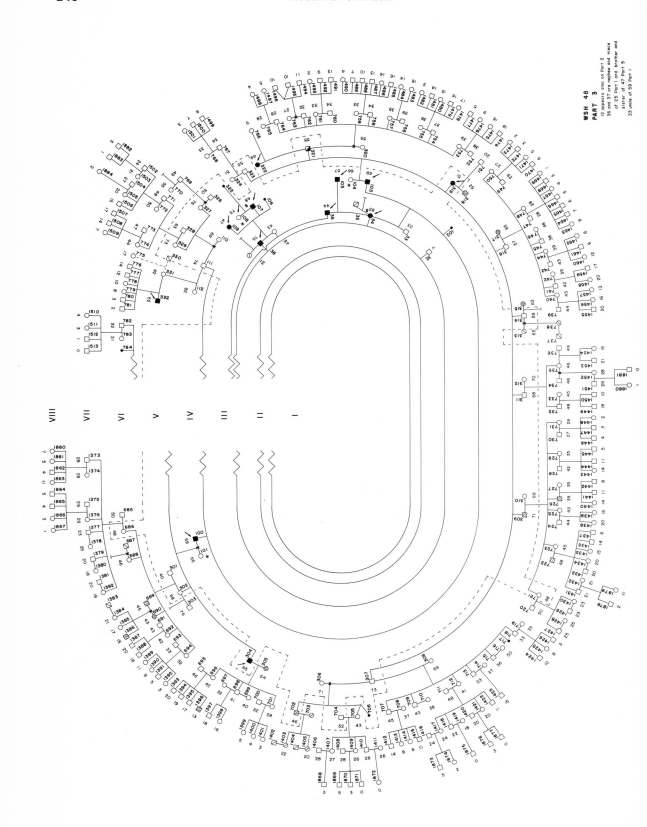

WSH 48
PART 3

12 appears also on Part 2
36 and 37 are nephew and niece
of 25 Part 1 and brother and
sister of 47 Part 5
33 uncle of 59 Part 1

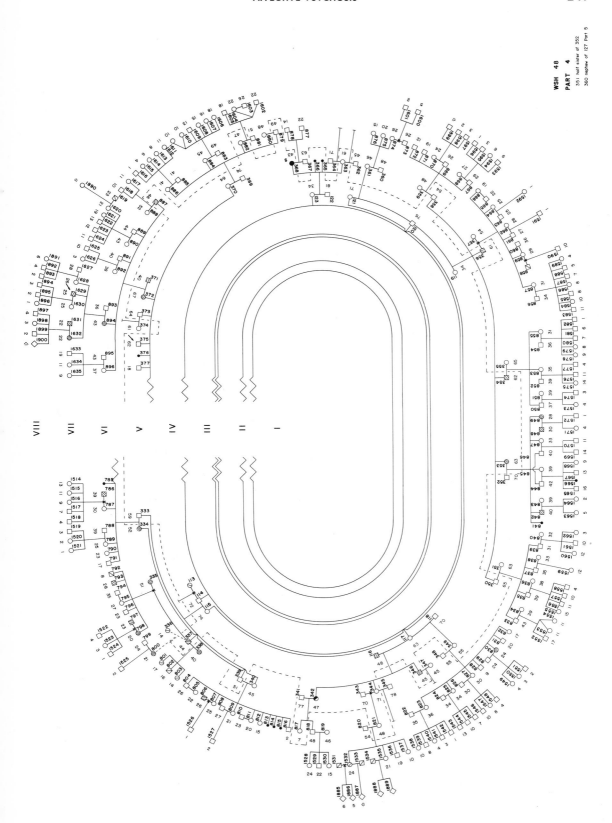

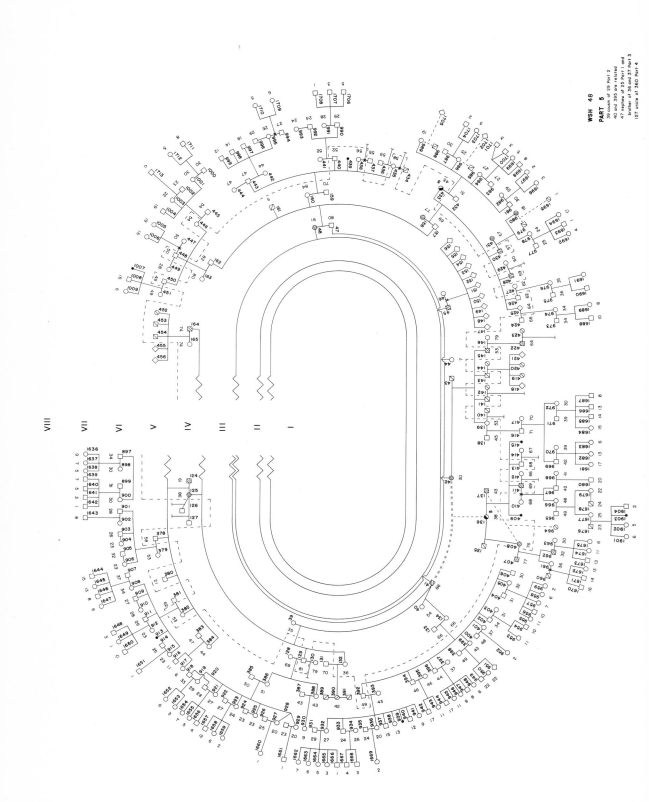

WSH 48

PART 5

39 cousin of 29 Part 2
40 and 395 are related
47 nephew of 25 Part 1 and
brother of 36 and 37 Part 3
127 uncle of 360 Part 4

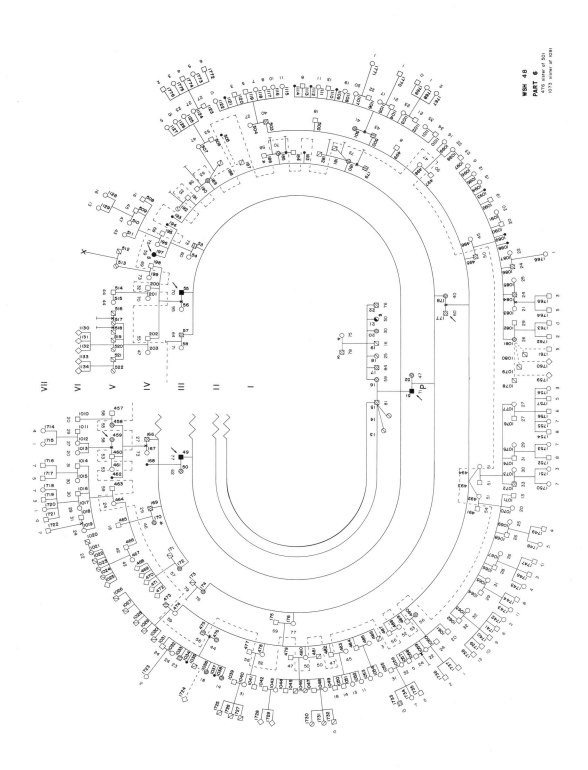

WSH 48
PART 6
476 sister of 501
1073 sister of 1091

WSH 48: The Proband

The proband (51), born 1857; died at age 71 of myocarditis. His early development was normal, although he was not considered "as bright" as the rest of the family. From childhood on he was subject to brief periods of unconsciousness, but with no convulsive movements. He worried excessively about his family after the death of his wife in 1905, but mental symptoms did not appear until 1914 when he became excited, talkative, violent and denudative, necessitating hospitalization at Warren State Hospital on 12/14/1914. He remained at Warren with a diagnosis of manic-depressive insanity, manic phase, until 2/26/1916, when he was discharged as restored. He had two more occurrences of manic-depressive psychosis, manic phase, with complete remission between episodes; one was for 12 months in 1923–1924, during which time he was hospitalized at a state mental hospital. He was hospitalized at Warren State Hospital during the last attack from 7/11/1927 until 4/1/1928. Classification: Manic-depressive reaction—manic type.

(52) wife of proband (51), born 1859; died at age 47 years of childbirth. She was described as "sexually immoral." Classification: Possible sociopathic personality disturbance.

Children

Daughter (174), born 1883; died at age 76 years of a stroke. Her "moral reputation was distinctly bad" according to relatives. In the last year of her life she was mentally unstable and "childish." Classification: Possible sociopathic personality disturbance; also, chronic brain syndrome of senium.

(177) husband of daughter (178), born 1884; died at age 60 years of cancer of the tongue. He used alcohol "since a boy, being occasionally drunk and very ugly at these times." He reportedly tried to "drown his sorrows in alcohol." The first attack of delirium tremens for which he was hospitalized for ten days was in July, 1927. After two months' partial abstinence he began to drink heavily and was again hospitalized. He was soon transferred to Warren State Hospital on 1/10/1928, with a diagnosis of alcoholism without psychosis. While hospitalized he was cooperative and showed fairly good insight, although he continued to blame his wife as being the cause of his drinking. Parole was granted on 5/29/1928, and he was never rehospitalized. Classification: Sociopathic personality disturbance—alcoholism (addiction).

Daughter (178), born 1888; died at age 40 years of tuberculosis of the hip. She was described as "a terrible woman to live with...a poor manager and a nag." Classification: Probable personality disorder.

(179) husband of daughter (180), born 1885; died of alcoholism, date of death unknown. Classification: Probable sociopathic personality disturbance—alcoholism (addiction).

Daughter (180), born 1890; described as having a bad "moral reputation." Classification: Possible sociopathic personality disturbance.

Daughter (185), born 1892. She was described as "not a good character...reputation of sexual irregularities." Classification: Possible sociopathic personality disturbance.

Daughter (189), born 1899. As a young woman was described as "a coarse girl of questionable reputation...was in a home for unmarried mothers." Classification: Probable sociopathic personality disturbance.

Grandchildren

(473) husband of granddaughter (474); described as an alcoholic. Classification: Probable sociopathic personality disturbance—alcoholism (addiction).

Grandson (475), born 1906; described as "an alcoholic...violent temper...nasty disposition." Alcoholism was "a problem for years." Classification: Sociopathic personality disturbance—alcoholism (addiction).

(476) wife of grandson (475), born 1918. She described herself as "a physical and mental wreck." She was chronically unhappy and often had "blue spells" because of her husband's alcoholism. Classification: Probable transient situational personality disturbance—adult situational reaction.

(490) wife of grandson (489), born 1906; described as "nervous." Classification: Possible psychoneurotic reaction.

Grandson (495), born 1912; described as "perennially unemployed and continually in need of financial assistance." Classification: Possible personality pattern disturbance—inadequate personality.

Grandson (500), born 1918. He was often unemployed and did not support his wife and family. Classification: Possible personality disorder.

(501) wife of grandson (500), born 1920. She was described as "often depressed or unhappy" and "had blue spells." She deserted her husband and children. Classification: Probable psychoneurotic reaction.

Grandson (503), born 1921. He said that he couldn't "stand being bossed." Consequently, he was usually unemployed and received welfare assistance. Classification: Probable personality disorder.

Great-Grandchildren

Great-grandson (1033), born 1939. He was described as "moody." He had a difficult time adjusting to work and to the family after his discharge from the service. Classification: Possible other transient situational personality disorder.

Great-granddaughter (1036), born 1944. She was living in a private charity home and was believed to have had an illegitimate child. Classification: Possible sociopathic personality disturbance.

Great-granddaughter (1038), born 1948. She was reportedly "a problem" at home and at school. Classification: Possible transient situational personality disorder—adjustment reaction of adolescence.

Great-grandson (1072), born 1929; described as a "drifter" who changed jobs often and seemed "to resent working." Classification: Probable personality disorder.

Great-granddaughter (1081), born 1936. She had three illegitimate children before marriage. Classification: Sociopathic personality disturbance.

Great-grandson (1084), born 1937. He was involved with the law as an adolescent and spent some time in a correctional institution. Classification: Probable sociopathic personality disturbance.

Great-grandson (1086), born 1938. He was involved with the law during adolescence and spent some time in a correctional institution. Classification: Probable sociopathic personality disturbance.

Great-Great-Grandchildren

Great-great-grandson (1733), born 1952; reportedly had "trouble adjusting to conditions," was on tranquilizers and missed school because of emotional problems. Classification: Possible personality trait disturbance—emotionally unstable personality.

Grandparents

Paternal grandmother (2), born 1790; died at age 66 years of typhoid fever. She was described as "irritable" and "excitable." Classification: Possible personality trait disturbance—emotionally unstable personality.

Maternal grandfather (3), born 1791; died at age 78 years of "heart trouble." He was described as "hot-tempered, rather shiftless and easy-going." Classification: Possible personality disorder.

Parents

Father (15), born 1807; died at age 81 years of apoplexy and cancer of the lip. He was described as an "exhorter of religion." He was not considered "well balanced" and was considered as "a joke" outside his own family. He was also described as an "even-tempered" man with no tendency to mood changes. Classification: Probable personality pattern disturbance—inadequate personality.

Mother (16), born 1821; died at age 59 years of cancer of the stomach. She was described as "excitable, nervous, rattle-headed...very peculiar" and as very decorative in her dress and very jealous of her husband without cause. Classification: Probable personality pattern disturbance—inadequate personality.

Aunts and Uncles

Paternal uncle (6), born 1812; died at age 87 years of "kidney trouble and carbuncle on the neck." He was described as a quick-tempered man, excitable and talkative, fond of arguments and a non-believer in religion. He would not have a physician in his last illness. Classification: Possible personality pattern disturbance—paranoid personality.

Paternal uncle (7), born 1814; died at age 50 years of suicide by hanging. He became run down physically, melancholic, apprehensive and thought that people were coming to burn him. His son and stepson enlisted in the Civil War which left him with no help on the farm at harvest time. He hired some hands, gave them conflicting instructions, then disappeared. He was found the next day where he had hanged himself. Classification: Probably with functional psychosis, psychotic-depressive reaction.

Maternal uncle (17), died at age 84 years of apoplexy. He was described as "jovial, easy-going and an incessant talker... he was very excitable, quick-tempered, 'rattleheaded' and an ardent prohibitionist and abolitionist." Probable personality trait disturbance—emotionally unstable personality.

Maternal aunt (20), died at age 30 years, cause of death unknown. She married but returned home shortly. She seemed "peculiar and worried, went to bed and died in a week." Classification: Possible psychoneurotic reaction.

Maternal aunt (21), died at age 50 years of suicide by hanging. She was of a suspicious nature, inclined to scold a good deal, was easily offended and was a "loud talker." About four years before her death she became "depressed, gloomy... worried constantly and thought things were 'all going wrong.'" She finally refused to see people and hanged herself. Classification: Probably with functional psychosis, psychotic-depressive reaction.

Maternal uncle (22), born 1839; died at age 76 years, cause of death unknown. He was described as "friendly but very sensitive... quick-tempered and not very observant." Classification: Possible psychoneurotic disorder.

Siblings

Paternal half sister (24), born 1830; died at age 80 years of paralysis of the throat. She had a stroke nine years before her death. She was childish, irritable, delusional and, during the last four years of her life, would run away from home. Classification: Chronic brain syndrome of senium.

(30) husband of sister (31), born 1830; died at age 88 years of "senile decay." Classification: Possible chronic brain syndrome of senium.

Sister (31), born 1839; died at age 58 years of a tumor. She was considered, from the age of 16, "very peculiar," suspicious and unreasonable. She always feared that someone was trying to steal her things and injure her in some way. She had three distinct periods of mental disturbance. The first episode occurred when she was a "young woman"—she remained in bed, cried a great deal, refused food, would not talk to people and would do no work. Ten years later, during the second attack, she was ugly, abusive, suspicious and apprehensive. About five years before her death her physician recommended that she be hospitalized at Warren State Hospital but she was never admitted. She told no one of her abdominal tumor for years as she feared surgery. Four months before her death she became very psychotic, and thought no one cared for her, feared everyone would harm her and believed the food was poisoned. She attempted suicide by cutting her wrists. Classification: Schizophrenic reaction—paranoid type.

Sister (34), born 1842; died at age 83 years of pneumonia. While a patient at a state mental hospital she was always "talkative, excitable, irritable, domineering and possessed of a vivid imagination." At age 32 years her husband and infant died. Some months later she became excited and boisterous and was admitted to a second state mental hospital for about a year. She remained well for 16 years, then became depressed and suicidal and was admitted to Warren State Hospital on 4/18/1891. She remained mute and suicidal until February, 1893, when she passed into a state of excitement which lasted a year. The depression that followed lasted until

1897, when she became apprehensive about her assumed wickedness and feared she would be killed. She was released in this condition in 1901 and remained at home until another period of excitement in 1914, when she was admitted to a state mental hospital where she remained until her death. Diagnosis at Warren State Hospital was manic-depressive psychosis. Classification: Schizophrenic reaction—schizo-affective type.

(36) husband of sister (35), born 1847; died at age 44 years at Warren State Hospital. For several years before admission to Warren State Hospital at age 35 years, psychotic spells of two weeks duration occurred about six times a year. While psychotic he believed he had no friends and that everyone was against him. At Warren State Hospital he was depressed, uncommunicative and apprehensive. Except for a short leave of absence, he was at Warren State Hospital until his death. Classification: Schizophrenic reaction—paranoid type.

Brother (38), born 1844; died at age 76 years of "cardiovascular renal complex" at Gowanda State Hospital, Helmuth, New York. First symptoms of a psychotic nature were in 1887 following an accident. He was bedridden for several months and during this time became "very excited." Ten years later he was admitted to Warren State Hospital, with a diagnosis of chronic mania. He had been irritable and "rattleheaded" since his accident, but after the death of his wife and the loss of some property he developed delusions of persecution and grandeur. He was paroled on 9/15/1902, admitted to Gowanda State Hospital on 12/11/1903, discharged on 5/4/1904 and readmitted on 3/25/1905, where he remained until his death in 1921. At Gowanda he had alternate periods of excitement followed by a quiet, tractable, agreeable state. Classification: Schizophrenic reaction—paranoid type.

Brother (41), born 1846; died at age 86 years of a cerebral hemorrhage. He was described as never melancholy but rather excitable and when upset would "storm the castle." The illegitimate child of his sister (42) was generally accepted to be his as his parents took that view. Classification: Possible personality disorder.

Sister (42), born 1851; accidentally burned to death at age 30 years. She was "never considered very intelligent—a woman of silly manners and few interests." Her illegitimate child was fathered by her brother (41). Classification: Probable sociopathic personality disturbance.

Brother (45), born 1847; age at death unknown. As a young man he was described as "shiftless" and "of poor judgment." At one time he thought he "could preach" and another time he "got the idea that he was a wonderful doctor." He deserted his wife and children and lived alone. For many years before his death he was "not considered sound mentally." Classification: Probable personality disorder.

Sister (48), born 1853; died at age 91 years of myocardial degenerative arteriosclerosis and senility. When interviewed at age 63 years she spoke as if depressed "in brief, low tones." She was reportedly worried about the mental illnesses of her siblings. Classification: Probable psychoneurotic disorder.

Brother (49), born 1856; died at age 77 years of chronic myocardial degeneration at a state mental hospital. He was normal, happily married and a good provider until age 50 years when he became melancholy and brooding. A year later he was admitted to the same hospital where he remained the rest of his life. At admission he was depressed and agitated. He gradually recovered from his depression and for about three months was normal. He then become overactive and destructive. Over the years the pattern of attacks continued with possible senile changes. Diagnosis and classification: Manic-depressive psychosis—mixed type.

(50) wife of brother (49), born 1858; died at age 62 years, cause of death unknown. She was described as a "woman of low character . . . quarrelsome, nagging nature . . . statements not reliable." Classification: Possible personality disorder.

Brother (53), born 1860; died at age 73 years of "heart failure." He was described as "irritable and excitable" and relatives thought for years that he would be "the next one to go off." When interviewed he answered questions irrelevantly and it was difficult to conclude the interview as he "went over things again and again." Classification: Probable personality pattern disturbance.

Brother (55), born 1862; died at age 70 years of acute cholecystitis. In 1920 he had his first psychotic episode when he deserted his wife, sold stock and machinery from his ranch and believed he was a real estate agent. In 1929 he became "irritable," talked a lot and "went West" as he believed he was "an undercover man." In July, 1932, he became restless and began carrying dangerous weapons as he "had trouble with people." He was subsequently hospitalized at a state mental hospital on 8/29/1932, where he died later in the year. While hospitalized he showed great circumstantiality in his speech, was very distractible and was diagnosed as manic-depressive, hypomania. Classification: Schizophrenic reaction—paranoid type.

Brother (57), born 1864; died at age 64 years of chronic nephritis. He was described as "queer at times and overtalkative; talked endlessly yet did not tell you anything." Classification: Possible personality disorder.

Nieces and Nephews

Half niece (60), born 1856; died at age 63 years of pulmonary tuberculosis. She was of a quiet, retiring disposition and, at age 50 years, had a "nervous breakdown." She was ill with pneumonia and remained in bed in a "semi-dazed" condition for four months. She was not depressed and never cried. Occasionally the figures on the wall paper and curtains would assume horrible shapes but she was aware that they were illusions. She had a second similar attack at age 56 years when she remained in bed for nine months. Her physician called the episodes attacks of neurasthenia. Classification: Probable psychoneurotic disorder—dissociative reaction.

Half nephew (63), born 1862; died at age 54 years of paresis and Bright's disease. He was reportedly hospitalized at a Nebraska state (mental) hospital in 1916. Classification: Probable chronic brain syndrome associated with central nervous system syphilis.

Half nephew (69), born 1854; died at age 59 years of tuberculosis of the lungs. He was described as "very high strung" and as "abusive" to his family. He was cruel to animals (he raised horses as a livelihood).

Classification: Probable personality trait disturbance—passive-aggressive personality.

Half niece (74), born 1859; died at age 80 years of coronary thrombosis. She was reportedly hypochondriacal. Classification: Probable psychoneurotic disorder.

Niece (97), born 1875; died at age 84 years of pneumonia at Warren State Hospital. She was always sensitive, shy and seclusive but in 1940 became definitely psychotic; she thought radio programs abused her reputation, that she was being seduced and that everything was a symbol of sex. She was hospitalized at Warren State Hospital on 3/23/1941, with a diagnosis of manic-depressive psychosis, and remained there until death in 1959. While hospitalized she exhibited no hallucinations but had many delusions of reference and paranoid ideas. Classification: Schizophrenic reaction—paranoid type.

Nephew (100), born 1865; died at age 69 years of hypostatic pneumonia. He was reportedly always a "shiftless, lazy fellow, naturally timid and suspicious." In 1899 he became depressed, jealous of his wife and imagined that people were stealing from him. A few months later, after threatening to kill his wife, he was committed to Warren State Hospital on 8/19/1899, and diagnosed as acute mania. On 9/23/1899 he escaped. He remained apprehensive and jealous when he returned home and was divorced by his wife. He spent the last nine years of his life at a county home. Classification: Schizophrenic reaction—paranoid type.

Nephew (103), born 1870; died at age 69 years of duodenal ulcers. He was considered to be "naturally queer," lazy, egotistical and an "endless talker" although often his comments were irrelevant. At age 32 years he became worried about the loss of some property and "wandered away from home." When found he would answer no questions and was committed to Warren State Hospital on 1/16/1903. While hospitalized he was highly religious but showed no delusions. He was taken home on 4/1/1903 and had no subsequent attacks of mental trouble. Classification: Schizophrenic reaction—paranoid type.

Nephew (105), 1879; died at age 57 years at Warren State Hospital of chronic myocarditis. As a boy he was considered peculiar; he was silly, lazy and foolish. At age 22 years he began talking about secret societies and how they would protect him. He began carrying a butcher knife and collecting rags which he burned in the night. He was at a state mental hospital for six months in 1901. He spent four months of 1903 at Warren State Hospital after he became threatening to neighbors. He was readmitted on 1/11/1906 and remained at Warren until his death in 1936. While hospitalized he was impulsively violent, difficult to manage, suicidal, childish and seclusive and mute at times. He was not delusional but did exhibit auditory hallucinations. He was first diagnosed as chronic mania, but rediagnosed in 1920 as dementia praecox. Classification: Schizophrenic reaction—hebephrenic type.

Nephew (107), born 1883; died at age 48 years of suicide by hanging. He was described as "goodnatured, jolly" but "inclined to worry considerably." He was hospitalized at Warren State Hospital for three months in 1930 because he was talkative, restless, noisy and unkempt. He had had previous manic attacks from which he recovered. After discharge from Warren State Hospital he suffered depressed episodes and suicided in 1931. Classification: Manic-depressive reaction—other.

(108) wife of nephew (107), born 1887; died at age 73 years of cancer of the stomach. She had been taking barbiturates for rheumatism for seven or eight years before she was admitted to a state mental hospital on 10/6/1938, with a drug reaction. Discharge was on 11/19/1938. Classification: Acute brain syndrome with drug intoxication.

Niece (109), born 1885; died at age 47 years of acute nephritis and pulmonary tuberculosis. Her mother died when she was 18 months of age; her father remarried when she was 10 years old, but soon separated. When he was committed to a mental hospital she lived with various relatives. Her psychosis began about one month previous to her admission to Warren State Hospital on 9/27/1911. She was later transferred to another mental hospital where she remained until death. While ill she was catatonic, disoriented, suicidal and destructive. She alternated between periods of mutism and excitement. She did have some periods when she was agreeable, neat, quiet and talked intelligently but was always a lit-

tle overactive. An original diagnosis of dementia praecox, catatonic type, was made but she was later diagnosed as chronic manic-depressive. Classification: Schizophrenic reaction—catatonic type.

(116) husband of niece (117), born 1855; died at age 48 years of "consumption." He was described as "irritable" and "quick-tempered" but did not remain angry for long. Classification: Possible personality trait disturbance.

(124) husband of niece (125), born 1864; died at age 61 years of erysipelas and chronic nephritis. He was described as "a lazy, good-for-nothing...better grammar than the average farmer . . . observant; is the sort who prefers talking to working." Classification: Possible personality disorder —inadequate personality.

Niece (125), born 1876. She suffered from "nervous spells" which were depressions lasting for several days to a week, preceded by a period of unusual happiness and elation. The spells began at about age 25 years. The family watched her carefully while she was depressed as they feared suicide. At age 86 years she was described as an "independent, hard-working, self-supporting person with a good sense of humor." Classification: Possible personality trait disturbance.

Niece (136), born 1865; died at age 38 years of suicide by hanging. She was reportedly the result of a brother/sister union and was raised by the grandmother. She was of a rather low-grade intelligence but had no mental problems until her 14-year-old daughter by her first husband became pregnant by her second husband. (136) became "so wrought up that she committed suicide." Classification: Probably with functional psychosis.

(137) husband of niece (136) and father of illegitimate child (964) by his 14-year-old stepdaughter (408); born 1871; died at age 43 years of typhoid fever. Classification: Possible sociopathic personality disturbance.

Nephew (145), born 1881; died at age 53 years of coronary disease. He reportedly had "trouble with alcohol." Classification: Possible sociopathic personality disturbance—alcoholism (addiction).

(158) wife of nephew (157), born 1879; died at age 77 years of arteriosclerotic heart disease. She reportedly had a "nervous con-

dition . . . rundown and tired . . . seclusive." Classification: Probable psychoneurotic disorder.

Nephew (164), born 1883; died at age 74 years of cancer of the prostate. He was reportedly immoral with his cousin. Classification: Possible sociopathic personality disturbance.

Nephew (166), born 1885; died at age 27 years, cause of death unknown. He reportedly "had wanderlust . . . when young he drank to excess, stole and was sexually immoral." His wife described him as "quick-tempered, quite talkative and always threatened to desert his family as soon as there was any trouble." He deserted his wife and children when the children were four and two years of age and "went West." Classification: Sociopathic personality disturbance.

Nephew (169), born 1889; died at age 29 years of "after effects of the flu." He was described as "mere trash . . . a rough harum-scarum sort of boy . . . never seemed to care about doing his work right . . . rattleheaded . . . jumped around and sang and danced in a peculiar, nervous way." Classification: Probable personality disorder.

(170) wife of nephew (169), born 1886; died at age 46 years of lobar pneumonia. She was described, when young, as a "lazy, good-for-nothing girl." As she grew older she was described as "domineering." Classification: Possible personality disorder.

Niece (172), born 1894; died at age 57 years of pneumonia. She was described as "sexually immoral" and as "quarrelsome." Classification: Possible sociopathic personality disturbance.

Niece (197), born 1890; died at age 59 years of coronary thrombosis. At age 15 years she had a "nervous breakdown" and was withdrawn, indifferent and quiet for one summer. In the fall she was nearly hit by a train, recovered immediately and returned to school. She became acutely ill physically and mentally about 10 days before admission to a state mental hospital on 3/24/1949, with a diagnosis of involutional psychosis, paranoid type. She was asocial, depressed, made suicide attempts, had an attitude of self-condemnation and had hallucinations and delusions. At times she was agitated. She expired showing no improvement in her mental condition. Clas-

sification: Schizophrenic reaction—paranoid type.

Distant Relatives

Half grandniece (209), born 1884. She "was considered neurotic" and a facial tic was observed during a 1916 interview. Classification: Possible psychoneurotic disorder.

(215) husband of half grandniece (216), born 1886; died at age 47 years of cancer of the pancreas. He was an alcoholic. Classification: Sociopathic personality disturbance—alcoholism (addiction).

Half grandniece (216), born 1888. Her own physician and those of a private hospital have diagnosed her as psychoneurotic. When interviewed at age 75 years she was well dressed, normal in appearance, pleasant in manners but very hypochondriacal. Classification: Probable psychoneurotic reaction—other.

(227) husband of half grandniece (228), born 1867. His whereabouts were unknown to the family for many years. He was known as a "schemer and gambler who lost all his money." Classification: Probable personality disorder.

Half grandniece (228), born 1877; died at age 67 years at Warren State Hospital of uremia. Her parents separated in 1904 and she lived with her mother. She worked in a factory until 1913, when she returned to her father's home to care for him in an illness. In 1917 a flu attack precipitated a mental disturbance during which she imagined that she had various ailments. She recovered completely from this attack. She married but separated because of her husband's gambling. In about 1940 she again began to imagine that she had numerous ailments, over which she worried constantly. She was involved in a legal matter after her employer died, which left her agitated and upset. She became depressed following her mother's death in 1945; she slept poorly, cried and maintained she was about to die. She was deluded but not hallucinated. Admission to Warren State Hospital was on 6/27/1945, where she remained until death later that year. Diagnosis was manic-depressive psychosis, depressed type. Classification: Schizophrenic reaction—paranoid type.

Half grandnephew (229), born 1891; died at age 69 years of general arteriosclerosis, multiple cardiovascular accidents. In 1950 he was depressed and had very high blood pressure. Classification: Possible chronic brain syndrome of senium.

(238) wife of half grandnephew (237), born 1892. At age 70 years she was described by an interviewer as "friendly, a very talkative person who would go into detail concerning the health of anyone about whom we requested information." She had many surgical operations and was described as "always complaining." She went "to the doctor a lot." Classification: Possible psychoneurotic disorder.

Half grandniece (241), born 1892. She "bossed the family" and was described as "not too well—nervous headaches." Classification: Possible psychoneurotic disorder.

Half grandnephew (250), born 1886. He and his wife separated because he "took no interest in making a living." The wife raised their son. Classification: Possible personality pattern disturbance—inadequate personality.

(260) wife of half grandnephew (259), born 1917. She had three hospitalizations in a state mental hospital for one month in 1951, for one month in 1957 and for two months in 1958. The diagnoses at the first two hospitalizations were schizophrenic reaction—catatonic type, and schizophrenic reaction—acute differentiated type. At the time of her third hospitalization she presented a picture of uncontrolled anxiety and marked depression following the death of her mother, whom she had nursed for many months, and a diagnosis of psychoneurotic disorder, depressive reaction was made. Classification: Schizophrenic reaction—acute undifferentiated type.

Half grandnephew (267), born 1892. When a young man he was described as "stubborn, disagreeable, extremely quarrelsome" and as having a "fiery temper." He was also described as "extremely lazy" and had to be urged continually to work. Classification: Probable personality disorder.

(268) wife of half grandnephew (267), born 1892; died at age 67 years of cerebral hemorrhage. She was described as "feeble-minded, possibly psychotic...extremely shiftless, untidy, dirty, profane and always antagonistic." Her children were placed in an orphanage after she abandoned them. Classification: Probably with functional psychosis.

(279) wife of grandnephew (278), born 1890; died at age 72 years of pneumonia at Warren State Hospital. Nervousness and anxiety caused her to quit her first job in a department store. In 1924, following two miscarriages, she became extremely upset and attempted suicide by poisoning. At this time she was visually and aurally hallucinated and was hospitalized at Warren State Hospital for five months in 1925 with a diagnosis of psychosis with psychopathic personality. She was normal until 1952, when she developed ideas of worthlessness, self-condemnation and sinfulness. She was again admitted to Warren State Hospital with a diagnosis of schizophrenic reaction, chronic undifferentiated type, and was released as recovered in 1953. In March, 1962 she developed pneumonia, which caused her anxiety and fear of death, with subsequent hospitalization at Warren State Hospital, where she died in January, 1963. Diagnosis at Warren at third hospitalization and classification: Schizophrenic reaction—chronic undifferentiated type.

Grandniece (281), born 1891. In 1912 she had some sort of "nervous spell" during which she became entirely rigid. In 1916 she was described as "weak physically" and as a "neurotic." Later she was described as "always sick or complaining of being sick." She was called a "radical" as she advocated "peculiar causes." Classification: Probable psychoneurotic disorder.

(283) wife of grandnephew (284), born 1903. She was divorced by (284) on grounds of lesbianism. She imagined enemies, was fearful of germs and had "staring spells." Her son believed she needed psychiatric care. Another family member insisted that the husband "cooked up a story about her being insane" in order to get a divorce, and described the son as "spoiled and self-centered." Classification: Possible schizophrenic reaction—paranoid type.

(290) wife of grandnephew (289), born 1878; died at age 78 years of bronchopneumonia. She was described as "nervous." Classification: Possible psychoneurotic disorder.

Grandniece (294), born 1903. As a child she was very sensitive. She quit teaching because "she was exhausted." In 1947 she was treated for a tumor of the womb, following which she had a depressed episode, and according to her family "never recovered." In 1955 she became so nervous and fidgety that she could not work. In 1956, after the death of her sister, she developed symptoms of anxiety, guilt feelings, vague ideas of reference, and was consequently hospitalized at a state mental hospital from 6/28/1957 until 5/19/1959. At age 60 she was still "getting along well." Diagnosis and classification: Involutional psychotic reaction.

Grandnephew (297), born 1891; died at age 61 years of pulmonary tuberculosis. When young he was described as "sensitive, melancholy, easily discouraged . . . jealous, reckless . . . occasionally drank to excess." Classification: Possible personality disorder.

Grandnephew (304), born 1898. His right eye was removed because of glaucoma in 1949; after this event he developed a disturbed episode for which he was hospitalized at a state mental hospital from March until June of that year. On 9/18/1951 he was admitted to a second state mental hospital with a diagnosis of psychoneurotic disorder, depressive type. He was still there on 9/5/1963 and was described as suspicious, irritable and subject to violent fits of temper. Classification: Schizophrenic reaction—paranoid type.

(305) wife of grandnephew (304), born 1899. She reportedly was devoted to her husband (304) and visited him frequently in the hospital even though the visits were unpleasant. An interviewer reported that, when discussing her husband's hospitalization, she became tearful and the interviewer considered her to be "somewhat depressed" but functioning adequately. Classification: Possible transient situational personality disorder—adult situational reaction.

Grandnephew (309), born 1892. At age 71 he was described as friendly and helpful but preoccupied with physical impairment resulting from strokes he had had. His memory was affected by his last stroke. Classification: Chronic brain syndrome associated with arteriosclerosis.

(315) wife of grandnephew (314), born 1900. The family had a "very low opinion of her" and called her an alcoholic. Classification: Probable sociopathic personality disturbance—alcoholism (addiction).

(317) wife of grandnephew (316), born 1898. She sought medical help for "nerves" as she had headaches at the back of the neck, would "get shaky and go to pieces" and was unhappy. Her physician stated that she had mild anxiety reactions which were not disabling, nor did they necessitate hospitalization. Classification: Psychoneurotic disorder—anxiety reaction.

(318) husband of grandniece (319), born 1903; died at age 52 years of congestive heart failure. He "went to pieces" after the death of his son and in 1953 reportedly sought psychiatric help for his "exaggerated depressive reaction." Classification: Probable psychoneurotic disorder—depressive reaction.

Grandniece (319), born 1902; died at age 51 years of arteriosclerotic heart disease. She had a "nervous breakdown" in 1935 and was hospitalized at a state mental hospital from 10/21/1935 until 12/4/1936, where she was diagnosed as manic-depressive psychosis—manic type. Little was known of the onset of the attack but she improved rapidly under psychotherapy. In 1951 she became nervous, claimed she could look into the future, had periods of uncontrolled laughter and swearing and was again admitted to the hospital with the same diagnosis. While hospitalized she was paranoid, grandiose, hallucinatory and hyperactive. She received 25 ECT treatments and was paroled much improved on 1/8/1952. In 1953 she was seen at a clinic with alleged gastrointestinal distress and complained of her husband's (318) nervousness. Classification: Manic-depressive reaction—manic type.

Grandnephew (321), born 1905. He was overweight, had heart trouble and a ruptured diaphragm. He was cheerful and helpful when interviewed, but when his grandchildren were mentioned he became tense and left the room. His wife stated that he was very short-tempered and flew into a rage over trifles. He was also described as suspicious, very hard to live with, and had beaten his wife several times. Classification: Possibly with functional psychosis, schizophrenic reaction.

(322) wife of grandnephew (321), born 1914. She reportedly was "always nervous" but became worse at age 33 years after the unfavorable outcome of a romantic episode with a soldier. At this time she was restless, couldn't sleep and was sent to a state hospital in New York on 12/17/1947. While hospitalized she exhibited somatic delusions and feelings of unreality. She revealed that in 1940 she became depressed after an accidental scalding of her baby. She also said that she became suspicious of imaginary advances by men after her divorce from her first husband. Diagnosis was manic-depressive psychosis, perplexed type, and she was paroled on 2/13/1948 and had no recurrence. At age 49 years she had hay fever and asthma. Classification: Schizophrenic reaction—paranoid type.

(332) husband of grandniece (331), born 1911; a patient at a state mental hospital in 1963, at age 52 years. His father died when he was four years old and he remembered but one event with his father, an affectionate one. His married life was "for the most part happy." Normally he described himself as energetic, nervous and fearful. In 1959 he was hospitalized at a Veterans Administration hospital with a "nervous condition" and again in July and August, 1960. First admission to the state mental hospital was from 3/3/1961 until 3/29/1961 with a diagnosis of primary behavior disorder, simple adult adjustment. Symptoms exhibited were pain in the head, depression and nervousness. Classification: Schizophrenic reaction—chronic undifferentiated type.

(334) wife of grandnephew (333), born 1911. She reportedly "had a nervous breakdown years ago and another just a few years ago." Both times she was treated at home. When interviewed at age 52 years she avoided talking about her mental symptoms. She was suspicious when first approached and thought the interviewers had come to take her grandchildren away. A state school reported her as "obviously quite retarded." The house and furniture were run down, cluttered and filthy. Classification: Probable psychoneurotic disorder.

(335) wife of grandnephew (337), born 1912. She deserted her family and had one child by the man with whom she ran away before divorcing (337). Classification: Sociopathic personality disturbance.

Grandnephew (337), born 1907; died at age 44 years of a coronary thrombosis. He attempted to raise the children he had by (335), who deserted him, and the child he had by the baby sitter (336), as well as the children by his second wife and her son by a previous marriage, but all were taken from him and placed in orphanages because of neglect. Classification: Possible sociopathic personality disturbance.

(338) wife of grandnephew (337), born 1923. She was reportedly "very nasty" to her children and did not always feed them. All her children and stepchildren were taken from her and placed in orphanages. Classification: Possible personality trait disturbance.

Grandniece (342), born 1889; died at age 47 years of cardiorenal vascular disease. She was described as normally "somewhat of a recluse." At menopause and after the death of her daughter she had a "mental illness" and had to be "taken care of by her family." When ill she remained in her room most of the time and was occasionally locked in. Classification: Probably with functional psychosis.

Grandnephew (346), born 1896; died at age 45 years of a hemorrhage and arteriosclerosis. He was considered "restless and unstable"; he had a bad temper and was "practically insane when mad." He had some strokes previous to his death. Classification: Probable personality trait disturbance.

Grandniece (353), born 1900. She reportedly had a "nervous disposition." Classification: Probable psychoneurotic disorder.

Grandnephew (354), born 1901. He was described as "nervous." Classification: Possible psychoneurotic disorder.

Grandnephew (356), born 1902. He was described as "a wanderer" and as having "itchy feet." He had "trouble with alcohol and would lose jobs because of it." He was also described as "never happy either before or after marriage." Classification: Personality pattern disturbance or sociopathic personality disturbance.

Grandniece (368), born 1911; died at age 43 years of a self-inflicted gunshot wound to the head. She became extremely meticulous and compulsive about her second baby's care immediately after its birth. She also had depressions during which she could not make small decisions. She saw a psychiatrist who recommended ECT but refused treatment as she knew nothing about ECT. Her husband, who denied his wife's trouble, let her make the decision. The psychiatrist, who saw her only on one occasion, on 8/24/1953, felt that her diagnosis was schizophrenic reaction, chronic undifferentiated type. She suicided a few months later. Classification: Schizophrenic reaction—chronic undifferentiated type.

(371) husband of grandniece (372), born 1883; died at age 40 years in a train accident. He was described as "a drifter and a heavy drinker who was drunk when killed by the train." Classification: Probable sociopathic personality disturbance—alcoholism (addiction).

Grandniece (372), born 1895. As an adolescent she reportedly had "nervous spells; would get blue, go away by herself, cry, desire to be alone." Classification: Transient situational personality disturbance—adjustment reaction of adolescence.

Grandnephew (372), born 1899. At age five years he developed "fainting spells" attended by slight jerking of the muscles. The spells subsided after age six years but at age 14 years he developed grand mal seizures. In November, 1925, at age 26 years, he was admitted to Warren State Hospital with a diagnosis of epilepsy—grand mal type, with psychotic reaction (schizophrenic reaction, paranoid type)—where he remained until 10/24/1929, when he was transferred to another hospital. At admission to Warren State Hospital he elicited a 10-year history of living "in a dream" for years with frank episodes of auditory and visual hallucinations. Classification: Chronic brain syndrome associated with convulsive disorder, with psychotic reaction. Possibly with functional psychosis, schizophrenia—paranoid type.

(407) husband of grandniece (408), born 1887; died at age 77 years of acute thrombosis. He was described as an alcoholic who "worked only when he had to" and as "always drunk." Classification: Sociopathic personality disturbance—alcoholism (addiction).

Grandniece (408), born 1888. At age 14

years she had an illegitimate child by her mother's second husband. After the birth of the child, she and the child were placed in an orphanage and the child was adopted out. She remained at the home as an employee for many years. She was "not considered mentally strong" and was subject to epilepsy and was retained as an employee "largely from the fact that she would not be able to protect herself if she were out in the world." At age 76 years she was described as senile. Classification: Possible personality pattern disturbance—inadequate personality.

Grandnephew (411), born 1895. At age 69 years he was described as with "no memory and childish" as he had "arteriosclerosis affecting the mind." Classification: Chronic brain syndrome of senium.

Grandnephew (422), born 1900. He reportedly "drinks a lot" and had "a nervous condition." Classification: Sociopathic personality disturbance—alcoholism (addiction); also, possible psychoneurotic reaction.

Grandnephew (428), born 1904. He was described as having "too many nerves" and as a "heavy drinker." When interviewed he described himself as a fairly heavy drinker but stated that he "had no trouble" with alcoholism. Classification: Probable sociopathic personality disturbance—alcoholism (addiction).

Grandnephew (430), born 1907. He was described at age 57 years as "nervous and not well at all...had parkinsonism... progressively worse." Classification: Probable psychoneurotic disorder.

(431) wife of grandnephew (430), born 1907. She was described as "neurotic." She complained of "aches and pains." Her daughter reportedly "left home as soon as possible to get away from her domineering control." Classification: Psychoneurotic disorder.

Grandniece (433), born 1914; died at age 45 years of suicide by hanging. At the time of her hanging she was despondent over the pregnancy of her 14-year-old daughter. Classification: Probably with functional psychosis, psychotic-depressive reaction.

Grandniece (458), born 1907. Her father deserted the family when she was four years of age. At age 14 years she reportedly had a "nervous breakdown" but was not hospitalized. She legally adopted her brother's children in 1956. Classification: Probable psychoneurotic disorder.

(459) wife of grandnephew (460), born 1904. She was hospitalized at a state mental hospital on 4/9/1949 as an inebriate and discharged as improved on 7/12/1950. Her children by (460) were adopted by (460)'s sister. Classification: Sociopathic personality disturbance — alcoholism (addiction).

(524) wife of half great-grandnephew (523), born 1906. She had chorea as a child. From early childhood until after menopause she was nervous, depressed, had many physical complaints and several abdominal operations. Her nervous condition subsided after menopause was completed. Classification: Probable psychoneurotic disorder.

Half great-grandnephew (543), born 1910. He had ulcers and was troubled by alcoholism but was "better since he joined Alcoholics Anonymous." Classification: Sociopathic personality disturbance — alcoholism (addiction).

(546) wife of half great-grandnephew (545), born 1917. She had multiple sclerosis, "crying spells" and was described as "thin and tense." Classification: Possible psychoneurotic disorder — depressive reaction.

(554) husband of half great-grandniece (555), born 1900. He was described in his previous wife's hospital record as "a spree drinker and a reckless driver." Classification: Possible sociopathic personality disturbance — alcoholism (addiction).

(561) wife of half great-grandnephew (562), born 1920. She was described as "cold and odd." Classification: Possible personality disorder.

(564) husband of half great-grandniece (565), born 1910. He deserted (565) when the children were small and was described as "no good, worked at nothing, lazy, and drank when he had the money." Classification: Sociopathic personality disturbance — alcoholism (addiction).

Half great-grandniece (579), born 1914. She described herself as "the nervous type." A relative stated that she was "hyperthyroid" and was nervous from that condition. Classification: Other transient situational personality disturbance.

Half great-grandnephew (581), born 1917. He was a missile engineer who reportedly had "worked at a lot of places" and was described as "nervous and fidgety . . . always on the go . . . had to be doing something." Classification: Probable personality disorder.

(584) wife of half great-grandnephew (583), born 1906. She was described as "nervous" but in fair health. Classification: Possible psychoneurotic disorder.

Half great-grandnephew (611), born 1914. He had a "drinking problem" but, after joining Alcoholics Anonymous, stopped drinking. Classification: Sociopathic personality disturbance — alcoholism (addiction).

Half great-grandnephew (614), born 1920. He had a "problem with alcohol" and although he joined Alcoholics Anonymous, he still had a problem at times. Classification: Sociopathic personality disturbance — alcoholism (addiction).

(632) husband of half great-grandniece (633), born 1908. He was described as "a bum" who worked sporadically. He was the second husband of (268) and, after her death in July, 1963, married (633), her daughter, in August of that year. Classification: Possible sociopathic personality disturbance.

Half great-grandniece (633), born 1921. She was at a state school for the retarded from 4/13/1931 until 11/26/1958, when she was transferred to a second state school. She was admitted when she failed to make an adjustment to public school and her mental retardation was noted. At the second state school she made an excellent adjustment and was described in the psychological evaluation as pleasant, cooperative, communicative but not talkative and as capable of functioning in the dull-normal range. She was also described as a "well adjusted woman." She married her mother's husband one month after the death of her mother. Classification: Personality disorder.

(644) husband of great-grandniece (645). He was a bigamist whose marriage to (645) was annulled shortly after it was performed. As a result he was in prison for five years. Classification: Sociopathic personality disturbance.

Great-grandniece (650), born 1920. She reportedly "frets a lot." Classification: Possible psychoneurotic disorder.

Great-grandniece (658), born 1933. She was described as "nervous — likes to keep busy." Classification: Possible psychoneurotic disorder.

Great-grandnephew (659), born 1923. He was described as a "spoiled, self-centered child" who, as an adult, "was still that way." He "played his father and mother against each other for what he could get." He was 30 years of age when his parents divorced. At age 39 years he was still single. Classification: Possible personality disorder.

Great-grandniece (677), born 1911. At age 45 years she said that she "had trouble with nerves" and was on tranquilizers for a time. After her children left home she said that she "had not enough to do, got bored and lazy." Classification: Probable psychoneurotic disturbance.

Great-grandnephew (679), born 1921. He reportedly "drinks a lot" and was married and divorced or separated twice. Classification: Probable sociopathic personality disturbance—alcoholism (addiction).

(689) husband of great-grandniece (690), born 1918. He was described as "a real mess—didn't work, drank heavily, was abusive to his family." His wife "thought he would change but after repeated separations she divorced him." He never made court-ordered support payments. Classification: Sociopathic personality disturbance—antisocial reaction.

Great-grandniece (690), born 1920. She was described as "somewhat of the black sheep of the family because of the poor marriage." She supported herself and her children by working as a waitress. Classification: Possible personality trait disturbance.

Great-grandnephew (702), born 1909. He lived with his father after the divorce of his parents. At age 46 years he was described as an alcoholic who was at one time hospitalized in a mental hospital (this could not be verified). Classification: Probable sociopathic personality trait disturbance—alcoholism (addiction).

(722) husband of great-grandniece, born 1915; at age 48 years an auto mechanic who "is a wonderful person" when sober but described as "mean and aggressive" after a few drinks. His children "live in fear of him," he had beaten his wife when inebriated and twice arrangements were made to have him committed for his alcoholism but the wife did not sign the final papers. Classification: Sociopathic personality disturbance—alcoholism (addiction).

Great-grandnephew (726), born 1923. As an adolescent he had few friends, "did not bother with the rest of the family" and spent a lot of time in his room reading. After time in the Navy and college, he was "a different person," became an electronic engineer and was involved in many community affairs. Classification: Transient situational personality disturbance—adjustment reaction of adolescence.

(786) husband of great-grandniece (787), born 1923. He reportedly "could not hold a job, partly because of liquor and partly because of stupidity." He was a patient at a mental health clinic for about three years. His IQ was 46 and he could neither read nor write. His family reported that he would laugh inappropriately and "had trouble with alcohol." Classification: Possible sociopathic personality disturbance—alcoholism (addiction).

Great-grandnephew (793), born 1935. He was raised in an orphanage after his mother deserted her family and his father and stepmother provided an inadequate home. Welfare records indicated that he was mentally defective, had a violent temper and was incapable of providing for his own needs. Classification: Possible personality trait disturbance.

(797) husband of great-grandniece (798), born 1939. He never provided well for his wife and family and deserted them before the last child was born. Classification: Personality pattern disturbance—inadequate personality.

Great-grandniece (798), born 1943. Her mother deserted the family and the father and stepmother provided an inadequate home from which the children had to be removed. At age six years she was hospitalized for rickets. Later she was placed in a foster home, then in an orphanage. While an eighth grade student she ran away and married (797), who later deserted her and three small children. At age 20 years she and her children were in a foster home where, with the help of the foster mother, she was able to keep the children clean and supervise them. Classification: Possible personality pattern disturbance.

Great-grandniece (800), born 1942. She was raised by her father and his wives (her mother was his children's baby sitter) until the home was broken up because of child neglect, then she was raised in various foster homes. She was described in welfare records as "very attractive, quite emotionally immature . . . and making a good effort to be an acceptable citizen." Classification: Possible transient situational personality disorder—adult situational reaction.

(806) husband of great-grandniece (807), born 1936. He deserted his wife before the birth of their child and was not heard from again. Classification: Probable personality trait disturbance.

Great-grandniece (830), born 1939. In November, 1960, a clinic report stated that she had a fairly severe anxiety made worse by her apprehension over her visual difficulties. Her problem was "functional on basis of personal inadequacy" and "she needed only encouragement in watching the progress of her vision." Classification: Transient situational personality disorder—adult situational reaction.

Great-grandnephew (842), born 1923. He reportedly was "nervous." Classification: Possible psychoneurotic reaction.

(848) husband of great-grandniece (849), born 1932. He was described as "inclined to be nervous." Classification: Possible psychoneurotic reaction.

Great-grandniece (849), born 1934. She was described as "sick a lot." She had "fainting spells during high school until after she married and had tumors removed from the uterus and rectum." Classification: Possible transient situational personality disorder—adjustment reaction of adolescence.

Great-grandnephew (887), born 1915. He reportedly "had trouble with alcohol" but did not imbibe after joining Alcoholics Anonymous. Classification: Sociopathic personality disturbance—alcoholism (addiction).

Great-grandniece (894), born 1919. She received medical treatment for nerves following the death of her husband and again during menopause. Classification: Transient situational personality disorder—adult situational reaction.

Great-grandnephew (962), born 1932. He put himself through high school and two years of college despite many family handicaps. His reply to a letter for family information sounded paranoidal in that he stated that any records of mental illness in his family were "false records" and "originated out of a 'political' atmosphere." Classification: Possible personality pattern disturbance—paranoid personality.

Great-grandniece (980), born 1946. She had an illegitimate child in 1963. The child was put up for adoption and at age 18 years she was making plans for college. She reportedly left home when quite young in order to get away from her mother's "domineering control." Classification: Probable transient situational personality disorder—adjustment reaction of adolescence.

Half great-great-grandnephew (1163), born 1934. When a young man "you could not talk to him or make him reason with you." He had a fear of cancer and heart trouble and at age 27 years had a "nervous breakdown." At age 29 years he was described as "irritable, moody and depressed." Classification: Probable psychoneurotic disorder.

Half great-great-grandniece (1193), born 1943. She was described as "wild and hard to handle." She had one illegitimate child before her marriage. Classification: Possible sociopathic personality disturbance.

Great-great-grandniece (1337), born 1946. At age 16 years she was at a state school. She was originally committed to a correctional school but failed to adjust and was referred to the state school. She was described diagnostically as a "mixture of neurotic conflict and character disturbance." The psychiatric report said there was an "exploitative narcissistic character embedded in her personality." She was a "willful, alternately subtly rejected and indulged child with above average intelligence, a facility in social relationship, a relative freedom from anxiety and an inner unconscious fantasy that nothing will ever do her any harm." She had a "problematic relationship" with her parents. Classification: Personality trait disturbance—emotionally unstable personality.

Great-great-grandnephew (1363), born 1938. He lived with his mother after his divorce and was described as a "mother's boy" which was reportedly the reason for his divorce. Classification: Possible personality pattern disturbance.

Great-great-grandnephew (1386), born 1948. He was a "problem to his mother" and was described as "just like his father . . .

irresponsible and should be disciplined." Classification: Probable transient situational personality disorder—adjustment reaction of adolescence.

Great-great-grandnephew (1396), born 1950. At age 13 years he was described as "brilliant" and reportedly spent most of his time reading. Because of his small stature and intellectual interests he did not socialize and received psychiatric help for problems in these areas. Classification: Probable personality pattern disturbance—schizoid personality.

Great-great-grandnephew (1629), born 1938. He had a history of ulcers, skin allergies and alcoholism and was a voluntary patient at a state hospital in 1964 because of his alcoholism. Classification: Sociopathic personality disturbance—alcoholism (addiction).

(1631) husband of great-great-grandniece (1632), born 1940. He reportedly "had trouble with alcohol." Classification: Possible sociopathic personality disturbance—alcoholism (addiction).

Great-great-grandniece (1632), born 1940. She was described as "nervous." Classification: Possible psychoneurotic disorder.

Family Summary

The proband, a paternal uncle, a maternal aunt, two sisters, three brothers, four nieces, four nephews, a half grandniece, five grandnieces and three grandnephews had psychotic disorders or probably or possibly so. Persons with psychotic disorders who married into the family included the husband of a sister, the wives of two half grandnephews, the wives of two grandnephews and the husband of a grandniece. Classifications of personality disorder were made for the wife of the proband, five daughters, two of their husbands, four grandsons and the husband and wife of a granddaughter and grandson, four great-grandsons, three great-granddaughters, a great-great-grandson, the paternal grandmother and the maternal grandfather, the father and mother, a paternal and a maternal uncle, four brothers, one sister, the wife of a psychotic brother, a half nephew, two nieces, four nephews, the husbands of three nieces, the wife of a nephew, one grand-

niece, seven grandnephews, and husbands of two grandnieces. Also, six wives of grandnephews, a half grandniece, a half grandnephew, the husbands of two half grandnieces, seven great-grandnieces, seven great-grandnephews, husbands of five great-grandnieces, two half great-grandnieces, four half great-grandnephews, three husbands of half great-grandnieces, the wife of a half great-grandnephew, a great-great-grandniece, four great-great-grandnephews, the husband of a great-great-grandniece and a half great-great-grandniece. A daughter with a possible personality disorder also was classified as chronic brain syndrome of senium. Others with this syndrome were a paternal half sister, a sister's husband, a half grandnephew and a grandnephew. One family member, a grandnephew, was classified chronic brain syndrome associated with arteriosclerosis. The wife of a nephew was hospitalized with acute brain syndrome with drug intoxication. A half nephew was possibly hospitalized with chronic brain syndrome associated with central nervous system syphilis. A grandnephew, an alcoholic, also was classified as with a possible psychoneurotic reaction. The neurotics were a sister, a maternal aunt and a maternal uncle, the wives of two grandsons, a nephew's wife, two half nieces, three grandnieces, two grandnephews, the husband of a grandniece, the wives of four grandnephews, three half grandnieces, the wife of a half grandnephew, three great-grandnieces, a great-grandnephew, the husband of a great-grandniece, the wives of three half great-grandnephews, a great-great-grandniece and a half great-great-grandnephew.

Controls

Brother (2) of (98), suicided at age 55 years. He was never hospitalized for mental problems. His family stated that his wife "drove him to suicide." Classification: Probably with functional psychosis.

Sister (4) of (98), born 1861; died at age 87 years of a coronary occlusion. She reportedly had "a very morbid disposition" and was described as "highly nervous" and as "emotionally disturbed from time to time." Classification: Probable psychoneurotic reaction.

Brother (1) of (170), born 1875. He reportedly was hypochondriacal and had "dizzy spells." Classification: Probable psychoneurotic reaction.

Brother (4) of (170), born 1883; died at age 73 years of a cerebral hemorrhage. He was described as "shiftless, a hard drinker" and as having "dizzy spells." Another informant stated, "Never saw him sober." Clas-

sification: Sociopathic personality disturbance — alcoholism (addiction).

See family pedigree, person 170.

See family pedigree, person 177.

Sister (7) of (177), born 1901. At age 61 years she was interviewed and described as "of a nervous, rigorous nature." Classification: Possible psychoneurotic reaction.

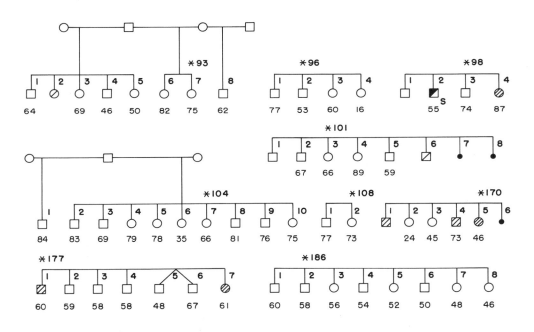

CONTROLS

W S H   48

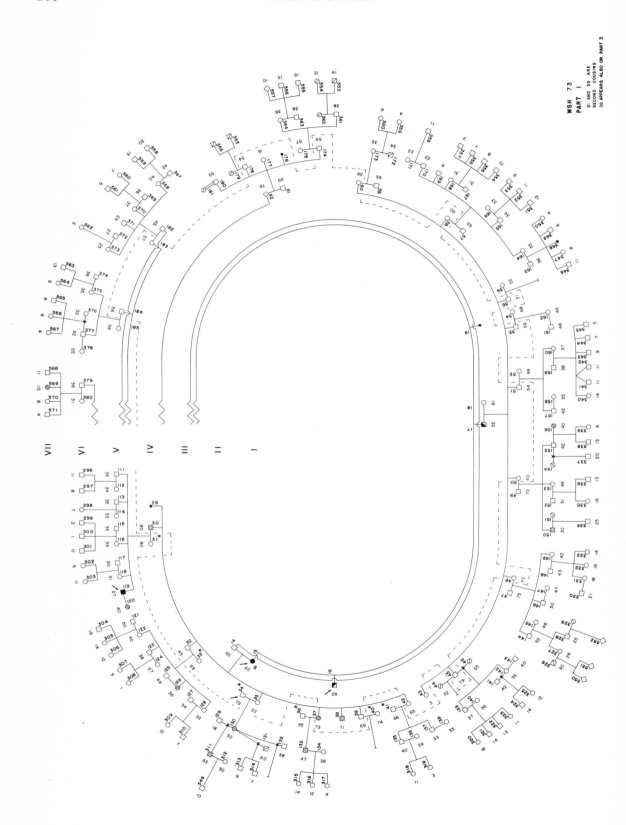

WSH 73
PART I
31 AND 33 ARE
SECOND COUSINS
36 APPEARS ALSO ON PART 3

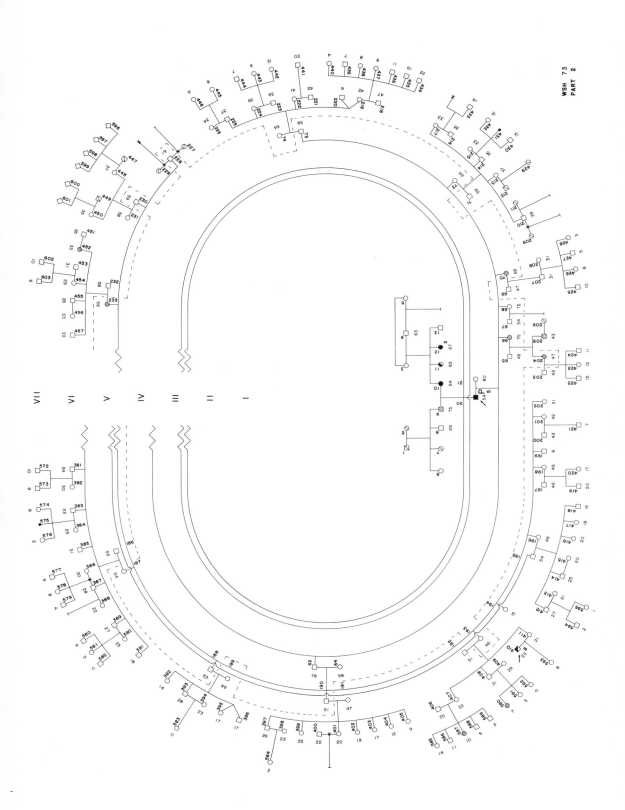

WSH 73
PART 2

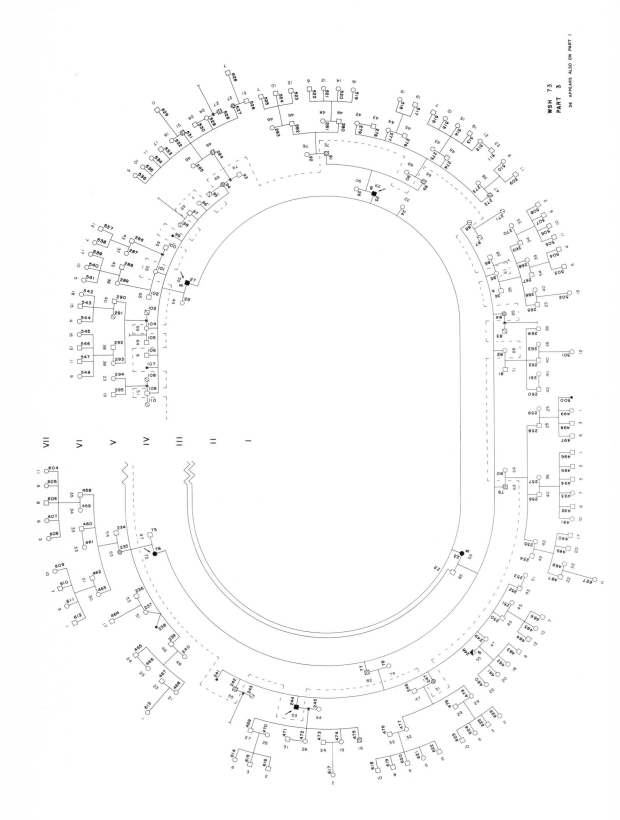

WSH 73
PART 3
36 APPEARS ALSO ON PART 1

WSH 73: The Proband

The proband (20), born 1860; died at age 54 years of suicide by hanging at Warren State Hospital. He was always a worrier. As a child, he worried excessively over ordinary problems. As an adult he did not socialize, had "terrific" headaches, was anxious and hypochondriacal. At age 48 years he had his first attack of severe depression during which he was suicidal. The depression lasted about three months and was preceded by a short period of overactivity, irritability and quarrelsomeness. In the spring of 1913 he became apprehensive about his health and attempted suicide. He spent three weeks in a private sanitarium, then was admitted to Warren State Hospital on 7/19/1913. He was not hallucinated and his delusions were of a hypochondriacal nature. He made several attempts at suicide before he succeeded. Diagnosis at Warren State Hospital and classification: Manic-depressive reaction — depressed type.

Children

Daughter (66), born 1887. She was described as "very high-tempered." She objected to the questions of the original interviewer "in a spirit of stubborn ugliness." At age 75 years she was "somewhat easily given to criticism... had strong opinions but no observable mental defects." Classification: Possible personality disorder.

Daughter (70), born 1893. She stated that she was somewhat depressed and nervous when overly tired. She had a "nervous twitch." Classification: Possible psychoneurotic disorder.

Grandchildren

Granddaughter (204), born 1915. She was described as "nervous from teaching" and as migrainous. Classification: Possible psychoneurotic disorder.

Grandson (205), born 1919. He was described as irresponsible and unable to handle money. His mother thought that "something must be wrong with him" as he wrote letters complaining of financial difficulty despite apparently good income. Classification: Possible personality pattern disturbance — inadequate personality.

Great-Grandchildren

(410) husband of great-granddaughter (411), born 1931; died at age 23 years of a self-inflicted gunshot wound to the head. As a youth he was "unstable... given to drinking." He was hospitalized at a county hospital from 5/5/54 until 5/10/54 with a diagnosis of psychoneurotic reaction, anxiety reaction. He had separated from his wife, but after hospitalization and an improvement in his condition they were reunited. Soon after, while under the influence of alcohol, he shot and killed his wife, his mother-in-law and himself. Classification: Probably with functional psychosis; possible personality disorder.

Great-Great-Grandchildren

Great-great-granddaughter (569), born 1952. She was seen by a psychiatrist because of irritability, nervousness, difficulty in sleeping and in getting along with playmates. The sessions were discontinued early but she did improve and later made a good adjustment. Her mother attributed the adjustment to the solution of the parents' marital difficulties. Classification: Transient situational personality disorder — adjustment reaction of childhood.

Great-great-granddaughter (587), born 1952. She was described as "high strung and nervous" and had a negative attitude toward school. Classification: Possible transient situational personality disorder — adjustment reaction of childhood.

Great-great-granddaughter (590), born 1955. She was described as "high-strung." Classification: Possible transient situational personality disorder — adjustment reaction of childhood.

Parents

Father (9), died at age 75 years of "stomach trouble." He was described as "devilish" and as a "rough, brutal man who would fly into a rage" at any displeasure. He was unkind to his wife and abused her verbally. Classification: Probable personality disorder.

Mother (10), born 1827; died at age 54 years of Bright's disease. She reportedly was "insane, ugly to her children and neglected them." "She would become angry and throw anything . . . was untidy in appearance and looked as though she never bathed." She seldom associated with people. Her moods were changeable in that she would be "pleasant one minute and call you obscene names in the next." She believed that "people were against her" and were stealing from her. At the time of her son's death she expressed no sorrow. She was rambling in conversation and would "talk about a half-dozen things at once." Classification: Schizophrenic reaction.

Aunts and Uncles

Maternal aunt (11), born 1830. Her natural disposition was "melancholy and serious" and she was inclined to be moody. At the time of menopause she had a "distinct attack of mental trouble for one year" during which she "had hysterical spells, complained of pain in her head and cried a great deal." She was well until about age 80 years when she again became nervous and easily excited. When interviewed at age 83 years she did not appear anxious or depressed but her memory was failing and she became confused in conversation. Classfication: Probably with functional psychosis — manic-depressive reaction.

Maternal aunt (12), born 1834; died at age 67 years of suicide by drinking carbolic acid. She was naturally "of a moody, almost morbid personality." At the time of menopause she developed delusions of poverty, insomnia and various somatic complaints. She was unable to do her work and complained of a pain in her head. She recovered after two years and was well except for brief periods of depression in the spring and fall of the year. Classification: With functional psychosis, involutional psychotic reaction.

Siblings

Sister (15), born 1854; died at age 62 years of a stroke. She was always considered "peculiar — would keep to herself." She was quick tempered, inclined to worry and had one attack of depression, the details of which are unknown, before her marriage. When interviewed at age 59 years she was in her third psychotic attack and was de-

luded, suicidal, homicidal, her memory was impaired and she ate and slept poorly. The same symptoms were present during the second attack, for which she was hospitalized at a state mental hospital from 3/5/1885 until 6/2/1885 with a diagnosis of acute melancholia. Classification: Schizophrenic reaction — paranoid type.

Brother (16), born 1853; died at age 28 years of dropsy. In 1871 he had an attack of "religious excitement" and was hospitalized, the details of which are unknown. He was again hospitalized on 2/6/1873, with a diagnosis of acute mania described again as "religious excitement." He was discharged 5/5/1873, and had no recurrence. Classification: Probable schizophrenic reaction — catatonic type.

Brother (17), born 1859; died at age 52 years of cancer of the mesentery. He reportedly had spells of depression, with one period of mild mental trouble. The details of his mental trouble are not known. Classification: Possibly with functional psychosis.

Sister (23), died at age 56 years. At about age 21 years she had "an attack of mental trouble lasting several months" during which she was "worried and melancholy," slept poorly, ate little and found it impossible to concentrate. She had neither delusions nor hallucinations. Three years later she had a similar attack. She became a "faith healer" and refused medical care for her family. In the winter of 1913 she attempted suicide by cutting her throat and injuring herself severely. Later, relatives stated that she was "insane for years" but never institutionalized. Classification: Schizophrenic reaction.

Brother (25), born 1864. He taught school as a young man but gave it up to start a business. The business was doing well but he thought his health was failing so he bought a farm. Soon after this he became depressed and melancholy and was hospitalized at a state mental hospital on 6/12/1893 with a diagnosis of chronic melancholia. He implored his brother to remove him from the hospital and complained so of homesickness that his brother took him from the hospital on 8/7/1893. On the way home he committed suicide by jumping from the roof of a building. Classification: Schizophrenic reaction.

Brother (27), born 1866; died at age 52

years at Warren State Hospital of myocarditis. At age 19 years he became excessively depressed for an unknown length of time. Two years later he again became depressed for a period of two years. During the second depression he was hospitalized at another state hospital from 10/26/1887 until 2/28/1888, with a diagnosis of chronic melancholia. He made several suicide attempts, one by drowning. He remained well for about 10 years, then became unduly elated and active for about one year. He was again normal for about 10 years and then, at about age 44, began another depression which became progressively worse until he was spending most of his time in bed. This gradually subsided and by September, 1914, he had become agitated and was hospitalized at Warren State Hospital with a diagnosis of manic-depressive psychosis. He remained hospitalized until death, expressing alternating periods of depression and agitation. Classification: Manic-depressive reaction—other.

Nieces and Nephews

Nephew (30), born 1882. He was always of normal mentality but when interviewed at age 80 years showed the memory impairment and rambling conversation of senility. Classification: Chronic brain syndrome of senility.

(34) husband of niece (35), born 1884. In 1927 he had influenza which slowed his memory and which was also followed by complaints of nervousness, pains in the head, dizziness, depression and thoughts of suicide and homicide. He was hospitalized at a state mental hospital from 1/15/1928 until 2/17/1928 with a diagnosis of postencephalitic neurasthenia. He did not work after that and was considered "disabled" by his family. When interviewed at age 79 years he was rambling and circumstantial in his conversation. Classification: Acute brain syndrome associated with infection.

Niece (37), born 1889. She was described in 1913 as "ambitious, sensible, neat and attractive" and as "decidedly nervous... restless, excited" and expressed herself "very vaguely." In 1962 she was described as highly excitable and anxious and in conversation would go from subject to subject or digress from the subject. There was a bit of projection in her attitude in that she claimed her sister was upset by the research, when in reality the sister was most cooperative. Classification: Probable psychoneurotic disorder; Possible personality disorder.

Nephew (38), born in 1891. He was described as always "odd." As a child he didn't play with other children and was very silent. When older he rarely worked because he "didn't feel like it" and would occasionally leave home for days at a time. He was called a "wanderer" and an alcoholic. Classification: Sociopathic personality disturbance.

Niece (76), born 1881; died at age 72 years of a cerebral hemorrhage. She was described as "like her mother...a 'Faith Healer.'" Prepsychotic symptoms began at about age 35 years. She harbored guilt feelings, maintained rigid thinking, was bizarre and eccentric in character and at times had delusions of reference and visual hallucinations. When she became abnormally suspicious and her ideas of persecution severe, she was hospitalized at a general hospital from 5/2/1938 until 8/8/1938, with a diagnosis of involutional psychosis, paranoid type. In 1949 she was diagnosed by a physician as with "cerebral arteriosclerosis, chronic myocarditis and mental." She made newspaper headlines because of her squalid living conditions and was subsequently hospitalized at a state mental hospital on 10/17/1952, with a diagnosis of chronic brain syndrome associated with cerebral arteriosclerosis with psychotic reaction. At admission she was described as anxious, irritable, belligerent, confused, paranoid, untidy and had delusions of reference. Over the years she had experienced several severe psychic traumas including the burning of her child, the death of her husband and the loss of money because of poor judgment. There was no improvement and she remained hospitalized until death. Classification: Schizophrenic reaction—paranoid type.

Nephew (77), born 1880. He showed some senile memory impairment in an interview at age 82 years. He stated that the men in his family were "heavy drinkers" but that "they could handle their drinks."

Classification: Possible sociopathic personality disturbance — alcoholism (addiction).

Nephew (79), born 1890; died at age 63 years of cancer of the esophagus. His wife stated that he would have lived longer if he hadn't drunk so heavily. Classification: Sociopathic personality disturbance — alcoholism (addiction).

Niece (84), born 1898. She was described as seclusive and uncommunicative. When an interview was attempted she refused to cooperate. Classification: Probable personality disorder; Possibly with functional psychoses.

Nephew (89), born 1887; died at age 66 years of acute cardiac failure and Parkinson's disease. He was described as "nervous." Classification: Possible psychoneurotic disorder.

Nephew (91), born 1890. He was described as "nervous" but when interviewed was interested, alert and apparently prosperous. Classification: Possible psychoneurotic disorder.

Niece (94), born 1894. She was described as "high-strung and nervous" but had received no medical attention for her nervousness. Classification: Probable psychoneurotic disorder.

Distant Relatives

Grandnephew (119), born 1935. On 6/30/1960 he was admitted to a Veterans Administration hospital with a diagnosis of schizophrenic reaction, undifferentiated type, in partial remission. This was a readmission as he had been discharged from the hospital on 5/19/1959 on an unauthorized leave. Details of hospitalizations are unknown. At the time of admission he was extremely suspicious and hostile and had delusions regarding his wife's fidelity. He talked of suicide but made no attempts. He was treated with drugs and showed some improvement. He escaped 7/18/1960 and on 9/9/1960 was living with his wife and "getting along fairly well." Classification: Schizophrenic reaction — paranoid type.

(120) wife of grandnephew (119), born 1922. She was 13 years older than her husband and her husband's case history stated that "she had a vivid imagination, was tor-menting and jealous and had a nervous breakdown in 1955." Classification: Probable psychoneurotic disorder; Possibly with functional psychosis.

Grandniece (126), born 1926. She was interviewed and described as "possibly immature in an hysterical sense" as she said that she was "very sensitive, worried over little things and brooded about things." Classification: Probable psychoneurotic disorder; Possible personality disorder.

Grandniece (130), born 1908. She was raised by her paternal grandmother as her mother died of tuberculosis the year (130) was born. She was described as "always had to be on the go," "temperamental, headstrong, possibly promiscuous" and as nervous and unhappy because of her unsuccessful marriages. Classification: Probable psychoneurotic disorder; Possible transient situational personality disorder.

Grandnephew (133), born 1915. He had a "nervous stomach" because of "pressure at work" and was described as an active suburbanite who was busy with civic activities and politics. Classification: Probable psychoneurotic disorder.

Grandnephew (150), born 1914; died at age 30 years when he was "lost at sea" while in the submarine service during World War II. He ran away from home at age 17 years and was described as the "black sheep" of his family. Classification: Possible personality disorder.

(156) wife of grandnephew (155), born 1924. She was described as "nervous." Classification: Possible psychoneurotic disorder.

Grandniece (233), born 1907. She was described by her family as "highly religious and narrow in her thinking — did not have friends or activities outside the church." When interviewed she expressed a great deal of hostility toward her sister because of their mother's hospitalization. The interviewer considered her to be a rigid, compulsive person. Classification: Possible personality trait disturbance — compulsive personality.

Grandniece (235), born 1909. She was interviewed and described herself as "a neurotic." Classification: Psychoneurotic disorder.

Grandnephew (242), born 1907. He was described as domineering and stingy with money. His attitude toward money was the cause of the short duration of his marriage. Classification: Possible personality disorder.

Grandnephew (244), born 1909. He had a history of sporadic employment, alcoholism and a bad conduct discharge from the Marines. In 1950 he began to express ideas of infidelity, was apprehensive about his children, was hallucinatory, had ideas of persecution and believed someone was poisoning his coffee. In December, 1953 he was jailed for firing a rifle at his wife's place of employment and subsequently admitted to a state mental hospital on 12/4/1953, where he remained until 4/20/1958 with a diagnosis of schizophrenic reaction, paranoid type, complicated by alcoholism. He was again hospitalized from 7/18/1962 until 9/13/1962 with the same diagnosis. At last information he was living alone in a small shack near his father's house. Classification: Schizophrenic reaction—paranoid type.

Grandniece (247), born 1911. At the time that her brother was hospitalized at a state mental hospital she wrote the governor of the state trying to get him released. She stated that she knew that his "drinks were doped...and who did dope them" and that she had the "evidence to go to the police." The hospital staff observed that she was "somewhat unstable." An interviewer described her as "basically a stable, hard-working woman of good intelligence...a very independent, proud woman." Classification: Possible personality pattern disturbance—paranoid personality.

(248) husband of grandniece (249), born 1907; died at age 55 years of suicide by shooting with a rifle. He was despondent over marital problems and probably under the influence of alcohol at the time of the shooting. Classification: Probably with functional psychosis; Possible psychoneurotic disorder—depressive reaction.

Grandnephew (272), born 1915. He was interviewed and described as reserved, possibly uneasy in social relationships and possibly with some mild maladjustments in the social area. Classification: Possible personality trait disturbance.

Grandnephew (284), born 1917. He was described as "inconsistent, bad-tempered, alcoholic, very nervous in handling his children...unstable at times, has tendency toward depression, can't hold a job." An interviewer estimated him to be non-psychotic but to possibly have a character disorder. Classification: Probable psychoneurotic disorder; Possible personality disorder.

Great-grandnephew (311), born 1930. He was described by the family as "flighty and unstable." He refused to be interviewed... insisted he knew little about the family and refused to talk about himself. Classification: Possible personality disorder.

Great-grandniece (452), born 1930. She was described as "artistic, nervous, sensitive, but in good health." Classification: Probable psychoneurotic disorder; Possible personality disorder.

Great-grandnephew (475), born 1946. He was placed in a private correctional institution for chronic truancy from 5/3/1962 until 5/11/1962. Classification: Transient situational personality disorder—adjustment reaction of adolescence.

Great-grandniece (527), born 1931. She described herself as nervous and said that she had trouble controlling her temper and handling her hostility. An interviewer estimated that she possibly had some psychoneurotic reactions in the form of headaches. Classification: Probable psychoneurotic disorder; Possible transient situational personality disorder.

(528) husband of great-grandniece (529), born 1936. He was described as "odd" and "immature." Classification: Possible personality disorder.

Great-grandnephew (531), born 1942. He left home while in the tenth grade, presumably because of intolerable treatment by his parents, and had an excellent record in the Navy. He was considered nervous by one informant. Classification: Probable transient situational personality disorder—adjustment reaction of adolescence; Possible psychoneurotic disorder.

Family Summary

The proband, the mother, a maternal aunt, two sisters, two brothers, a niece, and two grandnephews had psychoses, and a maternal aunt, two brothers, the husband of a grandniece and the husband of a great-granddaughter probably or possibly so. Personality disorders, or the possibility of such disorders, were found in a daughter, a grandson, three great-great-granddaughters, the father, three nephews, a niece, three grandnephews, two grandnieces, a great-grandniece, two great-grandnephews and the husband of a great-grandniece. A daughter, two nieces, two nephews, three grandnieces, two grandnephews, the wives of two grandnephews and two great-grandnieces were probably or possibly neurotic. A nephew was classified as chronic brain syndrome of senility. The husband of a niece

was classified as acute brain syndrome associated with infection.

Controls

Sister (1) of (34), born 1883. At age 79 years she was described as senile but was not hospitalized for her disability. Classification: Chronic brain syndrome of senium.

Brother (5) of (40), born 1901; died at age 55 years of "heart trouble." He reportedly "drank too much." Classification: Possible sociopathic personality disturbance—alcoholism (addiction).

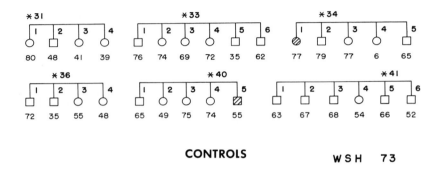

CONTROLS   **W S H   73**

WSH 79: The Proband

The proband (38), born 1866; died at age 77 years at Warren State Hospital of senility. He was described as "a glum, surly man ... weak-minded and easily led into trouble." He was also "a hard drinker, a quarrelsome, lazy" man who mistreated his wife. In the summer of 1912 he was promiscuous with a neighbor lady. In December he developed dizzy spells and couldn't work. He became worried and depressed and felt that his relationship with the neighbor had ruined his family and that people were trying to kill him and his family. He was prone to crying spells and attempted suicide three times. Admission to Warren State Hospital with a diagnosis of manic-depressive psychosis in one of limited mental ability was on 1/24/1913. He remained depressed for a year, then gradually improved and was discharged on 9/26/1917. He remained well until September, 1937, when he became worried, complained of prostate pains and developed unreasonable fear of punishment and death. He was returned to Warren State Hospital on 11/6/1937 with a diagnosis of manic-depressive, depressed type, and remained there until his death. At Warren State Hospital he thought he was being poisoned. His memory, attention and apprehension were impaired. Classification: Involutional psychotic reaction.

Child

Daughter (100), born 1903; died at age 17 years, cause of death unknown. She was described as "a queer child—nervous and fidgety" and as "impudent and indifferent." Classification: Possible psychoneurotic disorder.

Parents

Father (15), born 1838; died at age 91 years. At age 25 years he had an attack of mental trouble which lasted about one year. He became glum and refused to talk; he accused his wife, falsely, of having improper relations with the school teacher; he ran away and enlisted in the army where they refused to keep him "as he was crazy." He was restless and active, but not destructive or suicidal, and he may have had delusions of a persecutory nature. Gradually he returned to his normal state and no further episodes were reported. Classification: Schizophrenic reaction—paranoid type.

Mother (16), born 1838; died at age 62 years of apoplexy. Four years before her death she had an attack of apoplexy which paralyzed one side and left her without speech. Her mind became affected, although she did regain use of her paralyzed side. Classification: Chronic brain syndrome of senium.

Aunts and Uncles

Paternal aunt (9), born 1832. When interviewed at age 81 years she was "feeble, decrepit, complaining ... her mind was weak" and she had been delusional about "creeping paralysis" for 10 years. Classification: Chronic brain syndrome of senium.

Paternal uncle (14), born 1847. At age 66 years he was described as "a good-for-nothing" who would become a "worthless drunkard" if his sons didn't "keep him straight." Classification: Probable sociopathic personality disturbance—alcoholism (addiction).

Siblings

Sister (28), born 1858; died at age 66 years of diabetes. She was described as "neurotic—when things went wrong she would fly all to pieces." Classification: Probable psychoneurotic disorder.

Sister (35), born 1864; died at age 86 years of heart failure. She was described as nervous and irritable. She was married four times. Classification: Probable personality disorder.

Nieces and Nephews

(86) husband of niece (87), born 1886. He reportedly "drinks a lot, does not pay his bills and does not keep his word." When interviewed he impressed the interviewer as "a friendly, elderly man who appeared lonely and wanted very much to talk" and that he was aged but very much alert. Classification: Sociopathic personality disturbance.

(90) husband of niece (91), born 1872; froze to death while intoxicated at age 72 years. He was reportedly an alcoholic. Classification: Probable sociopathic personality disturbance—alcoholism (addiction).

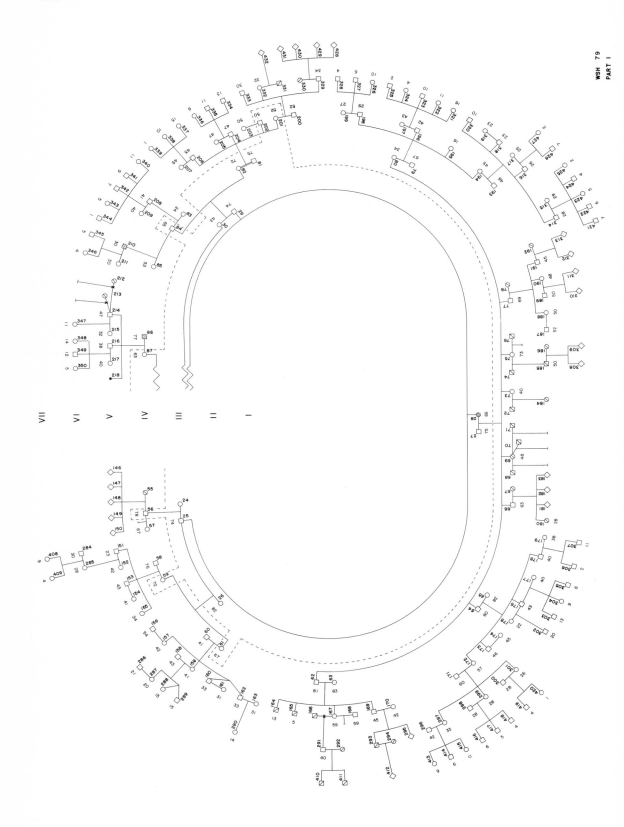

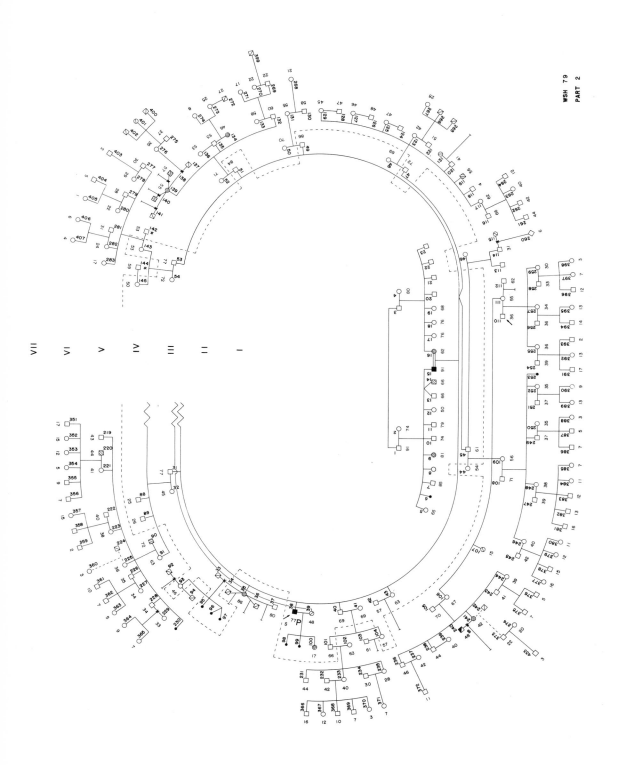

(110) husband of niece (111), born 1900; died at age 36 years of general paresis at a state mental hospital in Oklahoma. First mental symptoms began in December, 1935, when he became very nervous, badly disturbed and unable to take care of himself. He was hospitalized in May, 1936, and died a month later. Classification: Chronic brain syndrome associated with meningoencephalitic central system syphilis, with psychotic reaction.

Nephew (119), born 1907. He was reportedly an alcoholic whose whereabouts were unknown to the family. Classification: Sociopathic personality disturbance — alcoholism (addiction).

(134) wife of nephew (135), born 1908; died at age 46 years of injuries received in an automobile accident. She was known to have "blackouts" which were attributed to her menopause. Presumably, she fell asleep at the wheel and caused the accident in which she died. Classification: Possible psychoneurotic disorder; Possible transient situational personality disorder.

(138) husband of niece (139), born 1906. He was described as an alcoholic who was "cured" when he married a nurse after his divorce from (139). Classification: Probable sociopathic personality disorder — alcoholism (addiction).

Niece (139), born 1908. She was described as "flighty and high-tempered." She was married four times. Classification: Possible psychoneurotic disorder.

(140) husband of niece (139). He was described as "an alcoholic who remarried his first wife" after his divorce from (139). Classification: Probable sociopathic personality disorder — alcoholism (addiction).

Distant Relatives

Grandnephew (210), born 1932. He was described as a very nervous person who

nearly had a nervous breakdown during his first year of law school and could not complete his law degree. Classification: Probable psychoneurotic disorder.

(220) husband of grandniece (221), born 1911; died at age 44 years of a heart attack. He was known as a "drunken, shiftless pauper." Classification: Sociopathic personality disturbance — alcoholism (addiction).

(240) husband of grandniece (241), born 1914; suicided at age 48 years. Classification: Probably with functional psychosis.

Grandniece (241), born 1921. She was considered the "black sheep of the family" and her whereabouts were unknown. She was "unable to settle down and adjust to marriage — would live with men" but not marry. Classification: Sociopathic personality disturbance.

Family Summary

The proband and his father were psychotic, although the father was never hospitalized. The husband of a grandniece was probably psychotic as he suicided at age 48 years. The husband of another niece died in a mental hospital of general paresis. The mother and a paternal aunt were classified as with chronic brain syndrome of senium. No one was considered decidedly neurotic but a daughter, a sister, a niece, a grandnephew and the wife of a nephew were possibly or probably so. A paternal uncle, a nephew, the husband of three nieces and the husband of a grandniece were either alcoholic or probably so. A grandniece and the husband of a niece had personality disturbances and a sister had a probable personality disorder.

Controls

None noteworthy.

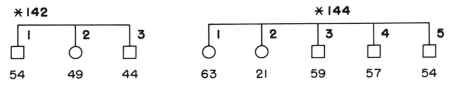

WSH 81: The Proband

Proband (23), born 1862; died at age 71 years at Warren State Hospital of chronic myocarditis. In 1902 he had a depression which he described as "the blues." Six years later he had another attack and was hospitalized at Warren State Hospital from 12/28/1908 until 9/14/1909 with a diagnosis of chronic mania. Ward notes at this hospitalization described him as introspective, complaining, nervous, restless and suicidal. In June, 1912, he became agitated, made desperate attempts at suicide and was again hospitalized at Warren State Hospital from 1/18/1913 until 6/24/1916 with a diagnosis of manic-depressive, depressed phase. While at home in care of his wife he continued to be melancholy, nervous and restless. He was found trying to shoot himself, then ran away. Subsequently he was caught and rehospitalized on 3/24/1918 at Warren State Hospital, where he remained until death; diagnosis was the same. Classification: Manic-depressive reaction — depressed type.

Children

Son (45), born 1890. At age 15 years he dropped out of school and at age 18 years, after an attempt to resume his schoolwork, he became despondent and was unable to study. When he returned home his depression cleared and he was well until the spring of 1913, when he became restless, deluded, aurally hallucinated and was a nuisance in the neighborhood. He was shortly admitted to Warren State Hospital with a diagnosis of dementia praecox. He was paroled 5/17/1914 and remained well for eight months, when he had to be hospitalized again. Diagnosis at the second admission on 7/23/1915 was also dementia praecox. He escaped from Warren State Hospital on 2/2/1916 and was never readmitted. Later an interviewer was advised not to try to contact him. His attitude toward his family was tyrannical and his main pastime was sitting by a window watching all who came to his house. Classification: Schizophrenic reaction — catatonic type.

Parents

Mother (13), born 1818; died at age 82 years of apoplexy. She was described as "stubborn and strong-willed . . . of an unhappy, discontented disposition." She had "sick headaches" all her life. Classification: Probable psychoneurotic disorder.

Aunts and Uncles

Paternal uncle (6), died at age 70 years when the little hut where he was chained because of his insanity caught fire and he burned to death. He was insane for several years before his death. Classification: Probably with functional psychosis; Possible chronic brain syndrome of senium.

Siblings

(25) husband of sister (26), born 1857; died at age 74 years of cirrhosis of the liver. He was hospitalized at Warren State Hospital from 9/5/1897 until 11/12/1900 with a diagnosis of melancholia. In July, 1897, he became depressed, confused and deluded and remained that way until December, 1898, when he became excited, restless and occasionally destructive. He was either depressed or excited until March, 1900, when he became dull and apathetic, in which condition he remained. He was never rehospitalized. Classification: Schizophrenic reaction — paranoid type.

Sister (28), born 1856; died at age 79 years of heart trouble. She was described as silly, childish, suspicious as well as inquisitive and answered the interviewer's questions with a nervous, inappropriate laugh. Classification: Probable personality disorder; Possibly with functional psychosis.

(29) husband of sister (30), born 1859; died at age 68 years of bronchopneumonia and paralysis agitans. He moved around from job to job a great deal because of a drinking problem. Classification: Sociopathic personality disturbance — alcoholism (addiction).

Sister (32), born 1862; died at age 64 years of chronic heart disease. She was described as suffering from a loss of memory and as cautious, suspicious, and lived "a life

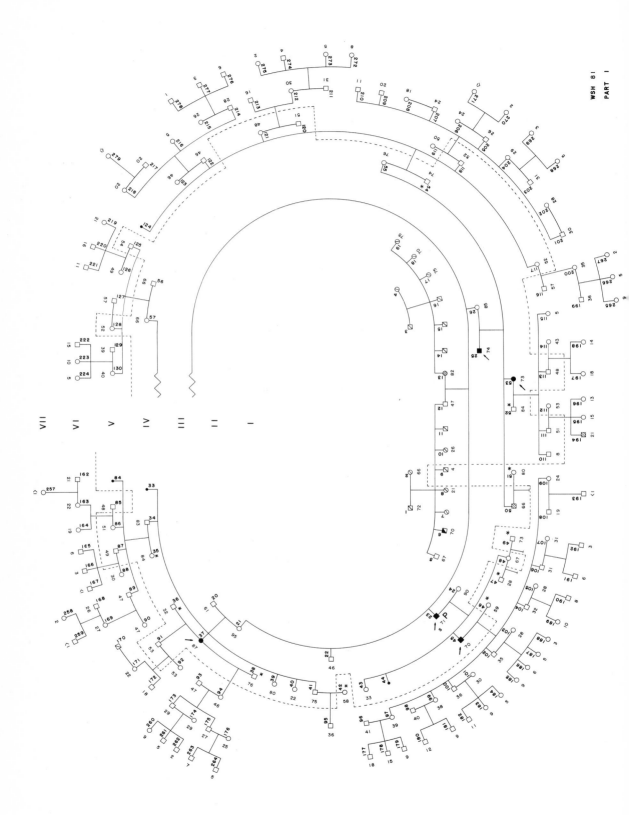

WSH 81

PART I

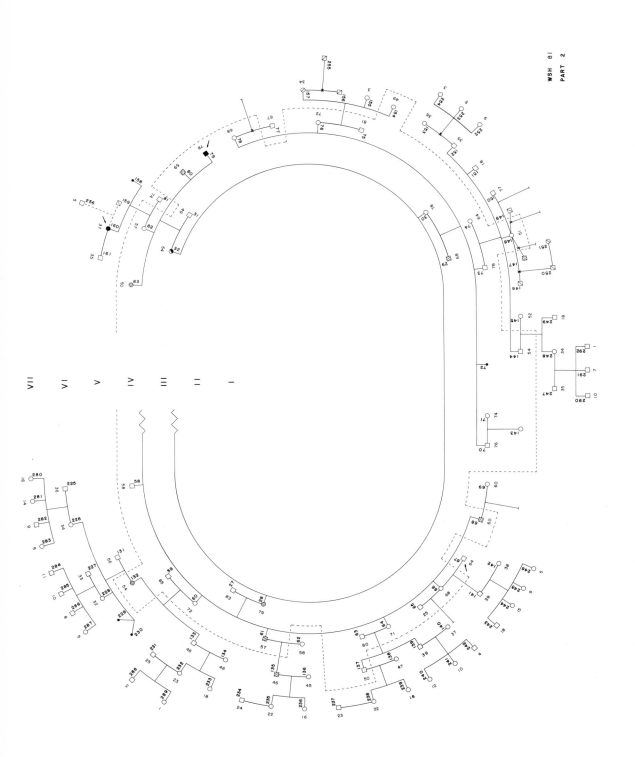

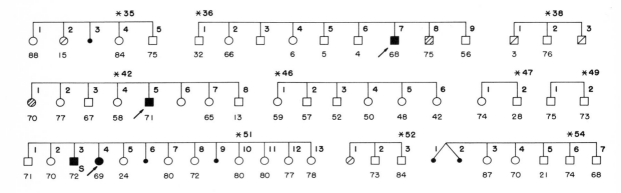

CONTROLS   **W S H   8 1**

Nieces and Nephews

apart from everyone else." She was considered both mentally deficient and mentally deranged." Classification: Probably with functional psychosis; Possible personality disorder.

Niece (37), born 1876. In 1963 she was a patient at a mental hospital in Illinois, where she was admitted on 2/11/1955. Diagnosis was chronic brain syndrome associated with senile brain disease. After the death of her second husband she continued to run their small grocery store alone. She was held up, slugged and robbed, and after that was always fearful of another hold-up. In 1954 she began to think that people were poisoning and gassing her. These ideas persisted in a clear, consistent way wherever she lived. Suicidal and homicidal tendencies were never present. Classification: Schizophrenic reaction—paranoid type.

Nephew (50), born 1879; died at age 66 years of cerebral arteriosclerosis with hemorrhage. He was described as "unduly self-centered and of an unstable disposition." Classification: Possible personality disorder.

Niece (53), born 1882; died at age 73 years of hypertensive heart disease. She was a pleasant, capable woman until age 32 years, when the death of a son because of osteomyelitis caused her to become very upset. She recovered and remained well until age 58 years, when she began to develop vague delusions of persecution and intermittent depressions. For one year she had aural and visual hallucinations, ideas of persecution and fears of killing herself and others. Hospitalization at a state mental hospital was from 11/13/1950 until 3/9/1951, with a diagnosis of involutional psychosis, paranoid type. Classification: Involutional psychotic reaction.

Nephew (61), born 1887; died at age 57 years of a heart attack. He was diabetic and considered by his family to be an alcoholic. Classification: Sociopathic personality disturbance—alcoholism (addiction).

(67) husband of niece (66), born 1896. On 10/30/1931 he was admitted voluntarily to a state mental hospital for diagnostic purposes. A diagnosis of neurosyphilis was made. He later developed arthritis. Classification: Chronic brain syndrome associated with meningovascular central nervous system syphilis, without qualifying phrase.

Nephew (68), born 1900. He worked as a lumberjack and was described as alcoholic and asthmatic. Classification: Sociopathic personality disturbance—alcoholism (addiction).

Nephew (80), born 1887; died at age 59 years of cancer of the stomach. The early study described him as bashful, unsociable and "not very bright." His family physician described him as "good material" for an emotional upset. Classification: Probable personality disorder.

Niece (83), born 1892; died at age 50 years of acute heart failure. She was always sickly and nervous and at age 21 years was described as "a hesitating, self-conscious girl who appeared vacant, apathetic and lacking in expression." She attempted teaching after graduation from normal school but proved inadequate both physically and in ability and had to discontinue. Classification: Personality trait disturbance — other.

Distant Relatives

Grandniece (132), born 1906. In 1958 she had an eye removed because of a tumor and was later described as "always nervous and a worrier." Classification: Personality trait disturbance — other.

Grandnephew (135), born 1914. He was described as overactive and accident prone. Classification: Possible psychoneurotic disorder.

(147) husband of grandniece (148), born 1907. He was described as "alcoholic." Classification: Sociopathic personality disturbance — alcoholism (addiction).

Grandniece (160), born 1924. In 1945, following the death of her mother, she became unsociable, lost interest in her personal appearance, wanted to stay in bed, did not want to feed herself and became generally indifferent. She was committed to a state mental hospital on 3/20/1948 with a diagnosis of dementia praecox, simple type. She went home on 3/6/1949, but was returned six months later. She eloped from the hospital on 2/25/1951, was returned 12/20/1951; eloped again 11/8/1954 and was not returned. When home she was a discipline problem for her father. An illegitimate male child was born to her on 2/27/1950. She was discharged as unimproved. Classification: Schizophrenic reaction — simple type.

Great-grandnephew (194), born 1939. He was described as a difficult child to raise and as an adult as "the super-salesman type." He got along well with people but his constant talking was described as monotonous. Classification: Possible personality disorder.

Family Summary

The proband, a son, two nieces, a nephew and a grandniece had a psychosis, and a sister and a paternal uncle probably were psychotic. A husband of a sister was also psychotic. All the psychotic individuals were hospitalized but only the proband made suicide attempts. The husband of a niece was hospitalized for observation with meningovascular syphilis. The mother was probably neurotic and a grandnephew possibly so. Personality disorders were found in a niece, three nephews, a grandniece, the husbands of a sister and of a grandniece. A sister probably had a personality disorder and a nephew and great-grandniece possibly so.

Controls

Brother (7) of (36), born 1885; died at age 68 years of cancer of the cecum. He was hospitalized twice at a state mental hospital with a diagnosis of manic-depressive reaction, manic type; once from December, 1936 until November, 1939 and again from April, 1943 until April, 1945. Classification: Manic-depressive reaction — manic type.

Brother (8) of (36), born 1887. At age 75 years his whereabouts and marital status were unknown. He was described as a disabled veteran of World War I (gas poisoning) and as unstable and a wanderer. Classification: Probable personality pattern disturbance — inadequate personality.

Sister (1) of (42), born 1881; died at age 70 years of a coronary occlusion. She was single and a music teacher who at age 35–40 years had a "slight nervous condition." Classification: Probable transient situational personality disorder — adult situational reaction.

Brother (5) of (42), born 1890; died at age 71 years of an acute myocardial infarction. He was a school superintendent who was first hospitalized for mental trouble on 5/14/1951, with a diagnosis of pre-senile melancholia with strong paranoid trends. He was discharged as improved on 8/3/1951, after electroconvulsive therapy. Onset of the illness began about one year before hospitalization when he became extremely anxious about his work responsibilities and very depressed with delusions concerning his health and threatened law suits. Hospitalization was at St. Francis Hospital, Pittsburgh, Pennsylvania. He reportedly had a "nervous breakdown" in

1940, at which time he was treated for a thyroid condition. Classification: Involutional psychotic reaction.

Brother (3) of (51), born 1870; died at age 72 years from a self-inflicted gunshot wound. He reportedly had a "problem with alcoholism: and, while intoxicated shot and killed his wife, his mother-in-law and himself." Classification: Schizophrenic reaction — paranoid type.

Sister (4) of (51), born 1871; died at age 69 years of apoplexy. She was first admitted to Warren State Hospital on 3/11/1908, with a diagnosis of chronic mania. Symptoms had been present for three years; she was abusive to her children, had a phobia about cleanliness and germs, was talkative (especially on religious matters), exalted, restless and overactive. She adjusted well at the hospital and was discharged as restored on 12/20/1908. She remained well, although extremely neat and particular about her personal appearance and house, until about 1935, when she again became excitable with the same phobia of germs. She accused her husband of infidelity and abused any woman she saw in the vicinity of their home. She also banged her head against the wall, then reported to the doctor that her husband beat her. Second hospitalization at Warren State Hospital was from 4/2/1937 until 7/23/1939, with a diagnosis of manic-depressive reaction, manic type. At parole she still had some of her paranoid convictions but was under good emotional control and was not hospitalized again. Classification: Schizophrenic reaction — paranoid type.

WSH 87: The Proband

Proband (34), born 1866; died at age 80 years of coronary thrombosis. At age 46, after 25 years of an unhappy marriage (she preferred living lavishly and her husband had several business failures), she became depressed and deluded; believed fuzz was growing on her face and that hair was growing on her child's face; eating and sleeping habits were disturbed and she lost 60 pounds. She attempted suicide by drowning and was subsequently hospitalized at Warren State Hospital on 1/9/1913, with a diagnosis of manic-depressive psychosis, depressed type. Hospital notes stated that she imagined she had committed a great sin and lost her soul as a result. She made a very good recovery, was paroled in 1915, and had no further difficulty. Classification: Involutional psychotic reaction.

(33) husband of proband (34), born 1860; died at age 70 years of cancer. He had a "severe nervous breakdown" in 1912. Previous to this he had several business failures. Classification: Probable psychoneurotic disorder.

Parents

Mother (12), born 1839; died at age 65 years of la grippe. At about age 50 years she became a "hard drinker." At the same time she developed epileptic seizures, grand mal type. Her mind was not impaired, except for the visual hallucination of her father sitting on a chair in her room at night, which persisted for the last six months of her life. Classification: Probable sociopathic personality disturbance — alcoholism (addiction); Possible chronic brain syndrome associated with convulsive disorder.

Aunts and Uncles

Maternal half aunt (22), had some sort of "nervous trouble" after menopause and was at a private sanitarium for a year or two. Classification: Probably with functional psychosis, involutional psychotic reaction.

Siblings

Brother (24), born 1850; died at age 27 years of pneumonia. At age 21 years he collapsed into unconsciousness while working in extreme heat. Two hours later he regained consciousness and no ill effects were noticed. A year later he began to exhibit strange ideas about politics and religion and to have "violent spells." He was at home for one year, then, in June, 1876, was hospitalized for a period of two years. While at home he had some insight into his violent spells and asked the family to stay away as he was not responsible for his behavior. The hospital described him as having a badly impaired memory, as touching things peculiarly and as talking to himself a great deal. He had syphilis. He was released from the hospital as restored and had no more mental trouble. Hospitalized diagnosis is unknown. Classification: Schizophrenic reaction — paranoid type.

Nieces and Nephews

Nephew (35), born 1873; died at age 70 years of "softening of the brain" while at a county home. Classification: Possible chronic brain syndrome of senium.

(44) wife of nephew (43), born 1886; died at age 69 years at Warren State Hospital of gastrointestinal hemorrhage. At age 18 years and again one year later she had attacks of extreme violence. She was hospitalized at Warren State Hospital on 2/1/1905, with the second attack, with diagnosis of acute mania. Six months later she was discharged as restored and was well for nine years until she married a "generally worthless" alcoholic man who was cruel and physically abusive. She again exhibited her previous symptoms of excitability and violent rages and was readmitted to Warren State Hospital on 4/5/1922, with a diagnosis of manic-depressive psychosis, manic phase. In 1940 she was re-diagnosed as dementia praecox, simple type, because of her deteriorated and apathetic condition which had persisted for 10 years. She was also resistive, silly, disoriented and her conversation was irrelevant. She was at Warren State Hospital until her death. Classification: Schizophrenic reaction — paranoid type.

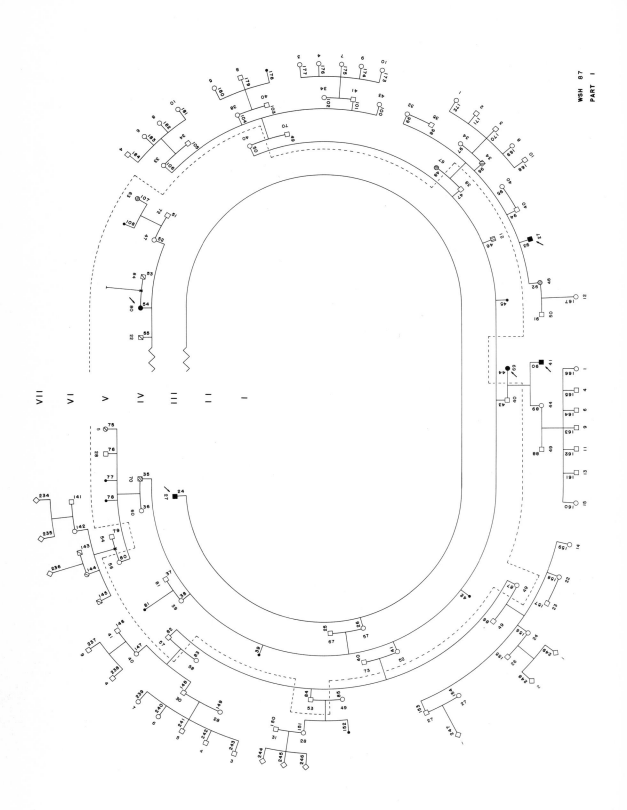

WSH 87
PART I

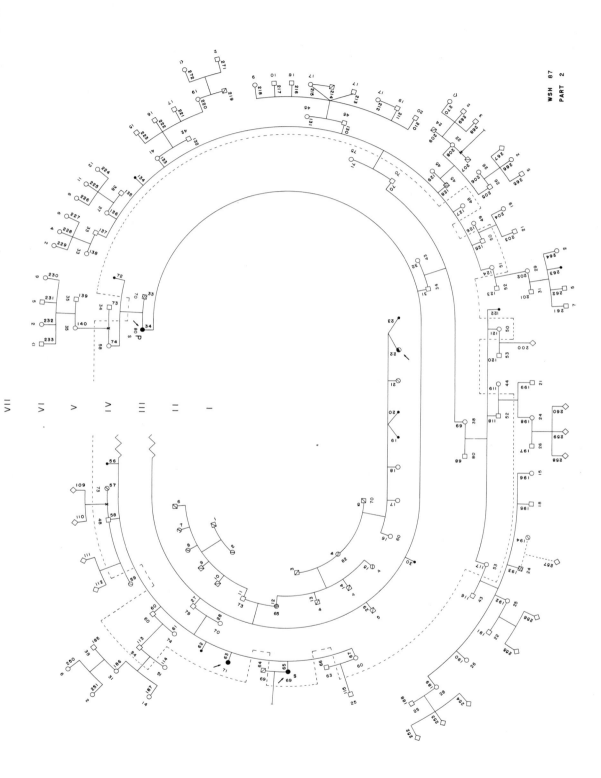

Nephew (46), born 1890; died at age 21 years of typhoid fever. He was described as "fast and sporty" and used alcohol to excess at times. Classification: Possible personality disorder.

(48) wife of nephew (47), born 1894. She was widowed at age 36 years and raised four children. In 1944 her oldest son became violent and was committed to Warren State Hospital, where he died the next month. She began threatening the Department of Health for hounding her son into a mental breakdown. The physician described her as emotionally unstable, difficult to control and possibly a borderline psychotic. Six months later her father died and her mentally ill mother was admitted to Warren State Hospital. The admitting physician described her as extremely unstable. Classification: Probable personality trait disturbance — emotionally unstable personality.

Niece (54), born 1878; died at age 80 years at Warren State Hospital of pneumonia. At age 66 years, after living seclusively in a hotel for years, she developed delusions that men were plotting against her and she became confused and fearful of going blind. Subsequently she was hospitalized at Warren State Hospital (12/31/1946) until her death.

At the hospital she was apathetic, disinterested, suspicious and fearful but aware that she was depressed and despondent. She was described by one physician as perhaps an "old paranoid praecox." Diagnosis at Warren State Hospital was senile psychosis, paranoid type. Classification: Schizophrenic reaction — paranoid type.

Niece (63), born 1891. At Warren State Hospital where she has been since 4/4/1917. Diagnosis at admission was unclassified — reaction of an unstable individual to mental stress (possible dementia praecox). She was always nervous, high strung and irritable, yet intelligent and very sociable. In 1916 she became illegitimately pregnant and had a criminal abortion in October of that year. Soon after this she developed the delusion that she had been married and that her ovaries had been removed; later she became visually and aurally hallucinated. After hospitalization her hallucinations became more prominent and she developed delusions of grandeur and persecution. She showed improvement and

parole was recommended four months after admission but she never went home. Classification: Schizophrenic reaction — paranoid type.

Niece (65), born 1894. At Warren State Hospital, where she has been since her second admission to Warren State Hospital on 10/29/1940, with a diagnosis of dementia praecox, paranoid type. Original admission to Warren State Hospital was on 9/25/1936 following a suicide attempt. She had been named the executor of her father's estate and, as the day to appear in court neared, she became increasingly anxious and made more than one suicide attempt. Her marriage of 18 years had been very stressful because of religious differences and financial instability. At admission she was overactive, delusional and aurally hallucinated; however, she made rapid recovery and was discharged to the custody of a sister on 6/8/1937. The sister was domineering and interfered continuously in her affairs. (65) reacted by threatening court action and pressing for medical examination of the sister (about six years later the sister was hospitalized at Warren State Hospital) which precipitated the second admission to Warren State Hospital. At the second admission she appeared to be deteriorated and chronically paranoid. Classification: Schizophrenic reaction — paranoid type.

Distant Relatives

Grandniece (90), born 1918. Her mother, a schizophrenic, was committed to Warren State Hospital when she was three years old; her father drowned when (90) was seven years old, and she was raised by her aunt. She was discharged, honorably, from the Army in 1946, then worked for her uncle until the uncle's death in 1956; after that she did not work. She had little interest in marriage because she "detests the responsibility" and "so many females are diseased." In 1957 she developed delusions of being poisoned and of having her phone tapped. She became suspicious and withdrawn and was hospitalized in Ohio in May, 1957. She refused to cooperate and left against advice on 6/13/1958, but was committed to a state mental hospital the same day with a diagnosis of schizophrenic reaction, paranoid type. She spent most of her time thinking of how to get away from the hospital and was paroled to her aunt on 9/24/1958. She was seen by an interviewer in 1959. It was the interviewer's impression that she had not adjusted to life outside the hospital. Classification: Schizophrenic reaction—paranoid type.

Grandniece (92), born 1913. She was reportedly "compulsively on the go." Classification: Possible personality trait disturbance—compulsive personality.

Grandnephew (93), born 1916; died at age 27 years at Warren State Hospital of acute catatonic excitement. He was always nervous—he never held a job for more than a short time and was rejected by the Air Force because of his nervousness. He had numerous abnormal sexual experiences at an early age about which he was very self-conscious. When he became old enough to be employed he held many jobs for short periods of time because he believed the other employees accused him of sexual perversion. Finally, he began to hear "voices," believed he was choking, said that he had radar in his teeth and jumped through a window, cutting himself, because he believed the house was about to blow up. The next day (4/3/1944) he was admitted to Warren State Hospital with a diagnosis of dementia praecox, paranoid type. While hospitalized he was fearful, quiet and affectless. Death occurred about one month after admission. Classification: Schizophrenic reaction—paranoid type.

Grandnephew (96), born 1927. He was a major in the United States Air Force. He reportedly was of a very nervous temperament and chewed his fingernails excessively. Classification: Probable psychoneurotic disorder.

Grandniece (107), born 1898. She told

an interviewer that she had been persecuted all her life because of her relatives in Warren State Hospital. She reportedly was also "very bitter and has some queer ideas." Classification: Possible personality disorder.

Grandnephew (128), born 1914. He was referred to as "always a problem" and "somewhat of a rebel." Classification: Possible personality disorder.

Great-grandnephew (193), born 1936. He was a bright honor student through grade eight but at age 14 years he became a problem boy and had been in correctional institutions since age 16 years. He had no special friends. He had been a model prisoner but was unable to overcome his impulsive stealing. Classification: Sociopathic personality disturbance—antisocial reaction.

Family Summary

The proband, a brother, three nieces, two grandnephews and the wife of a nephew had psychotic disorders and a maternal half aunt probably so. The proband and one of the psychotic nieces made suicide attempts. A grandnephew had a personality disorder, the mother and the wife of a nephew probably so. A nephew, a grandnephew and two grandnieces possibly had personality disorders. The proband's husband and a grandnephew were probably neurotic and a nephew was possibly suffering from chronic brain syndrome of senium. The proband's parents had seven children, 24 grandchildren, 42 great-grandchildren, 73 great-great-grandchildren and 39 great-great-great-grandchildren.

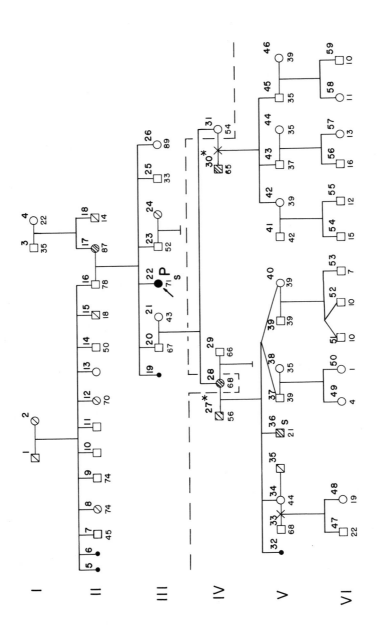

WSH 90: The Proband

The proband (22), born 1866; died at age 71 years of chronic myocarditis and manic-depressive psychosis. She was hospitalized eight times during her lifetime, each hospitalization diagnosed as manic-depressive, manic phase. The attacks were classic in nature (the first at age 26 years) with increased psychomotor activity, flight of ideas and marked distractibility with no symptoms in the interims. She made one suicide attempt in 1935 and "never slept well, even as a child." Dates and places of hospitalizations were as follows:

Warren State Hospital...........	2/23/1893 – 6/15/1893
" " "	8/16/1907 – 8/ 6/1908
" " "	10/15/1912 – 1/30/1913
" " "	3/28/1913 – 4/30/1913
The Sheppard and Enoch Pratt Hospital..........................	4/11/1924 – 5/17/1924
Eastern Shore State Hospital...	9/29/1926 – 10/12/1926
Burn Brae Hospital	10/12/1926 – unknown
The Sheppard and Enoch Pratt Hospital	10/28/1935 – 12/ 9/1935
Burn Brae Hospital..............	7/12/1936 – death (9/23/1936)

Classification: Manic-depressive reaction, manic type.

Parents

Mother (17), born 1836; died at age 87 years of arteriosclerosis. She was described as "inclined to be over-talkative, loud and pert... some acquaintances are inclined to consider her unbalanced... she manifested no abnormal or bizarre ideas..." Classification: Probable personality disorder; Possibly with functional psychosis.

Nieces and Nephews

(27) husband of niece (28), born 1890; died at age 56 years of hypertensive cardiac vascular disease. He reportedly had "trouble with alcohol—not alcoholic—just trouble." Classification: Possible sociopathic personality disturbance—alcoholism (addiction).

Niece (28), born 1892. She was described as "always on the go," an extraordinarily active woman who volunteered her

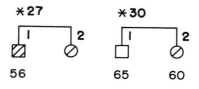

CONTROLS WSH 90

daughter's services as well as her own. Classification: Possible personality pattern disturbance—cyclothymic personality.

(30) husband of niece (31), born 1895. He had a history of alcoholism but "dried up" in 1938 with the help of Alcoholics Anonymous. Classification: Sociopathic personality disturbance—alcoholism (addiction).

Distant Relatives

Grandnephew (36), born 1918; died at age 21 years of illuminating gas poisoning—one gas jet was open in the kitchen. His death was reported as caused by pneumonia by his mother and sister and as a suicide by his cousin. Classification: Possible suicide.

Family Summary

The proband was the only frankly psychotic and hospitalized family member. The mother had a probable personality disorder or was possibly psychotic. A niece had a possible personality disorder and two nieces married alcoholic men (one but possibly so). A grandnephew may have committed suicide. The proband's parents had six children, two grandchildren, eight great-grandchildren and 13 great-great-grandchildren.

Controls

See family pedigree, person 27.

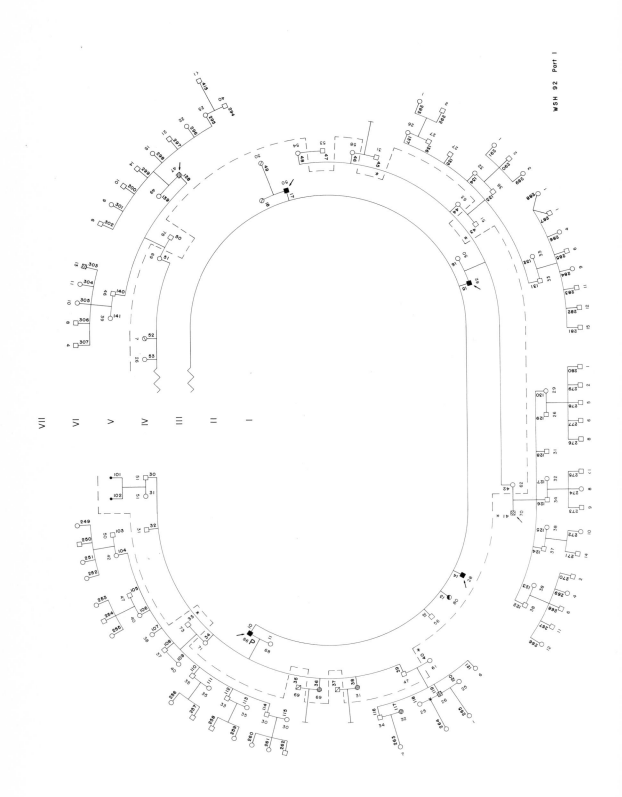

WSH 92 Part I

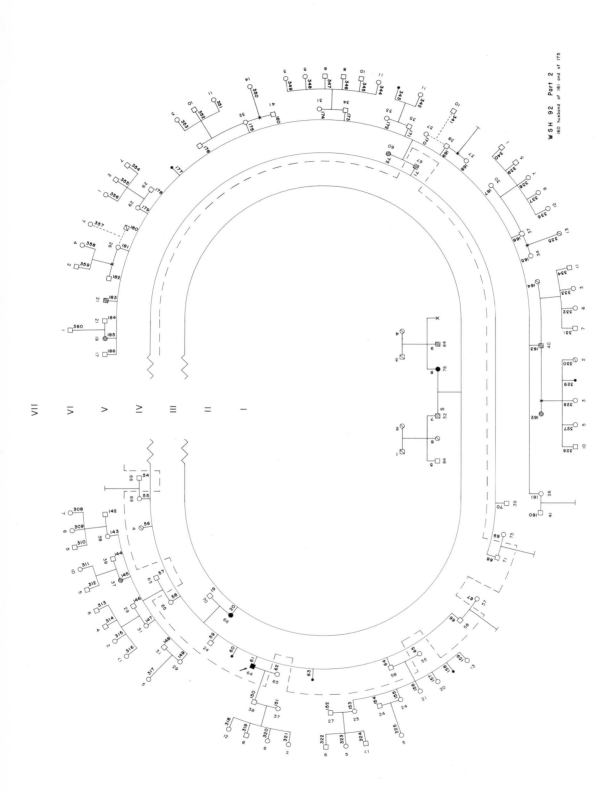

WSH 92 Part 2
160 husband of 161 and of 175

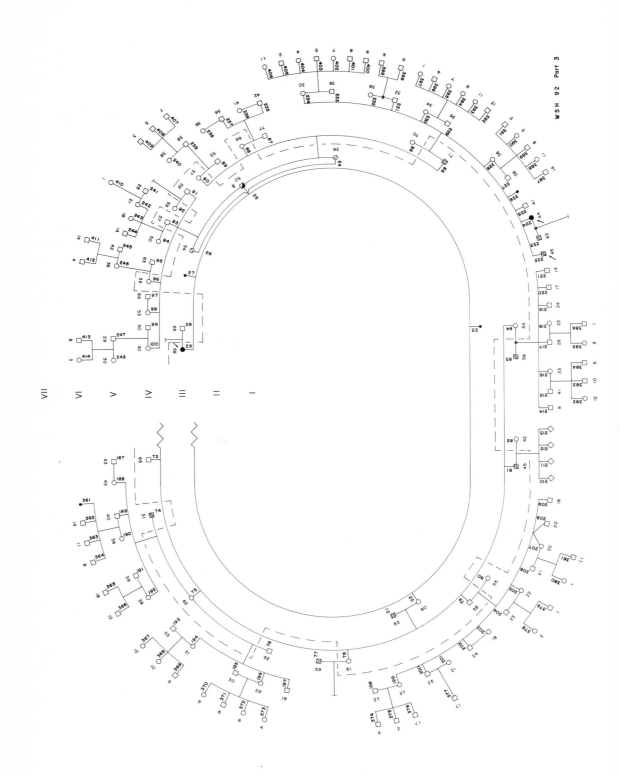

WSH 92 Part 3

WSH 92: The Proband

Proband (10), born 1847; died at age 86 years at Warren State Hospital of chronic myocarditis. He was described as a kind husband, solicitous father, successful businessman, and as sociable and fond of company until age 45 years when, following an attack of grippe, he became irritable, difficult in his business relationships, and began to sleep during the day as well as at night. Symptoms became worse (he became threatening to his family) and he was hospitalized at Warren State Hospital on 9/30/1897, with a diagnosis of acute mania. The course of his illness never changed and the statement that "he had periods of excitement every few months and at other times was quiet, orderly, occupied and mildly deluded" was true until his death. He was at home from 10/10/1898 until 7/8/1904. Concluding diagnosis at Warren State Hospital as of 7/31/1920 was manic-depressive, circular type. Classification: Manic-depressive reaction — other.

Children

Daughter (36), born 1891. She has resided in a rest home since the death of her husband, although her sister stated that she had no problem but was just "fat and lazy." Classification: Possible personality pattern disturbance — inadequate personality.

Daughter (38), born 1895; died at age 31 years of kidney trouble. She was described as a normal domestic when interviewed but welfare records reported her as persistently immoral. Classification: Sociopathic personality disturbance — anti-social reaction.

Grandchildren

(116) wife of (117), born 1929. She received psychiatric attention but was not hospitalized when she became mildly depressed after the death of her mother. Classification: Psychoneurotic disorder — depressive reaction, conversion reaction.

Grandson (119), born 1935. He was recognized by his mother as "very high-strung" and never as "steady" as his older

brothers. She described his first marriage as "either very happy or very miserable — never really got going." He did well in college, but quit because of his "forced" marriage and worked as a radio announcer. His second wife's family financed his Mexican divorce and his attendance at a drama school. Classification: Personality trait disturbance — emotionally unstable personality.

Parents

Father (7), born 1820; died at age 52 years of suicide preceded by an episode of painful neuralgia and the persistent harassment of his psychotic wife. Classification: Probable transient situational personality disorder — gross stress reaction.

Mother (8), born 1826; died at age 76 years of kidney trouble and catarrh. She reportedly had attacks of melancholia during her entire married life. She became violent after the death of her husband and later became silly and childish. Classification: Schizophrenic reaction — paranoid type.

Aunts and Uncles

Maternal uncle (9), born 1828; died at age 84 years of senility and dementia. He was described as "somewhat deranged for several years before he died." Classification: Chronic brain syndrome of senium.

Siblings

Sister (13), born 1851; died at age 80 years, cause of death unknown. The original study classified her as a neurotic. When interviewed she was despondent and fearful and suffering from nervousness and insomnia. She had an awkward, stiff gait which made it difficult for her to do her work as a domestic. Classification: Probably with functional psychosis.

Brother (14), born 1855; died at age 28 years at Warren State Hospital of "disease of the brain." He was hospitalized at Warren State Hospital on 5/14/1883 with a diagnosis of acute mania. This was his second attack of mania, which had begun about four months before admission. He had been melancholy for seven or eight years previous to the first attack of mania. Much of the time during his illness he had a great aversion to food, believing it would destroy him. He remained at Warren State Hospital until his death. Classification: Schizophrenic reaction — paranoid type.

Brother (15), born 1856; died at age 62 years at Warren State Hospital of purulent meningitis. He was admitted to Warren State Hospital on 12/8/1908 after an 11-month stay at a mental hospital in New York State. Diagnosis at Warren State Hospital was manic-depressive, manic phase. Symptoms reportedly developed "several years" before his admission and were characterized by periods of excitement followed by periods of depression. The hospital notes gave a 10-year history of delusions of persecution, hallucinations, threats of homicide, talking to himself and ideas of influence. He was paroled to his wife from 5/4/1912 until readmission on 6/24/1918, and remained at Warren State Hospital until death. Classification: Schizophrenic reaction — paranoid type.

Brother (17), born 1859; died at age 50 years at Warren State Hospital of tuberculosis. He was admitted to Warren State Hospital 7/12/1906 with acute melancholia. He had suffered an attack of melancholia without hospitalization eight years previous to admission. When ill he was confused, restless, untidy, delusional, silent and unsociable. He was never discharged from Warren State Hospital. Classification: Schizophrenic reaction — chronic undifferentiated type.

Sister (20), born 1860; died at age 66 years of chronic valvular heart disease. Neighbors stated that she would leave her home and wander around at night; she would also leave her family unattended a day or two at a time. The interviewer described her laugh as without mirth and she would give no information about her psychotic brother. Classification: With functional psychosis, probable schizophrenic reaction.

(21) husband of (22), born 1857; died at age 83 years of chronic myocarditis. He was described as a "drunken, good-for-nothing sport." Classification: Probable sociopathic personality disturbance — alcoholism (addiction).

Brother (25), born 1869; suicided at age 50 years of a self-inflicted revolver wound. He left his successful rig-building and contracting business to enter into an unsuccessful farming venture because of his wife's ailing health. His son believed that, as a consequence, he was depressed before his suicide, although he had no treatment for a depression at any time during his life. Classification: Probably with functional psychosis.

Sister (29), born 1872; died at age 58 years at Warren State Hospital of uremia and cancer. At age 20 years she had an attack of depression which lasted two months, but she was otherwise described as sociable, generous, sympathetic and industrious until shortly after her marriage, at age 46, to a feeble old man who was unable to work and support her. She became restless, agitated and much distressed over the idea that someone was trying to poison her and that she was going to be burned, hanged or electrocuted. She was admitted to Warren State Hospital on 10/6/1918 with a diagnosis of manic-depressive psychosis, depressed type. She was discharged one year later and lived comfortably until 4/1/1924 when she again became very restless, unhappy, depressed and self-accusatory, and was again admitted to Warren State Hospital on 4/10/1924, with a diagnosis of manic-depressive psychosis, depressed phase. She remained hospitalized until her death. Classification: Schizophrenic reaction — paranoid type.

Nieces and Nephews

(41) husband of niece (42), born 1891; died at age 70 years of a coronary. He was described as an alcoholic but that his drinking never interfered with his work. After retirement he suffered a coronary and later developed senile changes that made it impossible for him to be cared for at home and he was hospitalized at a Veterans Hospital. Classification: Chronic brain syndrome of senium.

Nephew (61), born 1897. A few weeks after his marriage he deserted his wife, who was expecting their child. His whereabouts were unknown for 10 years. Twenty-seven years later he went back to live with his wife on her farm. There was no apparent marital discord. At age 36 years he began having "nervous spells" which came on in late summer. With the onset of nervousness he would begin to drink, with resulting belligerence, and on occasion was arrested and jailed. First hospitalization for his "nervousness" was in August, 1949 (age 52 years). He remained hospitalized until 12/14/1949, with a diagnosis of mixed psychosis—schizothymic. Readmission to Warren State Hospital was on 6/6/1955, after two weeks of sleeplessness and overtalkativeness. He was also delusional and threatened to shoot people. Diagnosis at this hospitalization and classification: Schizophrenic reaction—paranoid type.

Nephew (71), born 1894. He was described as "always irresponsible . . . he and his wife would go away for months at a time leaving the children alone . . . couldn't understand how the children survived." Classification: Personality pattern disturbance—inadequate personality.

(72) wife of nephew (71), born 1901. A child-study department report stated that the "attitude of the family is one of indifference to the real problems involved." Classification: Personality pattern disturbance—inadequate personality.

(74) husband of (75), born 1892; died at age 31 years of shock following general burns received accidentally when opening a steam valve. At the time of his death he was serving a 20-year prison term for robbery. Classification: Sociopathic personality disturbance—antisocial reaction.

(77) husband of niece (78), born 1902. He was twice described as an alcoholic. Classification: Sociopathic personality disturbance—alcoholism (addiction).

Nephew (81), born 1904. He was described as "a sadistic person . . . jealous of his own children because they occupied so much of his wife's time . . . would mistreat them at every opportunity." He was also described as "unusual" but "never irrational" and as a "heavy drinker" at one time. Classification: Probable personality disorder, either personality trait disturbance, or sociopathic personality disturbance.

(83) husband of niece (84), born 1902. He was described by three informants as an alcoholic. Classification: Sociopathic personality disturbance—alcoholism (addiction).

Nephew (85), born 1891. He described himself as a "nervous" person who had sought medical attention for his nervousness. He had a history of asthma and of a "nervous breakdown" without hospitalization before marriage. Classification: Possible psychoneurotic disorder and psychophysiologic respiratory reaction, asthma.

Distant Relatives

Grandnephew (138), born 1914; completed college as an education major and worked as an assembly line supervisor. He was hospitalized in 1957 with the following diagnosis:

(1) Severe functional nervous disorder, manifested by epigastric distress, constipation and palpitations;
(2) Cancerophobia;
(3) Chronic anxiety state; and
(4) Rectal polyps, removed.

In describing his illness for the study he considered his fears exaggerated and his absence from work for months after his hospitalization as unreasonable. Classification: Psychoneurotic disorder—anxiety reaction.

Grandniece (145), born 1922. She was upset and "nervous" for two months following the birth of her second child, who was born a few days after the death of her father, to whom she was much attached. Classification: Psychoneurotic disorder—anxiety reaction.

(162) first wife of grandnephew (163). In 1953 her children were taken from her and placed in an orphanage (two of them later were adopted). She was described as "a filthy housekeeper . . . now lives with a colored man." Classification: Personality pattern disturbance—inadequate personality.

Grandnephew (163), born 1921. He was described as an "alcoholic—now reformed." In 1951 he was in criminal court for fraudulent conversion. Classification: Sociopathic personality disturbance—antisocial reaction.

Grandnephew (183), born 1940. He was described as "always in trouble from age ten . . . started by stealing bicycles." The correctional institution where he was most recently committed was his fourth such institutional commitment. Classification: Sociopathic personality disturbance.

Grandniece (185), born 1942. At age 19 years she was considered to have normal mental health; however, as an early adolescent she was a persistent truant and was committed to the Youth Development Center at Cambridge, Pennsylvania. Classification: Transient situational personality disorder – adjustment reaction of adolescence.

Grandnephew (222), born 1917. He was described by his parents as "a hard boy to raise . . . independent . . . always ran away from home." He was "restless, footloose, drank a lot and 'borrowed' cars." At age 36 years he developed epileptic seizures which later ceased. He had a colostomy which was subsequently closed, and at age 41 years he was hospitalized with a diagnosis of personality disorder, sociopathic personality disturbance and acute brain syndrome associated with alcoholism. Classification: Probable sociopathic personality disturbance – alcoholism (addiction).

(223) husband of grandniece (224), born 1900. He went on "drunks . . . periodic drunks." Classification: Possible sociopathic personality disturbance – alcoholism (addiction).

Grandniece (224), born 1918. At age 33 years she had an operation, following which she became irritable and began showing paranoid trends (excessive hand washing) and eventually stopped cooking for her husband for fear of poisoning him. She was admitted to St. Francis Hospital, Pittsburgh, Pennsylvania, on 2/1/1954. She showed marked improvement and was discharged on 3/25/54. Diagnosis at hospitalization and classification: Schizophrenic reaction – paranoid type.

Great-grandnephew (303), born 1948. At age eight years he was sent to a military school because he was "difficult." He was also described as "antisocial but highly intelligent." Classification: Transient situational personality disorder – adjustment reaction of childhood.

Family Summary

The proband, three brothers, one sister, a nephew and a grandniece had psychotic disorders and were hospitalized because of their illnesses. The mother and another sister were psychotic but not hospitalized and another brother (who suicided) and an additional sister were probably so. Psychoneurotic disorders were found in a grandniece and in a grandnephew, who was hospitalized. Another nephew was possibly neurotic, and a daughter, a grandson, the father, a nephew and a grandnephew probably, and a daughter possibly so. A maternal uncle and a niece's husband were classified as with chronic brain syndrome of senium and the niece's husband was hospitalized with this disability. A sister's husband, a niece's husband and a grandniece's husband were alcoholics. A daughter-in-law was neurotic and a nephew's wife, a niece's husband and a grandnephew's wife had personality disorders. The proband's parents had 12 children, 40 grandchildren, 86 great-grandchildren, 165 great-great-grandchildren and one great-great-great-grandchild.

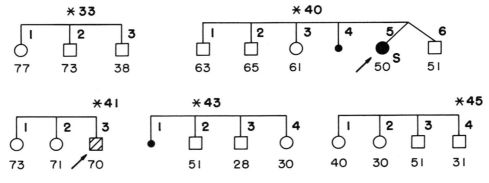

Controls

Sister (5) of (40), born 1910; died at age 50 years of suicide by jumping from a third floor apartment window. She was described as "not too happy as a child, although she (later) enjoyed parties and going out with boys." Her father died when she was three years of age and she was raised in "straitened circumstances" by her mother and older sister. She married, against the advice of her family, a man who was an alcoholic and "some sort of sexual deviate." Between the years of 1949 and 1959 she was hospitalized several times at a general hospital for neuropsychiatric treatment and made several suicide attempts. Diagnosis was emotional personality disorder, passive dependent type. Classification: Psychotic-depressive reaction.

See family pedigree, person 41.

SCHIZOPHRENIA
(EARLIER DIAGNOSED
AS AFFECTIVE PSYCHOSIS)

Thirty probands were considered at the time of reclassification as being schizophrenic, whereas the earlier diagnosis had been of a different disorder. Four of these had been unclassified during the 1912–1917 study, while the others had diagnoses of melancholia, mania, or manic-depressive psychosis (see Table 2–2). Recent reclassification led to the diagnosis of schizophrenia in all of these cases.

According to some characteristics, this group appeared to be intermediate between the more clearly affective and schizophrenic groups. In general, the parameters closely resembled those of the last group (schizophrenic), and in most tabulations these two groups are pooled.

The kinships presented here are: WSH 11, 14, 17, 18, 21, 25, 30, 33, 34, 44, 50, 53, 57, 58, 60, 64, 68, 71, 74, 75, 77, 84, 88, 89, 93, 94, 95, 96, 97 and 98.

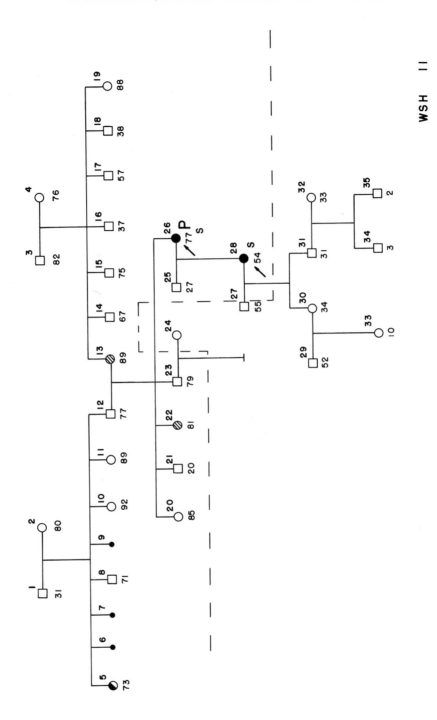

WSH 11: The Proband

Proband (26), born 1884; died at age 77 years of cerebral hemorrhage. She graduated as valedictorian from a private school at age 20 years. After six months of nurse's training she quit because of nervousness. At age 22 years she was widowed and left with a seven-weeks-old daughter. Although subject to "blue spells" she did not develop psychotic symptoms until October, 1914 at 30 years of age, when she became agitated, noisy and restless. She also developed delusions of poverty and made a suicide attempt by hanging with a towel. On 2/4/1915 she was admitted to a mental hospital with a diagnosis of dementia praecox, catatonic type. When discharged two months later she was unimproved, but soon recovered and remained well until late 1916, when she became irritable, fault-finding, expansive in her ideas and extravagant. She made arrangements for gynecological operations which were not necessary; she was talkative and flighty, unable to rest at night and unable to concentrate during the day. Second hospitalization was at Warren State Hospital from 1/13/1917 until 10/6/1917, with a diagnosis of manic-depressive psychosis, manic phase of the circular type. Third hospitalization was at a different state hospital from September, 1927 until October, 1931, with a diagnosis of manic-depressive psychosis — hypomania. Fourth hospitalization was at still another hospital from 6/1/1934 until she was transferred to a county home on 1/6/1952. Official discharge from the hospital was on 6/28/1955. Diagnosis was manic-depressive — manic phase, although the cardinal psychotic symptoms included many of those of a schizophrenic process. At various times she was noisy, destructive, disoriented, constantly talking with flight of ideas, distracted, manneristic, and had bizarre somatic complaints and was silly. Classification: Schizophrenic reaction — schizo-affective type.

Children

Daughter (28), born 1908. Her father died when she was seven weeks of age. She and her mother lived with her grandparents and other relatives. When she was six, and again when she was nine years of age, her mother was hospitalized with mental illness. Her first psychotic episode was at age 16 years. Immediately after graduation from high school she married a man described as "an intelligent, understanding person." The second psychotic episode developed at age 49 years when she became restless, expressed the idea that she was an FBI agent and attempted suicide by cutting her wrists and drinking poison. She was subsequently treated at a state hospital and then at a mental health clinic where her diagnosis was schizophrenia-paranoid, and idiopathic epilepsy with convulsive seizures, petit mal. The following year, on 3/7/1959, she was admitted to another state hospital with a diagnosis of schizophrenic reaction, schizo-affective type. On 8/25/1962 she was interviewed while home for a visit and described as "intelligent... handled herself well as far as social functioning was concerned." She still seemed actively psychotic and confided to the interviewer that she was a "non-paid informer for the FBI." In January, 1963 she went home on a trial visit and at last information had not returned to the hospital. Classification: Schizophrenic reaction.

Parents

Mother (13), born 1853; died at age 89 years, cause of death unknown. She was described as a "nervous, excitable, unstable woman" as well as "very loquacious." When interviewed she was found to be "hospitable and kind-hearted." Classification: Probable psychoneurotic disorder.

Aunts and Uncles

Paternal aunt (5), born 1847; died at age 73 years of cancer. She reportedly became "deranged and was insane for some time" at about age 35 years. She had no recurrence of her "insanity" and was described later as "lovable" but inclined to worry. Classifica-

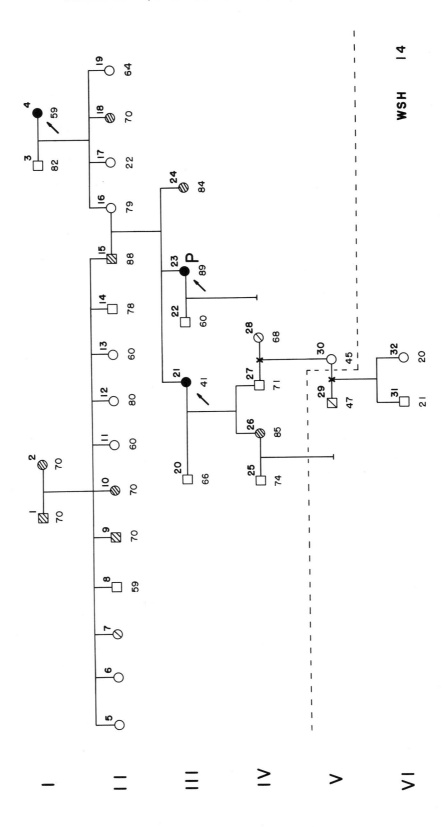

tion: Probably with functional psychosis, involutional psychotic reaction.

Siblings

Sister (22), born 1881. At age 81 years she was described as "sickly" with pernicious anemia, arthritis and gall bladder trouble. She reportedly had "hysterical ten-dencies." Classification: Psychoneurotic disorder.

Family Summary

The proband and her daughter had psychotic disorders and a paternal aunt probably so. The mother and a sister were neurotic.

WSH 14: The Proband

Proband (23), born 1859; died at age 84 years of chronic cardiovascular renal disease. She was reportedly "well educated, friendly, of perfectly normal mind" until after her marriage at age 28 years when she first developed symptoms of mental illness, although the symptoms were never described. At age 42 years she had an attack which lasted one week and had two additional "irrational periods" or "manic attacks" associated with physical illness before her admission to Warren State Hospital on 3/10/1917, with a diagnosis of cyclothymic reaction to stress and illness. She was discharged six months later and was never again hospitalized. She had been ill with the grippe while caring for her mother who also had the grippe, but who developed pneumonia and died just previous to her (23) admission to Warren State Hospital. Classification: Schizophrenic reaction— paranoid type.

Grandparents

Paternal grandfather (1); died at "over 70 years of age" of cancer of the face. He was described as "quiet and retiring—overly particular and nice about his work" as a carpenter and as "very quiet though not at all lovable." Classification: Possible personality trait disturbance— compulsive personality.

Paternal grandmother (2); died at age 70 years of hemorrhage of the lungs. She was described as "a very talkative woman who showed great determination...she had a quick temper and was hard to get on with...a great worker who saw to it that all her family worked very hard." Classification: Possible personality disorder.

Maternal grandmother (4), born 1821; died at age 59 years of "complication of diseases" at a state mental hospital. She was described as a "sociable, talkative, bright, capable woman who had excellent taste" and who married young. She "lost her health" soon after the birth of the proband's mother. She later "became insane" and was hospitalized at the state mental hospital on 10/1/1880, where she died two months later. She had delusions of persecution and "thought people were trying to kill her." Classification: Schizophrenic reaction.

Parents

Father (15), born 1828; died at age 88 years of la grippe. He was described as a "brutal, ugly-tempered man who went off into insane rages...swore and abused his family shockingly." Classification: Probable personality pattern disturbance—paranoid personality.

Aunts and Uncles

Paternal uncle (9); died "past 70" years of age of paralysis. He was described as with an "ugly, disagreeable disposition," was "abusive to his family" and "taunted his son and drove him from home when the son joined the church." Classification: Probable personality disorder.

Paternal aunt (10); died at age 70 years of cancer. In the years preceding her death she "became skeptical and bitter toward anything orthodox...quarrelsome and disagreeable." She intended to "disinherit her daughter and give the valuable property to strangers" but died before the plan could be executed. Classification: Probable personality disorder.

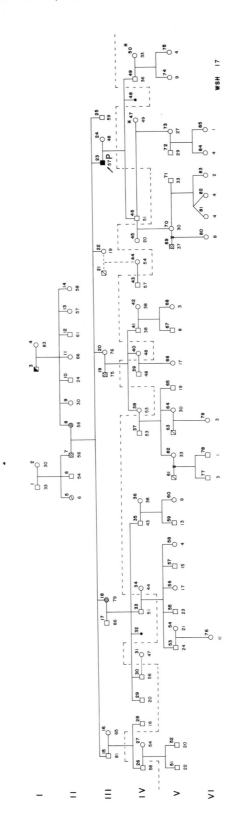

Maternal aunt (18); at age 70 years described as "very queer . . . not interested in her work . . . does not care for company." Classification: Probable personality disorder.

Siblings

Sister (21), born 1856; died at age 41 years of cancer of the breast at Warren State Hospital. She experienced an episode of incoherence which lasted about nine months after the birth of her first child at age 22 years. At age 33 years she was hospitalized at Warren State Hospital, with a diagnosis of acute mania, where she remained, except for a period of 16 months, until she died. Her illness was characterized by excitement, violence and occasionally talkativeness and destructiveness. Classification: Schizophrenic reaction — catatonic type.

Sister (24), born 1863; died at age 84 years of bronchopneumonia with contributory senility and malnutrition. In mid-life she was described as "in very delicate health and of a nervous disposition." Classification: Possible psychoneurotic reaction and possible chronic brain syndrome of senium.

Nieces and Nephews

Niece (26), born 1878; died at age 85 years of arteriosclerosis. She reportedly had "nervous trouble from time to time." At age 64 years she was described as "cooperative and helpful." Classification: Possible psychoneurotic disorder.

Family Summary

The proband, a sister and the maternal grandmother had psychotic disorders. Personality disorders were discovered in the paternal grandparents, the father, two aunts and an uncle. A sister and a niece were neurotic.

WSH 17: The Proband

Proband (23), born 1892; died at age 57 years of pneumonia. He was described as a generous, kind-hearted person who was an excellent workman (he was a cabinet maker). At about age 24 years he was given some highly desirable piecework to do. The promotion caused some gossip in the workshop. He consequently began to be suspicious of people and within two months had become so threatening to his coworkers that he was discharged from work. He became sleepless, dazed, confused and was hospitalized at Warren State Hospital from 1/22/1917 until 8/14/1917, with hallucinations and great apprehension. Diagnosis at Warren State Hospital was dementia praecox. He was greatly improved at discharge and was never again hospitalized. Classification: Schizophrenic reaction — paranoid type.

Grandchildren

(69) husband of granddaughter (70), born 1927. He was a high school graduate and laborer who was described as irresponsible and unable to hold a job. Classification: Possible personality disorder.

Grandparents

Maternal grandfather (3), born 1840. He was known to have a "violent, ungovernable temper" and was described as "insane and mentally ill" by various family members. Classification: Possibly with functional psychosis.

Parents

Father (7), born 1861. At age 56 years he was described as of a "nervous temperament." Classification: Possible psychoneurotic disorder.

Mother (8), born 1861. At age 56 years she was described as "emotionally unstable and high strung." She had a "complete nervous breakdown" after her daughter's death following an illegitimate pregnancy. Classification: Psychoneurotic disorder.

Siblings

Sister (18), born 1885. In 1955 she had a "nervous breakdown" and was "unconscious for two months." Her physician didn't expect her to live. Previously she had "spells" described in her hospital record when under treatment for a broken hip as generalized choreic convulsions. At age 79 years she was described as a helpful and cooperative informant. Classification: Probable psychoneurotic disorder.

(19) husband of sister (20), born 1889. A retired automobile factory worker who, relatives say, lost his job because of drinking; he "drank more after retirement." Classification: Sociopathic personality disturbance—alcoholism (addiction).

Family Summary

The proband had a psychotic disorder and the maternal grandfather possibly so. The father and mother and a sister were

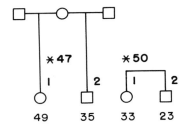

CONTROLS

W S H   I 7

neurotic. The husbands of a sister and of a granddaughter had personality disorders.

Controls

None noteworthy.

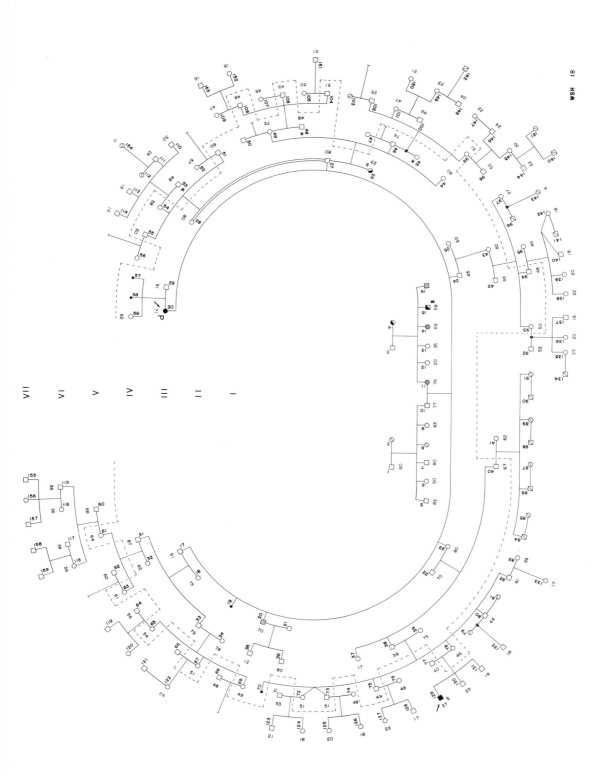

WSH 18: The Proband

Proband (30), born 1863; died at age 71 years of cardiorenal vascular disease. The first attack of mental illness occurred at age 14 years following typhoid fever. While ill she refused to talk to anyone and upon recovery was "slovenly and flighty." The second attack followed the birth of her first child when she became "excited, violent and destructive." This attack lasted five months with a gradual recovery. There was an 18-year interval before the next attack at age 40 years, when she was again "noisy, excited and destructive." During this attack she was hospitalized at Dunham's Sanitarium for three months. There were succeeding similar attacks lasting about six months each at ages 42, 43, 47 and 50 years for which she was hospitalized. On 11/8/1915 she was admitted to Warren State Hospital with a diagnosis of manic-depressive psychosis, manic phase, and was discharged in 1916 but rehospitalized at Warren in 1920 and again in 1923. There were three subsequent hospitalizations at other hospitals before her death. She was described as "quiet and gentle" between attacks. As her disease progressed she was occasionally mute; she developed paranoid ideas and at times had to be fed by nurses. Classification: Schizophrenic reaction—schizo-affective type.

Grandparents

Maternal grandmother (4). She was described as "insane" for years. Classification: Probably with functional psychosis.

Parents

Mother (11), born 1824; died at age 76 years of pneumonia. She was described as an intelligent, conscientious woman with remarkable business ability but also as "very peculiar." She was excitable and would "worry herself almost insane." She became "deranged" a year before her death. Classification: Probable chronic brain syndrome of senium.

Aunts and Uncles

Maternal aunt (14), died at age 69 years of grippe. She was reported "insane" for

two years before her death. Classification: Chronic brain syndrome of senium.

Maternal uncle (15); committed suicide by strangulation at age 58 years. He was described as a "queer" man who lived alone in the woods after his wife divorced him. Classification: Probably with functional psychosis.

Maternal uncle (16), born 1833; died at age 63 years of pneumonia. He was described as "queer . . . unsociable but a good worker . . . kind to his family but lacking in common sense." A year before his death he became insane. Classification: Probable chronic brain syndrome of senium.

Siblings

Brother (20), born 1849; died at age 70 years of a heart attack. He completed a business school course and worked as a farmer-bookkeeper. He reportedly was "very peculiar" and was "inclined to exaggerate and to get excited over schemes which never worked out." Classification: Possible personality trait disturbance—passive-aggressive personality.

(26) wife of brother (27), born 1860; died at age 23 years of suicide by poison. She had been despondent for a short time before her suicide and left a note not to blame her husband. Classification: Probably with functional psychosis, psychotic depressive reaction.

Distant Relatives

Great-grandnephew (129), born 1935. First symptoms of mental disturbance were at age 12 years when he became depressed and withdrawn. At age 20 years he received four months private treatment by a psychiatrist. Within the next year his father died in a car accident. He became mute and fearful, which necessitated hospitalization. At hospitalization he complained of distressing self-consciousness and lack of self-confidence. He made two suicide attempts while hospitalized and on medication. Insulin shock therapy brought about an improvement and he was released in custody of his mother after four months of hospitalization. Classification: Schizophrenic reaction—catatonic type.

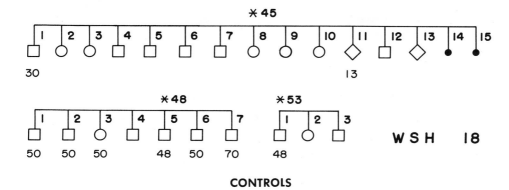

CONTROLS

Family Summary

The proband and a great-grandnephew had psychotic disorders and the maternal grandmother, a maternal uncle and the wife of a brother probably so. The mother, a maternal aunt and a maternal uncle were classified as chronic brain syndrome of senium. A brother had a possible personality disorder.

Controls

None noteworthy.

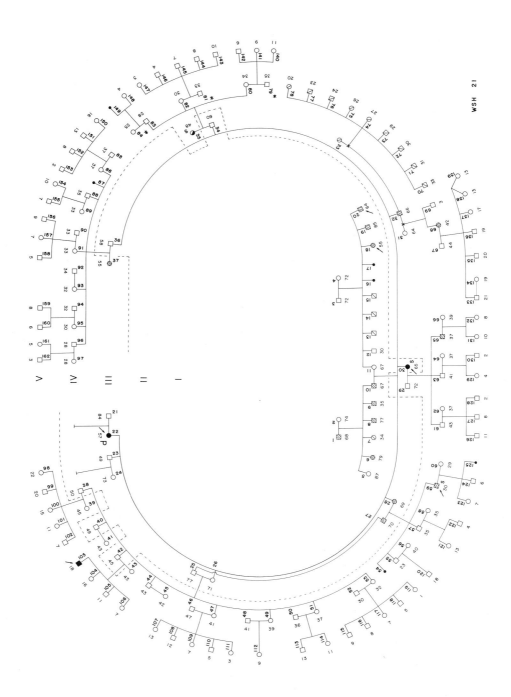

WSH 21

WSH 21: The Proband

Proband (22), born 1886; died at age 60 years at Warren State Hospital of pulmonary tuberculosis. She began showing mental symptoms slowly while hospitalized for "stomach trouble" at age 32 years. At admission to Warren State Hospital on 9/7/1916 she was described as "devoid of ideas, evasive, disinterested and auditorily hallucinated." A diagnosis of unclassified with a preference for schizophrenia, hebephrenic type, was made. She improved considerably and was discharged on 10/18/1919. Her family considered her to be normal for the next 15 years until she underwent an appendectomy, after which she displayed a marked agitated depressive reaction. She developed paranoid delusions and symptoms similar to those present at her first hospitalization and was readmitted on 7/18/1933. Diagnosis at second admission was atypical manic-depressive depression. Classification: Schizophrenic reaction — catatonic type.

Grandparents

Paternal grandfather (1); died at age 68 years of "dropsy" or "stroke." He was described as a "steady drinker" and also as "strong" and well until the day of his death. Classification: Possible sociopathic personality disturbance — alcoholism (addiction).

Parents

Father (10), born 1860; died at age 67 years of cellulitis of the neck. He was described as a "practical, thrifty farmer" yet "very easily worried." Classification: Possible psychoneurotic disorder.

Aunts and Uncles

Paternal aunt (6), born 1864; died at age 79 years of cardiac decompensation. She reportedly had a "very nervous temperament" and at one time had a "nervous breakdown" from which she completely recovered. Classification: Probable psychoneurotic reaction — other.

Paternal uncle (8), born 1862; died at age 77 years of a cerebral hemorrhage. He was described as "a steady drinker." Classification: Probable sociopathic personality disturbance — alcoholism (addiction).

Paternal uncle (9); described as "happy-go-lucky" and "a steady drinker." He left home after the death of his mother when he was 35 years of age and was never heard of again. Classification: Probable sociopathic personality disturbance — alcoholism (addiction).

Maternal aunt (18); died at age 55 years of carcinoma of the rectum. She was described as a "high strung, emotional woman" who, at age 28 years, after an emotional shock, was incapacitated for weeks with insomnia, anorexia and gastric disturbances. At age 50 years, after a hemorrhoidectomy, she "became obsessed with the idea of insanity" and "lost control over her thoughts." About three years later, on 10/16/1928, she was admitted to Warren State Hospital with a diagnosis of neurasthenia. She improved slightly and was released on 10/1/1929 for care in a general hospital. Classification: Psychoneurotic disorder — anxiety reaction.

Maternal uncle (19), born 1872; died at age 85 years of "softening of the brain." Classification: Possible chronic brain syndrome of senium.

Maternal uncle (20), born 1871; died at age 64 years of a cardiovascular accident at Warren State Hospital. He was well, except for "gas on his stomach for many years," until his first heart attack at age 52 years. Seven years later he had a stroke, followed in four weeks by a second stroke. After the second stroke he became delirious, overactive, untidy; he developed speech difficulties, memory defects, paranoid delusions and became suicidal. He was admitted to Warren State Hospital, where he remained until death. Classification: Chronic brain syndrome associated with circulatory disturbance — with psychotic reaction.

Siblings

(27) husband of sister (28), born 1890; died at age 70 years of cerebral thrombosis. The Army clinical record stated that he had "suffered from emotional illness" since age 57 years. Classification: Psychoneurotic disorder.

Sister (28), born 1893. She was interviewed at age 69 years and described as friendly and cooperative. She stated that her life had been "one problem after another with little happiness in-between." Classification: Psychoneurotic disorder.

Sister (30), born 1898. Her childhood was normal. She graduated from grade eight as valedictorian; however, she was forced to leave school and give up her teaching ambitions for economic reasons. In 1948, after a son returned from the military in an excited state and another son married, she had a depressive reaction and attempted suicide with sleeping pills. She reportedly had electroshock treatments as an outpatient at a mental hospital in 1952. In July, 1963, she became restless, sleepless, irritable and afraid to be alone; she thought she was losing her mind and had suicidal thoughts. When admitted to a mental hospital on 9/6/1963 she appeared depressed, apathetic and tense and felt guilty over her suicidal thoughts. She was paroled on 1/28/1964. When interviewed she was friendly and cooperative. The interviewer described her memory as "exceptional" and her mental health as "O.K." Classification: Involutional psychotic reaction.

Brother (32), born 1895. At last information, at age 66 years, he was working as a milk truck driver. He and his wife had separated; his "drinking" was reportedly one of the problems. Classification: Sociopathic personality disturbance — alcoholism (addiction).

(35) wife of brother (34), born 1905; died at age 48 years of suicide by hanging. She reportedly had periods of depression and feared being committed to a mental hospital. Classification: Probably with functional psychosis, paranoid reaction.

(37) wife of brother (36), born 1907. When interviewed at age 55 years she had a "series of hypochondriacal complaints"; she had difficulty during menopause when she experienced severe anxiety and had a spastic colon from age 35 years. Classification: Probable psychoneurotic disorder.

Nieces and Nephews

Nephew (59), born 1932. He was described as "always high strung and nervous." At age 15 years he attempted suicide by placing a gun to his head and pulling the trigger; miraculously, the firing pin was broken and the gun did not fire. He was first seen by a psychiatrist on a weekly basis at Army basic training camp after induction in January, 1953. Previous to this he had sought medical attention for his nervousness from his family physician. After six months in the service he received a neuropsychiatric discharge with a diagnosis of passive dependency reaction, chronic, severe, manifested by clinging, inefficiency and helplessness; predisposition, severe; lifetime history of dependency; stress, none; and incapacity, severe. He described his life as "a series of nervous breakdowns" as far back as he could remember. Classification: Personality trait disturbance.

Nephew (65), born 1925. He reportedly was "quite nervous" after returning from World War II. He was also described as a "nervous wreck" at that time. Classification: Probable psychoneurotic disorder.

Niece (68), born 1920. She was a housewife who reportedly "drank to the point of intoxication." When interviewed she was cooperative and her mental health "seemed O.K." Classification: Probable sociopathic personality disturbance — alcoholism (addiction).

Distant Relatives

Grandnephew (103), born 1944. Until age 14 years he was a "model boy." At age 15 years he began stealing his father's car, his school grades dropped and he exhibited mood swings from elation to depressed, "sleepy" periods. He fluctuated between being honest and extremely dishonest and felt no remorse or regret for his bizarre behavior. Admission to a state mental hospital was on 11/3/1961, with a diagnosis of schizophrenic reaction, schizo-affective type; parole was approved on 5/12/1962. Classification: Schizophrenic reaction — chronic undifferentiated type.

Family Summary

The proband, a sister and a grandnephew had psychotic disorders and a wife of a brother probably so. The father, a sister,

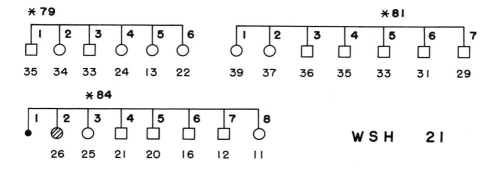

WSH   21

CONTROLS

a nephew, a paternal and a maternal aunt, the husband of a sister and the wife of a brother were neurotic. A maternal uncle was hospitalized with chronic brain syndrome associated with circulatory disturbance with psychotic reaction. Another maternal uncle was classified as with possible chronic brain syndrome of senium. Personality disorders were found in a brother, two paternal uncles, the paternal grandfather, a nephew and a niece.

Controls

Sister (2) of (84), born 1936. At age 26 years she was described as a "chronic complainer" whose complaints about her health had no physical basis. Classification: Probable psychoneurotic reaction.

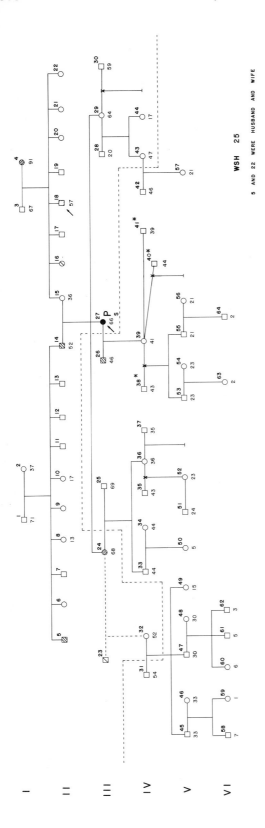

WSH 25

5 AND 22 WERE HUSBAND AND WIFE

WSH 25: The Proband

Proband (27), born 1895. She was reportedly moody, irritable and unmanageable as a child. At about age 20 years she became indifferent to her surroundings, depressed and withdrawn, and was admitted to a state mental hospital where she remained for six weeks. Diagnosis was dementia praecox, catatonic type. After her return home she remained indifferent and idle and attempted suicide by taking poison. Later that year she became irritable, abusive and violent and was admitted to Warren State Hospital on 1/21/1916. Delusions of a persecutory nature were present at the time of admission. Her other symptoms were described as typical of maniacal excitement and a diagnosis of manic-depressive psychosis, manic phase, circular form, was made. There was a subsequent hospitalization at Warren State Hospital in late 1926. In 1945 she became very nervous, worried, excited, had delusions of persecution, and was hospitalized at a state mental hospital for two years. She improved and at age 66 years was working as a domestic. Classification: Schizophrenic reaction — paranoid type.

(26) husband of proband (27), born 1894. He was a day laborer who was described as "constantly chasing women." He never made a home or living for his wife and deserted her after nine years of marriage. He returned many years later at age 46 years and tried to re-establish the marriage but she was not interested. His whereabouts were unknown after that. Classification: Probable sociopathic personality disturbance.

Grandparents

Maternal grandmother (4), born 1825; last known at age 91 years when she was described as a "senile psychotic." Classification: Possible chronic brain syndrome of senium.

Parents

Father (14), born 1861; died at age 52 years of cancer of the stomach. He was described as "a seclusive drinker," dis-

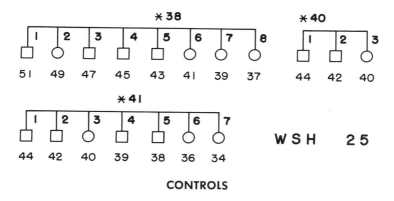

CONTROLS

agreeable, quick-tempered and also as discouraged and melancholy. He reportedly did not support his wife and children adequately. Classification: Possible personality pattern disturbance—inadequate personality.

Aunts and Uncles

Paternal uncle (5), born 1848; age and cause of death unknown. He was described as ill-tempered and easily intoxicated when younger and as chronically ill in old age. Classification: Possible personality pattern disturbance—inadequate personality.

Maternal uncle (18), born 1846; died at age 57 years of exhaustion of paresis at Warren State Hospital where he was a patient from 11/14/1902 until his death. The first symptoms of central nervous system syphilis began in 1901. Classification: Chronic brain syndrome associated with meningoencephalitic syphilis with psychotic reaction.

Siblings

Sister (24), born 1893; at age 68 years a housewife described as nervous, distractible and probably "not too bright." She thought she had ulcers but there was no medical evidence to substantiate her belief. A later interviewer described her as eccentric, but definitely not psychotic. Classification: Possible psychoneurotic disorder.

Family Summary

The proband was psychotic and a maternal uncle was hospitalized with a psychotic reaction to central nervous system syphilis. The maternal grandmother was classified as possible chronic brain syndrome of senium. A sister was neurotic. Personality disorders were found in the father, a paternal uncle and in the husband of the proband.

Controls

None noteworthy.

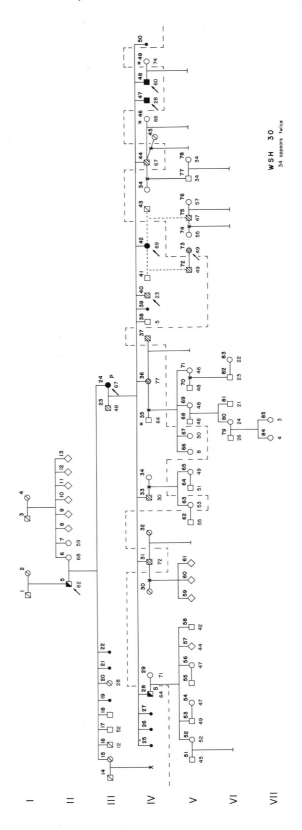

WSH 30
34 appears twice

WSH 30: The Proband

Proband (24), born 1863; died at age 67 years of acute cardiac dilatation at Warren State Hospital. She had a six-year history of periodic attacks of mania prior to her first admission to Warren State Hospital on 4/18/1887, with a diagnosis of periodic mania. She was discharged on 10/1/1887, but had seven subsequent hospitalizations, all less than two years in duration except the last which was from 8/12/1912 until her death on 10/13/1930. Diagnoses at the subsequent hospitalizations were acute mania, puerperal mania, periodic mania, periodic mania, recurrent mania, recurrent mania and manic-depressive psychosis—hypomanic phase. Each attack was characterized by excitement, restlessness, confusion and talkativeness. She had no periods of depression. She married at age 19 years and had 12 children and three miscarriages. Because of her illness and her husband's irresponsibility, the children were either put up for adoption or forced to become self-supporting at a very young age. Classification: Schizophrenic reaction—schizo-affective type.

(23) husband of proband (24), born 1858; died at age 48 years of pernicious anemia. He was described as "intelligent but shiftless." He was once a hotel owner but lost the hotel because of "shiftlessness and alcoholism"; he later worked as a carpenter. A daughter described him as "a drunkard who never did anything but drink." Classification: Sociopathic personality disturbance—alcoholism (addiction).

Children

Son (28), born 1883; died at age 64 years of bichloride of mercury poisoning. His death was ruled a suicide. He had "very little" education and worked variously as a wagon maker, a blacksmith and a teamster. He was self-supporting from age 12 years. He was described as "quiet... never surly or disagreeable" and very healthy mentally and physically until shortly before his death when he suffered a stroke. He then had to quit work and became depressed. Classification: Probably with functional psychosis.

Son (31), born 1884; died at age 72 years of hypostatic pneumonia and cancer. Although he had little education and was self-supporting from a young age, he became owner of a grocery and trucking business. He changed his name after his divorce from his first wife. When last seen by relatives he made unreasonable complaints about the service at a family picnic (he preferred to eat with many small dishes around him and there were too few at the picnic) and was described as "nervous" and as with "an inferiority complex." Classification: Probable psychoneurotic disorder.

Son (33), born 1885; last known at age 30 years when he deserted his wife and two children and "went West." When very young he was described as "rather wild and restless... wandered all over the country." He drank a good deal but later seemed to settle down and appeared "steadier and more ambitious." One family member described him as "light-hearted and full of fun." Classification: Probable sociopathic personality disturbance.

Daughter (36), born 1887. At age 77 years she was interviewed. She rather enjoyed telling how deprived she was in childhood and how hard she had to work then and later on. She bragged inoffensively about what she had achieved despite handicaps, as her foster mother, who made her work very hard and gave her little opportunity to attend school, died when she was 13 years of age and she was then on her own. When young she was described as "stubborn, easily excitable and not inclined to communicate her troubles or show her grief." She was unable to get along with her first husband and was very hostile toward her second husband. Classification: Possible personality trait disturbance.

(37) husband of daughter (36); died in 1938, age and cause of death unknown. He was a ship's cook and described as a "wanderer." Classification: Possible personality disorder.

Son (40), born 1893. He was reportedly hospitalized at a mental hospital in 1915, but no records could be located. At age 23 years, the last time any family member heard from him, he stated in a letter that he was very nervous. Classification: Probable psychoneurotic disorder.

Daughter (42), born 1895. At age 69 years she was a patient at Warren State Hospital, where she had been since age 25 years. This was her third hospitalization; the first was for nine months in 1917–1918 and the second from November, 1918 until February, 1920. She was adopted at age nine months into a "good home...with every possible advantage." As a child she was neat and industrious but abnormally sensitive and had prolonged crying spells. She was promiscuous in her sexual activities from age 14 years and had two illegitimate children before admission to Warren State Hospital. At age 16 years she had a period of excitement lasting four days; at ages 18 and 20 years she had other brief periods of excitement. About three days before her first hospitalization she became very active, noisy and destructive. At admission she was described as talkative, silly, distractible and indifferent to her surroundings. When last seen she was described as "quite old, less excited, did not remember people and was bedridden." Preferred diagnosis at Warren State Hospital was dementia praecox—catatonic type, with an alternative diagnosis of manic-depressive—manic type. Classification: Schizophrenic reaction—catatonic type.

Son (44), born 1897. At age 67 years he was described as "somewhat loud" and "what he said was not well organized" but there was "no reason to doubt his essential balance." He was considered "a little touched" at age 20 years when he wanted to marry a 60-year-old woman. Classification: Possible personality trait disturbance—schizoid personality.

Son (47), born 1899; died at age 28 years at Warren State Hospital of congestive edema of the lungs and chronic myocarditis. He was placed in the county home at age three years and supported himself as a laborer from age 13 years. At age 16 years his personality changed and he became insolent, unruly and easily dissatisfied. A few months later he became irrational and impulsive, developed persecutory delusions and began to wander around at night. He was sent to a county home on 11/9/1914, and transferred to Warren State Hospital in February, 1915. His course at the hospital was deteriorative and was marked by short periods of confusion and excitement. A diagnosis of catatonic dementia praecox was made. Eventually he took no food, held strange, stiff positions and died in 1927. Classification: Schizophrenic reaction—catatonic type.

Son (48), born 1901. He was adopted at age five weeks. There was no unnatural behavior observed during infancy or childhood. In June, 1917, at age 16 years, he became hallucinated and entertained ideas of reference. This episode cleared up but in October, 1917, he became suspicious, indifferent, talked irrationally, refused to sleep and was hallucinated. The episodes of peculiar behavior alternated with periods of "listless, stupid" behavior until he was hospitalized at Warren State Hospital in December, 1918, with a diagnosis of dementia praecox, hebephrenic type. From the time of discharge from Warren State Hospital in February, 1919, until about one week before his second admission on 1/17/1930, he was reasonably well with mild, restless periods occurring occasionally. He then became "disheveled, maniacal, destructive and profane." At admission he was quiet and cooperative and remained so until his parole in June, 1930. Diagnosis at the second hospitalization was manic-depressive psychosis—hypomanic phase. At age 60 years he was still out of the hospital and working as a janitor. Classification: Schizophrenic reaction—paranoid type.

Grandchildren

Grandson (72), born 1914. At age 49 years he was a carnival worker who was described as a "born gambler" and former alcoholic who quit drinking because of an ulcer. His family said that he always had "itchy feet" and his wife reported that he was not a very affectionate man and did not want children. Classification: Sociopathic personality disturbance.

(73) wife of grandson (72), born 1914. At age 49 years she was a carnival worker who had been hospitalized twice at a state mental hospital with a diagnosis of psychoneurotic reaction, anxiety reaction. The first hospitalization was from 2/28/1958 until 3/31/1958. She had been tense and fearful for many years and the death of her mother in December, 1957 greatly upset her. Her husband had to leave town with his carnival work almost immediately after her discharge. She again became tense and anxious with headaches and returned to the hospital where she remained for another five months. She was not rehospitalized. Clas-

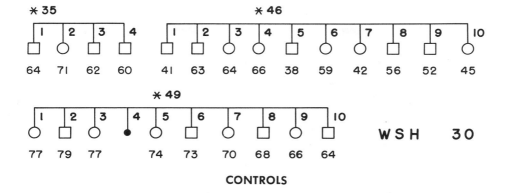

CONTROLS

sification: Psychoneurotic disorder—anxiety reaction.

Grandson (75), born 1916. He was adopted when very young by his mother's foster mother. At age 47 years he worked as a janitor and was described as "a worrier and very nervous . . . almost everything bothers him . . . no sense of humor . . . cannot understand when you are kidding him." Classification: Psychoneurotic disorder.

Parents

Father (5), died at age 62 years in Germany, of pneumonia. At middle age he became so upset and worried after his grist mill burned that he was hospitalized for two years in a mental hospital. He remained well after his return home. Classification: Probably with functional psychosis.

Family Summary

The proband, two sons and a daughter had psychotic reactions and another son and the father were probably psychotic. The husband of the proband, two sons, a daughter, a daughter's husband and a grandson had personality disorders. Two sons, a grandson and the wife of a grandson were neurotic.

Controls

None noteworthy.

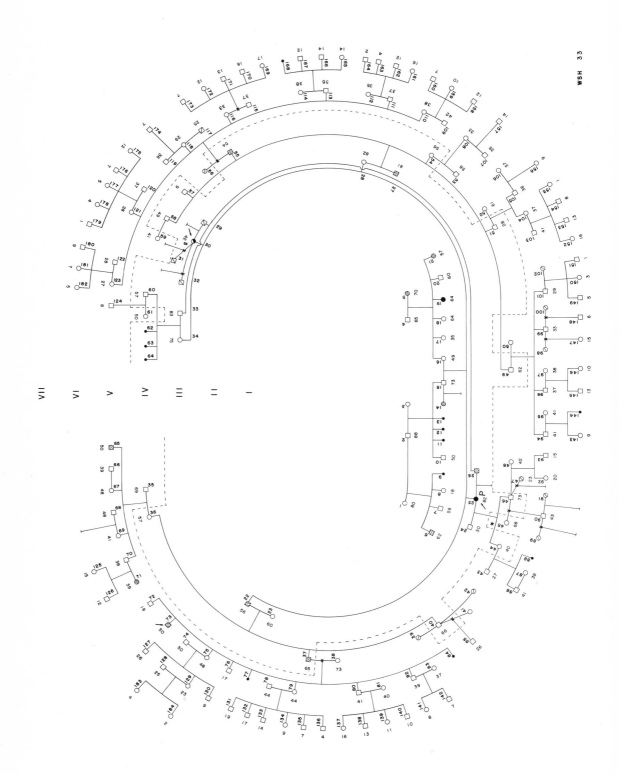

WSH 33

WSH 33: The Proband

The proband (25), born 1870; died at age 82 years at Warren State Hospital of cancer of the uterus. As an adolescent she was treated cruelly by her stepmother. She married at age 17 years and was described as "silly, flighty, loud, excitable and high-tempered" at the time of her marriage. About a year later, on 9/17/1888, she was admitted to Warren State Hospital in a state of depression and confusion. Three weeks previously she had become incoherent and had jumped out a window because she thought the house was on fire. Diagnosis at admission was melancholia. She was released as improved on 2/22/1889 and remained normal until early in 1895 when, while ill from a possible miscarriage, she was told of her husband's accidental death. She went into a "raving state" and was readmitted to Warren State Hospital on 4/9/1895. On admission she was excited, confused and destructive, but improved and was released on 1/1/1896. After the death of her first husband she became sexually promiscuous, but later married a brother of her sister's husband. In 1915 she attended a religious revival meeting during which she became very excited and imagined she could cure people. She was readmitted to Warren State Hospital where she remained until her death. At admission she was "noisy, untidy and playful." Diagnosis was manic-depressive, manic phase. She later developed many visual and auditory hallucinations as well as many delusions. Classification: Schizophrenic reaction—paranoid type.

(26) second husband of proband (25); died when "quite old" of tuberculosis. He was described as a "shiftless drunkard." Classification: Probable sociopathic personality disturbance—alcoholism (addiction).

Grandparents

Maternal grandmother (5); died at age 70 years, cause of death unknown. She reportedly had "ugly spells and an irritable, scolding personality." At age 45 years she had "collapsed" and was bedridden for nine years, but gradually recovered. The nature of the "collapse" was unknown. Classification: Psychoneurotic disorder.

Parents

(14) second wife of father (15). Her stepchildren hated her because she was harsh, irritable and verbally abusive. Classification: Possible personality trait disturbance—passive-aggressive personality.

Aunts and Uncles

Paternal half-uncle (6), born 1854. At age 62 years he was still single and described as a cranky, irritable fellow who drank to excess. He was also described as "a lazy, ineffectual man who never worked more than a week or two at a time." Classification: Personality pattern disturbance—inadequate personality.

Maternal aunt (19), died at age 64 years of a heart attack. As a young woman she was described as cheerful and good-natured as well as submissive and lacking in will power. Morphine was prescribed for a severe kidney problem during her third pregnancy. She became addicted and used it until three or four years before her death. As she grew older she became dull, inactive, and practically helpless. About three years before her death she developed an illness which she attributed to morphine and refused further use of the drug as she thought it would kill her. At this time she developed mild epileptiform seizures. She later became irritable and developed the delusion that there were prostitutes in her upstairs rooms and imagined that her husband was unfaithful. Classification: Schizophrenic reaction—paranoid type.

Maternal aunt (21), born 1859. When interviewed at age 57 years she was described as well-dressed, gracious and intelligent. Family members described her as nervous, peculiar and critical; when excited she would "lose control of herself and go into screaming spells." Classification: Personality trait disturbance—emotionally unstable personality.

Siblings

Brother (22), born 1868; died at age 56 years of a heart attack. He was described as "wild" when young; he drank heavily and was "jolly" although rather quick-tem-

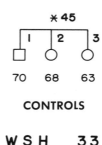

CONTROLS

W S H   33

pered. Classification: Probable transient situational personality disorder—adult situational reaction.

(27) husband of sister (28), born 1877; died at age 81 years of arteriosclerosis and uremia. His children could not please him as he was so quick-tempered; his daughter reported that "he drove his sons away." Classification: Possible personality trait disturbance—passive-aggressive personality.

Sister (30), born 1882; died at age 42 years of a heart attack. She was described as "deceitful and snobbish." At age 26 years she drank carbolic acid as a suicide attempt, although she was not depressed at the time. She reportedly had a goiter which "affected her mind and caused her death" at Mercer Sanitarium. Classification: Probably with functional psychosis, manic-depressive reaction—other.

Nieces and Nephews

Nephew (37), born 1890; died at age 65 years, cause of death unknown. He was described as the "black sheep of the family" and as wild, reckless and a heavy drinker. Classification: Sociopathic personality disturbance—anti-social reaction.

Nephew (55), born 1907. Family members described him as an alcoholic and a "drunk" who had "trouble with the law." At age 54 years he was described as bitter about his divorce and as permanently disabled by pelvic and leg injuries received in an accident four years previously. Classification: Sociopathic personality disturbance—alcoholism (addiction).

Distant Relatives

Grandnephew (65), born 1912. At age 50 years he was still single. He reportedly was alcoholic until about age 35 years. He was once tubercular which necessitated the removal of a lung lobe. Classification: Sociopathic personality disorder—alcoholism (addiction).

(71) wife of grandnephew (70), born 1923. At age 39 years she was described as obese and "quite nervous, probably due to hypothyroidism." Classification: Probable psychoneurotic disorder.

Grandnephew (73), born 1912. At age 50 years he had recently been released from an alcoholics' treatment center in New Jersey where he had been hospitalized for one year. He was living in a halfway house and working as an orderly in a hospital. Classification: Sociopathic personality disturbance—alcoholism (addiction).

Family Summary

The proband and a maternal aunt were psychotic and a sister probably so. The maternal grandmother and the wife of a grand-nephew were neurotic. Personality disorders were found in a husband of the proband, a wife of the father, a brother, a sister's husband, a paternal half uncle, a maternal aunt, two nephews and in two grand-nephews.

Controls

None noteworthy.

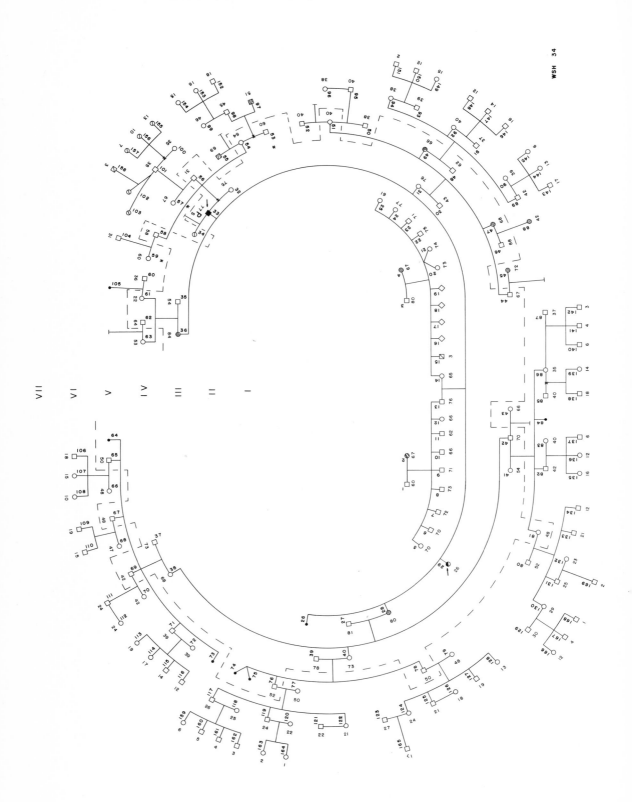

WSH 34

WSH 34: The Proband

The proband (33), born 1871; died at age 77 years of acute coronary insufficiency. He had a "common school" education with average progress. At age 21 years he was depressed for a period of one month with no suicidal tendencies. At age 23 years he had a second attack of depression during which he made several suicide attempts and also expressed his intention to kill his wife. At age 34 years he developed symptoms of sleeplessness and apathy which persisted until a few weeks before his admission to Warren State Hospital on 9/20/1915, when he became fearful, suicidal and homicidal. Three days before admission he attempted suicide by taking arsenic. Diagnosis at Warren State Hospital was manic-depressive psychosis, depressed phase. He was discharged on 12/21/1917 and never rehospitalized. His first wife left him in 1916 and he later remarried. Classification: Schizophrenic reaction — paranoid type.

Children

(55) husband of daughter (54), born 1855; died at age 69 years of cirrhosis of the liver. He was a railroad trainman who was retired from his employment because of "nerves." He was known to scream so that the neighbors complained. Classification: Sociopathic personality disturbance — alcoholism (addiction).

Grandchildren

Grandson (97), born 1910. He never married and reportedly sold his mother's home, which he had inherited, for money for "liquor and women." He was described by various family members as very obese and as an alcoholic; he described himself as the "black sheep" of the family. Classification: Sociopathic personality disturbance — alcoholism (addiction).

Grandparents

Paternal grandmother (2), died at age 67 years of apoplexy. She was described as a "lively, jolly" woman until six years before her death when she suffered the first of a series of strokes which left her paralyzed and emotionally disturbed. Classification: Chronic brain syndrome associated with arteriosclerosis.

Maternal grandmother (4), died at age 67 years a few days after her first stroke. She was described as "high strung," extremely energetic almost to the point of restlessness, rather irritable and quick tempered though never violent. Classification: Possible personality disorder.

Siblings

Sister (28), born 1863; died at age 80 years of a coronary embolism and arteriosclerosis. She was described as "very nervous — had goiter all her life." She had a "heart condition" the last 10 years of her life. Classification: Possible psychoneurotic disorder.

Sister (29), born 1865; died at age 26 years at Warren State Hospital of exhaustion following three weeks of acute excitement, of which one week was spent at Warren State Hospital. The onset of her mental illness was sudden; however, it did follow several months of failing physical health. Previous to the illnesses she was considered a "jolly girl" although irritable and obstinate at times. Classification: Possibly with functional psychosis, schizophrenic reaction — catatonic type.

Sister (36), born 1874; died at age 84 years of acute cardiac failure. She was described as of a "neurotic disposition . . . would worry easily and become exhausted physically and nervously." When in this exhausted condition she would moan for hours, then feel better. Classification: Psychoneurotic disorder.

Nieces and Nephews

(45) wife of nephew (44), born 1888. At age 72 years she described herself as "very nervous" although she had never been treated for nervousness. She was under treatment for heart trouble. Classification: Possible psychoneurotic disorder.

Niece (47), born 1892. She was described as very nervous and excitable. She,

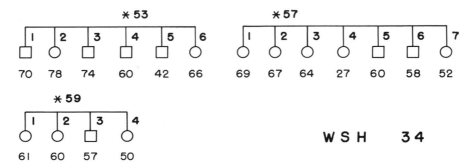

WSH 34

CONTROLS

her husband and daughter refused to be interviewed. Classification: Possible psychoneurotic disorder.

Niece (49), born 1894. At age 66 years she was described as very nervous and withdrawn. She refused to go out socially and depended upon her children for all her needs. The adjustment problems began after the death of her husband. She was urged to seek professional help but refused. An interview was attempted but she would not answer the door and was observed "peeping" out the window. Classification: Transient situational personality disorder—adjustment reaction of late life.

Distant Relatives

Grandniece (88), born 1918. At age 42 years she was single, lived at home with her parents and never went out without one of them accompanying her. Other family members considered her "peculiar" and stated that she made no attempt at socializing with people her own age. She had "back trouble" and received treatment regularly. Classification: Personality pattern disturbance—schizoid personality.

Family Summary

The proband had a psychotic disorder and a sister possibly so. Two sisters, a niece and the wife of a nephew were neurotic. The paternal grandmother was classified chronic brain syndrome associated with arteriosclerosis. Personality disorders were found in a niece, a grandson, the maternal grandmother, a grandniece and in the husband of a daughter.

Controls

None noteworthy.

WSH 44: The Proband

The proband (33), born 1864. She was always considered peculiar and lived a secluded life. She completed grade eight, then taught school for two years. She always lived at home and later occasionally worked as a domestic. After the death of her mother in 1907 she had episodes of depression lasting two or three months when she would lie in bed and not want to talk. She had a depression from May until July, 1914, then in the fall suddenly became excited. On December 22, 1914, she was admitted to Warren State Hospital. Diagnosis at Warren State Hospital was manic-depression — double form hypermania. At Warren she was noisy, talkative, confused, irrational, distractible, disoriented, had delusions of poisoning and of a spiritual world, visual illusions and hallucinations. She began to improve in April, 1915, and was released from Warren State Hospital on 8/19/1915. She was again hospitalized at Warren State Hospital from 4/29/1916 until 8/20/1920. When her sister was admitted to Warren State Hospital in 1930, the proband was reportedly "as peculiar as ever." Classification: Schizophrenic reaction — paranoid type.

Grandparents

Paternal grandfather (1), died at age 83 years of apoplexy. He was described as a severe, cruel man who kicked one of his sons so hard that the son's "mind was affected." Classification: Possible personality disorder.

Parents

Father (15), born 1827; died at age 75 years at Warren State Hospital, cause of death unknown. He reportedly was "always peculiar and was probably insane" for many years before his admission to the hospital at age 72 years. He was excitable, talkative, ugly, abusive to his wife, quarrelsome and drank to excess. His wife left him in 1866, returned briefly and left him permanently in 1873. At other times he was seclusive and uncommunicative. Warren State Hospital records described him as excited and deluded at admission and during his residence there he was generally exhilarated and restless, although at times he was rather quiet. He died three years after admission to Warren State Hospital. Classification: Chronic brain syndrome associated with cerebral arteriosclerosis.

Aunts and Uncles

Paternal uncle (6), died at age 66 years, immediate cause of death unknown. He was "out of his mind" for the year before his death and was very hard to manage as he continually wanted to run away. Classification: Probable chronic brain syndrome of senium.

Paternal uncle (7), died at age 73 years of tuberculosis. He reportedly was "insane for at least 25 years before his death." He believed someone was going to poison him and would eat no food until others had eaten of it. He also had a great fear that "the Catholics were going to injure him." His sister and her husband took him to a state mental hospital but the doctors were unable to persuade him to stay. He improved after that visit but was never quite normal. Classification: Schizophrenic reaction — paranoid type.

Maternal aunt (17), suicided at age 45 years by cutting her throat with a razor. She became depressed and worried about a year before her death. Her family feared suicide and tried to watch her closely. Classification: Probably with functional psychosis, manic-depressive reaction.

Maternal aunt (19), suicided at age 28 years by taking poison. She became depressed when her third child was a few weeks old; she refused to talk to people and expressed a wish to die. She suicided about five months later. Classification: Probably with functional psychosis, manic-depressive reaction.

Maternal aunt (20), died at age 70 years, cause of death unknown. She had two episodes of mental trouble. The first attack occurred when her youngest child was a baby. She became melancholy, seclusive and suicidal. The attack lasted for three years and she was hospitalized for a time in a state mental hospital. When she came home she was unusually happy and elated and remained well for 15 years, when she again

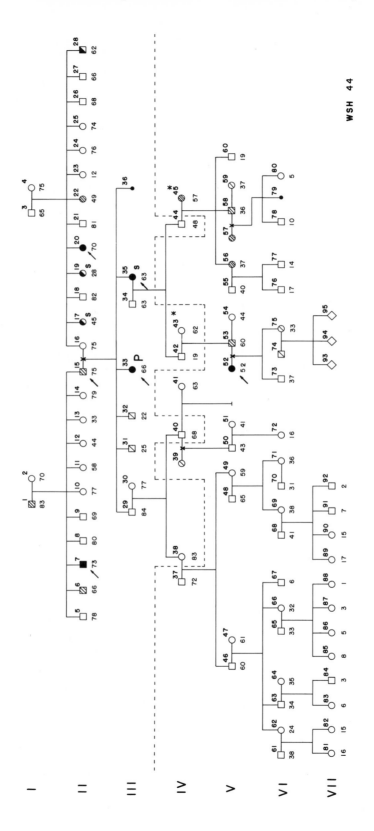

WSH 44

became depressed with feelings of unworthiness. She recovered from the attack and was normal until her death. Reportedly she was a spiritualist with mediumistic powers. Classification: Manic-depressive reaction, other.

Maternal aunt (22), died at age 49 years of a tumor. She reportedly was "a worrier who would have blues for days at a time." She was also a spiritualist who claimed mediumistic powers. Classification: Probable psychoneurotic disorder.

Maternal uncle (28); at age 62 years he had a period of depression and despondency. Classification: Probably with functional psychosis, psychotic-depressive reaction.

Siblings

Sister (35), born 1867; died at age 63 years of chronic myocarditis at Warren State Hospital, where she had been hospitalized for three months with a diagnosis of manic-depressive psychosis, depressed phase, third attack. She was described as always stubborn, domineering and complaining. At age 32 years she had a depression which lasted about one year, although she was profoundly depressed for only two or three months. At age 53 she was again depressed for a period of seven or eight months and made a suicide attempt by shooting herself. Five years later, following a period of slight overactivity, she developed another depression which lasted about eight months. One year before her admission to Warren State Hospital she again became depressed and attempted suicide by turning on the gas. In one year she lost 60 pounds. At Warren State Hospital she was quiet, indifferent and ate very little. Classification: Manic-depressive reaction, depressed type.

Nieces and Nephews

(45) wife of nephew (44), born 1903; at age 57 years described as "high strung and nervous." Classification: Psychoneurotic disorder.

Distant Relatives

(52) wife of grandnephew (53), born 1908. She was a homeless child of illegitimate birth who was abandoned by her mother when a baby. The Salvation Army and various families raised her. She was married at age 17 years and divorced three years later. The two children from this union were removed from the home because of neglect by the mother and physical abuse by the father. Her husband's relatives described her as a "low grade, feeble-minded woman"; however, the state hospital records, where she was hospitalized from 7/20/1953 until 7/9/1957 with a diagnosis of involutional psychosis—paranoid type, described her as of average intellectual capacity but almost deaf because of bilateral perforated ear drums. She was hospitalized after an arrest for making false accusations against her landlord and against children in the neighborhood. At discharge from the hospital she was again functioning at her normal level but in 1962 she reportedly wore a "lodestone" about her neck rather than wear her hearing aid as the "lodestone absorbs a considerable amount of radium from her system." Classification: Schizophrenic reaction—paranoid type.

Grandnephew (53), born 1904. At age 60 years he described himself as once "wild and irresponsible." He had a criminal record of burglary, larceny and child abuse in early adulthood. A probation officer described him as "lazy, incompetent and mentally ill." He later established a good reputation as a sober, industrious city employee with no mental problems. Classification: Transient situational personality disorder—adult situational reaction.

Grandniece (56), born 1925. At age 37 years she was described as "very nervous." The family refused permission to have her interviewed "because it would upset her—she's so nervous." Classification: Probable psychoneurotic disorder.

(57) wife of grandnephew (58), born 1926. She reportedly had a "nervous breakdown" after the death of her second child, who died in infancy. Classification: Possible psychoneurotic disorder.

Grandnephew (58), born 1927. He was described as of a nervous temperament and reportedly had a "nervous breakdown" at one time, although details were unknown, and he worked steadily as an electrical engineer. Classification: Probable psychoneurotic disorder.

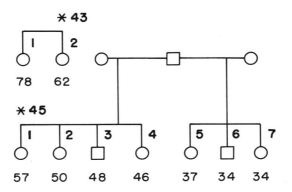

CONTROLS W S H   4 4

Family Summary

The proband, her sister, a maternal aunt, a paternal uncle and the wife of a grandnephew had psychotic disorders and two maternal aunts and a maternal uncle probably so. The father was hospitalized with a psychotic reaction to cerebral arteriosclerosis and a paternal uncle was classified as probable chronic brain syndrome of senium. A maternal aunt, a grandniece, a grandnephew, the wife of a nephew and the wife of a grandnephew were neurotic. Personality disorders were discovered in the paternal grandfather and in a grandnephew.

Controls

None noteworthy.

WSH 50: The Proband

The proband (41), born 1851; died at age 70 years of bronchopneumonia. She always had a bad temper but managed good control after her marriage at age 18 years. At age 20 years she developed symptoms of psychosis with extreme irritability and periods of mutism. She always did her housework erratically and was an inefficient and poor manager of her household. In the six years before commitment to Warren State Hospital, on 10/28/1911, with a diagnosis of dementia praecox, she was hypochondriacal, committed many acts of violence toward others and attempted suicide twice. While hospitalized she was generally indifferent and showed some deterioration. She was discharged from Warren State Hospital on 4/1/1914. There was no improvement in her mental health from then until her death. Classification: Schizophrenic reaction — paranoid type.

(40) husband of proband (41), born 1845; died at age 68 years of uremic poisoning. He was described variously as "a wonderful man," "a stubborn, ugly man" and as having "no regard for his wife . . . except as a workhorse." He and (41) "battled almost constantly." Classification: Possible personality disorder.

Children

Son (91), born 1874; died at age 55 years from exhaustion of mental disease. He was hospitalized on 5/13/1928, at a mental hospital with a diagnosis of cerebral spinal syphilis, and discharged as improved on 5/28/1928. On 5/3/1929, he was hospitalized at a state mental hospital where he died five days later. He was confused, disoriented and possibly suffering from a toxic psychosis. Classification: Chronic brain syndrome associated with central nervous system syphilis.

Daughter (95), born 1875; died at age 34 years of tuberculosis. She was described as "always jolly" and had a history of three illegitimate pregnancies by two men. Classification: Sociopathic personality disturbance — dyssocial reaction.

Daughter (99), born 1876. She had two illegitimate pregnancies before her marriage. Classification: Sociopathic personality disturbance.

Son (101), born 1878. At age 82 years he was described as "hard to get along with, prefers his own company" and as a "disliked, friendless" person who was always "very peculiar." He would sometimes "for months at a time be sulky and disagreeable and hardly speak." He did not abuse his children physically but refused to allow them to dress like other children and insisted that they quit school. Classification: Possibly with functional psychosis, manic-depressive reaction — other.

Daughter (113), born 1891. At 70 years of age she was described by an interviewer as friendly, cooperative and normal. When younger she had "hysterical spells," a bad temper and was described as "the most peculiar member of the family." Classification: Personality trait disturbance.

Grandchildren

Grandson (223), born 1900; suicided at age 62 years by carbon monoxide poisoning. An interview was attempted in 1961 but he refused to cooperate as he was upset over the death of his wife (224) of cancer earlier in the year. Classification: Probably with functional psychosis.

(225) third wife of grandson (223), born 1909. She was described as "an alcoholic and lifelong tramp." Classification: Sociopathic personality disturbance — alcoholism (addiction).

Great-Grandchildren

Great-granddaughter (460), born 1925. She reported that she was a very nervous person who had "difficulty with her nerves" at about age 35 years, but overcame her problem. Classification: Possible psychoneurotic disorder.

Great-granddaughter (476), born 1926. She was described as "high-strung" and suffered "severe emotional upsets during menstrual periods." Classification: Personality pattern disturbance — emotionally unstable personality.

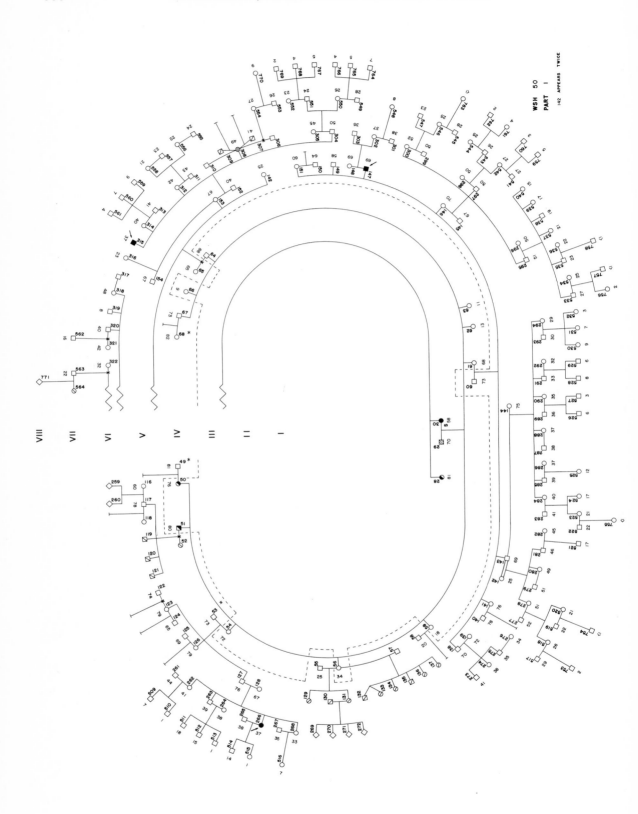

WSH 50
PART I

142 APPEARS TWICE

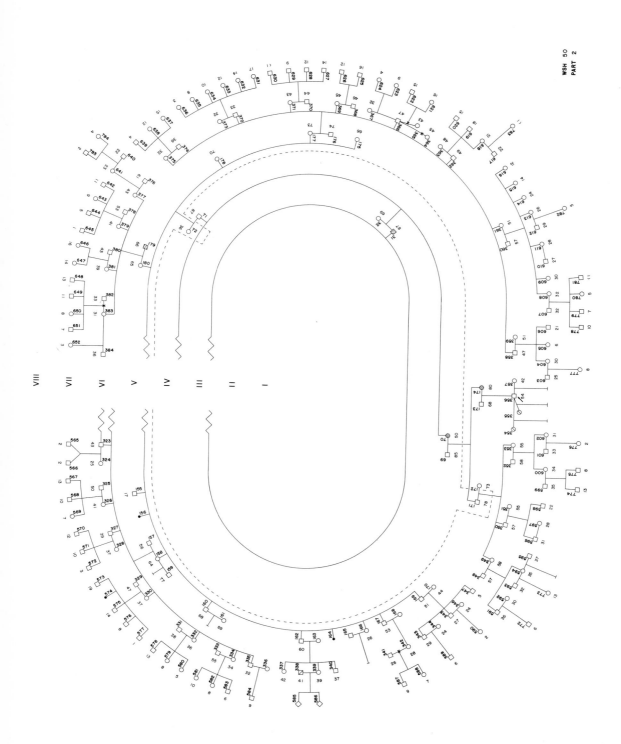

WSH 50
PART 2

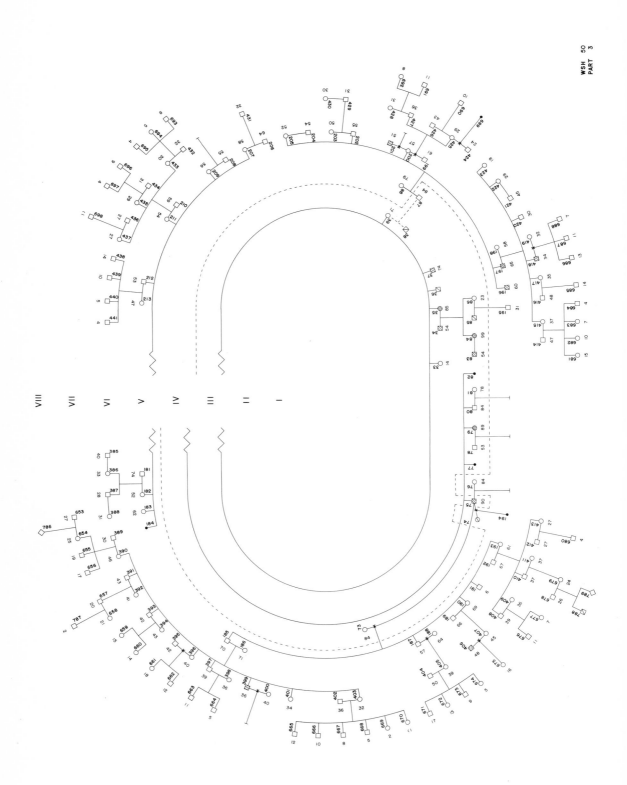

WSH 50
PART 3

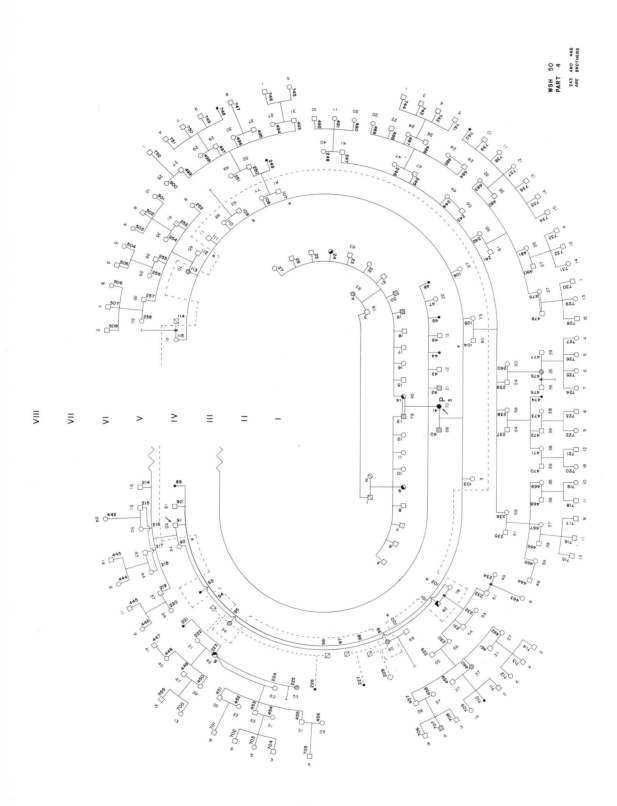

WSH 50
PART 4

243 AND 466
ARE BROTHERS

Great-great-grandchildren

Great-great-grandson (707), born 1955. He was of small stature and was described as a poor eater and a "pathological liar." Classification: Transient situational personality disturbance—adjustment reaction of childhood.

Grandparents

Maternal grandmother (4), born 1775; died at age 83 years, cause of death unknown. She was described as mentally "off by spells." Classification: Possibly with functional psychosis.

Parents

Father (13), died at age 77 years of "old age." He was regarded as "sound mentally" but "very nervous." Classification: Possible psychoneurotic reaction—other.

Mother (14), born 1812; died at age 45 years of complications of childbirth. She reportedly had "queer spells" lasting for several days during which she would "pout and sulk" and do little. One entire summer she was depressed and delusional and remained in bed. Classification: Probably with functional psychosis, schizophrenic reaction.

Aunts and Uncles

Paternal aunt (9). Facts about her were unknown, except that she "was always kept locked up" and no family members ever saw her. Classification: Probably with functional psychosis.

Maternal uncle (19); described as "a very heavy drinker" who had periods of amnesia lasting several days and one period of mental derangement. Classification: Sociopathic personality disturbance—alcoholism (addiction). Also, acute brain syndrome associated with alcohol intoxication.

Maternal uncle (20), reportedly a "very hard drinker" who lost his money and his father's estate and was eventually supported by the township. Classification: Sociopathic personality disturbance—alcoholism (addiction).

Maternal aunt (24), reportedly had "periods of mental derangement." Classification: Probably with functional psychosis.

Siblings

Sister (28), born 1830; died at age 81 years, cause of death unknown. All during her life she had "queer spells" when she wanted to drown herself in the river. She became "demented" in the last year of life. Classification: Probably with functional psychosis, schizophrenic reaction.

(29) husband of sister (30), born 1835; died at age 70 years of appendicitis. He drank "quite heavily" and was mean and abusive to his family when he did so. He was blamed for his wife's suicide as he "ran after other women." He also voluntarily went to war, leaving his wife to care for their 11 children. Classification: Probable sociopathic personality disturbance.

Sister (30), born 1833; died at age 58 years of suicide by hanging. She reportedly had "melancholy spells lasting two or three months at a time." She was also described as "a very lovely person" who "worried herself to death." Classification: Manic-depressive reaction—depressed type.

Brother (31), born 1834; died at age 87 years of a cerebral hemorrhage. He was always considered to be a "very peculiar man." Although in "comfortable circumstances," he ate and slept in one room and wore shabby clothes which he refused to remove when he went to bed. At age 82 he showed a mild degree of memory and apprehension impairment. Classification: Personality disorder.

(34) husband of sister (35), born 1842; died at age 54 years, cause of death unknown. He reportedly at one time "got to drinking to excess and ran away and left his family." He was an amputee. Classification: Possible personality disorder.

Sister (35), born 1836; died at age 85 years of cancer. She was described by her physician as "a neurotic woman with melancholy tendencies—if the least little thing occurred, would worry and brood...and remain in bed." Classification: Psychoneurotic reaction—other.

Brother (37), born 1846; died at age 74 years, cause of death unknown. At the time of death he was a patient at a county home where he was "recognized to be feeble-minded, being silly and incompetent from childhood." Classification: Possible personality pattern disturbance—schizoid personality.

Brother (42), born 1857; died at age 21 years when accidentally killed by a falling tree. He was described as "queer, contrary and mute at times." Classification: Probable personality pattern disturbance—schizoid personality.

Nieces and Nephews

Niece (50), born 1855; died at age 76 years of heart failure. She was generally known to be "insane." Classification: Probably with functional psychosis.

Nephew (51), born 1857; died at age 80 years of cancer of the bowels. He was generally known to be "insane." Classification: Probably with functional psychosis.

Niece (70), born 1864; died at age 50 years of shock following surgery. She was described as "a cruel, malicious, revengeful woman who caused a great deal of trouble." Classification: Probable personality disorder.

Nephew (75), born 1869; died at age 70 years of dehydration. He deserted his first wife in 1903 and remarried without a divorce in 1905. He served a prison sentence for bigamy. Classification: Possible sociopathic personality disturbance.

Niece (79), born 1872; reported at one time to be "abnormal" and at another as "going crazy," although she was never hospitalized. Classification: Possible personality disorder.

(83) husband of niece (84), born 1861; died at age 54 years of nephritis. He was reportedly an "invalid" and an "alcoholic." Classification: Sociopathic personality disturbance—alcoholism (addiction).

Niece (84), born 1860; died at age 99 years of cerebral sclerosis. She was described as "an unusually bright woman" who was also an alcoholic and "drank a fifth a day." Classification: Sociopathic personality disturbance—alcoholism

Distant Relatives

Grandnephew (147), born 1895. He was admitted to a Veterans Administration Hos-

pital on 11/12/1929, and was continuously hospitalized from that time. His diagnoses were schizophrenic reaction, paranoid type, chronic, severe and tuberculosis, pulmonary, minimal, inactive. Classification: Schizophrenic reaction—paranoid type.

Grandniece (174), born 1884. When interviewed at age 80 years she was generally cooperative but refused to talk about her son. She was described by family members as "moody and contrary with her husband ... finds fault with her neighbors" and "very difficult to please." There was continual "fussing and bickering" in the home. Classification: Probable personality pattern disturbance.

(179) husband of grandniece (180), born 1895. When interviewed at age 66 years it was suggested that he had either been drinking heavily or his memory was affected. He looked and acted depressed. His wife had died in the year preceding the interview. Classification: Possible transient situational personality disorder—adult situational reaction.

Grandnephew (196), born 1892; died at age 60 years of acute cardiac dilatation. A contributory cause of death: psychotic arteriosclerosis. Classification: Chronic brain syndrome associated with cerebral arteriosclerosis.

Grandnephew (197), born 1896. He had severe arthritis and in 1961 suffered a cardiovascular accident. Classification: Possible chronic brain syndrome associated with cerebral arteriosclerosis.

(201) husband of grandniece (200), born 1903. He was reportedly an alcoholic. Classification: Possible sociopathic personality disturbance—alcoholism (addiction).

Great-grandniece (266), born 1925. She had two similar episodes of mental disturbance during which she was restless, agitated, confused and apprehensive. The first episode was in 1960 when her husband was hospitalized for 3½ weeks with ulcers. She was treated with tranquilizers. The second episode began when she became depressed following the birth of a child on 10/5/1961. She was hospitalized two weeks later with a diagnosis of schizoid state. After a course of seven electroshock treatments she was discharged and made a good adjustment. Classification: Schizophrenic reaction—paranoid type.

Great-grandniece (308), born 1914. Her family was broken up when she was age 14

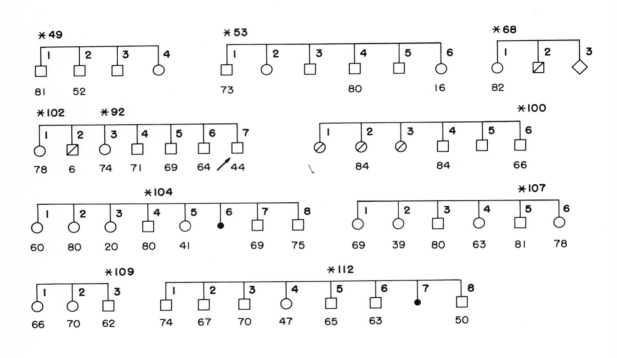

CONTROLS   W S H   50

years because of the death of her father and her mother's illness. At age 49 years she was interviewed and gave inaccurate, conflicting information, although she appeared "pretty well integrated" mentally. She had had several operations for cancer and complained frequently about her health. Classification: Possible personality disorder.

Great-grandnephew (315), born 1924. At age nine years his father died of tuberculosis. His mother remarried a short time later and he was sent to a boarding home as his stepfather had 16 children by a previous marriage, eight of whom lived with his mother and stepfather. He was hospitalized at a Veterans Administration Hospital on 1/30/1948, was transferred to another Veterans Administration Hospital in 1952, and at age 37 years was still hospitalized. Diagnosis and classification: Schizophrenic reaction — hebephrenic type.

Great-grandnephew (356), born 1909; died at age 54 years of bronchopneumonia. Syphilis was diagnosed in 1952 and he received two series of treatments. Late that year he developed a cancerphobia. Mental symptoms persisted and he was committed to a state mental hospital on 11/30/1953, with a diagnosis of chronic brain syndrome with central nervous system syphilis, meningoencephalitic, with psychotic reaction. He was paroled 1/24/1954, but was readmitted on 3/17/1954. He remained hospitalized with gradual deterioration until his death. Classification: Chronic brain syndrome associated with meningoencephalitic syphilis with psychotic reaction.

Great-grandnephew (399), born 1925; described as "nervous" and as an epileptic. Seizures began at age 21 years. Classification: Possible psychoneurotic disorder.

(406) husband of great-grandniece (407), born 1913. He was divorced by (407) because of his alcoholism. At last information he was with Alcoholics Anonymous and doing well. Classification: Sociopathic personality disturbance — alcoholism (addiction).

Great-grandnephew (418), born 1927.

He was a "problem child" and while in the service went A.W.O.L. several times. As an adult he was described as a "drifter" and as "just plain immoral." Classification: Sociopathic personality disturbance — antisocial reaction.

Family Summary

The proband, a son, a grandson, the mother, the maternal grandmother, a paternal and a maternal aunt, two sisters, a niece, a nephew, a grandnephew, a great-grandniece and a great-grandnephew had or probably or possibly had, psychotic disorders. A son and a great-grandnephew were hospitalized with central nervous system syphilis. Two great-grandnephews had psychotic reaction to arteriosclerosis. Personality disorders were found in the husband of the proband, three daughters, a great-granddaughter and a great-great-grandson. Such disorders were also found in two maternal uncles, three brothers, three nieces and a nephew, a grandniece, a great-grandniece and in a great-grandnephew as well as in the wife of a grandson, the husbands of two sisters, the husband of a niece, the husbands of two grandnieces and the husband of a great-grandniece. A sister, the father, a great-granddaughter and a great-grandnephew were neurotic.

Controls

Brother (7) of (102) and (92), born 1900; died at age 44 years of general paralysis of the insane at a state mental hospital where he was admitted on 9/30/1940, with a diagnosis of psychosis with syphilitic meningoencephalitis (general paralysis). After a series of antiluetic therapy he was furloughed, but he returned within two months and remained hospitalized until his death. Classification: Chronic brain syndrome associated with central nervous system syphilis.

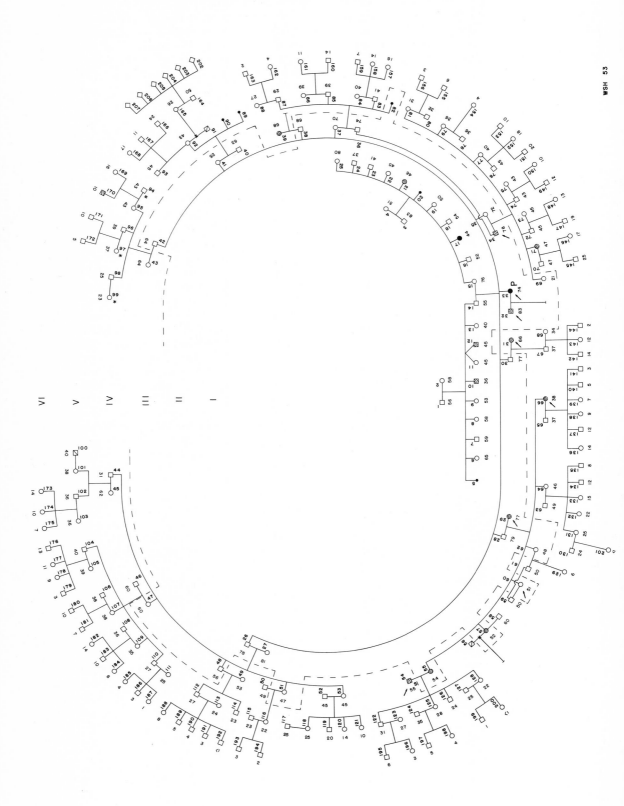

WSH 53

WSH 53: The Proband

The proband (33), born 1886; died at age 74 years of an acute coronary. She began to show behavioral changes two or three years previous to the onset of depression, for which she was hospitalized at Warren State Hospital on 10/19/1914. At Warren State Hospital she exhibited excited, obscene behavior, had delusions of persecution and developed some paranoid ideas against her husband and was diagnosed first as manic-depressive — manic phase, then as dementia praecox — paranoid type. She was paroled as improved on 6/15/1916, but for the next six years she was disagreeable and threatening to family and friends and was readmitted to Warren State Hospital on 9/1/1922, where she remained until death. At the time of her second admission to Warren State Hospital she was aurally hallucinated. Classification: Schizophrenic reaction — paranoid type.

(32) husband of the proband (33), born 1876; died at age 83 years of chronic myocarditis and generalized arteriosclerosis at a state mental hospital where he had been for five days because of general mental confusion. Classification: Chronic brain syndrome associated with cerebral arteriosclerosis.

Aunts and Uncles

Paternal uncle (10), born 1868; died at age 36 years of hemorrhage of the lungs. He occasionally drank to excess when he "got into a drinking crowd" and was imprisoned twice for stealing. Classification: Sociopathic personality disturbance — antisocial reaction.

Paternal uncle (12), born 1870; at age 45 years he was described as the "most excited and unstable of his family." Classification: Personality trait disturbance — emotionally unstable personality.

Maternal aunt (17), born 1858; died at age 44 years of apoplexy. At age 24 years, after the birth of her second child, she began to develop symptoms of psychosis and at age 30 years was placed in a county home where she remained until her death. At the county home she was described as "like a child" — her answers to questions were irrelevant, her memory poor

and powers of comprehension child-like. She was also extremely religious and had the delusion that she owned the home. The cause of her mental disorder was given as abuse by her husband, as he often beat her. Classification: Schizophrenic reaction — paranoid type.

Maternal aunt (21), born 1869; died at age 46 years of unknown causes. She was described as "rather light weight mentally." Classification: Possible personality disorder.

Siblings

(29) wife of brother (28), born 1885. She was forced to drop out of school at an early age to care for her younger siblings. She married at age 21 years but "didn't want to" and was a "nagging, easily irritated housewife" who had no interest in her housework. Reportedly, her marriage continued only as a result of the husband's "kindness and understanding." In 1955, after her fourth hernia operation in eight years, she became agitated, nervous, sleepless, thought no one was trying to help her and threatened suicide several times, but never made an actual suicide attempt. She was hospitalized at Warren State Hospital from June until September, 1955. The psychiatrist felt that, since she assumed family responsibilities at such a young age, she wanted others to care for her and to be free of responsibilities. Diagnosis at Warren State Hospital and classification: Psychoneurotic disorder — depressive reaction.

(31) wife of brother (30), born 1896. She quit high school because of nervousness and "a racy heart." At 20 she married a man 11 years her senior. Marital adjustment was good and she was pleased when she became pregnant, but one month after normal delivery of a healthy baby boy she claimed she felt weak all over, went to bed and remained there for 19 years, except for one month after returning from treatment at a university hospital. Her child was sent to a sibling and she had no responsibility in rearing him. While in bed she felt "wilted, worn out and weak all over." She did little moving while in bed as she was afraid it would affect her heart. She was hospitalized at Warren State Hospital, Warren, Pennsylvania, from 11/1/1942 until

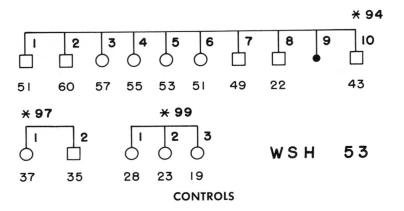

CONTROLS

4/20/1943. She showed no organic disorder and was diagnosed as psychoneurotic disorder, conversion reaction type. At age 66 years she was perfectly well, lived with her son and his family and babysat for her three grandchildren. Classification: Psychoneurotic disorder—conversion reaction.

(34) husband of sister (35), born 1880; died at age 78 years of cancer at Warren State Hospital. He was well until 1956, when he became confused, forgetful, failed to recognize family members and developed some delusions of persecution. He was admitted to Warren State Hospital on 4/18/1957, and remained there until death. Diagnosis at Warren State Hospital and classification: Chronic brain syndrome associated with cerebral arteriosclerosis.

(39) wife of brother (38), born 1894; at age 68 years described as "very nervous and shakes all over." The nervousness began after a gall bladder operation at age 65 years. Classification: Transient situational personality disorder—adjustment reaction of late life.

Nieces and Nephews

(54) husband of niece (55), born 1907. He was brought up by an overly strict mother and an alcoholic father. His school and work adjustments were fair but he was an irritable, abusive husband and father who drank excessively. On 4/7/1961, he was admitted to a state mental hospital following a suicide attempt (he shot himself through the mouth with a rifle) and returned home on a leave of absence in July, 1961. At last information he had his drinking under control and his family life was more pleasant. Classification: Personality trait disturbance—passive-aggressive personality.

Niece (55), born 1908; described at age 54 years as "wonderful but sometimes irritable, nervous and worried." She was described as only moderately sociable. Classification: Probable psychoneurotic disorder.

Niece (57), born 1910; described as "a very nervous person" who was seen by a psychiatrist for one session. Classification: Transient situational personality disorder—adjustment reaction of late life.

Niece (60), born 1911. She was hospitalized from 9/11/1944 until 11/28/1944, with syphilis of the central nervous system, tabes dorsalis, with no psychotic symptoms or antisocial conduct. She was hospitalized principally for fever therapy. Classification: Chronic brain syndrome associated with meningoencephalitic syphilis.

Niece (66), born 1924. She did not like school and completed grade seven at 17 years of age. She married at age 24 years but made an inadequate adjustment and soon became fearful, apprehensive and agitated with periods of faintness and screaming. She developed obsessive fears of injuring others and was hospitalized at Warren State Hospital from 3/27/1951 until 6/27/1951. At Warren State Hospital she was tense, apprehensive, rigid and anxious, but had no hallucinations or delusions. Diagnosis at Warren State Hospital was psychoneurosis, psychasthenia. Classification: Psychoneurotic reaction—other.

Niece (71), born 1915. At age 47 years she received outpatient psychiatric care at a psychiatric clinic. Diagnosis and classification: Psychoneurotic disorder—depressive reaction.

Distant Relatives

Grandnephew (170), born 1952. As a first grader he "clammed up and withdrew" after a teacher slapped him. He also developed a speech defect. At age 10 years, after speech therapy, he was described as "much better." Classification: Transient situational personality disorder—adjustment reaction of childhood.

Family Summary

The proband and a maternal aunt had psychotic disorders. Personality disorders were found in two paternal uncles and one maternal aunt, a niece, a grandnephew, the wife of a brother and the husband of a niece. Three nieces and the wives of two brothers were neurotic. One niece was treated for meningoencephalitic syphilis. The proband's husband and a sister's husband were hospitalized with mental problems associated with cerebral arteriosclerosis.

Controls

None noteworthy.

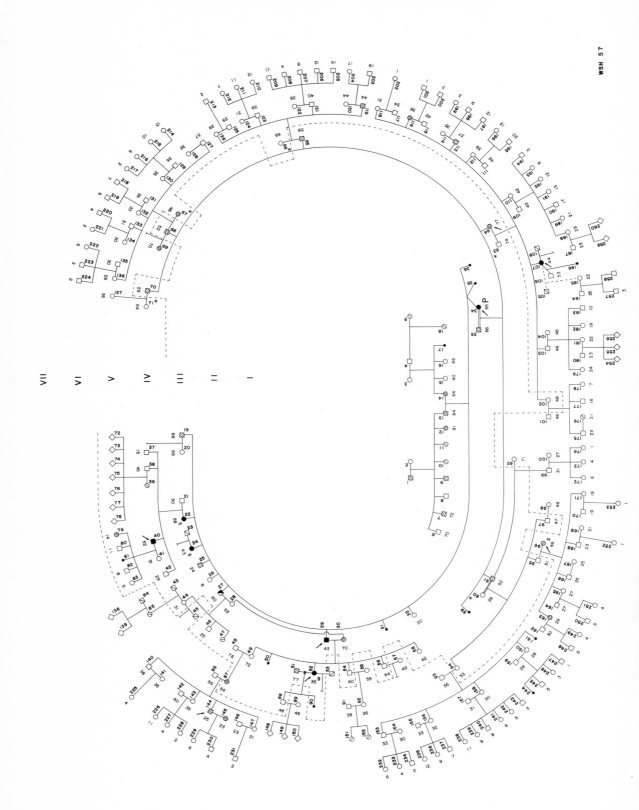

WSH 57: The Proband

The proband (34), born 1862; died at age 65 years at Warren State Hospital of myocarditis. She had her first episode of depression at age 20 years when, for a period of two months, she neglected her 13-week old child. After that, every two or three years she would have a period of depression or hyperactivity. At age 43 years, while "noisy, excited and emotional," she began to undress in front of a train and was admitted to Warren State Hospital on 9/4/1905. She was discharged as restored three months later. Diagnosis at this hospitalization was acute mania. In early 1914 she became very hyperactive, attacked her husband and fought with her children. She was subsequently institutionalized at Warren State Hospital from 6/11/1914 until 7/23/1915, with a diagnosis of manic-depressive insanity, manic phase. She was again hospitalized in a period of hyperactivity from 12/20/1919 until 2/24/1922, with a diagnosis of manic-depressive psychosis. She eventually developed delusions and hallucinations and remained hospitalized after her last admission on 2/15/1923. Classification: Schizophrenic reaction—schizo-affective type.

(33) husband of (34) and her first cousin once removed, born 1860; died at age 66 years, cause of death unknown. He was reportedly "peculiar" but in an "indefinite way." Classification: Possible personality disorder.

Children

Son (61), born 1885; died at age 52 years of a cerebral hemorrhage. He was an obese person who weighed over 300 pounds and was described as a heavy drinker. He also reportedly "had an uncontrollable temper." Other informants stated that he "drank to excess" and was once struck by lightning and "never got over it." Classification: Sociopathic personality disturbance —alcoholism (addiction).

Daughter (64), born 1887; was hospitalized at a state mental hospital for three months in 1964 with a diagnosis of chronic brain syndrome of senium. Before that, she was at a general hospital for one month. For two or three years before hospitalization she was "surly, jealous, disagreeable" and complained of being nervous and unable to eat. Classification: Probable chronic brain syndrome of senium.

Son (65), born 1890; died at age 59 years of cancer. He was described as "quiet and seclusive before strangers" but at home was "quiet and self-centered; had exaggerated ideas of his own importance." He was also described as "unreasonable and easily angered." Classification: Possible personality disorder.

(67) wife of son (68), born 1900; died at age 46 years of a heart condition. She reportedly was an alcoholic who "drank herself to death—hid gin bottles." Classification: Probable sociopathic personality disturbance—alcoholism (addiction).

Son (68), born 1895; accidentally drowned at age 52 years. He was described as "slow and easy-going" and as an alcoholic who "may have been drunk at drowning." Classification: Sociopathic personality disturbance—alcoholism (addiction).

(69) wife of son (68), born 1891. When interviewed at age 70 years she was described as "flamboyant . . . wore heavy jewelry and too frilly clothing for her age and used profanity fluently." She was suspected by her sister-in-law of conspiring in her husband's death (by drowning). Classification: Probable sociopathic personality disturbance.

Son (70), born 1897; died at age 29 years of tuberculosis. He was described as a "quiet fellow" and as "lazy, obstinate, quick-tempered, very determined in his opinions" and thought "he knew everything." Classification: Possible personality disorder.

Grandchildren

(96) wife of grandson (95), born 1912. She had a history of many surgical operations and outbursts of temper. At age 39 years she developed "spells" when she

would become nauseated and unconscious but was without convulsions. She became irritable, suspicious and attempted suicide with drugs. She was subsequently hospitalized at a state mental hospital for four months and found to have hallucinations and delusions from taking bromides. Her psychotic reactions were attributed to drug intoxication. At age 49 years she was still "nervous" and not considered entirely well by her family. Classification: Psychoneurotic disorder and acute brain syndrome associated with drug intoxication.

Granddaughter (107), born 1917. She had a "nervous breakdown" at age 17 years when she became depressed after the death of a boy friend. At age 22 years she suddenly became promiscuous and had an illegitimate child who was adopted by her parents. The illness which precipitated her admission to a state mental hospital in 1947 began following the death of her child of a heart problem at age 14 days. She became hysterical, refused to accept the reality of the child's death, was excited, overactive, violent and hallucinated. After 11 shock treatments and nine months of hospitalization she was sent home. Diagnosis was dementia praecox, catatonic type. In 1960 she was admitted to a general hospital for a month with a complaint of depression. She had been taking tranquilizers for anxiety and panic and had developed thoughts of suicide. She had menorrhagia for six months previous to hospitalization. Diagnoses were (1) schizophrenic reaction, schizo-affective type with depression, (2) personality trait disturbance, passive-aggressive personality, passive-dependent type, (3) menorrhagia, (4) anemia due to chronic blood loss. Classification: Schizophrenic reaction — paranoid type.

Grandson (113), born 1924. He reportedly was "sort of the nervous type" who would get "upset and discouraged" after a day of rebuffs in insurance selling. A psychologist who grew up with him described him as with a "neurasthenic type of personality." Classification: Probable psychoneurotic disorder.

Granddaughter (116), born 1925. She described herself and her family as "tense and nervous." The interviewer described her as anxious and "somewhat tense." Classification: Possible psychoneurotic disorder.

Grandson (119), born 1918. He was described as of a nervous temperament and reportedly had "blue spells." Classification: Possible psychoneurotic disorder.

Great-Grandchildren

Great-granddaughter (163), born 1932. She was described as "almost as bad as her mother." She was "tense, irritable" and temperamental. She was steadily employed as a telephone operator and was never treated for mental or emotional problems. Classification: Possible personality trait disturbance — emotionally unstable personality.

Grandparents

Paternal grandfather (1), who lived to be "quite an old man." He was described as "markedly alcoholic." Classification: Sociopathic personality disturbance — alcoholism (addiction).

Parents

Father (13), born 1814; died at age 84 years of "old age." As a young man he was regarded as "queer." At age 40 years he became greatly agitated over the location of a new schoolhouse and carried this grudge for years. He had vague ideas of persecution — "everyone's hand was agin him," and had a violent temper, at one time pursuing the proband with an ax. He was a notorious sex-offender and a heavy drinker, but always maintained a "mask of piety" and observed the religious customs as a Methodist preacher. When guests arrived at his home he would stay away from the house and have his wife bring his meals to the field. Classification: Sociopathic personality disturbance—dyssocial reaction.

Mother (14), born 1820; died at age 54 years of apoplexy. She was described as "lively and sociable" as a young girl but as "a broken-hearted woman" after her marriage. She was very industrious and it was through her manufacture of butter and cheese that the family was supported. Classification: Probable transient situational personality disturbance—gross stress reaction.

Aunts and Uncles

Paternal uncle (7), born 1805; died at age 72 years of catarrh of the stomach. He was described as "jealous of his wife" and had spells when he was "very angry and ugly." When young he "drank to excess." He had an episode of "great fear" and begged his children to pray for him. Classification: Sociopathic personality disturbance—alcoholism (addiction).

Paternal uncle (9). He reportedly "had the idea that he could preach." As he grew older he became childish and could not get along with his children. Classification: Possible personality disorder.

Paternal aunt (12), born 1820; died at age 91 years of "old age." She was regarded as "peculiar" and was subject to sick headaches. She also had "a bad temper... chased her granddaughter with a butcher knife." Classification: Probable personality disorder.

Siblings

Brother (19), born 1841; died at age 69 years of an ulcerated bladder. He was college educated and was a minister until he was "put out of the church" because his conduct was considered "unfitting for a minister." He sometimes preached when intoxicated and was once threatened with divorce by his wife because of adultery. In any situation of unusual responsibility he would become very excited and unable to handle the situation. Classification: Personality trait disturbance—other.

Sister (22), born 1843; died at age 58 years of self-inflicted burns. She had three attacks of mental illness, the first occurring after the birth of her first child at age 25 years. The family considered her out of her mind and she would shut herself up in a clothes closet so that people could not see her. The second attack occurred at age 42 years when she became uncommunicative and apprehensive. The third attack was at age 58 years when she continually thought that people were going to harm her. If not watched closely she would run into the woods and return naked. On some days she seemed almost normal and expressed regret for her behavior. She was left alone one day, as she seemed normal, and, while alone, saturated quilts with oil, ignited them and jumped into the flames. She died of the burns received. Classification: Schizophrenic reaction—catatonic type.

Sister (24), born 1845; died at age 43 years of suicide by poison. She was described as "almost a crank" on housekeeping. She did not want children but after menopause began to worry that she had none. Her mental trouble was of gradual onset but during the last four weeks of life she was "raving." She attempted to kill her husband, was noisy, active and apprehensive. She took poison because "the devil told her to do so." Classification: Schizophrenic reaction—catatonic type.

Brother (25), died at age 24 years of tuberculosis. He was described as a "tall, gaunt, eccentric fellow" who did little work but spent his time "tearing around the country—he was full of the devil." Classification: Possible personality disorder.

Brother (27), born 1855; died at age 60 years, cause of death unknown. He was a teacher who was dismissed because of "slovenly habits," then became a carpenter and gardener. He was described as "decidedly peculiar... showed a lack of balance and common sense." Classification: Probably with functional psychosis, schizophrenic disorder.

Brother (29), born 1857; died at age 43 years at Warren State Hospital of typhoid fever. He developed the first symptoms of mental illness at age 22 years, when he became indifferent to his surroundings and took every medicine "he could lay his hands on." His condition gradually improved but the second attack began at age 30 years, after his wife gave birth to their first child, when he became either talkative or withdrawn and would remain in bed. He finally became noisy, violent, deluded and denudative and was admitted to Warren State Hospital in 1899 with a diagnosis of acute mania. He often refused to eat or speak. After 15 months he was discharged but was readmitted three months later when he became dull and apathetic. Diagnosis at second hospitalization was chronic mania. Classification: Schizophrenic disorder—catatonic type.

(30) wife of brother (29), born 1861; died at age 70 years of myocarditis. She was described as "nervous" and when tired would "tremble all over." Classification: Psychoneurotic disorder—anxiety reaction.

Nieces and Nephews

Nephew (40), born 1874. At last information (at 52 years of age) he was reportedly a patient at a Veterans hospital. This could not be verified. He behaved "peculiarly" after age 30 years in that he believed people were "in league against him." About 10 years later his ideas of persecution, bad temper and noisy behavior caused him to lose his position and he was hospitalized at Warren State Hospital with a diagnosis of dementia praecox, paranoid type. He shortly escaped but was returned in 1915 after he threatened to kill his wife. He escaped again in 1916 and was readmitted in 1917. Classification: Schizophrenic reaction—paranoid type.

(51) husband of niece (52), born 1884. He was described as "ugly, taunting— would frequently remind (52) that her father was insane" and as "unreliable." Classification: Personality disorder.

Niece (52), born 1887; died at age 35 years of suicide by strychnine poisoning. She had her first symptoms of psychosis after the birth of her first child, at age 26 years, when she became depressed and irritable. She recovered after eight months but had another episode the following year with suicidal tendencies and was hospitalized at Warren State Hospital in 1914, with a diagnosis of manic-depressive psychosis, depressed phase, second attack. She was paroled in 1916 and was not readmitted. Seven years later she suicided. Classification: Manic-depressive reaction—depressed type.

Distant Relatives

Grandniece (79), born 1901; age 14 years at last information. She was described as "excitable and trembled when scared, which occurred frequently." Classification: Possible personality trait disturbance— emotionally unstable personality.

Grandniece (87), born 1907; died at age 54 years of multiple sclerosis. She was described as "neurotic and demanding... would scream and cry all the time lamenting the fact she was pregnant." Classification: Psychoneurotic disorder.

Great-grandnephew (144), born 1937. He was reared by a neurotic mother who did not want him. As a child he cried frequently and had temper tantrums. After the death of his father he had increasing trouble with his mother and wife and his wife claimed physical and sexual abuse. He developed an episode of severe abdominal pain and vomiting and, after medical tests revealed nothing wrong, he was hospitalized at a state mental hospital on 7/27/1957. He was found to be very immature, egocentric, jealous of his wife and lacking in insight. He was preoccupied with sex and the Rorschach revealed many anal responses, identification with and hostility toward women and evidence of poor emotional control. He was paroled on 11/12/1957. Diagnosis and classification: Personality trait disturbance—emotionally unstable personality and passive-aggressive personality.

(145) wife of great-grandnephew (144), born 1939. She was described in her husband's hospital records as "very immature and strongly dependent on her parents." She fought with (144), "clawing and scratching" him. She finally deserted her children and ran away with a married man. Classification: Probable personality disorder.

Family Summary

The proband, two sisters, a brother, a granddaughter, a nephew and a niece had psychotic disorders. A brother was probably psychotic. Two grandsons, a granddaughter, a grandniece and the wives of a brother and a grandson were neurotic. Personality disorders were found in the proband's husband, her paternal grandfather, four sons and two of their wives, the father and mother, two paternal uncles and a paternal aunt, two brothers, a grandniece, a great-granddaughter, a great-grandnephew, in the husband of a niece and in the wife of a great-grandnephew. A daughter was classified as with probable chronic brain syndrome of senium.

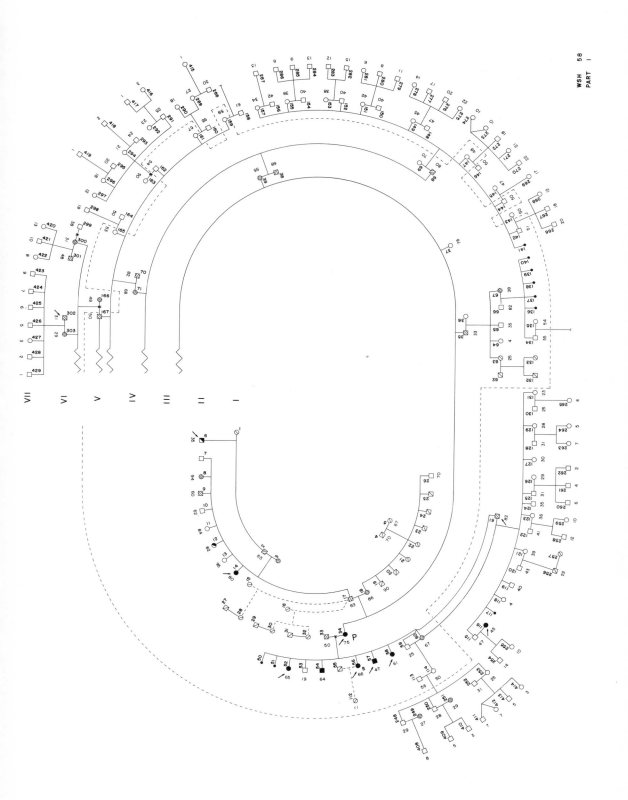

WSH 58
PART I

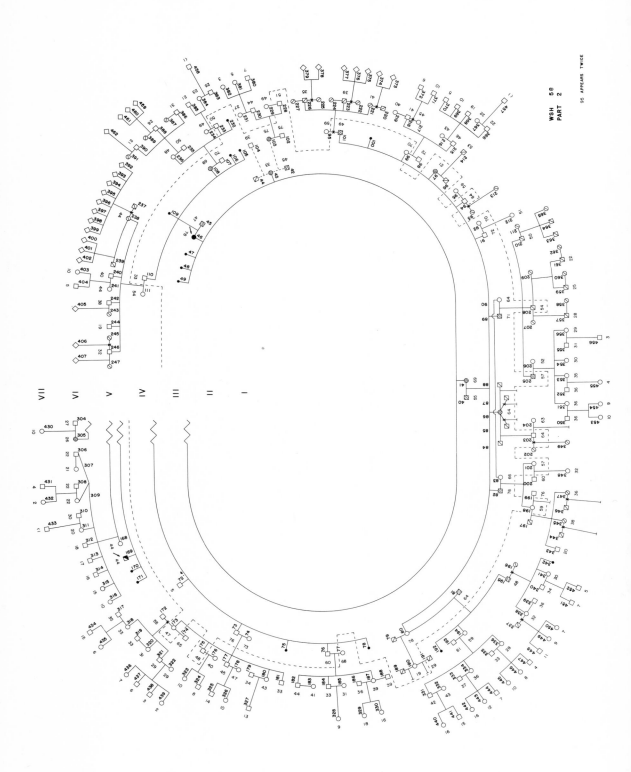

WSH 58
PART 2

95 APPEARS TWICE

WSH 58: The Proband

The proband (34), born 1854; died at age 75 years at Warren State Hospital of chronic myocarditis. She was described as very pretty and always "snobbish." At age 20 years, following an attack of typhoid fever, she was "nervous" and would talk and pray at night. She recovered and remained well until age 34 years when she became very talkative, destructive, irritable and developed auditory hallucinations and delusions of persecution (she believed people were stealing from her). She was hospitalized at Warren State Hospital from 6/28/1892 until 2/15/1893, where she rapidly improved. She was normal until 1896, when she developed another similar attack and was readmitted to the hospital. The attack lasted two months. Subsequent remissions between attacks became shorter and she became very deteriorated, with attacks of depression as well as of hyperactivity. Diagnosis at first hospitalization was acute mania and at the second hospitalization it was dementia praecox. Classification: Schizophrenic reaction—paranoid type.

(33) husband of proband (34), born 1849; at age 50 years deserted his wife and children and was never heard from again. He was described as the "black sheep" of an otherwise respectable family. He was an unfaithful husband, a good miner and a very clever thief. He was also reportedly "very frequently" intoxicated. Classification: Sociopathic personality disturbance.

Children

Daughter (52), born 1879; died at age 65 years at Warren State Hospital, of pulmonary tuberculosis. As a child she would pout and sulk. At age 21 years she began to imagine that she was to be married and would occasionally laugh without cause or strike someone with no provocation. She was admitted to Warren State Hospital on 8/28/1900, and found to have visual hallucinations about hell. She was discharged on 5/13/1901, but readmitted on 8/25/1902, when she again became unmanageable. She "saw the devil," was denudative, afraid of people and had an induced abortion for a probably imaginary pregnancy. She continued to deteriorate, with shorter periods of remission, and was sometimes deeply depressed and at other times confused and vicious. Diagnosis at Warren State Hospital was dementia praecox. Classification: Schizophrenic reaction—catatonic type.

Son (54), born 1881; died at age 64 years of influenza. He was described as "quite a heavy drinker" who changed jobs often and who had "spells" when he would not reply to questions and would "sit and laugh to himself." Affect was inappropriate. At times he would be noisy at night and would engage in bizarre activities, such as washing and rewashing clothes. He was never hospitalized. Classification: Schizophrenic reaction—paranoid type.

Daughter (56), born 1885; died at age 66 years at Warren State Hospital of arteriosclerotic heart disease. As a child she was reportedly "bad-tempered" and would "sneak and lie." At age 16 years she became "vicious" and was placed in a poorhouse for seven weeks, then transferred to Warren State Hospital on 11/12/1901. She had successive periods of depression, excitement and normality, but not necessarily in that order. She went home on 12/8/1906, became illegitimately pregnant, again developed symptoms of excitement and depression and was readmitted on 10/30/1907. On several occasions she attempted suicide. She escaped on 10/1/1915, was committed to another state mental hospital on 2/2/1916, and was transferred to Warren State Hospital on 3/4/1916, where she remained until her death. Diagnosis at Warren was acute mania, manic-depressive. Classification: Schizophrenic reaction—schizo-affective type.

Son (57), born 1888; died at age 47 years at Warren State Hospital of chronic myocarditis. He was always considered "mentally unbalanced" and "very peculiar" as he was silly, claimed that the Lord made promises to him and thought he had discovered perpetual motion. He also had tactile hallucinations of a hand touching his face. He was arrested on 1/22/1917, when he caused a disturbance by playing a mouth organ, running and jumping in the streets, and by playing a piano and singing in a hotel lobby. He was transferred to Warren

State Hospital on 1/30/1917, with a diagnosis of dementia praecox. He escaped on 1/31/1918, was returned on 7/5/1922 and paroled on 8/16/1924. He was readmitted on 8/5/1926 and remained at Warren until his death. A 1927 diagnosis at Warren was schizophrenia. Classification: Schizophrenic reaction.

Daughter (58), born 1890; died at age 61 years at Warren State Hospital of an acute coronary occlusion. Until age 25 years she was shy and quiet, then she developed the delusion that she was about to be married, became disorderly, would wander about and had periods of mutism. She spent six weeks in a county home, then was admitted to Warren State Hospital on 11/29/1916, and remained there until her death. Diagnosis at Warren was dementia praecox, hebephrenic type. While hospitalized she had aural and visual hallucinations, was incoherent, lacked insight and her affect and memory were impaired. She developed delusions of a bizarre, persecutory type. Classification: Schizophrenic reaction — paranoid type.

Daughter (60), born 1897. She reportedly was "scattered and difficult to follow" in conversation since age 37 years. An interviewer described her, at age 67 years, as easily distractible and rambling. She appeared indifferent to her personal appearance as well as to the appearance of her home. Classification: Probable personality pattern disturbance.

(61) husband of daughter (60), died at age 82 years at a state mental hospital of congestive heart failure. He was admitted 10 days prior to his death because of sleeplessness and confusion. He had hardening of the arteries. Classification: Chronic brain syndrome associated with cerebral arteriosclerosis.

Grandchildren

(116) wife of grandson (115), born about 1918; hospitalized at a mental hospital on 3/7/1964 with delusions of persecution and impaired insight and judgment. The hospital diagnosis was paranoid reaction with depressive element, for which she received eight electroshock treatments and was discharged 4/15/1964. Classification: Schizophrenic reaction — paranoid type.

Great-Grandchildren

(249) wife of great-grandson (248), born 1937. She was described as "nervous and excitable." Classification: Possible psychoneurotic reaction.

(251) wife of great-grandson (250), born 1935. She was described as "nervous and excitable." Classification: Possible psychoneurotic reaction.

Grandparents

Paternal grandfather (2), died at age 85 years, cause of death unknown. He reportedly was "silly in conversation, drank a good deal and stole sheep as well as household valuables from his neighbors." Classification: Probable sociopathic personality disturbance.

Paternal grandmother (3), described as "not very bright" and as a "scold." She would talk abusively of people, then be very pleasant to them in person. She also occasionally left home for a day or two after quarrels with her husband. Classification: Possible personality disorder.

Parents

Father (17), born 1829; died at age 83 years of "old age." He reportedly was "ugly tempered" and lied, drank, was illiterate and "quarrelsome." He was imprisoned in 1877 for theft. Classification: Sociopathic personality disturbance.

Mother (18), born 1829; died at age 86 years, cause of death unknown. She was described as "ignorant, profane, broken down mentally, demented" and with an uncontrollable temper. She directed the activities of the "Stewart gang of thieves." Classification: Sociopathic personality disturbance.

Aunts and Uncles

Paternal half uncle (6), died at age 35 years at a mental hospital in Philadelphia, Pennsylvania. He was well educated and a lawyer; however, he was known as "crazy John" and had spells of anger, when he became destructive, didn't work and "talked along religious lines." Family members attributed his "insanity" to a blow on the head received in a fight. Classification: Probably with functional psychosis, schizophrenic reaction.

Paternal aunt (8), born 1816; died at age 94 years from the effects of a fall. Her "mind was poor" the last 20 years of her life—she was "a scold," bad tempered, excitable and would desert her family for days at a time. She could not recognize people and had untidy habits. She was totally demented the last five years of her life. Classification: Probable chronic brain syndrome of senium.

Paternal uncle (9), died at age 60 years of gangrene. He was described as "simple-minded, a thief, entirely untrustworthy—a rascal who would beat you any way he could." Classification: Probable sociopathic personality disturbance.

Paternal aunt (12), born 1820; died at age 82 years of "old age." She was described as "a silly scold" who had "angry spells." She was peculiar, unintelligent and superstitious, and fancied she could see "signs" in the sky at times. She would leave her home for days at a time. Classification: Probably with functional psychosis, schizophrenic reaction.

Paternal aunt (14), born 1830; died at age 80 years of cancer of the stomach. She reportedly became "insane" at about age 25 years following the excitement of some revival meetings. After that she had no normal periods but imagined people talked about her, and she mumbled to herself and would scold passersby in an abusive fashion. She would wander away and stay in vacant houses. At one time she was hospitalized and was in a county home from 1906 until her death. Classification: Schizophrenic reaction.

Siblings

Brother (35), born 1855; died at age 33 years. He was shot to death while looting a house. He was described as "a thief and an alcoholic" and was imprisoned for larceny. Classification: Sociopathic personality disturbance.

(38) husband of sister (39), born 1851; died at age 68 years of a cardiovascular accident. He was described as "a drunken, lazy, dishonest, good-for-nothing man—too lazy to work." Classification: Personality pattern disturbance.

Sister (39), born 1861; died at age 55 years of diabetes. She was described as an "ignorant woman of rather bad temper and low moral reputation . . . ill-tempered . . . occasionally left her husband and lived with other men . . . didn't pay bills." She threatened her husband and assaulted him at times. Classification: Sociopathic personality disturbance.

(40) husband of sister (41), born 1857; died at age 55 years in a railroad accident while trespassing. He was described as "an ugly-tempered man and a heavy drinker." He would disappear for several months "when on a spree." Classification: Sociopathic personality disturbance—alcoholism (addiction).

Sister (41), born 1862; died at age 69 years, cause of death unknown. She was described as bad tempered and as having a bad reputation. She became violent when angry and once attempted to take her husband's life with a butcher knife. When angry with her husband she would "curse and swear and quarrel" with him for weeks. When she went into the surrounding towns to work she posed as a widow. She often separated from her husband for months at a time. Classification: Probable personality pattern disturbance—schizoid personality or paranoid personality.

(42) father of illegitimate child of (43), born 1849; died at age 45 years of a heart attack. He was reportedly "probably an alcoholic." Classification: Possible sociopathic personality disturbance—alcoholism (addiction).

Sister (43), born 1868; died at age 33 years of pneumonia. She reportedly would "fly into tantrums" over insignificant events. She had two illegitimate children, both of whom she gave to her sister. Classification: Possible personality disorder.

(45) husband of sister (46), born 1868; was age 47 years at last information, when he was described as a "heavy drinker." Classification: Possible sociopathic personality disturbance—alcoholism (addiction).

Sister (46), born 1871; died at age 78 years at a state mental hospital, of myocarditis. She was always "notorious" because of her hot temper and destructive tendencies. She had outbreaks of violence, frequently associated with menstrual periods, when she would break dishes, destroy furniture and attack her husband. She and her husband separated many times and she would go to live with other men. Attempts were made to hospitalize her, especially after she stabbed her husband in the forehead with a knife and abused her children, but she was not hospitalized until 10/25/1916, after she attacked her sister. At about age 32 years she began to have periods of idleness and indifference, as well as of violence, when she would break into senseless laughter. She also developed aural hallucinations and thought people were talking about her. Hospitalization was at Warren State Hospital, with a diagnosis of dementia praecox; some staff members considered her an imbecile with an "uncontrollable temper." She was transferred to another state mental hospital on 11/15/1917, and remained there until death in 1949. Classification: Schizophrenic reaction.

Nieces and Nephews

Niece (67), born 1884; died at age 38 years, cause of death unknown. She was described by her mother as "kind of nervous — like easily becomes delirious when ill." Her physician said "she is a poor, miserable, extremely nervous woman . . . one of your primary neurotics." Classification: Psychoneurotic disorder.

Nephew (68), born 1882; as a young man described as an alcoholic who was a good workman but lost jobs and spent time in jail because of his drinking. When interviewed at age 80 years he was found to be blind but had an excellent memory and was happy and friendly. Classification: Sociopathic personality disturbance — alcoholism (addiction).

(70) husband of niece (71), born 1876; died at age 82 years of lymphatic leukemia. He reportedly drank "to excess at times." Classification: Possible sociopathic personality disturbance — alcoholism (addiction).

Niece (71), born 1883; died at age 68 years of coronary thrombosis. She was the "only member of the family who could read or write." She had "nervous prostration" at one time and was described as a nervous, excitable woman who bit her fingernails

continually. Classification: Probable psychoneurotic reaction.

(81) husband of niece (80), born 1876; died at age 64 years of cancer of the kidneys. He was described as "a heavy drinker who beat his wife frequently." Classification: Possible sociopathic personality disturbance — alcoholism (addiction).

Nephew (82), born 1882; died at age 64 years of cancer. He was described as a "heavy drinker" and as an unusually ugly, mean and disagreeable man. He deserted his wife and children to live with another woman, although he later returned to his wife. Classification: Probable sociopathic personality disturbance — alcoholism (addiction).

Niece (86), born 1885; died at age 64 years of cancer. She was described as "nervous — faints easily." She was also described as "unreliable . . . reputation was bad . . . very crooked" and as "living in a house of ill fame." She had an "extreme temper." Classification: Probable sociopathic personality disturbance.

Nephew (89), born 1887; died at age 71 years of heart disease. He was described as "outspoken and gruff" and reportedly once "drank to excess" but later was "under a pledge of abstinence." Classification: Possible sociopathic personality disturbance — alcoholism (addiction).

Niece (97), born 1892; died at age 21 years following a miscarriage. She was described as "nervous and excitable like the rest of the family." Classification: Possible psychoneurotic reaction.

Nephew (101), born in 1901; was "killed by a train while trespassing on railroad property" at age 49 years. He was a "heavy drinker." Classification: Probable sociopathic personality disturbance — alcoholism (addiction).

Niece (103), born 1887. At age 75 years was described by an interviewer as "sharp-featured, terse in speech . . . evasive in discussing parentage." An early interviewer described her as "shows lack of emotion, eyes have a glassy stare, conversation a steady monotone . . . expressed self in rather stilted fashion." She was reared by a maternal aunt. Classification: Possible personality pattern disturbance — schizoid personality.

Niece (108), born 1894; described as

"neurotic," of an "hysterical temperament" and inclined to exaggerate any little physical ill. Classification: Probable psychoneurotic disorder.

Distant Relatives

(166) wife of grandnephew (167), born 1914. She had a common-law marriage to (167) for seven years, after which they separated. She was described as "nervous" and at age 49 years was under a doctor's care for her nervousness. Classification: Probable psychoneurotic disorder.

Grandnephew (167), born 1913. He was described as "nervous and always irritable." He deserted (166) after seven years of common-law marriage. Classification: Probable psychoneurotic disorder.

Grandnephew (169), born 1919. He had a "breakdown" at age 17 years and was treated with drugs at a private sanitarium. He was also treated at a mental hospital in Ohio (records had been destroyed), from which he was discharged on 11/30/1949. At age 44 years he was described as "much like a child—can't remember anything" and had never worked. Classification: Probably with functional psychosis, schizophrenic reaction.

Grandnephew (195), born 1906; died at age 48 years of cirrhosis of the liver. He was described as a "heavy drinker" with a history of much marital conflict. Classification: Probable sociopathic personality disturbance—alcoholism (addiction).

Grandnephew (205), born 1907; described at age 57 years as "very hostile." While being interviewed he yelled at his wife not to answer questions, but she ignored him and explained that "he was like that." As a child, beginning at age four years, he had "spells" during which he would fall over and was unable to speak, but had no convulsive movements. This problem was never diagnosed. Classification: Possible psychoneurotic disorder.

Great-grandniece (300), born 1932. Her parents separated when she was seven years of age. At age 31 years she described herself as nervous and high strung and was under doctor's care for her nervousness. Classification: Probable psychoneurotic disorder.

(301) husband of great-grandniece (300), born 1915. He reportedly was an alcoholic and had ulcers. He was incarcerated for non-support of his children by a previous marriage. Classification: Sociopathic personality disturbance—alcoholism (addiction).

(302) husband of great-grandniece (303), born 1932. He was described as lazy, usually unemployed and an alcoholic who was hospitalized for one week for his alcoholism. He had since been a member of Alcoholics Anonymous. Classification: Sociopathic personality disturbance—alcoholism (addiction).

Great-grandniece (303), born 1934. She had a speech defect as a child and at age 29 was treated "for nerves." She was about five years of age when her parents separated. Classification: Probable psychoneurotic disorder.

Great-grandniece (305), born 1937. She was about two years of age when her parents separated. At age 26 years she doctored for nerves. Classification: Probable psychoneurotic disorder.

Family Summary

The proband, three daughters, two sons, a grandson, a paternal aunt and a sister had psychotic disorders, and a paternal aunt, a paternal half uncle and a grandnephew had probable psychotic disorders. Personality disorders were found in the proband's husband, a daughter, each of the paternal grandparents, both parents, a paternal uncle, a brother, three sisters, four nephews, two nieces and in a grandnephew. They were also found in the husbands of four sisters, the husbands of two nieces and the husbands of two great-grandnieces. A paternal aunt and the husband of a daughter had chronic brain syndrome. Four nieces, two grandnephews, three great-grandnieces, the wives of two great-grandsons and the wife of a grandnephew were neurotic.

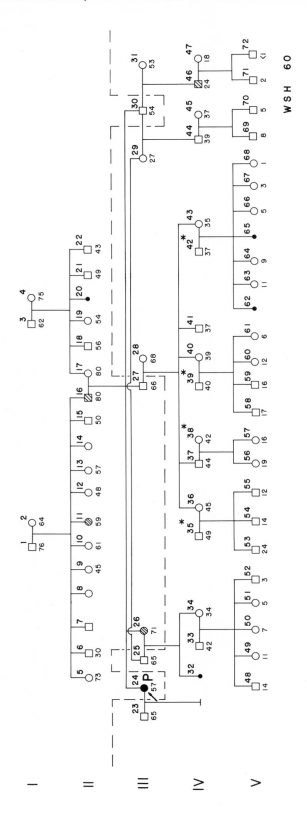

WSH 60

WSH 60: The Proband

The proband (24), born 1888; died at age 57 years at Warren State Hospital, of manic-depressive psychosis, manic phase. She was an active, outgoing person and a successful teacher who, within the year prior to her admission to Warren State Hospital on 12/10/1913, began to experience hyperactivity, disorientation, possible hallucinations, untidiness and elation. Diagnosis at this hospitalization was manic-depressive psychosis, manic phase. While hospitalized she developed paranoid ideas and bizarre delusions; she believed there were "dead men under her bed." After her discharge on 12/4/1914, she was normal until two days before her second admission to the hospital in 1945. At this time the welfare agency had removed a 12-year old girl, who had been with the patient and her husband for a number of years, from their home, refusing the adoption they had requested. The proband talked incessantly and appeared to be in constant motion. At the hospital she did not sleep, was incontinent, required tube feeding, and died within one week. Classification: Schizophrenic reaction—catatonic type.

Parents

Father (16), born 1861; died at age 80 years, cause of death unknown. He was described as a "steady drinker." Classification: Possible sociopathic personality disturbance—alcoholism (addiction).

Aunts and Uncles

Paternal aunt (11), born 1855; age at last information was 59 years. Before her marriage she was an unsuccessful seamstress. She was always subject to "blue spells" which would come on without cause and last two or three days. For a period of two years, following the death of her husband, she worried a great deal, cried frequently, took little interest in things and insisted that she "wanted to die." Classification: Probable psychoneurotic disorder—depressive reaction.

Siblings

Sister (26), born 1889. She was described as obese and as suffering from chronic insomnia. She was under treatment for her insomnia, but with no results. She and her husband were separated but not divorced. Classification: Probable psychoneurotic disorder.

Nieces and Nephews

Nephew (46), born 1936. As a child he stuttered noticeably. His father died when (46) was 14 years of age and his mother remarried three years later. His relationship with his stepfather was good. As an adult he had difficulty holding a job, although additional training alleviated this problem. His marriage was one of necessity and the resulting financial difficulties were very stressful for him and he was described as very nervous. Classification: Possible other transient situational personality disturbance.

Family Summary

The proband had a psychotic disorder. Her father was possibly alcoholic and a sister and paternal aunt were probably neurotic. A nephew had a transient personality disorder.

Controls

None noteworthy.

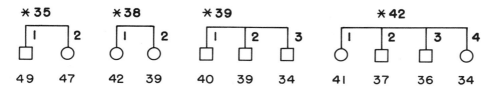

CONTROLS

W S H   6 0

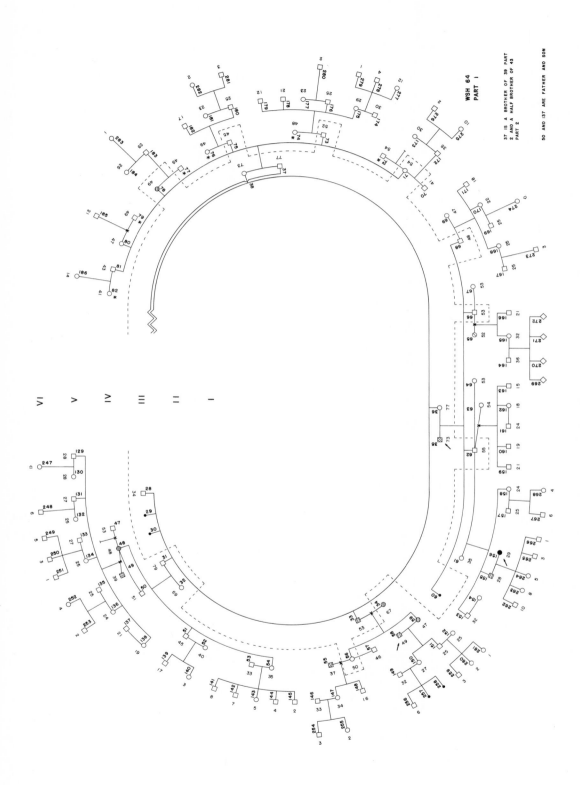

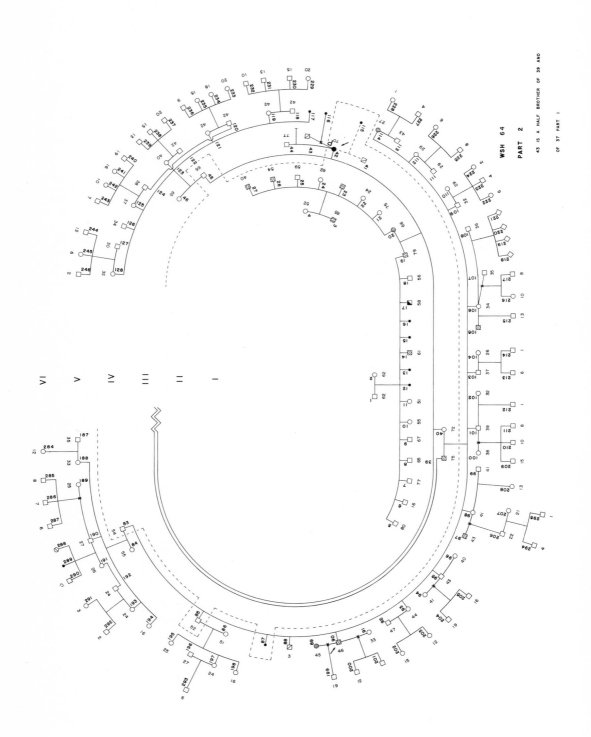

WSH 64

PART 2

43 IS A HALF BROTHER OF 39 AND OF 37 PART 1

WSH 64: The Proband

The proband (42), born 1892. She became a domestic after leaving school, where she reportedly made very poor progress. As a domestic she had at least 12 positions in seven years. She left each place of employment voluntarily. She gave birth to an illegitimate child on 12/28/1913. The delivery was difficult and the infant died a few days after birth. Four days following the delivery she "developed a maniacal state." At no time did she have a fever. The family could not retain the services of a nurse so she was hospitalized; at this time she became unmanageable and was committed to Warren State Hospital on 1/10/1914, with a diagnosis of manic-depressive psychosis. She was untidy, destructive, careless of personal appearance, refused to remain in bed, and showed a jocular reaction with sudden changes to brief periods of sadness. She was distractible, obscene and possibly hallucinated. She was discharged as improved on 10/23/1914. The second hospitalization at Warren State Hospital, from 5/18/1916 until 10/9/1916, with a diagnosis of manic-depressive, hypermanic phase — imbecility, followed her second confinement and was similar to the first psychotic break. She remained well and her history of psychosis was unknown to most of her friends and relatives. Classification: Schizophrenic reaction — catatonic type.

Grandparents

Maternal grandfather (3), born 1829; died at age 65 years. He was described as "a hard drinker" who became intoxicated every week or two. When intoxicated he became "very ugly." Classification: Probable sociopathic personality disturbance — alcoholism (addiction).

Parents

Father (19), born 1841; died at age 79 years. He was described as "very severe with his children ... unreasonably cross with them." He was also described, in old age, as "a broken-down, feeble man, both mentally and physically," his comprehension became poor and his conversation was apt to be irrelevant. Classification: Probable chronic brain syndrome of senium.

Mother (20), born 1857; died at age 66 years. She was described as "a talkative, emotional woman" who made "extravagant, vague and meaningless" statements to the interviewer. In 1902 she suffered an attack of "brain fever" and for a period of five weeks experienced severe headaches. For one week she was bedridden and delirious. It was observed that she was mentally deficient as well as emotionally unstable. Classification: Personality trait disturbance — emotionally unstable personality.

Aunts and Uncles

Paternal uncle (14), born 1853; age 61 years when interviewed. He had a "decided boasting tendency" and was described as a "hard drinker." Classification: Possible sociopathic personality disturbance — alcoholism (addiction).

Paternal uncle (17); age 58 years at last information. After he had typhoid fever he was "out of his mind" for almost a year. His recovery was very sudden and his health was otherwise normal. Classification: Probably with functional psychosis.

Maternal uncle (23), reportedly a "hard drinker." Classification: Possible sociopathic personality disturbance — alcoholism (addiction).

Maternal uncle (26), born 1860; age 54 years at last information. He was described as lazy and unstable and was reportedly in a home or institution in Canada in 1914, although this could not be verified. Classification: Possible personality disorder.

Maternal uncle (27); died at age 40 years, reportedly of cancer of the stomach, although other sources said that "whiskey was what really finished him." Classification: Probable sociopathic personality disturbance — alcoholism (addiction).

Siblings

Brother (33), born 1883; died at age 53 years of cancer. He left his wife in 1925 but supported her for 10 years until they were divorced. He moved around a great deal as he had "skipped bail" when he was in legal trouble; he was also described as a "con man." Classification: Sociopathic personality disturbance.

(35) husband of sister (36), born 1881; died at age 73 years of pneumonia. At age 59 years he was diagnosed as a psychoneurotic at the Warren State Hospital Clinic. At age 66 years he suffered a head injury when he fell over backwards on ice, striking his head on frozen ground. Two weeks later he had a convulsion, following which his speech became thick and peculiar. He later became confused and irritable. His adjustment was progressively impaired and he was admitted to Warren State Hospital on 2/24/1950, with a diagnosis of senile psychosis. He remained at the hospital until his death. Classification: Chronic brain syndrome associated with cerebral arteriosclerosis.

(39) husband of sister (40); age 75 years at last information. He was described as "physically fine but easily confused due to senility." He was also described as "exceptionally mean to the children when younger." Classification: Possible personality disorder.

Nieces and Nephews

Niece (48), born 1914. In 1938 she "suffered a nervous breakdown" when her second husband was drinking and could not support the family. She described her own condition as "crazier than a bed bug." Classification: Probable psychoneurotic reaction—other.

(49) husband of niece (48), born 1911. He was described as "no good" and was an alcoholic who did not support his family. Classification: Sociopathic personality disturbance—alcoholism (addiction).

(55) husband of niece (56), born 1897. He was described by his family as "flighty." In 1934 he left his job and "disappeared"; his whereabouts were unknown after this. Classification: Possible personality disorder.

(58) husband of niece (59), born 1908; died at age 49 years of cirrhosis of the liver. He was hospitalized at a state hospital from 8/3/1955 until 10/3/1955, with a diagnosis of psychosis due to alcohol, delirium tremens. For two weeks prior to admission he had been drinking beer day and night. An arrest warrant was obtained for disorderly conduct when he "talked rough, refused to wear clothes and threatened to rape his daughter." He also suffered from delusions and hallucinations, sleeplessness and was unable to work. While hospitalized the acute episode rapidly subsided; however, he remained somewhat suspicious. Classification: Sociopathic personality disturbance—alcoholism (addiction); also, acute brain syndrome associated with alcohol intoxication.

Niece (59), born 1915. She had "doctored for nerves" and was concerned that she had cancer when there was no medical basis for her fear. Classification: Probable psychoneurotic reaction.

Niece (78), born 1913. At the time of menopause she had severe emotional difficulties during which she was depressed and cried frequently. Classification: Transient situational personality disturbance—adult situational reaction.

(89) wife of nephew (90), born 1917. She had one child before her marriage to (90) and one later. She and (90) were divorced when the child was two years of age because of her promiscuity as well as his antisocial behavior. Classification: Sociopathic personality disturbance—antisocial reaction.

Nephew (90), born 1916. He had a history of kleptomania, several imprisonments for petit larceny and two arrests for indecent exposure. He was divorced from both his wives. He was voluntarily admitted to a state hospital on 2/12/1952, after an arrest for wife beating. A diagnosis of without mental disorder, psychopathic personality, asocial and amoral trends was made, and he was discharged on 3/20/1952. Classification: Sociopathic personality disturbance—antisocial reaction.

(97) husband of niece (98), born 1917. He was described as "no good" because of his alcoholism. Classification: Sociopathic personality disturbance—alcoholism (addiction).

(105) husband of niece (106), born 1926; died by drowning, details of his death unknown. He was an alcoholic. Classification: Sociopathic personality disturbance—alcoholism (addiction).

Niece (114), born 1935. She was reported to be a hypochondriac and "doctored for nerves." She was raising her husband's two children by his first marriage, as well as her own two children. She was near a "ner-

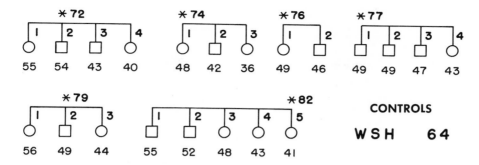

Distant Relatives

Grandnephew (155), born 1933; died at age 28 years from injuries received in an automobile accident. He was raised by his father's second wife after the death of his mother and the divorce of his father from the second wife. In 1962 he was incarcerated for forgery. Classification: Sociopathic personality disturbance.

(156) wife of grandnephew (155), born 1933. She was admitted to a state hospital on 2/20/1960, with a diagnosis of schizophrenia, undifferentiated type, where she remained. Several unsuccessful home care attempts had been made. Symptoms began about two years previous to admission when she became careless in her appearance, over-religious, began to wander away from home without a reasonable explanation and began to neglect her children. At last information she was hospitalized, remaining unspontaneous, somewhat seclusive, unsociable and preoccupied

vous breakdown" in 1961 but was reportedly "better after her husband died." Classification: Probable psychoneurotic reaction.

with religious beliefs. Classification: Schizophrenic reaction—chronic undifferentiated type.

Family Summary

The proband and the wife of a grandnephew were the only psychotic members of this family, although a paternal uncle was probably so but was never treated. Other hospitalized individuals included the husband of a sister with a psychosis associated with cerebral arteriosclerosis, the husband of a niece with acute alcoholism and a nephew who was admitted voluntarily with a diagnosis of personality disorder. Other personality disorders were found in the maternal grandfather, the mother, a paternal uncle, three maternal uncles, a brother, the husband of a sister, a niece, the wife of a nephew, the husbands of four nieces, and in a grandnephew. Three nieces were neurotic. The father was classified as with probable chronic brain syndrome of senium.

Controls

None noteworthy.

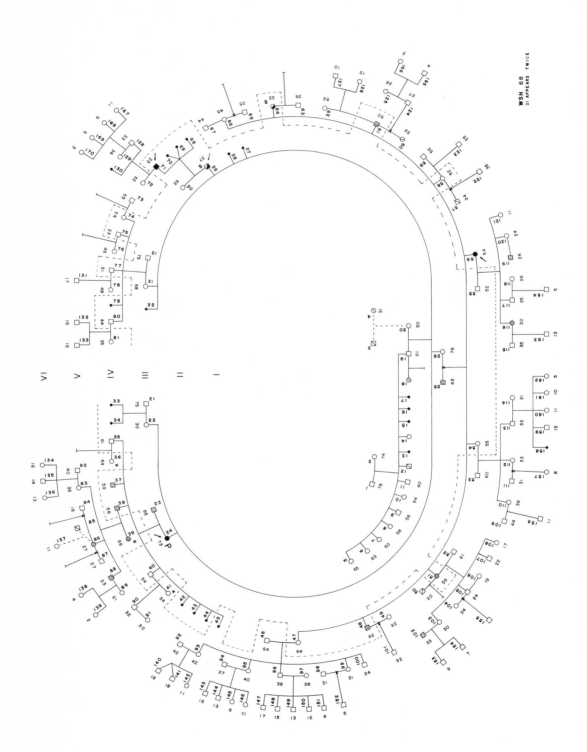

WSH 68
21 APPEARS TWICE

WSH 68: The Proband

The proband (24), born 1876; died at age 73 years at Warren State Hospital, of a strangulated hernia. She was originally admitted to the hospital on 8/5/1913, with a diagnosis of manic-depressive psychosis, depressed phase, and discharged on 8/27/1914. A second hospitalization with the same diagnosis was from 3/21/1923 until 9/1/1923. Symptoms at both psychotic episodes were similar; she appeared worried, unhappy, agitated, had suicidal tendencies and auditory and visual hallucinations. She was hospitalized a third time on 11/3/1949, and remained at Warren State Hospital until her death. Classification: Schizophrenic reaction—paranoid type.

(23) husband of proband (24), born 1874; died at age 65 years, cause of death unknown. He was described as "ugly, surly . . . sarcastic and proud." Classification: Possible personality disorder.

Children

Son (37), born 1901. He was interviewed and described as a suspicious, eccentric man who lived alone after his mother's death. Classification: Possible personality disorder.

Son (38), born 1904. He was very intoxicated when interviewed; however, although he drank daily, he was steadily employed. His wife described him as brutal and as a sex pervert. Classification: Sociopathic personality disorder—alcoholism (addiction).

(39) wife of son (38), born 1904. She was extremely intoxicated when interviewed and, although cooperative, she cried, laughed, was vulgar and profane and at one time threatened to throw the interviewer out of the house. She spent her days frequenting the local taverns and family members were unsuccessful in their attempts to get her to seek medical aid for her alcoholism. Classification: Sociopathic personality disturbance—alcoholism (addiction).

Grandchildren

Granddaughter (86), born 1933. Her first marriage lasted three weeks and was annulled. A year later she had an illegitimate child and the following year she married her second husband. This marriage ended in divorce after nine years. Classification: Possible personality disorder.

Grandson (88), born 1937. As an adolescent he had "trouble with the law." He was a heavy drinker but not considered an alcoholic by his family. He was brutal to his family and was arrested several times for wife beating. Classification: Sociopathic personality disturbance—antisocial reaction.

Siblings

(25) husband of sister (26), born about 1879 and listed as deceased on his wife's death certificate in 1956. He was a poor provider who deserted his family when his youngest child was six years of age. Classification: Sociopathic personality disturbance—antisocial reaction.

Brother (29), born 1883; died at age 37 years of myocarditis, pneumonia and diphtheria. He was always considered to be a "worrier" and following some financial difficulties regarding the purchase of a farm with an old claim against it, he became depressed and attempted suicide with a hatchet. He was hospitalized and died one month later. Classification: Probably with functional psychosis—psychotic-depressive reaction.

Nieces and Nephews

Nephew (48), born 1898; died at age 62 years of cancer. He and his wife separated several times and were finally divorced because of his alcoholism. Classification: Sociopathic personality disturbance—alcoholism (addiction).

Niece (51), born 1902. She was described by various family members as "nervous and talkative." When interviewed, she stated that she would give no information, then "talked a blue streak." Her ramblings had to be interpreted in order to get the information needed. During the interview her descriptions of illness and "sick spells" were given in detail. When describing surgery for "female trouble" she stated that she felt as if she had a "balloon on her head" which broke and "water or blood

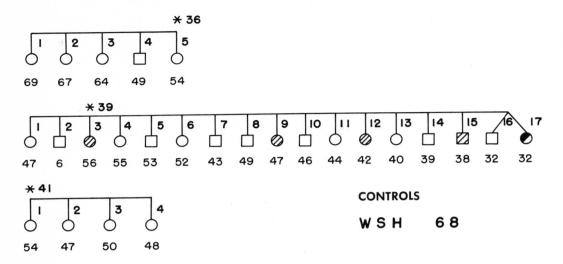

CONTROLS

W S H   6 8

flowed over her face and shoulders." No more than one family member could visit her at a time or she would become "nervous and collapse." Classification: Psychoneurotic disorder—conversion and anxiety reactions.

Niece (56), born 1906. In 1950, following the birth of her youngest child, she became "distraught and had a peculiar attitude toward the baby." Her mental problems necessitated two hospitalizations for psychiatric care: one from 9/10/1951 until 10/4/1951, discharged as restored on 9/4/1952; and a second from 9/8/1956 until 10/8/1956, again discharged as restored on 4/7/1958. When interviewed she refused to sign a release of her hospital records for a description of her illness but the diagnosis and classification were schizophrenic reaction—catatonic type.

Nephew (61), born 1910. At age 15 years he was considered incorrigible and delinquent and was charged with theft. The charges were dropped when the costs were paid. At age 20 years he was charged with fornication and bastardy; these charges were also dropped when the costs were paid. The sheriff's notes stated that he "hit the bottle, drank quite a bit." Classification: Sociopathic personality disturbance—antisocial reaction.

Niece (64), born 1913; suicided at age 22 years by shooting herself. Contributory causes of death were listed as melancholia and ill health. A short time before her suicide she had been injured in an automobile accident, after which she became "very

moody." Classification: Probably with functional psychosis, psychotic-depressive reaction.

Nephew (71), born 1913; died at age 23 years of pulmonary tuberculosis. He was always a "worrier" and worried over business matters associated with his occupation of farmer. In early 1929 he became elated, grandiose and expressed delusions of wealth. He was committed to a state mental hospital from 4/17/1929 until 10/26/1929, with a diagnosis of dementia praecox, hebephrenic type; he was described as disoriented, irrelevant, incoherent and untidy. In July, 1930, after recovering from pneumonia, he became incoherent and irrelevant in conversation; he wept one moment, laughed the next, and became inattentive and rather destructive. He was readmitted to the hospital with the same diagnosis as before, and remained there until his death. Classification: Schizophrenic reaction.

Distant Relatives

(102) husband of grandniece (103), born 1928. He was described as "a good worker but he drinks too much." He lost his car and his home because of his drinking, which, also reportedly, caused ulcers. Classification: Sociopathic personality disturbance—alcoholism (addiction).

Grandniece (116), born 1931. She had "doctored for nerves" for 12 years after her pregnancy at age 18 years. Classification: Probable psychoneurotic reaction.

(119) husband of grandniece (120), born 1935. His behavior was described as "erratic at times." Classification: Possible personality disorder.

Family Summary

The proband, a niece and a nephew had a psychotic disorder and a brother and a niece probably so. Those classified as, or perhaps, with personality disorders included two sons and a wife of one of the sons, the proband's husband, a granddaughter and a grandson, the husband of a sister, two nephews and the husbands of two grandnieces. A niece and a grandniece were neurotic.

Controls

See family pedigree, person 39.

Sister (9) of (39), born 1913. She reportedly was married and divorced four times and had a "drinking problem." Classification: Possible sociopathic personality disturbance — alcoholism (addiction).

Sister (12) of (39), born 1918. She was described as an alcoholic. Classification: Sociopathic personality disturbance — alcoholism (addiction).

Brother (15) of (39), born 1922. A son of his died of leukemia at age 15 years. At this time (15) began "drinking heavily." Classification: Possible sociopathic personality disturbance — alcoholism (addiction).

Sister (17) of (39), born 1928. She reportedly received treatment in a mental hospital shortly after her first marriage. In 1958 she applied for outpatient treatment but did not accept treatment as she was "feeling better about her problems." Classification: Possibly with functional psychosis.

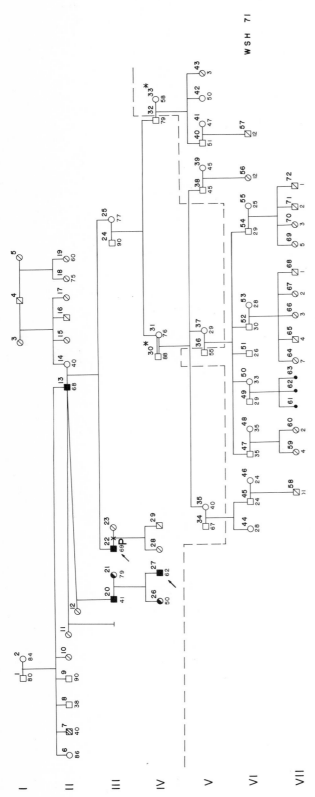

WSH 71: The Proband

The proband (22), born 1844; died at age 69 years at Warren State Hospital of pulmonary edema and chronic endocarditis. He was always considered "shiftless." He was hospitalized at Warren State Hospital from 4/17/1902 until 2/9/1903, and again, after a normal period of three years, from 3/6/1906 until 7/10/1906, with a diagnosis of acute mania. At each attack of mania he was hyperactive, destructive, incoherent and religiously excited. The third admission was on 11/29/1913. The attack persisted until he was completely enfeebled and he succumbed to weakness 11 days after admission. Final diagnosis at Warren State Hospital and classification: Schizophrenic reaction—catatonic type.

Parents

Father (13), died at age 68 years of "liver trouble." It was reported that, although he was of a naturally bright and lively disposition, he was subject to periods of mental disturbance lasting several months at a time. He was never hospitalized during these episodes and there was no regularity of interval between the attacks. During the episodes he would refuse to speak to anyone and could not work because of lack of concentration. He never attempted suicide. Classification: Manic-depressive reaction—other.

Aunts and Uncles

Paternal uncle (7), died at age 40 years of tuberculosis. "In young life" he had one attack of mental disturbance during which he was talkative and excited. Classification: Probable transient situational personality disorder; Possibly with functional psychosis.

Siblings

Paternal half brother (20), born 1856; died at age 41 years of inflammation of the brain. He experienced three or four periods of depression in his lifetime: the first was at about 18 years of age and the last began two

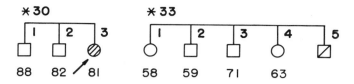

CONTROLS

weeks before his death. He always made a good recovery and was normal in the intervals between attacks. He would do no work, would read a little, but spent most of his time looking at the ceiling during a depressed period. He had no periods of mutism and never refused food. At times he imagined he had committed "the unpardonable sin" and spoke of suicide, although he never made an attempt. Classification: Manic-depressive reaction, depressed type.

(21) wife of half brother (20), born 1861; died at age 79 years of chronic interstitial nephritis. She was described as a nervous, excitable and rather peculiar woman who lived as a recluse in utter poverty with her schizophrenic son and probably psychotic daughter. A sizable estate, however, was left after her death. Not only did they live as recluses but also in separate areas of the house as they were afraid of getting germs from each other. Classification: Probably with functional psychosis, schizophrenic reaction—paranoid type; Possible personality pattern disturbance—paranoid personality.

Nieces and Nephews

Half niece (26), born 1883; died at age 50 years of acute bronchitis. She was described as "talkative and not a shut-in personality" although strangely lacking in interests and ambitions. She lived as a recluse with her mother and psychotic brother. Classification: Probably with functional psychosis, schizophrenic reaction—paranoid type; Possible personality pattern disturbance—paranoid personality.

Half nephew (27), born 1889; died at age 62 years at Warren State Hospital of myocardial failure. He attended college for two years and worked as a gardener. He was

W S H 71

hospitalized at Warren State Hospital from 12/27/1930 until 11/19/1934, with a diagnosis of psychoneurosis, hysterical type. While hospitalized he displayed characteristic hysterical phenomena, including one delirious episode with infantile conduct. He was readmitted on 9/10/1940. All but one month of the intervening time had been spent at a private mental hospital. At the time of the second admission he was a "clear-cut schizophrenic" and was diagnosed as schizophrenic reaction, hebephrenic type. He remained confused and hallucinated until his death. Classification: Schizophrenic reaction—paranoid type.

Family Summary

The proband, his father, a half brother and a half nephew had psychotic disorders, and a half niece and the half brother's wife were probably so affected. Only the proband and the half nephew were hospitalized with their psychoses. A paternal uncle had a probable psychotic disorder or was possibly psychotic.

Controls

Sister (3) of (30), born 1879. In 1960 she was a patient at a state mental hospital where she had been since 11/20/1958, when she was admitted because of memory impairment and suicide threats. Diagnosis was chronic brain syndrome with cerebral arteriosclerosis. She was confused, disoriented, belligerent, aurally hallucinated and had a systematized delusion regarding her mother and brother, who were deceased. Classification: Chronic brain syndrome associated with cerebral arteriosclerosis.

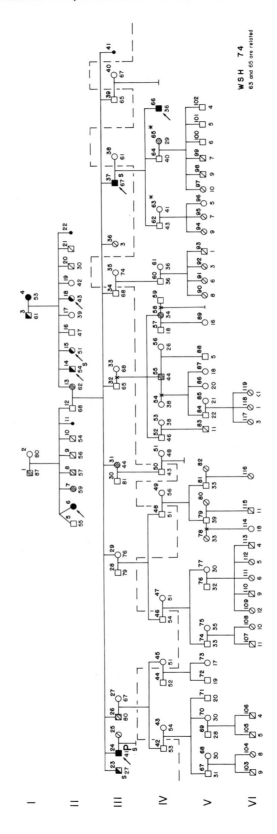

WSH 74
63 and 65 are related

WSH 74: The Proband

The proband (24), born 1878; died at age 41 years at Warren State Hospital of pulmonary tuberculosis and arthritis deformans. He was admitted to Warren State Hospital on 7/23/1913 with a diagnosis of manic-depressive, depressed type. For a year and a half before admission he had many hypochondriacal periods. He had experienced persecutory delusions and auditory hallucinations. He occasionally confined himself to his house and on one occasion attempted suicide by hanging from a bedpost. On several occasions he attempted to jump out the window. There was also a history of an attack of depression about seven years previous to hospitalization. At the time of admission his mental status disclosed depression, retardation, impairment of attention and memory and delusions of self-accusation, persecution and unworthiness. He remained hospitalized until death. The most recent diagnosis at Warren State Hospital and classification: Schizophrenic reaction—paranoid type.

Grandparents

Paternal grandfather (1), born 1806; died at age 87 years of old age. He was described as "a shiftless man of a disagreeable, hypochondriacal temperament." Although he was a strong, powerful man physically, he was always complaining and took a great deal of patent medicine. He continually moved from farm to farm. Classification: Probable psychoneurotic disorder; Possible personality disorder.

Maternal grandfather (3), born 1835; died at age 61 years of Bright's disease. He was reportedly "out of his mind" for two years in middle life, supposedly as a result of la grippe. Classification: Probable acute brain syndrome associated with infection; Possibly with functional psychosis.

Maternal grandmother (4), born 1837; died at age 53 years of la grippe. She reportedly "became insane at age 47 years and was never normal after that." She was oriented but despondent and oppressive, continually expecting some terrible disaster to come upon the family. She sometimes talked as if she imagined she saw people who were not in the room. Classification: With functional psychosis.

Parents

Mother (13), born 1857; died at age 62 years of a heart condition. She was described as "decidedly nervous." Her reaction to the interviewer was guarded and suspicious. Classification: Possible psychoneurotic disorder.

Aunts and Uncles

Paternal aunt (6), born 1848. She reportedly was "insane" from the time of adolescence; she was indifferent to her surroundings and remained in bed. Her whereabouts were unknown to the family but it was generally believed that she died in a mental hospital. Classification: With functional psychosis, probable schizophrenic reaction.

Paternal aunt (7), born 1854, was age 59 years at last information. She was described as "inclined to worry, nervous, moody, pessimistic and imagined that people did not care for her." She also imagined that her husband had said things about her or had mistreated her when in reality he had not. Classification: Probable psychoneurotic disorder; Possible personality pattern disturbance—paranoid personality.

Paternal uncle (18), born 1856. At interview he was described as "a dirty, grizzly man who became quite excited during conversation and was apt to lose the thread of his discourse." He was described by his wife as hypochondriacal. Classification: Probable psychoneurotic disorder; Possible personality disorder.

Maternal uncle (14), born 1859. At age 54 years he had maintained normal mental health but he reportedly was later hospitalized at a state mental hospital and still later committed suicide. Classification: Probably with functional psychosis.

Maternal aunt (15). At age 36 years she became "insane" for a time following an operation and was hospitalized in New York state. Eight years later she had another psychotic episode but was not hospitalized. Classification: Probably with functional psychosis; Possible chronic brain syndrome or psychoneurotic disorder.

Maternal aunt (18), born 1870. She reportedly had always been "peculiar." On 6/1/1897 she was hospitalized at Warren State Hospital with a diagnosis of acute mania, which was supposed to have been caused by la grippe. She was restless, excited, confused and disturbed at admission. At other times she was dull and obstinate. She gradually improved and was discharged on 7/30/1897. At age 43 years, during an interview, she stated that she had a recurrence of "mental trouble" several weeks previous to the birth of her last child in October, 1907, when she "imagined things." Her husband was killed about two weeks before the birth of this child. Classification: Probably with functional psychosis; Possible acute brain syndrome with psychotic reaction.

Siblings

Brother (23) born 1876; died at age 27 years. The cause of his death was reported as heart trouble, poisoning, a gunshot wound, suicide and murder. No death record could be located. He was considered a possible suicide. Classification: Possibly with functional psychosis.

Brother (26), born 1880. He was reportedly "always sick and always complaining" and "nervous and peculiar." Classification: Probable psychoneurotic disorder; Possible personality disorder.

Sister (31), born 1886; died at age 44 years of renal disease. She was described as "always ailing" and had "operation after operation." Classification: Possible psychoneurotic reaction, other.

Brother (37), born 1893. He developed periods of depression lasting months at a time, during which he made suicide attempts. He had one hospitalization from 10/22/1958 until 9/4/1959, when he was paroled in the custody of his wife. The attack for which he was hospitalized began in the summer of 1958, when he developed a fear of cancer of the stomach. Medical examination revealed no abnormality. Diagnosis and classification: Manic-depressive reaction—depressed type.

Nieces and Nephews

Nephew (55), born 1916. He was described as "wild" as a child. As an adult he changed jobs often because of "restlessness" and was described as "stubborn," with a bad temper. Classification: Possible personality disorder.

Niece (58), born 1926. She was described as "wild" and her occupation was reported to be "men and running around." She neglected her daughter and was "mean to her—not wanting her around." Classification: Possible sociopathic personality disturbance.

(65) wife of nephew (64), born 1931. She was on tranquilizers at the time of interview and in her seventh pregnancy, and already with six children, living and well, between ages four and ten years. She felt her nervous problem was the result of her pregnancy and the effect of her father-in-law's mental illness on the family. Classification: Possible transient situational personality disorder.

Nephew (66), born 1924. At age 20 years, while in the Philippine Islands during World War II, he developed a "head disease" for which he was hospitalized and evacuated to the United States, receiving a service-connected disability of anxiety reaction. In 1953 he was in an automobile accident, followed by a period of unconsciousness of unknown length. On 12/11/1954 he was admitted to a Veterans Administration facility with a diagnosis of schizophrenic reaction, undifferentiated type. At admission he was described as "silly, dull and flattened, withdrawn and vague." He heard voices calling him "crazy" and thought that the medicine and cigarettes were "doped." He also exhibited inappropriate laughter and had no insight into his condition. He remained hospitalized. Classification: Schizophrenic reaction—paranoid type.

Family Summary

The proband, a brother, a paternal aunt, the maternal grandmother and a nephew were psychotic, and all except the grandmother were hospitalized. A maternal uncle and two maternal aunts probably had psy-

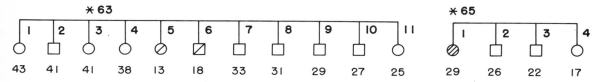

CONTROLS

WSH 74

63 and 65 are related

choses (the uncle suicided) and were hospitalized. A brother and the maternal grandfather were possibly psychotic, the brother a possible suicide. A paternal aunt, a paternal uncle, a brother, a sister, the mother, and the maternal grandfather were classified as with neurotic disorders. Personality dis-

orders included a nephew, a niece and the wife of a nephew.

Controls

See family pedigree, person 65.

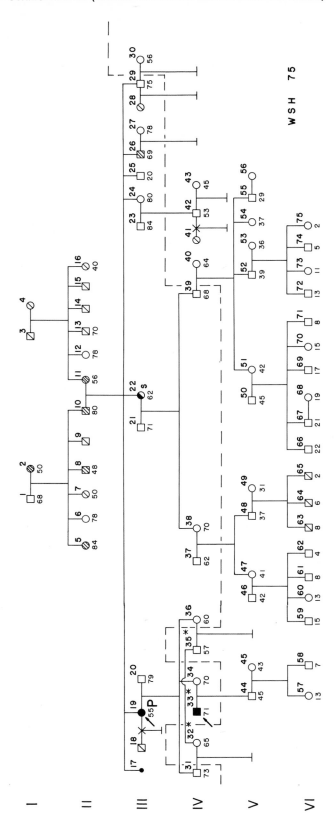

WSH 75: The Proband

The proband (19), born 1867; died at age 54 years of acute nephritis and anemia. She was married for a period of about one year when 15 years of age. She married again at age 21 years. As a girl she was "vivacious and lighthearted," but in late years was "inclined to worry." She was committed to Warren State Hospital on 10/9/1908 with a diagnosis of chronic melancholia. Symptoms were of a marked depression, emotional instability and delusions of a self-depreciatory and self-accusatory type. She made a good recovery at the end of seven months. She was "rather peculiar" and at times refused to speak to anyone while at home, but was essentially normal until April, 1912, when she became morose, quit work and would sit around in a depressed mood. Second admission to Warren State Hospital was on 7/8/1913, with a diagnosis of manic-depressive insanity, depressed phase. She had delusions of a self-accusatory type and was aurally hallucinated. She was paroled against advice on 11/15/1913 and was never again hospitalized. Classification: Schizophrenic reaction—paranoid type.

Children

(33) husband of daughter (34), born 1889. He was hospitalized twice when he developed spells of anxiety, slight depression, nervousness, insomnia and loss of appetite. The first admission was in 1943 with a diagnosis of involutional psychosis, paranoid type. The second hospitalization was made voluntarily and was from 1/15/1956 until 5/20/1956, with a diagnosis of manic-depressive psychosis, mixed type. Other observed symptoms during hospitalization were of "a flat and inappropriate affect, mannerisms, withdrawn and seclusive behavior, incoherency, flight of ideas, blocking, unrealistic and incongruous thinking, confusion and perplexity." Classification: Schizophrenic reaction.

Grandparents

Paternal grandmother (2), born 1802; died at age 50 years of apoplexy. She report- edly had a "seclusive, reticent disposition" and was described as a "stern, disagreeable woman who was hard to get along with." Classification: Possible personality pattern disturbance—paranoid personality.

Parents

Father (10), born 1845. He lived to be at least 80 years of age. He was described as "naturally distant and seclusive" but this was "not so marked as to call him a psychopathic personality." Classification: Possible personality pattern disturbance—schizoid personality.

Mother (11), born 1846; died at age 56 years of diabetes. She was described by her family as of a "pleasant, even temperament"; however, her family physician stated that "she was more peculiar than her husband...and subject to hysterical attacks." Classification: Possible transient situational personality disorder—adult situational reaction.

Aunts and Uncles

Paternal aunt (5), born 1829; was age 84 years when an interview was attempted. She refused admittance to the interviewer and gave misleading directions to the home of her brother. She was always considered "odd" and lived apart from people. Classification: Probable personality pattern disturbance—paranoid personality; Possibly with functional psychosis, schizophrenic reaction—paranoid type.

Paternal uncle (8), born 1837; died at age 75 years of apoplexy. He was called "peculiar" by his family and "crazy" by other acquaintances. At age 49 years, following some financial reverses, he became more moody, gloomy and taciturn than usual and spent a great deal of time in bed. About seven years later his judgment became noticeably impaired. He received a notice that the sheriff was going to take over his property. He purchased a gun and that night insisted he could hear the sheriff coming. That was the only history of possible hallucinations. He often refused to eat and seldom ate more than one meal a day. His conversation was often rambling and incoherent. He did not deteriorate and seemed to improve the last two years of his life. Classification: Probable personality pattern disturbance—inadequate personality or paranoid personality; Possibly with functional psychosis, schizophrenic reaction—chronic undifferentiated type.

Siblings

Sister (22), born 1868; died at age 62 years of angina pectoris and herpes zoster. She was described as of a "melancholy temperament and a gloomy, sensitive, seclusive nature." She had one "mental upset" which lasted several months and began previous to the birth of her first child when she was 22 years of age. During this episode she became indifferent to her surroundings and on one occasion attempted suicide. She rejected the child after its birth and relatives had to care for it. On another occasion she dressed up in her wedding gown and told her family that was how she wanted to be dressed when she died. Classification: Probably with functional psychosis, schizophrenic reaction; Possible psychoneurotic disorder—depressive reaction.

Brother (26), born 1881; died at age 69 years of coronary thrombosis. He had "a melancholy temperament and was inclined to have 'the blues' frequently." His wife described him as "the gentlest, most understanding person who ever lived." Classification: Possible psychoneurotic disorder—depressive reaction; or, personality trait disturbance—emotionally unstable personality.

Family Summary

The proband and her son-in-law were each psychotic and hospitalized. A sister probably had a psychotic episode during which she attempted suicide. A brother was possibly neurotic and the paternal grandmother, the father, the mother, a paternal aunt and a paternal uncle had personality disorders.

Controls

Sister (3) of (32) and (35), born 1900; completed grade 10 and was a housewife who had two children. She was admitted to Warren State Hospital on 6/13/1941, with a diagnosis of involutional psychosis, melancholia. She was normally "jolly, generous, laughing, agreeable and even-tempered," although "quite sensitive and inclined to keep her troubles to herself." Mental symptoms were thought to have been precipitated by bankruptcy proceedings filed by her husband in March, 1941, when she had prolonged crying spells and became quite pessimistic. Two weeks before admission she became deluded (thought she was to give birth to twins or triplets). The day before admission she attempted to drink a poisonous cattle spray. On 1/7/1942 she had improved sufficiently to be paroled. Recent informants state that she was never readmitted to the hospital and remained well mentally. Classification: Schizophrenic reaction—paranoid type.

Sister (5) of (32) and (35), twin of (6), born 1903. She was admitted to a state mental hospital on 9/12/1941, and discharged as improved in 1943. Her diagnosis was dementia praecox, paranoid type. She was readmitted on 2/20/1945 and on 3/1/1961 was still a patient under continuous hospital care. She was described as "chronically hallucinated, showing some degree of deterioration." Classification: Schizophrenic reaction—paranoid type.

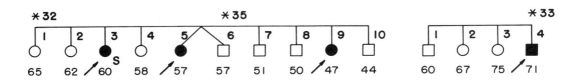

CONTROLS   WSH   75

Sister (9) of (32) and (35), born 1913. She married twice and there were two children by the first marriage, which ended in divorce, and none by the second. Her second husband left her after one year. On 2/10/1954, she was admitted to a state mental hospital because of bizarre behavior and somatic complaints. Premorbidly, she was described as "jolly and having been able to make friends easily." Onset of her mental symptoms was during the summer of 1952, when she began to verbalize paranoid feelings in regard to women in general and began to have bizarre somatic symptoms which were not based on physical disease. During hospitalization she received ECT and drug therapy and was well enough to begin a leave of absence on 8/14/1958. She was readmitted 3/1/1959 and remained hospitalized. Classification: Schizophrenic reaction—paranoid type.

See family pedigree, person 33.

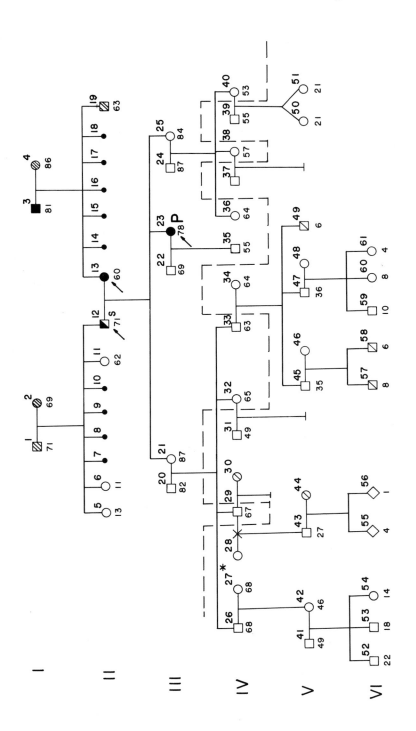

WSH 77

WSH 77: The Proband

The proband (23), born 1874; died at age 78 years of arteriosclerosis with mitral insufficiency. She was admitted twice to Warren State Hospital, from 5/2/1913 until 9/5/1913, and from 10/14/1923 until 12/19/1923. Diagnosis at each admission was manic-depressive psychosis, manic phase. Each psychotic episode was characterized by extreme overactivity, bizarre ideas about religion, delusions of persecution and auditory and visual hallucinations. She was described as "never quite well" both before and after the hospitalizations as she was seclusive and over-religious. She had unusual ideas of child care and refused to allow her child to associate with other children or to attend school, until she was legally forced to send him. Classification: Schizophrenic reaction — catatonic type.

Grandparents

Paternal grandfather (1), born 1815; died at age 71 years of cancer of the stomach. He was subject to "sick headaches" with vomiting every Sunday. These persisted through his entire life. Classification: Psychoneurotic disorder — conversion reaction.

Paternal grandmother (2), born 1821; died at age 69 years of la grippe. She was described as "nervous, irritable, petulant, very moody and eccentric." She had periods when she was more than usually depressed. At age 40 years, following a physical illness, she became addicted to morphine. The addiction was cured after about one year. Classification: Probable personality trait disturbance — passive-aggressive personality; Possibly with functional psychosis, schizophrenic reaction.

Maternal grandfather (3), born 1827; died at age 81 years of apoplexy. He was described as a lazy, determined, obstinate man easily excited about religion or politics. At about 50 years of age, for a span of two years, he had a period of religious enthusiasm, terminating in a mental breakdown. He was excited, talkative, restless, preached continually and at times would dance and sing wildly. Six years before his death he had an attack of hemiplegia which affected his left side and made him helpless. He was childish and demented the last three years of his life. Classification: With functional psychosis, probable schizophrenic reaction — catatonic type; also, chronic brain syndrome of senium.

Maternal grandmother (4), born 1810; died at age 86 years of dysentery. She was described as excitable, high strung and impulsive and as very much like (2). Classification: Probable personality trait disturbance — emotionally unstable personality; or, passive-aggressive personality.

Parents

Father (12), born 1848; died at age 71 years of a cerebral hemorrhage and arteriosclerosis. He was hospitalized at Warren State Hospital from 8/20/1910 until 11/18/1910, following a suicide attempt. For many years he was "gloomy and depressed" in the spring. At admission he believed he had committed a great crime and was eternally lost. He remained well after discharge from Warren State Hospital. Classification: Probably with functional psychosis — involutional psychotic reaction; Possible psychoneurotic disorder — depressive reaction.

Mother (13), born 1853; died at age 60 years of chronic myocarditis at Warren State Hospital. She was described as normally intelligent, interesting, lively, gay and an ardent and fanatical follower of a religious sect. In April, 1913, she became elated, loquacious, profane, obscene and homicidal. She burned her religious literature. She was hallucinated, delusional and suffered from insomnia. Admission to Warren State Hospital was on 4/29/1913, where she remained, unimproved, until her death nine days later. Diagnosis at Warren State Hospital was manic-depressive psychosis, manic phase. Classification: Schizophrenic reaction — catatonic type.

Aunts and Uncles

Maternal uncle (19), born 1850; age 63 years at last information. He had used alcohol to excess for many years and in 1906 he had an episode of "alcohol insanity," when

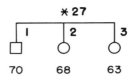

CONTROLS

W S H   7 7

he became violent, spoke to people who were not present and threatened to kill his wife because of her imagined infidelity. The hallucinations and delusions lasted about three weeks but he did not work for three or four months. After this psychotic episode he no longer used alcohol and was described as a man of "keen, clear and rather forceful intellect whose memory showed no sign of being impaired" at age 63 years. Classification: Sociopathic personality disturbance — alcoholism (addiction), and acute brain syndrome associated with alcohol intoxication.

Family Summary

The proband, her mother and her maternal grandfather were psychotic. Her father was probably so and he attempted suicide. The paternal grandfather had a psychoneurotic disorder. The paternal and maternal grandmothers had probable personality disorders. A maternal uncle was an alcoholic with an episode of alcoholic psychosis.

Controls

None noteworthy.

WSH 84: The Proband

The proband (39), born 1862; died at age 87 years of "old age." At age 22 years she suffered a depression. About four years later she suffered a second attack of mental disturbance when she talked all the time and was very active. From then on she had attacks of indefinite duration at various times. Admission to Warren State Hospital was on 2/6/1913, with a diagnosis of manic-depressive psychosis, manic phase. She remained hospitalized until 6/10/1919, with symptoms of some distractibility, flight of ideas, persistent delusions of a persecutory nature with some outbreaks of temper and foolish laughter. She earned her living as a seamstress after her release from Warren State Hospital and was remembered as "melancholy but talkative." As she became older she became bewildered and spent some time in a county home. Classification: Schizophrenic reaction — paranoid type.

Grandparents

Maternal grandfather (3), born 1806; died at age 50 years of bronchial trouble. He was described as "a quick-tempered man, a very hard drinker . . . was dead drunk frequently." Classification: Possible sociopathic personality disturbance — alcoholism (addiction).

Parents

Mother (16), born 1825; died at age 75 years of a stroke of paralysis. Every summer her daughter observed an unusual nervous activity similar to that observed in the proband. Classification: Probably with functional psychosis, manic-depressive reaction — manic type; Possible personality pattern disturbance — cyclothymic personality.

Aunts and Uncles

Maternal aunt (20), born 1829; died at age 84 years of a tumor of the womb and heart trouble. She was admitted to Warren State Hospital on 4/16/1889 with a diagnosis of melancholia. She believed she had caused her sister's death and that her soul was condemned. There was no change in her condition at Warren State Hospital, where she remained depressed, confused and very much worried. On 6/11/1896, she was taken home where she persisted in her delusions until her death, although she did keep them to herself the last five years of her life. Classification: Involutional psychotic reaction.

Siblings

Brother (30), born 1854; died at age 69 years of heart failure. He was described as quick tempered and of a roving disposition, although his physician and long-time acquaintance described him as normal and very intelligent. Classification: Possible personality disorder.

Sister (34), born 1857; died at age 77 years of general debility. She had attacks of mental disturbance from the age of 16 years when she would become disorderly and violent and careless of her appearance. Admissions at Warren State Hospital were from 7/18/1902 until 8/13/1904, and from 11/27/1911 until 6/10/1919, with diagnoses of periodic mania and of manic-depressive psychosis. Symptom descriptions during hospitalization frequently described her as "simple" or "childlike" between the periods of excitement. She became blind in old age. Classification: Schizophrenic reaction — catatonic type.

Sister (35), born 1858; died at age 70 years of general debility. She had periods of mental disturbance, which took the form of a depression, all her life from age 20 years. She was remembered as "odd" and "melancholy"; she wanted to be alone and often ate alone. She became blind in old age. Classification: Probably with functional psychosis.

Sister (43), born 1866; died at age 61 years of carcinoma of the rectum. She was reportedly mentally deficient and had an episode of "nervous prostration" in 1904. Details of her illness were unknown. Classification: Probably with functional psychosis; Possible psychoneurotic disorder.

(46) husband of sister (45), born 1869; died at age 77 years, cause unknown. He was described as an "alcoholic" and by another source as "able but alcoholic." Classification: Probable sociopathic personality disturbance — alcoholism (addiction).

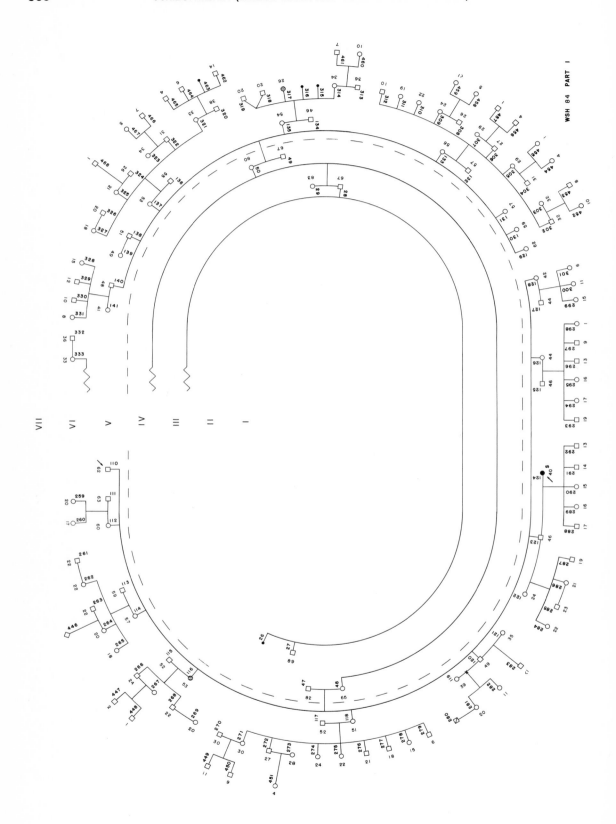

WSH 84 PART I

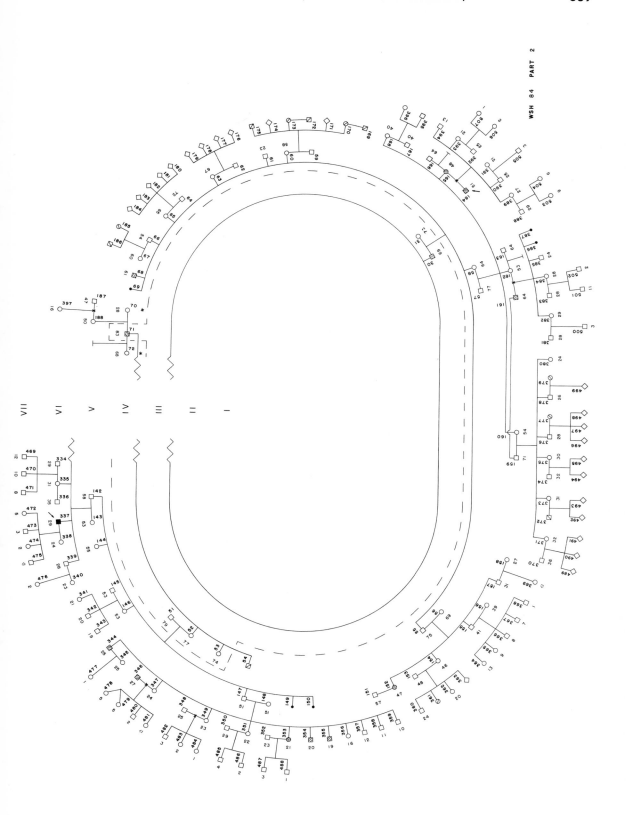

WSH 84 PART 2

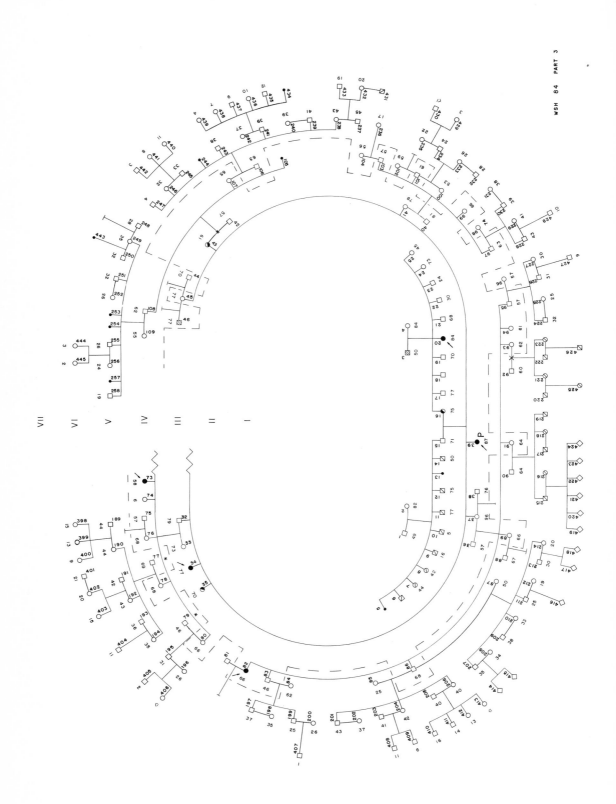

Nieces and Nephews

Nephew (68), born 1901; died at age 61 years of cardiorespiratory failure and bronchial asthma. He was considered a "bum" by his family as he would move from job to job and died in "skid row." Classification: Probable personality disorder.

Nephew (71), born 1878. He graduated from the Yale Divinity School and was a minister who took tranquilizers for what he described as "internal nervousness." Classification: Transient situational personality disorder — adult situational reaction.

Niece (73), born 1880; died at age 58 years of generalized arteriosclerosis. At age 33 years she had a "breakdown from overwork" but was not hospitalized. Ten years later, on 11/1/1923, she was admitted to a state mental hospital with a diagnosis of involutional melancholia. At admission she was depressed, anxious and suspicious. She showed gradual deterioration and eventually became disinterested in her environment, resistive, untidy and uncooperative to nursing care. Classification: Schizophrenic reaction — paranoid type.

Niece (82), born 1889; died at age 66 years of congestive heart failure. She completed a business course but could not work because she "couldn't apply what she had learned." She was admitted to Warren State Hospital on 2/4/1954, with a diagnosis of schizophrenic reaction, hebephrenic type. About a year before admission, although there was some speculation that symptoms had persisted for over 10 years, she began to see persons who were not there and claimed that she could talk to dead people. She began wandering at night, unclothed, although it was winter. She also had a somatic delusion in that she "could not figure where her blood was running to." Her delusional system was apparently satisfying to her. She remained at Warren State Hospital until her death. Classification: Schizophrenic reaction — paranoid type.

Distant Relatives

Grandnephew (110), born 1899. He was always considered to be mentally deficient. On 12/9/1944 he was admitted to a state mental hospital for 60 days because of window peeping, an uncontrollable temper and overactivity. Diagnosis was "without psychosis, mental deficiency." Classification: Mental deficiency.

Grandniece (116), born 1908. She had several operations and, following a hysterectomy, was "on the verge of a nervous breakdown" for a few months. Classification: Other transient situational personality disturbance.

(124) wife of grandnephew (123), born 1921. She developed delusions of persecution following a sterilization operation in 1948; these persisted in a mild way until December, 1956. She was hospitalized at a general hospital from 1/16/1957. Her condition became progressively worse and she was admitted to Warren State Hospital on 6/18/1957, with a diagnosis of schizophrenic reaction, paranoid type. While at Warren State Hospital she was described as "flat" and withdrawn, suicidal, suspicious and hostile. She claimed she'd been raped at the general hospital and that she had died the previous December. She believed that the Warren State Hospital staff could read her mind and that they were experimenting with her. She did not respond well to treatment and was still at Warren State Hospital on 4/16/1962. Classification: Schizophrenic reaction — paranoid type.

Grandniece (152), born 1914. She received medical treatment for "a little nervous condition" when she taught an overcrowded classroom but had no problem after that time. Classification: Possible psychoneurotic disorder.

(161) husband of grandniece (162), born 1898. He was described by his wife as "a child beater" and by his sister-in-law as a "sex maniac." Classification: Personality pattern disturbance, other.

(164) husband of grandniece (165), born 1911; (165) was his sixth wife. He had a two-way mirror installed through which he could observe women in the bathroom in the adjoining apartment. When this was discovered he was hospitalized for observation from 5/28/1957 until 9/11/1957. Psychiatric examination and psychologic testing revealed a psychoneurotic disorder, anxiety reaction with the possibility of some dissociation and symptomatic sexual deviation. Classification: Psychoneurotic disorder — anxiety reaction.

Grandniece (165), born 1914. She had a "nervous breakdown" reportedly because of trouble with her husband (164) and the

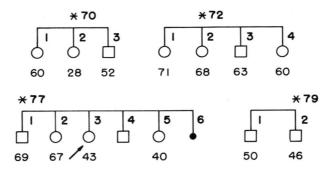

CONTROLS   W S H   8 4

beginning of menopause. She was treated by a general practitioner, recovered and had no recurrence of her trouble. Classification: Probable psychoneurotic disorder.

Great-grandniece (317), born 1935; at age 26 years employed as a full time baby sitter. She experienced a depression during puberty and later seemed to suffer a "personality lack," according to a recent informant. She was also described as nervous and unsociable. Classification: Transient situational personality disorder — adjustment reaction of adolescence.

Great-grandnephew (337), born 1932. On 6/26/1950 he had rather an abrupt onset of delusions. He was hospitalized from 6/30/1950 until 9/6/1950, with a diagnosis of schizophrenia, paranoid and catatonic. Hospitalization at a state mental hospital for prolonged care was advised but he maintained a satisfactory adjustment at home until 3/4/1953, when his symptoms recurred, and he was admitted to a state mental hospital on 3/26/1953. On admission he was bewildered but cooperative but on the next day he became very restless and lost contact with reality. He was discharged on 8/18/1953 and was not rehospitalized. Diagnosis and classification: Schizophrenic reaction — paranoid type.

Great-grandnephew (344), born 1936. He was a heavy drinker who was once tried for killing a man with his fist in a barroom brawl. He was exonerated because others had also struck the same individual. Classification: Sociopathic personality disturbance — alcoholism (addiction).

(346) husband of great-grandniece (347), born 1935. He never worked steadily and was considered to be "mentally affected" as well as an alcoholic. Classification: Sociopathic personality disturbance — alcoholism (addiction).

Great-grandniece (353), born 1940. She had "St. Vitus dance" at age six years and was later "quite nervous and upset easily." Classification: Other transient situational personality disturbance.

Great-grandnephew (354), born 1941. He was described as "quite wild" and irresponsible. He was arrested for stealing. Classification: Sociopathic personality disturbance — antisocial reaction.

Great-grandnephew (355), born 1942. He was described as "quite wild," irresponsible, and was arrested, with (354), for stealing. Classification: Sociopathic personality disturbance — antisocial reaction.

Family Summary

The proband, a maternal aunt, a sister, two nieces, and a great-grandnephew had psychotic disorders and were hospitalized. The mother and two sisters probably had psychotic disorders and the wife of a grandnephew was hospitalized with schizophrenia. A grandnephew was hospitalized in a mental hospital with mental deficiency. Only the wife of the grandnephew attempted suicide. Personality disorders were found in a nephew, a grandniece, three great-grandnephews, two great-grandnieces and probably or possibly in the maternal grandfather, a brother, and a nephew. One grandniece was probably neurotic and another possibly so. Two spouses had personality disorders (the husbands of a grandniece and of a great-grandniece) and a husband of a sister was probably an alcoholic. The husband of a grandniece was neurotic.

Controls

Sister (3) of (77), born 1896; died at age 43 years at a state mental hospital, of Huntington's chorea. Classification: Chronic brain syndrome associated with Huntington's chorea with psychotic reaction.

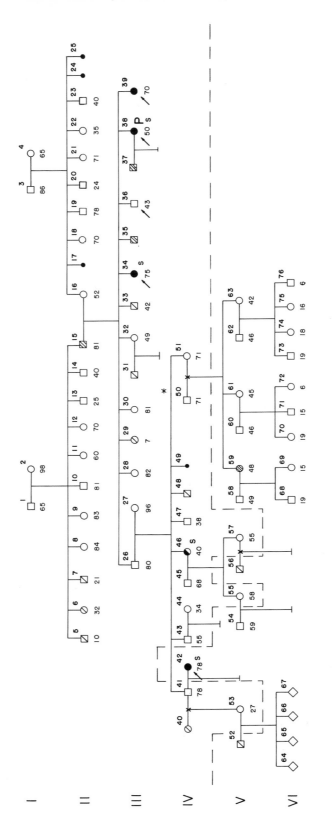

WSH 88

WSH 88: The Proband

Proband (38), born 1870; died at Warren State Hospital at age 50 years of chronic myocarditis. She was admitted to Warren State Hospital on 7/17/1912, with a diagnosis of unclassified psychosis following a suicide attempt by drinking carbolic acid. Her illness began after the death of her husband, when she became overly religious. She gradually became hypochondriacal, haughty, developed ideas of unworthiness and subsequently became markedly agitated and preoccupied with suicidal thoughts. She remained hospitalized, at times destructive, denudative and violent with no improvement in her mental condition, until her death. Final diagnosis at Warren State Hospital was dementia praecox, paranoid type. Classification: Schizophrenic reaction—paranoid type.

(37) husband of proband (38); died in 1909 of peritonitis. He reportedly had syphilis and was of a "neuropathic disposition." Classification: Possible personality disorder.

Parents

Father (15), born 1828; died at age 81 years of apoplexy. He reportedly was not neurotic or peculiar until, following a "stroke of paralysis," he became "affected" and had delusions of being burned. His family physician remembers him as an "odd, peculiar man who had the reputation of annoying women on the streets." Classification: Probable chronic brain syndrome; Possible personality disorder.

Siblings

Sister (34), born 1862; died at age 75 years of a coronary occlusion. In 1919, while working as a hat designer in Missouri, she suffered a mental upset (details unknown) and was hospitalized for one month. She was brought home for a few days, then admitted to Warren State Hospital on 7/29/1919, with a diagnosis of manic-depressive psychosis, involutional type. She had a history of "hysterical outbursts" and of luetic infection at age 35 years, for which she was treated (spinal findings were negative). Her mental illness was characterized by great agitation, apprehensiveness, depression, auto-accusatory delusions and suicide threats and attempts. She was a private patient at Warren State Hospital for four years and was then paroled to her relatives, contrary to the advice of the staff. She lived at home and worked in the millinery business, although not considered quite normal, until her death. Classification: Schizophrenic reaction—paranoid type.

Brother (35), born 1864; last known to be a painter of circus scenery in Sarasota, Florida. He was described as "selfish, irresponsible and alcoholic." Classification: Possible personality disorder.

Brother (36), born 1868; died at age 43 years at Warren State Hospital of dementia paralytica. Before hospitalization at Warren State Hospital on 8/21/1910, he was hospitalized for three weeks in Iowa. He suffered from loss of memory, exaggerated reflexes and from convulsions. Classification: Organic psychosis, type unspecified.

Sister (39), born 1875; died at age 70 years at Warren State Hospital of chronic myocarditis. At age 67 years, after the three sisters with whom she had lived had died and the family income, which at one time was substantial, was gone, a nurse friend persuaded her to enter Warren State Hospital (admitted 7/23/1943). She was afraid to stay alone, was incompetent and was so overactive that at times she would forget to eat. At Warren State Hospital she was flighty, overactive, overtalkative and distractible, yet her ideas were more or less depressive and she was often on the verge of tears. Diagnosis was manic-depressive psychosis, mixed type. She remained at Warren State Hospital until her death. Classification: Manic-depressive reaction—manic type.

Nieces and Nephews

(42) wife of nephew (41), born 1874; died at age 78 years following surgery for an intestinal obstruction. She was hospitalized at Warren State Hospital from July 31, 1952 until October, 1952. Diagnosis was unclassified psychosis. A suicide attempt (she slashed her right arm) precipitated her hos-

pitalization. Reportedly, her first marriage ended in divorce because of her extreme temper outbursts. Her pre-morbid personality was described as austere, rigid and domineering. The onset of her psychosis followed a stroke at age 67 years, when she developed delusions of infidelity and persecution involving her husband, a neighbor and a daughter-in-law. Classification: Paranoid reaction—paranoid state.

Niece (46), born 1881; suicided by drowning at age 40 years. She had suffered no emotional or mental upsets in her life; however, she was suffering from tic douloureux at the time of her suicide. Surgery for the neuralgia had been unsuccessful. Classification: Probably with functional psychosis.

Distant Relatives

Grandniece (59), born 1914. She was interviewed and was quite antagonistic. She insisted that the great-aunts hospitalized at Warren State Hospital were not mentally ill but had infections from hair dye. Classification: Possible personality pattern disturbance—paranoid personality.

Family Summary

The proband and two of her sisters were psychotic and hospitalized at Warren State Hospital. A brother, also hospitalized at Warren State Hospital, had an unspecified organic psychosis. Another brother, the proband's husband, the proband's father and a grandniece possibly had personality disorders. A niece suicided following unsuccessful surgery for the painful neuralgia of tic douloureux. A nephew's wife was hospitalized with a psychotic condition after attempting suicide. The proband and one sister also made suicide attempts. The proband's parents had 11 children, seven grandchildren, six great-grandchildren and 13 great-great-grandchildren.

Controls

None noteworthy.

CONTROLS

W S H   88

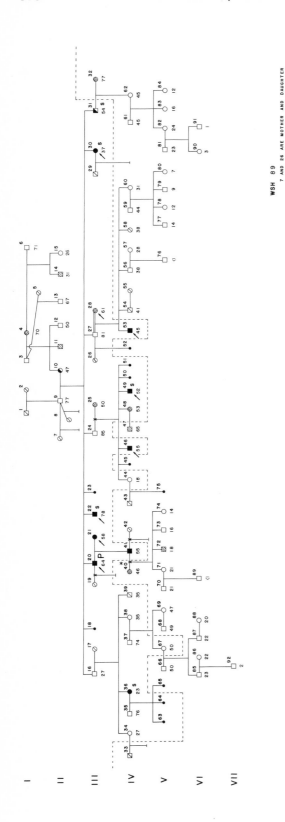

WSH 89

7 AND 26 ARE MOTHER AND DAUGHTER

WSH 89: The Proband

The proband (20), born 1868; died at age 64 years at Warren State Hospital of chronic myocarditis. At age 21 years he became so depressed, restless and suspicious that he was admitted to Warren State Hospital on 3/19/1891, with a diagnosis of periodic mania. He was discharged 1/1/1892. For the next 40 years he would alternate between episodes of confused, restless, noisy and excited behavior and periods of inactivity and indifference. Dates of admission and discharge and diagnoses at subsequent hospitalizations, all at Warren State Hospital, are listed below:

8/2/1892 – 3/23/1893   Chronic mania.

8/30/1894 – 11/5/1895   Acute mania.

10/23/1912 – 1/1/1915   Dementia praecox or episode in a constitutional defect (he did not show the deterioration expected in a dementia praecox at this time).

12/1/1918 – 10/28/1919   Manic-depressive, mixed type.

8/11/1920 – 2/27/1923   Manic-depressive insanity, mixed type (during this period he first developed auditory and visual hallucinations).

7/6/1923 – death   Manic-depressive insanity, atypical manic reaction, circular type.

During the later admissions he became increasingly disoriented. He was most probably mentally defective before he developed his other problems. Classification: Schizophrenic reaction – paranoid type with mental deficiency.

(21) wife of the proband (20), born 1869; died at age 58 years of cancer. She was described as "troublesome and fault-finding" throughout her life. She was also described as "simple-minded and poor in judgment." She had an uncontrollable temper and her marriage was characterized by quarreling and nagging. She was admitted to Warren State Hospital on 7/19/1915,

with a diagnosis of imbecile. Since she exhibited no symptoms of psychosis after admission, she was released in 1916. Little was known of her from 1916 until her death in 1926, except that she was a nuisance to those who lived near her. Classification: Schizophrenic reaction — paranoid type.

Children

(40) wife of son (41), born 1914. In 1956 her children were taken from her as she was considered an unfit parent. She had poor physical health and her promiscuity made her a real social problem. Classification: Sociopathic personality disturbance — antisocial reaction.

Son (41), born 1907. He spent most of his adolescence moving around the United States and Canada, but returned to Pennsylvania to marry. His marital life was very stormy (he threw knives at his wife, stuck forks into her, cut her hand with an ax and bit her child on the face). His wife finally had him arrested in 1947 after he attacked her with a poker and he was committed to a correctional institution (his third commitment since age 31) for assault and battery against his wife and brutal treatment and neglect of her children. The prison psychiatrist called him insecure and psychopathic. After his release, he became a "drifter," holding many jobs, most of which he quit because "the police were hounding him." He later married a faith healer and claimed that he could cure people himself. His physical health was noteworthy in that he developed ulcers during his adolescence. Classification: Schizophrenic reaction — paranoid type.

Grandchildren

Grandson (72), born 1944, a resident of a minimum security institution for delinquent boys. He was struck in the head by the poker his stepfather was swinging at his mother when three years of age. Consequently, his stepfather was incarcerated and his mother relieved of the children as an unfit parent. At age 12 years he exhibited behavior difficulties such as bed wetting, soiling, lying, speech difficulties and homosexuality and was placed in a children's home. Because of very frightening nightmares he was referred to the Warren State Hospital's outpatient clinic and found to be immature, mentally defective, insecure and uncertain in interpersonal relations. In 1957 he was described as having a schizoid or psychopathic personality. In 1961 he was transferred to a home for delinquent boys. Classification: Personality pattern disturbance — schizoid personality.

Grandparents

Maternal grandmother (4), died at age 70 years of catarrh and tuberculosis. She was very demented the last two years before her death. Earlier in her life she was considered feeble-minded. Classification: Chronic brain syndrome due to cerebral arteriosclerosis or in senium; Mental deficiency.

Parents

Mother (10), born 1846; died at age 47 years of marasmus. She was described as "mentally and morally...of low order." She was an alcoholic, "lazy, shiftless, and insane the last seven years of her life." She had convulsive attacks about once a week during the seven years of insanity. Classification: Probable chronic brain syndrome associated with convulsive disorder; Possibly with functional psychosis.

Aunts and Uncles

Maternal uncle (11) was described as dull, selfish and unable to care for his property. Classification: Possible personality pattern disturbance.

Maternal half uncle (14), born 1860. He was described as "below par in intelligence" and "ugly and disagreeable toward his wife." He had the "dirtiest and worst kept house in town." Classification: Probable personality disorder.

Siblings

Brother (22), born 1872; died at age 78 years, cause unknown. Little information was available about his life outside the hospital, but he was hospitalized from January,

1903 until January, 1904, and from June, 1910 until November, 1910. Diagnosis at each admission was imbecility. As a child he had "fits." In September, 1902 (at age 29 years) he began to have delusions, became violent and made several suicide attempts. His suicidal tendencies seemed to result from his guilt and anxiety over sexual intercourse with animals. He seemed to recover well and showed no further disturbance. Classification: Psychotic-depressive reaction.

(25) wife of brother (24), born 1885; died at age 50 years when strangled by her son (46) during a wild party. She was "always wild," was drunk most of the time and had many extra-marital affairs. Classification: Sociopathic personality disturbance—antisocial reaction.

(28) second wife of brother (27), born 1894; died at age 61 years at Warren State Hospital of pneumonia. She was always quick tempered, and could never attend public functions because she would become "nervous" and have to leave. At her son's wedding she became so "nervous" she had to be taken home. She was then unable to do her work, became more disoriented and developed delusions that she was being poisoned. Two years after her son's wedding she was admitted to Warren State Hospital (5/2/1955) and died 11 days later. Diagnosis and classification: Chronic brain syndrome associated with cerebral arteriosclerosis.

Sister (30), born 1880; suicided by hanging at age 37 years at Warren State Hospital. She was an alcoholic. At age 30 years (in 1910) she had a manic attack during which she attempted suicide by drinking carbolic acid. She recovered and was normal until March, 1913, when she became violent, homicidal, incoherent, developed delusions of persecution and had hallucinations. Admission to Warren State Hospital was on 4/3/1913. During the four years at Warren State Hospital she developed episodes of overactive posturing. Diagnosis at Warren State Hospital was manic-depressive, manic type. Classification: Schizophrenic reaction—catatonic type.

Brother (31), born 1882; suicided by hanging at age 54 years. He was retired on a disabled pension from his work as a railroad car inspector following a work accident.

Reportedly, his "inactivity, poor health and constantly nagging wife" depressed him. This depression preceded his death. Classification: Probably with functional psychosis, psychotic-depressive reaction.

(32) wife of brother (31), born 1883. She always had a variety of hypochondriacal complaints, which improved following her husband's (31) suicide. However, in later years she again developed her multiple complaints. Classification: Psychoneurotic disorder.

Nieces and Nephews

Niece (36), born 1890; died at age 23 years from a self-inflicted gunshot wound. In late childhood and adolescence she reportedly had "nervous spells during which she hardly knew anything." These cleared up following her marriage at age 18 years. At age 20 years she developed auditory hallucinations and would remain mute for days at a time. She would also run away from home and hide in the woods. After the birth of her third child she became more disturbed, attempted to kill the child, and eight months later she suicided. Classification: With functional psychosis, probable schizophrenic reaction.

Nephew (46), born 1905, a patient at a state mental hospital where he was admitted on 9/23/1934, with a diagnosis of psychosis with mental deficiency. Commitment to Farview followed sentencing to the penitentiary for eight to 16 years for the strangulation of his mother. He and his mother (who was promiscuous and alcoholic) were always antagonistic and he strangled her during a wild party. After the sentencing he became secluded, was mute and stared into space for hours. Latest diagnosis and classification: Schizophrenic reaction—catatonic type.

(47) husband of niece (48), born 1907. The interviewer found him hostile, suspicious and uncooperative. Classification: Personality pattern disturbance—paranoid personality.

Niece (48), born 1907. She lived in a small, dirty trailer set off in the bushes. The interviewer found her hostile and suspicious. Classification: Personality pattern disturbance—paranoid personality.

Nephew (49), born 1909. At age 25

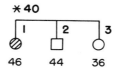

CONTROLS

WSH 89

years he discovered his mother's body after her murder and since then reportedly had been alcoholic and "upset." He was hospitalized at Warren State Hospital from 10/21/1939 until 1/3/1940, as a result of a suicide attempt with a razor after a woman with whom he'd been cohabitating refused to live with him any longer because of indebtedness. Diagnosis at this admission was alcoholic psychosis in a mental defective. Two years later he was hospitalized from 4/10/1942 until 6/6/1942 at an army station hospital with a diagnosis of dementia praecox, simple type. After his discharge from the army because of his depression and auditory hallucinations he was again hospitalized at Warren State Hospital from 6/13/1942 until 11/10/1942, with a diagnosis of psychosis with epidemic encephalitis. He made a marginal adjustment and was unemployed, living in poverty, after that. Classification: Schizophrenic reaction— simple type with mental deficiency.

Nephew (53), born 1912; died at age 45 years of a coronary thrombosis. As an adolescent he was sentenced to 19 months in a reformatory for car theft. At age 29 years he had influenza, later developing psychotic symptoms (irritability, auditory hallucinations, many somatic complaints and long periods of standing and staring into space). He was accused of arson, became very excited and was admitted to Warren State Hospital on 4/11/1941, with a diagnosis of dementia praecox, paranoid type. At Warren State Hospital his face was mask-like, his posture stiff and his diagnosis was changed to psychosis with epidemic encephalitis. He was released, improved, on 8/9/1941. Classification: Schizophrenic reaction— paranoid type.

Family Summary

The proband, a brother, a sister, a son, three nephews and a niece were frankly psychotic, another brother probably so, and the mother possibly so. Two of the siblings suicided and one brother and a nephew made suicide attempts. A niece and a grandson had personality disorders. The proband's second wife was psychotic. Two uncles, a daughter-in-law, a sister-in-law and a niece's husband had personality disorders, another sister-in-law was neurotic and a third had chronic brain syndrome associated with cerebral arteriosclerosis, as did the paternal grandmother. The proband's parents had nine children, 19 grandchildren, 18 great-grandchildren, five great-great-grandchildren and one great-great-great-grandchild.

Controls

See family pedigree, person 40.

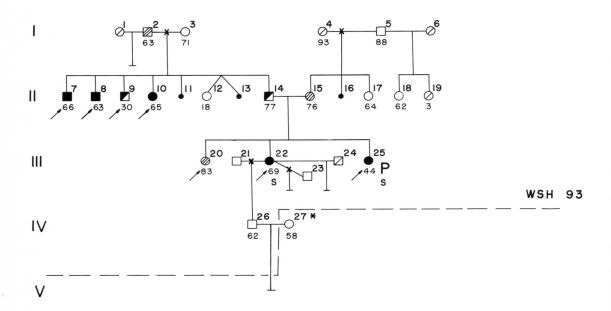

WSH 93: The Proband

Proband (25), born 1892; died at age 44 years of multiple injuries received when hit by an automobile. Her first period of mental disturbance was at age 14 years when she had a period of excitement followed by a period of depression, during which she made a suicide attempt. The following year she again had a period of excitement followed by a period of depression. The next year, during a period of excitement, she came in conflict with the law and was committed to Warren State Hospital on 8/24/1911, with a diagnosis of dementia praecox. She was paroled on 2/11/1912 as improved. Subsequent hospitalizations with diagnosis were as follows:

2/2/1914 – 12/19/1914	Manic-depressive, double form, hypomanic.
8/24/1915 – 4/7/1916	Manic-depressive reaction, double form.
6/9/1917 – 5/10/1919	Manic-depressive psychosis, double form – atypical type.
7/15/1919 – 3/20/1920	Manic-depressive psychosis, double form – atypical type.
9/30/1926 – 5/28/1930	Manic-depressive psychosis, manic phase.

Hyperactivity was the usual immediate cause of hospitalization. While hospitalized she would sometimes have periods of agitated depression, during which she spent most of her time picking her fingers. She would occasionally smile in an affected manner and would request the physician to give her a fatal dose of anesthetic or a poison. In February, 1917, while at home, she tried to induce her father and sister to assist her in killing her mother. She was never capable of self-support as she always showed judgment defect in her conduct and had no insight into her mental condition. Classification: Schizophrenic reaction – schizo-affective type.

Grandparents

Paternal grandfather (2), born 1811; died at age 63 years of apoplexy. He was extremely "close" with his money and an unusually hard worker. He reportedly "worked himself to death"; for example, he would build fences by moonlight after working all day. After the birth of their last child, his wife refused to live with him any longer. Classification: Personality trait disturbance – compulsive personality.

Parents

Father (14), born 1844; died at age 77 years of arteriosclerosis and chronic nephritis. He was described as "not quite right... selfish and miserly" and as penurious and inconsiderate of his family. Classification: Probably with functional psychosis.

Mother (15), born 1852; died at age 76 years of a ruptured aneurysm of the aorta. She reportedly had sudden emotional changes and was considered "peculiar." Classification: Personality pattern disturbance – paranoid personality.

Aunts and Uncles

Paternal uncle (7) born 1838; died at age 66 years at Warren State Hospital of nephritis. He was always considered "weak minded" but had no real mental problem until he returned from the Civil War, when he at times became flighty or ugly to his family. At admission to Warren State Hospital on 11/17/1885, with a diagnosis of acute mania, he was very much confused. The notes made during his 19 years at Warren State Hospital reveal a variety of moods; usually he was quiet, sometimes dull. He was always deluded and confused. He had a few excited periods after he had been there a few years, but was idle, listless and dull the last part of his life. He never married. Classification: Schizophrenic reaction – chronic undifferentiated type.

Paternal uncle (8) born 1840; died at age 63 years at Warren State Hospital of pulmonary tuberculosis. He never married. He was described as the "best fellow ever" until he developed symptoms of mental illness at about age 29 years. The symptoms persisted and in December, 1881, he became violent and was admitted to Warren State Hospital on 12/22/1881, with a diagnosis of chronic mania. A hospital note of 7/25/1903 described him as very much demented. Classification: Schizophrenic reaction – chronic undifferentiated type.

Paternal uncle (9) born 1841; died at age 30 years at a state mental hospital, cause of death unknown. There was little known about him except that he never married and was admitted to the hospital on 1/26/1869, with a diagnosis of chronic mania. He was hospitalized until his death. Classification: Probably with functional psychosis.

Paternal aunt (10) born 1847; died at age 65 years of chronic interstitial nephritis. She was always regarded as "silly and foolish" and as "a dependent girl with little mind of her own." She was married a short time but was turned out by her mother-in-law because of her negligence. She lost twins by self-induced abortion and later had an illegitimate child by a farm laborer at her parents' farm. She was admitted to Warren State Hospital on 11/15/1889, with a diagnosis of chronic mania. On admission she was confused but not deluded or hallucinated. She was transferred to another state hospital on 8/8/1894, but returned to Warren State Hospital on 8/26/1896 and remained there with steadily increasing dementia until her death. Classification: Schizophrenic reaction – chronic undifferentiated type.

Siblings

Sister (20) born 1874; died at age 83 years of an acute coronary accident at Warren State Hospital. She never married and did much toward supporting her family by working as a nurse. One of her employers stated that (20) had a nervous breakdown about 1910 and was "going home to rest up" because of a nervous breakdown in 1913. At the time of admission to Warren State Hospital on 1/8/1949, her nephew stated that (20) had been psychotic for at least 25 years.

Her mental disturbance seemed to go in cycles, with three months of depression followed by three months of overactivity. A diagnosis of manic-depressive psychosis, hypomania, with senile changes was made. In 1954 a revised diagnosis of chronic brain syndrome with senile brain disease was made. Classification: Probable chronic brain syndrome with arteriosclerosis; also, possible personality pattern disturbance – cyclothymic personality.

Sister (22) born 1876; died at age 69 years of suicide by drowning. At age 21 years she left nurse's training and married. A year later her husband left her with a child to support and enlisted in the armed services. He returned from the Cuban War but went directly to the Philippines, without seeing (22), where he died of malaria. She continued her nursing but developed a "nervous, hysterical condition, worn out mentally and physically." After six months' rest she completed training, then worked as a nurse. She remarried in 1908 and this husband deserted her after a year and a half of marriage. She "went home a nervous wreck" and was taken to Warren State Hospital on 7/19/1909. An admission note stated that she had had syphilis. Diagnosis was recurrent mania. She was discharged as restored on 12/1/1909. Subsequent hospitalizations were as follows, with a diagnosis of manic-depressive psychosis, manic phase, made each time:

12/27/1923 – 11/10/1924
3/10/1926 – 12/11/1926
11/4/1935 – 5/8/1936

Her psychosis was characterized by noisiness, talkativeness and resistiveness, although first symptoms were delusions of persecution with threats to neighbors. During her second psychotic episode she was convinced that the Catholics were against her. Classification: Schizophrenic reaction – paranoid type.

Family Summary

The proband, both her sisters, three paternal uncles and one paternal aunt were hospitalized with mental illnesses. The fa-

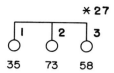

CONTROLS
W S H   93

ther was probably psychotic but never hospitalized; the mother and the paternal grandfather had personality disorders. The parents of the proband had three children and one grandchild. The proband never married and was childless.

Controls

None noteworthy.

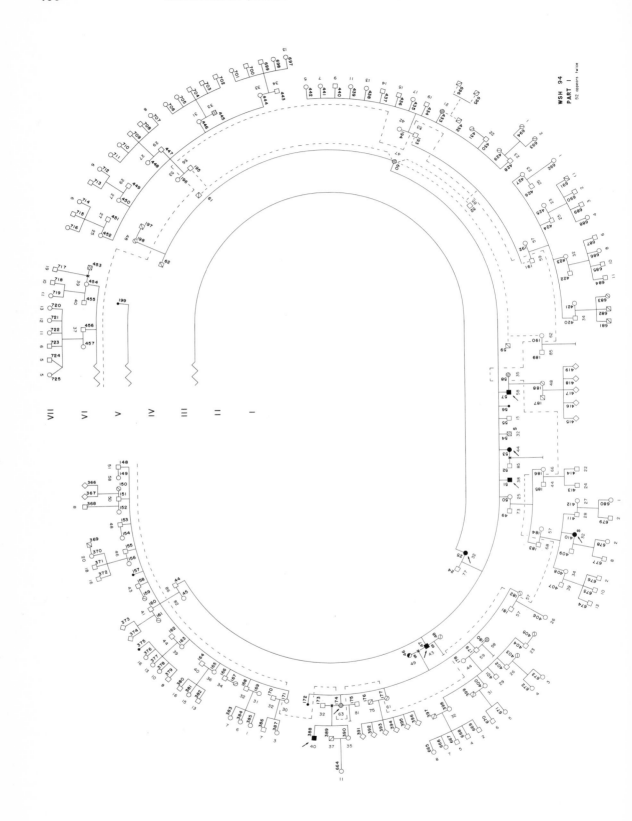

WSH 94
PART I
52 appears twice

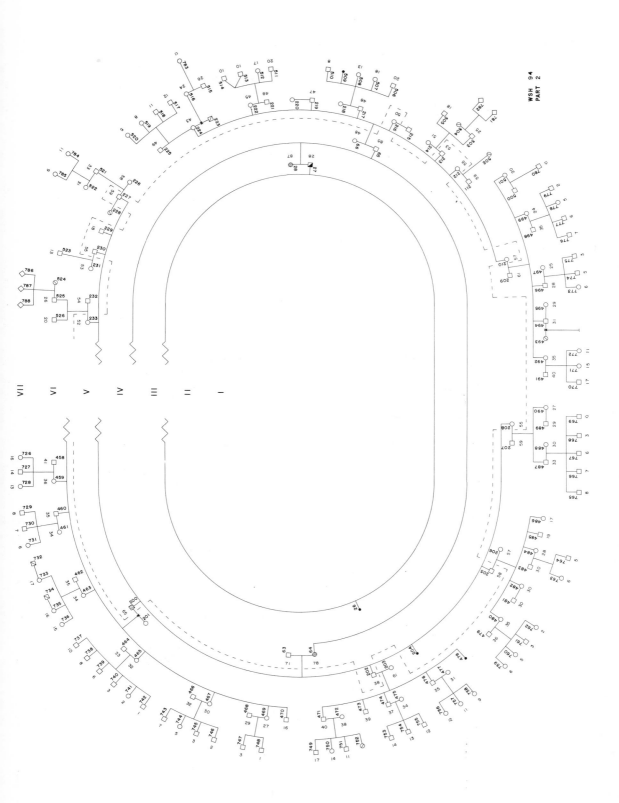

WSH 94
PART 2

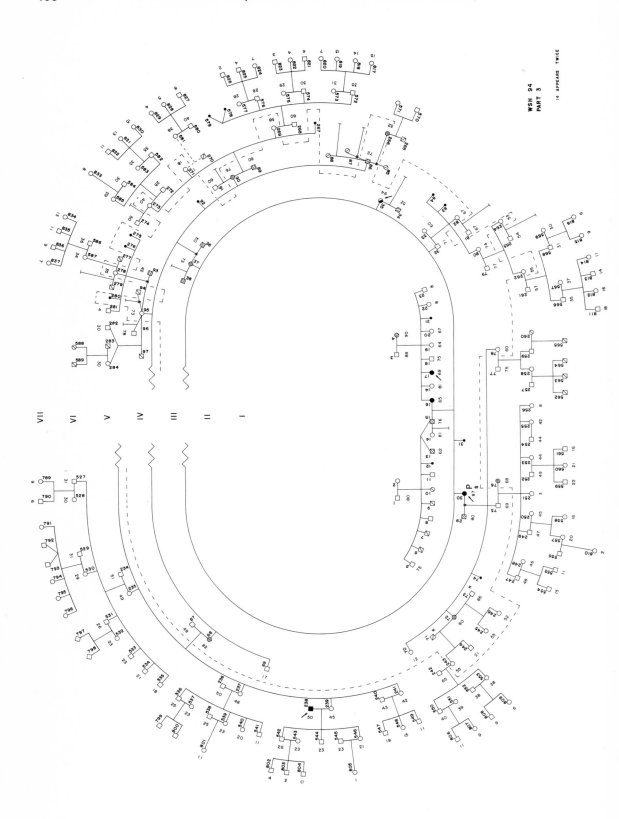

WSH 94
PART 3

14 APPEARS TWICE

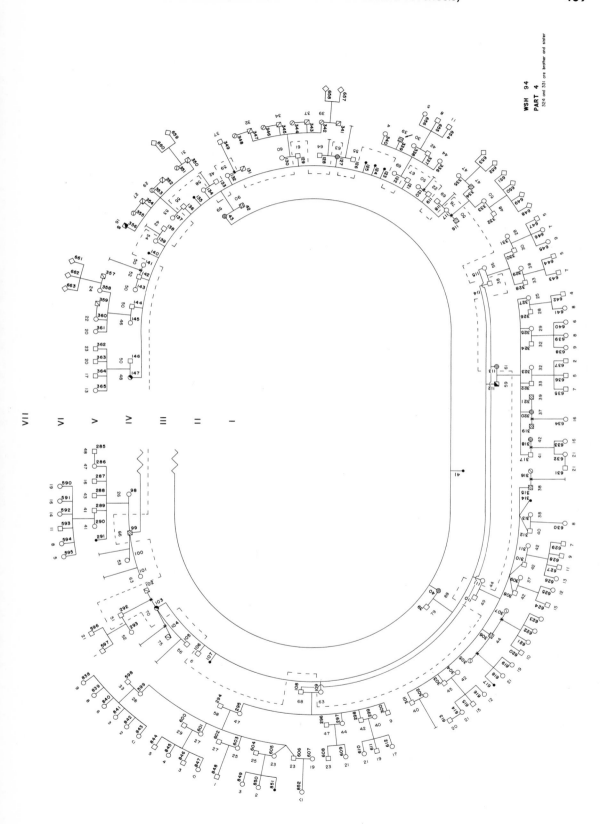

WSH 94
PART 4
324 and 331 are brother and sister

WSH 94: The Proband

The proband (30), born 1857; died at age 87 years of a cerebral embolism. She was always exceedingly hot tempered. The first symptoms of mental disorder began at about age 49 years, when she became unusually irritable and unstable for a day or two at a time. About three years later she "went crazy on religion" and attempted suicide three times. From then until her admission to Warren State Hospital on 7/23/1912, her behavior was abnormal. Diagnosis at Warren State Hospital was manic-depressive psychosis, depressed phase, involutional type. While hospitalized she was depressed, restless, worried, apprehensive and suicidal. She was discharged on 9/17/1914 as improved. Subsequent hospitalizations, during which her symptoms were similar to the above, or involved agitation with delusions of persecution, were as follows:

8/17/1922–7/15/1923	Diagnosis as above
1/16/1926–2/10/1926	Dementia praecox
2/10/1926–10/8/1927	Manic-depressive psychosis
1/6/1939–11/4/1942	Psychosis with arteriosclerosis

Classification: Schizophrenic reaction—paranoid type.

(29) husband of the proband (30), born 1857; died at age 80 years of chronic nephritis. He was described as "a silent gloomy man of rather an unsociable disposition." In 1922 he and the proband (30) separated and he went to live with one of his sons. Classification: Possible personality disorder.

Children

Daughter (72), born 1882, a housewife with an elementary school education. When interviewed she hinted at being "nervous" but refused to elaborate. She was described as "pretty close to a mental break during menopause." Classification: Probable psychoneurotic disorder, anxiety reaction; Possibly with functional psychosis.

Grandparents

Maternal grandmother (4), born 1813; died at age 90 years of apoplexy. She was described as "nervous and fretful, inclined to worry over little things." She also had frequent attacks of "fainting spells" which were reportedly caused by "defective circulation." Her death was sudden and occurred during one of her "fainting spells." Classification: Psychoneurotic disorder—anxiety reaction.

Parents

Father (15), born 1831; died at age 76 years of tuberculosis. He was described as "slow and rather dull mentally . . . was easily influenced, seemed to be lacking in will power and decision." Others reported that he "went crazy over religion." He became childish before he died and his judgment was somewhat impaired. Classification: Probable personality disorder.

Mother (16), born 1833; died at age 65 years of diabetes. She was described as "nervous and high-strung—used to fret over trifles." In 1858 she had a "sunstroke due to picking berries in the hot sun . . . became insane" and remained so for five months. During this episode she was at first violent and talkative, then gradually quieted down into a "kind of stupor." She never again regained her initiative and self-reliance, but did care for her family. Classification: Schizophrenic reaction—catatonic type.

Aunts and Uncles

Paternal uncle (13), twin to (15), the proband's father, born 1831; died at age 62 years of chronic diarrhea. He was a blacksmith and described as a "cranky, ill-natured man" with little sense of responsibility. He would go on an occasional "alcoholic spree" which would last for several weeks. His mind began to fail about six months before he died and he developed a "mania for iron and would pull a fence to pieces in order that he might have the nails." Classification: Sociopathic personality disturbance — alcoholism (addiction).

Maternal aunt (17), born 1836; died at age 69 years of cholelithiasis. She was a school teacher who was always considered "odd" and described as melancholy and solitary. At age 32 years she became "violently insane" and was cared for at home in a room built for this purpose. She was never again normal as she would talk in a strange manner, thought her food was poisoned and that people were trying to get rid of her. She married at age 40 years but remained with her husband for only six months, then returned to her parents' home. In 1898 she again became excited and disturbed and was admitted to Warren State Hospital on 11/14/1898, with a diagnosis of chronic mania. She remained at Warren State Hospital, excited, delusional, hallucinated, obscene and indifferent until her death. Classification: Schizophrenic reaction — paranoid type.

Siblings

Sister (25), born 1853; died at age 32 years of exhaustion from excitement at Warren State Hospital. She had always neglected her home and children and would never assume any responsibility. Also, nothing could cause her to worry. In December, 1884, when her tenth child was two weeks old, she became incoherent and had visual hallucinations of an elephant reaching down from the ceiling to get her. She became even worse and was admitted to Warren State Hospital on 3/28/1885, with a diagnosis of acute mania. Her condition remained stationary until her death two months later. Classification: Schizophrenic reaction — catatonic type.

Brother (27), born 1855; died at age 28 years of "brain fever." He was described as "a man with a hot temper" who "worried easily." About three weeks before his death he became restless and raving and remained so until his death. His condition was diagnosed by his physician as "brain fever." Alleged causes of the condition were injury to back, overwork and sunstroke. Classification: Probably with functional psychosis.

(28) wife of brother (27), born 1854; died at age 87 years of arteriosclerotic heart disease. She was described as "a woman of keen mentality and gracious disposition, but of a nervous temperament." Classification: Possible psychoneurotic disorder.

(34) husband of sister (35), born 1860; died at age 52 years of pneumonia. He was described as "indolent, lazy . . . cruel and abusive to his wife," also as "a restless fellow — cares of life didn't press him too much." Classification: Probable personality disorder.

Sister (35), born 1863; died at age 94 years, cause of death unknown. She was naturally of a quiet, calm disposition. In 1884, shortly before her marriage, she suffered a spinal injury and after this had "fits" every few weeks for four years. She reportedly was unable to bear children because of a childhood accident, the nature of which was unknown. In early 1910, she had an attack of influenza followed by an "attack of insanity" and she was hospitalized at a state mental hospital from 4/21/1910 until 5/23/1911, with a diagnosis of infective — exhaustive psychosis (infection delirium). At admission she stated that previous to her illness with influenza she had been melancholy and subject to nervous and emotional disturbances accompanying the menopause. The second episode of mental illness followed the death of her husband and was, as the first illness had been, characterized by restlessness, confusion, disorientation and flight of ideas. The second hospitalization, for which no diagnosis was recorded, was from 4/28/1912 until 1/11/1913. The third and fourth hospitalizations and diagnoses were as follows:

7/26/1921 — 9/29/1922   Manic-depressive psychosis, manic type.
6/23/1926 — 3/8/1957 (Death)   None recorded

Classification: Probably with functional psychosis.

(36) first husband of sister (37); died at age 50 years, cause of death unknown. He was described as "lazy, worthless, abusive to his wife — lived in squalid condition, filthy in language and habits." He could not stand erect because of a back injury received during a cyclone in 1884. He and (37) were divorced. Classification: Either personality pattern disturbance — inade-

quate personality; or, sociopathic personality disturbance.

Sister (37), born 1866; died at age 73 years of hypostatic pneumonia. She was described as "childish and emotional" and as having a speech defect. She deserted her husband and later entered into common-law marriage with another man. Classification: Probable sociopathic personality disturbance.

(38) second husband of sister (37). He was described as a "hard drinker" who "abused his first wife" although he and (37) got along well. Classification: Possible personality disorder.

Sister (40), born 1868; died at age 88 years of intracranial hemorrhage. She was described as "unstable, nervous and eager to discuss her nerves and ill health." Classification: Psychoneurotic disorder.

(42) husband of sister (43), born 1867; died at 90 years of age, cause of death unknown. He was described as a "kind father and husband when sober, but goes on drink bouts—then a raving maniac." Classification: Sociopathic personality disturbance—alcoholism (addiction).

Sister (43), born 1873; died at age 59 years of asthma. She was an unmarried mother at age 15 years (later the father of the child became her husband) and felt disgraced as a "fallen woman." As an extremely religious person she irritated her townspeople by her efforts to convert them. She felt "divinely protected" because her father "gave her to God." Classification: Probable personality pattern disturbance—other.

Nieces and Nephews

(46) first wife of nephew (47), born 1881; suicided at age 49 years by swallowing chloroform. She deserted (47) and her family when her youngest child was an infant. She was also described as promiscuous. She later remarried but had no children. Classification: Probably with functional psychosis.

Nephew (47), born 1872; died at age 43 years of myocarditis at Warren State Hospital. As a child he was normal but made poor progress in school. At age 24 years he developed a depression in which he cried easily,

was self-accusatory, begged to be burned up and was suspected of attempting suicide. He was hospitalized at Warren State Hospital on 5/4/1896, with a diagnosis of unclassified psychosis and discharged as restored on 4/1/1897. He remained well until October, 1914, although during this time his wife deserted him and their four small children. The second psychotic episode began with a depression, and he later developed excitement, hallucinations, destructiveness and nihilistic and suicidal tendencies. He was admitted to a county home in December, 1914, and in early January, 1915, after a symptom-free week, he was allowed to visit his family. While at home he chopped off his hand and was again admitted to Warren State Hospital on 1/27/1915, where he remained, his condition stationary and diagnosis unclassified, until his death. Classification: Schizophrenic reaction—paranoid type.

Nephew (51), born 1876; died at age 38 years of tuberculosis. He was naturally of a very quiet, even disposition and a thorough, reliable workman, called "the clock" because he was so steady and reliable in his work as a farm laborer. In the winter of 1907–1908, he began taking a patent medicine for an imaginary ailment which made him gay and talkative and occasionally produced delirium tremens. He gradually became "melancholy," then restless, violent and denudative, and was placed in a county home. He was there for three weeks, then admitted to Warren State Hospital on 8/6/1907, with a diagnosis of mania. On 1/23/1908, he was transferred again to the county home, although he was still depressed, confused and listless, and remained there until his death a few years later. The classification of acute brain syndrome associated with drug intoxication was considered but the preferred classification was schizophrenic reaction.

Niece (53), born 1878; died at age 44 years with a diagnosis of bronchopneumonia. She was described as naturally of a "light-headed disposition, silly and of inferior intelligence." On 1/1/1899, she began a manic attack in which she was overactive, denudative, bizarre and destructive. She attempted to kill her father but was not suicidal. She was hospitalized at Warren State Hospital on 1/29/1899, where she gradually improved and was discharged on 7/31/1900, as restored. After discharge from Warren State Hospital she was at times unusually restless and somewhat flighty in conversation but otherwise in normal mental health. When she discovered that her husband was the father of her sister's (60) illegitimate children, she left him (February, 1911). She then became nervous and uneasy and eventually violent, denudative, confused and silly and was readmitted to Warren State Hospital on 11/12/1911, where she remained, unimproved, until her death. While hospitalized she sometimes reacted to delusions and hallucinations. Classification: Schizophrenic reaction—catatonic type.

Nephew (54), born 1880; died at age 32 years. The coroner's verdict as to the cause of death was suicide since he was found dead, lying across railroad tracks with a revolver by his side. He would "go on hard drinking sprees and reportedly "drank like a fish." Classification: Probable sociopathic personality disturbance—alcoholism (addiction).

Nephew (57), born 1884; died at age 58 years of chronic myocarditis. He was always "irresponsible and simple minded." In November, 1916, he became excited and confused (he thought he was to be crucified for his sins) and was admitted to a county home, where he remained until his admission to Warren State Hospital on 12/11/1916, with a diagnosis of unclassified imbecility with dementia praecox. He had periods of religious exaltation with visual and auditory hallucinations, alternating with periods of worry and apathy. He remained at Warren State Hospital, where he was generally cooperative, with occasional "hollering spells" at night, until his death. Classification: Schizophrenic reaction—paranoid type.

(58) wife of nephew (57), born 1886; last known at age 35 years when she was convicted of bigamy as she married a "much older man" while still married to (57). Classification: Sociopathic personality disturbance.

Niece (60), born 1884; died at age 47 years of nephritis and malnutrition. She was described as "decidedly feebleminded" and as not knowing right from wrong. She was hired by her father (24) to care for her sister (53) who was ill with a psychotic disorder. While caring for her sister, she had four illegitimate children, two by her sister's husband (53). She was once hospitalized for hyperthyroidism and again with terminal illness, but never with a psychotic disorder. Classification: Sociopathic personality disturbance—dyssocial reaction.

Niece (64), born 1877; died at age 78 years of a coronary occlusion. She was described as "quick and decided in actions and speech . . . gives one the impression of a high nervous tension." She had severe headaches which lasted for days or weeks at a time. Classification: Probable psychoneurotic disorder.

Niece (68), born 1881; described as "quick-tempered . . . most nervous of the family." More recently she was described as exhibiting a "senile forgetfulness—memory impairment and mild disorientation—but was pleasant." Classification: Chronic brain syndrome of senium.

(76) wife of nephew (75), born 1894. When interviewed for the study she was hostile to the interviewer. She refused to answer her husband's questions when the interviewer was present and loudly and angrily left the room. Classification: Possible personality disturbance—either paranoid or schizoid personality.

Nephew (86), born 1885; died at age 72 years, cause of death unknown. As a young man he was "of a roving disposition" and "loose habits" who "squandered money recklessly." In later years he was blinded by a piece of steel. He had no history of treatment for a psychotic disorder. Classification: Probable personality disorder.

(89) first husband of niece (90), born 1879; died at age 60 years, cause of death unknown. He was described as a "hard drinker who abused his family." He reportedly had syphilis. Classification: Sociopathic personality disturbance—alcoholism (addiction).

Niece (90), born 1887; a housewife who was described in early life as "quiet, uncommunicative, brooding" and oversensitive. In late life she had a memory impairment. Classification: Probable psychoneurotic disorder; also, chronic brain syndrome of senium.

(93) first husband of niece (95), born 1881; died at age 42 years of a skull fracture received in an automobile accident. He reportedly was a "heavy drinker, an unfaithful

husband" and "abused his family." Classification: Sociopathic personality disturbance—alcoholism (addiction).

Nephew (99), born 1896; a retired janitor who had fair health except when he "drank too much." He was described as a "happy-go-lucky person to the point of callousness and irresponsibility." Classification: Sociopathic personality disturbance—alcoholism (addiction).

Niece (103), born 1892; a housewife who was described as a "household drudge—quiet, unassertive, honest and industrious but required supervision." When interviewed later she was described as "not obviously psychotic—but certainly eccentric—smacking her lips, closing her eyes tightly, staring around the room as she talked." Classification: Possibly with functional psychosis, schizophrenic reaction.

Nephew (112), born 1902; died at age 59 years of bronchial obstruction, bronchial asthma, and emphysema. He was described as "domineering, self-centered, abusive—had a violent temper. He was moody and depressed in the last year of his life." Classification: Possibly with functional psychosis.

(113) wife of nephew (112), born 1901. When interviewed for the study she was found to be a garrulous, unkempt woman who spoke with great sarcasm about her husband, daughter and son-in-law. Her home was dirty and disordered. (112) once tried to have her committed to a mental hospital, but the family opposed this and she was not treated. Classification: Probable personality pattern disturbance—schizoid personality; Possibly with functional psychosis.

(116) first husband of niece (117), born 1885. His whereabouts were last known at age 50 years. He was described as a "spendthrift" and "irresponsible." Classification: Probable sociopathic personality disturbance.

Niece (127), born 1901, a secretary who refused to be interviewed. Reportedly, after the death of her husband she was "lonely and anxious" and had a series of electroshock treatments for "depressive, obsessive, compulsive neurosis." Classification: Probable psychoneurotic disorder, depressive reaction.

Niece (147), born 1916, a nurse who had three "emotional upsets," twice following childbirth. The "upsets" were characterized by depression. Classification: Probably with functional psychosis.

More Distant Relatives

Grandniece (174), born 1901, a housewife who was raised by farmers who compelled her to do very heavy work and permitted little recreation. She was frequently beaten and ill-treated by them. As an adult she was always high-strung and nervous, particularly after marriage at 21 years of age. About five years before admission to Utica State Hospital on 1/26/1934, with a diagnosis of psychoneurosis, hysterical type, she became very depressed, suffered from severe frontal headaches and would occasionally have nervous spells of numbness all over. Her tongue would get thick, her hands would swell and her face became pale. The spells lasted from four hours to all day and were never accompanied by unconsciousness. She was divorced by her first husband. She was most cooperative with the study. Classification: Probable psychoneurotic reaction; Possibly with functional psychosis, schizophrenic reaction, chronic undifferentiated type.

(180) second wife of grandnephew (179), born 1906, a teacher who when interviewed for the study, although helpful and cooperative, laughed inappropriately during the interview. The interviewer considered the inappropriateness extreme. Classification: Probable personality pattern disturbance—schizoid personality.

Grandnephew (200), born 1898, a large-machine mechanic who had a heart problem since childhood. At one time, when he was taken out of school for a while because of his ill health, he became "rather blue and melancholy." Classification: Possible transient situational personality disorder—adjustment reaction of adolescence.

(238) husband of grandniece (239), born 1914. Psychiatric problems began while he was in Europe with the United States Armed Services. He wrote his wife accusing her of infidelity with no basis for his accusation. He was honorably discharged in Jan-

uary, 1944, but was observed by his wife to be indifferent to his children, highly oversexed and after six months had to quit his job because he believed he was being persecuted by his fellow employees. He feared going blind, was afraid to leave his wife alone, had stomach ailments with no medical basis and moved from job to job. First hospitalization was at a state mental hospital on 7/4/1948, after snapping his fingers and walking the floor all night. A diagnosis of dementia praecox, paranoid type, was made. He received combined pharmacological treatment, subcoma insulin therapy and electric convulsive therapy, and was paroled as recovered on 11/23/1948. Subsequent hospitalizations, each because of recurrent symptoms and all diagnosed as dementia praecox, paranoid type, were as follows:

2/1/1952 – 6/4/1952
12/11/1952 – 3/19/1953
12/6/1953 – 3/2/1954
9/30/1955 – 6/25/1958

Classification: Schizophrenic reaction – paranoid type.

Grandniece (266), born 1912, at age 52 years was a patient at a county home where she had been since age 32. She was described as of "dull normal mentality and perhaps somewhat nervous." At about the time of admission she had neurasthenia, but remained at the home chiefly because of negligence and never showing signs of psychosis. Classification: Possible personality disorder; also, mental deficiency.

Grandnephew (306), born 1920. At age 44 years he worked regularly as a plumber. Described as "no good – deserted both wives – not worth the room he occupied." Classification: Sociopathic personality disturbance.

Grandnephew (315), born 1926. He deserted his wife and was described by family members as "not dependable." Classification: Possible sociopathic personality disturbance.

(318) wife of grandnephew (317), born 1920. She was divorced by (317) after carrying on a prolonged affair that resulted in four pregnancies. Classification: Sociopathic personality disturbance – dyssocial reaction.

(319) first husband of grandniece (320); described as unfaithful, a migrant and usually unemployed. Classification: Sociopathic personality disturbance.

Grandniece (320), born 1925, a waitress who at age 15 years had a "nervous breakdown," during which she was "nervous, restless and cried for three months." She was not hospitalized. Classification: Probable psychoneurotic disorder.

(321) second husband of grandniece (320); described as "no good – hasn't worked a day in six years of marriage – sleeps day in, day out." Classification: Sociopathic personality disturbance.

Grandnephew (334), born 1917, an electrician who used alcohol to excess. Classification: Sociopathic personality disturbance – alcoholism (addiction).

Grandnephew (339), born 1925, a college graduate who worked as a precision laborer. He never married. In 1957 he was hospitalized at a Veterans Administration Hospital with an "emotional upset" which was worsened by his excessive use of alcohol. Classification: Probable psychoneurotic reaction; also, possible sociopathic personality disturbance – alcoholism (addiction).

Grandnephew (356), born 1939; suicided at age 16 years with an anesthetic which he stole from a hospital. Details of his previous mental condition were unknown. Classification: Probably with functional psychosis.

Great-grandnephew (388), born 1923; single and unemployable after he became psychotic and was hospitalized at a state mental hospital on 10/3/1945, with a diagnosis of schizophrenia. Other details of his illness were unknown, except that he was released from the hospital on 5/11/1946, on convalescent care, and was discharged on 5/17/1947. Classification: Schizophrenic reaction.

Great-grandniece (410), born 1930, a nurse whose last place of residence was in England. In 1954, following the birth of her first child, she became depressed and attempted suicide by slashing her wrist. One week later she again attempted suicide, this time with gas. She had four sessions with a psychiatrist and apparently made a good adjustment until she became preoccupied with religion and manifested many grandiose and paranoid delusions. She was hospitalized from 3/25/1957 until 5/23/1957 at Walter Reed Hospital with a diagnosis of

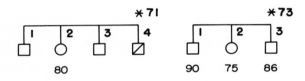

CONTROLS

W S H   94

schizophrenic reaction, paranoid type. She was then well until 2/10/1959, when she again developed symptoms of sleeplessness, inappropriate behavior, confusion of thought and paranoid ideas. She was again hospitalized, first at an Air Force Hospital Clinic on 3/8/1959, and 10 days later she transferred to a mental hospital. She improved to a point of almost complete remission and was discharged on 4/18/1959. Her child, who was mentally retarded, caused her a great deal of anxiety but once the child was institutionalized, she remained well. Some family members reported that she was "nervous" long before the birth of her first child, but there was no mention of symptoms of psychosis. Classification: Schizophrenic reaction—paranoid type.

Great-grandniece (433), born 1942, a housewife who lived with her two illegitimate sons and a male companion whom she "will marry someday." Classification: Sociopathic personality disturbance.

(445) husband of great-grandniece (446), born 1930. He was a Rehabilitation Bureau client because of his height (4 feet, 6 inches) handicap. The agency reported him to be a chronic complainer and considered his complaints to be psychosomatic. Classification: Personality pattern disturbance—other.

(453) first husband of great-grandniece (454), was discharged from the United States Army because of emotional instability. Classification: Probable personality trait disturbance—emotionally unstable personality.

Family Summary

The proband, her mother, one maternal aunt, one sister, three nephews, one niece, one great-grandniece, one great-grand-nephew and a husband of a grandniece had psychotic disorders. A brother, a sister, a grandnephew and the wife of a nephew had problems severe enough to be considered probably with a psychosis, and a niece possibly so. The maternal grandmother and a sister were psychoneurotic, and a daughter, three nieces and two grandnieces were probably or possibly neurotic, as was the wife of a brother. Those with a personality disorder were a paternal uncle, two nieces, a nephew, three grandnephews and a great-grandniece. The father, two sisters, two nephews and two grandnephews and a grandniece probably or possibly had a personality disorder. Two nieces (one of whom possibly had a personality disorder) were classified as with chronic brain syndrome of senium. The husbands of two sisters, of two nieces, of two grandnieces and one great-grandniece, and the wives of a nephew and a grandnephew, had personality disorders. The husbands of two sisters, of a niece and of a great-grandniece, and the wives of a son, a nephew, a grandnephew and the proband's husband, probably or possibly had personality disorders. The proband and a nephew made suicide attempts. The nephew's first wife suicided and the nephew's brother (also a nephew to the proband) was an alcoholic who possibly suicided. A great-grandnephew also committed suicide. The proband's parents had 11 children and 52 grandchildren. There were 119 great-grandchildren, 216 great-great-grandchildren, and 187 great-great-great-grandchildren. The proband had five children, 12 grandchildren, 13 great-grandchildren and five great-great-grandchildren, none of whom developed a psychosis.

Controls

None noteworthy.

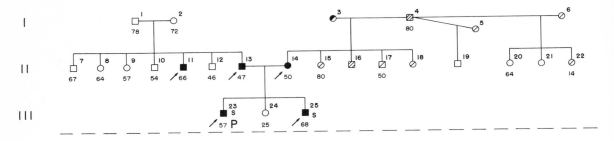

WSH 95

WSH 95: The Proband

The proband (23) born 1864; died at age 57 years at Warren State Hospital of chronic myocarditis. At age 21 years, following the death of his parents, he became overreligious. About four months before his admission to Warren State Hospital on 8/5/1889, he became greatly confused, suicidal, and thought that witches were going to burn him. Diagnosis at admission was acute mania. He was apathetic, depressed, silent and inactive for about a year and a half, then he improved suddenly and was discharged on 4/23/1891. He made a marginal adjustment at home for the next nine years. Occasionally he would remain in bed for a week with no apparent cause and would eat little, declaring there were lice in the food. When he worked, he was employed as a farm or mill laborer. An uncle was instrumental in getting him recommitted to Warren State Hospital on 2/8/1900. Diagnosis was again acute mania. He remained hospitalized until his death. He was often severely depressed and attempted suicide, was sometimes mildly excited, but never violent, and was in a severe depression for the two months preceding his death. Classification: Schizophrenic reaction—paranoid type.

Grandparents

Maternal grandmother (3); died of childbirth in 1840 at age 40 years. She was said to have died insane but no accurate description of her illness could be obtained. Classification: Probably with functional psychosis.

Maternal grandfather (4) was born in 1802; died at age 80 years of kidney trouble. He was described as a man "with an awful temper... would strike people without warning if they angered him" and as a "silent man, rarely speaking unless spoken to." He never received treatment for mental or emotional problems. Classification: Probable personality trait disturbance, passive-aggressive personality.

Parents

Father (13) born 1838; died at age 47 years of pneumonia. At age 15 years he became very much excited over an emotional religious sect. He became violent and was restrained in the county poor house for a short time. The psychotic episode lasted about one year and he never again had a psychotic break but was sociable and worked diligently as a farm laborer. Classification: Schizophrenic reaction.

Mother (14) died at age 50 years of tuberculosis. Her mother died at the time of (14)'s birth and she was raised by another family until age 21 years, when she returned to the home of her father, who had remarried. At her foster home she was forced to do work far beyond her strength and was not allowed to return to her father's home until she was 21 years of age. She had not been allowed to attend school regularly and several months of recuperation were needed for her to regain her physical health. When her son was four years old (about 1868) she tried to burn him as a piece of wood and was subsequently hospitalized at a state mental hospital for 13 months. After her release from the hospital she was quiet and reserved and did her own work but did not socialize. There were no additional hospitalizations. Classification: Schizophrenic reaction—chronic undifferentiated type.

Aunts and Uncles

Paternal uncle (11) born 1861; died at age 66 years of cardiac dilation. As a boy he was quiet and reserved. At age 16 years, for a period of three months, he would wander from place to place, was unpredictable and erratic in his behavior and would have sharp mood changes from overtalkativeness, with silly and flighty conversation, to days of depression or confusion. There was one more such episode lasting about three months before the third episode at age 26, when he was first hospitalized at Warren State Hospital (12/21/1886) with a diagnosis of periodic mania. He was discharged on 4/16/1887. A second hospitalization was at Warren State Hospital from 10/10/1914 until 5/19/1915, with a diagnosis of manic-depressive insanity, circular type. The third hospitalization was also at Warren State Hospital on 3/14/1916; diagnosis was again manic-depressive insanity, circular type. He remained at Warren State Hospital until his death. Each hospitalization was characterized by excitement, ideas of persecution, hypochondria and irritability. Classification: Schizophrenic reaction—chronic undifferentiated type.

Maternal uncle (16), date of birth and age at death unknown except that he died during the Civil War. He was single and a cabinet maker by trade. On at least one occasion he had delirium tremens. This occurred following a drinking spree over an unhappy love affair. Classification: Sociopathic personality disturbance—alcoholism (addiction); also, acute brain syndrome associated with alcohol intoxication.

Siblings

Brother (25) born 1873; died at age 68 years of senility at Warren State Hospital where he had been a patient for 41 years. Diagnosis at admission was acute mania. He became quite emaciated and remained ill, idle and unsociable for the first eight years of hospitalization, then he began to improve physically. He was suspicious and suicidal and had the delusion that a cancer or animal was crawling around in him. In later years he spent most of his time drawing pictures of this animal. Classification: Schizophrenic reaction—paranoid type.

Family Summary

The proband, both parents, a paternal uncle, a brother who made a suicide attempt, and probably the maternal grandmother had a psychotic disorder. The maternal grandfather and a paternal uncle had personality disorders. The proband's parents had three children and no grandchildren.

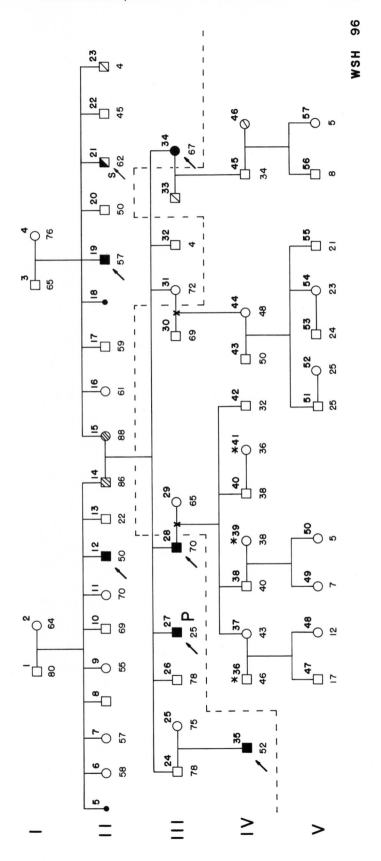

WSH 96

WSH 96: The Proband

The proband (27) born 1887; died at age 25 years at Warren State Hospital of abdominal tuberculosis. He had a normal childhood and as an adolescent was quiet, shy, hard working and did not date. He completed the "common" school at age 18 years and worked as a laborer. At age 23 years he was seriously ill with measles complicated by a severe cold which "settled in his stomach and bowels." He was never again well physically. A few months later he became apprehensive and overreligious. In early September of 1911, he became restless and destructive, was held in jail a few days, and admitted to Warren State Hospital on 9/12/1911 with a diagnosis of manic-depressive psychosis. The diagnosis was later of dementia praecox. He remained destructive, was filthy, careless, rarely spoke, and, when not confined to his bed, stood in one position for long periods of time. He became more emaciated and catatonic and subsequently succumbed from tuberculosis. Classification: Schizophrenic reaction—catatonic type.

Parents

Father (14) born 1855; died at age 86 years of heart trouble. He was a "silent, gloomy, serious" man, a hard drinker who had difficulty making a living because of "kidney trouble." Classification: Probable sociopathic personality disturbance—alcoholism (addiction).

Mother (15) born 1857; died at age 88 years of senility and arteriosclerosis. She "worried considerably" over the proband's illness and complained of heart pains. She was also described as listless and apathetic. Classification: Probable psychoneurotic disorder.

Aunts and Uncles

Paternal uncle (12) born 1839; died at age 50 years, cause of death unknown. He was a soldier during the Civil War and was knocked down and stunned by a shell. Although he sustained no physical injury, the shock was supposed to be the cause of the mental trouble he later developed at age 33

years, at which time he became excited and hallucinatory. After one year of hospitalization he was discharged as improved. Twelve years later, following a similar attack, he was admitted to Warren State Hospital on 4/21/1884, with a diagnosis of chronic mania. He became threatening and imagined that blood trickled down his side from war injuries. He also imagined that his body contained great mineral deposits and had other somatic complaints. He was discharged, unimproved, on 8/15/1889 and lived with his sister until his death. He was much improved mentally the last two years of his life, but never worked after the onset of his illness at age 33 years. Classification: Schizophrenic reaction—paranoid type.

Maternal uncle (19) born 1861; died at age 57 years of pneumonia at Warren State Hospital. He was a "bully" as a youth, but after fracturing his skull at age 25 years, he "joined the church and gave up drinking." Three years later he had an episode of nervousness, twitching and shaking of his hands, with hospitalization at Warren State Hospital on 3/18/1889. While hospitalized he was mildly depressed, suspicious, nervous and restless. He was discharged on 4/29/1889, unimproved. Four years later he complained of head pains and became so cross and irritable that he was readmitted to Warren State Hospital, where he remained, requiring seclusion because of excitement until he died. Classification: Schizophrenic reaction—paranoid type.

Maternal uncle (21) born 1863; died at age 62 years at Warren State Hospital of tuberculosis. He had always "worried over trifles and had many real and fancied pains." At age 59 years he suffered an 18-foot fall which required a 12-week hospitalization. He then became more and more depressed, made a suicide attempt and was subsequently admitted to Warren State Hospital on 11/19/1925. He remained apprehensive and depressed until his death. Classification: Probably with functional psychosis, psychotic-depressive reaction; also, chronic brain syndrome of senium.

Siblings

Brother (28) born 1889; died at age 70 years at a Veterans hospital of pulmonary tuberculosis. He had no evidence of mental

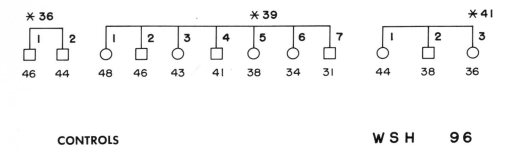

CONTROLS   **W S H   96**

disease until he returned from service with the armed forces in 1945 and accused his wife of infidelity, later obtaining a divorce. He had a nomadic existence until 1949, when he caused a disturbance in his hotel room because "spirits and spirit voices" were bothering him. He was hospitalized at a Veterans Administration hospital on 5/18/1949, with a diagnosis of arterio-sclerosis, cerebral with psychotic re-action, and was released in the custody of his family on 8/12/1949. He made a bor-derline adjustment until 1953, when he spent four weeks receiving electroconvul-sive therapy at a private sanitarium. When this therapy appeared to be insufficient he was transferred to a state mental hospital on 12/31/1953, where he remained, unim-proved, until his transfer on 3/15/1956 to a Veterans Administration hospital. At this hospital he was vague, rambling, incoherent and hallucinated. He felt that "they" double-crossed him and that he had no need for hospitalization. Affect was flat-tened and judgment affected. A diagnosis of involutional psychotic reaction, mixed type, moderate with depressive and para-noid features was made. His mental status improved somewhat but he had several bouts with pneumonia and chronic in-flammation of the lungs, and on 11/17/1959 a diagnosis of active pulmonary tubercu-losis was made and he was subsequently transferred to another hospital on 11/19/1959, where he remained until his death less than a month later. Classification: Schizophrenic reaction—paranoid type.

Sister (34) born 1896, at the time of the study a patient at a state mental hospital. The Finlayson Study described her as a shy,

retiring adolescent, pleasant and agreeable but decidedly bashful. She became ill in March, 1928, and was hospitalized from 3/16/1928 until 7/9/1928. She was hospi-talized because of paranoid delusional ideas, auditory hallucinations and misin-terpretation of her surroundings. Diagnosis was schizophrenic reaction, paranoid type. She was returned to the hospital on 9/16/1929 and transferred to another state hospital, where she remained suspicious, seclusive and almost continuously aurally hallucinated. She regressed, was de-teriorated and poorly oriented and at the time of the study it was impossible to carry on a conversation with her. Classification: Schizophrenic reaction—paranoid type.

Nieces and Nephews

Nephew (35) born 1912, had a psychot-ic break at age 18 years and was hospital-ized from 8/4/1930 until 12/31/1931. He was always of a temperamental nature and de-scribed by his family as "shy" and "not a good mixer." He and his mother were "very good pals." In May, 1930, he began to say "funny things." He thought his arm would reach a great distance, would pull the shades and search the house for knives to use for defense. He developed a heart pho-bia and would sit for hours in one position with his hand over his heart. At admission he showed marked psychomotor retarda-tion, had grandiose ideas, was at times de-nudative and was disoriented as to time, place and person. A diagnosis of dementia praecox, catatonic type, was made. He im-proved gradually and was released into the custody of his mother. He was never readmitted for mental illness. Classification: Schizophrenic reaction — catatonic type.

Family Summary

The proband, a paternal uncle, a maternal uncle, two siblings (a brother and a sister) and a nephew were classified as with a schizophrenic reaction and were hospitalized with their psychotic disorders. One hospitalized maternal uncle was probably psychotic. The father of the proband was an alcoholic and the mother a neurotic. There was one suicide attempt in a maternal uncle. The proband's parents had seven children and seven grandchildren.

Controls

None noteworthy.

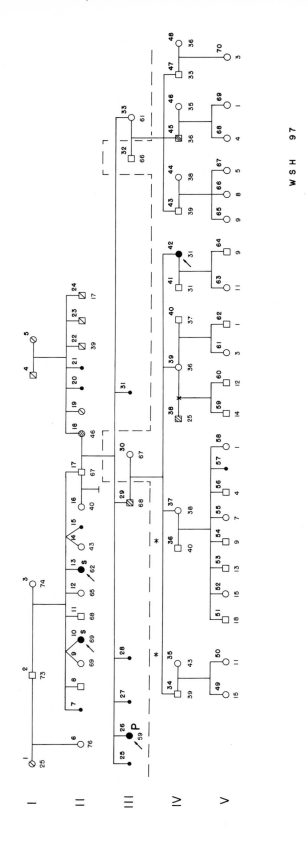

W S H   97

WSH 97: The Proband

The proband (26) born 1886; died at age 59 years at a state mental hospital of bronchopneumonia following a hip fracture. Early influences were said to have been "the best" for the proband. She attended school until 17 years of age (educational attainment unknown). She became psychotic at age 19 years and had six separate commitments, spending approximately 24 of her 59 years in mental hospitals. Her first symptoms began soon after the death of her mother, whom she cared for during the mother's terminal illness, when she became seclusive, introspective, depressed, melancholy, over-religious and emotional. She was admitted to Warren State Hospital on the five following dates with the following diagnoses:

4/13/1905 – 12/1/1905 – Acute melancholia
3/28/1910 – 11/7/1910 – Dementia praecox
9/17/1912 – 2/18/1914 – Manic-depressive psychosis
11/2/1914 – 9/20/1918 – Manic-depressive psychosis
9/21/1920 – 4/15/1924 – Manic-depressive psychosis

Following the fifth discharge from Warren State Hospital she worked as a domestic until she again became ill and was admitted, on 4/25/1931, to the state hospital, where she died. Diagnosis at admission was psychosis with anemia, but a more recent evaluation suggested a schizophrenic diagnosis. Classification: Schizophrenic reaction – paranoid type.

Parents

Father (17), born 1857; died at age 67 years of cancer of the stomach. He had an attack of "brain fever" at age 15 years; he was in bed for three months and then fully recovered. Classification: Acute brain syndrome associated with infection.

Mother (18), born 1858; died at age 46 years of tuberculosis. She was described as "very nervous" but with "good habits of life." Classification: Possible psychoneurotic disorder.

Aunts and Uncles

Paternal aunt (10), born 1843; married, one daughter, a former school teacher who, in 1901, became depressed and attempted

suicide by drowning. She was subsequently hospitalized for two or three months at a private sanitarium. Classification: Psychotic-depressive reaction.

Paternal aunt (13), born 1850; married with three children; a former school teacher who was well until her house was struck by lightning and the house and all her possessions burned. Following this she threatened suicide by hanging and was "mildly deranged." Fifteen years later, on 9/25/1906, following a suicide attempt by poisoning, she was admitted voluntarily to Warren State Hospital with a diagnosis of chronic mania. Ward notes described her as "dazed and confused and rather childish in actions." She was discharged as improved on 9/21/1907. When interviewed at age 62 years she was described as passive and childish. Classification: Schizophrenic reaction, probably hebephrenic type.

Siblings

Brother (29), born 1893, an optometrist, described by his sister as extremely thin and nervous and as suffering from insomnia and lack of appetite. He was constantly "on the go" and very active in his community; however, there was no history of treatment for mental or emotional trouble. Classification: Possible psychoneurotic disorder.

Nieces and Nephews

Husband (38) of niece (39), born 1924; history unknown from age 25 years. He was described as a selfish, nervous person who was agreeable socially. Classification: Possible personality disorder.

Niece (42), born 1930, a housewife, was admitted voluntarily to a private psychiatric hospital on 5/18/1958. Approximately two years before hospitalization, (42), who had always been a shy, self-conscious, withdrawn person, experienced a personality change. She took a position outside the home and apparently in an attempt to gain self-confidence, sought attention from other men, greatly jeopardizing her marriage. About a week before admission she became restless, impulsive and delusional. At admission affect was inappropriate. While hospitalized she became very confused and agitated and response to therapy was slow and

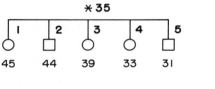

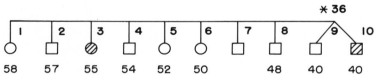

CONTROLS   W S H   97

incomplete. She was followed as an outpatient after her release on 8/30/1958. Hospital diagnosis and classification: Schizophrenic reaction, schizo-affective type.

Nephew (45), born 1926; died at age 36 years in an automobile accident; he was treated as an outpatient at a state mental hospital when 15 years of age. At the time of treatment he was on probation for stealing a car. Antisocial behavior began at age 14 years when he began to wander from home and hitchhike about the country. His home training was inadequate (the father turned the discipline over to the mother, who was unable to carry it out; furthermore, the mother was antagonistic toward (45)). His reactions were suggestive of a psychopathic personality and it was recommended that he obtain work at age 16 years. He became a pattern maker and received no further psychiatric help. Classification: Sociopathic personality disturbance, antisocial reaction.

Family Summary

The proband, two paternal aunts and one niece had psychotic disorders and were hospitalized for their illnesses. Both aunts attempted suicide. A nephew was treated for a personality disorder as an adolescent and a niece's husband was considered to possibly have a personality disorder. The mother was neurotic. The proband never married and was childless. The proband's parents had six children and seven grandchildren.

Controls

Sister (3) of (36), born 1906. She married three times but had no children and reportedly had a "nervous temperament." Classification: Possible psychoneurotic disorder.

Brother (10) of (36), born 1921. He worked, although irregularly, as an aircraft electronics maintenance technician. He was a poet of some reputation and had read considerably in psychology and psychiatry. When interviewed at age 40 years he stated that he "couldn't stand routine." Classification: Probable personality pattern disturbance — inadequate personality.

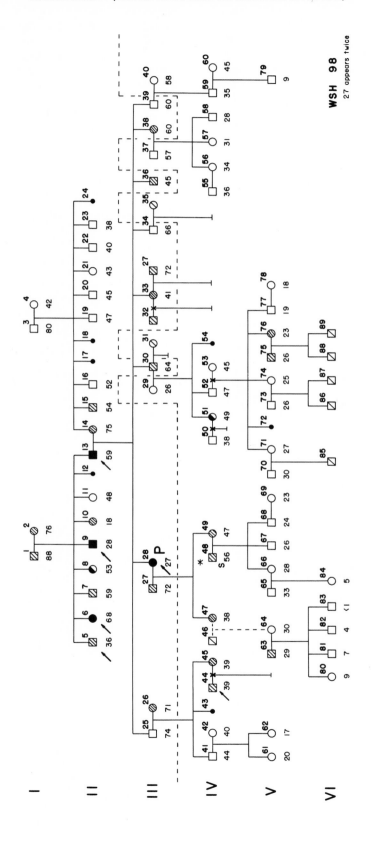

WSH 98

27 appears twice

WSH 98: The Proband

The proband (28), born 1888; died at age 27 years at Warren State Hospital of gangrene of the lung. She left school at age 14 years to work as a domestic until her marriage at age 21 years. Her paternal grandfather attempted several times to seduce her as a child. Married life was unhappy as her husband "drank" and neglected her. The husband and his father, who lived with them, also quarreled a great deal. About 10/1/1913, she became irritable, violent and destructive; her conversation was incoherent and irrelevant. She was also visually and auditorily hallucinated. She was hospitalized at Warren State Hospital with a diagnosis of manic-depressive, manic phase, from 1/4/1914, until her death. Just prior to admission she developed delusions of persecution and poisoning. Classification: Schizophrenic reaction—catatonic type.

(27) husband of proband (28), born 1882; age at last information was 72 years. At interview he was found to have a very poor memory and "slow and halting speech." Classification: Possible chronic brain syndrome of senium.

Children

Daughter (47), born 1911; accidentally drowned in a boating accident at age 38 years. She was four years old when her mother was hospitalized at Warren State Hospital. She then lived with her paternal grandmother and later with her maternal aunt. Her relationship to (46) was not entirely certain but he was presumably the father of her illegitimate daughter, although it reportedly "could have been two or three other men." Her death record listed (46) as her husband. Classification: Sociopathic personality disturbance.

(48) husband of daughter (49), born 1904. He was described as an alcoholic who at one time attempted suicide. Classification: Sociopathic personality disturbance—alcoholism (addiction).

Daughter (49), born 1913. She was two years of age when her mother was hospitalized and was raised by her paternal grandmother and a maternal aunt. She married at 16 years of age but separated from her husband 13 years later because of his alcoholism. At this time she received medication for "nerves" on two separate occasions. Classification: Possible transient situational personality disturbance—adult situational reaction.

Grandchildren

(63) husband of granddaughter (64), born 1932. He had a history of alcoholism and had served several prison sentences. He was described by a prison psychologist as an emotionally unstable and immature personality who was egocentric, alcoholic, irresponsible and with sex conflicts. He was diagnosed as non-psychotic and received counseling and work with AA. In 1962 he was on parole and seemed to be adjusting well. Classification: Sociopathic personality disturbance.

Grandparents

Paternal grandfather (1), died at age 88 years of "old age." He was described as an alcoholic and as "peculiar, lazy, shiftless . . . ugly, disagreeable to his wife." Classification: Sociopathic personality disturbance.

Paternal grandmother (2), died at age 76 years of apoplexy. She was an active woman who was the main financial support of the family; nevertheless, she was considered "queer" by those who knew her. When older she suffered three strokes, following which she became "irritable, childish and gradually demented." Classification: Chronic brain syndrome of senium.

Parents

Father (13), born 1854; died at age 57 years at Warren State Hospital, of septicemia and myocarditis. As a young man he was industrious and well. From age 38 years he was a "steady drinker." In early 1902, at age 48 years, he became excited, talkative, had vague ideas of persecution, slept little and "seemed to want to shoot someone." He was admitted to Warren State Hospital on 10/16/1902, where he remained until death. His condition was never diagnosed at Warren. Hospital notes described him as "deluded, noisy and careless" and later as "foolish and confused." At times he assaulted other patients. Another note, a few months before his death, described him as "standing in one position much of the time . . . filthy . . . very difficult to keep him dressed." Classification: Schizophrenic reaction—catatonic type.

Mother (14), born 1865; died at age 75 years of pulmonary embolus. She was considered an unreliable and untruthful informant, but industrious and hard working. She was sleepless and worried at the time of her husband's death. Classification: Possible psychoneurotic reaction.

Aunts and Uncles

Paternal uncle (5), born 1851; died at age 36 years of tuberculosis. He was admitted to Warren State Hospital on 9/23/1884 because of "intemperance"—he reportedly was intoxicated "practically all the time." Upon admission he was anxious and worried and for over two years he did not speak at all. He then became very talkative, restless and destructive. He escaped on 3/3/1887, and died three months later. Classification: Sociopathic personality disturbance—alcoholism (addiction).

Paternal aunt (6), born 1853; died at age 68 years of pulmonary tuberculosis at Warren State Hospital. She was described as always "decidedly peculiar." She denied that there was either mental illness or tuberculosis in the family when, in reality, her husband and daughter were tubercular and two of her siblings had been hospitalized at Warren with psychotic disorders. After the death of her daughter she became depressed, refused to eat or sleep and was occasionally destructive. She was not hallucinated but did have some "vague delusions" and was admitted to Warren State Hospital on 9/4/1914, where she remained until death. Admitting diagnosis at the hospital was undifferentiated depression with a concluding diagnosis of schizophrenia, catatonic type. Classification: With functional psychosis, probable schizophrenic reaction.

Paternal uncle (7), born 1855; age at last information was 59 years. He was described as an alcoholic. Classification: Sociopathic personality disturbance—alcoholism (addiction).

Paternal aunt (8), born 1861; age at last information was 53 years. She was described as a "very eccentric" woman who was very excitable, sometimes becoming almost hysterical. She also "imagined things that are not so." Classification: Probably with functional psychosis.

Paternal uncle (9), born 1862; died at age 28 years at Warren State Hospital of exhaustion. He was described as always a "peculiar, weak-minded fellow" who was always excitable and could never hold a job or get along with people. He was very religious. At one time he tried to shoot his brother and at another time thought he was drowning. He became violent and was admitted to Warren State Hospital on 11/14/1890, where he died two months later. Diagnosis at Warren was acute mania. Classification: Schizophrenic reaction.

Paternal aunt (10), died at age 18 years of pneumonia. She was described as always "cross and irritable" and "hard to get along with." Classification: Possible personality disorder.

Maternal uncle (15), born 1860; age at last information was 54 years. He was described as "a steady drinker all his life." After the death of his wife he drank even more and developed the idea that no one cared for him. His physician suspected that he had tuberculosis, but (15) tried to prove that he did not by using his tubercular wife's drinking cups and dishes. Classification: Sociopathic personality disturbance—alcoholism (addiction).

Siblings

(26) wife of brother (25), born 1890. She was interviewed and reported that she had had "several nervous breakdowns" and recalled two episodes, one following the birth of her first child at age 26 years. The second episode mentioned was in 1958, at age 68 years, when she was treated with tranquilizers and hospitalized in a general hospital for one week. At each episode she would become increasingly tense and nervous, developed "sick headaches" and went to bed. Classification: Psychoneurotic reaction.

Brother (30), born 1891; died at age 64 years of a heart attack. He was described as unable to hold a job and as "utterly worthless." He could not care for a wife and family, was very immoral and showed little interest in his children. Classification: Socio-pathic personality disturbance.

(32) husband of sister (33); whereabouts unknown since 1915. He was described as a "dissipated braggart." Classification: Possible personality disorder.

Sister (33), born 1893; died at age 41 years of cancer of the cervix. She was assaulted by her paternal grandfather as a child and continued her irregular behavior with many men even after she married. She divorced her first husband and married the proband's husband. She was described as "nervous and excitable and very loud and forward." Classification: Sociopathic personality disturbance.

Brother (36), born 1898; died at age 45 years of carcinoma of the lung. He was described as a "drifter" and as an alcoholic in early years. Classification: Sociopathic personality disturbance.

Sister (38), born 1900. She was interviewed in 1960 and described as an evasive informant who showed occasional aphasia. Classification: Possible chronic brain syndrome of senium.

Nieces and Nephews

(44) husband of niece (45), born 1921. In early life he was friendly, agreeable, and a good worker, but he became alcoholic and lost several jobs because of his drinking. He was arrested at different times for drunkenness, drunken driving and disorderly conduct. He was hospitalized from 7/17/1959 until 10/20/1959, and was described as a "rather typical non-psychotic alcoholic." Classification: Sociopathic personality disturbance—alcoholism (addiction).

Niece (45), born 1921. She eloped to marry (44) against her parents' wishes. The couple always lived with her parents until (44) became so alcoholic that the parents put them out. After (44) was hospitalized, (45) had a "nervous breakdown," lost weight, became tense and extremely nervous but received no treatment for her nervousness. Classification: Probable psychoneurotic reaction—other.

Niece (51), born 1913. After her mother's death, when she was six years of age, she and her brother were placed in an orphanage. She was interviewed in 1960. The interviewer reported that she did not understand the purpose of the interview

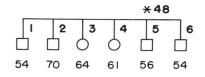

CONTROLS

W S H   9 8

and was very suspicious. Her brother described her as unstable, depressed and seclusive. She talked to herself. At one time her doctor recommended institutional care, but she was never hospitalized. At the time of interview her apartment was well kept but, on one occasion, an apartment manager had to ask her to move because she was noisy, profane, abusive and destructive. Classification: Probably with functional psychosis, schizophrenic reaction.

Distant Relatives

(75) husband of grandniece (76), born 1936. He was reportedly "doctoring for nervous trouble." Classification: Probable psychoneurotic reaction.

Grandniece (76), born 1939. She was reportedly "doctoring for nervous trouble." Classification: Probable psychoneurotic disorder.

Family Summary

The proband, her father, a paternal aunt and a paternal uncle had psychotic disorders and a paternal aunt and a niece probably so. Personality disorders were discovered in two daughters and in one of their husbands, in the paternal grandfather, two paternal uncles, a paternal aunt, a maternal uncle, two brothers, a sister, the husbands of a granddaughter, a sister and a niece. The husband, the paternal grandmother and a sister were classified as chronic brain syndrome of senium. The mother, a niece, a grandniece, her husband and the wife of a brother were possibly or probably psychotic.

Controls

None noteworthy.

SCHIZOPHRENIA

A total of 43 probands had conditions diagnosed as paranoia or dementia praecox during the 1912–1917 study and considered as schizophrenia upon reclassification (see Table 2–2). This is essentially half of the 89 probands from the 1912–1917 series.

The pedigree drawings and descriptive summaries in this group cover the following kinships: WSH 13, 16, 20, 22, 23, 24, 31, 32, 36, 37, 39, 40, 41, 42, 43, 45, 46, 47, 49, 51, 52, 54, 55, 56, 59, 61, 62, 63, 65, 66, 67, 69, 70, 72, 76, 78, 80, 82, 83, 85, 86, 91, and 99.

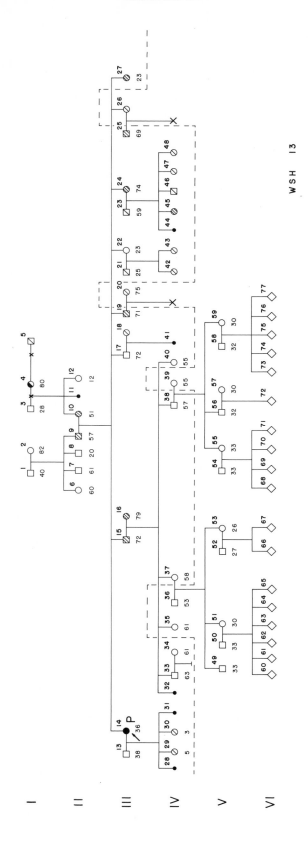

WSH 13

WSH 13: The Proband

Proband (14), born 1882; died at age 36 years of tuberculosis at Warren State Hospital. She was described as "kind, jovial and sympathetic" before her marriage and her "mental upsets" were associated with her pregnancies in that, after each pregnancy, she became "upset." While "upset" she would "wander away from home and was noisy at night." The onset of her psychosis was six years before admission to Warren State Hospital on 6/10/1916, where she remained until her death 26 months later. Diagnosis at Warren State Hospital was dementia praecox. At Warren State Hospital she had auditory and olfactory hallucinations, delusions of persecution and poisoning, religious "visions," and was manneristic and generally apathetic. Classification: Schizophrenic reaction—paranoid type.

Grandparents

Maternal grandmother (4), died at age 80 years of apoplexy. She was described as "overbearing, officious" and "had a temper that everyone feared." She was known as a "devil" in the community. She was also described as "a very worrisome woman but withal good-natured." Classification: Probably with functional psychosis.

Parents

Father (9), born 1859. At age 57 years he reportedly "had a violent temper and was an excessive drinker." Classification: Possible personality disorder.

Mother (10), born 1865. When interviewed at age 51 years she described herself as "very nervous and fearful." She had "abnormal superstitious ideas and was possessed with fear." She was also described as with a "violent, ungovernable temper, a jealous disposition and was quarrelsome, suspicious and unreasonable." Classification: Probable psychoneurotic disorder.

Siblings

Brother (15), born 1883; died at age 72 years of coronary thrombosis. He was a railroad shop employee who reportedly was "a very heavy drinker and a gambler." Classification: Possible sociopathic personality disturbance—alcoholism (addiction).

(16) wife of brother (15), born 1885. At about age 35 years she had tuberculosis and was described as "very nervous." At age 79 years she was considered to have no nervous symptoms. Classification: Possible psychoneurotic disorder.

Brother (19), born 1886; died at age 71 years of a heart attack. He reportedly had "the family trait of a violent temper and was a heavy drinker." Classification: Possible sociopathic personality disturbance—alcoholism (addiction).

Sister (24), born 1890. She reportedly always had "a violent temper." When interviewed at age 74 years she refused to give information on her own family but gave information on a brother and a sister. Classification: Possible personality disorder.

(25) husband of sister (26), born 1892; died at age 69 years of an accidental skull fracture. As a young man he was described as "very nervous" and with "a quick temper." He was found intoxicated and was charged with drunkenness on the day of his fatal accident; the circumstances surrounding his accident are uncertain. Classification: Possible psychoneurotic disorder.

Sister (27), born 1893. At age 23 years she reportedly was "very, very nervous" and had periods of exhibiting a horrible temper when she lost control of herself so completely and shook so violently that she had to be restrained. Classification: Probable psychoneurotic disorder.

Nieces and Nephews

Niece (45). At a 1965 interview with her mother, (45) was very hostile to the interviewer and continually interrupted the conversation. Classification: Possible personality disorder.

Family Summary

The proband had a psychotic disorder and the maternal grandmother probably so. Personality disorders were discovered in the father, two brothers, a sister and in a niece. The mother, a sister, the wife of a brother and the husband of a sister were neurotic.

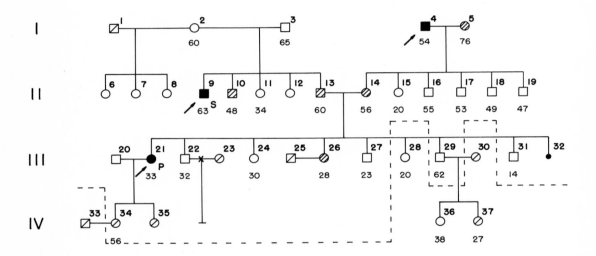

WSH   16

WSH 16: The Proband

Proband (21), born 1883; died at age 34 years at Warren State Hospital of chronic myocarditis following a period of catatonic excitement. She attended school until grade nine but was forced to leave because of "extreme nervousness." She was described as a "cheerful, happy woman" until about one year before admission to Warren State Hospital on 9/22/1916, when she had a period of excitement lasting approximately one month. She was normal for nine months, then became depressed and again excited. At admission to Warren State Hospital she was destructive, noisy, profane and confused; she had delusions of infidelity regarding her husband and bizarre delusions regarding her children. Diagnosis at Warren State Hospital was dementia praecox. She remained hospitalized until her death. Classification: Schizophrenic reaction—catatonic type.

Grandparents

Maternal grandfather (4), born 1835; died at age 54 years at Warren State Hospital of exhaustion of chronic mania. He was admitted to Warren State Hospital in February, 1888, in a confused and restless state. He remained hospitalized until September, when he went home much improved. The improvement was only temporary and he was readmitted in November; he died a year later. Classification: Schizophrenic reaction.

Maternal grandmother (5), born 1841. At age 76 years she was described as "a very nervous woman." Classification: Probable psychoneurotic disorder.

Parents

Father (13), died at age 60 years of apoplexy. He was described variously as "calm, easy-going, phlegmatic, . . . quiet and unsociable" and as "broken down with hard work." His townspeople considered his death to have been "due to alcohol." Clas-sification: Possible sociopathic personality disturbance—alcoholism (addiction).

Mother (14); interviewed and described at age 56 years as "nervous and unstable." The proband's hospital abstract described her as "neurotic and eccentric." Classification: Probable personality trait disturbance—emotionally unstable personality.

Aunts and Uncles

Paternal uncle (9), born 1854. He was committed to a state mental hospital on 6/29/1883, and released as improved on 4/12/1884. He had nursed a sick baby almost day and night in February, 1883. During this time he became nervous and excited. The child got well but (9) remained too upset to work. He refused to eat, resisted attention, was sleepless and thought he was going to die. On admission he was agitated and depressed. He once attempted suicide by hanging with a sheet. At age 63 years he was described as "very nervous and worries easily" and also as "insane." Classification: Manic-depressive reaction—mixed type.

Paternal uncle (10). At age 48 years he was described as "a heavy drinker," although steadily employed by an oil company. Classification: Probable sociopathic personality disturbance—alcoholism (addiction).

Siblings

Sister (26), born 1889. At age 28 years she was married but childless and described as "very nervous." Classification: Probable psychoneurotic disorder.

Family Summary

The proband, the maternal grandfather and a paternal uncle had psychotic disorders. The maternal grandmother and a sister were neurotic. Personality disorders were found in the father, the mother and in a paternal uncle.

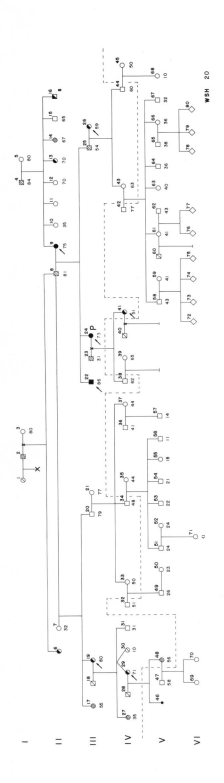

WSH 20: The Proband

Proband (24), born 1867; died at age 73 years of chronic myocarditis. There were seven admissions to sanitariums and mental hospitals during her lifetime, as well as treatment as a private patient for a period of six years. At different times in her illness she showed delusions and hallucinations, was untidy, denudative and noisy. She was never suicidal or homicidal. She first exhibited "mental impairment" before the birth of her daughter (41) in 1896. Diagnosis at her first hospitalization, which was at a private mental hospital from June, 1897 until February, 1898, was primary dementia. Diagnosis at Warren State Hospital, where she was hospitalized from 7/8/1916 until 3/4/1923, was dementia praecox—paranoid type. Classification: Schizophrenic reaction—paranoid type.

(23) husband of the proband (24), born 1865; last heard of at age 31 years. He was known to be unfaithful to his wife and as saying that his marriage and divorce were directed by the "spirits." Classification: Psychoneurotic reaction, other.

Children

Daughter (41), born 1896; died at age 51 years of hypostatic pneumonia. Her marriage was annulled. The death certificate stated that she was a patient at a private mental hospital for 18 years and nine months. Cause of death, other than the immediate cause, was debilitation and malnutrition. Schizophrenic make-up was listed as another existing condition. Classification: Probably with functional psychosis, schizophrenic reaction.

Grandparents

Paternal grandfather (2), born about 1800; age and cause of death unknown. He was described as a "violent-tempered man . . . ran away and left his wife . . . was an alcoholic." Classification: Probable sociopathic personality disturbance.

Maternal grandfather (4); died at age 84 years, cause unknown. He was described as "very eccentric, though not considered insane." Classification: Possible personality disorder.

Parents

Father (8), born 1824; died at age 81 years of "old age." He was a successful banker-manufacturer. His family described him as "a shrewd and sharp man" who "understood nothing but making money." He reportedly was so domineering that his whole family was afraid of him; yet, he also reportedly "indulged and ruined" his family. Classification: Probable personality disorder.

Mother (9), born 1836; died at age 75 years, cause of death unknown. She reportedly was "insane and suffered from migraines," was eccentric and believed in spiritualism. She spent the last 20 years of her life in hospitals. Classification: Schizophrenic reaction — paranoid type.

Aunts and Uncles

Paternal aunt (6); died at a very old age, cause of death unknown. She was described by her family as "peculiar" and by neighbors as "insane." Classification: Probably with functional psychosis.

Maternal aunt (13), born about 1846. At age 70 years it was reported that her "mind was not right ... she has been in many sanitariums." Classification: Probably with functional psychosis.

Maternal aunt (14), born 1850. At age 67 years she was described as always "very peculiar, a 'weakminded' woman, discontented with her lot in life and a social climber." Classification: Probable psychoneurotic disorder.

Maternal uncle (16), born 1855. He either committed suicide or was killed when a young man; the proband's case history stated that he committed suicide. Classification: Possibly with functional psychosis.

Siblings

Paternal half sister (17), born 1854; died at age 55 years of pneumonia. She never married and was described as "neurotic." Classification: Probable psychoneurotic disorder.

Paternal half sister (19), born 1856; died "in her 80's" of senility. At age 60 years she was described as "quite well preserved"; however, in later years she was committed to mental hospitals more than once. Classification: Possibly with functional psychosis.

Brother (22), born 1869; died at age 86 years, cause of death unknown. At age 31 years he began to show considerable depression but later became more paranoid, with feelings of persecution and excitement. Admission to a mental hospital was on 2/16/1909. He remained there, with no substantial improvement, until his death 46 years later. Classification: Schizophrenic reaction — paranoid type.

Brother (25), born 1873; died at age 54 years of a fractured skull received in a car accident. He was a college graduate and a successful banker who was described as "a sex offender, an alcoholic" and "lived a fast life." Classification: Sociopathic personality disturbance — antisocial reaction.

(26) wife of brother (25), born 1877; died at age 59 years of influenza. She reportedly was mentally ill for several years before her death and was hospitalized at a mental health sanitarium. Classification: Probably with functional psychosis.

Nieces and Nephews

Half niece (27), born 1878. At age 35 years she was described as "neurotic." Classification: Probable psychoneurotic disorder.

Half niece (29), born 1880; died at age 71 years of pneumonia at a mental health sanitarium. She had been hospitalized for seven months before her death and was described as "neurotic and temporarily insane." Classification: Probably with functional psychosis.

Distant Relatives

Half grandniece (48), born 1906. She did not answer questionnaires and refused to see an interviewer on three occasions. Her physician stated that she avoided doctors, refused medical advice even when seriously needed, and smoked and drank heavily. Classification: Probable sociopathic personality disturbance — alcoholism (addiction).

Family Summary

The proband, her mother and a brother had psychotic disorders and a daughter, a half sister, two aunts, an uncle, a half niece and the wife of a brother probably or possibly so. Personality disorders were discovered in the father, both grandfathers, a brother and in a half grandniece. A maternal aunt, a half sister, a half niece and the proband's husband were neurotic.

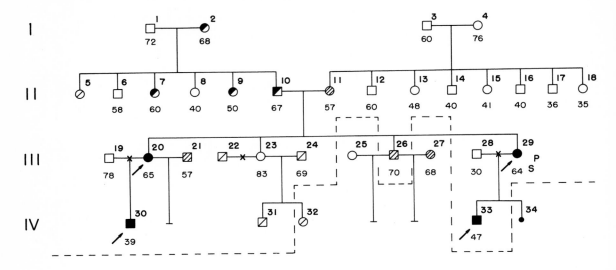

WSH 22

WSH 22: *The Proband*

Proband (29), born 1893; died at age 64 years at Warren State Hospital of hypertensive heart disease with coronary occlusion. She completed grade four at age 15 years and was known as a "peculiar" child. She was described as "quiet, mild and usually happy and cheerful" until her first pregnancy, when she became insanely jealous of her husband. Delivery of the baby was by caesarean section with convulsions preceding and following the surgery. She was unable to assume the responsibility of caring for the home and expressed suicidal and homicidal tendencies. First admission to Warren State Hospital was on 12/2/1916, about one year after the birth of her child and following a suicide attempt by poison. A diagnosis of dementia praecox was made. She was paroled on 10/13/1917, but was never able to adjust at home and was rehospitalized at Warren State Hospital for two years beginning on 11/9/1920. Diagnosis at this hospitalization was dementia praecox, paranoid type. In January, 1924, she suffered a minor head injury in a streetcar accident and refused to work after recovery from this accident. Subsequently she spent another two years at Warren State Hospital. Last admission to the hospital was on 2/26/1931. She remained at Warren State Hospital until her death about 27 years later. Diagnosis was consistently dementia praecox, paranoid type, and she was described as apathetic, vague, and disoriented for time and place. She was deluded and had queer somatopsychotic symptoms. Her conversation and ideas had a distinct paranoid coloring. Classification: Schizophrenic reaction—paranoid type.

Children

Son (33), born 1915. At age 47 years he was a patient at a state mental hospital and diagnosed as schizophrenic reaction, paranoid type, in a mental defective. He was admitted to a state school at age nine years and remained there until June, 1962, when he became delusional and abusive. He spent a short time at a general hospital before admission to the state mental hospital on 8/7/1962. Classification: Schizophrenic reaction—paranoid type.

Grandparents

Paternal grandmother (2), died at age 68 years of a stroke. She was described as "a peculiar, bad-tempered woman who was considered insane by the people who knew her." Classification: Probably with functional psychosis.

Parents

Father (10), died at age 67 years of tuberculosis. He did not work and would not provide for his family. He was described as "ugly, stingy" and was considered to be insane. He also reportedly had "ugly fits" during which he became raving and destructive. Classification: Probably with functional psychosis.

Mother (11), born 1860 and at age 57 described as "high strung, nervous" and an "emotionally unstable" woman. Classification: Possible psychoneurotic disorder.

Aunts and Uncles

Paternal aunt (7), died at age 60 years of stomach trouble. She was reportedly insane when she died. Classification: Possibly with functional psychosis.

Paternal aunt (9), died at age 50 years of kidney disease. She reportedly was insane for some time before her death. Classification: Probably with functional psychosis.

Siblings

Sister (20), born 1879; died at age 65 years at Warren State Hospital of a cardiovascular accident. She was a waitress and hotel maid previous to her marriage in her early twenties. On 1/12/1911, she was admitted to a state mental hospital with a diagnosis of dementia praecox and discharged as improved on 5/15/1912. At admission she was confused, suspicious and hallucinated. On 12/4/1924, she was admitted to Warren State Hospital with a diagnosis of manic-depressive psychosis, manic phase, in a possible mental defective. After release four months later she remained well until August, 1927, when she became loquacious, noisy, unkempt and denudative and was readmitted to Warren State Hospital on 10/8/1927. At Warren State Hospital the overproductive tendencies were varied by periods of muteness. There was a marked tendency towards posturing, affected conversation and baby talk and to flight of ideas. A diagnosis of manic-depressive psychosis, manic phase, was made. She remained hospitalized until death. Classification: Schizophrenic reaction—catatonic type.

(21) husband of sister (20), born 1880; died at age 57 years, cause of death unknown. He had little education and worked occasionally as a painter. In 1924 he was charged by (20) with an incestuous attack on a daughter by a previous marriage. The charge occurred at the time of (20)'s first commitment to Warren State Hospital and no indictment was made. He was imprisoned on a charge of vagrancy in 1935. Classification: Possible sociopathic personality disturbance.

Brother (26), born 1891; died at age 70 years of cancer of the lungs. He was described by family members as a wanderer who had been arrested for drunkenness and for disorderly conduct. He was also involved in a robbery. His second wife described him as a devoted and responsible husband who worked as a skilled laborer in the steel industry. Classification: Other transient situational personality disturbance.

(27) wife of brother (26), born 1898. At age 68 years she was interviewed and, although cooperative, her memory was described as "very bad." Classification: Chronic brain syndrome of senium.

Nieces and Nephews

Nephew (30), born 1906; died at age 39 years at Warren State Hospital of pulmonary tuberculosis. He was an itinerant laborer who was considered "peculiar" for several years before his admission to Warren State Hospital on 9/21/1935. He had the delusion that snakes resided in him "for some time" before his admission. He remained hospitalized with a diagnosis of schizophrenia until his death; the auditory hallucinations and lack of insight persisted but there was no evidence of progressive deterioration. Classification: Schizophrenic reaction—paranoid type.

Family Summary

The proband, her son, a sister and a nephew had psychotic disorders and the father, the paternal grandmother and two paternal aunts probably or possibly so. The mother was possibly neurotic. Personality disorders were found in a brother and in the husband of a sister. The wife of a brother was classified as with chronic brain syndrome of senium.

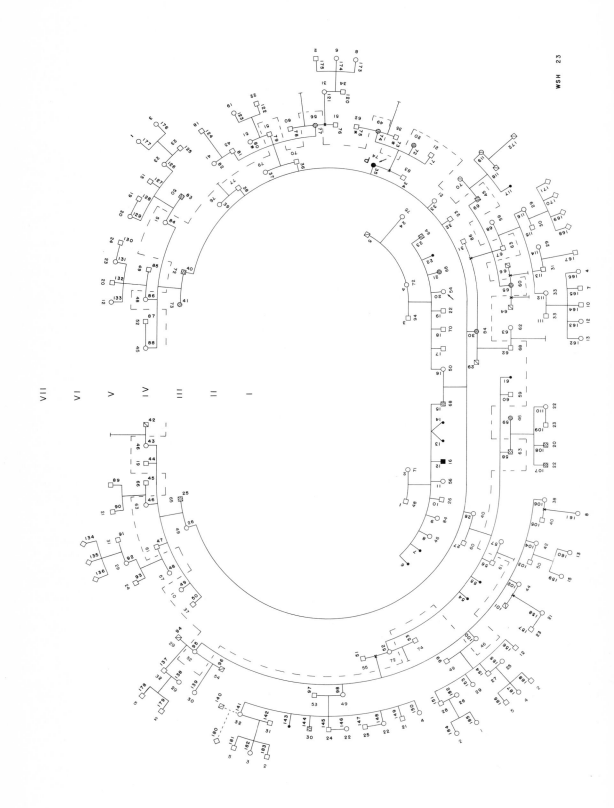

WSH 23: The Proband

Proband (35), born 1878; died at age 74 years at Warren State Hospital of coronary thrombosis. She had a normal life until age 35 years, when she developed delusions of poisoning and persecution and of influence. She began to have auditory and visual hallucinations. She had four admissions to Warren State Hospital, each with a diagnosis of dementia praecox—paranoid type. The admissions were in 1916, 1917, 1936 and 1945. Between the second and third admissions she was at a private hospital where she was discharged as unimproved. Classification: Schizophrenic reaction—paranoid type.

Children

Daughter (72), born 1906; died at age 20 years of puerperal infection following an abortion. She was a discipline problem for her father and aunt, with whom she lived until entering college. She was attending business college at the time of her death. Classification: Sociopathic personality disturbance.

Daughter (74), born 1912. At age 49 years she was employed as a domestic and stated that she was never treated for a mental disorder; however, after her first marriage she reportedly drank heavily and a letter from a private hospital states that she was hospitalized there for 11 days with a diagnosis of acute toxic delirium. Classification: Sociopathic personality disturbance—alcoholism (addiction).

Parents

Father (15), born 1834; died at age 68 years, cause of death unknown. He was described variously as "jolly in disposition . . . had a faculty for picking up friends easily" and as "reckless . . . gambled, went on occasional sprees." Classification: Possible personality disorder.

Aunts and Uncles

Paternal uncle (12), born 1841; died at age 16 years, cause of death unknown. He was described as a very serious boy and a good student who, at about age 16 years, became "mentally unbalanced" and took to his room, where he wore a bandage over his eyes and would allow no one but his sister to wait on him. Classification: Schizophrenic reaction.

Maternal aunt (20), born 1843; died at age 54 years at Warren State Hospital of exhaustion due to paretic mania. Diagnosis at admission on 8/5/1896 was paretic mania. At admission and throughout her hospitalization she was greatly disturbed and deluded with grandiose ideas. Classification: Chronic brain syndrome associated with meningoencephalitic syphilis—with psychotic reaction.

Maternal aunt (21), born 1848. She was a "recognized prostitute" who was arrested on several occasions for keeping a "disorderly house." Classification: Sociopathic personality disturbance—antisocial reaction.

Maternal uncle (23), born 1852. He was frequently arrested for drunkenness and was described as "ugly, profane and perhaps a thief." Classification: Sociopathic personality disturbance—alcoholism (addiction).

Siblings

(25) husband of sister (26), born 1866; died at age 65 years of cancer of the prostate. He was described as a "heavy drinker" by early informants but no mention of a drinking problem was made by later informants. Classification: Possible sociopathic personality disturbance—alcoholism (addiction).

Sister (30), born 1871; died at age 84 years of a heart condition. She was described as both "nervous" and "easy-going" in early life but later informants described her as a "trouble maker." She was interested in having the proband released from the hospital, then quickly tired of her care and tried to get other siblings to care for her, which caused much misunderstanding in the sibship. Classification: Personality pattern disturbance, other.

Brother (40), born 1889. His mother died when he was 18 months of age and he spent his childhood going from home to home. Even though his childhood was unsettled he maintained a close relationship

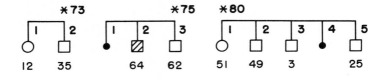

CONTROLS   W S H   2 3

with his siblings. At age 72 years he was known in the family as a "hypochondriac." He was always anxious about his health and changed doctors every few months. Classification: Psychoneurotic disorder—conversion reaction.

(41) wife of brother (40), born 1888. She reportedly had some mental problems following the untimely death of a 15-year-old grandson. She received no treatment for the problems so the grief was probably within normal limits. Classification: Possible psychoneurotic disorder—depressive reaction.

Nieces and Nephews

Nephew (58), born 1898, a retired railroad laborer. At age 63 years he was described as quite hostile about giving details of his own health. He had loss of sensation in his arms and legs for which there was no physical basis. He also had other psychosomatic symptoms and took tranquilizers and sleeping pills. His room was cluttered and filthy, for which he was most apologetic to the interviewer and explained that he couldn't keep it clean because of "weakness of arms." Classification: Psychoneurotic disorder—conversion reaction.

(59) wife of nephew (58); died at age 46 years of tuberculosis. She was described as a "prostitute" who "drank heavily." Classification: Sociopathic personality disturbance—antisocial reaction.

Niece (65), born 1899; died at age 60 years of leukemia. She was remembered as an "odd, nervous, domineering" woman with many physical complaints. Classification: Psychoneurotic reaction—other.

Nephew (69), born 1903; died at age 45 years of a heart attack. He reportedly was a drug addict and had been hospitalized for addiction. He also belonged to a criminal gang and served time in a penal institution. Classification: Sociopathic personality disturbance—drug addiction.

Niece (77), born 1905. When interviewed at age 56 years she "seemed complaining, querulous and went into every topic in the minutest detail." Classification: Possible personality trait disturbance.

(83) husband of niece (84), born 1911. He left a "banking career" to join the ministry and was ordained at age 45 years. He had difficulty with his parishes and was referred by the Bishop to a psychiatrist who found no evidence of psychosis. Classification: Personality trait disturbance—compulsive personality.

Distant Relatives

Grandnephew (107), born 1934. He completed grade seven and at age 22 years had no legal employment. He was an early juvenile delinquent and had arrests for armed robbery and for involvement in narcotics possession and trade. Classification: Sociopathic personality disturbance—antisocial reaction.

Grandnephew (108), born 1936. He had the same social problems as (107), except that his delinquency began at an earlier age. Classification: Sociopathic personality disturbance—antisocial reaction.

Family Summary

The proband and a paternal uncle had psychotic disorders. A maternal aunt was institutionalized with a psychotic reaction to central nervous system syphilis. Personality disorders were found in two daughters, the father, a sister, a maternal aunt and a maternal uncle, a nephew, a niece, two grand-nephews, the husband of a sister, the wife of a nephew and in the husband of a niece. A brother, a nephew, a niece and the wife of a brother were neurotic.

Controls

Brother (2) of (75), born 1897. He was described as "lazy and shiftless" and was divorced by his wife because of his irresponsibility. At age 64 he led a marginal existence as a part-time casual farm laborer. Classification: Probable personality pattern disturbance — inadequate personality.

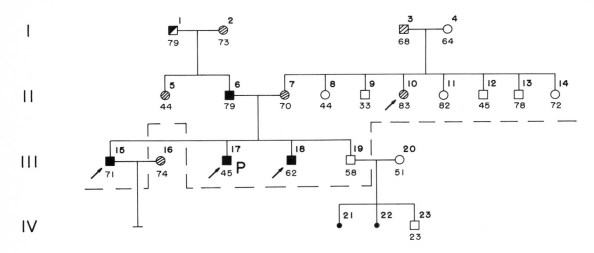

WSH   24

WSH 24: The Proband

Proband (17), born 1892; died at age 45 years at Warren State Hospital of pulmonary tuberculosis. He was recognized as "peculiar" and "dull" when still a young boy and had only reached grade six at age 16 years. When first admitted to Warren State Hospital on 8/9/1910, the commitment papers stated that he had been having "occasional queer spells for seven years," although no satisfactory account of the onset of his illness could be obtained. He was always of a restless, discontented nature and the butt of neighborhood jokes and taunts. At Warren State Hospital he was described as generally shy, unoccupied, careless and indifferent, but had several excited periods, developed delusions of persecution and became threatening and impulsive. Diagnosis at first hospitalization was dementia praecox. He was discharged on 4/8/1911, but was readmitted on 6/25/1912, with a diagnosis of hebephrenic dementia praecox. The second hospitalization lasted 15 months. The third hospitalization was from June, 1915 until March, 1918. The fourth admission was in 1922 and he remained hospitalized until his death 15 years later. He had continuing hallucinations of a religious nature, and an ever increasing defect in orientation for time, person and place. Conversation, while never voluntary, finally ceased and he became mute. Clas-

sification: Schizophrenic reaction—paranoid type.

Grandparents

Paternal grandfather (1), born 1837. At age 79 years he was described as always "mentally dull—very peculiar" and later as "overly religious" and "half a lunatic." In mid-life he reportedly had a period of mental derangement following some financial problems. Classification: Probably with functional psychosis, schizophrenic reaction—hebephrenic type. Also, possible mental deficiency.

Paternal grandmother (2), born 1843. At age 73 years she was described as "having become rather peculiar through living with (1), although she had never been mentally deranged." Classification: Possible personality disorder.

Maternal grandfather (3), born 1848. At age 68 years he was considered quick-tempered and rather eccentric. Classification: Possible personality disorder.

Parents

Father (6), born 1868; died at age 79 years of chronic myocarditis. He was described as "always defective and peculiar," over-religious and hopelessly incoherent in conversation. Classification: Schizophrenic reaction—chronic undifferentiated type.

Mother (7), born 1870; died at age 70 years of cancer of the bowels. She was described as high strung and scolding. Classification: Possible personality disorder.

Aunts and Uncles

Paternal aunt (5), born 1866. At age 44 years described as seclusive and peculiar. When interviewed she reportedly had a "silly, simpering manner" and would laugh inappropriately. Classification: Personality pattern disturbance—schizoid personality.

Maternal aunt (10), born 1877; died at age 83 years at Warren State Hospital of general physical deterioration. She was hospitalized at Warren on 2/2/1955, with a diagnosis of chronic brain syndrome with senile brain disease. The onset of her mental illness was gradual, and developed over a period of a year and a half, when she showed loss of memory and accused people of stealing from her. When younger she reportedly did practical nursing and was described as "intelligent with good knowledge and judgment." Classification: Chronic brain syndrome of senium.

Siblings

Brother (15), born 1890. At age 26 years he was described as "distinctly peculiar . . . and not very soundly balanced." He later became a mechanic who owned and operated a small gas station. He managed the gas station with no assistant, which involved working all day and half the night. The schedule did not bother him for several years but in the summer of 1949 he began to notice the lack of sleep, started to lose weight and became more and more depressed. He was admitted to a state mental hospital with a diagnosis of involutional psychosis—melancholia, on 8/28/1949, where he remained for about four months. After his return home from the hospital he managed his gas station, working only days. When interviewed at age 71 years the rambling irrelevancies in his conversation were more pronounced than expected in a senile individual; however, he seemed quite in control of the business aspects of his life. Classification: Involutional psychotic reaction.

(16) wife of (15), born 1887. She was a teacher who taught all her life. At age 74 years she was teaching retarded children and, although she showed a warm understanding of her pupils, she otherwise seemed a "tart, hostile person." She was quite tolerant of her husband. She had several facial tics but did not seem to be a nervous person. Classification: Possible psychoneurotic disorder.

Brother (18), born 1899. He attended school until age 16 years and reached the fifth grade. He had little ability and was described as rather lazy but good natured and agreeable, until the spring of 1914, when he began to imagine he was rich, had patents to sell and became a nuisance in the neighborhood with his efforts to sell his imaginary possessions. He settled down after a few months but in the spring of 1915 and in the spring of 1916 he again had outbreaks of restless activity. He became violent when his family tried to restrict his activities and was admitted to Warren State Hospital on 6/19/1916, with a diagnosis of imbecility and manic-depressive psychosis. He had five subsequent admissions to Warren State Hospital. The dates of admission and diagnoses were as follows:

5/20/1917—Imbecility
3/24/1922—Congenital deficiency (imbecile) with unclassified excitement
4/6/1936—Psychosis with mental deficiency
8/14/1944—Manic-depressive psychosis—depressed phase
3/16/1961—Schizophrenic reaction—paranoid type

He was grandiose, overactive and mildly antisocial during periods of excitement. He was drinking to excess before his 1936 admission. At the time of his sixth admission to Warren State Hospital he had cellulitis of both lower extremities and was of the opinion that his legs had been poisoned by socks washed along with paint rags. He was described as hostile, talkative, irrelevant and disoriented to time and place. At age 62 years, staff notes indicated that he probably would never be discharged from the hospital. Classification: Schizophrenic reaction—paranoid type.

Family Summary

The proband, two brothers and the father had psychotic disorders and the paternal grandfather probably so. A maternal

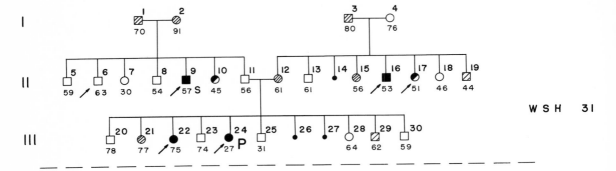

aunt was institutionalized with chronic brain syndrome of senium. Personality disorders were found in the paternal grandmother, maternal grandfather, mother and in a paternal aunt. The wife of a brother was probably neurotic.

WSH 31: The Proband

Proband (24), born 1888; died at age 27 years at Warren State Hospital of cerebrocervical meningitis. She was described as an obedient child but seclusive and serious; she never entered into activities with other children and showed an abnormal interest in religion. At puberty her serious, seclusive nature became more pronounced. In late 1910, she developed auditory, visual and tactile hallucinations and delusions of persecution and poisoning. Periods of apathy and indifference alternated with episodes of noisy, excited behavior. She was hospitalized at Warren State Hospital from January until November, 1911, with a diagnosis of dementia praecox. The second hospitalization was from late 1915 until her death on 4/13/1916. Her mental symptoms persisted between hospitalizations. Classification: Schizophrenic reaction — catatonic type.

Grandparents

Paternal grandfather (1), died at age 70 years of apoplexy. He was described as "essentially a quiet, distant man ... rather quick-tempered and of a saving nature." Classification: Possible personality pattern disturbance — schizoid personality.

Paternal grandmother (2), died at age 91 years of a "general breakdown" following a fracture of the left femur. She was described

as "not as quiet" as (1) but "apt to worry and become irritable." Classification: Possible psychoneurotic disorder.

Maternal grandfather (3), born 1815; died at age 80 years of a "general breakdown." He was described by his family as "high-tempered." Classification: Possible personality trait disturbance — emotionally unstable personality.

Parents

Mother (12), born 1859; died at age 61 years of uremia. At age 57 she was very difficult to interview because of her evasive answers and conditional replies. Her friend and a physician both described her as "peculiar" and commented that no one ever seemed to become acquainted with her. Classification: Probable personality pattern disturbance — paranoid personality.

Aunts and Uncles

Paternal uncle (6), born 1859. He completed one year of training at a teachers' college, and was a proprietor of a small grocery store. He was described as "quiet, agreeable and a hard-worker." In August, 1921, he developed diabetes mellitus. He refused to follow the physician's advice and, as his physical symptoms became worse, mental symptoms developed. An episode of confusion, marked suspiciousness and violence followed a period of depression, and he was admitted to Warren State Hospital on 10/25/1921, with a diagnosis of unclassified psychosis. After three and a half months of dietetic care he was released from the hospital, much improved. Classification: Acute brain syndrome associated with metabolic disturbance — diabetes.

Paternal uncle (9), born 1864; died at age 57 years of cancer. The management of the family farm had always been his responsibility. He had two attacks of depression. The first attack, with symptoms of apprehension, disturbed sleep, religious anxiety and one suicide attempt, began about two weeks before his admission to Warren State Hospital on 2/13/1906. He was discharged as restored on 10/29/1906, and remained normal until he again became depressed in April, 1911. Admission notes at his second hospitalization stated that he was depressed and apprehensive and thought "he cannot get better but is going to die." He also insisted he was unable to move but on persuasion was able to do so. He went home on 7/6/1911, and remained unhospitalized until his death. When interviewed at age 52 years he seemed normal although of a quiet, uncommunicative nature. Classification: Manic-depressive reaction—depressed type.

Paternal aunt (10), born 1869; died at age 45 years of heart disease and chronic arthritis. She was always of a "jolly nature" until age 44 years, when she became acutely ill with arthritis and was profoundly toxic. She became depressed, refused all food as she suspected it was poisoned and finally died of starvation. Classification: Probably with functional psychosis, psychotic-depressive reaction.

Maternal aunt (15), born 1860; described at age 56 years as "of a jolly, lively temperament but high strung and very quick-tempered and nervous." Classification: Possible personality trait disturbance—emotionally unstable personality.

Maternal uncle (16), born 1863. He was described as "naturally irritable, excitable, high-strung and very quick-tempered." At about age 44 years he became very jealous of his wife and developed delusions regarding her and her behavior. He also believed he was being watched by a detective. The delusions persisted, and on 1/3/1912, he was admitted to Warren State Hospital. While hospitalized he was cheerful, got along well and rarely mentioned his delusions, although his family said that he never did give up these ideas, even after his release on 4/29/1912. When interviewed at age 53 years he was talkative, alert, agreeable and presented a friendly attitude toward his wife. Classification: Schizophrenic reaction—paranoid type.

Maternal aunt (17), born 1867; died at Warren State Hospital at age 63 years. She never married and worked as a domestic. At about age 30 years she was hypnotized by an amateur hypnotist at a party, following which her personality began to change; she became careless in her appearance, her voice became coarse and she had at least one episode of supposed hallucinosis. She was described as "very stubborn and somewhat irritable but rather extrovert" before her personality change. In the spring of 1929 she suffered a cerebral hemorrhage. She was confused and semi-conscious for some time and later became very irritable, resistive and noisy. She was admitted to Warren State Hospital in November, 1929, where she died six months later. Diagnosis was psychosis with cerebral arteriosclerosis. Classification: Probably with functional psychosis, schizophrenic reaction.

Maternal uncle (19), born 1872. At age 44 years he was described as a heavy drinker who would become intoxicated for weeks at a time. He was arrested many times for drunkenness. When sober he was quiet with little to say. Classification: Sociopathic personality disturbance—alcoholism (addiction).

Siblings

Sister (21), born 1883; at 77 years described as "senile and tottery . . . hard to get along with." Classification: Chronic brain syndrome of senium.

Sister (22), born 1885; died at age 75 years at Warren State Hospital, of arteriosclerotic cardiovascular disease. She was described as very critical of people who did things well, yet was a perfectionist. She had six admissions to a mental health sanitarium from October, 1946 until September, 1953. Each admission was diagnosed as manic-depressive reaction—manic type. At each hospitalization she showed rapid improvement and would make an adequate adjustment until her next attack of overtalkativeness and overactivity. On 7/23/1954, she was admitted to Warren State Hospital and again described as overtalkative, irrelevant and overactive. She remained hospitalized until her death. Classification: Manic-depressive reaction—manic type.

Brother (29), born 1898. At age 62 years

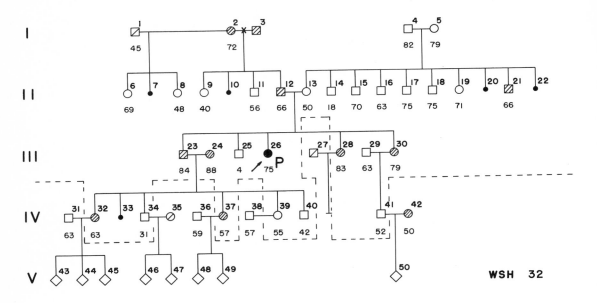

WSH 32

he was described as having numerous somatic complaints ascribed to his "nervousness." Classification: Psychoneurotic disorder.

Family Summary

The proband, a sister, a paternal uncle and a maternal uncle had psychotic disorders and a paternal and a maternal aunt probably so. A paternal uncle was hospitalized with a psychotic reaction to a metabolic disturbance (diabetes). The paternal grandmother and a brother were neurotic. Personality disorders were found in the paternal and maternal grandfathers, in the mother, a maternal aunt and in a maternal uncle. One sister was classified as chronic brain syndrome of senium.

WSH 32: The Proband

Proband (26), born 1875; died at age 75 years of a sub-arachnoid hemorrhage. She was described as always quiet, seclusive, uncommunicative, obstinate and contrary. She had some business school training and worked as a clerk, a postmistress and then as a domestic. At age 25 years she became restless and irritable, and developed ideas of persecution unassociated with any causal

event. She did have typhoid fever the same year but reportedly had a good convalescence. The mental symptoms subsided but recurred nine years later when she became increasingly irritable and violent, restless, noisy, obscene and developed many delusions and hallucinations. She was hospitalized at Warren State Hospital from 7/22/1915 until 7/16/1919, with a diagnosis of dementia praecox, paranoid type. She was discharged from Warren State Hospital against advice but was never rehospitalized. Classification: Schizophrenic reaction— paranoid type.

Grandparents

Paternal grandmother (2); died at age 72 years of apoplexy. She was described as a "disagreeable, vindictive woman who held grudges" by her daughter, and as "a fairly agreeable, pleasant woman" by her daughter-in-law. Classification: Possible personality disorder.

Paternal grandfather (3); died of heart trouble. He was the divorced first husband of the paternal grandmother and was described as quick tempered; he "would get so angry that he would be ready to kill people." Classification: Probable personality disorder.

Parents

Father (12); died at age 66 years of heart trouble. He was described as sarcastic, unscrupulous and particularly fond of practical jokes; he had a particular dislike for the proband. Classification: Probable personality disorder.

Aunts and Uncles

Maternal uncle (21), born 1850. He was last known at age 66 years when he was described as "good-natured, quiet and thrifty" although he drank to excess. Classification: Possible sociopathic personality disturbance—alcoholism (addiction).

Siblings

Brother (23), born 1871; died at age 84 years of cerebral thrombosis. He was described as accident prone and alcoholic "when younger." Classification: Possible transient situational personality disorder—adjustment reaction of adolescence.

(24) wife of brother (23), born 1874. She completed elementary school and was a housewife with no history of mental disorder until age 88 years, when she complained of fatigue and tiredness. The complaints developed about three months after a fall which incapacitated her for a short time. She was seen by a psychiatrist who described her as well oriented with no gross emotional disturbance and a clear sensorium. His diagnosis and classification: Chronic brain syndrome of senium and chronic brain syndrome associated with cerebral arteriosclerosis.

Sister (28), born 1877. She was a retired art teacher who married for the first time when in her 60's. As a young woman she was described as eccentric and seclusive. When interviewed at age 88 years she did not mention the proband, in whom she'd never shown an interest. Her husband died after five years of marriage. Classification: Possible personality pattern disturbance—schizoid personality.

Sister (30), born 1881. At age 79 years she was interviewed by a psychiatrist who described her as very suspicious and paranoid. She described herself as a "worry wart." (30) and (28) lived in (30)'s home. Classification: Probable personality pattern disturbance—schizoid personality.

Nieces and Nephews

Niece (32), born 1898. She was interviewed at age 63 years but was very reluctant to give information. She was suspicious and refused to discuss other family members beyond barest details. Her husband was quiet, reasonable, and tried to persuade his wife to answer questions. Classification: Possible personality disorder.

Niece (37), born 1904. She was a housewife who, when a study interview was attempted, refused to talk to the interviewer, was verbally abusive and threatened physical violence. There were no reports of treatment because of emotional disturbance. Classification: Probable personality pattern disturbance—schizoid personality.

(42) wife of nephew (41), born 1911. She refused to be interviewed for the study. The interviewer described her as very antagonistic. Classification: Possible personality pattern disturbance—paranoid personality.

Family Summary

The proband was the only psychotic member of this kinship. The wife of a brother had a psychotic reaction to arteriosclerosis and senility. Personality disorders were found in the 10 remaining psychiatrically noteworthy persons, including the paternal grandparents, the father, two sisters, a brother, a maternal uncle, two nieces and the wife of a nephew.

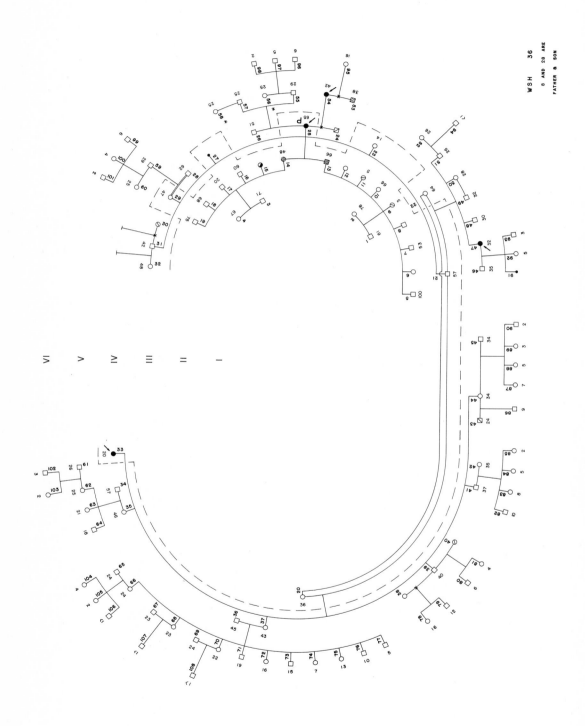

WSH 36

8 AND 28 ARE
FATHER & SON

WSH 36: The Proband

Proband (25), born 1897. She was a patient at Warren State Hospital from 4/10/1915 until 9/30/1915, with a diagnosis of dementia praecox. At discharge she was described as very much improved: less withdrawn, more sociable and talkative. After her marriage and the birth of a daughter she was hospitalized at another state hospital for four months. Throughout the following years she had financial and marital trouble, divorce, and the care of her second husband during a long terminal illness. In 1955 she was again hospitalized with a diagnosis of manic-depressive psychosis, depressed type. She was hospitalized for two months. At age 65 years she was interviewed at her brother's home, which she had owned and he had taken over. She did not volunteer information about her hospital commitments nor those of her daughter and, although not too happy with her living arrangements, did not want to be a burden to her sons. She was described by the interviewer as "poised, calm, well adjusted, with no psychotic or emotional abnormalities noted during a lengthy interview." Classification: Schizophrenic reaction — paranoid type.

Children

Daughter (54), born 1919. At age 42 years she was in a family–home care program supervised by a state mental hospital. She completed grade eight and was a bus operator. Her first hospitalization was from 7/15/1933 until 6/22/1936, for symptoms characterized by severe depression, agitation and marked mental retardation. She was again admitted on 11/15/1944, and had been released several times to convalescent or family care, but her outside adjustment was usually of short duration and she was returned to the hospital. Classification: Manic-depressive reaction — depressed type.

(53) husband of daughter (54), born 1909. He reportedly was verbally and physically abusive to (54). Classification: Possible personality trait disturbance — passive-aggressive personality.

Parents

Father (13), born 1871; died at age 66 years of arteriosclerosis. He reportedly was "disagreeable, not to be trusted and drank a lot." Classification: Sociopathic personality disturbance — alcoholism (addiction).

Mother (14), born 1873; died at age 48 years of arteriosclerosis. She was described as a "neurotic, unprincipled woman who lied deliberately." Classification: Personality trait disturbance — emotionally unstable personality.

Aunts and Uncles

Maternal aunt (15), born 1857; died "at an elderly age," cause of death unknown. She had a period of mental disturbance after the birth of her first child and less severe attacks following the births of her third and fifth children. She was never hospitalized during the attacks. Classification: Possibly with functional psychosis.

Nieces and Nephews

Niece (33), born 1913; died at age 20 years of pulmonary tuberculosis. At age 16 years she became disturbed after the death of her mother. The disturbance was characterized by untidiness, seclusiveness, bad temper and attacks on her stepmother. She was admitted to a state mental hospital on 12/15/1931, and stayed there until her death on 8/9/1933. On admission she was irritable and resistive and during hospitalization she was overactive, destructive and assaultive. Her mental condition was unchanged at the time of her death. Classification: Schizophrenic reaction — paranoid type.

Niece (47), born 1930. She was a patient at a state mental hospital from June until November, 1957, following the birth of a daughter. She had been depressed on one previous occasion following the loss of a child at birth. At age 32 years she described herself as "fine" and said that she "had gotten an understanding" of herself. Diagnosis and classification: Schizophrenic reaction — catatonic type.

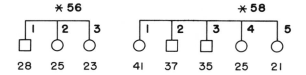

CONTROLS   W S H   36

Family Summary

The proband, her daughter and two nieces had psychotic disorders and a maternal aunt possibly so. The father, the mother and the husband of a daughter had personality disorders.

Controls

None noteworthy.

WSH 37: The Proband

Proband (22), born 1874; died at age 52 years of cerebral hemorrhage. She was a teacher before her marriage. Although always considered "slightly peculiar" she got along well until her child was about two years of age and it became apparent that the child was an idiot. She became anxious about the child and developed auditory hallucinations and vague persecutory delusions centering around her child. Admission to Warren State Hospital was on 6/28/1915, with a diagnosis of dementia praecox, paranoid type. She showed little insight into the death of her defective child in 1916. Her husband and sister cared for her after her release from Warren State Hospital on 9/14/1916. Classification: Schizophrenic reaction — paranoid type.

Grandparents

Paternal grandfather (1), died at age 59 years of miliary tuberculosis. He was described as "a man of mild disposition and temperate habits" who became silly and childish during his last year of life. The condition was described by an interviewer as "a psychosis of organic etiology." Classification: Chronic brain syndrome of senium.

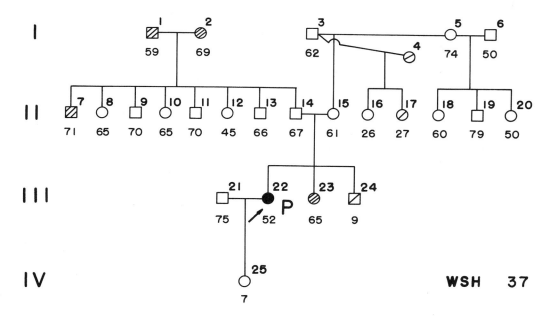

Paternal grandmother (2), died at age 69 years, cause of death unknown. She was described as "a chronic complainer and a scold" and as irritable and nagging. Classification: Possible personality disorder.

Aunts and Uncles

Paternal uncle (7), born 1829; died at age 71 years of "creeping paralysis." He was an ambitious and successful farmer who became "demented" in the six months prior to his death. Classification: Chronic brain syndrome of senium.

Siblings

Sister (23), born 1876; died at age 65 years of diabetes mellitus and exophthalmic goiter. She was described as "shy and self-contained . . . difficult to become acquainted with . . . intelligent but eccentric." She was intense in her dislikes and had few friends because of her superior attitude. She taught school until the proband was admitted to Warren State Hospital, when she assumed the care of the proband's retarded, spastic child. After the proband's release from Warren State Hospital, (23) cared for her until the proband's death. She was an inmate at a county home for three years prior to her death and was considered "a mental case" the last few months. Classification: Probable personality pattern disturbance—paranoid or schizoid personality.

Family Summary

The proband had a psychotic disorder and was hospitalized for treatment. The paternal grandmother and a sister had personality disorders. The paternal grandfather and a paternal uncle were classified as with chronic brain syndrome of senium.

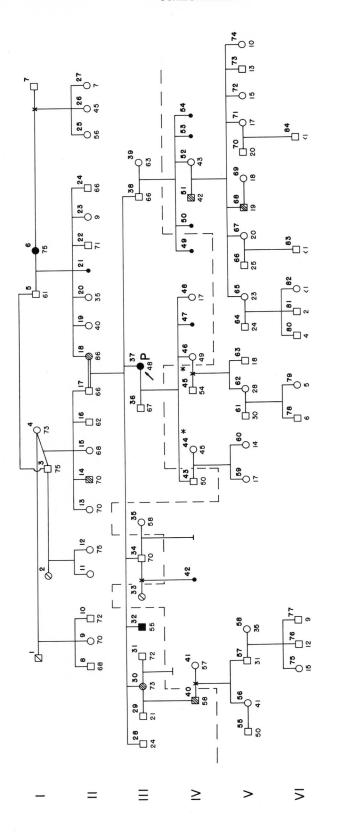

WSH 39: The Proband

Proband (37), born 1892; died at age 48 years of chronic myocarditis. She made "not much progress" in school and had "fits" until 10 years of age. In 1914, following a miscarriage, she developed delusions of persecution and poisoning and denied being the mother of her children. Admission to Warren State Hospital was on 6/25/1915, where she remained for eight years. Diagnosis was dementia praecox engrafted on mental deficiency. She remained at home for five years, then spent 11 years at a county home before her next hospitalization at Warren State Hospital on 3/5/1940, with a diagnosis of dementia praecox, paranoid type. At admission she was greatly incapacitated because of a heart condition. She gradually improved physically and mentally until 9/21/1940, when she was paroled to the county authorities. She died within five months after parole. Classification: Schizophrenic reaction—paranoid type.

Grandparents

Maternal grandmother (6), died at age 75 years of "hemorrhages from the bowels." She reportedly had been "insane" for a great many years before her death, although the age of onset was indefinite. She had many delusions of persecution, would remain in her room and refuse to talk or eat as she imagined that the food was "no good" and that people were coming to steal things from her. Classification: Paranoid state.

Parents

Mother (18), first cousin of her spouse, the proband's father (17), born 1855; died at age 86 years of unknown causes. She was described variously as peculiar, hypochondriacal, a poor manager, very excitable and subject to "awful nervous spells." Classification: Personality trait disturbance—emotionally unstable personality.

Aunts and Uncles

Paternal uncle (14), born 1846; at age 70 years he was described as an "odd, surly man, who drank to excess." He was described by an interviewer as "shaky and tremulous" and referred to himself as "a terrible drinker." Classification: Sociopathic personality disturbance—alcoholism (addiction).

Siblings

Sister (30), born 1876; died at age 73 years of chronic myocarditis and hypertension. She described herself as "terribly nervous"; however, she received no treatment for her nervousness. She and her husband raised the proband's children. Classification: Psychoneurotic disorder.

Brother (32), born 1879; died at age 55 years of chronic Bright's disease. All informants referred to him as "queer," "feebleminded" or "stupid." He lived alone in a shack and was reportedly a heavy drinker. He was also described as "not sane ... he began to show symptoms of mental trouble at the age of 25 years." Classification: Schizophrenic reaction—paranoid type.

Nieces and Nephews

Nephew (40), born 1894; died at age 58 years of chronic myocarditis and asthma. He attended school until 16 years of age but did not reach the eighth grade. He was described as "very cruel" to his wife and deserted her. He was also described as a heavy drinker, perhaps an alcoholic. Classification: Sociopathic personality disturbance—antisocial reaction and alcoholism (addiction).

(51) husband of niece (52), born 1918. He became diabetic at age 30 years. After he became mentally ill with diabetes, he spent two months totally blind and was reportedly severely depressed at that time. He recovered completely from the blindness and depression. Classification: Transient situational personality disorder—adult situational reaction.

Distant Relatives

Grandnephew (68), born 1941. He was rejected from the armed services because of a "nervous disorder which affected his heart." Classification: Probable psychoneurotic disorder.

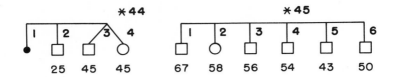

CONTROLS   W S H   39

Family Summary

The proband, a brother and the maternal grandmother had psychotic disorders. The mother, a paternal uncle, a nephew and the husband of a niece had personality disorders. A sister was neurotic and a grandnephew probably so.

Controls

None noteworthy.

WSH 40

WSH 40: The Proband

The proband (27), born 1883; died at age 40 years of tuberculosis. As a youth she was serious and reserved, exceedingly careful in her own conduct and highly critical of others. She once refused to submit to a gynecological examination which seemed necessary because she was afraid "people would talk and say she had gone there for some other reason." She married at age 29 and her subsequent pregnancy was considered the precipitating cause of her mental illness. While pregnant she became extremely critical of others, began to withdraw from her surroundings, developed some delusions of persecution and exhibited some violence toward her mother. She was admitted to a sanitarium on 10/23/1914, with a diagnosis of amentia following childbirth and was discharged a month later as improved. After a recurrence of violence she was committed to Warren State Hospital on 7/30/1915, with a diagnosis of dementia praecox. While at Warren State Hospital she was apathetic, uncommunicative, seclusive and expressed some hallucinatory activity and persecutory thought. She remained hospitalized until she died. Classification: Schizophrenic reaction—paranoid type.

(26) husband of proband (27); birth and death dates unknown. He was described by the proband's sister as a "stinker." Classification: Possible personality disorder.

Aunts and Uncles

Paternal aunt (9), born 1851. She was normal and well at age 64 years. Her mother stated that she had "nervous spells" which, with further questioning, proved to be little more than a natural reaction to trouble or illness. Classification: Possible psychoneurotic disturbance.

Maternal half uncle (24), born 1881; age and cause of death unknown. He was reported to be mentally deficient but was "steady, reliable and able to support himself." As a child he was easily excited and apprehensive but was "more controlled" as an adult. Classification: Possible transient situational personality disturbance—adjustment reaction of childhood.

Siblings

(28) husband of sister (29), born 1887. At age 74 years he was described as a retired oil field worker in poor, failing health. He was described as "a real stinker" by his sister-in-law. Classification: Possible personality disorder.

Nieces and Nephews

Niece (53), born 1918. At age 43 years she had "trouble with nerves due to meno-pause." Classification: Psychoneurotic disorder.

Family Summary

The proband was the only family member with a psychotic disorder. A niece was classified as neurotic and a paternal aunt possibly so. A maternal half uncle, the proband's husband and the husband of a sister were possibly with personality disorders.

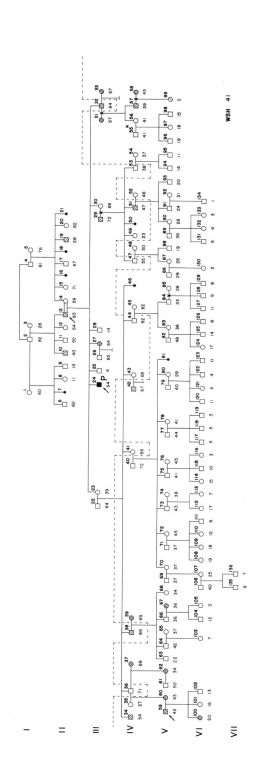

WSH 41

WSH 41: The Proband

The proband (24), born 1875; died at age 64 years of pneumonia at Warren State Hospital. At age 25 years he was hit on the head by a falling tree and was unconscious for several hours. No unusual behavior was observed after this but about eight years later he complained of being drugged by people who wanted to obtain money from him. A few years later he became quiet, seclusive, developed persecutory delusions and imagined that his family was not related to him. He was admitted to Warren State Hospital on 4/10/1915, and died there 24 years later. Diagnosis at Warren was dementia praecox, paranoid type. He remained deluded and hallucinated until death. Classification: Schizophrenic reaction—paranoid type.

Parents

Father (13), first cousin of the proband's mother (14), born 1844; died in 1927 of cerebral hemorrhage. He was described as the "really peculiar" member of his family. He was "always odd," but grew worse, becoming emotional (given to crying spells), excitable and high tempered. He spent much time and money trying to locate oil with a fake instrument. Once he beat a balky horse to death. He was admitted to Warren State Hospital from a county home at age 83 years of age with a diagnosis of psychosis with cerebral arteriosclerosis. At admission he was disoriented, attention was poor and his memory for recent events was nil. He died a short time after admission to Warren. Classification: Probable psychoneurotic disorder.

Aunts and Uncles

Paternal uncle (10); died at age 40 years of tuberculosis. He was a cooper and barber described as "versatile...witty...an accomplished penman." He reportedly "drank a great deal" and was "loose in his relations with women." Classification: Possible personality disorder.

Maternal uncle (19); died at age 28 years of injuries received when kicked by a horse. He was described as a very prosperous storekeeper, unscrupulous, and very much disliked by the people of the town, although "on the surface he was an agreeable man." Classification: Probable personality disorder.

Siblings

Sister (27), born 1881; died at age 64 years of diabetes. She was inclined to become excited or worried rather easily and was described as "a little nervous." Classification: Probable psychoneurotic disorder.

(29) husband of sister (30), born 1888. At age 72 years he was described as an alcoholic who had been unemployed for at least 15 years because of his drinking. Classification: Sociopathic personality disturbance — alcoholism (addiction).

(31) wife of brother (32), born 1905. She deserted (32) and their two children when the children were five and three years of age. At 35 years of age she was described as a "complaining woman who thought life had treated her roughly." Classification: Sociopathic personality disturbance.

Brother (32), born 1896; died at age 64 years of obstructive jaundice. He drank daily, but excessively only on weekends. His drinking was the cause of marital stress in his first marriage. His second marriage was turbulent; however, this wife drank with him. He had little interest in his children. Classification: Sociopathic personality disturbance — alcoholism (addiction).

(33) wife of brother (32), born 1895; described as "a fairly heavy drinker." Classification: Possible sociopathic personality disturbance — alcoholism (addiction).

Nieces and Nephews

Nephew (34), born 1890; died at age 54 years of a cerebral brain hemorrhage. He was retarded. He also had epileptic seizures every two or three years following an attack of scarlet fever when young. Described as "set in his ways," he had difficulty adjusting to the death of his father. Classification: Probable transient situational personality disturbance — adjustment reaction of late life.

(37) wife of nephew (36), born 1893; described as "bossy, mean and domineering ... won't do anything for herself." She

had crippling arthritis. Classification: Probable personality trait disturbance.

Nephew (38), born 1893. At age 69 years he was described as "embittered over the death of his youngest son." In 1935 he had a "peculiar episode" during which he was bedridden for two weeks with dizziness and nausea. The episode was attributed to an incorrect glasses fit. He was extremely active in community affairs. Classification: Possible psychoneurotic disorder.

(39) wife of nephew (38), born 1893; reportedly had some depression during menopause. Classification: Probable transient situational personality disorder — adjustment reaction of late life.

(42) husband of niece (43), born 1883; died at age 67 years of arteriosclerotic heart disease. He was described as lazy, a gambler and a drinker. Classification: Sociopathic personality disturbance.

Nephew (51), born 1915. He was described as an alcoholic who had lost many jobs and much business because of his drinking. His lack of interest in his children and family caused much marital discord. Classification: Sociopathic personality disturbance — alcoholism (addiction).

Nephew (57), born 1923; at age 39 years he was serving a seven-to-15-year term for burglary at a correctional institution where he was incarcerated on 9/4/1962. At the correctional institution he was classified as a schizoid personality with possible paranoid tendencies as he was not hallucinated and had no well-defined delusional symptoms. His mother deserted the family when he was three years of age, after which he spent four years in an orphanage and several years in a home for boys. He had numerous arrests for vagrancy, deserted from the army and eventually received a dishonorable discharge. He also had a record of one rape and four burglaries (two with assault). The correctional institution staff believed him to be a potential custodial and security problem. Classification: Sociopathic personality disturbance — antisocial reaction.

(58) wife of nephew (57), born 1933. She married (57) when she was pregnant by someone else whom she had known but 11 days. Her marriage to (57) was her third marriage, the first two ending in divorce. The institutional records of (58) state that she stabbed (57) and claimed the stabbing was a suicide attempt by (57). Classification: Probable personality disorder.

Distant Relatives

(59) husband of grandniece (60), born 1919. He was first hospitalized for nervous jerks of his shoulders and arms at a Veterans Administration Hospital in May, 1961, at age 42 years. He ran away from this hospital and was subsequently hospitalized at another veterans' facility in December, 1961. He was also treated for "nervousness" and muscle twitching at Veterans Administration hospitals. Final diagnosis was psychoneurotic disorder, anxiety reaction, chronic, in partial remission; precipitating stress; unhealthy family situation; premorbid personality, long-standing history of anxiety; numerous hospitalizations for treatment of nervous conditions in Veterans Administration hospitals. Upon admission and during treatment he was found to be "friendly, cooperative, well oriented and not psychotic" although his wife had had him arrested for threatening to kill her while on leave of absence from the hospital. He was released on 7/25/1962. Classification: Psychoneurotic disorder—anxiety reaction.

Grandniece (60), born 1919. She was one year old when her mother died. Her childhood was reportedly very unhappy as she lived with an aunt until five years old, then with her father and stepmother who was a "domineering, bossy" woman. At age 43 years she was interviewed and found to be very "talkative, dramatic, anxious and tense." The interviewer found it impossible to ascertain whether or not this was a temporary condition due to her husband's hospitalization. The hospital reported that her attitude toward her husband's hospitalization had been "unreasonable." Classification: Probable transient situational personality disorder—adult situational reaction.

Grandniece (62), born 1928. At age 34 years she was described as obese, a "nymphomaniac" who was often "remorseful and lonely." When young she rebelled against all parental control and was promiscuous from the age of 12 or 13 years. At age 26 years she "ran off" with a person sought by the police and was apprehended as an accessory in his crimes. Classification: Probable transient situational personality disorder—adjustment reaction of adolescence.

(67) wife of grandnephew (66), born

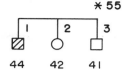

CONTROLS
W S H   4 I

1926. She was described as "a hostile person who dominated her husband" and as "a hostile, aggressive person with poor social relationships." She quarreled with relatives and neighbors and was obsessive about being clean. Classification: Personality trait disturbance—passive-aggressive personality.

Great-grandniece (100), born 1941; a college student described as "depressed, disturbed about father's (59) illness ... feels rather worthless." Classification: Other transient situational personality disturbance.

Family Summary

The proband was the only family member with a psychotic disorder. The proband's father was hospitalized in old age with a psychotic reaction to arteriosclerosis, although he was probably neurotic most of his life. Other neurotics were a sister, a nephew and the husband of a grandniece. Personality disorders were found in two uncles, a brother, three nephews, two grandnieces and a great-grandniece. They were also found in a sister's husband, the wives of two brothers, the wives of three nephews, the husband of a niece and in the wife of a grandnephew.

Controls

Brother (1) of (55), born 1918. He was married three times. He married for the first time at age 19 years and reportedly "drank and ran around for a time while young." Classification: Possible transient situational personality disorder—adjustment reaction of adolescence.

WSH 42: The Proband

The proband (38), born 1895; died at age 33 years at Warren State Hospital of an acute intestinal obstruction. He was admitted to Warren on 4/7/1914, with a diagnosis of dementia praecox, catatonic type, and remained there until death. First symptoms of mental illness appeared during the winter of 1912, when he was observed to laugh to himself and stare in a senseless fashion. Gradually there was a profound change of character; there were bizarre acts, mannerisms, inaccessibility, loss of mental and physical ability and marked disturbances of judgment. Classification: Schizophrenic reaction—catatonic type.

Grandparents

Maternal grandfather (3), died at age 79 years of unknown causes. At one time he reportedly became agitated, worried and suicidal. He possibly had other similar attacks. Classification: Probably with functional psychosis, involutional psychotic reaction.

Maternal grandmother (4), died at age 71 years of dropsy. At about age 40 years she had a depression lasting several months from which she recovered completely. Classification: Probably with functional psychosis.

Parents

Mother (15), born 1852; died at age 83 years, cause of death unknown. She reportedly had a period of "melancholy" at 18 years of age when she believed she was going to die in two weeks. About one month before the birth of the proband, at age 41 years, she became "convinced that the child would never be born." She suffered regularly from nightmares and chronic insomnia. Classification: Psychoneurotic disorder—anxiety reaction.

Father (14) and mother (15) were second cousins.

Aunts and Uncles

Maternal aunt (19), born 1859; died at age 29 years of tuberculosis. She experienced one episode during which she thought she had committed some sin and would not "die right." Classification: Possible psychoneurotic disorder.

Maternal uncle (24), born 1872; died at age 64 years of mitral stenosis. At age 22 years he had a period of mental trouble during which he would not work but would remain in his room and whistle and sing. He also attempted to poison his family. After his recovery he "went west" and remained estranged from his family. Classification: Probably with functional psychosis.

Siblings

Sister (27), born 1879; died at age 54 years of lobar pneumonia. She was reported to be normal by everyone except her physician, who stated that she had consulted him about visual and auditory hallucinations. She realized that they were imaginary and became fearful of her mental soundness. Classification: Probably with functional psychosis.

Sister (29), born 1881. At age 80 years she was described as "always a sickly woman—stomach trouble." When younger she was described as "sensitive, retiring, quick to fancy people were making slighting remarks about her—did not like to attend meetings or large social gatherings." Classification: Personality pattern disturbance—schizoid personality.

Brother (32), born 1886; died at age 23 years at Warren State Hospital of a self-inflicted gunshot wound to the head. He was admitted to Warren after the suicide attempt on 3/24/1909, and lived for one week. Premorbidly he was gentle, quiet and good natured. A short time before the suicide he began to brood, became self-centered, had delusions of persecution and transitory hallucinations and illusions. Classification: Schizophrenic reaction—paranoid type.

Brother (35), born 1890; died at age 53 years of carcinoma of the gall bladder. At age 19 years he expressed the wish that he wanted to die as the "Almighty God had rejected him" and subsequently attempted suicide by choking himself and cutting his arteries. He was hospitalized at Warren State Hospital from November, 1909 until April, 1910. Although he improved while hospitalized, he was never again normal. Classification: Schizophrenic reaction.

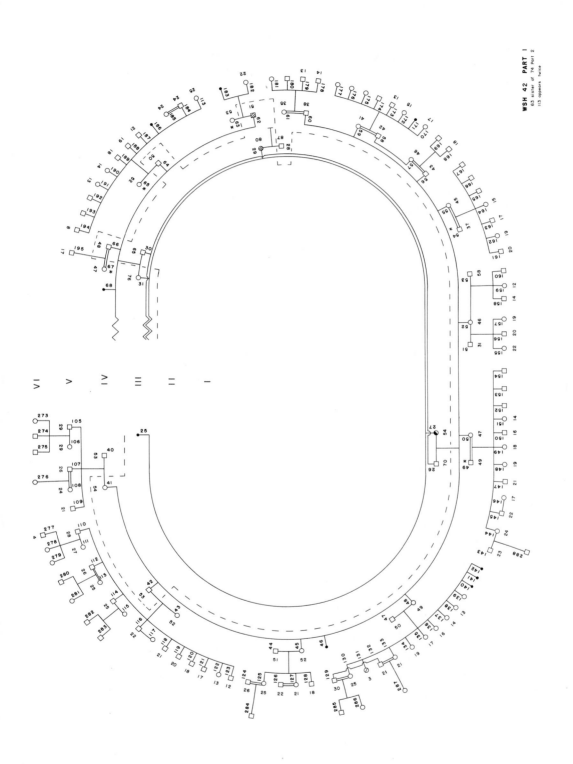

WSH 42 PART 1
63 sister of 74 Part 2
113 appears twice

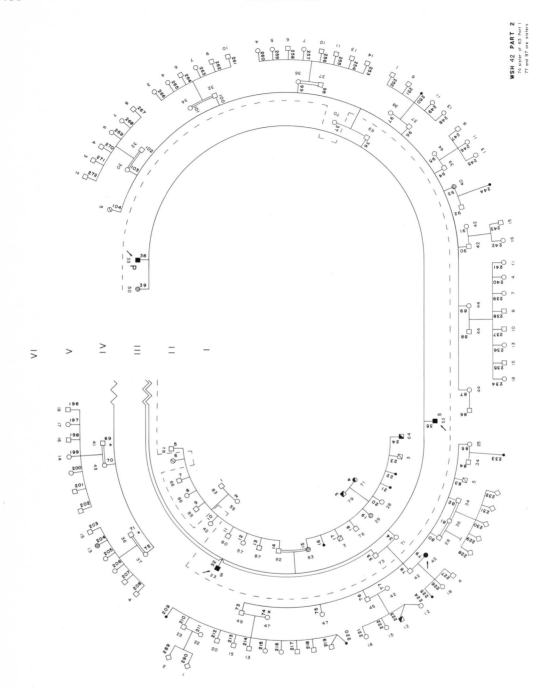

WSH 42 PART 2
74 sister of 63 Part I
77 and 97 are sisters

Sister (39), born 1898; died at age 50 years of carcinoma of the ovary. She was described as of a "sullen nature, inclined to be indifferent and was a persistent bed-wetter." Classification: Probable personality disorder—schizoid personality.

Nieces and Nephews

Nephew (62), born 1910. He described himself as "nervous" and with a "nervous stomach." Classification: Psychoneurotic reaction—other.

(79) wife of nephew (78), born 1919.

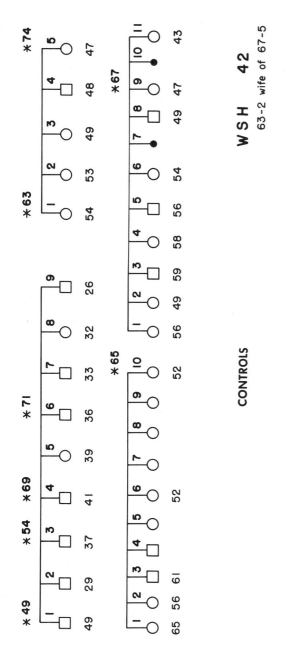

which followed a neck injury received in a fall. She was not hospitalized for her symptoms of "worry and melancholy," but was taken to a chiropractor who "cured her." Classification: Psychoneurotic disorder—depressive reaction.

Distant Relatives

Grandniece (204), born 1948. At age 11 years she had an emotional upset during which she would "scream and yell" at the slightest cause. She could not get along with her teacher and would wake at night screaming that the teacher was after her. The upset subsided when she changed schools and teachers. Classification: Transient situational personality disturbance—adjustment reaction of childhood.

Grandnephew (223), born 1949. (221), (223) and his twin (224) were all mentally deficient and were cared for at home. None of the three ever talked, were unable to dress or feed themselves and were not toilet trained. (223), at age 12 years, was observed by an interviewer to frequently engage in a rhythmical rolling motion in which he would rock back and forth until his head and shoulders were on the floor and his legs were extended straight into the air. After a moment or two of this he would get up. He also had episodes of twirling with six or eight revolutions before he quit. If interrupted he would begin his rocking behavior. His father, noting the interviewer's concern, said "He does that all the time." Classification: Probably with functional pyschosis, schizophrenic reaction—childhood type.

Family Summary

The proband, two brothers and the wife of a nephew had psychotic disorders and the maternal grandparents, a maternal uncle, a sister and a grandnephew probably so. The mother, a maternal aunt, a nephew and a niece were classified as neurotic. Personality disorders were found in two sisters and a grandniece.

Controls

None noteworthy.

She had an acutely excited reaction after a childbirth in 1943 and was hospitalized for a month at a mental health sanitarium. Her illness was described as "might have been just a sort of reactive depression or ... a little splitting of the personality." Classification: Schizophrenic reaction—acute undifferentiated type.

Niece (93), born 1921. She had a depressed period lasting two months in 1957,

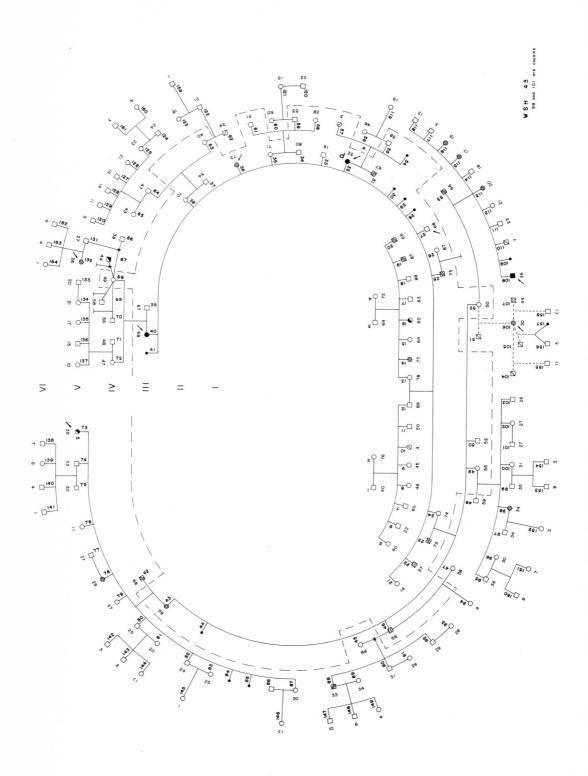

WSH 43
99 and 101 are cousins

WSH 43: The Proband

The proband (32), born 1882; died at age 32 years of carcinoma of the cervix. In her youth she was considered "ambitious and industrious." In December, 1909, following the accidental death of her youngest child, she became melancholy and inattentive to her household duties. She would stare into space for long periods of time and dwelt a great deal on the idea that she was losing her mind. This condition subsided somewhat, then remained unchanged until late 1912 when, following some religious meetings, she became excited, violent, developed ideas of persecution, poisoning, infidelity, reference and visual and tactile hallucinations. She was hospitalized at a private hospital from 12/28/1912 until 3/11/1913. An attempt was made to have her resume her household duties but she was so engrossed with her hallucinations that she paid little attention to her work or personal appearance and was admitted to Warren State Hospital on 11/4/1914, with a diagnosis of constitutional inferiority (mental age, 10½ years) with superimposed dementia praecox of the paranoid type. She was discharged from Warren on 12/20/1915, and had no subsequent hospitalizations for mental illness. Classification: Schizophrenic reaction—paranoid type.

(31) husband of the proband (32), born 1877; died at age 67 years of a coronary occlusion. He reportedly was a "heavy drinker, irresponsible" and "did not have a good name in the community." Classification: Sociopathic personality disturbance—alcoholism (addiction).

Aunts and Uncles

Maternal aunt (14), died at age 77 years of "old age." She was delusional, her memory was poor and she had a tendency to wander during the last three years of her life. Classification: Chronic brain syndrome of senium.

Maternal aunt (16), born 1860; died at age 60 years of asthma. She reportedly was considered "crazy" and retarded by friends and family as she would "get angry spells when she would talk and scold and complain of people talking about her. She would also have laughing spells." Classification: Probably with functional psychosis.

Maternal uncle (19), born 1845; died at age 87 years, possibly of delirium tremens. He was an alcoholic who furnished little support for the family. When intoxicated he was ugly and disagreeable but was otherwise "pleasant and jolly." He had periods of delirium tremens. Classification: Sociopathic personality disturbance—alcoholism (addiction).

Maternal uncle (20), born 1847; died at age 66 years of injuries received in an accident. He reportedly "never amounted to anything as he spent everything he earned for liquor." Classification: Sociopathic personality disturbance—alcoholism (addiction).

Siblings

Brother (22), born 1870; died at age 37 years of exhaustion with chronic catarrhal enteritis. He was described as "an odd, peculiar fellow, very quiet and rather melancholy." Classification: Probable personality pattern disturbance—schizoid personality.

(23) husband of sister (24), born 1873; died at age 75 years of a coronary occlusion. He was described as "a heavy drinker" and "crazy," as well as irresponsible. Classification: Sociopathic personality disturbance—alcoholism (addiction).

Brother (25), born 1875; died at age 73 years of cardiorenal disease. He was described by some as "selfish and negligent" and his physician said that he could not be considered normal. Classification: Probable personality disorder.

Brother (27), born 1877; died at age 68 years at a state mental hospital, of chronic myocarditis. As an infant he had "brain fever" followed by a convulsive disorder. He was subsequently considered retarded by his family and kept at home with his parents. After their deaths he lived at his sister's but never adjusted to the change. He was committed to the state hospital on 6/5/1941, when his relatives complained that he burned things, threatened violence to members of the family, neglected his appearance and feared that all strangers were after him. Diagnosis was psychosis with mental deficiency. Classification: Chronic brain syndrome of unknown cause with psychotic reaction; also, mental deficiency, severe.

Sister (36), born 1888; died at age 73 years of arteriosclerotic heart disease. Her family considered her retarded. She was treated at a general hospital in March, 1960, for severe hypothyroidism. After the death of her sister in 1961 she grieved and lost an excessive amount of weight. She was again hospitalized and remained so until her death. While hospitalized she expressed fears that men were trying to beat her and that visitors and hospital personnel (principally male) were after her. Classification: Probable chronic brain syndrome of senium.

Sister (40), born 1893. At age 66 years, shortly after the death of her husband, she was hospitalized with symptoms of a depression; she lost interest in all activities, showed considerable psychomotor retardation and often reverted to "babyish" mannerisms. She received 10 electroconvulsive therapy treatments and subsequently had an amazing and dramatic recovery. At age 68 years she appeared "emotionally and socially well adjusted." Classification: Psychotic-depressive reaction.

Nieces and Nephews

(42) husband of niece (43), born 1894. He was described as "a heavy drinker, irresponsible, boisterous and mean to his children." He was also a nuisance in the local taverns. Classification: Sociopathic personality disturbance—alcoholism (addiction).

Niece (43), born 1903. She had convulsions in infancy and was considered mentally retarded. All of her children were removed from the home because she (and her husband) drank heavily and ignored the children. At age 59 years she was described as emotionally stable. Classification: Sociopathic personality disturbance—alcoholism (addiction).

Nephew (46), born 1906. He was divorced by his first wife because of alcoholism and non-support. His second wife had him arrested for the same reasons. At age 52 years he quit drinking and at age 56 years he was described as "settled down." Classification: Sociopathic personality disturbance—alcoholism (addiction).

(53) husband of niece (52), born 1906; described as "unreliable, a heavy drinker and a disorderly person." He was imprisoned twice on larceny charges and on another occasion for alcoholism. Classification: Sociopathic personality disturbance.

(67) husband of niece (68), born 1908. He was divorced by (68) in 1952 after seven weeks of marriage because of cruelty. A psychologist working in a marriage clinic diagnosed him as schizophrenic. He was described by a colleague, a chemistry professor, as an introvert. Classification: Probably with functional psychosis, schizophrenic reaction.

Distant Relatives

Grandniece (73), born 1923. She left her alcoholic parents' home at age 16 years, after which she took some of her brothers and sisters to live with her and helped support them. When the younger siblings became self-supporting she lived alone. She was admitted to the psychiatric division of a general hospital on 5/9/1959, after attempting suicide by taking an overdose of sleeping pills and gassing herself. A diagnosis of depressive reaction and character disorder was made; she was given electric shock treatments and released on 6/9/1959. On 8/13/1962, after another suicide attempt by taking an overdose of medication, she was again hospitalized. Diagnosis was depressive reaction and she was released three days later. Classification: Probable psychoneurotic disorder—depressive reaction.

Grandniece (78), born 1933. At age 29 years she described herself as emotionally unstable and was under the care of a "nerve doctor." She was very hostile toward her parents and blamed them for her nervousness. Classification: Probable psychoneurotic disorder.

Grandnephew (88), born 1929. He reportedly had a nervous stomach, severe headaches, and was described by the interviewer as "highly suspicious, almost chronically angry" and exhibited inappropriate affect. Classification: Probable personality pattern disturbance—paranoid personality.

Grandniece (98), born 1927. She reportedly took medication for nervousness, although she never consulted a physician or had prescribed medication. At age 34 years the interviewer described her as "fairly dependent and immature." Classification: Probable psychoneurotic disorder.

Grandniece (106), born 1931. At age 30 years she and the fourth of her four illegitimate children lived with the father of the child in conditions described by the interviewer as "those of severe deprivation."

She spent two years at a correctional institution during adolescence because of "corrupt behavior." As an adult she had a history of promiscuity with minor boys. She was hospitalized at a state mental hospital from 5/20/1960 until 8/5/1960, with a diagnosis of sociopathic personality disturbance with sexual promiscuity. Classification: Sociopathic personality disturbance.

(107) father of illegitimate child of grandniece (106), born 1918. He was separated, but not divorced from his wife and lived with (106) on public assistance as he claimed that arthritis and other physical defects prevented him from employment; however, he did a great deal of hunting and fishing. He had tried to collect disability pension from the army but was always turned down. An interviewer described him at age 44 years as of borderline intelligence, friendly and in good mental health. Classification: Possible personality pattern disturbance—inadequate personality.

Grandnephew (108), born 1936. He attended special classes for the mentally retarded in public school and at age 26 years was regularly employed as a factory worker. He was hospitalized at a state mental hospital from 11/14/1952 until 12/13/1952, with a diagnosis of psychosis with mental deficiency—period of excitement. He had two shock treatments while hospitalized and showed significant improvement while under treatment. Classification: Schizophrenic reaction—paranoid type (with mental deficiency).

Grandniece (113), born 1942. She was committed to an institution for the retarded on 5/1/1959, as she was "becoming promiscuous" and was difficult to manage. At the school the clinical psychologist reported that she may have been educationally retarded but she was not intellectually retarded. Further testing revealed her IQ to be 93. She was described as "emotionally infantile, dependent, hostile and self-punishing." She was placed in a foster home on 1/16/1961, but returned on 5/5/1962 because of illness. Diagnosis at the school was adjustment reaction of childhood and adolescence. Classification: Personality trait disturbance—emotionally unstable.

Grandniece (115), born 1945. She attended special classes for the mentally retarded while in public school. In June, 1961, she was admitted to a state school because

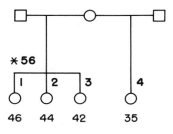

CONTROLS
W S H   43

of "running around with boys." Classification: Transient situational personality disorder—adjustment reaction of adolescence.

Grandniece (116), born 1947. In public school she was placed in special classes for the retarded. She was admitted to a state school in June, 1961, because she was "running around with boys." Classification: Transient situational personality disorder—adjustment reaction of adolescence.

(132) wife of grandnephew (131), born 1935. In April, 1961, she was examined by a psychiatrist, then hospitalized for five days at a general hospital because of nervous tension. She was prescribed tranquilizers. With the tranquilizers and after a move from a cramped apartment to a new, modern house she appeared well at age 26 years. Classification: Psychoneurotic disorder—anxiety reaction.

Family Summary

The proband, a sister and a grandnephew had psychotic disorders, and a maternal aunt and the husband of a niece probably so. A sister and a maternal aunt were classified as chronic brain syndrome of senium. A brother was hospitalized with a psychotic reaction to an unknown cause. Personality disorders were found in the proband's husband, two maternal uncles, two brothers, a niece, a nephew, four grandnieces, a grandnephew, a sister's husband, the husbands of two nieces and in the father of a grandniece's illegitimate child. Three grandnieces and the wife of a grandnephew were neurotic.

Controls

None noteworthy.

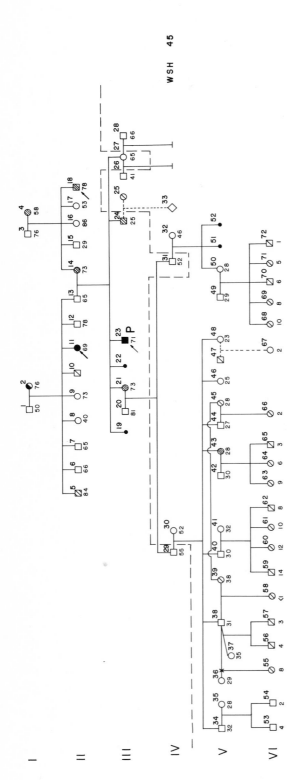

WSH 45: The Proband

The proband (23), born 1888; died at age 71 years at Warren State Hospital of malnutrition and fractures of left wrist and hip. He was admitted to Warren on 3/15/1915, and remained there until his death. Previous to his hospitalization he was seclusive, ambitious, hyper-religious and over-scrupulous. While hospitalized he was described as "reluctant to talk, disinterested and seclusive." He did not answer questions readily and his facial expression was blank. He developed delusions of persecution, ideas of reference and auditory hallucinations. Diagnosis throughout his hospitalization was dementia praecox, hebephrenic type. Classification: Schizophrenic reaction—paranoid type.

Grandparents

Paternal grandmother (2), born 1810; died at age 76 years of la grippe. She was insane at the age of 35 years for a period of six weeks and was always quick tempered and excitable. Classification: Probably with functional psychosis.

Maternal grandmother (4), born 1821; died at age 58 years of rheumatism. She was described as quick tempered and rather fretful, although intelligent and capable. Classification: Possible personality trait disturbance.

Parents

Mother (14), born 1854; died at age 73 years of diabetes mellitus. She was described as neither very intelligent nor very capable. She had "spells of nervous jerking" all her life and had a "hasty temper." In conversation she would wander in a fragmentary manner from one subject to another. Classification: Possible personality pattern disturbance.

Aunts and Uncles

Paternal uncle (5), born 1830; died at age 74 years, cause of death unknown. He was described as a religious crank who neglected his work and responsibilities to study the Bible. Classification: Personality pattern disturbance.

Paternal aunt (11), born 1847. At age 69 years she appeared to be in good health; however, at age 35 years she became very apprehensive at night, imagined strange noises, became over-religious and turned against her husband (she wanted to kill him). She was hospitalized at Warren State Hospital for three months and was much improved when discharged. She had no subsequent attacks. Classification: Schizophrenic reaction—paranoid type.

Maternal uncle (18), born 1859; died at age 78 years at Warren State Hospital of chronic myocarditis; psychosis with cerebral arteriosclerosis. At age 57 years he was described as "slovenly in appearance, his air one of self-importance, but he was communicative and friendly." He was a college graduate, a surveyor, who owned oil properties, from which he derived the income that supported him. Classification: Chronic brain syndrome associated with cerebral arteriosclerosis.

Siblings

Sister (21), born 1884; died at age 73 years of cerebral thrombosis. She was described as nervous. Classification: Possible psychoneurotic disorder.

Brother (24), born 1892; died at age 25 years of pulmonary tuberculosis. He completed grade three at age 13 years and had a record of "spasms." He was described as a "wild, heedless fellow." Classification: Possible personality disorder.

Distant Relatives

Grandniece (43), born 1931. At age 28 years she was described by the physician as "jumpy—quite a pusher" who was a bit on the compulsive side and had a minor anxiety neurosis for which she had prescribed medication. Classification: Psychoneurotic disorder—anxiety reaction.

Family Summary

The proband and a paternal aunt had psychotic disorders and the paternal grandmother probably so. A maternal uncle was psychotic with cerebral arteriosclerosis. Personality disorders were found in the mother, the maternal grandmother, a paternal uncle and in a brother. A sister and a grandniece were neurotic.

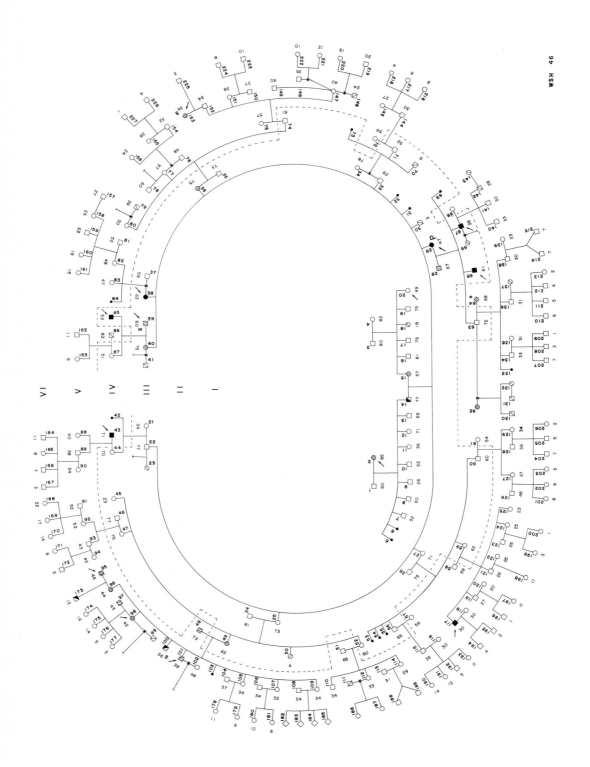

WSH 46

WSH 46: The Proband

The proband (29), born 1867; died at age 47 years of arteriosclerotic epilepsy at Warren State Hospital. She made excellent progress in school and when she finished high school she taught school for two years. She was normal until age 33 years, when she began to grow irritable and quarrelsome, neglected her family and became over-religious and hallucinated. About 15 years later, two weeks before her admission to Warren State Hospital on 1/11/1915, she became irrational and fearful. Diagnosis at Warren State Hospital was dementia praecox, paranoid type. She died at the hospital six months after admission. Classification: Schizophrenic reaction—paranoid type.

(28) husband of the proband (29), born 1865; died at age 67 years of a cerebral hemorrhage. He was described as "ignorant, simple-minded" but "domineering" and as a "real mean tyrant." Classification: Personality trait disturbance—passive-aggressive personality.

Children

(62) wife of son (63). Unknown except that she was an alcoholic. Classification: Possible sociopathic personality disturbance—alcoholism (addiction).

(64) wife of son (63). At age 68 years she was described as often depressed and unhappy. She "doctored a lot." Classification: Probable psychoneurotic disorder.

Son (65), born 1891; died at age 61 years of coronary thrombosis at Warren State Hospital. He would wander about the country and be gone as long as five years before his family would hear from him. He was admitted to Warren State Hospital in 1944 at age 52 years, although his first disappearance was at age 19 years. At admission he was disoriented for time, place and person and was hallucinated. He thought he was receiving messages from the Federal Bureau of Investigation and that the Axis was about to destroy Erie, Pennsylvania, by radio-television. Diagnosis at Warren was dementia praecox, paranoid type. Classification: Schizophrenic reaction—paranoid type.

Son (67), born 1899; died at age 38 years at a state mental hospital, of locomotor ataxia. At about age 36 years he became depressed and easily upset and his physician treated him for syphilis. A year later, when he developed grandiose ideas of great wealth and became hallucinated, he was admitted to the hospital, where he died a year later. Diagnosis was psychosis with syphilitic meningoencephalitis. His delusions and hallucinations were bizarre and he was uncooperative and assaultive, rather unlike the confused reaction observed in a disturbed organic psychosis. Classification: Schizophrenic reaction—paranoid type; Also, chronic brain syndrome associated with meningoencephalitic syphilis.

Grandparents

Paternal grandmother (2), born 1807; died at age 85 years at Warren State Hospital, where she had been for four years. She gradually became demented after age 75 years. Classification: Chronic brain syndrome of senium.

Parents

Father (14), died at age 77 years, cause unknown. He was always considered peculiar in that he was overly religious and had very poor judgment. About three years before his death he became "demented." Classification: Probably with functional psychosis—schizophrenia.

Mother (15), died at age 57 years of apoplexy. At age 38 years she had her first stroke, which left her speech affected and her left side helpless. She had several more strokes during the last three years of life and became physically helpless and emotionally unstable. Classification: Chronic brain syndrome associated with cerebral arteriosclerosis.

Aunts and Uncles

Maternal aunt (20), born 1848; died at age 49 years of erysipelas at Warren State Hospital. She developed epilepsy at age 16 years and gradually became so "demented" that she was hospitalized at Warren in 1893 at age 45 years. At the hospital she was periodically excited with screaming spells, and was untidy and destructive. Classification: Chronic brain syndrome associated with convulsive disorder with psychotic reaction.

Siblings

Sister (36), born 1879; died at age 75 years of cancer of the kidney. She was described as "the dreamer type" and would sit for long intervals looking at nothing. Classification: Possible personality pattern disturbance — schizoid personality.

Sister (38), born 1883; died at age 63 years of mammary carcinoma at Warren State Hospital. At age 33 years she was hospitalized at a state mental hospital where she remained for 11 years. Diagnosis at this hospital was paranoia. Symptoms of mental disorder began about two years before admission. Admission to Warren State Hospital was at age 57 years. At the hospital she expressed bizarre religious delusions of a paranoid nature and was destructive to clothing and bed clothes. Diagnosis at Warren was dementia praecox — paranoid type. Classification: Schizophrenic reaction — paranoid type.

(39) husband of sister (40), born 1879; died at age 60 years of suicide by shooting. He was a physician who took drugs to alleviate depression. At age 43 years he was hospitalized at Warren State Hospital for three months for drug addiction. He had been treated four years previously at a private hospital. Classification: Sociopathic personality disturbance — drug addiction.

Sister (40), born 1888. She was described in the hospital records of her husband and son as subject to "periodical hysterical outbreaks" and as "unstable emotionally." Classification: Probable personality disorder.

Nieces and Nephews

(43) husband of niece (44), born 1899. At age 18 years he had a depression following a revival meeting. The depression would recur from time to time but he was not hospitalized until 1940 at age 51 years after he expressed suicidal ideas. Diagnosis at a state mental hospital was dementia praecox, paranoid type. At admission he was confused, agitated and worried about religion. An adenoma of the thyroid was removed with subsequent improvement in his condition and he was paroled six months after admission. Readmission to the hospital was in 1947, with a diagnosis of manic-depressive psychosis, depressed type. He returned to the hospital for short stays in 1950, 1955 and 1957. On each occasion he had excellent remissions after a course of electroshock therapy. Classification: Schizophrenic reaction — schizo-affective type.

(48) husband of niece (49), born 1875; died at age 73 years of arteriosclerosis. After his retirement he drank very heavily. Classification: Sociopathic personality disturbance — alcoholism (addiction).

Niece (49), born 1893; died at age 62 years of a cerebral accident. As she grew older she reportedly used to "sit on the floor; didn't have sense enough to turn the knob to get out." Classification: Possible chronic brain syndrome associated with cerebral arteriosclerosis.

Nephew (85), born 1911. At age 53 years (in 1964) he was a patient at a state mental hospital where he was first admitted on 7/25/1933 with a diagnosis of dementia praecox. He had five subsequent admissions to the same hospital with diagnoses of dementia praecox, hebephrenic type, and dementia praecox, paranoid type. He graduated from high school with honor at age 17 years. He matriculated at college, where he remained three months, then returned home because of homesickness. At age 18 he left home, but phoned home for assistance in returning. The next year he left home again and was arrested for riding a freight car. At age 22 he became depressed and was convinced he was going to die. He was placed in a private sanitarium but had to be removed after three days because of his noisy and destructive behavior. When home again he jumped from a three-story window and was subsequently admitted to the state hospital for the first time. At admission he was noisy, hyperactive, impulsive, manneristic and incoherent and irrelevant in conversation. As his illness progressed he became suspicious, seclusive and delusional with marked attention and affect impairment. Classification: Schizophrenic reaction — paranoid type.

Distant Relatives

(95) husband of grandniece (96), born 1917; reportedly was once hospitalized for alcoholism. Classification: Sociopathic personality disturbance — alcoholism (addiction).

Grandniece (96), born 1918; described as in very poor health because she was both diabetic and a periodic alcoholic. Classification: Sociopathic personality disturbance—alcoholism (addiction).

(97) husband of grandniece (98), born 1916; died at age 43 years of acute coronary occlusion. He was described as a "heavy drinker" who went on "sprees" by one informant but a drinking problem was not mentioned by another. Classification: Possible sociopathic personality disturbance—alcoholism (addiction).

Grandniece (98), born 1920. In 1960 she was hospitalized for one month at a state mental hospital, for "drinking and nerves." Classification: Sociopathic personality disturbance—alcoholism (addiction).

Grandnephew (100), born 1923. At age 36 years he was found dead in his room with the gas on. It was never established whether his death was the result of murder or suicide. He completed two years of medical school and worked as a boat inspector. Classification: Probably with functional psychosis.

Grandnephew (101), born 1924. He completed two years of college and worked as a shipyard apprentice. He was hospitalized for six months for ulcers, kidney trouble and alcoholism. Classification: Sociopathic personality disturbance—alcoholism (addiction).

Grandnephew (117), born 1930. He was admitted to a state mental hospital at age 19 years when he became disorderly, restless, indifferent, untidy and suffered from bizarre delusions. He was diagnosed as dementia praecox, catatonic type, and treated with electroshock therapy. He was paroled after nine months' stay and at age 30 years had not been rehospitalized. In 1955 he was interviewed and stated that he had no recurrence of mental symptoms but had some fainting attacks which had been diagnosed as petit mal seizures. Classification: Schizophrenic reaction—catatonic type.

(153) wife of grandnephew (152), born 1926. She had an "extremely nervous condition" at age 13 years but was not treated. She married at age 19 years and divorced her husband three years later as he was "inconsiderate." She married again at age 24 years and this three-year marriage was terminated because of the husband's drinking and physical abuse. She married the third time at age 31 years, which proved to be

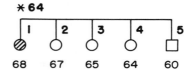

CONTROLS
W S H 46

another unhappy marriage. Four years later she was hospitalized following a suicide attempt. Diagnosis was immaturity reaction with depressive and acting-out tendencies. She was hospitalized for one month. Classification: Psychoneurotic disorder—depressive reaction.

Great-grandnephew (173), born 1950. He reportedly was withdrawn and had psychological problems. Relatives believed his problems were caused by his parents' alcoholism. An aunt, when describing his problems, said that once when she was visiting the home he sat on top of the refrigerator and would neither speak nor come down but "just huddled there." Classification: Probably with functional psychosis.

Family Summary

The proband, two sons, a sister, a nephew, a grandnephew and the husband of a niece had psychotic disorders and were hospitalized. The father, a grandnephew and a great-grandnephew were probably psychotic. The paternal grandmother was hospitalized with chronic brain syndrome of senium and the mother and a niece were classified as chronic brain syndrome associated with cerebral arteriosclerosis. One psychotic son also had chronic brain syndrome associated with meningoencephalitic syphilis. A maternal aunt was hospitalized with a psychotic reaction to a convulsive disorder. Personality disorders were found in two sisters, two grandnieces, a grandnephew, the husband of the proband, the wife of a son, the husband of a sister, the husband of a niece and in the husbands of two grandnieces. The wife of a son and the wife of a grandnephew were neurotic.

Controls

See family pedigree, person 64.

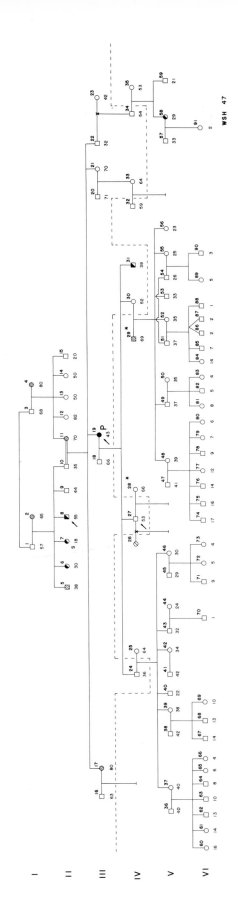

WSH 47

478

I

II

III

IV

V

VI

WSH 47: The Proband

The proband (19), born 1878; died at age 43 years of bronchial pneumonia at Warren State Hospital. At age 32 years she experienced a gradual change in her disposition until she was unable to do any housework and was eventually, for about eight months previous to her admission to Warren State Hospital on 1/5/1915, completely indifferent to her surroundings. In addition to her mental symptoms she had tremors and movements of her hands and head which the doctors at Warren considered to be choreic in nature. From the time of admission to Warren State Hospital until her death, she gradually deteriorated until she was mute and helpless. Diagnosis at Warren State Hospital was dementia praecox. Classification: Schizophrenic reaction—catatonic type.

Children

Son (27), born 1898; died at age 53 years of pneumonia and organic brain disease. In February, 1932, he was ill for three weeks with a cold and fever and it was difficult to rouse him. After the illness there was weakness in his back and legs and his speech became slurred. From 1935 until his admission to a Veterans Administration hospital, he felt "blue and depressed." Diagnosis was psychosis with organic disease, encephalitis lethargica. From the time of admission until his death he displayed progressive emotional and intellectual deterioration and eventually became completely helpless. Classification: Chronic brain syndrome associated with encephalitis with psychotic reaction.

(29) husband of daughter (30), born 1893. He was described as "grouchy and odd" by family members. An interviewer seemed to be of the same opinion. Classification: Personality disorder.

Son (31), born 1901; died at age 39 years of injuries received when hit by a car. He was admitted to a state school on 9/3/1937, with a diagnosis of mental retardation, introvert personality. There was evidence of cerebral injury. A few years before admission to the school he fell from a house, sustaining a head injury. After that there were perceptible physical and personality changes as he became tremorous, seclusive and unresponsive. Classification: Probably with functional psychosis, schizophrenic reaction—chronic undifferentiated type; also, chronic brain syndrome associated with trauma; also, mental deficiency.

Grandparents

Paternal grandmother (2); died at age 65 years, cause of death unknown. She was described as "unintelligent, shiftless, ugly, disagreeable...fond of bemoaning her fate." Classification: Probable personality disorder.

Maternal grandmother (4); died at age 80 years of apoplexy; described as a "scold." Classification: Possible personality disorder.

Parents

Mother (11), born 1845; at age 70 years described as a former school teacher who was a poor manager and housekeeper, "stubborn and ugly tempered" and had little insight into the proband's illness. Classification: Probable personality disorder.

Aunts and Uncles

Paternal uncle (5); died at age 38 years of pneumonia. He was described by his physician as "reckless...unintelligent" and by others as "blundering, clumsy... never accomplished much." Classification: Possible personality pattern disturbance—inadequate personality.

Paternal aunt (6), died at age 30 years, exact cause of death unknown. About one year before her death she became despondent and took to her bed. She would hardly speak and took no interest in her surroundings. Her legs were doubled up in an unnatural way and she did not seem normal mentally. Classification: Probably with functional psychosis.

Paternal aunt (7), a "bright, smart" girl who committed suicide at age 18 years. Classification: Probably with functional psychosis.

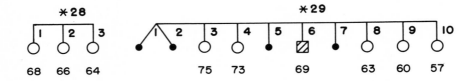

CONTROLS   W S H   4 7

Paternal uncle (8), born 1870. At age 55 years he was a patient at a state mental hospital with a diagnosis of psychosis—senile dementia. He was reportedly "feeble-minded" from birth. Deafness occurred at age 12 years as a result of scarlet fever. The hospital described him as totally deaf, childish, quiet and rather suspicious. Classification: Probably with functional psychosis—schizophrenia.

Siblings

Sister (17), born 1874; died at age 80 years of cancer of the neck and cheek. She was described as of a social disposition and as "nervous and high tempered." Classification: Probable psychoneurotic disorder.

Distant Relatives

Grandniece (58), born 1933. She was interviewed on two different occasions and reacted in an angry, resentful and evasive manner. She was under treatment by a psychiatrist and was apparently making a marginal adjustment with the aid of a tranquilizer prescription and monthly sessions with her psychiatrist. She had an hysterical quality in her voice and manner and reportedly had been treated with ECT. Classification: Probably with functional psychosis.

Family Summary

The proband had a psychotic disorder and a son, a grandniece, two paternal aunts and a paternal uncle probably so. One son was hospitalized with a psychotic reaction to encephalitis. A sister was neurotic. Personality disorders were found in the mother, both grandmothers, a paternal uncle and in the husband of a daughter.

Controls

See family pedigree, person 29.

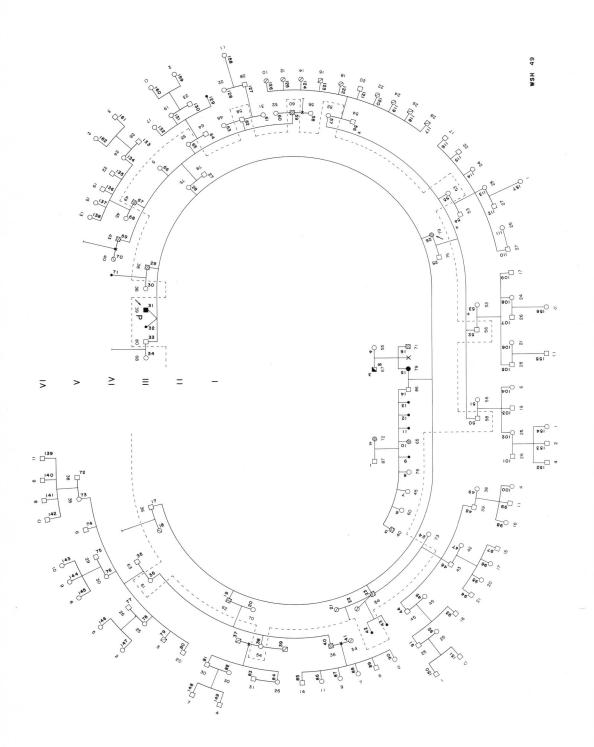

WSH 49

WSH 49: The Proband

The proband (31), born 1886; died at age 39 years of heart dilatation during an epileptic seizure. At age 15 years he became depressed and worried about his health (he dislocated his left shoulder and it was never reduced) and his habit of masturbation. By age 17 years he was so worried and excited that he was admitted to Warren State Hospital on 8/17/1903. He had a total of six admissions to Warren from then until he escaped on 9/9/1917, for a total of 113 months of hospitalization. The original diagnosis at Warren State Hospital was chronic mania; later it was changed to dementia praecox. Hospital notes described him as depressed, confused, suspicious and on a few occasions, violent and impulsive. He had delusions of persecution and auditory hallucinations. Classification: Schizophrenic reaction—paranoid type.

Grandparents

Paternal grandmother (2), born 1804; died at age 72 years of heart trouble. She was described as "quiet and upset nervously" at the time of menopause. Classification: Possible transient situational personality disorder—adjustment reaction of late life.

Maternal grandfather (3), suicided by drowning in a well at age 67 years. At age 65 years he developed a "melancholy pattern" in which he "sat about idle, answers were unintelligible, muttered to himself." Classification: Probably with functional psychosis, involutional psychotic reaction.

Parents

Mother (15), born 1845; died at age 79 years of arteriosclerosis. She was psychotic from age 40 years; she thought the water was poisoned, screamed often, accused her husband of infidelity, had periods of seclusive, apathetic behavior and other periods of noisy disturbance. Classification: Schizophrenic reaction—paranoid type.

Aunts and Uncles

Paternal uncle (5), died at age 40 years in a railroad accident. He had periods of drinking which would last for several days, but had no hallucinatory episodes. Classification: Possible sociopathic personality disturbance—alcoholism (addiction).

Paternal aunt (10), born 1851. At age 65 years she was described as "probably neurotic" as she had spells in which "her arm would fly up and she would scream." In later years she spent much time in bed. Classification: Probable psychoneurotic disorder.

Maternal uncle (16), born 1845; at age 71 years described as a "broken down old man, physically and mentally," and as "very emotional." Classification: Probable chronic brain syndrome of senium.

Siblings

Brother (19), born 1872; died at age 62 years of an obstruction of the common bile duct. He drank "rather large quantities of alcohol" and was "nervous" to the point where it interfered with his work (as a telegrapher) because of a hand tremor. Classification: Probable psychoneurotic disorder.

Brother (23), born 1874; died at age 54 years of "dope and alcohol." He was a dentist who was very successful until he became alcoholic and addicted to narcotics. Classification: Sociopathic personality disturbance—alcoholism (addiction); also, drug addiction.

Sister (26), born 1876; died at age 79 years of cerebral hemorrhage. In "her 70's" she "became queer" and was admitted to a county home with "loss of memory." Classification: Possible chronic brain syndrome of senium.

Brother (29), born 1882. He was a heavy drinker who disappeared at age 38 years after his wife died in childbirth. Classification: Possible sociopathic personality disturbance—alcoholism (addiction).

Nieces and Nephews

Nephew (40), born 1926. He was divorced by his wife because of his alcoholism and was described by family members as "a drunkard." Classification: Sociopathic personality disturbance—alcoholism (addiction).

Nephew (59), born 1902; described as "nervous and a heavy drinker." Classification: Possible psychoneurotic disorder.

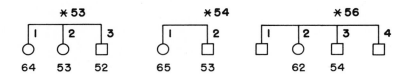

CONTROLS

W S H   4 9

Nephew (67), born 1913; died at age 49 years of subdural hemorrhage after a fall downstairs. He was described as "an occasional drinker" and as "more than an occasional drinker." Classification: Possible sociopathic personality disturbance—alcoholism (addiction).

Nephew (69), born 1919; described as nervous and as a very heavy drinker. Classification: Possible psychoneurotic disorder.

Family Summary

The proband and the mother had psychotic disorders and the maternal grandfather probably so. A sister and a maternal uncle were classified as with chronic brain syndrome of senium. Personality disorders were found in the paternal grandmother, a paternal uncle, two brothers and in two nephews. A paternal aunt, a brother and two nephews were neurotic.

Controls

None noteworthy.

WSH 51

WSH 51: The Proband

The proband (19), born 1888; died at age 72 years of a myocardial infarction and pneumonia at Warren State Hospital. The onset of his psychosis was at age 20 years and he was hospitalized at age 26 years, first for two weeks at a general hospital, then for a week at a state mental hospital; and on 3/6/1914 he was admitted to Warren State Hospital, where he remained until his death 48½ years later. Diagnosis at Warren State Hospital was dementia praecox—hebephrenic type. Symptoms included stereotyped movements, bizarre grimaces, signs with his hands and mutism at times lasting for months. Classification: Schizophrenic reaction—catatonic type.

Grandparents

Maternal grandfather (3), born 1819; died at age 80 years of "general debility." He was described as "an ugly, violent-tempered, domineering old man and a heavy drinker . . . when angry and intoxicated he would threaten to kill his children and attempted to choke them." Classification: Sociopathic personality disturbance—alcoholism (addiction); also, personality trait disturbance—passive-aggressive personality.

Parents

Mother (10), born 1856; died at age 86 years of a cerebral hemorrhage. She was described as a "distinctly neurotic woman . . . inclined to exaggerate and make extravagant statements . . . lacked stability." In conversation she went into great detail and could not remain on the subject. Classification: Probable psychoneurotic disorder.

Aunts and Uncles

Maternal uncle (11), born 1848; died at age 59 years of a skull fracture received in an accidental fall. He was normally pleasant and agreeable but reportedly an alcoholic "of the spree type" until 10 years before his death when he stopped drinking. On one occasion he had delirium tremens, became apprehensive and imagined someone was after him. Classification: Acute brain syndrome associated with alcoholic intoxication; also, sociopathic personality disturbance — alcoholism (addiction).

Maternal uncle (14), born 1859; died an accidental death while intoxicated at age 50 years. He reportedly was drunk every weekend. Classification: Sociopathic personality disturbance — alcoholism (addiction).

Maternal uncle (15), born 1862; died at age 68 years, cause of death unknown. He was described as "a good-for-nothing drunkard" who never supported his family. Classification: Sociopathic personality disturbance — alcoholism (addiction).

Maternal aunt (16), born 1865; died at age 80 years of "old age." She reportedly would drink "all she could get her hands on . . . usually had a bottle in her stocking" and would not hesitate to "ask a man on the street for 25¢ to buy booze." Classification: Sociopathic personality disturbance — alcoholism (addiction).

Siblings

Brother (23), born 1894; died at age 67 years of undetermined natural causes. When interviewed at age 65 years he admitted that he used to drink a great deal and sometimes became mean while doing so. His children reported discord in the home because of his former drinking habits. Classification: Sociopathic personality disturbance — alcoholism (addiction).

Nieces and Nephews

(32) wife of nephew (31), born 1929. She was described as "somewhat anxious" and reportedly "doctors a lot for her nerves." Classification: Probable psychoneurotic reaction — other.

(33) husband of niece (34), born 1901. His wife worked most of their married life to provide the bare necessities; he would use his salary for unnecessary items and wine, leaving the family without food. When interviewed at age 62 years he was sloppily dressed but cooperative, and had worked but a few months of the past five years. He had completed grade 11 and was an electrician by trade. Classification: Sociopathic personality disturbance — alcoholism (addiction).

(38) wife of nephew (37), born 1926. She had a stroke in 1958 which left her with some paralysis and resulted in a personality change. Although never a good housekeeper, she became worse after the stroke and began to leave home for a week or two at a time. She was hospitalized at a general hospital from 9/6/1961 until 9/16/1961 for alcoholism and physical ailments related to her stroke. Classification: Sociopathic personality disturbance — alcoholism (addiction).

(52) wife of nephew (51), born 1943. As a child she lived in an orphanage, then was moved from aunt to aunt and made suicide attempts at 14 and 15 years of age. She made a good adjustment after her marriage and at 19 years of age was described by the interviewer as "easy going, relaxed and with a good sense of humor." Classification: Personality trait disturbance — passive-aggressive personality.

Distant Relatives

Grandnephew (69), born 1949. At age 14 years his uncontrollable temper was of concern to his parents, who asked the interviewer for advice about it. He had on one occasion become so angry that he hit his younger sister on the head with a spatula, causing a scalp wound with profuse bleeding. Classification: Probable personality trait disturbance — passive-aggressive personality.

Family Summary

The proband had the only psychotic disorder in this pedigree. The mother and the wife of a nephew were neurotic. Personality disorders were listed for the maternal grandfather, three maternal uncles, a maternal aunt, one brother, a grandnephew, the husband of a niece and the wives of two nephews.

Controls

See family pedigree, person 37.

Brother (2) of (52), born 1936. His mother died when he was 14 years of age. He always had serious adjustment prob-

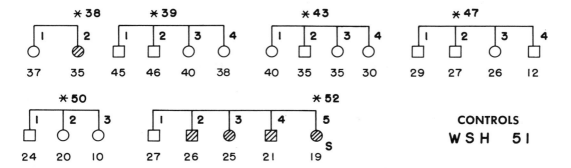

lems. In April, 1953, he was placed in a home for delinquent boys and was in and out of penal institutions continuously after that. At age 26 years he was described as "married young and was supported by his wife." Classification: Sociopathic personality disturbance—antisocial reaction.

Sister (3) of (52), born 1937. Her mother died when she was 13 years of age. At age 16 years she was attending a trade school but had problems of lack of interest in school, obesity (she weighed 250 pounds) and she was domineering with other students and friends. At this time she was referred to a psychiatric clinic; no reports were available. At age 25 years she was hap-

pily married to the 51-year-old father of the illegitimate child she had at age 21 years. Classification: Personality trait disturbance—passive-aggressive personality.

Brother (4) of (52), born 1941. His mother died when he was nine years of age. He then lived in a home for boys, in foster homes and with friends and relatives, but nowhere did he make an adequate adjustment. His work record was irregular. He had a violent temper, was abusive to his wife and was described as "irresponsible and immature." Classification: Sociopathic personality disturbance—antisocial reaction.

See family pedigree, person 52.

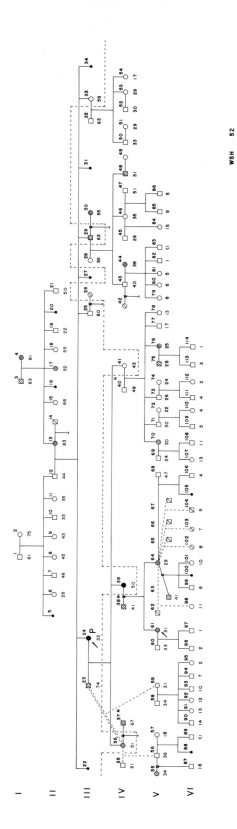

WSH 52

WSH 52: The Proband

The proband (24), born 1892; died at age 33 years of tuberculosis at Warren State Hospital, where she had been since age 22 years. She was considered well until early July, 1914, when she became loud, unruly and could not sleep. She also developed the delusion that her husband would injure her children and kill her mother. On 7/24/1914, she set fire to the house and subsequently was admitted to Warren State Hospital with a diagnosis of dementia praecox. At Warren, catatonic symptoms became pronounced and she became apathetic, stuporous and occasionally mute. Classification: Schizophrenic reaction—catatonic type.

(23) husband of proband (24), born 1888. He was described as "an intelligent man from a degenerate family." After the death of the proband, he fathered a child by his daughter, then remarried and had five children who had to be removed from the home because of parental neglect. At age 74 years he was described by an interviewer as friendly and cooperative, but all information received was furnished by his second wife. Classification: Sociopathic personality disturbance.

Children

Daughter (36), born 1911. At age 15 years she was married one month before the birth of her first child. The marriage was fraudulent as the man used the name of his brother in the marriage certificate. They did not live together as man and wife, but she went home to live with her father and stepmother. Five years later she gave birth to a second child which was fathered by her father. She later remarried but had to support herself by working in a bubble gum factory. At age 51 years she was still employed at the factory, where she was a foreman. She had divorced her husband, after giving him money to establish a home. She inherited a home from an elderly couple whom she had cared for in their later years. Classification: Transient situational personality disorder—adjustment reaction of adolescence.

(37) husband of daughter (36), born 1897. He was a laborer and truck driver who was never able to hold a job or provide for (36). He was also described as a heavy drinker but the drinking was not the cause of his chronic unemployment. Classification: Sociopathic personality disturbance.

(38) husband of daughter (39), born 1908; died at age 41 years of a coronary occlusion. He was a heavy drinker and an alcoholic. Classification: Sociopathic personality disturbance—alcoholism (addiction).

Daughter (39), born 1912. She was placed in a foster home when her mother was institutionalized; later she returned to live with her father and stepmother. On 3/13/1957, she was referred to a Portland, Oregon, psychiatrist for psychiatric evaluation as the welfare commission had observed peculiarities in her behavior in their contacts with her in regard to obtaining public assistance. It was the psychiatrist's impression that she had a schizophrenic reaction of chronic undifferentiated type, with somatic delusions and paranoid ideation. When interviewed at age 50 years she vacillated from complete cooperation to lack of acknowledgment of a question. When she did attempt a reply, she couldn't make up her mind as to an answer. Classification: Schizophrenic reaction—chronic undifferentiated type.

Grandchildren

(55) wife of grandson (56), born 1928; at age 34 years described as "a heavy drinker—steps out constantly." She had custody of their son. Classification: Sociopathic personality disturbance.

Granddaughter (61), born 1931. She was a patient at a state mental hospital from 8/2/1940 until 1/1/1941, with complaints of visual disturbance and school failure. Her oculist had diagnosed her sight problem as an hysterical loss of vision. She received psychotherapy and was not returned from a visit to her father on 1/1/1941; her condition had improved under therapy. As an adolescent she had an episode of paralysis of one arm, which later disappeared. As an adult she made a satisfactory adjustment, although she was described as high strung and nervous. Classification: Psychoneurotic disorder—conversion reaction.

(63) husband of granddaughter (64), born 1911. He married (64) when she feared

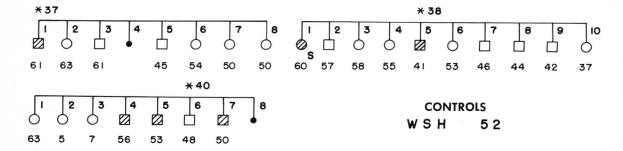

CONTROLS

W S H   5 2

she was pregnant by (62), which was the case. He was never able to support (64) because of his gambling and drinking. Classification: Possible personality disorder.

Granddaughter (64), born 1933. At age 29 years she was interviewed and proved to be cooperative. She was described as very obese due to a "glandular balance" and was under a physician's care for the condition; the obesity did not interfere with her work as a licensed practical nurse. Four of her nine children were illegitimate, three of whom were adopted and the fourth was placed in a foster home. Of the remaining five children, two died in infancy, one was adopted, one was in a foster home and the youngest lived with her. Classification: Sociopathic personality disturbance—antisocial reaction.

Granddaughter (70), born 1931; died at age 20 years of a crushed chest and fractured skull received in an automobile accident. She was described as "nervous—worried frequently." Classification: Probable psychoneurotic reaction.

(75) husband of granddaughter (76), born 1934. At age 28 years he was described as severely crippled from polio, and as an epileptic who had a "vicious temper" during his attacks. Classification: Personality trait disturbance—emotionally unstable personality.

Granddaughter (76), born 1937; described at age 25 years as "nervous, a worrier and very thin." Classification: Possible psychoneurotic disorder.

Grandparents

Maternal grandfather (3), born 1833; described as always "peculiar." At age 83

years he was described as "forgetful." Classification: Possible personality disorder.

Maternal grandmother (4), born 1826; died at age 81 years of pneumonia. She was described as "a distinctly neurotic, excitable woman who quarreled constantly with her husband." Classification: Psychoneurotic reaction—other.

Parents

Mother (13), born 1868; died at age 83 years of cancer of the lungs. She was described as "lacking in mental balance" and by her physician as "pugnacious, dishonest and hysterical." Classification: Psychoneurotic disorder—conversion reaction.

Aunts and Uncles

Maternal aunt (17), died at age 52 years, nine days after an operation for a tumor. She reportedly was of an "excitable disposition." Classification: Possible personality disorder.

Siblings

Brother (29), born 1898; described at age 63 years as very odd and eccentric, bordering on mental illness. Classification: Probable personality pattern disturbance—schizoid personality.

(30) wife of brother (29), born 1908. In 1920 she was committed to a correctional school on a charge of incorrigibility. In 1927 she was sent from there to a state school. She had an IQ of 54. She completed the vocational training course there and was

discharged on 7/11/1947. Classification: Sociopathic personality disturbance.

Nieces and Nephews

(44) wife of nephew (43), born 1925. At age 38 years she had many somatic complaints and was extremely nervous. Classification: Psychoneurotic disorder.

Nephew (48), born 1930. He was described as "a bum," an "odd ball" and as mentally retarded. He had difficulty holding a job and was last known to be traveling with a circus as a roustabout. He had been arrested several times for a variety of offenses, including burglary. Classification: Sociopathic personality disturbance—antisocial reaction.

Family Summary

The proband and a daughter had psychotic disorders. The mother, the maternal grandmother, three granddaughters and the wife of a nephew were neurotic. Personality disorders were found in a daughter, a granddaughter, the maternal grandfather, a mater-nal aunt, a brother, a nephew, the proband's husband, the husbands of two daughters, the wife of a grandson, the husbands of two granddaughters and in the wife of a brother.

Controls

See family pedigree, person (37).

Sister (1) of (38), born 1900; died at age 60 years of a compound fracture of the skull. The physician who signed the death certificate stated "one can only surmise whether it was accidental or suicide." Classification: Possibly with functional psychosis.

See family pedigree, person (38).

Brother (4) of (40), born 1906. At age 56 years he was described as "probably an alcoholic." Classification: Sociopathic personality disturbance—alcoholism (addiction).

Brother (5) of (40), born 1909. At age 53 years he was described as an alcoholic. Classification: Sociopathic personality disturbance—alcoholism (addiction).

Brother (7) of (40), born 1912. At age 50 years he was described as an alcoholic who had a history of arrests. Classification: Sociopathic personality disturbance—alcoholism (addiction).

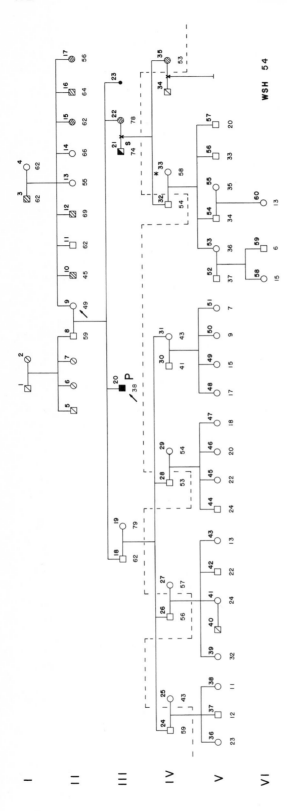

WSH 54

WSH 54: The Proband

The proband (20), born 1882; died at age 38 years of ulcers of the stomach at Farview State Hospital, Waymart, Pennsylvania. He had little education and worked as a track layer in a mine until his aggressive behavior caused him to lose his job. His first symptoms of bad temper and aggression appeared about two years before his hospitalization at Warren State Hospital on 10/14/1911. While at Warren State Hospital he had periods of screaming alternating with periods of withdrawal and melancholia. He became very suspicious and seclusive and was very abusive to doctors and attendants. Diagnosis at Warren State Hospital was dementia praecox—paranoid type. He was transferred to Farview State Hospital on 9/25/1917 as a dangerous patient and remained there until his death. Classification: Schizophrenic reaction—paranoid type.

Grandparents

Maternal grandfather (3), died at age 62 years of ulcers of the stomach; described as "a short-sighted, stubborn man who never took advice from others." Classification: Possible personality pattern disturbance—inadequate personality.

Parents

Mother (9), born 1859; died at age 49 years of epilepsy. She developed convulsions at age eight years. The attacks were ascribed to some camphor she had eaten. Her next seizures were at age 16 years, with no known precipitating cause. The intervals between seizures decreased until she had them about three times a month. Her mind began to deteriorate and she was hospitalized at Warren State Hospital in 1902 for about one year. While hospitalized she was confused and deluded. Her husband cared for her at home the last five years of her life. Classification: Chronic brain syndrome associated with convulsive disorder, with psychotic reaction.

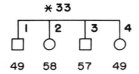

CONTROLS
WSH 54

Aunts and Uncles

Maternal uncle (10), died at age 45 years of alcoholism. Classification: Sociopathic personality disturbance — alcoholism (addiction).

Maternal uncle (12), born 1844; died at age 69 years of general debility caused by over-drinking. The last few months of his life he was very feeble and childish. Classification: Sociopathic personality disturbance — alcoholism (addiction).

Maternal aunt (15), died at age 62 years, cause of death unknown. She reportedly "complained and lamented a good deal" after her husband's death and her physical health failed. Classification: Possible personality pattern disturbance — inadequate personality.

Maternal uncle (16), born 1851; at 64 years of age described as a farm laborer who spent money impulsively and had very poor judgment. Classification: Possible personality pattern disturbance — inadequate personality.

Maternal aunt (17), born 1859; was age 56 years and well at last information. Until the time of menopause she had sick headaches accompanied by nausea. The headaches usually occurred at the time of menstrual periods. Classification: Possible psychoneurotic disorder.

Siblings

(21) husband of sister (22), born 1883;

died at age 74 years of a self-inflicted bullet wound. He was separated from his wife at the time of his death and had lived with another woman for four or five years. He was despondent before his death. Classification: Probably with functional psychosis.

Sister (22), born 1885; died at age 78 years, cause unknown. She was interviewed and described as friendly and helpful although she suffered from severe headaches. Classification: Possible psychoneurotic disorder.

Nieces and Nephews

Niece (35), born 1911; described at age 53 years as "always nervous — works like a horse." Classification: Possible psychoneurotic disorder.

Family Summary

The proband had a psychotic disorder and the husband of a sister probably so. The mother was hospitalized with a psychotic reaction to a convulsive disorder. A maternal aunt, a niece and a sister were possibly neurotic. Personality disorders were found in the maternal grandfather, three maternal uncles and in one maternal aunt.

Controls

None noteworthy.

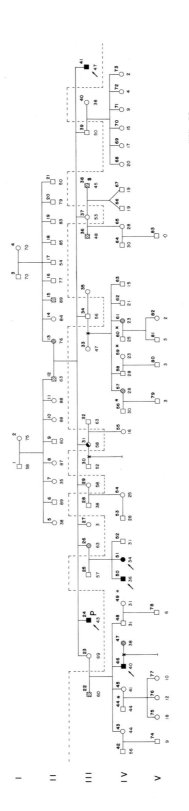

WSH 55

WSH 55: The Proband

The proband (24), born 12/21/1895; died at age 57 years at Warren State Hospital of pneumonia. He was reportedly "always dull." At age 16 years he developed "peculiar ideas" in that he became confused, imagined the devil was in his room and insisted on carrying a knife. He was admitted to Warren State Hospital on 6/13/1914, with a diagnosis of dementia praecox. Symptoms at admission were destructiveness, diminished affect, delusions and fragmentary and neologistic speech. He remained at Warren, with little improvement, until his death. Classification: Schizophrenic reaction — paranoid type.

Parents

Father (12), born 1867; died at age 63 years of cancer. He was described as "intelligent and thrifty but quick-tempered and impatient." His treatment of his children was reportedly "quite brutal." Classification: Probable personality disorder.

Mother (13), born 1871; died at age 76 years of a cerebral hemorrhage. She was described as "a weak rather inefficient woman . . . talked in nervous agitated whispers . . . a fussy disposition." She accused her husband of infidelity and was firmly convinced that his abusive treatment of the proband caused the proband's mental illness. Classification: Probable personality disorder.

Aunts and Uncles

Maternal uncle (15), died at age 89 years of senility. Classification: Chronic brain syndrome of senium.

Siblings

(22) husband of sister (23), born 1889; died at age 60 years of a cerebral hemorrhage. He never provided adequately for his family and lived away from home half of the time. He was described as "never paid a bill . . . was easily hurt . . . and always had a guilty conscience." Classification: Personality disorder.

Sister (26), born 1898; described as "compulsively clean." Classification: Possible personality disorder — compulsive personality.

Sister (31), born 1905. She was interviewed twice at age 58 years and was described as extremely talkative; she expressed a firm belief that demons inhabited the bodies of psychotics and alcoholics and claimed that she had the power to heal by the "laying on of the hands." She talked continuously throughout her lengthy interviews and spoke frantically of the "power of God." Classification: Probably with functional psychosis.

(36) husband of sister (37), born 1892; died at age 48 years of accidental carbon monoxide poisoning. He was an alcoholic and was drunk at the time of his death. Classification: Sociopathic personality disturbance — alcoholism (addiction).

(38) husband of sister (37), born 1902; died at age 45 years of suicide by carbon monoxide poisoning. He suicided after an eight-day argument with his wife. He was described as a "very heavy drinker" and was considered alcoholic. Classification: Sociopathic personality disturbance — alcoholism (addiction).

Brother (41), born 1914. He began drinking at age 13 years and, except for the time spent in the army and as a prisoner of war, drank regularly after that, sometimes as much as a gallon of wine or a pint of whiskey at a time. In 1947, he became apprehensive and fearful for his life (believed a gang was after him and that hunters were shooting at him rather than at game). He later developed auditory hallucinations, including homosexual accusations, and depression of mood. He was hospitalized as an alcoholic from 7/11/1949 to 7/20/1949, and was admitted to Warren State Hospital on 10/23/1949, with a diagnosis of dementia praecox, paranoid type, and psychosis due to alcohol, acute hallucinosis. He was discharged from Warren State Hospital on 3/26/1950, but was readmitted on 7/7/1952, still suffering from alcoholism and auditory hallucinations. Between commitments he had been arrested several times for disorderly conduct, drunkenness and passing bad checks. Diagnosis at second admission to Warren was paranoid schizophrenia with secondary alcoholism. He was transferred to a Veterans Hospital

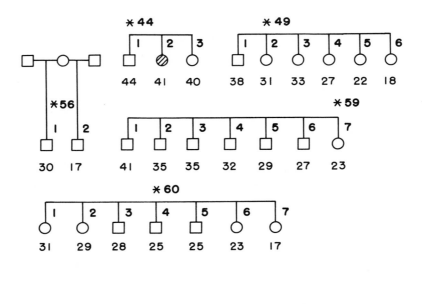

CONTROLS   **W S H   5 5**

Nieces and Nephews

Nephew (46), born 1920. He was unemployed since 1950 (he had worked as a factory laborer) and was divorced in 1953 because of his alcoholism and "inability to handle everyday problems." On 5/12/1954, he was admitted to a state mental hospital because of his excessive use of alcohol, belligerent behavior and nervousness. At the hospital he was delusional, suspicious, had fixed ideas and was diagnosed as a paranoid schizophrenic. At age 40 years he was on leave from the hospital and living with his mother. He was described as "aggressive, incontinent" and a "real skid row alcoholic." Classification: Schizophrenic reaction—paranoid type.

(47) wife of nephew (46), born 1922; described as a "heavy drinker...a good match for (46)...they were both alike." Classification: Sociopathic personality disturbance—alcoholism (addiction).

Nephew (50), born 1925; completed one year of college and worked as a laborer, when employed. While serving in the navy during World War II he reportedly sustained a head injury (hit on the head by a falling coconut). His father, a pediatrician, reported that he was afflicted with acute catatonia since his Navy discharge on 5/15/1946. On March 21, 1949, he began psychotherapy and in 1954 he was admitted to a Veterans Hospital where he was at age 36 years. Diagnosis at the Veterans Hospital and classification: Schizophrenic reaction—catatonic type.

Niece (51), born 1927. She became mentally ill during her first year of college. She was hospitalized at a general hospital on 3/23/1946, suffering from schizophrenia. She was transferred to another hospital where she was at age 34 years. She was preoccupied and assaultive during her entire illness. Diagnosis at the hospital and classification: Schizophrenic reaction—hebephrenic type.

Niece (57), born 1933; described herself as "high strung." Interviewer's notes corroborated her description. Classification: Probable psychoneurotic disorder.

on 1/9/1961 and was still there at age 47 years. Classification: Schizophrenic reaction—paranoid type.

Niece (61), born 1938; described as "exceptionally nervous" by her family. She was somewhat reluctant to cooperate in an interview and "appeared very nervous." Classification: Probable psychoneurotic disorder.

Family Summary

The proband, a brother, two nephews and a niece had psychotic disorders and one sister was probably psychotic. The father and the mother, a sister, the husbands of three sisters and the wife of a nephew had personality disorders or probably or possibly so. A maternal uncle was classified as chronic brain syndrome of senium and two nieces were probably neurotic.

Controls

Sister (2) of (44), born 1919. As a child she was very nervous and often refused to eat. Her siblings had asked her to see a psychiatrist because of her nervousness; they "don't know how her husband takes it." Her children often came to the aunt's home in tears because of their mother's behavior. Classification: Personality trait disturbance—emotionally unstable personality.

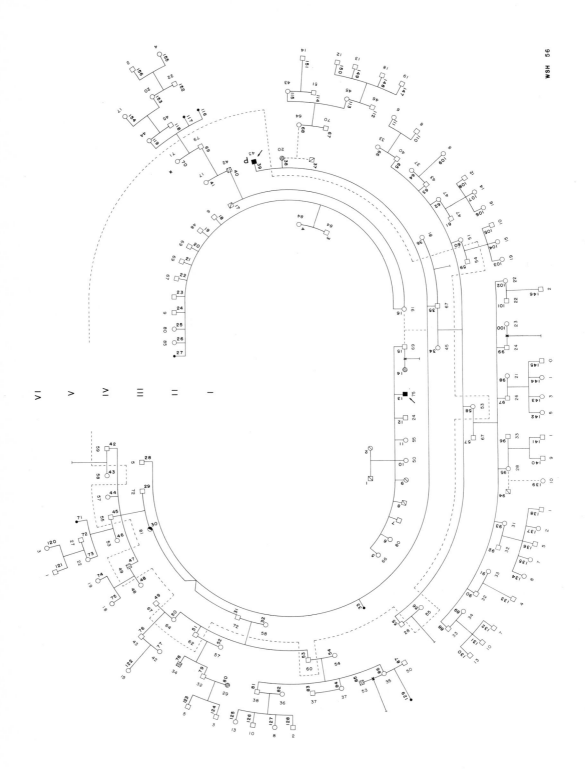

WSH 56

WSH 56: The Proband

The proband (39), born 1883; died at age 43 years at Warren State Hospital, of acute dilation of the heart. He was considered normal and industrious until age 27 years, when he had a nervous breakdown. At admission to Warren State Hospital four years later he had delusions of influence and persecution and visual hallucinations. Diagnosis was dementia praecox, paranoid type, and he remained at Warren, unimproved, until death. Classification: Schizophrenic reaction—paranoid type.

Parents

(14) first wife of father (15); deserted (15) and went west to Minnesota with another man as his common-law wife. Classification: Probable sociopathic personality disorder.

Aunts and Uncles

Paternal uncle (13), born 1826; died at age 75 years, cause of death unknown. He was hospitalized at a state mental hospital at ages 26, 34 and 41 years, suffering from "recurring episodes of excited, mischievous behavior and possibly some depression." Classification: With functional psychosis, probably manic-depressive reaction—other.

Siblings

Sister (30), born 1872; died at age 81 years of a coronary occlusion. She reportedly had a "nervous breakdown" at age 48 years but was not hospitalized for treatment. Classification: Probably with functional psychosis, involutional psychotic reaction.

Sister (38), born 1880; died at age 20 years of measles. She was described as "a nice person" and as "wild." Her death was reported as a possible suicide by one family member. Classification: Sociopathic personality disturbance.

Maternal half brother (40), born 1863; died at age 42 years of an accidental death. He was an alcoholic who, on one occasion, had delirium tremens. Classification: Socio-

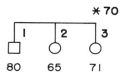

CONTROLS

WSH 56

pathic personality disturbance—alcoholism (addiction).

Nieces and Nephews

Nephew (47), born 1913; described as having "moody periods." Classification: Possible psychoneurotic disorder.

Distant Relatives

Grandnephew (78), born 1928. He was described as a "heavy drinker, possibly an alcoholic . . . didn't care to work at one job very long—seemed to become bored." He reportedly felt that his parents favored his brother although this was denied by the parents. Classification: Personality pattern disturbance—inadequate personality.

(80) wife of grandnephew (79), born 1933; she had consulted a doctor for "a mild nervous condition." Classification: Psychoneurotic disorder—anxiety reaction.

(85) husband of grandniece (86), born 1909; reportedly an alcoholic. Classification: Sociopathic personality disturbance—alcoholism (addiction).

Family Summary

The proband and a paternal uncle had psychotic disorders and a sister probably so. A nephew and the wife of a grandnephew were neurotic and a sister, a half brother, a grandnephew, the husband of a grandniece and the first wife of the father were classified as with personality disorders.

Controls

None noteworthy.

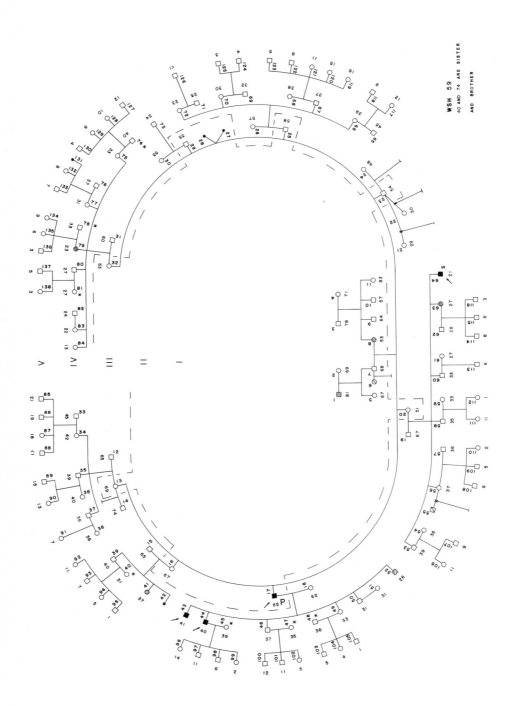

WSH 59
40 AND 74 ARE SISTER
AND BROTHER

WSH 59: The Proband

The proband (17), born 1895; died at age 65 years of coronary thrombosis. He was admitted to Warren State Hospital on 3/30/1914, with a psychosis characterized by transitory periods of excitement, looseness of thought, auditory hallucinations, persecutory delusions and diminished affect. Onset of symptoms was two weeks before admission and a diagnosis of dementia praecox was made. He was released from the hospital six months after admission and was never hospitalized again. He later married and became a prosperous farmer with no further psychotic episodes. Classification: Schizophrenic reaction—catatonic type.

Children

Son (43), born 1919. He was hospitalized twice, once from 7/31/1936 until 9/16/1937, and again from 9/22/1939 until 10/30/1941. Diagnosis at the first admission was dementia praecox, and was schizophrenia, hebephrenic type, at the second. His symptoms, which persisted after his release from the hospital were seclusiveness, irrelevancy in conversation, poor judgment in purchases and eating at odd hours. On occasion he became so disturbed that his family considered returning him to the hospital, but he improved spontaneously and could be kept at home. Classification: Schizophrenic reaction—paranoid type.

Son (44), born 1920. He was hospitalized at a state mental hospital from 8/16/1944 until 5/8/1945, with a diagnosis of dementia praecox, paranoid type. At admission he was demanding, belligerent, irritable, showed a marked loss of affect, his emotional reactions were unpredictable and he was subject to short periods of catatonic stupor. Shortly after release from the hospital he married a widow with two children. He was steadily employed and considered a good, reliable worker after that. At one time during a critical illness he became depressed, but as his physical condition improved his depression left him. Classification: Schizophrenic reaction—paranoid type.

Son (52), born 1934. He was described as "single, read a great deal and was not very active socially." He had recurrent stomach ulcers beginning at age 17 years. Classification: Probable personality pattern disturbance—schizoid personality.

Grandparents

Paternal grandfather (1), born 1832; died at age 81 years of a "general senile breakdown." He was normal until a few years before his death, when he began to wander from home, his conversation became rambling and, during the last year of life, it was necessary for him to have an attendant at night. Classification: Chronic brain syndrome of senium.

Parents

Mother (8), born 1867; died at age 53 years of cirrhosis of the liver. She was "weary and weak" and "flustery" to the point of nervousness, although she was suffering from anemia. Later descriptions seemed to discount the nervousness and indicated that she was in normal mental health. Classification: Probable psychoneurotic disorder.

Nieces and Nephews

Niece (41), born 1923. She was seen weekly by a psychiatrist for a six-month period at age 18 years because of "tension and loss of a boy friend." She was interviewed in 1960 and described as "very anxious" and very dependent on her parents. She spoke very freely of her former "blue spells" and suicidal thoughts. Classification: Psychoneurotic disorder—anxiety reaction.

Niece (63), born 1933. She had a "nervous breakdown" at age 21 years, but was not hospitalized. She developed severe persistent allergies at age 19 years. Classification: Probable psychoneurotic disorder.

Nephew (64), born 1939, a patient at a state mental hospital with a diagnosis of schizophrenic reaction, paranoid type. He was admitted on 11/7/1958, because of agitation, distorted sense of values and irrational, unpredictable behavior. He

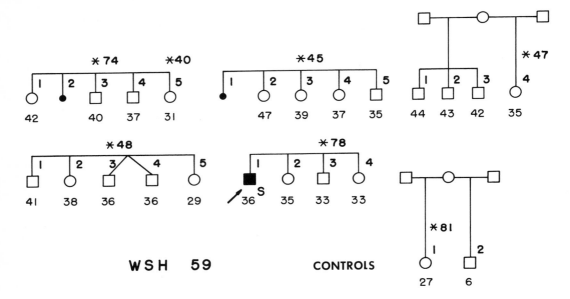

WSH   59   **CONTROLS**

attributed his behavior to the dictates of God. Symptoms began five years prior to hospitalization. While hospitalized he had suicidal thoughts and made attempts to follow them through. Classification: Schizophrenic reaction—paranoid type.

Niece (79), born 1932. In 1960 she received medical attention for tenseness and insomnia, as well as for a kidney infection. When interviewed her affect was somewhat flat. Classification: Transient situational personality disorder—adult situational reaction.

Family Summary

The proband, two sons and a nephew had psychotic disorders. Another son had a probable personality disorder, as did a niece. The mother and two nieces were neurotic. The paternal grandfather was classified as chronic brain syndrome of senium.

Controls

Brother (1) of (78), born 1925. At age 36 years he was a patient at a Veterans Administration Hospital, with a diagnosis of schizophrenic reaction, catatonic type—chronic and convulsive state, grand mal. He failed to make an adjustment after entering high school and left school in the tenth grade to enter the United States Navy. He "fell" overboard from his ship on 12/13/1944, after making several verbal threats of suicide and after having expressed paranoid ideas. He was hospitalized almost continuously after that, with brief unsuccessful stays at home. Classification: Schizophrenic reaction—catatonic type.

WSH 61: The Proband

The proband (46), born 1882; died at age 74 years of myocardial degeneration. She was admitted to Warren State Hospital on 12/2/1913, with a diagnosis of dementia praecox. The onset of the psychosis occurred in August, 1913, following a hospitalization for labor inducement because of uremic convulsions. She was violent, restless and noisy and aurally and visually hallucinated. She later developed delusions of poisoning. Discharge from Warren was on 10/31/1914. She made an adequate adjustment after leaving the hospital and was never again hospitalized for a mental disorder. Classification: Schizophrenic reaction—paranoid type.

Grandparents

Maternal grandfather (3), born 1810; died at age 84 years of grippe and pneumonia. He was reportedly a "very heavy drinker" who had a very unpleasant disposition. While drinking "he would become very ugly...many times chased his wife and family out of the house with a butcher knife." Classification: Sociopathic personality disturbance—alcoholism (addiction).

Parents

Father (10), born 1839; died at age 63 years of apoplexy. He was described as "quite content to let his wife do the work and support the family while he sat and talked and read." He was a "steady drinker ...a great braggart...conceited." He had an infected leg, perhaps a syphilitic infection, which prevented his working. Classification: Personality pattern disturbance—inadequate personality.

Aunts and Uncles

Paternal uncle (6), died at age 55 years of Bright's disease. He was "a barber who drank too heavily to follow up the trade regularly." Each time his children gave him money to start a business again "he would get to drinking, get into debt, and have to give up the shop." Classification: Socio-pathic personality disturbance—alcoholism (addiction).

Maternal uncle (16), born 1845; suicided by shooting himself at age 40 years. He was described by one informant as "one of the queerest men I ever met." He shot himself while intoxicated after his wife refused to go out with him. Classification: Probably with functional psychosis, schizophrenic reaction.

Maternal aunt (17), born 1850; died at Warren State Hospital at age 62 years of cancer. She had "a very hard life" as she was married twice, had eight children, and neither husband provided for the family. In 1888 she suffered a fall and was unconscious for 10 days, but no other mental symptoms were observed at that time. About five years later she developed vague ideas of persecution. The symptoms persisted and gradually became more severe until, shortly before admission to Warren State Hospital on 12/14/1898, she had a definite psychotic break and was hallucinated, emotional, noisy and often refused to talk. She was taken home on 5/10/1899, but returned to the hospital on 1/19/1900. Diagnosis was acute mania. Her condition remained stationary and she remained at Warren State Hospital until her daughters took her home one week before death to care for her in her terminal illness. Classification: Schizophrenic reaction.

Siblings

(21) husband of sister (22), born 1864; died at age 25 years of an accidental death while intoxicated. Classification: Possible sociopathic personality disturbance—alcoholism (addiction).

Sister (22), born 1865; died at age 74 years, cause of death unknown. Her physician reported that she showed a slight neurotic tendency. Classification: Possible psychoneurotic reaction.

(23) husband of sister (22), born 1858; died at age 81 years of apoplexy. He had a "nervous breakdown" in 1922 and was hospitalized for observation in a general hospital. Classification: Possible psychoneurotic reaction.

Sister (25), born 1867; died at age 52 years at Warren State Hospital of tuberculosis of the lungs. As a child she was of

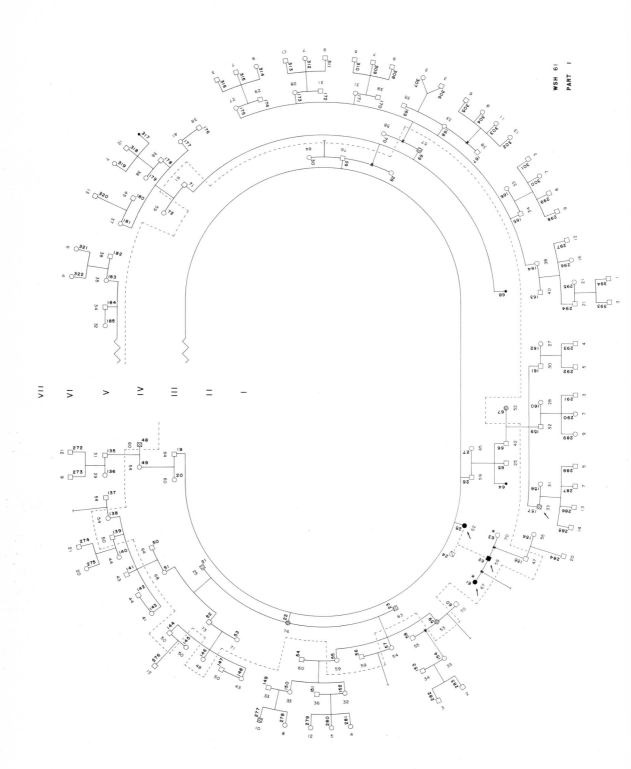

WSH 61
PART I

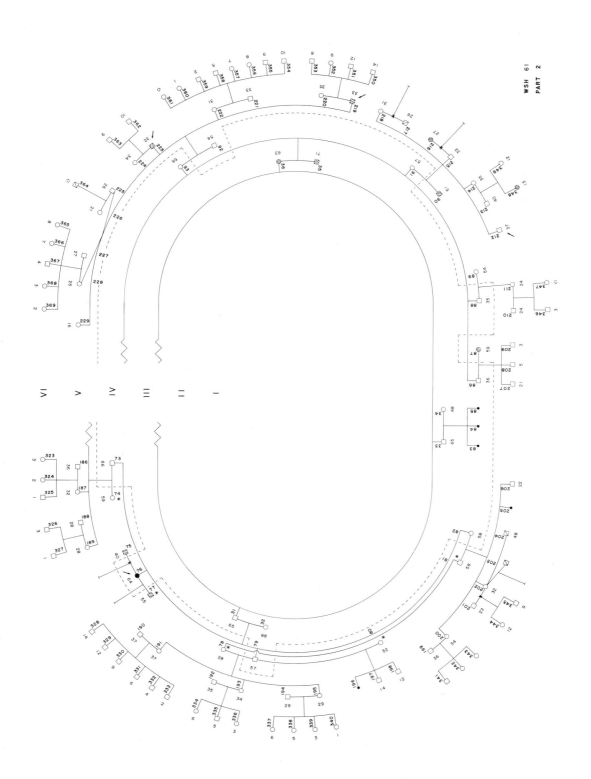

WSH 61
PART 2

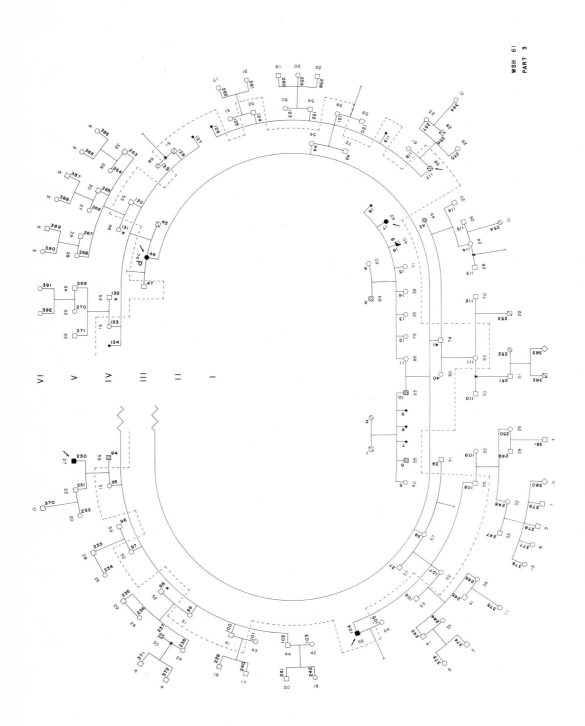

WSH 61
PART 3

average ability but would frequently run away from school. At age 20 years she had an illegitimate child but refused the father's marriage proposal. Ten years later she converted to Catholicism and became deeply religious. From then on she devoted all her time and attention to the church. She was admitted to Warren State Hospital on 11/27/1907, with a diagnosis of dementia praecox. About two years before admission she became more irritable and unreasonable than was ordinary for her and about one week before admission she became markedly deranged: she was noisy, excited and had numerous delusions. She remained at Warren State Hospital until her death. While hospitalized she developed a "marked paranoid tendency" and feelings of superiority and self-assurance. Classification: Schizophrenic reaction—paranoid type.

(35) husband of sister (36), born 1866; died at age 71 years of cirrhosis of the liver with alcoholism as a contributing factor. Classification: Sociopathic personality disturbance—alcoholism (addiction).

Sister (36), born 1875; died at age 63 years of rheumatic heart disease. She was described as "the most neurotic member of this fraternity"; however, her home conditions were considered to be at least partially responsible for her neurosis. Classification: Transient situational personality disturbance—adult situational reaction.

(42) wife of brother (41), born 1911. She cooperated with the interviewer only to verify the date of her husband's death. Neighbors consider her "queer" but not abnormal. Classification: Possible personality disorder.

Nieces and Nephews

(48) husband of niece (49), born 1900. He has changed jobs often and at one time was considered an alcoholic. He remarried after the death of (49) and became "more dependable and better adjusted." Classification: Sociopathic personality disturbance—alcoholism (addiction).

Niece (59), born 1907. She was described as "always somewhat nervous and excitable." She was hospitalized at a general hospital for four days in 1960 because of an "hysterical attack," although the hospital records stated the diagnosis as "acute heart attack—angina." Classification: Possible psychoneurotic reaction—other.

(61) wife of nephew (62), born 1892; died at age 67 years at Warren State Hospital of uremia. Her marriage lasted only a short time. At age 36 years she developed persecutory delusions which persisted and led to her admission to a general hospital on 5/11/1938. She was forcibly transferred to Warren State Hospital on 6/29/1938, where she remained until death. Diagnosis at Warren was paranoid condition. Prominent in her symptomatology were delusions that organized political gangs and religious organizations were persecuting her. Classification: Schizophrenic reaction—paranoid type.

Nephew (62), born 1887; died at age 59 years at Warren State Hospital, of acute cardiac dilation. He was a "jolly, good-natured, competent" youth who became very hot tempered and unpleasant in his early twenties. He began to think he could converse with dead people, accused people of poisoning him, and greatly exaggerated his self-importance. He was admitted to Warren State Hospital on 12/16/1914 and, because laboratory tests indicated syphilis, was diagnosed as general paralysis of the insane and paresis. However, further laboratory findings in 1922 and 1927 did not suggest syphilitic infection, yet he retained his symptoms until death. Classification: Schizophrenic reaction—paranoid type.

(67) wife of nephew (66), born 1908. She was described as neurotic in her son's Warren State Hospital case history and reportedly received psychiatric aid in 1947. Classification: Psychoneurotic reaction—other.

Nephew (69), born 1890; died at age 57 years of apoplexy. He was described as headstrong and quick tempered and as "rather wild." In 1917 he reportedly drank "too much for a boy his age." In 1939 he was divorced by his first wife because of his alcoholism. Classification: Sociopathic personality disturbance—alcoholism (addiction).

(75) husband of niece (76), born 1876. His whereabouts were unknown after age 40 years when he was divorced by (76) for his alcoholism; they were married but three months. Classification: Sociopathic personality disturbance—alcoholism (addiction).

Niece (76), born 1896. Normally she was a calm, self-assured person who was strong willed, sociable and friendly. Her first episode of mental illness developed in April, 1936, when she became overly active and elated and became careless about her home. She was not violent but was noisy and denudative. She was admitted to a Chicago hospital and shortly transferred to a state mental hospital on 4/18/1936, where she was diagnosed as manic-depressive reaction, manic type. She was discharged as recovered on 12/11/1936. A second hospitalization, to another state hospital, followed and was preceded by the appearance of psychotic symptoms for a period of four weeks, when she became fanatically religious and imagined that she was to have an immaculate conception. She also imagined that she and her husband were sister and brother rather than wife and husband and wanted to become a nun. She was not violent or suicidal but was denudative. Diagnosis was again manic-depressive psychosis, manic type, and she was discharged as recovered on 1/28/1947. At age 64 years she was interested and cooperative and appeared fully recovered. She reported unhospitalized psychotic episodes in 1941 and in 1952 and another hospitalization in 1950, which could not be verified. Classification: Schizophrenic reaction — catatonic type.

(77) husband of niece (76), born 1905. He began to drink heavily in 1935. After that he was divorced twice because of his alcoholism and married a third time to a wife who reportedly drank with him. Classification: Sociopathic personality disturbance — alcoholism (addiction).

(87) wife of nephew (86), born 1901. She was described as "very nervous." Classification: Psychoneurotic reaction — other.

(90) husband of niece (91), born 1902; died at age 51 years of coronary heart disease. He and (91) had numerous separations. He served one year in a workhouse for theft. Classification: Sociopathic personality disturbance.

(94) husband of niece (95), born 1902. He was treated in 1956 for a "nervous condition" which he described as diagnosed as an "endocrine imbalance." Classification: Probable psychoneurotic reaction.

Nephew (104), born 1896; died at age 58 years of an acute coronary occlusion. He was described as a "plodder" who was subject to nightmares and sleepwalking. He was hospitalized four times at Warren State Hospital from 1946 until 1954. Each admission was preceded by a week of overactive and overtalkative behavior, with religious delusions of a grandiose and bizarre nature and hallucinations. Affect at each psychotic episode was inappropriate — either flat or euphoric. Behavior ranged from uncooperative to combative and destructive. He responded well to electroconvulsive therapy at each hospitalization. Diagnosis at the first hospitalization was unclassified. At subsequent hospitalizations there was no agreement on diagnosis, although clinic directors diagnosed him as schizophrenic. Classification: Schizophrenic reaction — paranoid type.

Nephew (117), born 1902; died at age 58 years of a coronary occlusion. He was hospitalized in 1955 at a city psychiatric hospital with a diagnosis of global aphasia — etiology unknown. Classification: Possible chronic brain syndrome of senium.

Distant Relatives

Grandnephew (157), born 1927. He had a long history of poor mental health, including a sporadic work record, a "somewhat nomadic existence," alcoholism, sexual deviation and severe anxiety. He was first admitted to a state mental hospital on 7/21/1953. He was diagnosed as psychoneurosis, anxiety state, in a passive-aggressive personality, and released on 10/20/1953 as improved. He returned regularly for outpatient psychotherapy until he had a recurrence of anxiety symptoms and reentered the hospital on 5/10/1954. He was discharged on 11/18/1954, after receiving carbon dioxide treatments and psychotherapy. Classification: Sociopathic personality disturbance — alcoholism (addiction) and sexual deviation; also, psychoneurotic disorder — anxiety reaction.

Grandnephew (212), born 1923. His early school life was punctuated with stealing and truancy; he once maliciously killed two of his household pets. As an adult he threatened to murder family friends, molested young children and expressed a desire to have intercourse with his grandmother, mother and sister. Prior to his first admission to a state mental hospital he spent at least five months in correctional institutions for juveniles. When he was admitted on 12/16/1938, his past medical history and symptomatology led to a diagnosis of psychosis with epidemic encephalitis. He escaped from the hospital on 1/1/1946, spent two years in the army and received an honorable discharge in January, 1950. He was soon recalled to active duty but was hospitalized at an army hospital with a diagnosis of schizophrenia. He was described as "vague, confused . . . marked flattening of affect." He was discharged in March, 1951, and worked sporadically as a laborer until his second admission to the state mental hospital on 8/22/1955, with a diagnosis of chronic brain syndrome with epidemic encephalitis. He remained hospitalized. Classification: Chronic brain syndrome associated with epidemic encephalitis, with psychotic reaction.

(216) wife of grandnephew (215), born 1932. She was described as "extremely nervous, always on the go." Her divorce was attributed to her hyperactivity. Classification: Psychoneurotic reaction — other.

Grandnephew (219), born 1926. He was admitted to a state mental hospital on 9/24/1959, suffering from depression, physical maladies and extreme nervousness. He was diagnosed as psychoneurotic depressive reaction and discharged as improved on 11/17/1959. Poor physical health and a cold family atmosphere were listed as factors contributing to his mental disorder. Classification: Psychoneurotic disorder — depressive reaction.

Grandnephew (223), born 1930. He entered a state mental hospital on 12/20/1961 because of drug addiction following a series of operations for intestinal disorders which appeared to have had a psychosomatic origin. Classification: Sociopathic personality disturbance — drug addiction.

Grandnephew (230), born 1935. He reacted to several work lay-offs beginning in December, 1960, by becoming withdrawn and depressed. He became preoccupied with bizarre religious ideas, and developed delusions and hallucinations. He was admitted to a state mental hospital on 4/2/1963, with a diagnosis of schizophrenic reaction, paranoid type. At last information he was still in the hospital, where he remained disinterested in ward activities and aloof but cooperative. Classification: Schizophrenic reaction — paranoid type.

(237) husband of grandniece (238), born 1931. He was divorced by his first wife because of his gambling, drinking and nonsupport. Classification: Sociopathic personality disturbance — antisocial behavior.

Great-grandnephew (277), born 1950. He was described as "emotional" and the family reportedly consulted the school psychologist. Classification: Possible transient situational personality disorder — adjustment reaction of childhood.

Great-grandniece (348), born 1946. She reportedly was very "high-strung and nervous when 7–8 years old," when her family was having financial difficulties. Classification: Possible transient situational personality disorder — adjustment reaction of childhood.

Family Summary

The proband, an aunt, a sister, two nephews, a niece and a grandnephew had psychotic disorders and were hospitalized with their illnesses, as was the wife of a nephew. A maternal uncle suicided and was probably psychotic. A grandnephew was hospitalized with a psychotic reaction to encephalitis. Personality disorders were found in the paternal grandfather, the father, a paternal uncle, a sister, a nephew, two grandnephews (both of whom were hospitalized with their disorders), a great-grandnephew and a great-grandniece. Also with personality disorders were the husbands of two sisters, the wife of a brother, the husbands of four nieces and the husband of a grandniece. A sister, a niece and a grandnephew were neurotic. The grandnephew was hospitalized with his neurosis. Also neurotic were the husbands of a sister and a niece, and the wives of two nephews and a grandnephew. One nephew was hospitalized with chronic brain syndrome of senium. One of the grandnephews hospitalized with a personality disorder also had a psychoneurotic disorder (anxiety reaction).

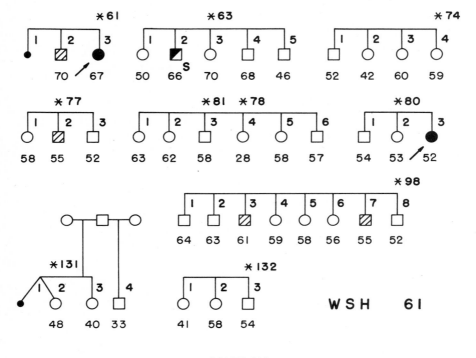

CONTROLS

W S H   6 1

Controls

Brother (2) of (61), born 1891; described as an "alcoholic, otherwise normal." Classification: Sociopathic personality disturbance—alcoholism (addiction).

See family pedigree, person 61.

Brother (2) of (63), born 1890; died at age 66 years of suicide by shooting. The death certificate listed "ill health" as a contributory cause of death, although the nature of the illness was not listed. Classification: Probably with functional psychosis.

See family pedigree, person 77.

Sister (3) of (80), born 1911. She was always pampered by her mother and always lived with her, refusing to work, even after having four illegitimate children. She was seen at a mental hospital, as an outpatient in February, 1946. In August, 1946, she became hallucinated and was hospitalized on 10/30/1946, where she remained until September, 1947. She was rehospitalized in March, 1949, and paroled a month later. Diagnosis was dementia praecox, simple type. At age 51 years she had not been rehospitalized and was reported by her family as "doing well." Classification: Schizophrenic reaction—paranoid type.

Brother (3) of (98), born 1900. He spent one and a half years in a reformatory when a teenager. When interviewed at age 61 years he was described as nervous and stated that he was on tranquilizers. Classification: Transient situational personality disturbance—adjustment reaction of adolescence.

Brother (7) of (98), born 1906. He was in a juvenile correctional institution as a teenager but had no adjustment problems after that. Classification: Transient situational personality disturbance—adjustment reaction of adolescence.

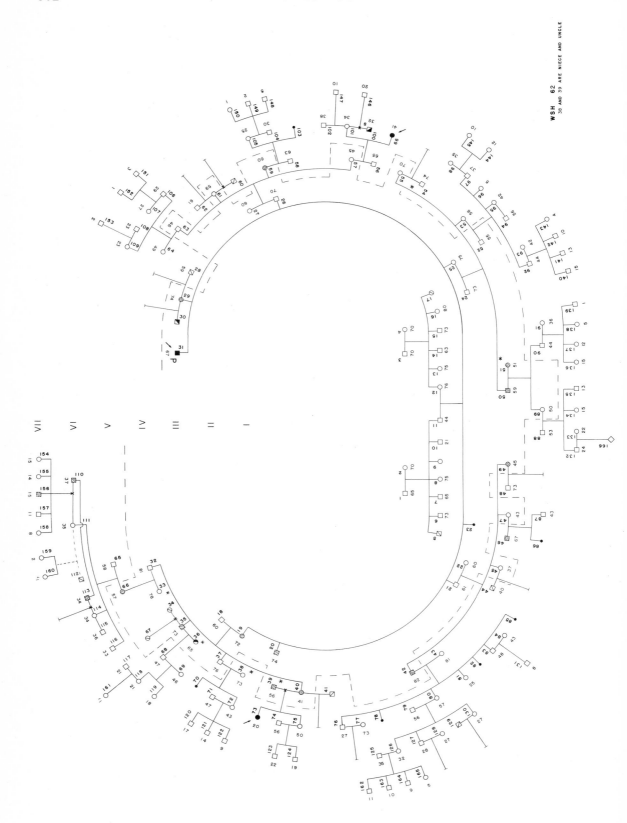

WSH 62
38 AND 39 ARE NIECE AND UNCLE

WSH 62: The Proband

The proband (31), born 1867; died at age 68 years at Warren State Hospital, of chronic myocarditis. There was a change in personality with confusion of thought, inability to concentrate, memory failure and delusional activity a few years prior to his admittance to Warren State Hospital on 12/5/1913. He was discharged as unimproved on 11/15/1916, and was readmitted on 1/10/1920, after threatening his brother and disturbing the neighbors. He remained at Warren until his death. Through the years he maintained that he should not be in the hospital and had delusions of persecution. He was also hallucinated and seclusive. Diagnosis at Warren was dementia praecox. Classification: Schizophrenic reaction—paranoid type.

Siblings

Sister (19), born 1852; died at age 72 years of heart disease. She was considered extremely difficult to get along with and was described as "neurotic" and a "scold." Classification: Possible personality pattern disturbance—schizoid personality.

Brother (20), born 1854; died at age 74 years of angina pectoris. He was described as a "rather odd character" and as "seclusive" and "stubborn." Classification: Possible personality pattern disturbance—schizoid personality.

Sister (29), born 1864; died at age 74 years of chronic myocarditis. She reportedly always caused trouble in the family and seemed to be highly unreasonable. She became more peculiar in her later years. Classification: Personality pattern disturbance—paranoid personality.

(30) husband of sister (29), born 1863, date of death unknown. He reportedly had a "nervous breakdown." Classification: Possibly with functional psychosis.

Nieces and Nephews

Nephew (35), born 1876; died at age 73 years of a cerebral hemorrhage. At one time he held a responsible position with a flour-milling company. Apparently the business failed in 1934, following which he was non-communicative and depressed. Later he worked as an attendant at a miniature golf course. Classification: Probable psychoneurotic disorder—depressive reaction.

(36) wife of nephew (35), born 1886; died at age 65 years of multiple myeloma. At the time of menopause she developed an "overactive imagination" and suspected her husband of "trying to take their son away from her." Classification: Possibly with functional psychosis, involutional psychotic reaction.

(39) husband of niece (40), born 1881; died at age 56 years of nephritis. He was a minister who, until he went into the ministry, was a heavy drinker. Classification: Possible transient situational personality disturbance.

Niece (40), born 1888; age at last information was 41 years. She was described as a "wild girl" who drank a lot and had a reputation for promiscuity. Classification: Sociopathic personality disturbance.

Nephew (42), born 1880. He was an alcoholic from age 14 years until age 52 years, but at last information had not had a drink for 30 years. Classification: Sociopathic personality disturbance—alcoholism (addiction).

(46) husband of niece (47), born 1879; died at age 67 years of cerebral thrombosis. He was reportedly an alcoholic. Classification: Sociopathic personality disturbance—alcoholism (addiction).

Niece (49), born 1900; died at age 45 years of cancer. She was described as extremely nervous and suffered some sort of seizures which were not diagnosed as epilepsy. Classification: Probable psychoneurotic disorder.

Nephew (50), born 1887; died at age 59 years of a heart attack. He reportedly "drank excessively." Classification: Sociopathic personality disturbance—alcoholism (addiction).

(51) wife of nephew (50), born 1893; died at age 51 years of encephalitis. She reportedly "drank excessively." Classification: Sociopathic personality disturbance—alcoholism (addiction).

Niece (59), born 1899; died at age 60 years of cancer. She was described as extremely nervous and compulsive. Classification: Psychoneurotic disorder.

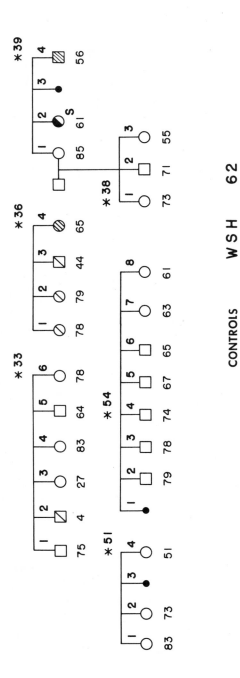

CONTROLS   W S H   6 2

Distant Relatives

Grandniece (66), born 1904. She had a "nervous breakdown" during the winter of 1960–1961, but was not hospitalized and reportedly made a good recovery. She also had mental trouble during menopause, when she had periods of depression. Classification: Probable psychoneurotic disorder — depressive reaction.

Grandniece (73), born 1909; died at age 20 years at a state mental hospital of pellagra. She was first diagnosed as suffering from pellagra in 1926, and was treated with some success. Symptoms began again in June, 1929, and became steadily worse. She was hospitalized in July, 1929, with a diagnosis of pellagra and hebephrenic dementia praecox. In August, 1929, she was admitted to the state hospital. Hospital notes stated that her thoughts were of a suicidal nature. There was no evidence of hallucinations and her behavior was neither assaultive nor threatening. Photographs show a facial expression of profound depression. Classification: Schizophrenic reaction.

Grandniece (99), born 1920; a patient at a state mental hospital at age 41 years. Her mental break followed the death of her idolized mother and the remarriage of her father and the birth of children in this marriage. She was moody, withdrawn, nervous and depressed and received shock treatments in 1948, 1951 and 1952; however, under treatment her condition became worse and she was hospitalized on 10/31/1952, with a diagnosis of dementia praecox, paranoid type. She improved with hospitalization. Classification: Schizophrenic reaction — paranoid type.

(100) husband of grandniece (101), born 1923; unknown except that he suicided at age 32 years. Classification: Probably with functional psychosis.

(110) husband of great-grandniece (111), born 1924. He was described as a moderately heavy drinker and as emotionally unstable. He received custody of their five children after he and his wife were separated. Classification: Personality trait disturbance — emotionally unstable personality.

(113) husband of great-grandniece (114), born 1927. He was reportedly alcoholic and abusive during his marriage to (114). Classification: Sociopathic personality disturbance — alcoholism (addiction).

Great-great-grandnephew (156), born 1949. He was a diabetic whose condition was not well controlled because of an emotional problem. Classification: Transient situational personality disturbance — adjustment reaction of adolescence.

Family Summary

The proband and two grandnieces had psychotic disorders and the husband of a sister, the wife of a nephew and the husband of a grandniece possibly or probably so. Personality disorders were discovered in two sisters and a brother, in a niece and two nephews and in a great-great-grandnephew. Personality disorders were also found in the husbands of two nieces, the wife of a nephew and the husbands of two great-grandnieces. A nephew, two nieces and a grandniece were neurotic.

Controls

See family pedigree, person 36.

Sister (2) of (39), born 1876; died at age 61 years of suicide by a gunshot wound to the head. She reportedly was "always peculiar and a constant problem." At the time of her death she had had a "nervous breakdown" and "should have been hospitalized." Classification: Probably with functional psychosis.

See family pedigree, person 39.

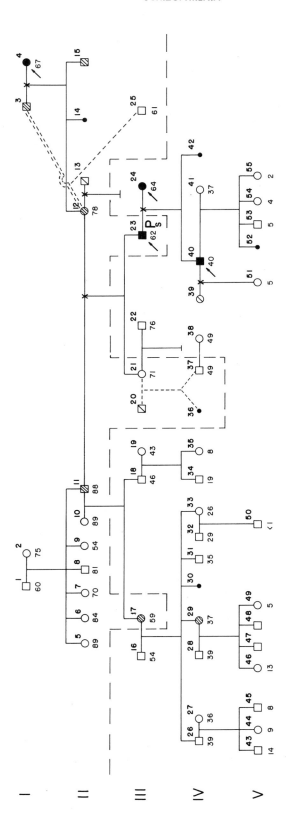

WSH 63

WSH 63: The Proband

The proband (23), born 1892; died at age 62 years of cancer. Shortly after leaving school at age 15 years his behavior became peculiar in that he would leave home for varying periods of time with no explanation of his actions, he expressed ideas that someone was trying to injure him and that he felt like killing someone. After being jailed more than once for his bizarre behavior he was admitted to Warren State Hospital on 6/13/1908 with a diagnosis of adolescent insanity. He was discharged after one year and remained at home for five years. During this time he married and divorced. He was readmitted on 9/28/1913 because of overactivity and a threatening attitude toward his family. Diagnosis at this hospitalization, which lasted until 9/8/1915, was manic-depressive psychosis. While hospitalized he attempted suicide on three different occasions. His third hospitalization, following 10 years of excessive alcoholism, was from 7/5/1946 until 9/14/1949. Because of the predominance of ideas of unworthiness, rather marked depression and slowing of psychomotor activities, he was diagnosed as manic-depressive — depressed phase. At the time of his fourth admission to Warren State Hospital in 1953 he was hallucinated and very fearful of threatening voices. A diagnosis of schizophrenic reaction was made. He remained at Warren State Hospital until his death. Classification: Schizophrenic reaction — paranoid type.

(24) wife of proband (23), born 1897; a patient at Warren State Hospital at age 64 years. At the time of her admission to Warren in 1947, it was noted that she had symptoms of mental illness for five years. She was hallucinated, noisy and overactive. Diagnosis at the hospital and classification: Schizophrenic reaction — paranoid type.

Children

Son (40), born 1921. His work record was irregular and there was marital discord in both marriages. He was hospitalized from 1946 to 1947; this admission was preceded by an arrest for felonious assault. He refused to sign a release for information from that hospital. An interviewer described him as rambling, opinionated and garrulous and his mental health as questionable or perhaps actually paranoid. No hospital abstract was received from the hospital but the medical superintendent did say that (40) was hospitalized as mentally ill and during examination found to be psychotic. Classification: Schizophrenic reaction — paranoid type.

Grandparents

Maternal grandfather (3), born 1846; age at last information was 69 years. He was described as the "one odd member" of a "good family." He did not get along with his neighbors and, although considered honest, was thought to be decidedly peculiar. He was the father of his daughter's (12) illegitimate child (25). Classification: Personality disorder.

Maternal grandmother (4), born 1848; died at age 67 years of unknown causes. She was admitted to Warren State Hospital on 11/12/1889, with a diagnosis of acute mania. She had exhibited symptoms for 19 years prior to her commitment but had become violent only two days before hospitalization. She was discharged on 4/19/1922. In 1915 she was a patient at a county home and suffering from Bright's disease. Classification: With functional psychosis, probable schizophrenic reaction.

Parents

Father (11), born 1868; died at age 88 years of chronic myocarditis. He reportedly always had a "very bad temper." He was described as cross and ugly and given to "fits of pouting" when he would speak to no one. He divorced (12) after three years of marriage on the grounds of desertion. He was confused, noisy and destructive in his last three years of life. Classification: Personality disorder; also, chronic brain syndrome of senium.

Mother (12), born 1871; died at age 78 years of cancer. She left (11) after three years of marriage to live with her father. She and her father left their home suddenly, in the night, and moved to another area of the state. Their child (25) was reportedly born during this trip. She was described by the interviewer as "sickly and indifferent" and described by her neighbors as "peculiar, anxious and seclusive." She was unable to do her work and would "imagine things" at times. Classification: Personality disorder.

Aunts and Uncles

Maternal uncle (15). He reportedly took up many occupations and would not remain in one place for any length of time. He also had exalted ideas of his own abilities. Classification: Probable personality disorder.

Siblings

Paternal half sister (17), born 1902. Her interviewer described her as of limited intelligence and commented that her self-styled nervousness, for which she took medication, was on a neurotic level. Classification: Psychoneurotic reaction.

Distant Relatives

Half niece (29), born 1924. She suffered from St. Vitus dance as a child and was so nervous that she would "chew the skin off her knuckles." She was a well-adjusted adult. Classification: Possible transient situational personality disturbance—adjustment reaction of childhood.

Family Summary

The proband, his wife, their son and the maternal grandmother had psychotic disorders. Personality disorders were found in the maternal grandfather, the father and the mother and in a maternal uncle. A paternal half sister was neurotic. A half niece had a transient adjustment reaction as a child and the father, who had a personality disorder, also was classified as with chronic brain syndrome of senium.

WSH 65

WSH 65: The Proband

The proband (29), born 1884; died at age 47 years at Warren State Hospital of bronchopneumonia. He was hospitalized at Warren on 6/4/1913. At the time of admission he was suffering from auditory and visual hallucinations, delusions of persecution and ideas of influence. The diagnosis made was dementia praecox, hebephrenic form. His condition remained the same until his discharge on 3/17/1915; however, he was readmitted on 9/24/1915 because he was thought to be dangerous. He had not injured anyone but he had collected and sharpened all the knives he could obtain and threatened his family. Except for two escapes, he was in continuous residence at the hospital, where he remained seclusive and apathetic with persecutory delusions. Classification: Schizophrenic reaction — paranoid type.

Parents

Father (8), born 1849; died at age 83 years of influenza. He was described as "irritable, petulant and moody." He worried constantly and would often, if something displeased him, pout and sulk for a week without speaking to anyone. Classification: Personality trait disturbance — emotionally unstable personality.

Siblings

Brother (22), born 1878; died at age 65 years of a coronary thrombosis and cancer of the rectum. He was a blacksmith by trade but worked as a laborer as his alcoholism interfered with his social and economic adjustment. He left home in 1915 and his whereabouts were unknown until 1935, when he arrived home and announced that he was home to stay. His family supported him until his death in 1944. Classification: Personality pattern disturbance — inadequate personality.

Brother (32), born 1889; died at age 66 years at Warren State Hospital, of gastrointestinal hemorrhage. He was admitted to Warren on 5/11/1942, following the death of his mother and the subsequent inability of

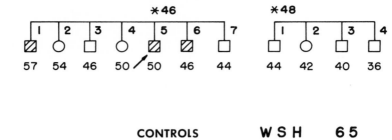

CONTROLS   W S H   6 5

other relatives to care for him. He remained hospitalized until his death. Diagnosis at Warren State Hospital was without psychosis, mental deficiency. He was described as a congenital defective with occasional temper tantrums but no marked mood swings. Classification: Mental deficiency.

Nieces and Nephews

(46) husband of niece (47), born 1910. He did many types of work, although he was primarily a bartender, and changed jobs frequently. He was discharged from the army in World War II after only six months in the service because of an anxiety reaction. His most recent diagnosis at a Veterans Administration hospital was psychoneurosis, anxiety reaction manifested by urticaria and neurodermatitis. Diagnosis by the interviewer, a staff psychiatrist, and classification: Psychoneurotic disorder—anxiety reaction.

(56) wife of nephew (55), born 1919. She deserted her husband and children in 1960. Friends and relatives were at a loss to explain her actions. Her psychiatrist reported that, at the time he saw her, she presented an anxiety reaction based on an adult maladjustment, in the nature of an immaturity reaction. Classification: Personality pattern disturbance—inadequate personality.

Family Summary

The proband was the only family member with a psychotic disorder. A brother was also hospitalized at Warren State Hospital for many years, but was a mental defective. The husband of a niece was a hospitalized neurotic. The father, a brother and the wife of a nephew had personality disorders.

Controls

Brother (1) of (46), born 1900; died at age 57 years of cirrhosis of the liver. He reportedly was an alcoholic. Classification: Probable sociopathic personality disturbance—alcoholism (addiction).

See family pedigree, person 46.

Brother (6) of (46), born 1916; described as a "drifter" whose whereabouts were unknown. He was never able to "hold a steady job." Classification: Possible personality disorder.

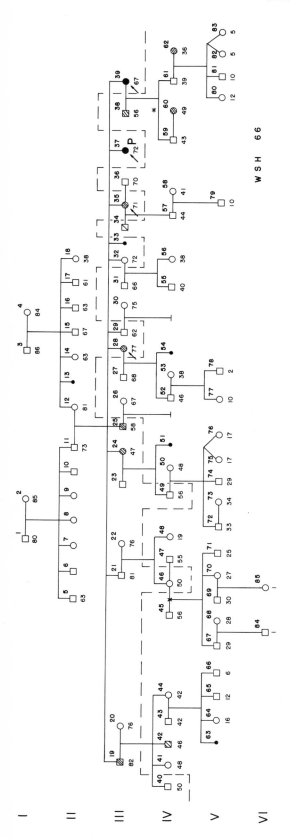

WSH 66

WSH 66: The Proband

The proband (37), born 1892, was a patient at Warren State Hospital, except for a period of two months, from 11/28/1913 until the time of the study. Symptoms began about five years before admission when she became cross and disagreeable, developed many vague physical complaints and had episodes of hysterical crying with numbness and choking sensations. Hospital admission notes described her symptoms as "delusions, grimacing, stereotype movements and negativism, suggesting a diagnosis of dementia praecox, hebephrenic type." In 1922, staff notes described her as mute, untidy and destructive. She remained severely demented. Classification: Schizophrenic reaction—catatonic type.

Siblings

Brother (19), born 1878. As an adolescent he had to drop out of school because of "a worn out nervous system." He apparently made a good adjustment in later life. Classification: Transient situational personality disturbance—adjustment reaction of adolescence.

Sister (24), born 1880; died at age 47 years of tuberculosis of the spine. At age 19 years she reportedly suffered a "nervous breakdown" and was in bed for 10 weeks. Classification: Psychoneurotic disorder.

Brother (25), born 1883; died at age 58 years of a coronary attack. He was a chaplain during World War I and, after the war, he spent two years recuperating as his "nerves were shattered." He did not return to the ministry but worked as a carpenter. Classification: Psychoneurotic reaction—other.

Sister (28), born 1883. She was hospitalized for a nervous disorder for about one year at age 19 or 20. Her brother remembers her as "bawling all the time" during this episode. Classification: Transient situational personality disorder—adjustment reaction of adolescence.

Sister (35), born 1890. She was hospitalized for a nervous problem at about age 16 years. When interviewed she appeared to be an extremely nervous person with little control over her anxieties. She felt extremely guilty over the family's apparent desertion of the proband. Classification: Psychoneurotic disorder—anxiety reaction.

(38) husband of sister (39), born 1895; died at age 56 years of angina pectoris. He was described both as "terribly spoiled" and as "a henpecked little man." In the early months of his marriage he locked (39) in their apartment while he was at work. Classification: Personality disorder.

Sister (39), born 1893. She was described as "always nervous." Her marriage was full of strife and she and her husband at times contemplated a separation. During the early months of her marriage (38) locked her in their apartment while he worked. At the time of World War II, when her two sons were in the armed services, she went to bed for several months and for one month did not bathe. She was subsequently hospitalized at a private sanitarium for two weeks. Diagnosis at hospitalization was depressive state. When interviewed she was seen as pathologically talkative, terribly anxious and tense. Classification: Manic-depressive reaction—depressed type.

Nieces and Nephews

Nephew (42), born 1914. He was interviewed by a Warren State Hospital staff psychiatrist and considered to be very introverted, perhaps even schizoid. He went out little and spent most of his time at his ham radio; however, he made a good adjustment at his work. Classification: Personality pattern disturbance—schizoid personality.

(60) wife of nephew (59), born 1911. She was described by an interviewer as "an immature person with migraine headaches and multiple physical complaints which appear to be the result of emotional disturbance." Classification: Psychoneurotic disorder—anxiety reaction.

(62) wife of nephew (61), born 1924. She was described by the interviewer as "a talkative, nervous person . . . constantly yelling at the children" and busy doing community work. She was an abandoned baby and was adopted at an early age. As a child she suffered from St. Vitus dance and as an adult still considered herself nervous, although she had no medical attention for nervous complaints. Her mother-in-law, who was at one time hospitalized with a psychotic disorder, lived in the home and

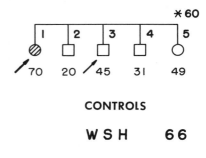

CONTROLS

W S H   6 6

was a disrupting force in the family. Classification: Possible psychoneurotic reaction.

Family Summary

The proband and a sister had psychotic disorders and were hospitalized with their illnesses. Two additional sisters were hospitalized as adolescents with psychoneurotic reactions. A brother and the wives of two nephews were also classified as neurotic. Personality disorders were found in a brother, a sister, the husband of the psychotic sister and in a nephew.

Controls

Sister (1) of (60), born 1893. In 1918 she was treated at a general hospital for a "nervous breakdown" which was attributed to overwork in caring for her siblings after the death of her mother, and then bearing the responsibility of nursing her father, who had cancer. She was not hospitalized for long and was still well at age 70 years. Classification: Probable psychoneurotic disorder.

Brother (3), born 1901; died at age 45 years of cancer of the brain. He was hospitalized for a short time in May, 1944, before he was admitted to a state mental hospital where he underwent brain surgery and a glioma in the left frontal region was subtotally removed. He was released from the hospital on 8/23/1944, but returned in May, 1945. In 1946 he was transferred to a county home, where he died. Classification:

Chronic brain syndrome associated with new growth, with psychotic reaction.

WSH 67: The Proband

The proband (29), born 1878; died at age 69 years of angina pectoris. He developed his first symptoms of mental illness at about age 28 years, when he developed noises of ringing and snapping in his ears, and became very restless. In 1907, at age 29, he was admitted to Warren State Hospital with a diagnosis of paranoia. He escaped nine months later and was readmitted in 1913. He escaped again in 1917, was readmitted in 1918 and escaped again in 1922. His family remembered him as "quiet and peculiar." He had symptoms of apathy, neologisms, delusions and hallucinations and after his first admission received a diagnosis of dementia praecox. Classification: Schizophrenic reaction—paranoid type.

Parents

Father (8), born 1844; died at age 57 years of apoplexy. He was reportedly a "peculiar" man and people "made fun of him." Others said that he was not "peculiar" in any way. He was also described as "cranky" and because of "lack of shrewdness" made bad financial investments. Classification: Possible personality pattern disturbance—inadequate personality.

Mother (9), born 1842; died at age 87 years, cause of death unknown. At age 72 years she showed some mental deterioration; her answers to questions were often irrelevant and she was querulous and complaining. Classification: Possible chronic brain syndrome of senium.

Aunts and Uncles

Maternal uncle (13), born 1832; died at age 79 years of apoplexy. He was described as "very much set in his ways, none of his children could get along with him." He was also described as "obstinate and bullheaded." Classification: Possible personality disorder.

Maternal uncle (17), born 1836; last heard of at 77 years of age, when he was described as a "querulous old man; irritable, peevish and subject to unreasonable prejudices." He was also hypochondriacal and took patent medicines for stomach trouble, palpitations of the heart and various other disorders. In all probability, as a younger, active man he had no peculiarities. Classification: Probable chronic brain syndrome of senium.

Maternal uncle (18), born 1838; died at age 76 years of cancer of the stomach. As a young man he was in the army and after that "never settled down in one place." He was considered a "drinking man," was a steady indulger and occasionally became intoxicated. Classification: Possible sociopathic personality disturbance—alcoholism (addiction).

Maternal uncle (20), born 1846; died at age 67 years, cause of death unknown. He kept house and brought up his child alone after the death of his wife. In later years he was described as "weak, passive and prematurely old." Classification: Possible chronic brain syndrome of senium.

Siblings

Brother (33), born 1880; died at age 45 years in a coal mining accident. He was described as "an ignorant man who did not always pay his bills and whose violent temper occasionally got him into major scrapes." Classification: Possible personality trait disturbance—emotionally unstable personality.

Nieces and Nephews

Niece (48), born 1892. She was described as a "pill taker" who imagined she was "going to die every day and who felt sick when nothing was wrong." Classification: Probable psychoneurotic reaction—other.

Niece (74), born 1898. (74) was four years of age when her mother died. She lived at various times with her maternal grandparents, her father and stepmother and with a maternal aunt. She was described as always very high strung and prone to worry unnecessarily. She had gall

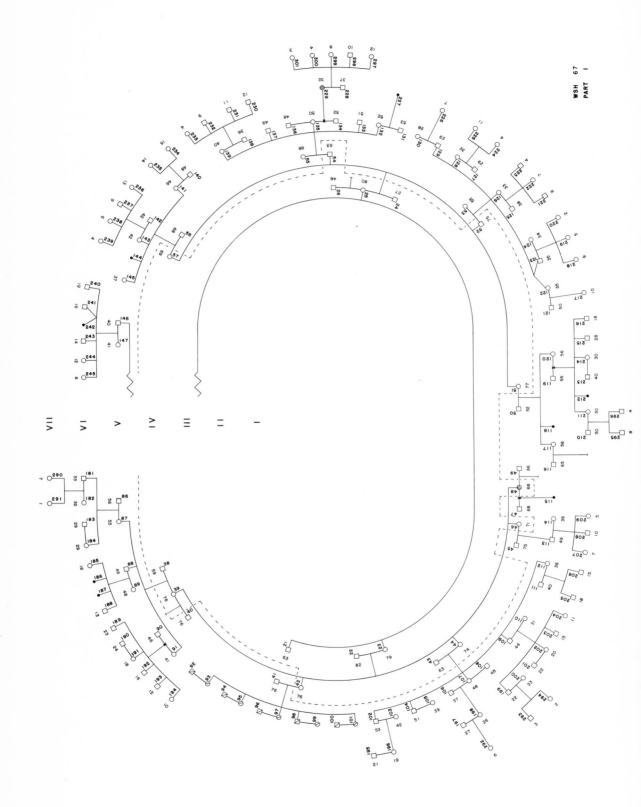

WSH 67
PART I

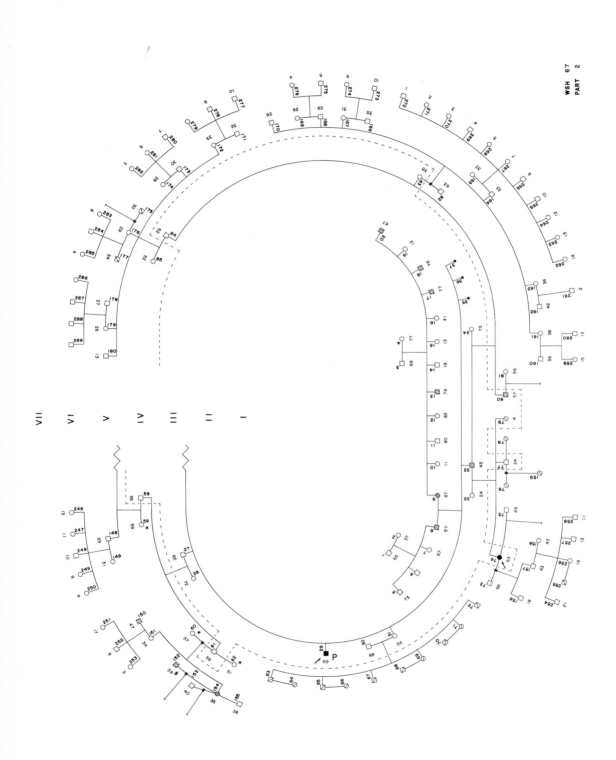

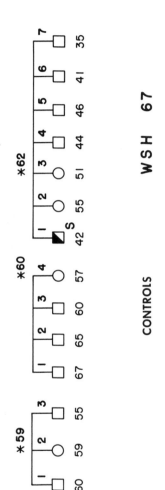

bladder surgery in August, 1950; and, following surgery, became depressed, fatigued and afraid of losing her mind. She was subsequently hospitalized for psychiatric treatment from 1/30/1951 until 3/3/1951. She remained well and unhospitalized after treatment. Classification: Involutional psychotic reaction.

Nephew (80), born 1906. His own statement was that he had not worked since rejection by the military draft as 4-F during World War II (age about 37 years). His wife (they were childless) had always been employed. Various relatives described him as "palsied from an accident" and as having "trouble with nerves." The interviewer considered symptoms of depression and neurasthenia. Classification: Personality pattern disturbance—inadequate personality.

Distant Relatives

(150) husband of grandniece (151), born 1917. He had ulcers and had a stomach resection. He was described as very nervous, very high strung, accident prone and took tranquilizers. Classification: Psychoneurotic reaction.

(152) husband of grandniece (154), born 1925. His marriage lasted but a few months because of his alcoholism. He made at least one suicide attempt. Classification: Sociopathic personality disorder—alcoholism (addiction).

Grandniece (154), born 1927. She always had problems making friends and was always withdrawn. She changed jobs frequently and, after her second divorce, was seen at a state mental health clinic for 30 visits between 9/27/1955 and 6/19/1956. The diagnostic impression at the clinic was personality trait disturbance, passive-aggressive personality. The clinic treatment was followed up by one and a half years of treatment by a psychologist. At last information she and her third husband were receiving marital counseling. Classification: Personality trait disturbance, passive-aggressive personality.

Great-grandniece (229), born 1929. She was described as a "nervous girl." She also had "spinal trouble." Classification: Possible psychoneurotic disorder.

Family Summary

The proband and a niece had psychotic disorders and a nephew possibly so. Personality disorders were located in the father, two maternal uncles, a brother, a grandniece and in one of the grandniece's husbands. The mother and two maternal uncles were classified as chronic brain syndrome of senium. A niece, a great-grandniece and the husband of a grandniece were neurotic.

Controls

Brother (1) of (62), born 1907; died at age 42 years of a self-inflicted gunshot wound to the head. His death was described as an accident that occurred while cleaning a rifle; however, the death certificate listed the death as a suicide. Classification: Probably with functional psychosis.

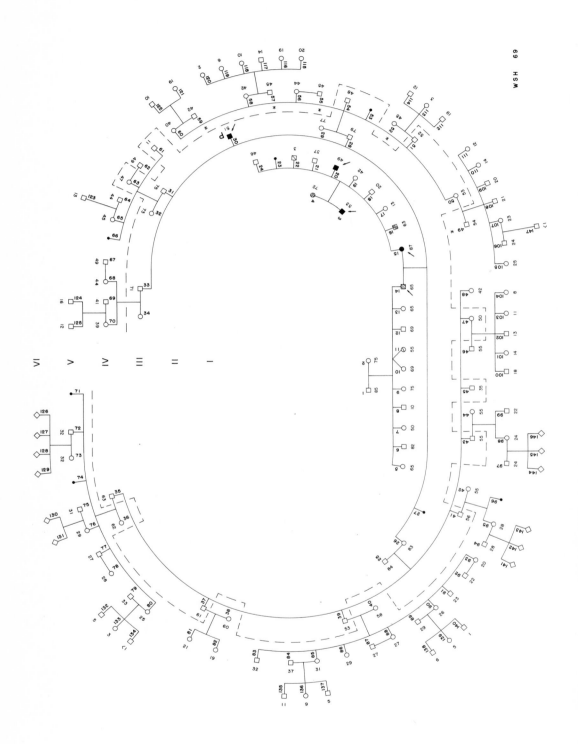

WSH 69: The Proband

The proband (30), born 1883; died at age 52 years at Warren State Hospital of cancer. At about age 20 years he was apprehended while attempting a robbery and imprisoned for 18 months. In September, 1910, he became "mentally unbalanced" and was placed in a county home for two months. He later developed delusions of a persecutory type and was again retained at the county home from February, 1911 until July, 1912. He was never well after his release and his mother, fearing for his, as well as her safety, had him arrested on 1/3/1913. He was retained in jail until admission to Warren State Hospital on 4/12/1913, where he remained until death. Diagnosis at Warren State Hospital was dementia praecox, paranoid type. Classification: Schizophrenic reaction—paranoid type.

Grandparents

Maternal grandfather (3), born 1821; died at age 53 years at a state mental hospital, cause of death unknown. He was described as sociable and pleasant and a successful farmer until much of his property was destroyed by a fire which spread from a small brush fire he had started. He then became a "raving maniac" and the "terror of the neighborhood" as he would frighten people by flourishing a razor at them and "preach" in a loud voice as if addressing an audience. He made an attempt on his wife's life and was subsequently hospitalized for one year (5/18/1869 until 5/11/1870). He was normal until February, 1874, when he again became restless, excitable, sleepless and drank to excess. He was rehospitalized and remained so, with increasing symptoms, until his death. Diagnosis at both hospitalizations was mania. Classification: Schizophrenic reaction—paranoid type.

Maternal grandmother (4), born 1830; died at age 72 years of apoplexy. She was described as "always high tempered and independent" but as a "normal woman in active life." As she grew older she imagined people were slighting her and she became difficult to please. Classification: Possible psychoneurotic reaction.

Parents

Father (14), born 1849; died at age 65 years at a county home, cause of death unknown. In March, 1887, he had an episode of amnesia, during which he wandered about in a dazed manner for four days and later had no memory of his actions. In December of the same year, while working on the railroad, he fell, striking his head on a rail. He was not unconscious but had severe neck and head pains and was paralyzed on the right side. He recovered physically but never recovered his power of speech. He spent 10 months in 1888 and 1889 at a state mental hospital. The next four years he did light work at home with his mother, who cared for him until her death. He was then admitted to Warren State Hospital on 12/17/1891, in a state of mild depression. On 8/8/1894, he was transferred to the hospital for the chronically insane and remained there until he was readmitted to Warren State Hospital on 9/17/1896, with a diagnosis of chronic mania. In January, 1897, he developed petit mal epilepsy. On 4/26/1900, he was transferred to a county home where he remained until his death. Recent considerations of his mental condition suggest that he may have been suffering from brain damage due to head injuries and was non-psychotic. Classification: Probable chronic brain syndrome associated with circulatory disturbance other than arteriosclerosis. Possible schizophrenic reaction—chronic undifferentiated type.

Mother (15), born 1851; died at age 87 years of myocarditis. She was described as "nervous and peculiar" from girlhood and as often haughty and unreasonable. At age 28 years she developed a psychosis which lasted for about one year. She was hospitalized at the time with a diagnosis of acute delirious mania. The onset of the psychosis occurred while she was still confined to bed, following the birth of her second child. She threatened suicide but made no attempt. She had almost complete responsibility for supporting and rearing her children and, although thought to be peculiar, was always considered able by friends and family. Classification: Schizophrenic reaction—paranoid type.

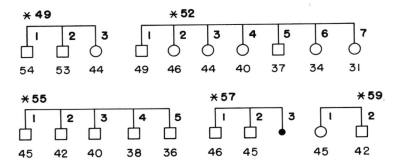

CONTROLS   W S H   6 9

Aunts and Uncles

Maternal uncle (16), born 1849; died at age 63 years of apoplexy. He was described as "grossly alcoholic" and as "always drunk and never sober." When intoxicated he was abusive to his children. Classification: Sociopathic personality disturbance — alcoholism (addiction).

Maternal uncle (20), born 1864; died at age 49 years of myocarditis. He was normal, successful, even tempered and sociable until about age 40 when, following the death of his mother, he moved to a hotel. Shortly after moving to the hotel he became irritable, refused to go to bed, made foolish financial investments and became incoherent in conversation. Three months later he was hospitalized at Warren State Hospital, where he remained until death. Diagnosis at Warren was acute mania. He showed intermittent but steady deterioration while hospitalized. Classification: Schizophrenic reaction — catatonic type.

Family Summary

The proband, his mother, his maternal grandfather and a maternal uncle were hospitalized with psychotic disorders. The father was possibly psychotic and the maternal grandmother possibly neurotic. Another maternal uncle was an alcoholic.

Controls

None noteworthy.

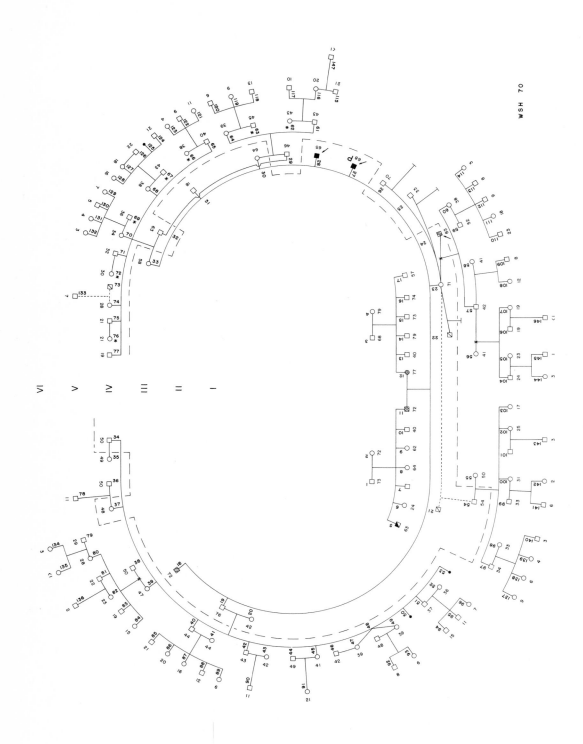

WSH 70

WSH 70: The Proband

The proband (27), born 1892. He was admitted to Warren State Hospital, on 5/19/1913, with a diagnosis of dementia praecox, catatonic form. He was described as always bashful but pleasant, agreeable and a good workman, although lacking in initiative. In 1910 he became indifferent in attitude, would sit without speaking for long periods of time, had periods of silly laughing and became incoherent in conversation. He became progressively worse and at the time of hospitalization was completely disoriented, had delusions of poisoning, visual hallucinations and was quite apathetic emotionally. He remained at Warren State Hospital and in 1960 was described as totally detached from almost all reality; contact was made with extreme difficulty and for only a few seconds. Classification: Schizophrenic reaction—catatonic type.

Parents

Father (11), born 1855; died at age 72 years of chronic myocarditis. Rather than live with his family, he lived in a shack near the mines and came home only on Sunday. At one time, in mid-life, he suffered from asthma for about four years. It was during this time that his personality changed and he became impatient and disagreeable. Classification: Personality disorder.

Mother (12), born 1862; died at age 77 years of "the flu." She was described as nervous and irritable and impossible to interview as she gave irrelevant answers to questions and jumped from subject to subject in conversation. Classification: Possible psychoneurotic disorder.

Aunts and Uncles

Paternal uncle (5), born 1841. He was killed by a falling stone while building a house at age 63. He was described as a capable and industrious carpenter and lumberman but of a neurotic temperament. There was an episode of "psychosis" when "scared in the war." Classification: Probably with functional psychosis, schizophrenia; Possible psychoneurotic disorder.

Siblings

Brother (18), born 1884; died at age 72 years of a cerebral hemorrhage. When young he was described as "lacking aggression" and as "very inept socially." As a child he would run and hide when visitors arrived and as a young adult he went out only occasionally with other young men and never socialized with women. His father, whom he feared, had to secure his jobs for him. He was never hospitalized for any reason. Classification: Probable personality pattern disturbance—schizoid personality.

(24) husband of sister (23), born 1877; died at age 83 years at Warren State Hospital of carcinoma of the penis. In February, 1960, he suffered a stroke (his second), following which his memory became impaired and his intellectual functions were greatly reduced. He eventually became confused, unkempt, disoriented and confused and was hospitalized at Warren State Hospital on 11/6/1960, where he died a month later. Diagnosis at Warren and classification: Chronic brain syndrome associated with cerebral arteriosclerosis.

Brother (28), born 1894; died at age 65 years of a malignant tumor of the abdomen. He was hospitalized at a Veterans Administration hospital from 1/26/1940 until 10/7/1942, with a diagnosis of dementia praecox, paranoid type. Details of his illness were unknown. Classification: Schizophrenic reaction—paranoid type.

Family Summary

The proband and his brother had psychotic disorders and were hospitalized with their illnesses. A paternal uncle was probably psychotic. The husband of a sister developed a psychotic reaction to cerebral arteriosclerosis and was hospitalized. The mother, the father and a brother had personality disorders.

Controls

Sister (3) of (67), born 2/19/1918. She was hospitalized at Warren State Hospital from 1/6/1960 until 4/26/1960, with a diagnosis of schizophrenic reaction, paranoid type. Although shy, she made an adequate

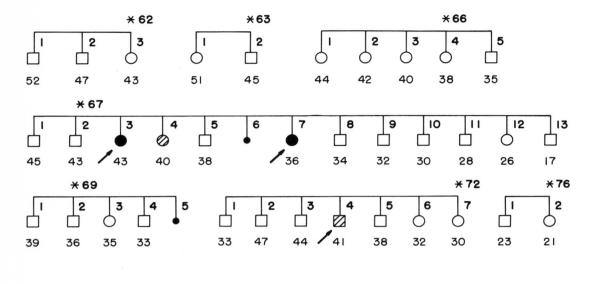

CONTROLS WSH 70

adjustment until about one month before admission, when she developed the delusion that she had given birth to a child by God and that her former employer was trying to "dope" her. She also developed auditory hallucinations. She improved after chemotherapy (ECT caused her to become confused and denudative). At discharge she was friendly, relevant and unable to remember the delusion she had had at admission. Classification: Schizophrenic reaction—paranoid type.

Sister (7) of (67), born 1925, a housewife with six children. She was admitted to a state mental hospital on 3/8/1960 because of fear of being controlled by radar, fear of "Russians" and fear of her husband. She believed that radar moved items in her house. About two years before admission she had an episode of suspiciousness and anxiety that lasted about two weeks. In January, 1960, when her sister (3) was admitted to a state mental hospital, (7) became anxious, fearful, hyperreligious and withdrawn. After ECT and chemotherapy she was granted a leave of absence as her paranoid delusions had subsided and her conversation was rational and realistic. Diagnosis at the hospital and classification: Schizophrenic reaction—paranoid type.

Brother (4) of (72), born 1923. Married but no children. He was hospitalized at a state mental hospital from 4/11/1960 until

7/8/1960 with a diagnosis of psychoneurotic disorder, conversion reaction. Symptoms first began about four months after his marriage when he had a "convulsive seizure." He continued to have the seizures, which were not typical of epilepsy, about once a month and no medication helped. Each attack was preceded by a severe headache. Once or twice he was hallucinated during an attack. During hospitalization his attacks subsided and he was taken off medication. A year later he was still well. Classification: Psychoneurotic disorder—conversion reaction.

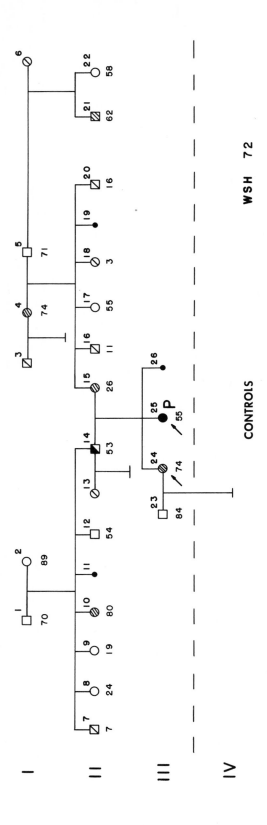

WSH 72: The Proband

The proband (25), born 1892. She was admitted to Warren State Hospital on 9/26/1913, and died there at age 55 years in a diabetic coma. She had a long history of behavior disorder, including excessive profanity as a child and fictitious tales of attempted rape as an adolescent. She accused her maternal step-grandfather of criminal assault and after he was cleared of the charge she was committed to a county home, where she later accused the superintendent of "the same misdeed." At the county home she once accused the attendants of giving her a bath in maggots. After her admission to Warren State Hospital she was described as "perfectly helpless as to personal duties" and showed "disorientation . . . disturbance of apprehension, attention and memory." First diagnosis at Warren State Hospital was dementia praecox superimposed on a constitutional defect. Later diagnoses were a probable psychosis, mental retardation and strong sexual tendencies. Classification: Schizophrenic reaction—paranoid type.

Grandparents

Maternal grandmother (4), born 1839; died at age 74 years of pneumonia. In early years she had a "tendency to worry" and was quick tempered, as well as vivacious and pleasure loving. Because of her vivacity she was not happy with her sedate first husband. At the time of menopause she was "peevish and fretful" and during an attack of grippe, she several times imagined that her son-in-law, who was staying at the home, was spying on her. Classification: Probable personality trait disturbance—compulsive personality; Possible transient situational personality disorder—adjustment reaction of late life.

Parents

Father (14), born 1853; died at age 53 years of stomach trouble. He had typhoid fever at the age of 19 years and was "never the same after that." He was never em-

ployed regularly; he was considered lazy and "had no ability to look ahead or plan for the future." The last three or four years of his life were spent in a county home, where he complained of severe headaches, became suicidal, refused to talk to anyone and did not know relatives who came to visit him. The proband's hospital abstract stated that "the father was insane." Classification: Probably with functional psychosis, schizophrenia; Possible chronic or acute brain syndrome associated with infection.

Mother (15), born 1868; died at age 26 years from illness following childbirth. She was described as "of good reputation." She was not considered to be "excitable or neurotic" but was "rather peculiar . . . used to dress oddly." She was also described as "thrifty" and as "passionately fond of her husband until her death." Classification: Possible personality pattern disturbance—schizoid personality.

Aunts and Uncles

Paternal aunt (10), born 1857; died "in her eighties" of heart trouble. She was described as "decidedly mentally deficient with a poor memory and an aversion for work." Classification: Possible personality pattern disturbance—inadequate personality.

Maternal half uncle (21), born 1852; date of death unknown. In August, 1913, he had a paralytic stroke which left him "quite helpless." In early life he was described as "decidedly peculiar." He was "comical in his manner and never took life very seriously." Classification: Probable personality pattern disturbance—inadequate personality.

Siblings

Sister (24), born 1888. She attempted many occupations, including dressmaking, millinery, saleswork and factory labor, but was only "capable in housework." She spent several years as a domestic, then ran off with her cousin's husband, whom she eventually married. On 6/27/1929, she voluntarily entered a state mental hospital for observation and was diagnosed as not insane, but with psychoneurosis. Her medical history was punctuated with minor physical illnesses. She was also described as a high-grade moron with a wretched family history, and having numerous psychoneurotic symptoms that seemed to predominate. Classification: Psychoneurotic disorder—conversion reaction.

Family Summary

The proband was the only psychotic person in this family, although the father was probably psychotic and a sister was hospitalized with a psychoneurotic reaction. The maternal grandmother, the mother, a maternal uncle and a paternal aunt may have had personality disorders.

WSH 76: The Proband

The proband (36), born 1891; died at age 23 years at Warren State Hospital of pleurisy and pulmonary tuberculosis. The patient was described as a strong, normal child until age seven years when, following a fall from a horse, he developed "fits." He continued to have "fits" (the nature of which are unknown). The "fits" persisted for two years. At age 14 years he suffered another fall and bumped his head, but was not unconscious. This fall was followed by severe frontal headaches. The first symptoms of psychosis occurred at age 17 years, with a noticeable change of disposition. Other symptoms were alcoholic excesses, a general indifference in attitude, inability to hold a position, irrelevant laughter, delusions of poisoning and persecution and hallucinations, with auditory, visual, tactile and possibly olfactory and gustatory reactions to the hallucinations. Admission to Warren State Hospital was on 4/8/1913, with a diagnosis of dementia praecox, hebephrenic type. He remained at Warren until death. Classification: Schizophrenic reaction — paranoid type.

Grandparents

Maternal grandmother (4), born 1817; died at age 86 years of apoplexy. She had six strokes, the first occurring 10 years before her death. She was psychotic the last three years of her life. She frequently thought she saw crowds of people outside her window; she also thought someone was trying to get her property and would leave the house to search for objects she believed had been taken. Once she tried to kill her son-in-law because of some imaginary wrong he had done her. Classification: Chronic brain syndrome of senium.

Parents

Father (20), born 1830; died at age 82 years of uremia nephritis. He was described as an odd, eccentric man who preferred "reading about and discussing religion to working." At age 66 years he developed the delusion that he had swallowed a lizard and could feel it bite his stomach. He maintained the delusion until death. For the last four years of his life he was blind. Classification: Personality disorder; also, probable chronic brain syndrome of senium or possibly with functional psychosis.

Mother (21), born 1849; died at age 79 years of cancer of the colon. She had "fits" until nine years of age. As an adult she was described as "peculiar, nervous, quarrelsome, illiterate, manneristic, suspicious and perhaps with persecutory ideas." When interviewed she gave conflicting replies to the questions. Classification: Probably with functional psychosis, schizophrenic reaction — chronic undifferentiated type.

(22) first husband of mother (21). He was described as a "shiftless, good-fornothing farmer and a habitual drunkard." Classification: Possible sociopathic personality disturbance — alcoholism (addiction).

(23) second husband of mother (21); died at age 30 years of a broken neck received in an accident. He was described as "shiftless and incapable." Classification: Possible personality pattern disturbance — inadequate personality.

Aunts and Uncles

Paternal uncle (11), died at age 75 years. He was described as a "hard drinker." Classification: Possible sociopathic personality disturbance — alcoholism (addiction).

Paternal uncle (12); died at age 50 years. He was described as a "hard drinker." Classification: Possible sociopathic personality disorder — alcoholism (addiction).

Paternal uncle (18), born 1837; aged 76 years when interviewed. He was described as "feeble, both physically and mentally." He could not remember the names of all his brothers and sisters and found it difficult to give information on people he could remember. He was still working as a carpenter but worked slowly because of a coarse tremor of his head and hands that developed at about age 66 years. His residence was in a state of general disorder and untidiness. Classification: Probable chronic brain syndrome of senium; Possible personality pattern disturbance — inadequate personality.

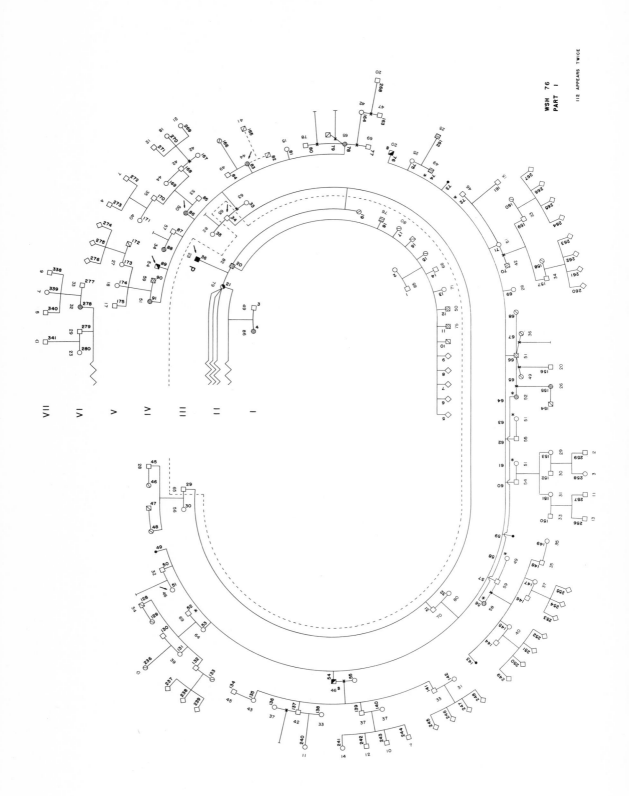

WSH 76
PART I

112 APPEARS TWICE

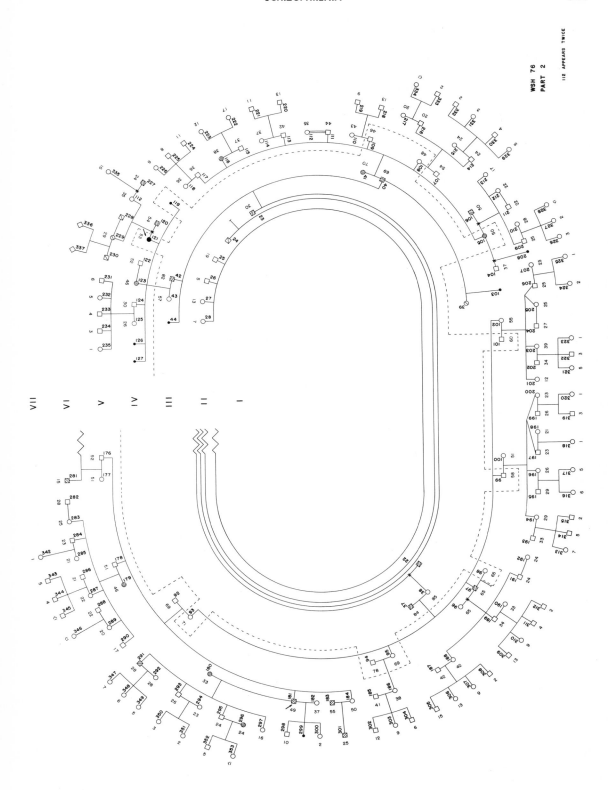

Half Siblings

Paternal half brother (34), born 1876; died at age 65 years of bronchopneumonia and dementia paralytica at a state hospital in Massachusetts. He was hospitalized from 8/30/1941 until his death on 11/5/1941, with a diagnosis of psychosis with syphilitic encephalitis. About a year and a half before admission he became confused and unable to care for himself. He had epileptiform seizures for several years preceding hospitalization. Reportedly, his confusion began following a fall during a seizure, at which time he struck his head. Classification: Chronic brain syndrome associated with meningoencephalitic central nervous system syphilis, with psychotic reaction.

(37) husband of maternal half sister (38), born 1859; died at age 84 years of myocardial failure and senility. Classification: Possible chronic brain syndrome of senium.

Maternal half brother (40), born 1879; died at age 69 years of acute cardiac dilation. He had epileptic seizures until age 12 years. He gave his wife and young children little financial help after he and his second wife were separated. Classification: Possible personality disorder.

(41) wife of maternal half brother (40), born 1890. She reportedly raised her family well in spite of hardships. At about age 69 years she had "nerve pills" prescribed as she had "three spells" during which she was nervous and worried. Classification: Probable psychoneurotic disorder.

Maternal half brother (42), born 1878; when interviewed at age 82 years he was very confused and "unable to make up his mind about anything." He was always considered to be mentally deficient. Classification: Possible chronic brain syndrome of senium.

Nieces and Nephews

(51) wife of half nephew (50), born 1900; died at age 46 years of acute cardiac dilation and cancer of the rectum at a state hospital in California, where she had been since 7/15/1926. She was normal until age two years when she had "brain fever," after which her parents noticed that she was mentally deficient. She was married at age

20 years but only remained with her husband a very short time. Admission notes stated, "Excitable at times; nervous, dull, sly . . . restless and depressed; will laugh and cry without apparent cause; wanders from home." At the hospital she was described as "indifferent, not actually resistant, but mentally inert; consciousness indefinite and vague." There were "vague general reactions as though of some secondary mental condition." There was no diagnosis given but a later superintendent suggested that it would have been mental retardation, post-encephalitic. Classification: Chronic brain syndrome associated with other intracranial infection, with behavioral reaction; also, mental deficiency.

Half nephew (54), born 1903; suicided by cyanide poisoning at age 46 years. He had suffered a severe accident two years previous to his death and was near death for a year. At the time of his death he was suffering from chronic osteomyelitis of the left tibia. Classification: Probably with functional psychosis; Possible psychoneurotic disorder — depressive reaction.

(56) wife of half nephew (57), born 1906. When interviewed in 1965 she had just lost her husband of 21 years (her second husband). She was described by the interviewer as either dull intellectually or considerably deteriorated, as her memory was so poor that she could give little information. She looked considerably older than her 58 years. She was described by relatives as "a very sweet person" and as sexually promiscuous. Classification: Possible sociopathic personality disturbance — antisocial reaction.

(64) wife of half nephew (66), born 1912. She was described as being sexually promiscuous. Classification: Possible sociopathic personality disturbance — antisocial reaction.

Half nephew (66), born 1909. At last information he was in a federal penitentiary for transporting a female across state boundaries for immoral purposes (his daughter). He claimed the charge was false since his daughter was a prostitute. At age 14 years his father had him committed to a correctional institution for truancy and incorrigibility. Four years later he was arrested for suspicion of rape, but was given a probationary sentence when he married the girl. He had subsequent prison terms for driving an automobile without the owner's permission; for attempted grand theft; for theft, and for grand theft. Classification: Sociopathic personality disturbance—antisocial reaction.

(70) husband of half niece (71), born 1901. While married to (71) she supported him most of the time. Though he recovered from a motorcycle accident, he continued to remain at home with his wife caring for him. The interviewer commented "He sounds like a passive-dependent individual." Classification: Possible personality pattern disturbance—schizoid personality.

(74) husband of half niece (75), born 1913. When interviewed he was hostile and uncooperative and considered "passive-dependent" by the interviewer. Classification: Possible personality trait disturbance, passive-aggressive personality.

Half nephew (76), born 1917; suicided at age 20 years with a gunshot wound to the head. He had been in a serious accident and had been told he had but six months to live at the time of the suicide. Classification: Probably with functional psychosis; Possible psychoneurotic disorder—depressive reaction.

Half niece (78), born 1897. In 1928 her daughter was in temporary foster care and (78) was described as "not always truthful" and displaying considerable "imagination." Eleven years later she was interviewed in connection with a niece who was receiving assistance. At this time she made a good impression and had apparently made a good marriage. Classification: Possible transient situational personality disorder.

Half niece (83), born 1900; died at age 44 years of bronchopneumonia and malnutrition at a state mental hospital. She died nine days after being admitted with undiagnosed psychosis. She had never been considered normal mentally, had spent some time in a reformatory and before she died she was receiving treatment for fractures and injuries received when hit by an automobile. Classification: Probable sociopathic personality disturbance; Possibly with functional psychosis.

Half niece (86), born 1902. She was at a psychiatric hospital for observation from 8/7/1922 until 8/16/1922. A diagnosis of conduct disorder without psychosis in an individual of low mental level (IQ 79) was made. She was referred to the

hospital from the Industrial School for Girls, where she was placed because of deceitfulness and irresponsibility. Classification: Sociopathic personality disturbance.

(88) wife of half nephew (87), born 1904; died at age 34 years of acute dilation of the heart, chronic alcoholism and delirium tremens. Classification: Sociopathic personality disturbance—alcoholism (addiction).

Half nephew (89), born 1907. He had average intelligence but completed only the third grade because of his failure to adjust. He was hospitalized at a state hospital from 7/25/1939 until he escaped on 6/14/1940. He had episodes of depression, thoughts of suicide and had a history of intemperate use of alcohol. Diagnosis at admission was "without psychosis, psychopathic personality, mixed types." Later, a determined diagnosis was dementia praecox, simple type. He was never rehospitalized and worked as a roofer and janitor. Classification: Probably with functional psychosis; Possible sociopathic personality disturbance.

(90) husband of half niece (91), born 1902. He was reportedly an alcoholic and a gambler. Classification: Sociopathic personality disturbance.

Half niece (91), born 1910. When an adolescent she was in the Industrial School for Girls for one year for drunkenness and accosting men. In 1937 her oldest child was removed from the home because of the drunkenness of the parents. She would appear at the welfare office when drunk to the point of falling off her chair and going to sleep. When seen by welfare workers in 1943, she was described as "vague, of limited intelligence and as evasive and contradictory in her statements." More recently she was "doing well" and working as a nursemaid. Classification: Sociopathic personality disturbance.

Half nephew (97), born 1895. He was once "practically an alcoholic" who stopped drinking. Classification: Possible sociopathic personality disturbance—alcoholism (addiction).

Half niece (105), born 1910. She was raised by her mother after the father deserted the family. She was ill most of her life; she had spinal meningitis, erysipelas, cancer of the breast and lost one eye. When interviewed her memory was impaired and she was extremely anxious that the information she gave did not cause discord among the siblings. Classification: Possible psychoneurotic disorder.

(106) husband of half niece (105), born 1910. Reported to be alcoholic or a heavy weekend drinker. Classification: Possible sociopathic personality disturbance—alcoholism (addiction).

Half niece (116), born 1922. She was described as "jittery" during an interview and commented that her whole family was "nervous" and that she "was the worst." Classification: Probable psychoneurotic disorder.

(120) husband of half niece (121), born 1906. He was described as "no good—always in trouble" and "he drank." When (120) and (121) were divorced, he received custody of the child. Classification: Probable personality disorder.

Half niece (121), born 1907. She was a patient at a state mental hospital from 10/21/1949 until 7/1/1953, with a diagnosis of psychoneurosis due to neurotic addiction. She had numerous hospitalizations with physical complaints which were out of proportion to her disability, but was not rehospitalized for mental illness. Classification: Schizophrenic reaction—chronic undifferentiated type.

Half niece (123), born 1914. She was described as "drinking and is close to being an alcoholic." She was also described as "sick—has the doctor quite a bit." Classification: Possible personality disorder.

Distant Relatives

Half grandniece (155), born 1930. Her father found her living in a house of prostitution. She lived with him thereafter until both were arrested in connection with a car theft. Classification: Sociopathic personality disturbance.

Half grandnephew (162), born 1938. His mother died when he was three years old. He received day-care in a nursery school until his father remarried a year later. As an adult he was unable to hold a job. Classification: Possible personality pattern disturbance—inadequate personality.

(179) wife of half grandnephew (178). She "went to the doctor for her nerves" while caring for her husband, who had been in an accident. Classification: Transient situational personality disturbance—gross stress reaction.

(180) wife of half grandnephew (181), born 1913; died at age 33 years of lymphatic leukemia and chronic nephritis. A description of hypochondriasis was given by the family doctor. Classification: Possible psychoneurotic disorder.

Half grandnephew (181), born 1911. He was hospitalized twice for alcoholism, once at a state mental hospital and once at an Alcoholics Anonymous hospital. Classification: Sociopathic personality disturbance—alcoholism (addiction).

(183) husband of half grandniece (184), born 1908. He had sought medical help for "nervous exhaustion." Classification: Probable psychoneurotic disorder.

(227) husband of half grandniece (112), born 1922. He could neither read nor write. School guidance records listed IQ scores of 73 in 1930 and 54 in 1933. He was described as "a lazy, good-for-nothing" and as "often in scrapes—a no-good." Classification: Probable mental deficiency; Possible personality disorder.

Great half grandniece (278), born 1928. She reportedly "tends to be nervous" and

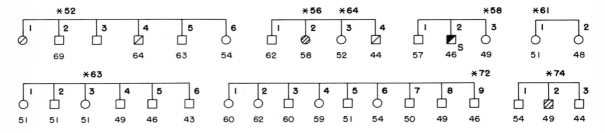

"goes to the doctor" because of her nervousness. Classification: Possible psychoneurotic disorder.

Great half grandnephew (281), born 1945. He was described as "accident prone . . . he's banged up a lot." Classification: Possible psychoneurotic disorder.

Great half grandnephew (291), born 1932. He was described by his family as "awful nervous" and as "drunk every time I see him." He once tried to strangle his wife while intoxicated. Classification: Probable sociopathic personality disorder—alcoholism (addiction); Possible psychoneurotic disorder.

(296) wife of great half grandnephew (295), born 1936. She said she was nervous and had "shingles" every time she had a baby. Her physician said nothing about her nervousness. Classification: Probable psychoneurotic disorder; Possible personality disorder.

Great half grandnephew (301), born 1938. He was described by various persons as "he never worked, has a terrible temper, just not all there"; an "odd person," and had "blue spells." He worked as a folksinger and when interviewed "made a good impression and talked well." Classification: Probable personality disorder; Possible psychoneurotic disorder.

Family Summary

The proband and a half niece were psychotic and were hospitalized with their illnesses. A half nephew was probably psychotic and was hospitalized. Other hospitalized individuals were a half brother and the wife of a half nephew with organic psychoses, two half nieces with personality disorders and a half grandnephew who was an alcoholic. Two half nephews who suicided were classified as probably with functional psychosis. The mother was in all probability a schizophrenic. The maternal grandmother, the father (who also had a personality disorder), a paternal uncle, a maternal half brother, and the husband of a maternal half sister were classified as chronic brain syndrome of senium. Those with personality disorder classifications included the mother's first and second husbands, two paternal uncles, a maternal half brother, three wives of half nephews, two half nephews, three half nieces, five husbands of half nieces, one half grandniece, a half grandnephew, the husband of a half grandniece, the wife of a half grandnephew, and two great half grandnephews. Neurotics, or probably or possibly so, were the wife of a maternal half brother, two half nieces, the wife and the husband of a half grandnephew and of a half grandniece, a great half grandniece, a great half grandnephew and the wife of a great half grandnephew.

Controls

See family pedigree, person (56).

Brother (2) of (58), born 1893; died at age 46 years of suicide by carbon monoxide poisoning. He was described as an alcoholic who "used alcohol as an anti-depressant," but was never treated for alcoholism. His family believed that he was inebriated at the time of his death and the death was, therefore, accidental; however, the verdict of the coroner's inquest was suicide. Classification: Probably with functional psychosis.

See family pedigree, person (74).

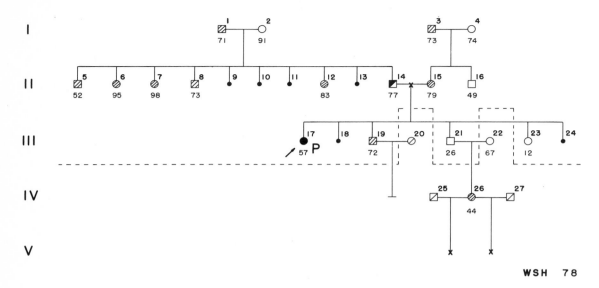

WSH   78

WSH 78: The Proband

The proband (17), born 1887; died at age 57 years of cancer of the stomach. She was a normal child who had a change in disposition at puberty, when she became odd, peculiar, introspective, seclusive, stubborn and self-willed. At age 26 years she became restless and over-religious, and developed the delusion that she was hypnotized and that her whole family was against her. She also thought that electric currents were going through her body. Admission to Warren State Hospital was on 1/18/1913, two weeks after the onset of the psychotic symptoms, and she was diagnosed as dementia praecox. She was bedridden at Warren from 1928 until she died in 1944. Classification: Schizophrenic reaction—hebephrenic type.

Grandparents

Paternal grandfather (1), born 1820; died at age 71 years of congestion of the brain and dropsy. About two years preceding death he developed severe head pains, had several attacks of delirium and became aphasic. Classification: Chronic brain syndrome of senium.

Maternal grandfather (3), born 1838; died at age 73 years of heart failure. He had migraine headaches all his life and was described as "a high-strung, nervous man

. . . had a fiery temper." Classification: Probable psychoneurotic disorder; Possible psychoneurotic disorder.

Parents

Father (14), born 1850; died at age 77 years of angina pectoris. At age 50 years he took a medical course and became an army physician. He was described by various family members as "vague, childish, with a lack of reason and good judgment . . . self-centered, petty and inclined to interpret things bearing no relation to him as direct acts against himself." He never got along well with people. He drank to excess, was arrested twice and made false accusations concerning his wife's behavior. Classification: Probably with functional psychosis, schizophrenic reaction, chronic undifferentiated type; Possible sociopathic personality disturbance—antisocial reaction.

Mother (15), born 1868; died at age 79 years of diffusive vascular disease. She was subject to sick headaches all her life and, while studying in medical school and caring for her children, was a "nervous wreck." Her in-laws considered her "unbalanced"; she showed pronounced favoritism among her children and was cruel to them. She and her husband were unhappy together and after the birth of their last child they separated. Classification: Personality trait disturbance—passive-aggressive personality.

Aunts and Uncles

Paternal uncle (5), born 1846; died at age 52 years of tuberculosis. From age 25 years he was a "hard and steady drinker" who was easily affected by even a glass of liquor. Classification: Possible sociopathic personality disturbance—alcoholism (addiction).

Paternal aunt (6), born 1847; died at age 95 years of general arteriosclerosis. She was described as a typical, single, elderly woman of refined taste and interests whose family had suffered financial reverses. When interviewed her steady stream of invectives against her sister-in-law and the proband's mother was checked every now and then with an apologetic remark. Her thinly veiled hostility, aggressiveness, shallow affect, bitterness and vindictiveness were described as a "narrow, shallow, conventional morality and judgment" by the interviewer. Classification: Probable personality trait disturbance—passive-aggressive personality.

Paternal aunt (7), born 1852; died at age 98 years of arteriosclerotic heart disease. She was described as the "most peculiar of the three sisters," (6), (7) and (12), and was never employed outside the home. Classification: Probable personality disorder.

Paternal uncle (8), born 1857; died at age 73 years of chronic myocarditis. He was regarded as rather erratic and peculiar. He lived with a married woman for a period of several years. He also used alcohol to excess, but gave it up completely later in his life. Classification: Probable sociopathic personality disturbance.

Paternal aunt (12), born 1859; died at age 83 years of cancer of the uterus. She was interviewed and described as "double-faced and insincere." She made absurd, extravagant statements and seemed very conceited. Classification: Personality trait disturbance—passive-aggressive personality.

Siblings

Brother (19), born 1890; died at age 72 years. He reportedly was always "stubborn, wayward" and "difficult." He never kept a position for any length of time and deserted the navy soon after he enlisted. He was in poor health and was unemployed after World War I, during which he was gassed in combat. Classification: Personality disorder.

Nieces and Nephews

Niece (26), born 1919. Her father was killed in action in World War II before she was born. She stated in a letter in 1963, while refusing to cooperate in the study, "My own history would bore you as I am only mildly a neurotic normal . . . presumably no psychotic tendencies are evident." Classification: Possible psychoneurotic disorder.

Family Summary

The proband was psychotic and the father probably so. The mother, a brother, three paternal aunts and two paternal uncles were classified as with some sort of personality disorder. The maternal grandfather and the only niece may have been neurotic. The paternal grandfather was classified as with chronic brain syndrome of senium.

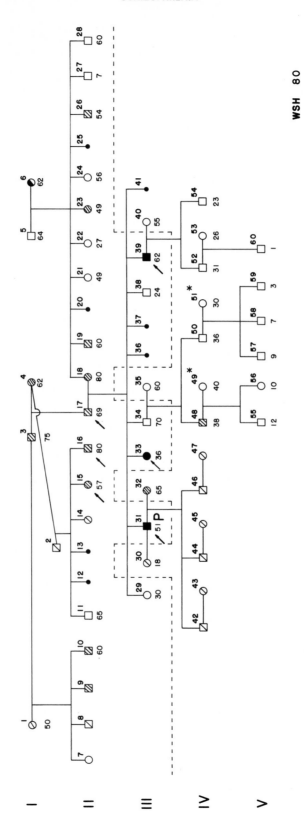

WSH 80: The Proband

The proband (31), born 1889; died at age 51 years of chronic myocardial heart disease. He received a scholarship to college, which he used for three and a half years, then became "lazy and dissatisfied." He had no interest in the jobs he subsequently obtained and was generally aimless and indifferent. In 1912 he became restless and agitated and was admitted to Warren State Hospital on 10/19/1912. He had no conduct disorders but was unable to concentrate, was untidy, apathetic, depressed and diagnosed as dementia praecox, hebephrenic form. He escaped 4/20/1913, one month before he was to be paroled to his sister, which he did not want. He later married for the second time, but no record of his mental health after his escape was available as his wife was uncooperative with the study. Classification: Schizophrenic reaction—simple type.

(32) wife of proband (31). When interviewed she was very suspicious and refused to give information because it "was against her religion." The interviewer described her as "one of the oddest persons she had ever met." She put their children in an orphanage after the proband died. She never visited them, or had them visit her. Classification: Possible personality pattern disturbance—paranoid personality or schizoid personality.

Parents

Father (17), born 1865; died at age 69 years of acute myocarditis. He began using opium at age 22 years, which he soon replaced with morphine. When he went to Oppenheimer Institute for a cure in 1910, he was using 50 grains per day. The permanence of his cure was doubtful as he was unstable, irritable and "something of a braggart." Classification: Sociopathic personality disturbance, drug addiction; also, possible psychoneurotic disorder.

Mother (18), born 1867; died at age 80 years of arteriosclerotic heart disease and fracture of the hip. Before her marriage she was a bright, vivacious and attractive girl, who, it was suggested, in other circumstances might have been "an unusually estimable and capable woman." In actuality, she was described as passive, listless, dull, indifferent and with little ambition. Classification: Possible personality pattern disturbance—inadequate personality.

Grandparents

Paternal grandfather (3), died at age 75 years of paralysis. He was said to have been an ugly-tempered man who did no work for many years before his death, although he was in good health. Classification: Possible personality disorder.

Paternal grandmother (4), born 1830; died at age 62 years of pneumonia. She was described as an intelligent and industrious woman who was subject to frequent, severe headaches. At age 55 years she began to use morphine, which she used until her death. Classification: Possible sociopathic personality disturbance—drug addiction.

Maternal grandmother (6), born 1844; died at age 62 years of paralysis. At the time of menopause she had kidney trouble and was sick in bed. While ill she became mentally deranged for two or three weeks. She talked a great deal, her answers to questions were irrelevant and she thought she was back in Ireland. Three years before her death she again became deranged; she was restless, indifferent to her surroundings, had somatic delusions and appeared silly and foolish. Classification: Probably with functional psychosis; Possible psychoneurotic disorder.

Aunts and Uncles

Paternal half uncle (9), born 1862, age at death unknown. He was described as an agreeable, upright man, who late in life seemed to undergo a personality change and became irritable, disagreeable, dishonest, unreliable and a heavy drinker. Classification: Sociopathic personality disturbance—alcoholism (addiction).

Paternal half uncle (10), born 1844; died at age 60 years. He was described as "a drunken tramp" whose whereabouts were generally unknown to the family. Classification: Sociopathic personality disturbance—alcoholism (addiction).

Paternal half aunt (15), born 1856. At age 57 years she was in a mental institution

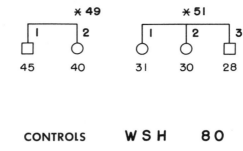

CONTROLS   W S H   8 0

in New York state, where she had been since age 52. She suffered from headaches with delirium every month and was described as a very artistic person. At age 25 years she began using morphine. She became so unreliable and troublesome that she was eventually hospitalized. Classification: Probable psychoneurotic disorder; Possibly with functional psychosis.

Paternal half uncle (16), born 1852; died at age 80 years. At age 40 years he began to drink to excess. Four years later he was institutionalized for a cure which lasted a year or two, then he relapsed into his former alcoholic habits. Classification: Sociopathic personality disturbance — alcoholism (addiction).

Maternal uncle (19), born 1862; died at age 60 years of a stroke. He became prominent in his community through politics but was called a "dead beat" because he did not pay his bills. Classification: Possible sociopathic personality disturbance.

Maternal aunt (23), born 1879; died at age 49 years of apoplexy. She complained of frequent headaches over one eye, which were described as "nervous headaches." She was described as obese, deceitful, unreliable and "had the aspirin habit." Classification: Probable psychoneurotic disorder.

Maternal uncle (26), born 1880; died at age 54 years of cancer of the prostate. Reportedly his "fondness for cleanliness and fear of germs was ridiculous to the extreme." Classification: Possible psychoneurotic disorder.

Siblings

Sister (33), born 1891; died at age 36 years of tuberculosis. She never seemed to outgrow her childish ways. She was backward in school, nervous, fidgety and excitable. At age 16 years she began acting strangely and talked to imaginary people. In July, 1912, after a possible sunstroke, she became aurally and visually hallucinated (she saw angels and her deceased grandmother). She was admitted to Warren State Hospital on 1/13/1913, with a diagnosis of dementia praecox in an imbecile. From 1/26/1919 until 6/30/1927, she was a patient at a state mental hospital where she was considered psychotic and mentally deficient. Classification: Schizophrenic reaction — paranoid type; also, mental deficiency.

Brother (39), born 1902. As a boy he was "dull, stupid and sleepy" and was given little attention or affection by his mother. His marriage was happy but adjustment to business failures and loss of a job in the 1940's was very difficult for him. He resented his wife's friends and employment, and in 1951, after his mother's death, he became hysterical and collapsed with severe chest pains. He was hospitalized five times but no heart ailment could be diagnosed. He had crying spells of depression and fear, believed he was dying and wanted his wife to sit up with him day and night. He became dependent upon narcotics and barbiturates. He was hospitalized at a state mental hospital from 9/6/1955 until 5/20/1958. After treatment he was no longer depressed and was concerned only with his somatic complaints. Diagnosis and classification: Involutional psychotic reaction.

Nieces and Nephews

Nephew (48), born 1926. He had a distinguished service record in World War II and was described as "nervous when he came back from the war." Classification: Possible situational personality disturbance—gross stress reaction.

Family Summary

The proband, a sister and a brother had psychotic disorders and were hospitalized. The maternal grandmother was probably psychotic. Personality disorders were found in the father, three paternal half uncles and probably or possibly in the wife of the proband, the mother, the paternal grand-

parents, a maternal uncle and a nephew. A paternal half aunt and a maternal aunt were probably neurotic and a maternal uncle possibly so. Among the personality disorders were two cases of drug addiction. The psychotic brother also developed a dependence upon narcotics and barbiturates. The three additional personality disorders were classified as alcohol addiction.

Controls

None noteworthy.

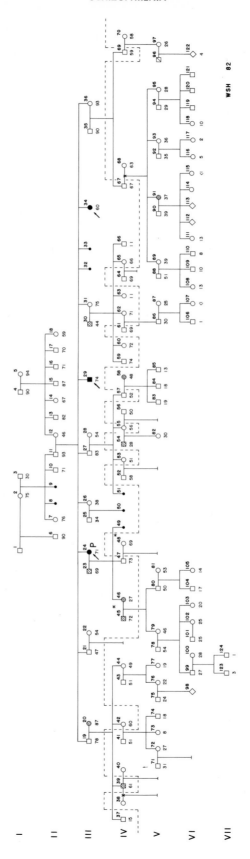

WSH 82

WSH 82: The Proband

The proband (24), born 1859; died at age 72 years at Warren State Hospital of diabetes. Although the eldest daughter, she was always "babyish" in her behavior and from childhood was nervous, fidgety, over-talkative and self-centered. In 1905 she developed delusions of persecution in that she believed her character was being attacked and that there were sewing machines in her head. She developed auditory hallucinations and became deaf. The condition persisted and she was hospitalized at Warren State Hospital from 11/10/1909 until 9/30/1912. Her paranoid thoughts continued and she was readmitted on 2/22/1913, where she remained, hypochondriacal and suspicious, until her death. Classification: Schizophrenic reaction—paranoid type.

(23) husband of proband (24), born 1860; died at age 69 years of cancer. He was described as "gay, loose principled, drank to excess and went with women of poor reputation." Classification: Possible sociopathic personality disturbance.

Children

(45) husband of daughter (46), born 1890. He was described as much like his wife's father. He had to leave his home for a time to avoid the consequences of a forged check. Classification: Possible transient situational personality disorder.

Daughter (46), born 1887; died at age 27 years of typhus. She reportedly was of an hysterical temperament; when she laughed she easily lost control of herself and would cry for an hour. At age 25 she had an episode of emotional trouble when she was despondent and melancholy. Classification: Probable psychoneurotic disorder.

Siblings

(2) wife of brother (19), born 1869; died at age 87 years of carcinoma of the bladder. A year before her death she became mentally confused and was placed in a rest home. Classification: Probable chronic brain syndrome in senium.

Brother (29), born 1862; died at age 74 years of a urinary tract infection at a state hospital. As a boy he was considered very bright but had little recreation and as he grew older he did not date girls. His first attack of mental disturbance was at age 20 years, when he became restless, noisy and was at times depressed. The next attack occurred in 1889 and he was hospitalized from 4/3/1889 until 9/1/1889, with a diagnosis of melancholia. He was readmitted with a third attack on 1/25/1894, with a diagnosis of primary dementia and discharged as recovered on 8/18/1894. There was a third admission in 1902, with a diagnosis of primary dementia. Subsequent admissions for mental disturbance were as follows:

12/23/1906 – 6/5/1908
1/16/1909 – 2/24/1910
7/18/1916 – 12/24/1918
9/12/1920 – 7/1/1936

His attacks of psychosis were either of excitement or depression. He made apparently complete recoveries between attacks, showing at best some eccentricities. His hallucinations were of a religious nature; he sometimes showed an elation of mood and was silly and superficial. Diagnosis at the state hospital was consistently manic-depressive psychosis. Classification: Schizophrenic reaction, schizo-affective type.

(30) husband of sister (31), born 1859; died at age 44 years of gastritis. He reportedly was an alcoholic. Classification: Possible sociopathic personality disturbance—alcoholism (addiction).

Sister (34), born 1870; died at age 60 years at a state hospital of chronic myocarditis. In 1903 she cared for her brother during his terminal illness with cancer. She worried much about him and after his death she developed delusions of persecution and ideas of annoyance (she thought someone was placing machinery in her body and electricity on her head). She was treated at a private hospital for six months and was returned partially recovered. After (29) was hospitalized she became very frightened and was admitted to a state mental hospital on 4/21/1907, with a diagnosis of dementia praecox, paranoid form, where she remained until her death.

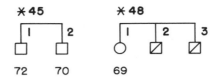

She was generally depressed but was at times excited. She persisted in her delusions of persecution. Classification: Schizophrenic reaction—paranoid type.

Nieces and Nephews

Nephew (39), born 1902. He was a retired army physician and was described as "brusk, unfriendly, always in a hurry, and alcoholic." His disposition apparently changed following his second marriage. When interviewed he was described as obese, florid in complexion, possibly inebriated, and as angry and hostile toward the project. Classification: Possible sociopathic personality disturbance—alcoholism (addiction).

(54) husband of niece (55); died at age 28 years, cause unknown. He was described as an unemployed, independently wealthy "playboy" who was considered to be an alcoholic. Classification: Sociopathic personality disturbance—alcoholism (addiction).

(58) wife of nephew (57), born 1913. She was described as "ill" and as having what the interviewer interpreted as compulsive behavior. Later she was described as an alcoholic. Classification: Sociopathic personality disturbance—alcoholism (addiction).

Distant Relatives

Grandniece (91), born 1927. Reportedly, she was always flighty, smoked to excess and had "stomach trouble" which had to be corrected periodically by careful diet. Classification: Possible psychoneurotic disorder.

Family Summary

The proband, a brother and a sister were psychotic and hospitalized. A daughter was probably a neurotic, a grandniece possibly so and a nephew possibly an alcoholic. The husband of a niece and the wife of a nephew were alcoholics and the husband of a sister was possibly an alcoholic. The wife of a brother was classified as probably with chronic brain syndrome in senium. The proband's husband and a son-in-law were classified as with possible sociopathic personality disturbances.

Controls

None noteworthy.

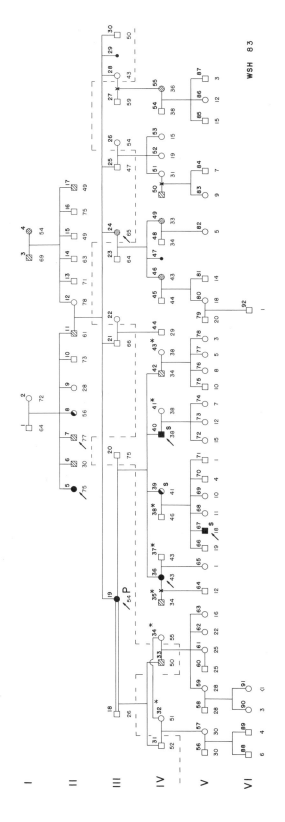

WSH 83

WSH 83: The Proband

The proband (19), born 1889; died at age 54 years at Warren State Hospital of an accidental skull fracture that occurred when she was pulled off a bench onto the floor by another patient. She was described as "always more reticent and diffident than other children of the family." Her first husband, and first cousin once removed, died in June, 1912, following a long terminal illness. Soon after his death she had a period of overactive religious interest followed by a marked depression and was subsequently hospitalized at Warren State Hospital from 1/31/1913 until 7/29/1913, with a diagnosis of manic-depressive psychosis, mixed type, or dementia praecox, catatonic type, with the latter diagnosis preferred. She remained well until 1916, when she had another "religious panic." She had no more trouble until 1931, when she again became hypomanic, then depressed, and was hospitalized at Warren from 2/3/1931 until 11/22/1932. Subsequent admissions were during depressions from 1/18/1936 until 6/24/1936, and from 12/9/1938 until death. When ill, whether in or out of the hospital, she was depressed with short periods of excitement which were considered too numerous to report in hospital notes. Diagnosis at Warren State Hospital after the first admission was consistently manic-depressive psychosis, depressed type. Classification: Schizophrenic reaction —catatonic type.

Children

Son (33), born 1910. After the death of his father and the hospitalization of his mother he lived with his paternal grandparents. He had a "nervous breakdown" in 1944, reportedly caused by exhaustion from overwork. He remained in bed for two weeks and gradually resumed activities with complete recovery in one year. He was later described as "very religious." Classification: Probable psychoneurotic disorder, depressive reaction; Possibly with functional psychosis, psychotic-depressive reaction.

(35) husband of daughter (36), born 1918; died at age 34 years of severe burns.

He was described by his sister as "lovable," by his wife as "inadequate" and as a possible drug addict. He contracted malaria during World War II and became an alcoholic after release from the armed services. He either flunked or quit pharmacy school but kept up the pretense of attending. Classification: Sociopathic personality disturbance — alcoholism (addiction); also, possible drug addiction.

Daughter (36), born 1922. Her early home life was poverty stricken, the discipline strict but kind. Her mother was hospitalized during most of her adolescent years and her father died when she was 18 years old. Another family raised her "through high school" and provided a nurse's training course. She was unhappily married and neglected her baby after its birth. When she and the baby's father were divorced, he was awarded custody of the child. After his death, the child was given to the paternal grandparents. In 1950 she was hospitalized for psychiatric treatment at a Veterans Administration hospital and on 1/18/1952 she was transferred to another Veterans Administration hospital with a diagnosis of schizophrenic reaction, undifferentiated, chronic, in partial remission. She reacted with fear and increased disorganization to electroshock therapy but showed gradual improvement with individual therapy and was released on 4/22/1955. Ten years later she appeared well, although still a clinic patient, and was happily married. Classification: Schizophrenic reaction — paranoid type.

Daughter (39), born 1924. She suffered poverty and severe deprivation during childhood. Her mother was hospitalized often during her adolescence and her father died when she was aged 16 years. At age 15, during a period when she was kept from school to keep house for the family while her mother was at Warren State Hospital, she had a depression. After the birth of her second child she suffered a depression and made a suicide attempt by drinking Lysol. She was later described as "nervous and shiftless" and was considered overweight and talkative, but with no indication of anxiety or tension when interviewed. She was preoccupied with an irregular religious denomination and gave the impression of mild instability. Classification: Probably with functional psychosis, psychotic-depressive reaction.

Son (40), born 1926. His mother's hospitalization occurred when he was four, nine and 11 years of age, and his father died when he was aged 14 years; his mother died two years later. Until age 13 years he had a strong desire to be a woman. After the death of his father he was depressed for a week and considered suicide. In 1950 he became despondent and preoccupied with religion for a few weeks (God talked to him) and in March, 1952, he began to think that his family and coworkers were against him, he developed auditory hallucinations and became unable to concentrate. He improved markedly following ECT and insulin therapy at Warren State Hospital from 3/10/1952 until 9/9/1952. The second admission to Warren State Hospital (9/4/1959) was an emergency because he was arrested for shaking up a boy as "the voice told him to." He had been delusional for months and remained hospitalized until 6/28/1960. The third hospitalization at Warren State Hospital, from 12/9/1963 until 3/25/1964, was precipitated by the delusions of grandeur he developed when he became very upset by the assassination of President Kennedy. He made a suicide attempt after his wife filed for divorce in 1963. Last admission to Warren State Hospital was on 1/12/1965, where he remained. Diagnosis and classification: Schizophrenic reaction — paranoid type.

Son (42), born 1928. He lived with an aunt after the hospitalization of his mother when he was four years old; his father died when he was 11 and he was self-supporting from age 13 years. He was a bed-wetter until age 12 years and as a youth suffered "spells of depression." Classification: Probable psychoneurotic disorder, depressive reaction; Possible transient situational personality disturbance, adjustment reaction of childhood.

Grandchild

Grandson (67), born 1946. He was a frankly unwanted child whose mother, when he was two months old, attempted suicide. He failed the first and tenth grades, school adjustments were always borderline and he was considered stubborn and difficult to discipline. At age 12 years he was seen at a child guidance center because of enuresis and "peculiar behavior" but the parents did not cooperate with the psychiatrist. At age 17 years, when a girl friend refused to go steady with him, he became quite upset and depressed, appeared distracted and confused, lost his appetite, began experiencing auditory hallucinations and made two suicide attempts, one by taking an overdose of medication and another by drinking iodine. He spent four days at a general hospital and was admitted to Warren State Hospital on 6/12/1963. He went home on 7/26/1964 but was soon returned. Diagnosis and classification: Schizophrenic reaction — paranoid type.

Grandparents

Maternal grandfather (3), born 1845; died at age 69 years of valvular disease of the heart. He was described as "always rather flighty, worrying and losing control of himself easily; said to be nervous." Classification: Probable psychoneurotic disorder. Possible personality trait disturbance — emotionally unstable personality.

Maternal grandmother (4), born 1851; died at age 54 years of cancer. She was described as a "trouble maker" and as a "gossip." Classification: Possible personality disorder.

Parents

Father (11), born 1865; died at age 61 years of bulbar paralysis. He was described as a "stern, rather silent man" and as "austere, stingy, penurious, high-strung, a worrier, highly pitched, very intense and at times unstable." He was also described as "a hard worker, sound thinker and business success." At age 40 years he was injured when he fell and was caught upon silo doors, where he hung by his neck until rescued. In his middle fifties he began to have small strokes and subsequently became irrational, confused, irritable, despondent and suicidal. He stuttered, had a tremor, his memory failed and he was occasionally hallucinated; however, he was cared for at home. Classification: Probable

personality disorder; also, chronic brain syndrome of senium.

Aunts and Uncles

Paternal aunt (5), born 1861; died at age 75 years at Warren State Hospital. She had the following hospitalizations and diagnoses:

4/16/1887–
       8/1/1887 — Acute mania
1/18/1893–
       4/17/1893 — Acute mania
2/25/1894–
       4/17/1894 — Periodic mania
2/10/1897–
       5/6/1897 — Periodic mania
5/24/1931– death
       — Manic-depressive psychosis, manic phase

At her first admission there was a reference made to one earlier episode of mild excitement in 1880. Between attacks she was "cheerful, happy-go-lucky, and a good mixer." The first four hospitalized attacks were characterized by restlessness, confusion, untidiness and occasional destructiveness. Two months before her fifth admission to Warren State Hospital she became ill with influenza and, after being well mentally for 35 years, became flighty, distracted, noisy and overactive. Classification: Manic-depressive reaction — manic type.

Paternal uncle (6), born 1870; died at age 30 years of dropsy. He was described as "always delicate, suffered much from rheumatism." He had no occupation. Classification: Possible psychoneurotic disorder.

Paternal uncle (7), born 1872; died at Warren State Hospital at age 77 years of chronic myocarditis and cerebral arteriosclerosis. He was considered peculiar by his community after he offered boys whiskey when in charge of a Boy Scout camp. He was also considered to have poor judgment in that he consistently made unsuccessful purchases in the stock market and at one time set up a roadside produce stand on a little-traveled road. In 1928 he suffered a stroke. In early 1945 he suffered a slight concussion in an automobile accident. In

November of 1945 he suffered another concussion when hit by an automobile. He returned to work but quit within a month because "his head bothered him." In the spring of 1948 he developed periods of silence followed by excessive talking. He became excessively worried, expressing death wishes, and was admitted to Warren State Hospital on 6/10/1948, where he remained until death. Diagnosis and classification: Chronic brain syndrome with cerebral arteriosclerosis.

Paternal aunt (8), born 1875; died at age 56 years of pneumonia. She was described in various sources as "psychotic but never committed . . . mentally ill over worry over money . . . had a period of mental disturbance . . . but could not furnish details," and that she "imagined things that weren't there, but was o.k. later." Classification: Probably with functional psychosis. Possible psychoneurotic disorder.

Maternal uncle (17), born 1892; died at age 49 years of carcinoma of the colon. In 1933 he lost his electrical equipment–radio store and became an unsuccessful real estate broker who was actually supported by his wife. After his financial losses he was described as a "broken man" who was not depressed but rationalized his financial difficulties by blaming General Motors for taking his inventions and by always being on the verge of a major real estate deal which did not materialize. Classification: Probable psychoneurotic disorder—depressive reaction. Possible transient situational personality disturbance—adult situational reaction.

Siblings

Sister (24), born 1895. In 1925, after the death of her second child at age 15 days, she experienced a depressive episode which cleared spontaneously in about six weeks. She was well until December, 1955, when she experienced an acute anxiety episode with agitated depression, during which she would cry for no reason, found it difficult to concentrate and neglected her housework. She was hospitalized at a general hospital in February, 1956, for 13 days, was given sedation and was in good remission for two to six weeks; then her anxiety returned in marked depression. She did not hallucinate and was never delusional. On 6/8/1956, she was admitted to a state mental hospital with a diagnosis of psychoneurosis, where she remained until 10/25/1956. She remained well and was most appreciative of the help received at the hospital when interviewed several years later. Classification: Psychoneurotic disorder—depressive reaction.

Nieces and Nephews

Niece (46), born 1917. In 1959, following the death of her mother-in-law and the illegitimate pregnancy of her daughter, she sought medical help "for nerves." Classification: Possible transient situational personality disorder—adult situational reaction.

Niece (49), born 1927. She had medication prescribed for "nerves" but no psychiatric care. Classification: Possible psychoneurotic reaction or personality disorder.

(50) husband of niece (51). For a period of a year and a half, while working an eight-hour office day, he also worked another eight-hour evening job with no vacation during the period. He began to have "blackouts," was briefly hospitalized and advised to discontinue his excessive work load. He was alcoholic after release from the United States Army and later had trouble with the police over a call-girl episode. Classification: Probable other transient situational personality disturbance. Possible sociopathic personality disturbance.

Niece (55), born 1924. She reported nervous indigestion and headaches until 13 years of age, when she "learned to worry less." Classification: Probable transient situational personality disorder—adjustment reaction to adolescence.

Family Summary

The proband, three of her children (one probably so), a grandson and two paternal aunts were psychotic (one probably so). A son, a daughter and the grandson made suicide attempts. A paternal uncle was hospitalized with a psychotic reaction to cerebral arteriosclerosis and a sister was a hospitalized neurotic. Two sons, the maternal grandfather, a paternal uncle, a maternal uncle and a niece were probably or possibly

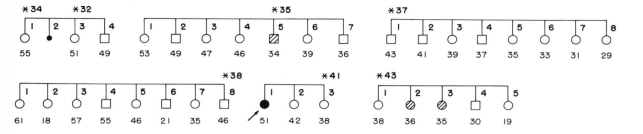

CONTROLS   W S H   8 3

neurotic. Two nieces had transient personality disorders and a husband of a niece
probably so. The father had a psychotic reaction to senility and probably a personality
disorder; the maternal grandmother possibly a personality disorder. One son-in-law
was an alcoholic and possibly a drug addict.

Controls

See family pedigree, person (35).

Sister (1) of (41), born 1915; a patient at
a state mental hospital in February, 1966,
where she was admitted on 6/25/1956, with
a diagnosis of mental deficiency with psychosis. At age two years she had poliomye-
litis with residual paralysis. She attended
school until age 16 years and reached the
third grade. During the 10 years preceding
her hospitalization at Warren she became
progressively more seclusive and apathetic.
Classification: Schizophrenic   reaction—
chronic undifferentiated type.

Sister (2) of (43), born 1927. She had
five children born within four years and was
"doctoring for nerves" when she had a sterilization operation, which further upset her.
Classification: Possible psychoneurotic disorder.

Sister (3) of (43), born 1928. She was
described as "always sullen and temperamental"; she did not get along well with
people. Classification: Possible sociopathic
personality disturbance.

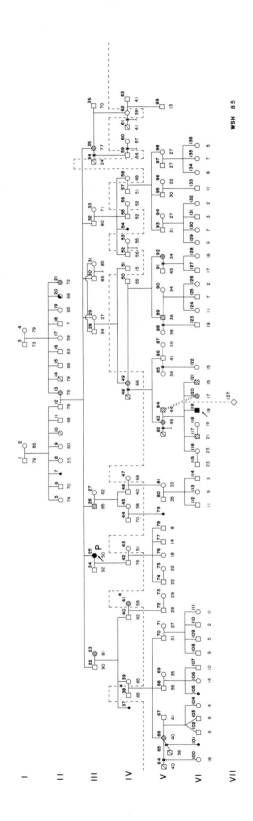

WSH 85

WSH 85: The Proband

The proband (25), born 1865; died at age 50 years at Warren State Hospital of chronic myocarditis. She was described as a "fairly intelligent, vivacious girl" and her husband described her as "friendly and pleasant but quick-tempered, nervous, hysterical and easily upset." The first symptoms of mental disorder were observed at age 39 years, when she developed intense headaches, inability to sleep and visual hallucinations. On 5/20/1905, she was admitted to Warren State Hospital with a diagnosis of acute mania based on symptoms of withdrawal, mutism and delusions of persecution alternating with episodes of quarrelsomeness and constant talking. She was taken home on 8/23/1905, but was entirely mute for three or four years and her delusions of persecution persisted. She was again hospitalized at Warren State Hospital from 6/27/1912 until her death on 6/18/1915, with a diagnosis of dementia praecox. She was generally dull, indifferent and unoccupied and occasionally mute or emotional and tearful. Classification: Schizophrenic reaction—catatonic type.

Parents

Mother (13), born 1843; died at age 75 years of pneumonia. She was described as a "nervous, emotional woman... lacking in initiative and will power... with no powers of discrimination." Classification: Probable psychoneurotic disorder; possible personality disorder.

Aunts and Uncles

Maternal aunt (20), born 1844; was aged 69 years in 1913, the time of last information. She reportedly had "a period of mental derangement" at the time of menopause. Classification: Probably with functional psychosis, involutional psychotic reaction. Possible transient situational personality disorder—adjustment reaction of late life.

Maternal aunt (21), born 1841; aged 72 years at time of last information. She was described as "a terrible talker... over-confident of her own opinions... gets a little mixed up at times." Classification: Possible personality disorder.

Siblings

(23) wife of brother (22), born 1870; died at age 81 years of arteriosclerosis. She was described as "high-strung and nervous." Classification: Probable psychoneurotic disorder.

Brother (26), born 1866; died at age 85 years of cardiac asthma. He reportedly drank to excess, at least on weekends and "sometimes several months at a time." He also changed jobs frequently. Classification: Sociopathic personality disturbance—alcoholism (addiction).

Sister (35), born 1883. She was described by an interviewer as fidgety and nervous and said that "her nerves were about worn out." Classification: Possible psychoneurotic disorder.

Nieces and Nephews

(41) wife of nephew (40), born 1901. She was interviewed and found to be neurotic with vague complaints with no apparent physical basis. Classification: Probable psychoneurotic disorder.

Niece (49), born 1894. Her mother died when she was six years of age and, after her father's death five years later, she was placed in an orphanage until released to live with very strict relatives. She married and divorced a man much older than herself to get away from the uncle's home. Her second marriage was very happy. When interviewed she said that she couldn't rest and doctored for her nerves, and never felt really well. Classification: Psychoneurotic disorder.

Distant Relatives

Grandniece (66), born 1920. She reportedly was "nervous, lost weight but refused to see a doctor" at one time. Classification: Possible psychoneurotic disorder.

Grandniece (83), born 1911. She was described by public welfare workers as "very nervous" and inadequate in making decisions. She knew of her husband's inces-

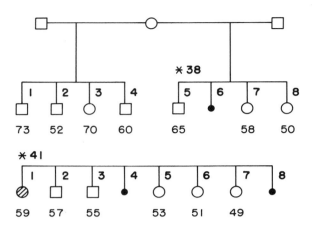

CONTROLS   **W S H   8 5**

tuous contacts with their daughter but did nothing to interfere. A Warren State Hospital interviewer thought she may have had a mild mental deficiency rather than a mental disorder. Classification: Personality pattern disturbance—inadequate personality.

(84) husband of grandniece (83), born 1916. He was imprisoned when it was discovered that he had impregnated his 14-year-old daughter. The psychologist described him as "a dependent, emotionally immature and rather poorly controlled first offender of average intellectual capacity." Psychiatrically, "he had a reactive depression with genuine guilt feelings." At age 26 years he developed spasmodic torticollis which was thought to be largely psychogenic in origin. His father had deserted his mother when (84) was a baby and his mother was later hospitalized for two years with a psychosis. Classification: Sociopathic personality disturbance—dyssocial reaction.

Grandnephew (89), born 1924. As a child he had ulcers and later had nervous stomach trouble. When he learned of his child's congenital hip dislocation he became extremely depressed and would weep about it. Classification: Psychoneurotic disorder.

Grandniece (92); age 34 at last information. She had five operations and was "extremely nervous" with symptoms of insomnia, irritability and depression, for which she received shots. Classification: Psychoneurotic disorder.

Great-grandnephew (117), born 1939. He was arrested for breaking into a cottage and stealing beer but behaved well during probation and after that time. The incident occurred when he was distressed by the plight of his sister, who had been impregnated by their father. Classification: Transient situational personality disturbance—adjustment reaction of adolescence.

Great-grandnephew (119), born 1941. He was always shy and self-conscious. Within two months after enlisting in the United States Navy, at age 18 years, he was found to be delusional during an examination for a cold and was hospitalized with a diagnosis of schizophrenic reaction, paranoid type. Upon admission on 9/23/1959, he was "blocked and confused." He thought someone was going to kill him, heard bells ringing and remained awake at night to "avoid being killed." He also thought there was something wrong with the food. He improved on drug therapy and was discharged on 2/19/1966. Classification: Schizophrenic reaction—paranoid type.

Great-grandniece (120), born 1943. The school nurse discovered that she was five months pregnant at age 15 years. Her father was responsible and was convicted of incestuous statutory rape. She was reportedly not "too deeply disturbed over the incident," put the child up for adoption and returned home. Latest information was that she was again pregnant. Classification: Probable transient situational personality disorder—adjustment reaction of adolescence.

Great-grandnephew (121), born 1945. He had convulsive spells which were not epileptic by EEG examination. He was advised not to return to school because of his convulsive spells and borderline IQ of 67. Classification: Probable transient situational personality disorder—adjustment reaction of adolescence.

Family Summary

The proband and a great-grandnephew were psychotic and hospitalized with their problems. One maternal aunt probably had an involutional psychotic reaction. A niece, a grandnephew and two grandnieces were neurotic and the mother and a sister were probably so. A brother, a grandniece and two great-grandnephews had personality disorders; a maternal aunt and a great-grandniece possibly or probably were so affected. The wives of a brother and of a nephew were probably neurotic and the husband of a grandniece had a personality disorder. The parents had seven children, 14 grandchildren, 18 great-grandchildren, 35 great-great-grandchildren and one great-great-great-grandchild.

Controls

See family pedigree, person (41).

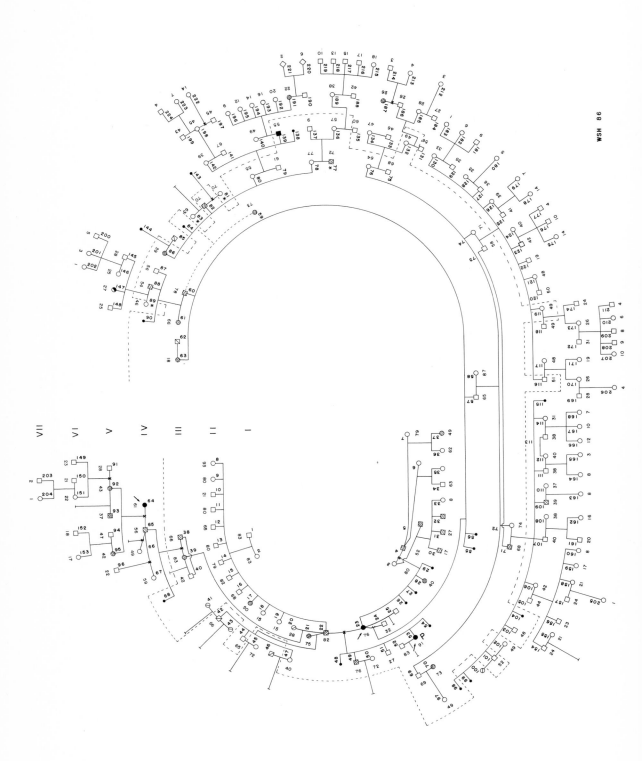

WSH 86

WSH 86: The Proband

The proband (53), born 1866; died at age 72 years at Warren State Hospital of arteriosclerosis. Her mother and father separated when she was one year of age and she did not live with her family until her father remarried when she was eight years old. She was reportedly the victim of her father's incestuous acts from an early age. Between the ages of four and 12 she had "frequent fits," during which she would lose consciousness. At age 21 she married a farmer. It was a contented marriage, although she often wore her husband's clothes and always worked outside like a man rather than do housework. Nothing was known about the onset of her psychosis but she was admitted to Warren State Hospital on 9/27/1912, as a mental defective with dementia praecox (preferred diagnosis) of paresis. She had a slightly positive Wasserman and the right pupil was slightly smaller than the left and reacted sluggishly. Her illness was characterized by delusions of persecution, hyper-religiosity and auditory and visual hallucinations. She was very helpful and pleasant in the wards but remained at Warren State Hospital until her death. Classification: Schizophrenic reaction—paranoid type.

Grandparents

Maternal grandfather (4) died at age 52 years, cause of death unknown. He left Ireland when a young man after breaking the laws of celibacy while training for the priesthood. He later became a petty lawyer and farmer. Classification: Sociopathic personality disturbance—dyssocial reaction.

(5) second husband of maternal grandmother (3). He was reportedly a "hard drinker" and a man of "bad reputation." He and (4) once traded wives. Classification: Sociopathic personality disturbance.

Parents

(21) third wife of father (22), born 1870; died at age 75 years of lobar pneumonia. It was doubted that (22) fathered the children born to (21) during their marriage, although (44) considered (22) to be his father. Classification: Sociopathic personality disturbance—dyssocial reaction.

Father (22), born 1829; died at age 82 years of pneumonia. He was described as "not very bright" and as a man with "loose morals." His daughter, the proband, was the victim of his incestuous acts from an early age. Classification: Sociopathic personality disturbance—sexual deviation.

Mother (23), born 1839; died at age 76 years at Warren State Hospital of chronic myocarditis. She was from a family notorious for their bad criminal and moral reputations. She was first admitted to Warren on 9/27/1883, with a diagnosis of acute mania. She had developed delusions about some property she thought she ought to have and became noisy and quarrelsome. She was discharged two years later, as improved. The next three Warren State Hospital hospitalizations and diagnoses, each with symptoms much like those at the first hospitalization, were as follows:

5/4/1890–
         9/4/1890—Chronic mania
2/20/1892–
         9/29/1892—Unknown
6/13/1903–
         11/3/1915—death
           Chronic mania

Previous to her fourth admission she made threats of violence. Classification: Schizophrenic reaction—paranoid type.

Aunts and Uncles

Paternal aunt (17) died at age 50 years of heart trouble. She was reportedly sexually promiscuous and "generally had a bad reputation." Classification: Sociopathic personality disturbance—dyssocial reaction.

Maternal aunt (28), died at age 40 years, cause unknown. She became a "hard drinker" after her first husband's death and spent her whole pension on alcohol. She ran her house like an "immoral resort" and was decidedly promiscuous. Classification: Sociopathic personality disturbance—sexual deviation.

Maternal half uncle (30), died at age 17 years of a bee sting received while stealing honey. He reportedly was "of a rough nature and a trouble maker." Classification:

Possible personality disorder.

Maternal half uncle (31), died at age 27 years of tuberculosis. He was reportedly a "hard drinker and a man of loose morals." Classification: Possible personality disorder.

Maternal half uncle (32), described as a "vicious imbecile" and as a "criminalistic imbecile." He was a chronic thief and was incarcerated at least three times. Classification: Sociopathic personality disturbance—dyssocial reaction.

Maternal half aunt (37), born 1864; age at last information was 49 years. She was described as "nervous because she had to run a boarding house." Classification: Possible psychoneurotic disorder.

Siblings

(38) husband of half sister (39), born 1874; died at age 66 years of heart trouble. He was reportedly a "lazy, good-for-nothing man" who did not support his family. Classification: Probable personality disorder.

Paternal half sister (39), born 1878; described by her family physician as "one of those harum-scarum women." Classification: Possible personality disorder.

Brother (49), born 1863; died at age 76 years of a coronary occlusion. He was described by his stepchildren as an alcoholic who often beat his wife. He was also described as accident prone. Classification: Sociopathic personality disturbance—alcoholism (addiction).

(59) common-law wife of (60), born 1871; died at age 73 years of myocardial failure. She separated from (60) at age 28 years and entered into a legal marriage. She was described as "neat, ambitious, and liked things clean." She reportedly had a violent temper, especially during the last years of her life, and occasionally chased her son-in-law with a butcher knife. Classification: Sociopathic personality disturbance—dyssocial reaction.

Maternal half brother (60), born 1857; died at age 78 years of a prostatic adenoma. He was described as an alcoholic, as illiterate and unpleasant, and as "a man of careless personal appearance and loose moral character." Classification: Sociopathic personality disturbance.

(61) wife of half brother (60), born 1867; died at age 66 years of cancer. She was described as "lazy, ignorant, untidy, whose three-room house was dirty and disorderly." Classification: Possible personality pattern disturbance—inadequate personality.

Maternal half sister (63), born 1858; murdered at age 18 years while on a sleigh ride. She was called a "tramp" who married at age 16 years. Classification: Sociopathic personality disturbance—antisocial reaction.

Nieces and Nephews

(64) wife of half nephew (65), born 1897; died at age 61 years at Warren State Hospital of arteriosclerosis. At age 18 years she married an alcoholic whom she divorced after nine years because of his alcoholic habits and physical abuse. Her next two marriages, one of which was to (65), each failed after a short duration. In 1936 she stopped attending dances, parties and movies, all of which she had attended previously, because they were "evil." She also had a "nervous spell," during which her hands shook and her body was covered with blisters. She had visions of Christ and said that he spoke to her and directed her activities. She carried an ice pick and flashlight as she feared her first husband, who was to be released from a penitentiary. Admission to Warren State Hospital was on 9/26/1936, with a diagnosis of mixed psychoneurosis. She was apathetic, sad and aurally and visually hallucinated. There was no release or parole from Warren State Hospital. Classification: Schizophrenic reaction—paranoid type.

Half nephew (65), born 1897; died at age 56 years of heart trouble. At age 15 years he was sent to a boys' reformatory for breaking into a grocery store. He was an alcoholic and at one time was convicted of rape and accused of incest. He had no further convictions after his release from prison in 1936. After age 40 years he suffered from asthma or silicosis. Classification: Sociopathic personality disturbance—sexual deviation.

(70) wife of half nephew (69), born 1887; reportedly had nervous trouble all her life. Classification: Psychoneurotic reaction.

(71) husband of half niece (72), born 1886; died at age 68 years of an acute coro-

nary thrombosis. He was reported to be an alcoholic. Classification: Possible socio-pathic personality disturbance—alcoholism (addiction).

(77) husband of half niece (78), born 1882; died at age 72 years of a stroke and pneumonia. While in elementary school he had migraine headaches that were painful enough to cause him to faint. He later out-grew them. Classification: Transient situa-tional personality disturbance—adjustment reaction of childhood.

Half nephew (82), born 1891. At age 19 years he lost his right arm in an accident. He was a heavy drinker, mistreated his wife and killed a man with his car while drunk. He reportedly had a vicious temper and was extremely antagonistic to family members. Classification: Sociopathic personality dis-turbance—alcoholism (addiction).

Half niece (86), born 1898; last known at age 39 years. She was arrested for truancy as a schoolgirl and was described as "boy-crazy" and as a trouble-maker who tried to break up the marriages of her own siblings. She was also described as a heavy drinker and as always dirty and unkempt. Classifica-tion: Sociopathic personality disturbance—alcoholism (addiction).

Half nephew (88), born 1907. He was interviewed and seemed to have some mildly paranoid ideas and the attitude of one who "never got the breaks." Classifica-tion: Possible personality disorder.

Distant Relatives

Half grandniece (92), born 1918. She was raised by her grandmother (39). She and her second husband (93), a paraplegic, quarreled constantly. During one of the quarrels, she struck him and her husband filed assault and battery charges against her. Shortly after a stressful period in 1961, during which time she hit a child while driv-ing an uninsured car, her daughter became illegitimately pregnant, she was meno-pausal and her husband demanded continu-ous care, her husband tried to have her com-mitted to a state mental hospital but failed. She did receive treatment at an outpatient clinic, where her psychiatrist diagnosed her as psychoneurotic. Classification: Psy-choneurotic disorder.

(93) husband of half grandniece (92), born 1924. He was a career army man who,

either as the result of a war injury or mul-tiple sclerosis, was a paraplegic. He was also an alcoholic, surly, sullen and hated his wife bitterly. Classification: Sociopathic personality disturbance—alcoholism (ad-diction).

(95) half grandniece, born 1919. Her parents were divorced when she was five years of age and she grew up in various foster homes. At age 15 she had an illegal abortion. She spent the next several years in state training schools and was under the control of the juvenile court because of delinquency and immorality. She made a good adjustment while under supervision and had no further treatment or commit-ments. Classification: Sociopathic personal-ity disturbance.

Half grandnephew (109), born 1921. He had rheumatic fever in 1938, which left him with a heart murmur. While in the armed service he had "blue spells" and was "ner-vous" but had no breakdown. He also had nervous indigestion for years. Classifica-tion: Probable psychoneurotic disorder.

Half grandnephew (139), born 1906. As a child he had convulsions. He was a mental defective who had little or no training. When he did secure work he complained that his employers and supervisors picked on him and he would consequently lose his job. He had many somatic complaints, was hallucinated for music and sounds, and was described in welfare records as "belliger-ent, demanding, and irrational." A psychi-atric report in 1945 diagnosed him as schizophrenic, paranoid type, with mental deficiency. He made a borderline adjust-ment to society and because of no overt an-tisocial behavior was not committed. Clas-sification: Schizophrenic reaction—para-noid type; mental deficiency.

Half grandniece (147), born 1934. She was a mute who never attended school. There was nothing organically wrong and she was considered to possibly be an un-treated childhood schizophrenic. Classifica-tion: Probably with functional psychosis, schizophrenic reaction—childhood type.

(187) wife of half grandnephew (186), born 1934. She had two illegitimate chil-dren and two by her husband. One of the il-legitimate children was born while she was married to her husband. Classification: So-ciopathic personality disturbance—dysso-cial reaction.

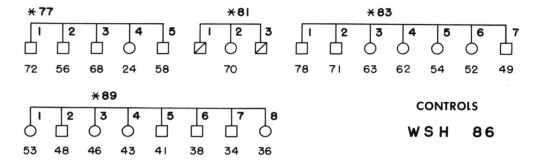

Half grandniece (191), born 1939. She was illegitimately pregnant twice, once before her marriage and once while married. Two of the children were committed as mentally retarded and (191) was to be committed also. Classification: Sociopathic personality disturbance — dyssocial reaction; also, mental deficiency.

Family Summary

The proband, her mother and a half grandnephew had a psychosis and a half grandniece probably so. Only the proband and her mother were hospitalized. A half grandniece was neurotic, a half grandnephew probably so and a half aunt possibly so. Many persons on the pedigree were considered to have personality disorders; included were the maternal grandfather, the father, a paternal aunt, a maternal aunt, three maternal half uncles (two but possibly so), a brother, a half brother, two half sisters (one but possibly so), three half nephews (one possibly so), one half niece and two half grandnieces. Noteworthy spouses include a hospitalized psychotic wife of a half nephew, a neurotic wife of a half nephew, and the following with personality disorders: the second husband of the maternal grandmother, the third wife of the father, the husband of a half sister (probably so), both the common-law wife and the legal wife of a half brother, two husbands of half nieces (one but possibly so), the husband of a half grandniece and the wife of a half grandnephew. The parents had five children, and the mother and father each had five additional children by other marriages, no grandchildren by the proband and her siblings, but 14 grandchildren, 35 great-grandchildren and 25 great-great-grandchildren by half siblings of the proband.

Controls

None noteworthy.

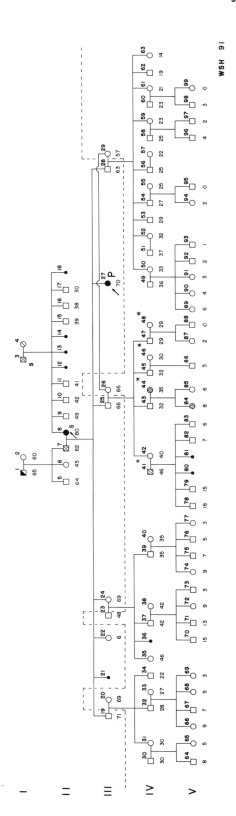

WSH 91

WSH 91: The Proband

The proband (27), born 1895, was still a patient at Warren State Hospital on 12/12/1966 after 54 years of continuous hospitalization (admission was on 12/6/1912). She was a friendly, cheerful girl until age 17 years, when she became slower in her work, unable to sleep and was mute at times. Her memory and intellect became impaired, she developed delusions of a religious nature and was subsequently admitted to Warren State Hospital with a diagnosis of dementia praecox, hebephrenic type. Her illness while hospitalized was characterized by bizarre delusions and hallucinations and episodes of overactivity and loquaciousness alternating with periods of mutism and apathy. Classification: Schizophrenic reaction—catatonic type.

Parents

Father (7), born 1854; died at age 62 years, cause of death unknown. He was described as "close and stingy." At about age 56 years he became worried and despondent, "cried over loss of money in an unwise sale," complained a great deal of not feeling well and was worried over home conditions. Classification: Probable psychoneurotic disorder—depressive reaction. Possible transient situational personality disorder—adjustment reaction of late life.

Mother (8), born 1863; died at age 80 years at Warren State Hospital of cerebral arteriosclerosis. She was a bright, vivacious girl when young and was well until after the birth of the proband, when she developed delusions and hallucinations of a religious variety. On one occasion she attempted suicide. At the beginning of her illness she was rather violent and excitable at times but later became dull, indifferent, unsociable and showed no emotional affect, either of elation or despondency. She was at Warren State Hospital from 1935 until her death eight years later. Classification: Schizophrenic reaction—chronic undifferentiated type.

Grandparents

Paternal grandfather (1), born 1822; died at age 65 years of "a general break-

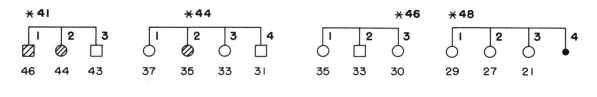

down." He was admitted voluntarily to a mental hospital in Germany at about age 40 years, which was the first of two admissions to mental hospitals. When old he was described as "quite odd." Classification: Probably with functional psychosis. Possible psychoneurotic disorder.

Maternal grandfather (3), born 1839, committed suicide, date and manner of which were unknown. Family members said that worry over home troubles caused him to commit suicide, that his natural disposition was cheerful and jovial and that he was not inclined to be despondent. He had been "drinking very hard" previous to his death. Classification: Probable transient situational disorder. Possibly with functional psychosis.

Nieces and Nephews

(41) husband of niece (42), born 1914. He was rejected for military service during World War II because of psychoneurosis. Classification: Probable psychoneurotic disorder.

(44) wife of nephew (43), born 1925. She was described as never at home and always has to be doing something. She was "not affectionate with children...oldest daughter is probably emotionally disturbed." A visiting nurse thought that her behavior was an exaggerated reaction to her dying husband and severely ill baby (the baby had meningitis with residual severe retardation). Neighbors described her as

"hard to get along with." Classification: Probable psychoneurotic disorder. Possible transient situational personality disorder — gross stress reaction.

Distant Relatives

Grandniece (84), born 1952, reportedly failed first grade because of an emotional disturbance. Classification: Possible transient situational personality disorder — adjustment reaction of childhood.

Family Summary

The proband and the proband's mother were hospitalized with psychotic disorders and the paternal grandfather was probably so affected. The proband's father was probably neurotic as were two persons who married a niece and a nephew of the proband. A grandniece may have had a transient personality disorder. The proband's parents had seven children, 20 grandchildren and 36 great-grandchildren.

Controls

See family pedigree, person (41).
Sister (2) of (41), born 1916. She was described at age 44 years as "the nervous type." Classification: Possible psychoneurotic disorder.
See family pedigree, person (44).

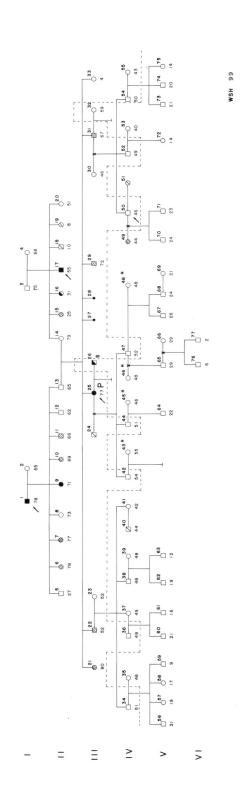

WSH 99

WSH 99: The Proband

The proband (25), born 1883. She was deserted by her husband in 1910 but was exceedingly industrious and managed to support herself and three small children. Her psychosis had an abrupt onset and was credited to overwork, worry, and excitement incidental to some religious meetings. Hospitalization at Warren State Hospital was from 11/28/1913 until 9/2/1916, with a diagnosis of dementia praecox. The principal characteristics of her illness were a hyper-religious trend, distractibility, hallucinations, delusions and variability of moods. She was never rehospitalized and was in good mental health at age 77 years. Classification: Schizophrenic reaction—paranoid type.

(26) second husband of (25), was married to (25) for six years then committed suicide over his mother's grave. Classification: Probably with functional psychosis.

Grandparents

Paternal grandfather (1), born 1813; died at age 78 years of cholera. He was hospitalized at Warren State Hospital from 9/5/1883 until 4/29/1884, with a diagnosis of acute mania. Admission notes stated that he was "greatly confused, restless, suspicious, unintelligent and run-down physically." He began to improve shortly after admission and remained normal, except that he slept a great deal the remainder of his life. Classification: Schizophrenic reaction—paranoid type.

Aunts and Uncles

Paternal aunt (6), born 1836; age at last information was 76 years. She was described as a "little excitable and nervous." Classification: Possible psychoneurotic reaction.

Paternal aunt (7), born 1837; age at last information was 77 years. She always talked of having conversations with her deceased friends and relatives. She also claimed to see imaginary lights which were "a warning of an approaching death." Classification: Personality pattern disturbance—schizoid personality.

Paternal aunt (9), born 1843; age at last information was 71 years. In 1911–1912 she was hospitalized for malaria. While hospitalized she developed a mental disturbance which persisted until the time of last information (at least two and a half years). She was talkative, restless, imagined that she had a great deal of money, was irritable and her flighty conversation was entirely along religious lines. She was not delusional but had what she called "presentments." Classification: Schizophrenic reaction—paranoid type.

Paternal aunt (10), born 1845; age at last information was 69 years. About 1906 she had surgery for cancer of the face. At this time she "worried and complained a great deal, talked of little except the fact that she had a cancer, was emotional and did not do her work." She would see few people and at times almost refused to talk to people. This attack lasted for one year. Classification: Personality trait disturbance—emotionally unstable personality.

Paternal uncle (11), born 1848; age at last information was 66 years. He drank to excess all his life and was described as "prematurely senile" and as a "harmless old soldier" who talked continuously about "the War" and his experiences in it. Classification: Sociopathic personality disturbance—alcoholism (addiction).

Maternal aunt (15), died at age 25 years of cancer. At age three years she was afflicted with a paralysis of both legs and one arm. The use of one leg and the arm was recovered, but one leg remained paralyzed, which necessitated the use of crutches for the remainder of her life. She was described as "nervous." Classification: Possible psychoneurotic reaction.

Maternal aunt (16), died at age 31 years of tuberculosis. Two years before her death she had a "mental upset" which lasted several months. The upset reportedly followed an illness described as inflammation of the uterus. At the time of the mental disturbance she could tolerate no noise and if she heard someone approaching she became apprehensive that they were coming for her. Classification: Probably with functional psychosis.

Maternal uncle (17), born 1859; aged 55 years at last information. About 1899, and again in 1911, he was worried, depressed, stuporous and had delusions of persecution. From 2/4/1911 until 5/4/1911, he was hospitalized at Warren State Hospital with a diagnosis of involutional melancholia. While hospitalized he sometimes threatened suicide but made no suicidal attempts. The first psychotic episode was reportedly precipitated by financial failures. In 1914 he apparently was still not normal but had not been hospitalized. Classification: Schizophrenic reaction—paranoid type.

Siblings

Sister (21), born 1879; age at last information was 80 years. She was reportedly "very nervous" and refused to be interviewed. Classification: Personality trait disturbance—emotionally unstable personality.

Brother (22), born 1880; died at age 52 years of a gunshot wound inflicted by his son after (22) had beaten his wife to death. He drank to excess and was abusive to his family. Classification: Sociopathic personality disturbance.

Brother (29), born 1888; age at last information was 72 years. He was a retired boatman and physically disabled. He was described as "a heavy drinker," as an alcoholic and as an "extremely surly and disagreeable person." Classification: Sociopathic personality disturbance—alcoholism (addiction).

Brother (31), born 1889; died at age 67 years of pulmonary tuberculosis. He reportedly drank excessively, was abusive to his children and was divorced by his first wife for cruelty. Classification: Sociopathic personality disturbance.

Nieces and Nephews

(49) wife of nephew (50), born 1919. She reportedly had been married twice since her divorce from (50). She had one child before her marriage and two while married to (50), all three of whom she abandoned. She was described as "defective" and as a "street walker." Classification: Sociopathic personality disturbance.

Family Summary

The proband, a maternal uncle and the paternal grandfather were psychotic and

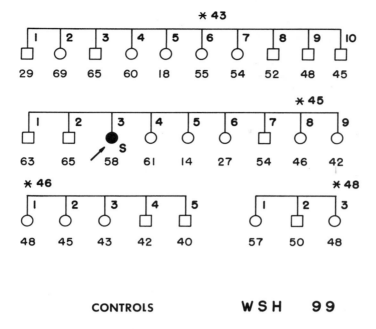

CONTROLS WSH 99

hospitalized with their illnesses. A paternal aunt, also psychotic, was never hospitalized. The proband's second husband suicided. Both he and a maternal aunt were classified as probably with functional psychosis. Personality disorders were found in two paternal aunts, a paternal uncle, a sister, three brothers and the wife of a nephew. A maternal aunt and a paternal aunt were possibly neurotic.

Controls

Sister (3) of (45), born 1897; died at age 58 years, cause of death unknown. She was admitted to a state mental hospital on 9/10/1936. About four or five months before admission, at the beginning of her sixth pregnancy (she had seven children and at least one miscarriage), she developed the delusion that she had syphilis and the phobia that there were bugs crawling in her. She also felt worthless and depressed and attempted to kill herself and her small child by walking, with caution, on railroad tracks. Diagnosis at the state hospital was dementia praecox. She remained quite ill until April, 1938, when she began to improve and was discharged in 1939 to the supervision of an aunt and uncle. She was never again hospitalized. Classification: Schizophrenic reaction—paranoid type.

INDEX

The letter "t" following a page number indicates a table.

9/4/73   114304

19⁰⁰   25%